OXFORD STUDIES IN EUROPEAN LAW

Series Editors

PAUL CRAIG

Professor of English Law at St John's College, Oxford

GRÁINNE DE BÚRCA

Professor of Law at New York University School of Law

Judging European Democracy

OXFORD STUDIES IN EUROPEAN LAW

Series Editors

Paul Craig, Professor of English Law at St John's College, Oxford and
Gráinne de Búrca, Professor of Law at New York University School of Law

The aim of this series is to publish important and original research on EU law. The focus is on scholarly monographs, with a particular emphasis on those which are interdisciplinary in nature. Edited collections of essays will also be included where they are appropriate. The series is wide in scope and aims to cover studies of particular areas of substantive and of institutional law, historical works, theoretical studies, and analyses of current debates, as well as questions of perennial interest such as the relationship between national and EU law and the novel forms of governance emerging in and beyond Europe. The fact that many of the works are interdisciplinary will make the series of interest to all those concerned with the governance and operation of the EU.

OTHER TITLES IN THIS SERIES

EU Values Before the Court of Justice
Foundations, Potential, Risks
Luke Dimitrios Spieker

Postnational Constitutionalism
Europe and the Time of Law
Paul Linden-Retek

The Legislative Priority Rule and the EU Internal Market for Goods
A Constitutional Approach
Eadaoin Ní Chaoimh

The Jurisprudence of Constitutional Conflict in the European Union
Ana Bobić

Reflexive Governance in EU Equality Law
Emma Lantschner

Enhanced Cooperation and European Tax Law
Caroline Heber

Legal Pluralism in European Contract Law
Vanessa Mak

Europe's Passive Virtues
Deference to National Authorities in EU Free Movement Law
Jan Zglinski

Accountability in EU Security and Defence
The Law and Practice of Peacebuilding
Carolyn Moser

Accountability in the Economic and Monetary Union
Foundations, Policy, and Governance
Menelaos Markakis

Official Secrets and Oversight in the EU
Law and Practices of Classified Information
Vigjilenca Abazi

Risk Regulation in the Internal Market
Lessons from Agricultural Biotechnology
Maria Weimer

EU Health Law & Policy
The Expansion of EU Power in Public Health and Health Care
Anniek de Ruijter

The Horizontal Effect of Fundamental Rights in the European Union
A Constitutional Analysis
Eleni Frantziou

EU Powers Under External Pressure
How the EU's External Actions Alter its Internal Structures
Christina Eckes

Frontex and Human Rights
Responsibility in 'Multi- Actor Situations' under the ECHR and EU Public Liability Law
Melanie Fink

EU Equality Law
The First Fundamental Rights Policy of the EU
Elise Muir

Subnational Authorities in EU Law
Michèle Finck

Judging European Democracy

The Role and Legitimacy of National Constitutional Courts in the EU

NIK DE BOER

OXFORD
UNIVERSITY PRESS

OXFORD
UNIVERSITY PRESS

Great Clarendon Street, Oxford, OX2 6DP,
United Kingdom

Oxford University Press is a department of the University of Oxford.
It furthers the University's objective of excellence in research, scholarship,
and education by publishing worldwide. Oxford is a registered trade mark of
Oxford University Press in the UK and in certain other countries

First Edition published in 2023

Published in the United States of America by Oxford University Press
198 Madison Avenue, New York, NY 10016, United States of America

British Library Cataloguing in Publication Data

Data available

Library of Congress Control Number is on file at the Library of Congress

ISBN 978–0–19–284523–8

DOI: 10.1093/oso/9780192845238.001.0001

Printed and bound in the UK by
TJ Books Limited

For Hannah

Series Editors' Preface

The role and legitimacy of national constitutional courts in the European Union (EU) is a central issue within EU law, and also more generally within EU studies written from the perspective of political science and international relations. There is a large literature that explores case law of national constitutional courts in relation to EU regulations, directives, and decisions, and to decisions of the Court of the Justice of the European Union (CJEU).

The German Federal Constitutional Court has played a very significant role in this respect, and its decisions have been praised and critiqued by scholars from varying perspectives. There have, however, been numerous other decisions by national constitutional courts that have taken issue with aspects of EU law or CJEU decisions. The scholarship has generated theory and counter-theory. Conceptions of constitutional pluralism have been advanced to justify the stance of national constitutional courts, and this theory has in turn been challenged on normative and empirical grounds.

There is also, as is well known, a very extensive literature on the legitimacy of constitutional review within the nation state. There is discourse justifying rights-based constraints enforced by courts whereby primary legislation can be invalidated for non-compliance with protections contained in a Bill of Rights. This is in turn opposed by those who argue that such review is counter-majoritarian, more especially given the prevalence of reasonable disagreement as to what, in more concrete terms, the meaning accorded to such rights should be.

Nik de Boer's book is a welcome addition to this literature, which addresses the role and legitimacy of national constitutional courts in the EU. The principal focal point of the study is, as indicated by the title, the role of such national constitutional courts when viewed from a democratic perspective. It is a strength of this work that analysis of the role of such courts at the EU level is judged against detailed examination of the contending arguments for constitutional review at the national level. His view about this debate then shapes, formally and substantively, the argument at the EU level. The central thesis is that national constitutional courts' review of EU law can risk constraining and narrowing democratic debate over the EU's constitutional underpinnings. The consequence is that national constitutional courts 'risk taking sides in good faith political disagreements among elected legislators about constitutional questions relating to the EU, thus distorting, rather than protecting, the democratic decision-making process'. The consequence then is that decisions about the EU's future are taken out of the hands of democratically elected bodies, with judges becoming the final arbiters of these issues.

There is no doubt that the book will spark further debate as to the legitimacy and role of national constitutional courts in the EU. The focal point of the study is important and will be of interest to all those concerned with the EU and the respective roles played by political and legal institutions in shaping its development.

Paul Craig and Gráinne de Búrca

Acknowledgements

The current book is the result of several years of research that I originally started for my doctoral dissertation at the Amsterdam Centre for European Law and Governance (ACELG) of the University of Amsterdam's Law Faculty. I had set out to transform the dissertation into a book in the Spring of 2020. But then the coronavirus pandemic intervened and as creches shut, my partner and I found ourselves with a one-year-old toddler stuck in a one-bedroom apartment. This obviously made writing a book, or doing any kind of work for that matter, somewhat difficult. Then, on 5 May 2020, while Europe was still in the middle of lockdown, the German Constitutional Court ruled that the European Central Bank's Public Sector Purchase Programme (PSPP) was *ultra vires*. I found out about this news while sitting on the edge of a sandpit in which my son was playing. Seeing the subsequent flood of commentaries on the judgment, without having much time to write myself, was not great for my stress levels. I also soon realized that the book project, with the German Constitutional Court's EU-related case law as its main object, would have to include a new chapter on the *PSPP* ruling and the coronavirus pandemic. That chapter—Chapter 7 in the book—is in a way still incomplete, as a number of cases discussed there were still pending for final decision at the time of writing. This book, however, was substantively concluded in August 2022. Subsequent developments are not taken into account.

Completing this work would not have been possible without the aid of many wonderful colleagues and friends. I am grateful to the University of Amsterdam and its Law Faculty for providing me with the opportunity to embark on this research project and turn it into a book. I owe a special debt to my doctoral supervisors Leonard Besselink, Deirdre Curtin, and Ingo Venzke for inspiration and guidance through the many stages of this research project. Christina Eckes, Martijn Hesselink, Jan Komárek, Franz Mayer, Marc de Wilde, and Bruno de Witte assessed the original doctoral dissertation and provided very helpful advice on how to transform the thesis into a book.

I am immensely grateful to Will Bateman, Leonard Besselink, Matteo Bonelli, Kas de Goede, Niels Graaf, Jens van 't Klooster, Michał Krajewski, Karsten Meijer, Tomi Tuominen, and Mattias Wendel for reading and commenting on parts of the book manuscript. I would also like to thank Jens van 't Klooster for permission to restate ideas in Chapter 7 of this book that we originally developed in 'The ECB, the Courts and the Issue of Democratic Legitimacy after Weiss' (2020) 57 Common Market Law Review 1689. A huge thank you to Alice Garner for excellent language editing, as well as to Caroline Valia-Kollery for the final copy-edit. Thanks also to Lila Blankestijn, Sarah el Galta, and Olga Kortz for invaluable research assistance.

Stimulating research visits abroad significantly enriched this research. I am grateful to Sacha Prechal for hosting me at the European Court of Justice, to Mark Tushnet for his willingness to act as my Faculty advisor for a stay as Visiting Researcher at Harvard Law School, and to Mattias Kumm for hosting me for a research stay at the Berlin Social Science Centre (WZB). A significant part of this research project builds on interviews conducted with politicians, civil servants, legal representatives in relevant cases before the German Constitutional Court, as well as constitutional court judges. I am immensely grateful for their willingness to participate in this project. For the research visits and conducting the interviews, I wish to acknowledge the financial support of ACCESS Europe and the Amsterdam University Fund.

My colleagues and students at the University of Amsterdam's Law Faculty and beyond have provided many stimulating discussions and daily inspiration. Thanks especially to Veit Bader, Ursus Eijkelenberg, Maarten Hillebrandt, Chris Koedooder, Christophe Majastre, Anne van Mulligen, Jan-Herman Reestman, Benjamin van Rooij, Anniek de Ruijter and Jerfi Uzman for the many conversations and inspiration. Parts of this work were presented and discussed at various occasions and locations. Thanks to all those who provided input at some point on this work.

I am also thankful to the series editors Paul Craig and Gráinne de Búrca for including this book in their Oxford Studies in European Law series, to the three anonymous reviewers of the original manuscript and book proposal for helpful advice, and to Lane Berger, Alex Flach, Charlotte Holloway, David Lipp, Amy Marchant, Kathrynn Plunkett, and John Smallman at OUP for their patience and support in making this book a reality.

Finally, I am grateful to my family and friends for support. My brother Walt and sister Lorijn for their encouragement throughout the many years that writing this book took. My parents, Anneke and Wim, for always supporting me in my endeavours, believing in my ability to bring this project to completion, and providing me with all the resources to do this. Samuel and Harry for joy, laughter, and love. The greatest debt I certainly owe to Hannah, my travelling companion in life who made the past years better in every way. I could not have completed this project without her and she will be happy to see it done. The book is dedicated to her.

Summary Contents

Detailed Contents

Table of Cases

NATIONAL COURTS

Austria

Belgium

Czech Republic

Denmark

Estonia

France

Germany

Ireland

Italy

Table of Legislation

EU PRIMARY LAW

EU SECONDARY LAW

INTERNATIONAL TREATIES (INCLUDING EU-RELATED TREATIES)

UNITED KINGDOM

List of Abbreviations

AfD	Alternative for Germany (*Alternative für Deutschland*)
AG	Advocate General
APP	Asset Purchasing Programme
art	Article
BDI	Federation of German Industries
CDU	Christian Democratic Union of Germany (*Christlich Demokratische Union Deutschlands*)
CDU/CSU	Christian democratic political alliance of the CDU and CSU
ch	Chapter
Charter	Charter of Fundamental Rights of the European Union
CJEU	The Court of the Justice of the European Union
Commission	European Commission
CSU	Christian Social Union in Bavaria (*Christlich-Soziale Union in Bayern*)
EAW	European Arrest Warrant
EC Treaty	Treaty establishing the European Community
ECB	European Central Bank
Ecofin	Economic and Financial Affairs Council
ed(s)	Editor(s)
edn	Edition
EEC Treaty	Treaty establishing the European Economic Community
EFSF	European Financial Stability Facility
EFSM	European Financial Stabilisation Mechanism
EMF	European Monetary Fund
EMS	European Monetary System
EMU	Economic and Monetary Union
EP	European Parliament
ESCB	European System of Central Banks
ESM	European Stability Mechanism
ESMFinG	Act for Financial Participation in the European Stability Mechanism
EU	European Union
EUZBBG	Act on Cooperation between the Federal Government and the German Bundestag in European Union Matters
FDP	Free Democratic Party (*Freie Demokratische Partei*)
GDR	German Democratic Republic
GFCC	German Federal Constitutional Court
GNI	gross national income
IGA	intergovernmental agreement
IGC	Intergovernmental Conference
IMF	International Monetary Fund

JCC	Joint Constitutional Committee of the *Bundestag* and *Bundesrat*
MFF	Multiannual Financial Framework
NGEU	Next Generation EU
OJ	Official Journal of the European Union
OMT	Outright Monetary Transactions
ORD	Own Resources Decision
para	paragraph
PDS	Party of Democratic Socialism (*Partei des Demokratischen Sozialismus*)
PEPP	Pandemic Emergency Purchase Programme
PSPP	Public Sector Purchasing Programme
QE	quantitative easing
SED	Socialist Unity Party (*Sozialistische Einheitspartei Deutschlands*)
SGP	Stability and Growth Pact
SMP	Securities Markets Programme
SPD	Social Democratic Party of Germany (*Sozialdemokratische Partei Deutschlands*)
SPV	special purpose vehicle
SRF	Single Resolution Fund
SRM	Single Resolution Mechanism
SSM	Single Supervisory Mechanism
StabMechG	Act on the Assumption of Guarantees in Connection with a European Stabilisation Mechanism
SURE	European instrument for temporary Support to mitigate Unemployment Risks in an Emergency
TEC	Treaty Establishing the European Community
TEU	Treaty on European Union
TFEU	Treaty on the Functioning of the European Union
TSCG	Treaty on Stability, Coordination and Governance in the Economic and Monetary Union
UK	United Kingdom
US	United States of America
WASG	Electoral Alternative for Labour and Social Justice (*Arbeit und soziale Gerechtigkeit – Die Wahlalternative*)

1
Introduction

On 5 May 2020, the red-robed judges of the German Federal Constitutional Court (GFCC) shocked Europe. In a ruling on the Public Sector Purchasing Programme (PSPP), a quantitative easing programme of the European Central Bank (ECB), they concluded that the Central Bank had failed to substantiate the programme's proportionality.[1] As a result, the German judges ruled that the PSPP was *ultra vires*, that is, beyond the scope of the Central Bank's competences. In reaching that conclusion they set aside the judgment of the Court of Justice of the EU (CJEU), which had previously upheld the programme, as 'simply not comprehensible' and 'objectively arbitrary'. Having long retained the right to rule on the scope of the EU's competences, the German judges had always refrained from taking the ultimate step of declaring EU law inapplicable within the German legal order. This time was different. The judgment led to a flood of criticism among commentators across Europe, both in the popular media as well as among legal experts.[2] Some held that the judgment threatened the existence of the euro.[3] Martin Sandbu of the *Financial Times* called the verdict a 'bomb under the EU legal order'.[4] In the same newspaper, Martin Wolf went so far as to state that future historians might mark the ruling 'as the decisive turning point in Europe's history towards disintegration'.[5]

That so much seemed to depend on a ruling by eight German judges was not a completely unfamiliar scenario. On 12 September 2012, it looked as though the fate of European integration also lay in the hands of Germany's constitutional judges. On that day, the GFCC ruled on the constitutionality of Germany's participation in two legal instruments adopted to solve the euro area's ongoing sovereign debt crisis: the European Stability Mechanism (ESM) and the Treaty on Stability, Coordination and Governance in the Economic and Monetary Union (TSCG or

[1] Bundesverfassungsgericht, judgment of 5 May 2020, 2 BvR 859/15 (*PSPP*).

[2] An overview of several commentaries is provided in Franz Mayer, 'The Ultra Vires Ruling: Deconstructing the German Federal Constitutional Court's PSPP Decision of 5 May 2020' (2021) 16 European Constitutional Law Review 733.

[3] Willem H Buiter, 'Germany's Judges Declare War on the ECB' (*Project Syndicate*, 6 May 2020) <www.project-syndicate.org/commentary/german-constitution-court-ecb-pspp-ruling-by-willem-h-buiter-2020-05> accessed 1 August 2022; Katharina Pistor, 'Germany's Constitutional Court Goes Rogue' (*Project Syndicate*, 8 May 2020) <www.project-syndicate.org> accessed 1 August 2022.

[4] Martin Sandbu, 'German Court Has Set a Bomb under the EU Legal Order' *Financial Times* (5 May 2020) <www.ft.com/content/79484c01-b66b-4f81-bdc6-fd4def940821> accessed 1 August 2022.

[5] Martin Wolf, 'German Court Decides to Take Back Control with ECB Ruling' *Financial Times* (16 May 2020) <www.ft.com/content/37825304-9428-11ea-af4b-499244625ac4> accessed 1 August 2022.

Judging European Democracy. Nik de Boer, Oxford University Press. © Nik de Boer 2023.
DOI: 10.1093/oso/9780192845238.003.0001

Fiscal Compact).[6] The EU's political leaders had agreed both legal instruments amidst persisting fears as to whether the EU would be able to adequately address the euro crisis.[7] Yet both instruments were controversial and fiercely opposed by those who felt the measures presented an undesirable and even illegal step in further European integration. The case before the GFCC was the result of no less than 37,000 constitutional complaints by German citizens, who essentially argued that both instruments violated the overall budgetary responsibility of Germany's parliament, the *Bundestag*.[8]

Had the GFCC decided that Germany's participation in the two instruments was unconstitutional, it would have delivered a significant blow to the EU's attempts at solving the euro crisis. Germany's participation was indispensable for the success of the ESM and the TSCG. The GFCC's constitutional review thus made 'the world look at Karlsruhe', as one commentator aptly put it.[9] When the German Court ruled that the ESM and TSCG were compatible with the German constitution—its Basic Law—the news was discussed in newspapers all over Europe and the borrowing costs for Spanish and Italian ten-year bonds fell, while the euro gained in value relative to the dollar.[10] Yet despite the GFCC's approval of the two measures, the Court reiterated a number of constitutional limitations on future European integration. That the *Bundestag* could not transfer its budgetary responsibility to a European institution created a constitutional obstacle for proposals seeking to centralize substantial parts of the Member States' budgets in order to make the monetary union more sustainable.[11] In addition, the case served as an important reminder of how national constitutional courts can exert a powerful influence over the constitutional development of the EU, given their role of authoritatively interpreting the constitution within their respective national legal orders.

[6] Treaty establishing the European Stability Mechanism, 27 September 2012, <https://eur-lex.europa.eu/legal-content/EN/TXT/PDF/?uri=CELEX:42012A0202(01)&from=EN> accessed 2 August 2022; Treaty on Stability, Coordination and Governance, <www.consilium.europa.eu/media/20399/st00tscg26_en12.pdf> accessed 2 August 2022.

[7] More precisely, the Fiscal Compact was adopted by twenty-five Member States. The ESM is an intergovernmental treaty concluded by the euro area Member States.

[8] Mattias Wendel, 'Judicial Restraint and the Return to Openness: The Decision of the German Federal Constitutional Court on the ESM and the Fiscal Treaty of 12 September 2012' (2013) 14 German Law Journal 21, 21 and 24.

[9] ibid 21; see also Thomas Darnstädt, 'Das überforderte Gericht' *Spiegel Online* (12 September 2012) <www.spiegel.de/politik/deutschland/kommentar-zum-esm-urteil-das-ueberforderte-gericht-a-855377.html> accessed 1 August 2022.

[10] See Quentin Peel, 'German Court Backs ESM Bailout Fund' *Financial Times* (Berlin, 12 September 2012); 'German Court Backs Eurozone's ESM Bailout Fund' (*BBC.com*, 12 September 2012) <www.bbc.com/news/world-europe-19567867> accessed 1 August 2022; 'Griechische Anleger feiern ESM-Urteil' *Spiegel Online* (12 September 2012) <www.spiegel.de/> accessed 1 August 2022.

[11] Bundesverfassungsgericht, judgment of 12 September 2012, 2 BvR 1390/12 (*ESM* interim judgment) para 210. On the economics of monetary unions in general, see Paul de Grauwe, *Economics of Monetary Union* (Oxford University Press 2014) 3–22 and 109–33.

The GFCC's *ESM* and *PSPP* judgments are part of a growing body of case law by constitutional courts from the EU Member States. In these cases, constitutional courts have reviewed EU Treaties and related legal instruments, as well as secondary EU law and decisions by EU institutions on their compatibility with national constitutional law. In relation to the euro crisis alone, the GFCC addressed constitutional concerns in no less than ten judgments.[12] Outside Germany, constitutional courts in Austria,[13] Belgium,[14] Estonia,[15] France,[16] Ireland,[17] Portugal,[18] Poland,[19] and Slovenia[20] have assessed the constitutionality of the EU's euro crisis measures.[21] Beyond the crisis, constitutional courts have raised concerns about diverse legal instruments such as the Framework Decision on the European Arrest Warrant,[22] the Treaty of Lisbon,[23] and the Data Retention Directive.[24] These EU-related judgments by national constitutional courts are of key importance. They address fundamental issues within the EU's constitutional order, namely the EU's

[12] Bundesverfassungsgericht, judgment of 7 September 2011, 2 BvR 987/10 (*EFSF*); Bundesverfassungsgericht, judgment of 28 February 2012, 2 BvE 8/11 (*the 9er Committee* case); Bundesverfassungsgericht, judgment of 19 June 2012, 2 BvE 4/11; Bundesverfassungsgericht, judgment of 12 September 2012, 2 BvR 1390/12 (*ESM* interim judgment); Bundesverfassungsgericht, 18 March 2014, 2 BvR 1390/12 (*ESM* final judgment); Bundesverfassungsgericht, order of 14 January 2014, 2 BvR 2728/13 (*OMT* reference); Bundesverfassungsgericht, judgment of 21 June 2016, 2 BvR 2728/13 (*OMT* final); Bundesverfassungsgericht, order of 18 July 2017, 2 BvR 859/15 (*PSPP* reference); Bundesverfassungsgericht, judgment of 30 July 2019, 2 BvR 1685/14 (*Banking union*); BVerfG, *PSPP* (n 1).

[13] Constitutional Court of Austria (*Österreichischer Verfassungsgerichtshof*), decision SV 2/12-18 of 16 March 2013 and decision SV 1/2013-15 of 3 October 2013.

[14] Belgian Constitutional Court No 62/2016, 28 April 2016 (*Fiscal Compact*).

[15] Supreme Court of Estonia (*Riigikohus*), Judgment (*en banc*) of 12 July 2012, Case no 3-4-1-6-12.

[16] French Constitutional Council (*Conseil constitutionnel*), case 2012-653 DC, decision of 9 August 2012 (Treaty on Stability, Coordination and Governance in the Economic and Monetary Union).

[17] Supreme Court of Ireland, judgment of 31 July 2012, *Pringle v Government of Ireland, Ireland and the Attorney General* [2012] IESC 47.

[18] See, on the several judgments, Mariana Canotilho, Teresa Violante, and Rui Lanceiro, 'Austerity Measures under Judicial Scrutiny: The Portuguese Constitutional Case-Law' (2015) 11 European Constitutional Law Review 155.

[19] Polish Constitutional Tribunal, judgment of 26 June 2013, K 33/12.

[20] Constitutional Court of the Republic of Slovenia, judgment of 3 February 2011, Case U-I-178/10-18.

[21] For overviews, see Federico Fabbrini, 'The Euro-Crisis and the Courts: Judicial Review and the Political Process in Comparative Perspective' (2014) 32 Berkeley Journal of International Law 64; Jan-Herman Reestman, 'Legitimacy through Adjudication: The ESM Treaty and the Fiscal Compact before the National Courts' in Thomas Beukers, Bruno De Witte, and Claire Kilpatrick (eds), *Constitutional Change through Euro-crisis Law* (Cambridge University Press 2017).

[22] Council Framework Decision 2002/584/JHA of 13 June 2002 on the European arrest warrant and the surrender procedures between Member States [2002] OJ L190/1. See, on its review, Jan Komárek, 'European Constitutionalism and the European Arrest Warrant: In Search of the Limits of "Contrapunctual Principles"' (2007) 44 Common Market Law Review 9.

[23] See, for an overview, Mattias Wendel, 'Lisbon Before the Courts: Comparative Perspectives' (2011) 7 European Constitutional Law Review 96.

[24] See *inter alia* Bundesverfassungsgericht, judgment of 2 March 2010, 1 BvR 256/08 (*Data-retention*); Constitutional Court of the Czech Republic (Ústavní soud), judgment of 22 March 2011, Pl ÚS 24/10 (*Data Retention*); Constitutional Court of Austria (*Österreichischer Verfassungsgerichtshof*), decision G 47/2012-49 of 27 June 2014 (*Data Retention*).

democratic legitimacy, the protection of persons' fundamental rights and freedoms, the division of competences between the EU and the Member States, as well as the place of national sovereignty within the EU.[25] Through these judgments, national constitutional courts impose constitutional limits on European integration and shape the EU's future development.

Yet is this a role that the national constitutional courts should fulfil? Are constitutional courts the institutions that should decide questions of such fundamental constitutional importance for the EU and, if so, in which situations? It could be considered that something has gone badly wrong when the fate of Europe's monetary union depends on the decision of eight German constitutional judges.[26] Democratic grounds would seem to favour that decisions which have major constitutional importance for the EU should be left to political institutions that represent Europe's citizens and can be held accountable by them. On the other hand, constitutional safeguards may be crucial in crisis-ridden Europe. Since the euro crisis especially, there have been mounting concerns about democratic shortcomings in the EU's decision-making process.[27] Challenges before national constitutional courts have often raised such concerns, and national constitutional courts have in fact claimed to protect democracy in the Member States.

This book explores the above conundrum systematically by scrutinizing the possible tensions between democratic legitimacy and the national constitutional courts' review of European law. The book aims to understand the democratic legitimacy of the national constitutional courts' role in relation to the EU. It asks how we should assess the democratic legitimacy of the national constitutional courts' review of EU Treaties and related legal instruments, as well as secondary EU law on their compatibility with national constitutional law. In doing so, this book offers a unique combination of analysis based on constitutional and political theory, with an in-depth case study of the GFCC's EU-related case law on German and EU politics.

[25] See also Mattias Wendel, 'Comparative Reasoning and the Making of a Common Constitutional Law: EU-Related Decisions of National Constitutional Courts in a Transnational Perspective' (2013) 11 International Journal of Constitutional Law 981, 982.

[26] See, on this point, also Franz Mayer, 'Rebel Without a Cause? A Critical Analysis of the German Constitutional Court's OMT Reference' (2014) 15 German Law Journal 111, 134–36. Mayer stated at page 135, among other things, that 'The reasonable thing to do would be to clearly state that in the Euro crisis, we have reached the limits of what law and lawyers can do and that the decisions have to be taken by those who are democratically elected and who will be held accountable'.

[27] For such democratic concerns, see eg Deirdre Curtin, 'Challenging Executive Dominance in European Democracy' (2014) 77 Modern Law Review 1; Mark Dawson and Floris de Witte, 'Constitutional Balance in the EU after the Euro-Crisis' [2013] The Modern Law Review 817; Jonathan White, 'Emergency Europe' (2015) 63 Political Studies 300. Explicit in calling for national constitutional resistance is Agustín José Menéndez, 'The Existential Crisis of the European Union' (2013) 14 German Law Journal 453.

1. Democratic Legitimacy and National Constitutional Courts in the EU

1.1 Democratic Legitimacy and Judicial Review

Concerns about the democratic legitimacy of constitutional courts are not new. They connect to long-standing debates about the democratic legitimacy of constitutional courts in the domestic context and, in particular, to democratic concerns about the power of such courts to strike down democratically adopted legislation on constitutional grounds. The democratic legitimacy of judicial review of legislation (hereafter simply: judicial review) is contested because it gives judges the power to strike down legislation adopted by democratically elected legislators if those judges deem that the legislation violates constitutional norms. For political systems in which democracy is thought to be of key importance in making legitimate laws, this 'counter-majoritarian difficulty' raises a normative problem.[28] According to a number of scholars, allowing courts to override democratically elected legislatures and giving courts ultimate authority to decide constitutional issues is undemocratic and lacks a compelling justification.[29]

The problem relates to two characteristics of constitutional law: entrenchment and indeterminacy. Entrenchment entails that constitutional legal norms are more difficult to change than ordinary legal norms and makes a constitution function as a body of higher law. For example, changing the constitution would require a supermajority of some sort in parliament or a constitutional convention. Indeterminacy entails that the meaning of most constitutional norms is highly indeterminate, often deliberately so, and hence gives broad discretion to those authorized to interpret such norms.[30] For example, constitutional norms such as 'everyone has the right to life'[31] or 'human dignity shall be inviolable'[32] leave open a wide variety of possible interpretations. They ostensibly also require their interpreter to make complex moral judgements.

[28] The notion stems from the work of Alexander Bickel: Alexander Bickel, *The Least Dangerous Branch: The Supreme Court at the Bar of Politics* (2nd edn, Bobbs-Merrill 1986) 16–23.

[29] See in particular Jeremy Waldron, *Law and Disagreement* (Oxford University Press 1999); Jeremy Waldron, 'The Core of the Case Against Judicial Review' (2006) 115 The Yale Law Journal 1346; Richard Bellamy, *Political Constitutionalism: A Republican Defence of the Constitutionality of Democracy* (Cambridge University Press 2007); Mark Tushnet, *Taking the Constitution Away from the Courts* (Princeton University Press 2000).

[30] The problem of indeterminacy is not restricted to constitutional law but may be understood as a general feature of legal norms. For a critical discussion of this debate, see eg Gerald J Postema, *Legal Philosophy in the Twentieth Century: The Common Law World* (Springer 2011) ch 6.

[31] Art 2 of the Charter of Fundamental Rights of the European Union.

[32] Art 1(1) BL for the Federal Republic of Germany (Christian Tomuschat and others, in cooperation with the Language Service of the German Bundestag tr) <www.btg-bestellservice.de/pdf/80201000.pdf> accessed 1 August 2022).

Entrenchment is often considered a key feature of constitutionalism. Constitutions generally fulfil three important functions. First, they constitute the political community as such, by establishing public authority and enabling certain institutions to produce law. Secondly, they divide public authority between different institutions and, in federal states, between different levels of government. Thirdly, they subject public authority to substantive limits, usually and most importantly, in the form of fundamental rights.[33] A common conception of constitutionalism holds that the exercise of political authority should be subject to legal limits, namely those limits enshrined in constitutional law. Entrenchment of constitutional law against ordinary legislative change is meant to ensure that political power is subject to such legal limits, a purpose that would be defeated if those in power could easily change the limits to their rule.[34]

The entrenchment of constitutional norms stands in tension with democracy, however, because it limits the scope for ordinary democratic law-making. This is so especially where the constitution subjects the authority of democratically elected legislatures to constitutional limits. Entrenchment of constitutional law entails that constitutional norms are not subject to political contestation and democratic decision-making in the same way as ordinary legal norms.[35] They subject the decisions of present democratic majorities to a political decision made in the past. This temporal problem raises a democratic concern even if constitutional norms seem determinate in their meaning: even where constitutional norms appear to state clearly how they should be applied in a particular case, they still privilege a past political decision over the potentially different wishes of later elected democratic majorities.[36]

If the constitutional norms are also indeterminate, judicial review entails that judges have the power to make key interpretive choices regarding the meaning of

[33] The three functions obviously overlap. Some authors also identify a fourth function of constitutions, an expressive function, which is the idea that constitutions also express the fundamental values or identity of a particular society. See Leonard FM Besselink and others, *National Constitutional Avenues for Further EU Integration* (Study requested by the European Parliament's Committee on Legal Affairs and Constitutional Affairs Committee of the European Parliament, DG for Internal Policies Study 2014) 9 <www.europarl.europa.eu/RegData/etudes/etudes/join/2014/493046/IPOL-JURI_ET(2014)493046_EN.pdf> accessed 1 August 2022; Maartje de Visser, *Constitutional Review in Europe: A Comparative Analysis* (Hart 2014) 1. On the three functions, see also Jeremy Waldron, 'Constitutionalism: A Skeptical View' in Jeremy Waldron (ed), *Political Political Theory* (Harvard University Press 2016).

[34] On this point, see Wil Waluchow, 'Constitutionalism' in Edward N Zalta (ed), *The Stanford Encyclopedia of Philosophy* (Winter 2012 edition); Jon Elster, 'Introduction' in Jon Elster and Rune Slagstad (eds), *Constitutionalism and Democracy* (Cambridge University Press 1988); Waldron, *Law and Disagreement* (n 29) 221; Bellamy, *Political Constitutionalism* (n 29) 1.

[35] To use Jeremy Waldron's words, constitutional provisions are 'compounded with an immunity against legislative change'. Waldron, *Law and Disagreement* (n 29) 221.

[36] It is unclear whether any legal norm can have such a clear determinate meaning, it is probably only a matter of degree. See eg the work of Ingo Venzke who in the context of international law argues how the meaning of legal norms is the product of interpretive practice: Ingo Venzke, *How Interpretation Makes International Law* (Oxford University Press 2012).

the constitution over and above the interpretive choices of the democratic legislative majority. For example, judges would be authorized to determine whether the protection of human dignity and the right to life are compatible with legislation authorizing abortion,[37] or whether the citizens' right to vote is compatible with legislation that authorizes a transfer of law-making authority to a supranational body.[38]

For these reasons, a key issue is how and whether judicial review can be considered legitimate, given that democratic decision-making is normally essential in making legitimate laws. To justify judicial review, two questions need to be answered. The first is: why is it legitimate to subject the democratic process to constitutional constraints? This question is primarily concerned with the normative relationship between democracy and other values. The second question is: why should courts be authorized to enforce and interpret these constraints rather than the legislature itself or some other institution? This second question is concerned with whether the institution of judicial review provides a better means to achieve the normatively desired outcome—whatever we think this outcome is—in comparison with a system in which this task is left to the legislature itself or perhaps to some other institution. It is primarily a question of comparative institutional analysis that must be rooted in empirical research. Normative arguments concerning the appropriate constraints on political authority do not necessarily entail that judges should enforce these constraints. Even if one accepts a demanding theory of justice that warrants significant constitutional constraints on any decision-making process, it is still necessary to demonstrate why courts and not the legislature itself—or possibly some other institution—are best placed to enforce these constraints. In fact, giving judges the ultimate say in interpreting and enforcing the constitution runs the risk that these constitutional judges may themselves become an unchecked power.[39]

In this book I argue that constitutional democracies face a fundamental difficulty. On the one hand, democratic legitimacy requires that certain preconditions are fulfilled. Not only must there be a democratic procedure in which people have an equal right to participate, but people must also be sufficiently free to begin with, in order to participate as free and equal in this collective decision-making process. The point of constitutionalism may be seen as ensuring these preconditions for democratic legitimacy. On the other hand, it seems impossible to fully determine what these preconditions are in a manner that is both uncontroversial and that removes all reasonable interpretive disagreement. As I argue, the best we can

[37] See eg Bundesverfassungsgericht, judgment of 25 February 1975, 1 BvF 1/74 (*Schwangerschaftsabbruch I*); Bundesverfassungsgericht, judgment of 28 May 1992, 2 BvF 2/90 (*Schwangerschaftsabbruch II*).

[38] As the German constitutional court assessed in Bundesverfassungsgericht, judgment of 12 October 1993, 2 BvR 2134/92 (*Maastricht*) (translation in [1994] 1 CMLR 57) and several subsequent EU-related judgments.

[39] Waldron, 'Constitutionalism: A Skeptical View' (n 33) 41–42. On these points see also Bickel, *The Least Dangerous Branch* (n 28) 3–4.

hope for is that a democratic society ensures ongoing deliberation about the preconditions for a democratically legitimate process. Judicial review may be a better way to ensure such deliberation, instead of leaving constitutional questions to the legislature themselves.[40] Yet, an evaluation of the democratic legitimacy of judicial review must be based on an empirically informed assessment of the comparative abilities of legislatures and constitutional courts.

1.2 National Constitutional Courts and the EU

On the face of it, democratic objections also apply to the role of national constitutional courts in relation to the EU. As guardians of their respective national constitutions, constitutional courts can constrain the leeway of elected politicians to adopt EU law and to take further steps in European integration. Where they hold a new EU Treaty or a piece of secondary EU legislation to be incompatible with the national constitution and declare it inapplicable with their respective national legal order, they override the assessment of the political institutions that chose to adopt these instruments. In the EU context, this democratic concern may be seen as particularly pressing, because the national constitutional courts' judgments have potential repercussions for the course of EU politics as a whole. They can affect citizens throughout the EU, a fact vividly illustrated by the markets' reaction to the GFCC's *ESM* judgment. In this vein, a number of scholars have criticized the EU-related case law of certain national constitutional courts as democratically problematic.[41] Others have stressed the problem that national constitutional review of EU law undermines the uniformity and effectiveness of EU law, and with it, the stability of the EU legal order.[42] More recently, some scholars have also warned about

[40] For support of such a vision see Jan Komárek, 'National Constitutional Courts in the European Constitutional Democracy' (2014) 12 International Journal of Constitutional Law 525.

[41] eg Christoph Schönberger criticized the GFCC's judgment on the Lisbon Treaty because: 'Fundamental decisions on the development of the European integration [*sic*] must be taken by political institutions, not by unaccountable courts, even if they are constitutional ones. Future transfers of powers to the European Union should, therefore, be left to the parliamentary majorities the Court itself cannot praise enough as the main expression of democratic legitimacy.' Christoph Schönberger, 'Lisbon in Karlsruhe: Maastricht's Epigonies at Sea' (2009) 10 German Law Journal 1201, 1210. Christian Tomuschat criticized the Court as not feeling bound by 'any doctrine of judicial self-restraint.' See Christian Tomuschat, 'The Ruling of the German Constitutional Court on the Treaty of Lisbon' (2009) 10 German Law Journal 1259, 1259. See also eg Mayer, 'Rebel Without a Cause?' (n 26); Christoph Möllers, 'Legalität, Legitimität und Legitimation des Bundesverfassungsgerichts' in Matthias Jestaedt and others (eds), *Das entgrenzte Gericht* (Suhrkamp 2011) 281.

[42] Among others, R Daniel Kelemen, 'On the Unsustainability of Constitutional Pluralism' (2016) 23 Maastricht Journal of European and Comparative Law 136; R Daniel Kelemen and others, 'National Courts Cannot Override CJEU Judgments: A Joint Statement in Defense of the EU Legal Order' (*VerfBlog*, 26 May 2020) <https://verfassungsblog.de/national-courts-cannot-override-cjeu-judgments/> accessed 1 August 2022; Joseph HH Weiler, *The Constitution of Europe: 'Do the New Clothes Have an Emperor?' And Other Essays on European Integration* (Cambridge University Press 1999) ch 9; Jürgen Basedow and others, 'European Integration: Quo Vadis? A Critical Commentary on the PSPP Judgment of the German Federal Constitutional Court of May 5, 2020' (2021) 19 International Journal of Constitutional Law 188.

the dangers of abuse by the politically captured constitutional courts of the increasingly authoritarian regimes in Poland and Hungary. These courts have started to invoke constitutional limits to European law in order to ignore unwelcome obligations under EU law and judgments of the CJEU.[43]

Still, a significant body of EU constitutional scholarship puts the national constitutional courts' review of European law in a more positive light. The debate is nuanced, and several authors who argue for the positive potential of national constitutional review of European law have criticized specific rulings by national constitutional courts.[44] Nonetheless, an influential narrative is that the national constitutional courts' EU-related case law can benefit the legitimacy of the EU. Much of this scholarship is also distinctly court-centred. It commonly focuses on conflicts between the CJEU and national constitutional courts without addressing the role of political institutions. It largely leaves aside the tension between democratic legitimacy and the role of constitutional courts. The book instead systematically explores the tension between democratic legitimacy and the role of constitutional courts and enquires whether it is not more democratically legitimate to leave decisions on issues of major constitutional importance for the EU to political institutions.

Within the existing scholarly debate, the GFCC's *Maastricht-Urteil* of 1993 proved to be a catalyst for extensive discussions on the national constitutional courts' role within the EU, as well as about the nature of the EU legal order more generally.[45] In their constitutional assessment of the Treaty of Maastricht, the German judges insisted on several constitutional limitations to European integration, despite ultimately judging the Treaty to be compatible with the German constitution. The Court held that the EU's democratic legitimacy primarily derived from national parliaments, which put in doubt the EU's ability to become fully democratic and rejected the competence of the EU institutions—including the CJEU—to determine the scope of their own competences.

One of the influential ideas that emerged in the wake of the *Maastricht-Urteil* was that of constitutional pluralism.[46] The *Maastricht-Urteil* conflicted with the

[43] R Daniel Kelemen and Laurent Pech, 'The Uses and Abuses of Constitutional Pluralism: Undermining the Rule of Law in the Name of Constitutional Identity in Hungary and Poland' (2019) 21 Cambridge Yearbook of European Legal Studies 59; Federico Fabbrini and András Sajó, 'The Dangers of Constitutional Identity' (2019) 25 European Law Journal 457.

[44] Mattias Kumm, 'Rebel Without a Good Cause: Karlsruhe's Misguided Attempt to Draw the CJEU into a Game of "Chicken" and What the CJEU Might Do About It' (2014) 15 German Law Journal 203; Miguel Maduro, 'Some Preliminary Remarks on the PSPP Decision of the German Constitutional Court' (*Verfassungsblog*, 6 May 2020) <https://verfassungsblog.de> accessed 21 July 2020.

[45] BVerfG, *Maastricht* (n 38). On its reception, seeJulio Baquero Cruz, 'The Legacy of the Maastricht-Urteil and the Pluralist Movement' (2008) 14(4) European Law Journal 389.

[46] The idea of constitutional pluralism is widely seen as connected to the *Maastricht* judgment. See, in this sense, particularly Baquero Cruz, 'The Legacy of the Maastricht-Urteil' (n 45); as well as Matej Avbelj and Jan Komárek, 'Introduction' in Matej Avbelj and Jan Komárek (eds), *Constitutional Pluralism in the European Union and Beyond* (Hart Oxford 2012) 1. It was first pioneered by Neil MacCormick, although primarily as a theory for understanding the nature of the EU legal order, rather than as a normative idea about how the EU legal order should be seen. See Neil MacCormick, 'The

basic principles of the EU legal order articulated by the CJEU: namely that the EU's legal authority derives from the European legal order itself, not from the Member States' constitutions; that EU law takes precedence over conflicting national law, even if of constitutional rank; and that the CJEU is the sole authority competent to assess the validity of EU law.[47] Faced with the GFCC's challenge to the primacy of EU law, constitutional pluralists have argued that the relationship between EU law and national constitutional law should not be understood in the hierarchical terms put forward by the CJEU: EU law should not always have primacy over conflicting national constitutional law.[48] In certain cases, national constitutional courts would be justified in reviewing EU law on constitutional grounds.

The national constitutional courts' review of European law has been justified on several related grounds. One idea is that the national constitutional courts' review can help ensure respect for the national constitutional identities of the Member States, understood as basic constitutional norms specific to a Member State.[49] Relatedly, some have argued that the constitutional courts can function as a check on the EU's powers, guarding against the concentration of public power at the EU level and ensuring adequate control.[50] In addition, some scholars contend that the possibility of constitutional conflict opens a space for contestation and dialogue in which the respective constitutional claims of the EU and the Member States can be addressed. This would allow the EU legal order to better accommodate a diversity

Maastricht-Urteil: Sovereignty Now' (1995) 1 European Law Journal 259; Neil MacCormick, 'Beyond the Sovereign State' (1993) 56 Modern Law Review 1. A further influential statement on constitutional pluralism is Neil Walker, 'The Idea of Constitutional Pluralism' (2002) 65 The Modern Law Review 317. On the influence of constitutional pluralism Joseph HH Weiler noted in 2012: 'Constitutional Pluralism is today the only party membership card which will guarantee a seat at the high tables of the public law professoriate.' Joseph HH Weiler, 'Prologue: Global and Pluralist Constitutionalism—Some Doubts' in Gráinne de Búrca and JHH Weiler (eds), *The Worlds of European Constitutionalism* (Cambridge University Press 2012) 8. Martin Loughlin stated in a similar fashion: 'Since 2002, the concept of constitutional pluralism has been actively promoted, invariably with a positive inflection, and it now seems to have achieved the status of a school, perhaps even a sect.' Martin Loughlin, 'Constitutional Pluralism: An Oxymoron?' (2014) 3 Global Constitutionalism 9, 22.

[47] Case 26/62 *NV Algemene Transporten Expeditie Onderneming van Gend en Loos v Nederlandse Administratie der Belastingen* [1963] ECR 3; Case 6/64 *Flaminio Costa v ENEL* [1964] ECR 585; Case 11/70 *Internationale Handelsgesellschaft mbH v Einfuhr- und Vorratsstelle für Getreide und Futtermittel* [1970] ECR 01125; Case C–314/85 *Foto-Frost v Hauptzollamt Lübeck-Ost* [1987] ECR 4199; Case C–399/11 *Stefano Melloni v Ministerio Fiscal* [2013] EU:C:2013:107; Court of Justice of the European Union Press Release 58/20, Press release following the judgment of the German Constitutional Court of 5 May 2020 (8 May 2020).

[48] See the works of MacCormick and Walker referred to in n 46. A more recent restatement is Neil Walker, 'Constitutional Pluralism Revisited' (2016) 22 European Law Journal 333.

[49] Armin Von Bogdandy and Stephan Schill, 'Overcoming Absolute Primacy: Respect for National Identity under the Lisbon Treaty' (2011) 48 Common Market Law Review 1417.

[50] Miguel Poiares Maduro, 'Contrapunctual Law: Europe's Constitutional Pluralism in Action' in Neil Walker (ed), *Sovereignty in Transition* (Hart Publishing 2003) 522–23; Miguel Poiares Maduro, 'Europe and the Constitution: What If This Is as Good as It Gets?' in Joseph HH Weiler and Marlene Wind (eds), *European Constitutionalism Beyond the State* (Cambridge University Press 2003) 74; Bogdandy and Schill, 'Overcoming Absolute Primacy' (n 49) 1452–53; Henry G Schermers, 'The Scales in Balance: National Constitutional Court v. Court of Justice' [1990] Common Market Law Review 97.

of reasonable constitutional viewpoints.[51] Yet another idea is that the national constitutional courts' EU-related case law is justified on democratic grounds.[52] In this respect, scholars have argued that the national constitutional courts' review is a justified response to pressing concerns about the democratic quality of the EU's decision-making process.

One such democratic justification is that constitutional courts protect the achievement of democracy in the nation-state. The courts check whether the EU's exercise of authority remains within the scope of its transferred competences and prevent the further transfer of too many powers to the EU. In this manner, they avoid the erosion of state authority and ensure that the nation-states remain the key source of legitimation for the EU. This in turn is said to be necessary, because the social preconditions of democracy have not been realized at the EU level: namely a sufficient sense of shared identity or a European-wide public sphere that allows meaningful political communication between citizens beyond borders.[53] Prior to Brexit, similar ideas had even found their way into political debate in the United Kingdom, despite the fact that UK courts traditionally have limited powers in reviewing legislation. Still, the UK government proposed bestowing on a UK court the power to review EU law similar to the GFCC's, in order to protect the sovereignty of the UK parliament.[54]

A related idea is that the national constitutional courts can refuse the application of EU law for democratic reasons if EU law conflicts with a national constitutional provision that is 'sufficiently clear and specific, and reflects a national commitment to something constitutionally essential'.[55] Another argument is that

[51] For such views, see Matej Avbelj, 'Constitutional Pluralism and Authoritarianism' (2020) 21 German Law Journal 1023; Marta Cartabia, 'Europe and Rights: Taking Dialogue Seriously' [2009] European Constitutional Law Review 5; Gareth Davies, 'Brexit and the Free Movement of Workers: A Plea for National Legal Assertiveness' (2016) 41 European Law Review 925; Tom Flynn, 'Constitutional Pluralism and Loyal Opposition' (2021) 19 International Journal of Constitutional Law 241; Nico Krisch, *Beyond Constitutionalism: The Pluralist Structure of Postnational Law* (Oxford University Press 2010); Maduro, 'Contrapunctual Law' (n 50); Aida Torres Pérez, *Conflicts of Rights in the European Union, A Theory of Supranational Adjudication* (Oxford University Press 2009); Andreas Voßkuhle, 'Multilevel Cooperation of the European Constitutional Courts: Der Europäische Verfassungsgerichtsverbund' (2010) 6 European Constitutional Law Review 175. In a more agonistic sense, based on Chantal Mouffe, Giuseppe Martinico has argued that 'constitutional conflicts are functional to the transformation of EU law'. Giuseppe Martinico, 'The 'Polemical' Spirit of European Constitutional Law: On the Importance of Conflicts in EU Law' (2015) 16(6) German Law Journal 1343, 1356.

[52] In a more general sense, see Komárek, 'National Constitutional Courts' (n 40) 525.

[53] In this direction, see Dieter Grimm, 'The Role of National Constitutional Courts in European Democracy' in Dieter Grimm (ed), *The Constitution of European Democracy* (Oxford University Press 2017)>; Peter Lindseth, *Power and Legitimacy: Reconciling Europe and the Nation-State* (Oxford University Press 2010) 133–87; Paul Kirchhof, 'Deutsches Verfassungsrecht und Europäisches Gemeinschaftsrecht' [1991] Europarecht-Beiheft 1 11; Sven Simon and Hannes Rathke, '"Simply Not Comprehensible." Why?' (2020) 21 German Law Journal 950.

[54] On this issue, see Jeff King, 'On the Proposal for a UK Constitutional Court' (*UK Constitutional Law Blog*, 8 February 2016) <https://ukconstitutionallaw.org/> accessed 1 August 2022; Mike Gordon, 'The UK's Sovereignty Uncertainty' (*UK Constitutional Law Blog*, 11 February 2016) <https://ukconstitutionallaw.org/> accessed 1 August 2022.

[55] Mattias Kumm, 'The Jurisprudence of Constitutional Conflict: Constitutional Supremacy in Europe before and after the Constitutional Treaty' (2005) 11 European Law Journal 262; Mattias

the constitutional courts' review functions as a catalyst for, or as an alternative to, public debate.[56] In yet another sense, some scholars contend that the national constitutional courts pressure the EU to become more democratic, for example by enhancing the transparency of the EU's decision-making processes and ensuring better participation of national parliaments in EU affairs.[57]

Still missing in these justifications of the national constitutional courts' role, however, is a systematic exploration of the democratic concerns that the courts' review raises and of the courts' legitimacy compared to that of political institutions in deciding issues of constitutional importance for the EU. The lack of attention to this issue is understandable in light of the EU's historical development. For a long time, a main issue for scholars has been to explain and justify the primacy of EU law over conflicting national law, this primacy being a remarkable development in itself.[58] The idea of constitutional pluralism can be understood as a third way between the absolute primacy of EU law over national law and its wholesale rejection. EU legal primacy could be accepted to a large extent, but in light of the EU's democratic legitimacy problems, EU law could not justify setting aside cherished principles of national constitutional law.[59] In addition, the extent to which the CJEU's doctrine of primacy empowered the ordinary judiciary at the expense of national legislatures may have pushed democratic concerns about the role of national constitutional courts to the background. The CJEU's *Simmenthal* judgment required all national courts to review national legislation on its compatibility with EU law and this requirement applied also to Member States where courts had little or no powers to engage in judicial review of legislation, as well as to Member States that

Kumm and Victor Ferreres Comella, 'The Primacy Clause of the Constitutional Treaty and the Future of Constitutional Conflict in the European Union' (2005) 3 International Journal of Constitutional Law 473; Mattias Kumm, 'The Moral Point of Constitutional Pluralism' in Julie Dickson and Pavlos Eleftheriadis (eds), *Philosophical Foundations of European Union Law* (Oxford University Press 2012); Mattias Kumm, 'Rethinking Constitutional Authority: On the Structure and Limits of Constitutional Pluralism' in Matej Avbelj and Jan Komárek (eds), *Constitutional Pluralism in the European Union and Beyond* (Hart Publishing 2012).

[56] Matthias Herdegen, 'Maastricht and the German Constitutional Court—Constitutional Restraints for an Ever Closer Union' (1994) 31 Common Market Law Review 235, 249. Mattias Kumm also suggests that the national constitutional courts have acted 'as contributors to and facilitators of democratic deliberations in their respective political orders'. Kumm, 'The Jurisprudence of Constitutional Conflict' (n 55) 292.

[57] Eyal Benvenisti and George W Downs, 'The Democratizing Effects of Transjudicial Coordination' (2012) 8 Utrecht Law Review 158.

[58] Joseph HH Weiler, 'Van Gend En Loos: The Individual as Subject and Object and the Dilemma of European Legitimacy' (2014) 12 International Journal of Constitutional Law 94; Morten Rasmussen, 'Revolutionizing European Law: A History of the Van Gend En Loos Judgment' (2014) 12 International Journal of Constitutional Law 136.

[59] This strategy of justification is most explicit in the work of Mattias Kumm, see the references in n 55. The title of the piece by Bogdandy and Schill, 'Overcoming Absolute Primacy' (n 49) hints at the same strategy.

reserved the function of judicial review of legislation for a specialized constitutional court.[60]

Yet, the national constitutional courts' role in relation to the EU may be seen as democratically problematic itself. Where a constitutional court holds a provision of EU law inapplicable within its national legal order, it subjects the EU legislature to a constitutional constraint. Similarly, where a constitutional court objects to the ratification of a new EU Treaty on constitutional grounds, it subjects the decision-making of both the Treaty drafters and the national legislature to a constitutional check. And no matter how undemocratic one thinks the EU is, its democratic shortcomings do not make the national constitutional courts any more democratic. Even despite a perceived democratic deficit of the EU's decision-making process, it is not obvious that judges should play a fundamental role in determining the core constitutional principles of the EU legal order. Granting this role to the national courts may simply entail that the authority to shape EU constitutional law shifts from an imperfect political process at the EU level to an even more democratically troublesome game of constitutional courts.

Thus, rather than simply asserting that national constitutional identities should be respected, one must also address who should determine what respect for national constitutional identity entails. Rather than only valuing dialogues about the EU's constitutional foundations, one must also ask who should do the talking. And in light of democratic concerns about the role of constitutional courts, one must wonder whether one can really expect these courts to facilitate democratic deliberation or strengthen the democratic quality of the EU's decision-making process, without constraining political discussion over the most desirable institutional architecture for the EU and its further development.

2. The Project of This Book

This book takes up democratic concerns about the role of constitutional courts and their comparative institutional legitimacy to assess these courts' role in relation to the EU. In light of democratic concerns about the institutional position of these courts, the question arises of whether national constitutional courts should not leave constitutional questions concerning the EU to political institutions.

The book's central question is thus how the democratic legitimacy of the national constitutional courts' review of European law should be assessed. By addressing this problem, the book aims to move beyond the existing scholarship in

60 Case 106/77 Simmenthal [1978] ECR 629; Monica Claes, 'The National Courts' Mandate in the European Constitution' (PhD thesis, Maastricht University 2004) 61–101. At the time, this was of course still Community law. See also Jan Komárek, 'The Place of Constitutional Courts in the EU' (2013) 9 European Constitutional Law Review 420.

three ways. First, and as already discussed, it brings democratic concerns about the role of constitutional courts to the fore in assessing their legitimate role in relation to the EU. The book systematically explores this problem by bringing the rich insights on democratic concerns about judicial review from the domestic context to shed light on the role of the constitutional courts in relation to the EU.

Secondly, through its focus on the transnational context of the EU, the book aims to contribute to the understanding of the democratically legitimate role of constitutional courts in a changing legal context. Most theoretical scholarship on the legitimacy of judicial review has been developed within the framework of a single nation-state.[61] It does not address a situation where law-making competences are transferred to a supranational entity. In addition, such scholarship is based on the assumption that a democratic procedure is firmly established, something still controversial in the EU.[62] This book furthers our understanding about how democratic considerations inform the normative assessment of the constitutional courts' role in a transnational context, where public authority is transferred to a supranational organization that is considered to suffer from various democratic legitimacy problems.

Thirdly, the book contributes to a more empirically informed understanding of the constitutional courts' role in relation to political institutions. Although the case law of national constitutional courts has sparked a significant body of scholarship, little is known about the impact of the constitutional courts' judgments on EU-related politics.[63] As I argue, insights into this impact allow for a better understanding of the democratic legitimacy of the national constitutional courts' review of European law. The book offers such insights through a detailed case study of the GFCC's role in relation to the EU. This analysis is integrated within the overall argument of the book, as it tests the arguments and assumptions in the theoretical debate on the legitimacy of judicial review. In this way, the book offers a unique combination of theoretical analysis and a detailed case study of Europe's most influential and authoritative constitutional court.

For the purposes of this work, the notion 'national constitutional court' is understood in a broad sense: it refers to all EU Member States' highest courts that have the competence to constitutionally review legislation. This definition captures both specialized constitutional courts in which the function of constitutional

[61] See eg the seminal works of Ronald Dworkin, *Taking Rights Seriously* (Duckworth 1977); Ronald Dworkin, 'The Forum of Principle' (1981) 56 New York University Law Review 469; Christopher F Zurn, *Deliberative Democracy and the Institutions of Judicial Review* (Cambridge University Press 2007); Waldron, 'The Core of the Case Against Judicial Review' (n 29); Bellamy, *Political Constitutionalism* (n 29).

[62] See eg the conditions in Waldron, 'The Core of the Case Against Judicial Review' (n 29).

[63] Bill Davies has made an important contribution in this respect, by offering an analysis of the reception of EU law within Germany and the GFCC's resistance during the period 1949–79. Bill Davies, *Resisting the European Court of Justice. West Germany's Confrontation with European Law, 1949–1979* (Cambridge University Press 2012).

review is concentrated and national highest courts with a wider jurisdiction. The term European law is used as a broad notion that includes EU-related legal instruments that strictly fall outside the scope of the EU Treaties but nonetheless clearly concern the EU. Particularly during the euro crisis, EU Member States adopted a number of legal instruments and treaties which lie outside the EU legal framework.[64] Examples are the ESM and the TSCG. In addition, in this book the term European law also refers to European Treaties before their formal entry into force. For example, the review of the Maastricht and Lisbon Treaties by the GFCC counts as the review of European law, even though the Treaties had not entered into force at the time of review. The term EU law is used more narrowly, namely to refer to the primary and secondary EU law in force that falls within the scope of the EU Treaty framework.

The book focuses on judicial review of legislative action. I consider the legitimacy of the national constitutional courts' review of European law and consider review of EU Treaties, EU-related treaties, and similar instruments that require ratification, as well as EU primary law and secondary legislation after ratification. Although many interesting questions can be raised about judicial review of executive action, I treat these mostly as outside the scope of this research. That said, I do take into account that the executive dominates the EU political process and address how this affects the legitimacy of the national constitutional courts' review. Furthermore, I also consider the role of the CJEU in the interpretation of EU law and address whether the national constitutional courts' review may be considered as a response to the CJEU's expansive case law. A final exception is that Chapter 7 does discuss judicial review of the ECB's actions in quite some detail. The reason is that the GFCC's *PSPP* ruling is a crucial part of the German Court's EU-related case law and the story of this book, while an appreciation of that case is incomplete without close consideration of the ECB's actions and the role of judicial review.

The range of this book restricts the argument to constitutional courts that are independent and operate in reasonably well-functioning Member State democracies. I take the analysis of this book to apply to such constitutional courts. The position of some politically captured courts that operate in Member States where a process of democratic and constitutional backsliding has taken place is treated as a special case largely outside the scope of this research.[65]

[64] Case C–370/12 *Thomas Pringle v Government of Ireland* [2012] EU:C:2012:756. On this issue, see Bruno de Witte, 'Using International Law in the Euro Crisis' (2013) ARENA Working Paper <www.arena.uio.no> accessed 1 August 2022. Some of the instruments are not even treaties under public international law. For example, the European Financial Stability Facility was registered as a company under Luxembourg law. The founding Member States concluded a framework agreement regarding its use but that was not a treaty as such.

[65] See, on these developments, eg Wojciech Sadurski, *Poland's Constitutional Breakdown* (Oxford University Press 2019); Stanislaw Biernat, 'How Far Is It from Warsaw to Luxembourg and Karlsruhe: The Impact of the PSPP Judgment on Poland' (2020) 21 German Law Journal 1104; Gábor Halmai, 'Abuse of Constitutional Identity. The Hungarian Constitutional Court on Interpretation of Article E) (2) of the Fundamental Law' (2018) 43 Review of Central and East European Law 23.

In assessing the democratic legitimacy of the national constitutional courts' review of European law, the book has three main objectives. As the first and primary aim, the book strives to better understand these courts' legitimate role in relation to the EU in a way that takes into account concerns about the democratic legitimacy of these courts. Shedding light on this aspect of the courts' institutional position allows one to see existing scholarship on the role of these courts in a new light. In this respect, the book departs from, and offers a fresh criticism of, constitutional pluralism. Pluralists tend to applaud the contestation and supposed dialogue that result from national judicial resistance to European law. The book shows how pluralists have insufficiently considered that the national constitutional courts' review can limit legitimate political disagreement on constitutional questions and distort political debate, whereas political institutions are often better placed to legitimately address such constitutional disagreements.

Secondly, by offering a normative assessment of the national constitutional courts' role, the book aims to contribute to accounts of how national constitutional courts should use their review powers when they deal with European law.

Thirdly, the book aims to inform ideas for institutional design. Particularly for Member States without strong judicial institutions for constitutional review, this work aims to help understand whether setting up such institutions can contribute to enhancing the legitimacy of the EU legal order and in what manner such institutions should be designed.[66] For Member States with strong constitutional courts, the book aims to help understand whether these institutions should change, or how other institutions may better respond to the courts' rulings in accordance with the demands of democratic legitimacy.

3. Outline of the Argument and Approach

The book's main argument is that the national constitutional courts' review of European law frequently risks constraining and narrowing democratic debate over the EU's constitutional underpinnings. The national constitutional courts

[66] In the Netherlands, for example, there is ongoing discussion about the introduction of judicial review on the basis of the constitution. See in particular the legislative proposal to this effect: *Kamerstukken II*, 2001–2002, 28 331, nr 2 (legislative proposal by MP Halsema); *Kamerstukken II*, 2001–2002, 28 331, nr 3 (Explanatory memorandum—legislative proposal by MP Halsema). The most recent development is that the Dutch government is now also in favour of judicial constitutional review, see the Letter of the Dutch Minister of the Interior and Kingdom Relations and the Minister for Legal Protection of 1 July 2022, 2022–0000321093 <www.rijksoverheid.nl/documenten/kamerstukken/2022/07/01/kamerbrief-over-hoofdlijnen-constitutionele-toetsing> accessed 2 August 2022. Occasionally, it is argued that judicial review should be introduced to allow judicial review of European law. See eg Frits Bakker and Kees Sterk, 'Laat Rechters de Grondrechten van Burgers Beschermen' *NRC Next* (7 March 2014) <www.nrc.nl/nieuws/2014/03/07/laat-rechters-de-grondrechten-van-burgers-bescherm-1353312-a40579> accessed 1 August 2022; Wetenschappelijke Raad voor het Regeringsbeleid, *Europa in Nederland* (Amsterdam University Press 2007).

risk taking sides in good faith political disagreements among elected legislators about constitutional questions relating to the EU, thus distorting, rather than protecting, the democratic decision-making process. Their review threatens to take essential decisions about the EU's future out of the hands of democratically elected bodies and makes judges the final arbiters of these issues in a manner that is difficult to justify in democratic terms. In this respect, the book challenges the body of scholarship that puts the national constitutional courts' review in a more positive light. Instead, national constitutional courts should adopt less intrusive forms of review. In this respect, the book highlights how the GFCC's review has helped to strengthen parliamentary oversight of EU decision-making, although other aspects of that Court's review raise serious democratic concerns.

My argument consists of four stages. The first stage is presented in Chapter 2, which critically discusses the ongoing debate about the democratic legitimacy of judicial review within the national context. This discussion considers key arguments for and against judicial review and forms the backdrop for understanding the role of constitutional courts in relation to the EU. I argue that democracy offers the best way to legitimize binding law where democracy is understood as a political procedure based on deliberation and equal political participation. This leads me to reject the view of legal constitutionalists. Legal constitutionalists justify constitutional constraints on democratic decision-making in the form of fundamental rights as necessary moral side-constraints that no democratic decision can legitimately violate. In this view, constitutional judges are better placed to protect rights than potentially oppressive democratic majorities.[67] The difficulty with this approach is that both the justification to give certain rights special constitutional protection and the proper interpretation of these rights are subject to reasonable disagreement. Reasonable people can disagree about which rights should be protected as fundamental rights, how different rights relate to each other, how they should be balanced in terms of conflict, and how they should be balanced against other considerations. Even where people agree in the abstract that certain rights merit special protection, they are still likely to disagree about their proper interpretation.

This problem has led political constitutionalists to reject judicial review in favour of majoritarian democracy. Political constitutionalists, such as Jeremy Waldron, Mark Tushnet, and Richard Bellamy, argue that rights and justice are subject to reasonable disagreement and consequently require justification in a decision-making process to which all citizens can contribute on the basis of political equality.[68] This

67 I take Ronald Dworkin and John Rawls as important proponents of this approach, see Dworkin, *Taking Rights Seriously* (n 61) 131–49; Ronald Dworkin, *A Matter of Principle* (Harvard University Press 1985) 9–70; Ronald Dworkin, *Freedom's Law: The Moral Reading of the American Constitution* (Oxford University Press 1996); John Rawls, *Political Liberalism* (Columbia University Press 2005).

68 See eg Bellamy, *Political Constitutionalism* (n 29); Waldron, 'The Core of the Case Against Judicial Review' (n 29); Jeremy Waldron, 'A Right-Based Critique of Constitutional Rights' (1993) 13 Oxford Journal of Legal Studies 18; Tushnet, *Taking the Constitution Away* (n 29). The idea is also reflected

is precisely what the democratic process aims to achieve, whereas judicial review allows judges to decide contested moral issues and override reasonable democratic majorities. In this respect, political constitutionalists criticize how legal and political philosophers often paint a degraded picture of legislative practice and an idealized picture of adjudication in order to defend judicial review.[69] Instead, political constitutionalists portray the democratic process as one in which the people's representatives deliberate in good faith on the common good. Courts are no better placed than legislatures to decide on fundamental rights, while legislative decision-making is much more democratic than judicial decision-making.

Other scholars, such as Jürgen Habermas and John Hart Ely, have sought to justify judicial review in democratic terms.[70] Here, the argument is that judicial review is not undemocratic after all, because it aims to protect the preconditions of a legitimate democratic process. This justification for judicial review would supposedly solve the problem that democratically unaccountable judges decide contested moral issues. Instead, courts would merely guarantee that such issues could be decided democratically. The challenge to this position is, nonetheless, that the preconditions for a legitimate democratic process are also subject to reasonable disagreement.

My argument in this book builds on an analysis of these different positions and follows Habermas' idea of the co-originality of public and private autonomy: democracy presupposes not just the protection of political rights such as the right to vote, freedom of expression, and freedom of assembly, but also the protection of liberal rights. Citizens can only meaningfully exercise their public autonomy and consider themselves authors of the law where they have a sufficient degree of freedom. On this understanding, a constitution institutionalizes the preconditions for legitimate democratic will-formation, both by setting up a democratic procedure and protecting liberal rights. A key problem, nonetheless, is that it seems impossible to fully articulate these preconditions in the abstract, outside the democratic process, because they leave open a wide variety of different reasonable interpretations. Given reasonable disagreements about the form and content of these preconditions, the constitution itself must also be the object of political debate.

in Habermas' theory of deliberative democracy: Jürgen Habermas, *Between Facts and Norms* (Polity Press 1996).

[69] This is a prominent theme also in Jeremy Waldron, *The Dignity of Legislation* (Cambridge University Press 1999). In that book, however, Waldron puts forward a picture of legislation that is explicitly idealized. At page 2, he states: 'I want us to see the process of legislation—at its best—as something like the following: the representatives of the community come together to settle solemnly and explicitly on common schemes and measures that can stand in the name of them all, and they do so in a way that openly acknowledges and respects (rather than conceals) the inevitable differences of opinion and principle among them.'

[70] John Hart Ely, *Democracy and Distrust: A Theory of Judicial Review* (Harvard University Press 1980); Zurn, *Deliberative Democracy* (n 61).

Habermas' co-originality thesis entails that the preconditions for democratic legitimacy must themselves be subject to ongoing political deliberation.

The justification for judicial review, therefore, cannot be that a constitutional court simply safeguards the preconditions for a legitimate democratic process, as these preconditions must themselves be part of democratic politics. Rather the justification must be that judicial review better ensures that deliberation takes place on the preconditions for a democratically legitimate procedure compared to a political system where this task is left to the legislature itself.

I argue that this leaves two main routes to justify judicial review of legislation. The first proceeds through a comparison of the actual deliberations of legislatures and constitutional courts. In this respect, it could be argued that just as the proponents of judicial review have been criticized for idealizing the role of courts, so too critics of judicial review have idealized the democratic process. If actual legislative debates rarely engage constitutional questions, one may prefer the deliberations of the courtrooms to the irrationality of the democratic process. For these reasons, I argue that the debate over judicial review should pay more attention to how legislatures and constitutional courts function in practice and in specific contexts, rather than trying to assess the democratic legitimacy of judicial review as a question of political philosophy. Such enquiries should assess how legislatures address constitutional issues, how legislatures' deliberations compare with the decisions and reasoning of courts, and how courts' review of legislation influences subsequent legislative deliberations. The outcomes of such analyses are likely to be context dependent. Assessments of the legitimacy of judicial review are likely to change over time, country, and context.[71]

A second route to justifying judicial review is to argue that judicial review should take a minimal or weaker form. Prodded by the fierce attacks of political constitutionalists on judicial review, a number of authors argue that proportionality review is still legitimate in ensuring the reasonableness of the democratic process. Proponents of this view thus accept reasonable disagreement about rights but claim that proportionality review ensures that democratic justifications remain reasonable and hence legitimate.[72] Another idea is weak-form judicial review, a form of judicial review where courts are competent to question the constitutionality of

[71] eg in Germany, Ulrich Haltern has argued that the constitutional distribution of powers is outdated and no longer fits its now mature democracy. Ulrich R Haltern, 'High Time for a Check-up: Progressivism, Populism and Constitutional Review in Germany' (1996) No 4/96 Jean Monnet Working Papers <https://jeanmonnetprogram.org/archive/papers/96/9605ind.html>, accessed 1 August 2022.

[72] Mattias Kumm, 'Institutionalising Socratic Contestation: The Rationalist Human Rights Paradigm, Legitimate Authority and the Point of Judicial Review' (2007) 1 European Journal of Legal Studies 1; Eoin Daly, 'Republicanizing Rights?: Proportionality, Justification, and Non-Domination' in Ester Herlin-Karnell, Matthias Klatt, and Héctor A Morales Zúñiga (eds), *Constitutionalism Justified: Rainer Forst in Discourse* (Oxford University Press 2019); Tom Hickey, 'The Republican Core of the Case for Judicial Review' (2019) 17 International Journal of Constitutional Law 288; Kai Möller, *The Global Model of Constitutional Rights* (Oxford University Press 2012).

legislation but leave the final decision to legislatures. Weak-form review is accepted by political constitutionalists because it is not subject to the main democratic objections that stronger forms of judicial review face. Instead, weak-form review allows ongoing discourse between courts and legislatures about the constitution, can help address unintended or unanticipated constitutional problems of legislation, and gives citizens the ability to contest legislation before independent courts on constitutional grounds. Nonetheless, the argument for weak-form review still assumes that legislatures will seriously consider constitutional questions.[73]

The second stage of this book's development is presented in Chapter 3. This chapter investigates the implications of the arguments developed in Chapter 2, for the context of the EU through a discussion of the EU-related case law of national constitutional courts. As in the national context, the national constitutional courts' review of European law raises a democratic concern, because it subjects political decision-making to constitutional constraints. Yet, the assessment of the democratically legitimate role of the national constitutional courts in relation to the EU has to take into account specific features of the EU context. One is that the EU is said to suffer from various democratic legitimacy problems. According to some, this justifies that national constitutional courts review European law with the aim of correcting the EU's democratic shortcomings. Another is that the institutional setting in which the constitutional courts' review takes place differs considerably from that of the domestic context. Within the EU context, political institutions at different levels of governance may be involved in law-making, depending on the specific European legal instrument under review.

Chapter 3 addresses the significance of these factors for the democratically legitimate role of the national constitutional courts in relation to the EU. The idea that national constitutional courts should aim to correct the EU's democratic shortcomings runs into a problem analogous to that within the national context: there is reasonable disagreement about what democracy means in relation to the EU. For example, one central bone of contention is whether the EU should be understood as an association of sovereign democratic states in which democratic legitimacy derives primarily from the nation-states, or that the EU should turn into a Europe-wide democracy itself, where democratized EU institutions carry the main burden of legitimation.[74] Such disagreement about how democratic principles are best realized within the EU complicates the idea that national constitutional courts should address the democratic shortcomings of the EU. Review by national

[73] Richard Bellamy, 'Democracy as Public Law: The Case of Constitutional Rights' (2013) 14 German Law Journal 1017.

[74] See, for different positions, eg Richard Bellamy, 'A European Republic of Sovereign States: Sovereignty, Republicanism and the European Union' (2017) 16 European Journal of Political Theory 188; Andreas Føllesdal and Simon Hix, 'Why There Is a Democratic Deficit in the EU: A Response to Majone and Moravscik' (2006) 44 Journal of Common Market Studies 533; Jürgen Habermas, 'Democracy in Europe: Why the Development of the EU into a Transnational Democracy Is Necessary and How It Is Possible' (2015) 21 European Law Journal 546.

constitutional courts risks constraining legitimate political debate over how democracy is best realized within the EU. A legitimate role for the national courts in this respect would hence be limited and be focused on aspects of the EU's democratic legitimacy problems that are beyond reasonable disagreement.

A different way to justify the national constitutional courts' review of European law is to claim that it ensures careful deliberation of the constitutional issues raised by European integration, a task that political institutions supposedly do not adequately fulfil themselves. The courts' role could be justified in this way where they catalyse deliberation outside the courts, or because they provide a superior forum for deliberation on constitutional questions compared to the political branches of government. This argument is analogous to the argument for judicial review in the domestic context developed in Chapter 2. Within the EU context, this justification could gain further strength from the democratic legitimacy problems of the EU's decision-making process. These problems arguably reduce the capability of the political institutions involved in making European law to deliberate on its constitutional implications. Yet to assess this justification for the role of national constitutional courts in the EU context, it is again crucial to understand the comparative institutional setting. This requires an assessment of how political institutions address constitutional issues within the EU context, of how these deliberations compare to the judgments of the national constitutional courts, and of how these courts' rulings impact on the deliberations and decision-making of political institutions. In relation to the main grounds on which national constitutional courts have reviewed European law, Chapter 3 discusses whether and how such review raises democratic concerns, and how a fuller understanding of the comparative institutional setting should allow for a better assessment of the legitimate role of these courts.

As the third stage, the book takes up these issues of comparative institutional legitimacy in a qualitative case study of the GFCC around three key constitutional episodes: the adoption and ratification process of the Maastricht Treaty, the euro crisis, and the Covid-19 crisis, including the aftermath of the *PSPP* ruling. This case study sets out to test the arguments raised in the theoretical debate in actual constitutional and political practice. The German Court was selected as a central case study because it is Europe's most authoritative constitutional court and the protagonist in most discussions on the role of the national constitutional courts in relation to the EU. The GFCC has the most elaborate and sophisticated line of case law on the EU, which has a significant influence on other Member States' constitutional courts and plays a central role in the academic debate.[75] The case study

[75] See eg Niels Petersen and Konstantin Chatziathanasiou, *Primacy's Twilight?* (European Parliament 2021) PE 692.276 <www.europarl.europa.eu/thinktank/en/document/IPOL_STU(2021)692276> accessed 1 August 2022; Luke Dimitrios Spieker, 'Framing and Managing Constitutional Identity Conflicts: How to Stabilize the Modus Vivendi between the Court of Justice and National Constitutional Courts' [2020] Common Market Law Review 361.

is to a large extent based on an extensive analysis of parliamentary debates; EU policy documents; and twenty-six interviews with politicians, civil servants, legal representatives in relevant cases before the GFCC, as well as constitutional court judges. The in-depth study of the GFCC allowed for research into extensive parliamentary debates and policy documents, a close consideration of different political arguments, and a good understanding of context, as well as a study of the GFCC's role over time. Naturally, the focus on the GFCC limits the overall generalizability of the findings. The case study does not exhaust the possible range of institutional settings in which national constitutional review can take place or all the grounds on the basis of which such review occurs, an issue taken into account in the overall conclusions.

The main finding from the case study is that the GFCC's review restricts the room for legitimate political disagreement regarding European integration in a way that is difficult to justify democratically. Chapter 4 starts with the GFCC's review of the Maastricht Treaty, which formed the basis for the Court's subsequent approach to European integration. The *Maastricht-Urteil* introduced *ultra vires* review and elaborately assessed the democratic credentials of the EU against a sovereigntist interpretation of democracy. The case has been a source of inspiration for constitutional courts beyond Germany and is of key importance in the academic debate on the role of national constitutional courts and the EU's constitutional architecture more generally.[76] One justification for the GFCC's judgment is that, despite all its shortcomings, the Court still discussed the constitutional implications of the Treaty and raised issues that political institutions had failed to consider. The chapter shows that this argument is difficult to sustain. The constitutional implications of this Treaty and its democratic deficiencies in particular, were amply discussed in the Treaty negotiations and the German ratification debates.

Instead, I argue, somewhat provocatively, that in this setting the GFCC's role is better understood as judicial Euroscepticism. The Court provided an additional forum for those critical of European integration to voice their concerns. In contrast to the German parliament, the GFCC opted for a national interpretation of the principle of democracy and identified several constitutional limitations to further European integration. By reviewing the Maastricht Treaty in this way, the Court may have contributed to further public debate on European integration, because there was little opposition to European integration as such within Germany's political institutions. The GFCC allowed for a more critical viewpoint, both by providing access to the Court as well as incorporating Euro-critical elements in its own judgment. In this manner, the court proceedings did lead to the consideration of some new issues, whereas the Court's judgment was still sufficiently open so

[76] The *Maastricht-Urteil* is generally seen as having provided the starting point for ideas of constitutional pluralism; see eg Cruz, 'The Legacy of the Maastricht-Urteil' (n 45); Avbelj and Komárek, 'Introduction' (n 46).

as not to constrain decision-making within the political branches. Furthermore, in the aftermath of the *Maastricht* judgment, the GFCC adopted a more Euro-friendly stance.

In the long term, the outlook has proved to be more troublesome, as discussed in Chapter 5's consideration of the euro crisis. In 2009, the GFCC returned to the main tenets of the *Maastricht-Urteil* with a ruling on the Lisbon Treaty that appeared even more restrictive for further European integration. During the euro crisis, the German Court subsequently reviewed several legal instruments in relatively quick succession. Yet, within this context the GFCC did constrain decision-making within the political branches. The Court's rulings reinforced and reified a particular type of politics. A politics in which budgetary discipline and the retention of German budgetary sovereignty is of overriding importance; in which financial assistance is given only under strict conditions; and in which the transference of more competences to the EU in economic and fiscal policy is cast as undemocratic, even if pleas for such transfers are rooted in democratic grounds.

Chapter 6, nonetheless, considers a more positive side of the GFCC's case law and discusses how the GFCC helped to ensure better parliamentary oversight of the executive operating in EU affairs. Through its insistence on strong information and participation rights in EU affairs for the German parliament, the GFCC helped counter a move in the crisis towards executive dominance and aided the safeguarding of space for democratic politics.

Chapter 7 discusses the *PSPP* judgment of 5 May 2020 and its repercussions in the broader context of the EU's response to the Covid-19 pandemic. As the German Court's first ever *ultra vires* judgment, the *PSPP* ruling is a further sign that the tension between the GFCC's case law and the course of European integration has become increasingly untenable. Yet, despite the significant escalation of this *ultra vires* ruling, the chapter shows how the weak remedy employed by the Court left the resolution of the constitutional concern to Germany's elected politicians. Such weak review allows national constitutional courts to signal constitutional problems relating to European integration, but leaves their resolution to the political branches, which is welcome from a democratic perspective. In addition, and unlike during the euro crisis, elected politicians openly criticized the GFCC's case law, introducing appropriate democratic contestation. However, whether the *PSPP* ruling marks a turn in the GFCC's dealings with EU law remains to be seen. The case law of the Karlsruhe judges continues to influence the development of European integration. Such influence is visible in the legal design of Next Generation EU (NGEU), a massive new recovery package of €750 billion adopted to combat the economic effects of the pandemic. Chapter 7 also discusses how the design of this new instrument indicates that constitutional concerns about budgetary sovereignty and possible *ultra vires* rulings have not disappeared.

As the fourth and final stage, the concluding chapter discusses the book's main findings and their implications. The Conclusion discusses what the case study suggests for the legitimate role of national constitutional courts in the EU more generally. It thus debates how the findings can contribute to a theory of legitimate constitutional interpretation and how they can inform ideas for the institutional design of constitutional review of European law. The Conclusion suggests that weaker and more limited review by national constitutional courts holds the promise of promoting legitimate democratic politics instead of constraining it.

2
Judicial Review and Democratic Legitimacy

1. Introduction

The current chapter addresses how we should assess the democratic legitimacy of judicial review of legislation within the domestic context. This is done in order to understand the democratic legitimacy of the national constitutional courts' review of European law. Chapter 3 subsequently draws out the implications for the role of national constitutional courts in relation to the European Union (EU).

Judicial review of legislation poses a democratic challenge because it allows democratically unaccountable courts to override the decisions of democratically elected legislatures. Although judicial review is a feature of many contemporary liberal democracies, its legitimacy remains contested for this reason.[1] The democratic concern is clearest in systems with so-called *strong-form* judicial review as opposed to systems with *weak-form* judicial review. In systems with strong-form judicial review, courts have the power to not apply legislation, to modify the legislation's effects, or, in some systems, to declare it invalid altogether if they judge that the legislation violates constitutional law.[2] Coupled with constitutional entrenchment, strong-form judicial review means that judges have the power to override ordinary parliamentary majorities, because the court's interpretations cannot be reversed in the ordinary legislative procedure. This usually entails that courts have an important role in interpreting constitutional law and in controlling whether legislation complies with constitutional law.[3] The democratic concern is less pressing in systems with *weak-form* judicial review. In such systems, courts do have the power

[1] Democratic concerns about judicial review have not resonated equally in different countries. In the US, the debate has been termed an 'academic obsession'. See Barry Friedman, 'The Birth of an Academic Obsession: The History of the Countermajoritarian Difficulty, Part Five' (2002) 112 The Yale Law Journal 153. The scholarly focus on this issue is partly explained by the lack of an explicit constitutional basis for judicial review in the US constitution. The basis for the exercise of judicial review was laid down by the Supreme Court itself in *Marbury v Madison*, 5 US (1 Cranch) 137 (1803). In Germany, by contrast, the explicit constitutional basis for the constitutional court's authority and its review of legislation appear to have limited concerns about its legitimacy. Christoph Möllers, 'Legalität, Legitimität und Legitimation des Bundesverfassungsgerichts' in Matthias Jestaedt and others (eds), *Das entgrenzte Gericht* (Suhrkamp 2011).

[2] Mark Tushnet, *Weak Courts, Strong Rights* (Princeton University Press 2008) xi and 33–36; Jeremy Waldron, 'The Core of the Case Against Judicial Review' (2006) 115 The Yale Law Journal 1346, 1353–59. Tushnet defines strong-form review as 'a system in which judicial interpretations of the Constitution are final and unrevisable by ordinary legislative majorities'.

[3] Waldron, 'The Core of the Case Against Judicial Review' (n 2) 1348–50. Below I offer some reasons on why courts may possibly not have the final say.

Judging European Democracy. Nik de Boer, Oxford University Press. © Nik de Boer 2023.
DOI: 10.1093/oso/9780192845238.003.0002

to assess ordinary legislation on conformity with constitutional norms, but do not have the final say on whether such legislation complies with those constitutional provisions.[4] Henceforth, I use the term 'judicial review' to refer to strong-form judicial review, unless otherwise stated.[5]

In assessing the legitimacy of judicial review, I employ the notion of legitimacy in a normative sense. I understand legitimacy to concern political legitimacy, which refers to the moral justification of political, or public, authority.[6] Assessing the legitimacy of judicial review can be aimed at institutional design—whether judges should have this power and if so in what form—as well as at developing an account of when and how courts should use their power to review legislation.[7] In this chapter I discuss both institutional proposals as well as accounts of how judges should use their review powers. I assess their comparative legitimacy, that is, I discuss what forms of judicial review are more legitimate compared to others.

As stated in the Introduction to this book, justifications of judicial review must address two issues. The first concerns whether it is legitimate to subject the democratic process to constitutional constraints and why. The second issue has to do with who should enforce and interpret any such constraints. Should this be left to courts or rather the legislature itself or some other institution? This second issue concerns whether judicial review provides a better way to achieve a normatively desired outcome—whatever this outcome is—in comparison to a system in which this task is left to the legislature itself or another institution. The first of these questions I shall call hereafter the *constitutional question*, the second I shall call the

4 Tushnet, *Weak Courts, Strong Rights* (n 2) ix and 18–42.

5 Although strong-form judicial review raises the clearest democratic concern, the extent to which this is a problem depends also on the difficulty of changing the constitution and on how judges use their powers. Strong-form judicial review is more problematic in democratic terms, where the constitution is very difficult to change. Furthermore, even in a system where judges have strong review powers and the constitution is heavily entrenched against change, judicial review may not pose a clear democratic problem where courts use their powers sparsely and mostly defer to the judgment of the legislature. The democratic objection to judicial review is therefore a function of three aspects of a legal system: (i) the degree of constitutional entrenchment, (ii) the strength and scope of judicial review powers, and (iii) how those review powers are exercised. See, for similar considerations, Larry D Kramer, *The People Themselves* (Oxford University Press 2006) 249–53; Richard H Fallon, 'The Core of an Uneasy Case for Judicial Review' (2008) 121 Harvard Law Review 1693.

6 See eg Richard H Fallon, 'Legitimacy and the Constitution' (2005) 118 Harvard Law Review 1787, 1796–801; Fabienne Peter, 'Political Legitimacy' in Edward N Zalta (ed), *The Stanford Encyclopedia of Philosophy* (Summer 2010 edition) <https://plato.stanford.edu/archives/sum2010/entries/legitimacy/>. accessed 1 August 2022; Tom Christiano, 'Authority' in Edward N Zalta (ed), *The Stanford Encyclopedia of Philosophy* (Spring 2013 edition) <https://plato.stanford.edu/archives/spr2013/entries/authority/> accessed 1 August 2022.

7 Arguments aimed at institutional design appear to rest more firmly on the idea that particular characteristics of institutions will lead to certain results. Conversely, theories aimed at interpretation will have to understand these results as a consequence of contingent—interpretive—choices. Both approaches require ideas about possible change. Those who argue for a different institutional design must assume that their arguments can convince the persons in charge of changing the constitution, whereas those who put forward an argument about judicial or legislative interpretation must assume that their arguments can convince judges or legislators. It is not clear what kind of argument should be preferred, unless one thinks that no form of judicial review can ever be legitimate.

institutional question. My principal claim in this chapter is that making the debate over the democratic legitimacy of judicial review more informed by insights into the actual functioning of courts and legislatures is a way to bring it forward. Different perspectives on the democratic legitimacy of judicial review rely on diverging empirical assumptions about the functioning of these institutions that require further research.

There are roughly three main ways to approach the legitimacy of judicial review. The first approach is commonly referred to as legal constitutionalism, which I discuss in section 1, on the basis of the work of John Rawls and Ronald Dworkin. On this view, majoritarian democratic processes are legitimate only insofar as they are subject to constitutional constraints in the form of fundamental rights, which ensure that democratic procedures do not result in certain substantively unjust outcomes. Judicial review protects these moral values enshrined in the constitution against potentially oppressive democratic majorities.[8] A key difficulty with this approach is that these moral values are subject to reasonable disagreement. Even if we agree on a high level of abstraction that democratic decision-making cannot legitimately violate certain rights, reasonable disagreements are still likely when we try to ascertain what this requires in concrete situations.

The second and opposed position is to reject judicial review and constitutional limitations on democratic government as undemocratic.[9] Along such lines, political constitutionalists argue that reasonable disagreements about justice and rights should be settled democratically. Democracy treats citizens as political equals and safeguards the taking of collective decisions after a process of deliberation that gives equal weight to citizens' respective views.[10] Constitutionalizing legal norms removes them from ordinary democratic debate, and judicial review empowers judges to decide contested moral issues against the position of democratic majorities. A difficulty with this approach is that it potentially leaves majoritarian democratic decision-making devoid of constraints necessary to safeguard its legitimacy.

[8] I take Ronald Dworkin and John Rawls as important proponents of this approach. See Ronald Dworkin, *Taking Rights Seriously* (Duckworth 1977) 131–49; Ronald Dworkin, *A Matter of Principle* (Harvard University Press 1985) 9–70; Ronald Dworkin, *Freedom's Law: The Moral Reading of the American Constitution* (Oxford University Press 1996); John Rawls, *Political Liberalism* (Columbia University Press 2005).

[9] Not all judicial review sceptics argue against constitutional constraints on democratic authority as such. See Frank I Michelman, 'Why Not Just Say No? An Essay on the Obduracy of Constitutional Fixation' (2014) 94 Boston University Law Review 1141. Richard Bellamy, however, rejects legal constitutionalism in favour of political constitutionalism, where 'the democratic process *is* the constitution'. Richard Bellamy, *Political Constitutionalism: A Republican Defence of the Constitutionality of Democracy* (Cambridge University Press 2007) 5.

[10] See eg Jeremy Waldron, *Law and Disagreement* (Oxford University Press 1999); Waldron, 'The Core of the Case Against Judicial Review' (n 2); Bellamy, *Political Constitutionalism* (n 9); Richard Bellamy, 'Political Constitutionalism and the Human Rights Act' (2011) 9 International Journal of Constitutional Law 86; Richard Bellamy, 'The Democratic Legitimacy of International Human Rights Conventions: Political Constitutionalism and the European Convention on Human Rights' (2014) 25 European Journal of International Law 1019.

For example, if the legitimacy of law depends on democratic procedures, it is difficult to accept majority decisions to abolish the democratic process as democratically legitimate. In addition, certain constitutional rights, such as freedom of speech and freedom of assembly, are obviously connected to democratic ideals, as they enable vibrant public debate. Beyond that, the mere fact that a majority of citizens favour a particular law seems insufficient to establish its legitimacy. For instance, if a democratic majority treats racial minorities with contempt or is unwilling to take their interests into account, it is hard to see why these minorities should accept the majority's decision as legitimate.

The third approach is to opt for a solution that holds the middle ground between these other two approaches, namely to justify constitutional constraints and judicial review in democratic terms. On this reading judicial review is not undemocratic after all, because it aims to protect democracy or democratic values. Jürgen Habermas and John Hart Ely, for example, articulate a version of constitutionalism and judicial review that focuses on preserving the preconditions of the democratic process. Nonetheless, such process-oriented judicial review is likely to still require from courts that they rule on issues of political morality, subject to significant reasonable disagreement.

Through a critical discussion of these different approaches, this chapter develops the following argument. On the one hand, there is no fundamental opposition between democracy and the ideals of constitutionalism. The point of constitutionalism can be understood as safeguarding the preconditions for democratic legitimacy. On the other hand, the dilemma is that it seems impossible to fully articulate constitutional limits in a way that would both be uncontroversial and at the same time do away with all good-faith interpretive disagreement. I contend that this fundamental difficulty is well captured by Habermas' idea of the co-originality of private and public autonomy. He argues that fundamental rights are preconditions for a deliberative democratic process, as they make legitimate democratic will-formation possible. Yet, they also require further specification in the democratic process. This idea ultimately emphasizes the limits of political philosophy in answering the relationship between constitutionalism and democracy: it is impossible to develop a fully adequate set of fundamental rights outside the democratic process and, consequently, it is even impossible to objectively determine when our decision-making procedures are fully democratically legitimate. The best we can achieve is that every instance of legislation is accompanied by good-faith deliberation on whether such legislation is compatible with the preconditions for a legitimate democratic process. In addition, citizens must always be able to contest the outcome of legislative procedures on the basis that it violates these preconditions.

The upshot of this argument is that an assessment of judicial review's legitimacy is context-dependent and crucially hinges on addressing *the institutional question*. An assessment of the democratic legitimacy of judicial review requires a comparison of how legislatures and constitutional courts actually deliberate on whether legislation is compatible with its preconditions and by asking each time which institution does a better job. Different normative theories of judicial review, ranging from the positive to the more sceptical, are informed by assumptions about the respective qualities of courts and legislatures. Yet, it is less clear to what extent these assumptions reflect how legislatures and courts actually function in practice.[11] To advance the debate on the democratic legitimacy of judicial review, it is thus necessary to gain further insight into the functioning of these institutions when it comes to deciding constitutional issues. Such work should assess how legislatures deliberate about constitutional issues in practice, how these deliberations compare with the decisions and reasoning of courts, as well as how judicial review of legislation influences subsequent legislative deliberations.[12] This book further explores that idea in relation to the EU and also does the work of comparing institutions itself in a case study on the German Federal Constitutional Court (GFCC).

My argument in this chapter proceeds in the following manner. Section 2 first discusses and criticizes the legal constitutionalist's justification of judicial review and constitutionalism based on the work of John Rawls and Ronald Dworkin. Section 3 subsequently discusses why democracy is a legitimate way to resolve reasonable disagreements about rights. Section 4 explores whether a justification of judicial review rooted in the value of democracy can nonetheless be justified. Here I discuss the idea of precommitment and procedural justifications of judicial review, ultimately drawing on the work of Habermas, and stressing the need for further enquiries into the functioning of legislatures and constitutional courts. Section 5 discusses why political constitutionalists, such as Jeremy Waldron, Richard Bellamy, and Mark Tushnet, reject judicial review by challenging the view that courts are better placed than legislatures to decide constitutional issues. I explain why their arguments do not rule out the legitimacy of judicial review completely, and how their case rests on assumptions about the deliberative qualities of legislatures that are insufficiently backed up. Section 6 details which forms of judicial review are less problematic from a democratic viewpoint and offers a case for weak-form judicial review. Yet, I consider that the assessment of the legitimacy of judicial review ultimately can only be fully addressed when the actual functioning of courts and legislatures is better understood. Despite democratic objections, strong-form judicial review can still be considered justified when it ensures that constitutional issues are the subject of serious deliberation in a particular political system. Section 7 sums up the argument. Parts of this chapter reflect well-known

[11] Exceptions are probably Tushnet, *Weak Courts, Strong Rights* (n 2); Larry D Kramer, 'Popular Constitutionalism, circa 2004' (2004) 92 California Law Review 959; Alec Stone Sweet, *Governing with Judges: Constitutional Politics in Europe* (Oxford University Press 2000).

[12] A synthesis of a significant body of empirical research about the deliberative quality of parliamentary debates and the possible effects of institutional settings can be found in Jürg Steiner, *The Foundations of Deliberative Democracy: Empirical Research and Normative Implications* (Cambridge University Press 2012).

positions in the academic debate. I aimed to keep the discussion relatively short but elaborate enough to keep the argument accessible to those less acquainted with this literature.

2. Legal Constitutionalism and its Challenges

Constitutionalism commonly refers to the idea that the exercise of political authority should be subject to legal limits, namely subject to those limits entrenched in constitutional law.[13] The legitimacy of subjecting the democratic decision-making process to such constitutional limits and leaving their enforcement to courts is often based on outcome-related considerations. In this vein, legal constitutionalists generally justify judicial review and constitutionalism in the following manner. First, they justify subjecting the democratic process to a set of constitutional constraints in the form of fundamental rights as a requirement of legitimacy. Such legal limits are supposed to ensure that democratic decision-making does not result in certain substantively unjust outcomes, namely an infringement of fundamental rights.[14] On this understanding, constitutional constraints are justified pre-politically and not in the democratic process itself. Secondly, it is thought best to leave the enforcement and interpretation of these constitutional constraints to the judiciary, because independent judges are more likely to reach correct outcomes when interpreting these constitutional norms. There are many variations of these arguments, but here I focus on the works of John Rawls and Ronald Dworkin as two key examples of this sort of approach.[15] Political constitutionalists, however, point out that legal constitutionalism pays insufficient attention to reasonable disagreement over justice and rights.

2.1 Legitimation by Constitution

The idea that a constitution is a precondition for the legitimate exercise of political power is a central tenet of John Rawls' liberal political theory. He proposes the 'liberal principle of legitimacy', which entails that:

[13] See Introduction, section 1.1.

[14] See Bellamy, *Political Constitutionalism* (n 9) 3; Waldron, 'The Core of the Case Against Judicial Review' (n 2) 1348–51; Jeremy Waldron, 'Democracy' in David Estlund (ed), *The Oxford Handbook of Political Philosophy* (Oxford University Press 2012) 198 <https://doi.org/10.1093/oxfordhb/9780195376692.013.0010> accessed 2 August 2022.

[15] A more elaborate treatment of various theories can be found in Bellamy, *Political Constitutionalism* (n 9); Christopher F Zurn, 'Deliberative Democracy and Constitutional Review' (2002) 21 Law and Philosophy 467; Christopher F Zurn, *Deliberative Democracy and the Institutions of Judicial Review* (Cambridge University Press 2007).

> [O]ur exercise of political power is fully proper only when it is exercised in accordance with a constitution the essentials of which all citizens as free and equal may reasonably be expected to endorse in the light of principles and ideals acceptable to their common human reason.[16]

In Rawls' view the constitution specifies certain conditions that the exercise of political power has to satisfy in order to be legitimate. Ordinary legislation adopted by democratically elected majorities has to comply with the limits of the constitution. This idea has been referred to as 'legitimation by constitution'. It proposes that the exercise of political power by a majority of citizens is justifiable to dissenters if it conforms to a constitution that can be subject to hypothetical consent.[17]

Rawls argues that such a constitution contains two types of principles. First, principles that structure the form of government and the political process, namely 'the powers of the legislature, executive and the judiciary' and 'the scope of majority rule'.[18] Secondly, a set of basic rights and liberties that the legislative majority must respect. These are the standard civil and political liberties familiar in liberal democracies 'such as the right to vote and to participate in politics, liberty of conscience, freedom of thought and of association, as well as the protections of the rule of law'.[19] Because the constitution contains the conditions with which political authority must comply in order to be legitimate in the first place, the constitution is itself removed from the political agenda. It fixes the content of basic rights and liberties 'once and for all' and takes them 'off the political agenda', which entails that they are no longer considered suitable for majoritarian decision-making.[20] In this sense, constitutional rights are pre-political.

Rawls deems that such a constitutional framework can legitimate coercive political power under circumstances of reasonable pluralism. This 'fact of reasonable pluralism' means that modern democratic societies are characterized by a diversity of opposing and irreconcilable reasonable religious, philosophical, and moral doctrines.[21] Reasonable pluralism is 'a permanent feature of the public culture of democracy' and 'the inevitable outcome of free human reason'.[22] As a result, 'a continuing shared understanding on one comprehensive religious, philosophical, or moral doctrine can be maintained only by the oppressive use of state power'.[23] A conception of legitimacy committed to treating citizens as free and equal is consequently limited in the range of substantive criteria that can be used for assessing the legitimacy of a decision-making procedure.

[16] Rawls, *Political Liberalism* (n 8) 137.
[17] Michelman, 'Why Not Just Say No?' (n 9) 1145–47.
[18] Rawls, *Political Liberalism* (n 8) 227.
[19] ibid 227.
[20] ibid 151, fn 16 on that page, 161, and 232–33.
[21] ibid xvi and 3–4.
[22] ibid 36–37.
[23] ibid 37.

Rawls argues that people can reasonably disagree about moral and ethical issues, because of the so-called 'burdens of judgment'.[24] These are 'the many hazards involved in the correct (and conscientious) exercise of our powers of reason and judgment in the ordinary course of political life'.[25] Important examples are that the evidence relating to a particular case is often complex and difficult to assess; that different people disagree about the weight to be given to different kinds of normative considerations; that our moral and political concepts suffer from a degree of indeterminacy; that people's different experiences affect their judgments on moral issues; that there are different kinds of normative issues on each side of a moral issue, which render it difficult to make an overall assessment; and that 'any system of social institutions is limited in the values it can admit so that some selection must be made from the full range of moral and political values that might be realized'.[26]

The challenge is to find out how citizens can still accept the legitimacy of coercive political power, despite their deep, but reasonable disagreement over moral and ethical questions. Rawls' answer is a political conception of justice that he believes all citizens can reasonably agree to, despite them disagreeing over what the good life is. The justification for subjecting democratic decision-making to a set of pre-political basic rights and liberties is that they reflect minimal requirements of justice. Rawls regards the content of this conception of justice as 'expressed in terms of certain fundamental ideas seen as implicit in the public political culture of a democratic society'.[27]

In Rawls' work, constitutional constraints on majoritarian democratic decision-making are thus justified pre-politically. Their justification derives from a hypothetical rational agreement on requirements of justice that can be the object of an overlapping consensus.[28] To understand what the requirements of justice are,

[24] ibid 54–55.

[25] ibid 55–56.

[26] ibid 56–57.

[27] ibid 13.

[28] The pre-political nature of Rawls' constitutional framework can be nuanced in at least two respects. Firstly, Rawls does acknowledge the possibility of some disagreement over constitutional issues. He contends that 'whether the constitutional essentials covering the basic freedoms are satisfied is more or less visible on the face of constitutional arrangements and how these can be seen to work in practice', Rawls, *Political Liberalism* (n 8) 229. This entails an agreement at least on 'the main outlines' or its 'central range', but not on all details (ibid 230 and 237). Rawls also submits that the list of constitutional rights should be settled at the stage of a constitutional convention, as well as further specified in the later legislative and adjudicative stages where parts of the veil of ignorance are successively lifted. The delegates to the constitutional convention decide on the adoption of a constitution in light of 'general knowledge of how political and social institutions work, together with the general facts about existing social circumstances' (ibid 336 and 334–40, more generally 293 and 298). Secondly, Rawls maintains that the constitution is an expression of 'the people's constituent power' and must be 'democratically ratified' (ibid 231–32). See on these points also Hugh Baxter, *Habermas: The Discourse Theory of Law and Democracy* (Stanford University Press 2011) 76–82. Yet overall, it appears that a constitution's democratic mode of enactment is not decisive, as Rawls maintains that '[t]he idea of right and just constitutions and basic laws is always ascertained by the most reasonable political conception of justice and not by the results of an actual political process', Rawls, *Political Liberalism* (n 8) 233.

Rawls offers an argument that consists of two stages. The first stage is that the requirements of justice are those that would be agreed to by free and equal citizens in what Rawls calls the *original position*.[29] This original position is a hypothetical situation in which citizens' representatives are situated as free and equal. They decide on a rational basis about the principles of justice that are to order their society, without their having any knowledge concerning their particular situation, such as their conception of the good life, their race, or social position.[30] According to Rawls, the parties in the original position would choose a set of basic liberties and accord them priority over other political decisions.[31] A key reason is that these rights protect a basic sphere of liberty necessary for persons to live a life according to their conception of the good life, whatever that conception may be.[32] The second stage is that this conception of justice can gain the support of what Rawls calls a reasonable overlapping consensus. This entails that citizens in an actual democratic society can each support the conception of justice from within their respective reasonable comprehensive doctrines. Because the conception of justice can gain allegiance from a diverse body of citizens with different comprehensive conceptions, a society governed by it will be stable.[33] Based on these arguments, Rawls holds that a reasonable consensus on matters of justice is possible, which legitimates the subjection of majoritarian democratic decision-making to constitutional constraints, despite pervasive reasonable disagreement in a democratic society.

A similar line of thought emerges from the work of Ronald Dworkin, who also considers constitutional rights as pre-political constraints on decision-making by democratically elected majorities. He rejects the majoritarian conception of democracy according to which political decisions must merely reflect the wishes

[29] This is the central argument of John Rawls, *A Theory of Justice (Revised Edition)* (Oxford University Press 1999).

[30] ibid.

[31] These are to be further specified at what Rawls calls the stage of the constitutional convention, a stage where a just governmental structure is chosen. The veil of ignorance is partially lifted and the representatives have the additional knowledge of particular circumstances of their society. See eg Rawls, *Political Liberalism* (n 8) 334–40.

[32] I leave out Rawls' arguments for why parties in the original position adopt the political liberties, which rests on the idea that protection of a set of political liberties and a system of representative government allow citizens to develop their capacity for a sense of justice. See ibid 315–24 and 289–371 more generally. The argument for the political liberties is complex; for more explanation see Joshua Cohen, 'For a Democratic Society' in Samuel Freeman (ed), *The Cambridge Companion to Rawls* (Cambridge University Press 2002) 104–11 <www.cambridge.org/core/books/cambridge-companion-to-rawls/for-a-democratic-society/F7F537FEA632E8FE066BEF451BEB73FE> accessed 1 August 2022. For reasons of readability I have also simplified the argument for the other basic liberties a little here. Rawls holds that the parties in the original position represent persons that have both a determinate conception of the good, as well as a capacity for a conception of the good. This is 'the capacity to form, to revise, and rationally to pursue such a conception, that is, a conception of what we regard for us as a worthwhile human life', Rawls, *Political Liberalism* (n 8) 302. Persons also have a higher-order interest in developing and exercising this capacity and to think of themselves as affirming their way of life 'in accordance with the full, deliberate, and reasoned exercise of our intellectual and moral powers' (ibid 313). This requires that persons must be allowed 'to fall into error and to make mistakes', for which they require freedom of conscience (ibid 314).

[33] ibid 35–40.

of the majority. Instead, he maintains that the United States (US) constitution is committed to 'the constitutional conception of democracy', where the aim is 'that collective decisions be made by political institutions whose structure, composition and practices treat all members of the community, as individuals, with equal concern and respect'.[34] The constitutional conception of democracy thus 'presupposes democratic conditions'.[35] The equal status of all citizens is 'the essence of democracy'[36] and requires the protection of rights that safeguard that status. Respecting citizens' equal status demands that citizens take part in collective decisions, that political processes treat them with equal concern, but also that citizens are accorded moral independence, which enables them to form and reflect on their own ethical, moral, and political judgements.[37] These presupposed democratic conditions—citizens' equal status—circumscribe the legitimate scope of majoritarianism, as majoritarianism does not by itself guarantee citizens' equal moral status.[38] Non-majoritarian decision-making that protects democratic conditions is therefore not contrary to democracy, but rather improves democracy. The crucial issue is rather whether the non-majoritarian decision correctly identifies the democratic conditions.[39]

2.2 Constitutional Courts as Forums of Principle

The idea of legitimation by constitution requires that an institution verify whether the exercise of political power conforms to the constitution. To assess whether a law is legitimate, it must be established that it complies with the constitution.[40] Judicial review is one mechanism to provide this 'service'. Rawls' and Dworkin's arguments in favour of judicial review rest on a rather negative view of majoritarian democratic politics and the concomitant idea that courts are better placed to decide constitutional issues.

In this respect Dworkin is most explicit. Rawls is more careful to embrace judicial review, although similar ideas emerge in his work.[41] Dworkin submits that

[34] Dworkin, *Freedom's Law* (n 8) 17.
[35] ibid 23.
[36] ibid 17.
[37] ibid 25–26.
[38] ibid 23.
[39] ibid 32–34.
[40] Michelman, 'Why Not Just Say No?' (n 9) 1156–57.
[41] Rawls is hesitant to fully endorse judicial review. He submits there is no universally best way to protect fundamental rights and thinks that such a solution should be tied to historical conditions and the political culture of a particular legal system. See Rawls, *Political Liberalism* (n 8) 234–35 and 240. See also Frank I Michelman, 'Rawls on Constitutionalism and Constitutional Law' in Samuel Freeman (ed), *The Cambridge Companion to Rawls* (Cambridge University Press 2002) 403–04 <www.cambridge.org/core/books/cambridge-companion-to-rawls/rawls-on-constitutionalism-and-constitutional-law/FBA9020B735ABF87E59624FEE30BA14F> accessed 1 August 2022. Ronald Dworkin more explicitly embraces judicial review, albeit in the context of US constitutionalism: Ronald Dworkin, *Law's Empire* (Hart Publishing 1998) 355–57.

constitutional courts function as 'forums of principle'. Unlike legislators, constitutional judges come to their decisions on the basis of moral argument and are therefore better placed to decide the moral issues that inevitably come up in constitutional cases:

> Judicial review insures that the most fundamental issues of political morality will finally be set out and debated as issues of principle and not simply issues of political power, a transformation that cannot succeed, in any case not fully, within the legislature itself.[42]

Rawls similarly contends that in a system with judicial review a constitutional court would be 'an exemplar of public reason'.[43] When applying the constitutional provisions on rights and governmental structures, such a court would be expected to reason only on the basis of the political principles that the constitution aims to protect and promote.[44] This use of public reason aims to ensure that the constitution's application is guided by the principles that free and equal citizens may reasonably be expected to endorse.

According to Dworkin, the electoral accountability of legislatures instead makes them less suitable to decide rights issues. In Dworkin's view it is typical of rights disputes 'that the interests of those in political control of the various institutions of the government have been both homogeneous and hostile'.[45] Legislatures are responsive to the majority's demands, whereas the majority is thought not to take rights seriously.[46] The underlying idea is that political majorities are less likely to base their decisions on moral arguments but more so on the self-interest and prejudices of the persons they represent.[47] This gives rise to the threat of the so-called 'tyranny of the majority': minorities run the risk of having their fundamental interests disregarded by oppressive majorities.[48] Rawls similarly suggests that issues of power and narrow self-interest will influence ordinary democratic processes more

[42] Ronald Dworkin, 'The Forum of Principle' (1981) 56 New York University Law Review 469, 517. Dworkin does acknowledge that judges may also make incorrect decisions about matters of rights. He thinks, however, that this threat should not be exaggerated, as any decision that proves very unpopular will be eroded in the long run, either because of lacking public compliance or because of political influence in the nomination of judges. See Dworkin, *Taking Rights Seriously* (n 8) 148.

[43] Rawls, *Political Liberalism* (n 8) 231–40.

[44] In addition, public reason encompasses 'guidelines of enquiry: principles of reasoning and rules of evidence in the light of which citizens are to decide whether substantive principles properly apply and to identify laws and policies that best satisfy them', ibid 224.

[45] Dworkin, *Taking Rights Seriously* (n 8) 143.

[46] Dworkin submits: 'Of course the comfort of the majority will require some accommodation for minorities but only to the extent necessary to preserve order; and that is usually an accommodation that falls short of recognizing their rights', ibid 146.

[47] See, for reasoning along these lines, Dworkin, *A Matter of Principle* (n 8) 24–25; Dworkin, 'The Forum of Principle' (n 42) 500–16; Dworkin, *Taking Rights Seriously* (n 8) ch 5. Dworkin expects public debate before a referendum or a legislative decision to be of low quality; see also his later work: Dworkin, *Freedom's Law* (n 8) 344.

[48] The issue is discussed in Waldron, *Law and Disagreement* (n 10) 13–14.

easily.[49] Moreover, as Dworkin submits, giving legislative majorities the power to decide issues of rights makes them judges in their own cause. By virtue of their independence, judges are consequently better able to reach correct outcomes in deciding rights issues than the political majorities in the legislature.[50]

In addition, both Dworkin and Rawls claim that judicial review has a positive effect on public debate and a nation's constitutional culture. Rawls submits that a constitutional court gives 'public reason vividness and vitality in the public forum' and often 'forces political discussion to take a principled form so as to address the constitutional question in line with the political values of justice and public reason'.[51] Dworkin likewise maintains:

> When an issue is seen as constitutional, however, and as one that will ultimately be resolved by courts applying general constitutional principles, the quality of public argument is often improved, because the argument concentrates from the start on questions of political morality. Legislators often feel compelled to argue for the constitutionality and not the just the popularity of measures they support, and Presidents or governors who veto a law cite constitutional arguments to justify their decision. When a constitutional issue has been decided by the Supreme Court, and is important enough so that it can be expected to be elaborated, expanded, contracted, or even reversed, by future decisions, a sustained national debate begins, in newspapers and other media, in law schools and classrooms, in public meetings and around dinner tables.[52]

In sum, Dworkin and Rawls support judicial review, because courts are better equipped than legislatures to tackle issues of moral principle and because judicial review will improve the moral quality of public debate.

2.3 The Problem of Reasonable Disagreement

A major criticism brought forward by political constitutionalists such as Jeremy Waldron and Richard Bellamy is that legal constitutionalism ignores pervasive and reasonable disagreement about matters of rights and justice. Such disagreement challenges the legal constitutionalist's justification for constitutionalism and judicial review, because it is supposed to be based on a reasonable consensus on requirements of justice.[53]

[49] Rawls, *Political Liberalism* (n 8) 233 and 237–38.

[50] Dworkin, *Law's Empire* (n 41) 375.

[51] Rawls, *Political Liberalism* (n 8) 233 and 239.

[52] Dworkin, *Freedom's Law* (n 8) 345.

[53] One can debate the extent to which Rawls does acknowledge the possibility of disagreement on constitutional issues. Rawls admits that judges may disagree with one another 'in the details of their understanding of the constitution', Rawls, *Political Liberalism* (n 8) 237. However, he does submit that

Rawls gives an important place to moral disagreements. Yet, he argues that despite citizens' disagreements about moral issues, they can nonetheless arrive at a reasonable consensus on issues of justice that in turn would justify higher constitutional law. In fact, this agreement on higher constitutional law is seen as an answer to disagreement in society. The conformity of legal norms to the constitution gives dissenters a reason to accept them even if they disagree with the prevailing views of the current majority of their fellow citizens.

Political constitutionalists instead invoke Rawls' idea of the 'burdens of judgment' to explain why reasonable disagreement also exists about matters of justice and rights rather than merely about conceptions of the good life.[54] These burdens matter not just when people evaluate questions about the good life, but also when they evaluate issues of justice. If it is true, for example, that the evidence bearing on a normative issue is 'conflicting and complex', that we may disagree about the weight of different normative considerations that are relevant, and that '[t]o some extent all our concepts, and not only moral and political concepts, are vague and subject to hard cases',[55] then we would expect people to reasonably disagree about the requirements of justice as well. They would reasonably disagree about what it entails to treat people as free and as equals, about how that requirement should be translated to the design of a hypothetical 'original position', what rights people should have, and how those rights should be interpreted in concrete cases.[56]

As Jeremy Waldron forcefully argues, given the burdens of judgment, reasonable disagreement about justice is a feature of modern democratic societies in a much more fundamental way than Rawls admits.[57] Waldron contends that the politics of actual societies 'are dedicated quite explicitly to grappling with fundamental

they will agree on the 'central range' of the basic rights. He also states that the basic rights and liberties that 'can be specified in but one way, modulo relatively small variations', ibid 228. See also n 28 above.

[54] Waldron, *Law and Disagreement* (n 10); Bellamy, *Political Constitutionalism* (n 9).

[55] Rawls, *Political Liberalism* (n 8) 56.

[56] Waldron, *Law and Disagreement* (n 10) 149–63. For a similar criticism of the pre-political nature of Rawls' constitutional framework see Jürgen Habermas, *The Inclusion of the Other: Studies in Political Theory* (The MIT Press 1998) 69–70. In this respect I also found the discussion useful in Raymond Geuss, *Philosophy and Real Politics* (Princeton University Press 2008). A powerful criticism of the supposed neutrality of Rawls' basic liberties is HLA Hart, 'Rawls on Liberty and Its Priority' (Oxford University Press 1983).

[57] See also Cohen, 'For a Democratic Society' (n 32) 129–31. Rawls cannot really claim that his conception of justice stands above such disagreements because, in developing his conception of justice, Rawls draws heavily on our present judgements about justice. Rawls' method to achieve a state of reflective equilibrium entails that the conception of justice is not so much discovered but is *constructed* from what is already there. See Thomas W Pogge, *Realizing Rawls* (Cornell University Press 1989) 268–69. Rawls appears to acknowledge these issues in his 'Reply to Habermas' in Rawls, *Political Liberalism* (n 8). There he expresses caution about the place of the original position and the principles of justice it leads to. He states that it may be incorrect that the principles agreed to in the original position are the most reasonable ones: 'We must check it against the fixed points of our considered judgments at different levels of generality' (381). He also states that the primary aim of 'justice as fairness' is 'to be presented to and understood by the audience in civil society for its citizens to consider' (384). At page 401 he states that '[t]he ideal of a just constitution is always something to be worked toward'.

*dis*agreements about justice'.[58] Once we accept the pervasiveness of disagreement about questions of justice and rights in democratic societies, it becomes very difficult to accept that constitutional principles are the result of a reasonable consensus on principles of justice and that it would be legitimate to remove those principles from further political debate. Rather, it seems that we must allow room for reasonable disagreements concerning issues of justice and rights in political debate. This also puts into doubt the idea that judges in a democratic system should have the last word in deciding difficult questions of moral principle. The existence of reasonable disagreement about justice and rights makes it implausible that judges can base themselves on the 'correct' view of what justice requires.[59]

Historical evidence appears to confirm that constitutional provisions are often subject to considerable disagreement. For example, Stone Sweet notes how the drafting of rights provisions in European constitutions 'proved to be the most difficult aspect of constitutional negotiations in all countries' and 'each party was allowed to enshrine its own preferred set of rights, usually watered down somewhat by the "horse-trading", thus giving partial victories to everyone'.[60] The fact that constitutional courts in different countries have handed down opposing judgments on similar issues such as the right to abortion provides another example of rights disagreement.[61] Jürgen Habermas offers the additional argument that ideas about the required protection of fundamental rights have historically evolved in light of the experiences and demands expressed by affected citizens themselves. He cites the struggle for women's equal status as an example and concludes that:

> [T]he individual rights that are meant to guarantee to women the autonomy to pursue their lives in the private sphere cannot even be adequately formulated unless the affected persons themselves first articulate and justify in public debate those aspects that are relevant to equal or unequal treatment in typical cases.[62]

Moreover, even if we could agree that a certain set of rights best accords with the requirements of justice, we would still be faced with disagreement on the level of interpretation. The constitutionalized standards of these rights cannot by themselves settle their proper interpretation. Agreement lies in the abstract definition of the higher norms but runs out when these have to be made more concrete. How

[58] Waldron, *Law and Disagreement* (n 10) 158.

[59] Bellamy, *Political Constitutionalism* (n 9) 4.

[60] Sweet, *Governing with Judges* (n 11) 39.

[61] Compare, eg, US Supreme Court, *Roe v Wade*, 410 US 113 (1973), in which the decision to have an abortion was judged part of the right of personal privacy, with the appraisal by the GFCC. The GFCC judged in 1974 that the right to life of the unborn prevailed over the mother's right to free development of her personality. This required that the 'condemnation of abortion must be clearly expressed in the legal order'. Bundesverfassungsgericht, judgment of 25 February 1975, 1 BvF 1/74 (*Schwangerschaftsabbruch I*). Translation from Vicki Jackson and Mark Tushnet, *Comparative Constitutional Law* (Foundation Press 2014) 113.

[62] Habermas, *The Inclusion of the Other* (n 56) 264, also 67–73.

particular rights are to be protected and how they should be balanced against other considerations will therefore be a matter of reasonable disagreement. Frank Michelman states the problem thus:

> It seems evident that no liberally-satisfactory such standard can possibly be framed with both sufficient breadth to serve as widely acceptable clause in a public contract on legitimacy, and at the same time sufficient closure to fend off good-faith interpretative controversy at the point of application; not 'freedom of expression;' not 'arbitrary arrest;' no, not even 'torture,' to take the extreme case.[63]

This problem of interpretive disagreement puts the idea of 'legitimation by constitution' into doubt. That idea depended on the expectation that the legitimacy of legal norms could be verified in light of its conformity to a set of higher constitutional norms. Interpretive disagreement, however, suggests that this is not wholly possible. Legitimation by constitution also requires an institutional mechanism by which interpretive disagreements can be settled. This mechanism could be a court that gives authoritative interpretations of the constitution, but this solution runs into democratic objections.[64]

3. Democratic Legitimacy as an Answer to Reasonable Disagreement

A response to the problem of reasonable disagreement is to move away from substantive questions about justice and rights to the question of what constitutes a legitimate *procedure* to settle disagreements. In this vein, Jeremy Waldron argues that there are two tasks in political philosophy. Not only must political philosophers occupy themselves with the question of what justice is, they must also theorize about how we can take legitimate political action where we disagree about justice.[65] In theorizing about the latter, they need to take into account the circumstances of politics, consisting of 'the felt need among the members of a certain group for a common framework or decision or course of action on some matter, even in the face of disagreement about what that framework, decision or action should be'.[66] Given these circumstances of politics, a crucial concern in political philosophy should be to reflect 'on the purposes for which, and the procedures by which,

[63] Frank I Michelman, 'Legitimacy, The Social Turn and Constitutional Review: What Political Liberalism Suggests' (2015) 98 Kritische Vierteljahresschrift für Gesetzgebung und Rechtswissenschaft 183, 195.

[64] ibid.

[65] Waldron, *Law and Disagreement* (n 10) 1–4. The idea is reiterated in Jeremy Waldron, 'Political Political Theory: An Inaugural Lecture' (2013) 21 The Journal of Political Philosophy 1.

[66] Waldron, *Law and Disagreement* (n 10) 102; Bellamy, *Political Constitutionalism* (n 9) 20–26.

communities settle on a single set of institutions even in the face of disagreement about so much that we rightly regard as important'.[67] Various democratic theorists have argued that democracy offers a fair procedure to resolve reasonable disagreements about justice. This is the case because democracy allows citizens to decide on the collective norms that they will be subject to through a public process of exchanging reasons and arguments.[68] The idea put forward in theories of deliberative democracy especially is that the legitimacy of the law depends on an *actual* process of reason-giving and public argumentation among equal citizens aimed at reaching mutually acceptable decisions.[69] Political constitutionalists argue in addition that majoritarian decision-making is a fair way to take collective decisions when there is reasonable disagreement about what the best decision is.

3.1 Democratic Participation

A first reason to consider democratic procedures as a fair way to resolve reasonable disagreements is that they allow citizens to participate as political equals in collective decision-making processes. There are fundamentally two reasons for valuing political participation. The instrumental justification is that only a sufficiently participatory political system safeguards an inclusion of all views and interests of the citizens and therefore can only produce decisions acceptable to its citizens.[70] The intrinsic justification is that only a political system that gives its citizens an equal right to participate in the decision-making process of the decisions by which they are bound, treats its citizens as equals. Such a system respects citizens' equal worth as autonomous individuals capable of reasoning on matters of public interest and gives their views equal weight.[71]

[67] Waldron, *Law and Disagreement* (n 10) 3.

[68] Bellamy, *Political Constitutionalism* (n 9); Amy Gutman and Dennis Thompson, *Democracy and Disagreement* (The Belknap Press of Harvard University Press 1996); Bernard Manin, 'On Legitimacy and Political Deliberation' (1987) 15 Political Theory 338; Waldron, *Law and Disagreement* (n 10).

[69] Habermas expresses the idea that for legal norms it is the democratic process that serves as the basis of its legitimacy: 'only those statutes may claim legitimacy that can meet with the assent (Zustimmung) of all citizens in a discursive process of legislation that in turn has been legally constituted.' Jürgen Habermas, *Between Facts and Norms* (Polity Press 1996) 110. See also Gutman and Thompson, *Democracy and Disagreement* (n 68) 5. Joshua Cohen expresses the idea in the following manner: 'The notion of a deliberative democracy is rooted in the intuitive ideal of a democratic association in which the justification of the terms and conditions of association proceeds through public argument and reasoning among equal citizens.' Joshua Cohen, 'Deliberation and Democratic Legitimacy' in James Bohman and William Rehg (eds), Deliberative Democracy: Essays on Reason and Politics (The MIT Press 1997) 72.

[70] Joshua Cohen, 'Procedure and Substance in Deliberative Democracy' in James Bohman and William Rehg (eds), *Deliberative Democracy: Essays on Reason and Politics* (The MIT Press 1997) 422–23; Habermas, *Between Facts and Norms* (n 69) 170.

[71] See Waldron, *Law and Disagreement* (n 10) 249–52; Jeremy Waldron, 'A Right-Based Critique of Constitutional Rights' (1993) 13 Oxford Journal of Legal Studies 18; Bellamy, *Political Constitutionalism* (n 9) chs 4 and 6. Bellamy also explains the importance of democracy by linking it to the republican ideal of freedom as non-domination, which I will not discuss further here.

In practice, modern-day democracy requires a division of labour and is primarily representative in nature. Habermas develops this idea of a division of labour in currently existing democracies by drawing a distinction between the 'strong public sphere' and 'weak public spheres'. The 'strong public sphere' consists of the governmental institutions where actual law-making takes place. Participation of citizens here is achieved by a system of representation: 'the parliamentary principle of establishing representative bodies for deliberation and decision making'.[72] Citizens choose their representatives in regular competitive elections on the basis of political equality.

The 'weak public spheres' are the non-governmental associations of civil society. The ideal on Habermas' model is that the formation of ideas in the weak public sphere feeds into the law-making process of the strong public sphere. The weak public spheres must 'detect and identify problems' as well as 'convincingly and *influentially* thematize them, furnish them with possible solutions, and dramatize them in such a way that they are taken up and dealt with in parliamentary complexes'.[73] This public opinion is then to be picked up in the strong public sphere to be transformed into binding laws.[74]

These two mechanisms of participation both serve two goals. First, they provide mechanisms to hold those equipped with political power accountable. They are mechanisms to ensure that actors equipped with political power justify and explain their decisions to citizens. These citizens can then make a retrospective assessment of those decisions and their justifications, and possibly accompany that behaviour with sanctions.[75] Secondly, both mechanisms are ways for citizens to contribute prospectively to democratic will-formation and ensure the responsiveness of the strong public sphere to the views of citizens.

3.2 Deliberation

A conception of deliberative democracy still demands that the justification of political decisions rests on reasons with a particular quality: they must be public reasons. The key to justifying decisions in the deliberative process is that citizens 'appeal to reasons that are shared, or could be shared, by their fellow citizens'.[76] This principle of public reasoning is rooted in the idea that participants in the political

[72] Habermas, *Between Facts and Norms* (n 69) 170.
[73] ibid 359 and ch 8.
[74] Zurn, *Deliberative Democracy and the Institutions of Judicial Review* (n 15) 241; Habermas, *Between Facts and Norms* (n 69) 171.
[75] Here I rely on Mark Bovens, 'Analysing and Assessing Accountability: A Conceptual Framework' (2007) 13 European Law Journal 447, 450, and 453.
[76] Gutman and Thompson, *Democracy and Disagreement* (n 68) 25.

process should recognize each other as free and as equals, and therefore should appeal to reasons that could be shared by others.[77]

The idea of public reasoning often serves to contrast the deliberative conception of democracy with so-called aggregative conceptions of democracy. On an aggregative conception, the existing preferences and interests of citizens are taken as given. An aggregative democratic process serves to give equal consideration to these preferences and interests, for example in the form of simple majority rule. On the deliberative conception, the existing preferences and interests of citizens need to be justified as well.[78] Central to this idea is the notion that citizens are able to revise their preferences in the process of deliberation and that they appeal to reasons acceptable to others.[79]

Countering the idea that democracy as a simple process of majority voting is sufficient to provide the resulting decisions with legitimacy, deliberative democrats offer the strong argument that 'the nature of the moral claims and the quality of the moral arguments that are made before a vote is taken'[80] are crucial. If, for example, a person's vote is based on faulty information, it is difficult to see what force the vote could have against someone who is affected in his vital interests by the resulting decision. Rather, a deliberative conception of democracy in which citizens publicly justify decisions towards each other on the basis of reasons that others could accept, in which they learn from each other's positions, and in which they take each other's claims into account, is best in line with the idea that citizens are to be seen as moral agents who deserve equal respect.[81]

The requirement of public reasoning limits the possible range of legitimate substantive outcomes that the political system can produce. Nonetheless, a thick, substantive reading of what these public reasons are should be avoided.[82] If one tries to specify in the abstract the content of public reasons, the risk is ending up with a Rawlsian-like conception of justice and reproducing the problem of disagreement to which democracy was supposed to provide an answer. Rawls, after all, argues that his conception is the result of a *reasonable* consensus on matters of justice that supplies the content for his idea of public reason.[83]

Several less demanding criteria have been articulated to distinguish public reasons from non-public reasons. Examples of private reasons are self-interested reasons, prejudice, assertions of power, reasons that appeal to the interests of a

[77] Cohen, 'Procedure and Substance in Deliberative Democracy' (n 70) 413–14.

[78] Amy Gutman and Dennis Thompson, *Why Deliberative Democracy?* (Princeton University Press 2004) 13–14; Cohen, 'Procedure and Substance in Deliberative Democracy' (n 70) 411.

[79] Cohen, 'Deliberation and Democratic Legitimacy' (n 69) 75–79.

[80] Gutman and Thompson, *Democracy and Disagreement* (n 68) 32.

[81] ibid 39–51.

[82] See also Bellamy, *Political Constitutionalism* (n 9) ch 5.

[83] In this sense I follow Bellamy's interpretation of Rawls: Bellamy, *Political Constitutionalism* (n 9) 184–88. Perhaps a more procedural, less substantive, reading of Rawls' idea of public reason is also possible.

particular group over that of others, but also reasons that appeal to a particular religious authority that could not be shared by all.[84] Some authors have usefully distinguished between self-regarding, other-regarding, and ideal-regarding justifications. Self-regarding justifications refer to the interests of the speaker herself or the group that she represents. Other-regarding justifications refer to the interests of groups or persons other than those of the speaker herself or the group she represents. Ideal-regarding justifications refer to ideals or abstract moral principles. From the perspective of deliberative democracy, speakers should justify their demands also on the basis of ideal or other-regarding justifications, whereas mere self-regarding justifications are generally not acceptable grounds for political decisions because other citizens cannot share them as an appropriate justification.[85] Self-interest can have a place in deliberation only in a 'suitably constrained' manner, which generally means that the admissibility of self-interest considerations was itself decided in a process of deliberation and mutual justification.[86] Finally, it is usually argued that deliberation should take place in good faith or be truthful. This means that the participants in a democratic discourse must genuinely believe themselves the claims they are making.[87]

3.3 Political Equality and Majoritarianism

Political constitutionalists such as Waldron and Bellamy do not see majoritarianism as tyrannical, but argue instead that it offers a fair decision-making process under circumstances of disagreement. Recall that the tyranny of the majority is thought to arise if citizens vote solely on the basis of their self-interest without seriously considering the interests of fellow citizens. Minorities would therefore run the risk of having their fundamental interests disregarded by oppressive majorities.[88] Courts that protect rights could then be regarded as necessary to remedy this shortcoming of the democratic process, even if citizens can reasonably disagree about the proper protection of rights. Yet, the situation is different if legislatures do

[84] Simone Chambers, 'Behind Closed Doors: Publicity, Secrecy, and the Quality of Deliberation' [2004] The Journal of Political Philosophy 389, 391–92; Dennis Thompson, 'Deliberative Democratic Theory and Empirical Political Science' (2008) 11 Annual Review of Political Science 497, 504; Rawls, *Political Liberalism* (n 8) 58.

[85] Daniel Naurin, 'Dressed for Politics' (PhD thesis, Göteborg University 2004) 62–64. This idea could be seen as the more general demand of reciprocity, which is key in justifying norms to others; see Rainer Forst, *The Right to Justification* (Columbia University Press 2012) 79–121.

[86] Jane Mansbridge and others, 'The Place of Self-Interest and the Role of Power in Deliberative Democracy' (2010) 18 The Journal of Political Philosophy 64. See further on this issue also Steiner, *The Foundations of Deliberative Democracy* (n 12) ch 3.

[87] Jürg Steiner and others, *Deliberative Politics in Action: Analyzing Parliamentary Discourse* (Cambridge University Press 2004) 19–20; Steiner, *The Foundations of Deliberative Democracy* (n 12) 153–58.

[88] See section 2.2 above.

in fact deliberate about rights and the problem is rights disagreement, not neglect of rights considerations at all.[89] Such an idea of deliberation must posit the idea of consensus as a regulative ideal, because it demands that citizens aim to convince each other and appeal to reasons that could be shared by others. However, given the circumstances of politics it is unrealistic to expect that the outcome of such deliberations should be consensus.[90]

Instead, Waldron and Bellamy argue that decision-making by a majority among elected legislators is a fair way to take collective decisions under circumstances of reasonable disagreement. This idea rests on the premise that democratic elections ensure that majority decision-making among elected legislators is a reasonable approximation of majority decision-making 'among the citizenry as a whole'.[91] In these conditions, Waldron and Bellamy contend that majority decision-making is fair. It can be seen to give proper respect to the fact that people have different views about justice and the common good. Majority decision-making also gives equal weight to each individual opinion and therefore respects the value of political equality. In addition, it is neutral between different contested outcomes, in the sense that it does not favour any outcome that is the subject of disagreement. A decision-making rule that requires a heightened majority, such as a two-thirds majority, favours those who wish to keep the status quo. Conversely, a rule that would require less than a majority appears to favour those who want to change the status quo.[92] Waldron and Bellamy also argue that the misgivings of legal constitutionalists against majority decision-making are selective, because courts often decide by majority as well.[93] Judges, however, lack a good claim to represent citizens in the way that legislators do.

Still, it is not the mere fact that a legislative majority supports a political decision which makes it legitimate. The idea is rather that the prior deliberation plays an important role and changes the nature of the voting process.[94] Legitimacy requires that collective decisions be justified in a process of argumentation in which all citizens have an equal right to participate and that is concluded by a vote.[95] The

[89] Bellamy, *Political Constitutionalism* (n 9) 37–38; Waldron, *Law and Disagreement* (n 10) 13–15; Waldron, 'The Core of the Case Against Judicial Review' (n 2) 1395–401; Jeremy Waldron, 'Rights and Majorities: Rousseau Revisited' in Jeremy Waldron (ed), *Liberal Rights* (Cambridge University Press 1993).

[90] Waldron, *Law and Disagreement* (n 10) 91–93. Some theorists of deliberative democracy do see deliberation ideally as aimed at creating consensus. For a discussion of some different views see Steiner, *The Foundations of Deliberative Democracy* (n 12) 139–43.

[91] Waldron, 'The Core of the Case Against Judicial Review' (n 2) 1388–89.

[92] Waldron, *Law and Disagreement* (n 10) 108–14; Waldron, 'The Core of the Case Against Judicial Review' (n 2) 1387–88; Waldron, 'Democracy' (n 14); Bellamy, *Political Constitutionalism* (n 9) 227; Kenneth O May, 'A Set of Independent Necessary and Sufficient Conditions for Simple Majority Decision' (1952) 10 Econometrica 680.

[93] Waldron, 'The Core of the Case Against Judicial Review' (n 2) 1391–92; Bellamy, *Political Constitutionalism* (n 9) 38.

[94] Cohen, 'Deliberation and Democratic Legitimacy' (n 69) 75.

[95] Manin, 'On Legitimacy and Political Deliberation' (n 68) 359–62; Habermas, *Between Facts and Norms* (n 69) 304 and 472–77.

legitimacy of a majority decision depends in this respect on the idea that the 'approval of the greatest number reflects, in that context, the greater strength of one set of arguments compared to others'.[96] This presumes that the views of the losing minority were taken into consideration and that in the future those in the minority may convince their fellow citizens.[97] In sum, majoritarian decision-making is a legitimate way to take collective decisions under the circumstances of politics, where coupled with a democratic process of deliberation and contestation over different views about justice and rights.

4. Reconciling Democracy and Judicial Review?

The previous discussion on why democracy offers a fair procedure to resolve reasonable disagreements about justice and rights leaves open the possibility that judicial review is nonetheless justified for democratic reasons. Various arguments exist for this position: some defend judicial decision-making as democratic in itself; others justify it for upholding democratic decisions made in the past or as a way to protect the democratic nature of the political process. In this section, I consider these attempts to reconcile democracy and judicial review and discuss why they are ultimately unconvincing. I devote most attention to a third view, namely the idea that judicial review is justified to protect the democratic process. This position has been articulated by Ely and Habermas. It resembles the views of Rawls and Dworkin but has a more procedural orientation. Such a procedural defence of judicial review is nonetheless subject to the same objection of reasonable disagreement.

4.1 Judicial Review as Participation

One supposedly democratic justification for judicial review is that the judicial process allows for a better form of citizens' participation than the ordinary political process. A first argument is that courts are also subject to the participatory mechanisms of elections and public opinion, albeit in a different way. Thus, one could argue that constitutional judges have democratic qualities, because they are appointed by representative institutions.[98] Therefore they have a derived democratic legitimacy. Similarly, it could be argued that constitutional courts are also subject to, and need to take account of, public opinion.[99]

96 Manin, 'On Legitimacy and Political Deliberation' (n 68) 359–60.

97 Richard Bellamy, 'Democracy as Public Law: The Case of Constitutional Rights' (2013) 14 German Law Journal 1017, 1031–32; Tom Hickey, 'The Republican Core of the Case for Judicial Review' (2019) 17 International Journal of Constitutional Law 288, 296–97.

98 Christopher L Eisgruber, *Constitutional Self-Government* (Harvard University Press 2007) 3–4.

99 See eg Barry Friedman, *The Will of the People* (Farrar, Straus and Giroux 2010).

The question of the way in which constitutional adjudication reflects decision-making in the democratic process has been the subject of a substantial amount of research in the US.[100] Authors in this field have argued that the US Supreme Court must often work together with the US President and Congress in order to shape constitutional law.[101] Already in 1957, Robert Dahl wrote that the views of the US Supreme Court are never for long out of line with the views of the legislative majority. The main reason is that the US President can bring the views of the Supreme Court in line with the views of the legislative majority, by appointing judges of his/her political colour on the Supreme Court.[102] Subsequent research by social scientists has largely affirmed this conclusion, leading to a general consensus that the 'courts have not been a strong or consistent countermajoritarian force in American politics'.[103]

Although this provides a degree of democratic legitimacy to judicial decision-making, on comparison, courts are likely to score less on the participatory scoreboard than legislatures. Courts have at best a derived participatory legitimacy, which is weaker than a directly elected legislature, even if we admit that legislative elections are from perfect. It is therefore unclear why on this basis courts should be in a position to override democratic legislative majorities.[104] This argument also applies to specialized constitutional courts. Some authors maintain that, for democratic reasons, it is also crucial to distinguish between systems with specialized constitutional courts, in which the function of judicial review is concentrated, and those where ordinary courts have this power.[105] In the so-called American model of judicial review, ordinary courts can declare a law unconstitutional if the issue arises in a concrete case between litigants. Most European countries, however, have vested sole power for judicial review in a separate institution, the specialized constitutional court.[106] Within this model only the constitutional court deals with

[100] Kramer, 'Popular Constitutionalism' (n 11) 967.

[101] ibid 970.

[102] Robert Dahl, 'Decision-Making in a Democracy: The Supreme Court as a National Policy-Maker' (1957) 6 Journal of Public Law 279, 279.

[103] Kramer, 'Popular Constitutionalism' (n 11) 971.

[104] Richard Bellamy, 'The Democratic Qualities of Courts: A Critical Analysis of Three Arguments' (2013) 49(3) Representation 343–44; Waldron, 'The Core of the Case Against Judicial Review' (n 2) 1386–95.

[105] See, for a discussion in this direction, although he invokes multiple reasons, Jan Komárek, 'National Constitutional Courts in the European Constitutional Democracy' (2014) 12 International Journal of Constitutional Law 525.

[106] The set-up was inspired by the ideas of Hans Kelsen, 'Judicial Review of Legislation: A Comparative Study of the Austrian and American Constitution' (1942) 4 Journal of Politics 183; Hans Kelsen, 'La Garantie juridictionelle de la constitution (la justice constitutionnelle)' [1928] Revue de droit public 197.The specialized constitutional court model has proved very influential in Europe. Specialized constitutional courts were established in Austria (re-established in 1945), Italy (1948), Germany (1949), France (1958), and Belgium (1985). Portugal (1976) and Spain (1978) established such courts following the overthrow of authoritarian regimes and their transition into democracies. After the collapse of the Soviet Union, most Eastern and Central European states also established specialized constitutional courts. Lithuania, Latvia, the Czech Republic, Hungary, Poland, Romania, Slovakia, and Slovenia all founded a specialized constitutional court. See Alec Stone Sweet, 'Why Europe Rejected American Judicial Review—and Why It May Not Matter' (2002) 101 Michigan Law Review 2744, 2745.

constitutional questions. In addition, several of these constitutional courts have jurisdiction to review the constitutionality of laws before they come into effect in abstract review proceedings. An important reason for vesting the power of judicial review in a specialized constitutional court is that it allows for a different type of political legitimation compared to the ordinary judiciary.[107] Specialized constitutional courts thus stand apart from both the ordinary judiciary and the legislature. They are described as occupying a space somewhere in between the judicial and the political.[108] Yet, even if they are more democratic than ordinary courts, specialized constitutional courts still have weaker democratic credentials than elected legislatures.

A second argument is that constitutional adjudication provides an additional avenue for citizens to participate in political decision-making. Constitutional litigation by individuals and public interest groups may be an additional way for these groups to bring their viewpoints into the political sphere.[109]

However, as pointed out by critics of this argument, this democratic justification for judicial review runs into two problems. The first is that litigants in judicial proceedings are not the decision-makers. They can present their views and arguments to judges, but ultimately the judges make the final decision. Secondly, the access to litigation is likely to be uneven. Only litigants with substantial resources are likely to be able to bring their case successfully before a court. Compared to the legislative process, the ideal of political equality is likely to be more imperfectly realized in judicial proceedings, despite the imperfections of the legislative process.[110]

The opportunity for individuals to challenge legislation in the courts may be important for those who struggle to get their voice heard in ordinary politics, while the procedure could also signal unintended effects of legislation on their position.[111] Yet, these arguments only justify judicial review in a weak form. They do not support that courts should be in a position to override the views of democratic

The trajectory of France is different, where the *Conseil constitutionnel* was originally founded to protect the dominance of the executive, but only later developed a rights-based type of review. See Sweet, *Governing with Judges* (n 11) 41.

[107] Sweet, *Governing with Judges* (n 11) 40; Möllers, 'Legalität, Legitimität und Legitimation' (n 1) 320–23; Victor Ferreres Comella, 'The Rise of Specialized Constitutional Courts' in Tom Ginsburg and Rosalind Dixon (eds), Comparative Constitutional Law (Edward Elgar 2011) 270–71. Ferreres Comella notes that many countries preferred a specialized constitutional court because the function of constitutional review was thought to require a particular democratic legitimacy. A specialized constitutional court would allow for a more democratic appointment procedure of its judges in comparison with ordinary judges as well as more limited durations of their tenure.

[108] Sweet, *Governing with Judges* (n 11) 31–49; Sweet, 'Why Europe Rejected American Judicial Review' (n 106) 2270; Möllers, 'Legalität, Legitimität und Legitimation' (n 1) 312–13 and 320–28.

[109] Aileen Kavanagh, 'Participation and Judicial Review: A Reply to Jeremy Waldron' (2003) 22 Law and Philosophy 451.

[110] Bellamy, 'The Democratic Qualities of Courts' (n 104); Waldron, 'The Core of the Case Against Judicial Review' (n 2) 1386–95.

[111] Kavanagh, 'Participation and Judicial Review' (n 109) 479–83.

majorities. Rather they justify that majorities reconsider their views in light of arguments not yet sufficiently addressed in the legislative process or in light of the legislation's unintended effects. These arguments are therefore compatible with courts playing a signalling function while legislatures retain the last word. For the participatory argument to support judicial review in strong form, it seems that the normal routes of democratic participation must be blocked.[112] Where that is not the case, the idea that courts would be better than legislatures at allowing citizens to partake in the decisions that govern them also conflicts with cherished ideas about judicial independence and the frequently articulated notion that judicial review exists to protect us from the pathologies of democratic decision-making. That courts do allow for some degree of participation by citizens is better seen as a counterbalance to the political power they unavoidably exercise in interpreting the constitution. Moreover, even if it could be established that courts had better participatory qualities than legislatures, we might still think that this should lead us to improve the workings of representative democracy rather than to take it as a case for judicial review.

4.2 Precommitment

A different way of attempting to reconcile democracy and judicial review is to argue that judicial review does no more than enforce a democratic decision made in the past. On this understanding, the constitution and the authorization of judicial review are precommitments made by a nation's citizens in the past that limit present democratic majorities.[113] Still, because the constitution stems from a democratic decision made by citizens themselves in a referendum or by their elected representatives, neither the constitutional constraints it imposes on democratic decision-making nor the judicial review it authorizes are undemocratic.

This justification for constitutionalism and judicial review is problematic for two key reasons. First, because the precommitment limits the ability of subsequent democratic majorities to decide on constitutional matters themselves.[114] It is doubtful that democracy includes the idea that prior generations should be able to make an agreement that still binds current citizens in the present, when the latter had no possibility to participate in making that agreement themselves.[115] To

[112] Waldron, 'The Core of the Case Against Judicial Review' (n 2) 1395.

[113] For an argument in this direction: Samuel Freeman, 'Constitutional Democracy and the Legitimacy of Judicial Review' (1990) 9 Law and Philosophy 327, 353–54.

[114] See also Waldron, *Law and Disagreement* (n 10); Jeremy Waldron, 'Constitutionalism: A Skeptical View' in Jeremy Waldron (ed), *Political Political Theory* (Harvard University Press 2016).

[115] This problem was raised by Thomas Jefferson, 'Letter to Samuel Kercheval' (12 July 1816) <https://founders.archives.gov/> accessed 1 August 2022. See also Richard Bellamy, *Liberalism and Pluralism* (Routledge 1999) 65; Möllers, 'Legalität, Legitimität und Legitimation' (n 1) 331–33. Möllers notes that this problem in the German context is less pressing compared to that of the US because most German

a certain extent, this critique applies not just to the constitution, but also to other democratically enacted legislation. After all, a significant amount of the legislation currently in force is likely to have been decided before many citizens were born or achieved the voting age. Nonetheless, an ordinary democratic majority could still change this legislation when they change their mind. This does not hold for constitutional law entrenched against legislative change. As long as the constitution remains in place, one can only assume that it is still supported by a political minority sufficiently large to block constitutional change.

The second problem is that a precommitment can only settle constitutional controversies where the constitutional norms are sufficiently specific. This is problematic where the norms are highly indeterminate, which is usually the case with rights provisions and other constitutional norms. Even if we agree at time A that the precommitment of a particular right would be important, it cannot settle subsequent reasonable disagreement at time B about how this right should be interpreted. Judicial review rather reserves this judgment to the judges on a constitutional court.[116]

The justification for entrenching constitutional norms and judicial review therefore cannot simply rely on the argument that these have been democratically enacted. Additional reasons must be given. For example, it could be argued that the constitutional norms are just or produce stability. However, such reasons for entrenching particular constitutional norms are in turn subject to reasonable disagreement and always drafted in a particular historical and social context. When faced with a conflict between the legislature's majority decision to adopt a particular law and a constitutional norm, it is not immediately clear why one should privilege the views of the constitution's drafters over that of current legislators, who are arguably in a much better position to take new developments into consideration, and are presumably as intelligent as the constitution's drafters.[117]

constitutional provisions can be amended relatively easily. An exception, however, is the so-called eternity clause of Article 79(3) of the German Basic Law.

[116] See, along these lines, Waldron, *Law and Disagreement* (n 10) 260–66. For the German context: Möllers, 'Legalität, Legitimität und Legitimation' (n 1) 329–30. The idea of 'originalism' can be seen as an attempt to remedy this problem of indeterminacy and still save the idea of precommitment. The idea there is to track down the historical intentions of the constitution's drafters or accepted understandings at that time. This, however, opens up a host of new problems, such as which intentions should count; whose intentions should count; how we should interpret these intentions; and what we should do if the intentions prove incomplete, absent, indeterminate, or conflicting. In particular, there is an apparent conflict between the open-ended nature of constitutional provisions and the more concrete intentions held by its drafters. The open-ended nature of these provisions seems to be evidence that the constitution's framers meant its interpretation to require moral judgement. These are familiar criticisms of originalism. See eg Dworkin, 'The Forum of Principle' (n 42) 476–95. For similar thoughts in the context of international law, see Ingo Venzke, *How Interpretation Makes International Law* (Oxford University Press 2012) 3–4.

[117] See Mark Tushnet, *Taking the Constitution Away from the Courts* (Princeton University Press 2000) 33–35. A similar argument is offered by Waldron, *Law and Disagreement* (n 10) 270–75.

4.3 Judicial Review to Protect the Democratic Process

A more convincing justification for subjecting the democratic process to constitutional constraints and judicial review is to argue that they enable rather than constrain democracy.[118] The best-known version of such a justification for judicial review is Ely's 'participation-oriented, representation-reinforcing approach'.[119] Ely argues that judicial review should be aimed at clearing the channels of political change and at facilitating the representation of minorities.[120] In this sense, judicial review should protect free speech and the right to vote in order to maintain an open political process.[121] In addition, judicial review should protect minorities that cannot protect themselves through the political process, because widespread prejudice prevents political majorities from taking their interests seriously.[122] Ely claims that courts are better qualified at performing such a representation-reinforcing approach than legislatures themselves. As relative outsiders, judges do not need to worry about staying in office and, by definition, prejudiced majorities will not seriously consider the interests of minorities.[123]

In a similar vein, Habermas justifies the function of a constitution and judicial review with reference to the democratic process. He argues that there is an internal connection between the idea of deliberative democracy and the protection of constitutional rights as a whole, not just political rights. In his view, a constitution embodies the institutional conditions for democratic will-formation.[124] Constitutional rights are not to be seen as pre-political liberties externally imposed on the democratic process, nor solely as the result of a process of political self-determination. Rather, conceptually they are co-original with democracy. They institutionalize the possibility of democratic will-formation, but at the same time need to be specified in the democratic process. Habermas calls this idea the co-originality of private and public autonomy. Public autonomy refers to the freedom of persons to participate in collective political decisions. Private autonomy refers to a sphere in which persons can freely determine their own actions. Habermas' argument is that citizens can only exercise their public autonomy if they are sufficiently

[118] Stephen Holmes argues to this effect, as: '[t]he dead should not govern the living; but they can make it easier for the living to govern themselves'. Stephen Holmes, 'Precommitment and Disagreement' in Jon Elster and Rune Slagstad (eds), *Constitutionalism and Democracy* (Cambridge University Press 1988) 240.

[119] John Hart Ely, *Democracy and Distrust: A Theory of Judicial Review* (Harvard University Press 1980) 87. Ely's approach was based on footnote four of Justice Stone's opinion in US Supreme Court, *United States v Carolene Products Co*, 304 US 144 (1938).

[120] Ely, *Democracy and Distrust* (n 119) 74.

[121] ibid 105–34.

[122] ibid 135–79.

[123] '[I]ns have a way of wanting to make sure the out stays out', ibid 106, and further 88 and 102–03 and for the second point 151.

[124] Habermas, *The Inclusion of the Other* (n 56) 248. A similar view is expressed, albeit much more briefly, by Manin, 'On Legitimacy and Political Deliberation' (n 68) 362. Waldron appears to share such a view in Waldron, *Law and Disagreement* (n 10) 282–85.

free to begin with. In order to consider themselves the authors of the law when they exercise their public autonomy, citizens must possess a sufficient degree of private autonomy.[125] Only under such circumstances is it possible to assume that citizens' approval for a particular law is based on reasons and not the result of force or coercion. Yet, in order to specify the rights that need to be protected, citizens also need public autonomy.[126] Private and public autonomy are therefore co-original:

> This mutual presupposition expresses the intuition that, on the one hand, citizens can make adequate use of their public autonomy only if, on the basis of their equally protected private autonomy, they are sufficiently independent; but that, on the other hand, they can arrive at a consensual regulation of their private autonomy only if they make adequate use of their political autonomy as enfranchised citizens.[127]

On this basis, Habermas argues that democratic legitimacy presupposes both rights that guarantee citizens' private autonomy, as well as rights that safeguard their opportunities for political participation.[128] These rights all need to be further specified in the political process itself and in a context-dependent way.[129] That is also the case for those rights that protect citizens' political rights. So, for example, in the political process it needs to be specified how political rights such as freedom of assembly, freedom of association, and freedom of expression are to be protected. Habermas understands 'the catalogues of human and civil rights found in our historic constitutions as context-dependent readings of the *same* system of rights'.[130] He also maintains that 'every constitution is a living project that can *endure* only as an ongoing interpretation continually carried forward at all levels of the production of law'.[131]

In Habermas' political philosophy, the function of a constitution is thus understood in procedural terms. It lays down the political procedures by which citizens can adopt democratically legitimate law, and democratic legitimacy presupposes safeguarding rights both to private autonomy as well as to public autonomy.

However, if Habermas' co-originality idea aims to overcome a tension between the protection of a set of liberal rights and democracy, then it surely fails. On the contrary, Habermas shows how the tension between democracy and liberal rights

[125] Habermas, *The Inclusion of the Other* (n 56) 259–61. See also the discussion in Kenneth Baynes, 'Democracy and the Rechtsstaat: Habermas' Faktizität und Geltung' in Stephen K White (ed), The Cambridge *Companion* to Habermas (Cambridge University Press 1995).

[126] Zurn, *Deliberative Democracy and the Institutions of Judicial Review* (n 15) 232.

[127] Habermas, *The Inclusion of the Other* (n 56) 261.

[128] See generally, and for further details on the different rights, Habermas, *Between Facts and Norms* (n 69) 118–31.

[129] ibid 125.

[130] ibid 128.

[131] ibid 129.

cannot be eliminated, because it is reproduced at this fundamental level. His co-originality thesis leads to the following problem: not only is it impossible to develop a fully adequate definition of a set of liberal rights outside the democratic process, it is also impossible to determine when our decision-making procedures are truly democratic.

Suppose, for example, that a particular country wants to adopt a new democratic constitution. If we take Habermas' co-originality thesis seriously, we would not really know where to start. We would think that the country's constitution has to include a set of rights in order for it to be democratic at all. But we would need to specify these rights in a democratic process because, according to the co-originality thesis, these rights cannot be specified outside a democratic process. However, before we have specified what these rights mean, we cannot be sure that we really have a legitimate democratic process. Therefore, it is unclear how we should go about designing this constitution.

A second example illustrates the same point. Imagine now that the country's constitution has been established. Its democratically elected legislature adopts a piece of legislation by majority in the ordinary legislative process. A citizen in the losing minority subsequently complains that the piece of legislation violates her right to privacy that is enshrined in the constitution. She argues that the piece of legislation therefore cannot be considered legitimate, because it violates a key right that is supposed to be a part of a legitimate democratic process to begin with. The legislature on the other hand argues that the piece of legislation is actually a further specification of the right to privacy. The co-originality thesis cannot tell us which side should win.

In both examples it is unclear how Habermas' co-originality thesis would help in addressing these questions. Rather, it suggests the opposite, namely that it is impossible to answer these questions as a matter of political philosophy. In designing and interpreting a constitution, we have to specify a certain conception of rights in a process that we think is democratic and that sufficiently protects the rights that are part of its preconditions. We cannot claim that the resulting conception is correct because that would require a vantage point we do not have. At best we can claim that we reasonably believe it to be correct until someone shows why it is not. In this vein, a constitutional settlement can be seen only as a temporary stabilization between the conflicting ideals of democratic majority rule and liberal rights that should always be open to future contestation.[132] The constitution is, as Habermas states himself, an 'unfinished project'.[133]

[132] In developing these thoughts, I found the insights of Chantal Mouffe useful, although I do not share her conception of democracy. See Chantal Mouffe, *The Democratic Paradox* (Verso 2000) 17–34 and 80–105. See similarly Baxter, *Habermas: The Discourse Theory* (n 28) 73–74. I believe Habermas acknowledges these points in Jürgen Habermas, 'Constitutional Democracy: A Paradoxical Union of Contradictory Principles?' [2011] Political Theory 766.

[133] Habermas, *Between Facts and Norms* (n 69) 384.

For such reasons it is also difficult to determine what Habermas' co-originality thesis entails for the democratic legitimacy of judicial review. In his view, constitutional courts are to guard the conditions of procedural legitimacy, 'namely to ensure that the process of lawmaking takes place under the legitimating conditions of *deliberative politics*'.[134] But is not entirely clear what that role entails. On the one hand, Habermas suggests a limited role for constitutional courts that focuses on a 'reasoned analysis' requirement, where the 'standard of judgment is the discursive character of opinion- and will-formation, in particular the question whether the legislative decision turned on reasons that can be publicly advocated or on private interests that cannot be declared in the framework of parliamentary negotiations'.[135] On the other hand, it seems that Habermas justifies quite a demanding theory of constitutional adjudication. Constitutional adjudication can be directed at the full set of constitutional rights, not just those that safeguard public autonomy but also those that safeguard private autonomy.[136] As Christopher Zurn puts it in an interpretation of Habermas' theory:

> According to Habermas, the function of constitutional review can be summarized as simply guaranteeing the procedural fairness and openness of democratic processes. Yet, concretely, the tasks involved are manifold: keeping open the channels of political change, guaranteeing that individuals' civil, membership, legal, political, and social rights are respected, scrutinizing the constitutional quality and propriety of the reasons justifying governmental action, and ensuring that the channels of influence from independent civil society public spheres to the strong public sphere remain unobstructed and undistorted by administrative, economic, and social powers.[137]

Habermas appears to maintain that this function of constitutional review can be performed by judges and does not lead to problems, because it is aimed at the application of already justified constitutional norms and does not itself require further justification of the content of the system of rights. And because judges are specialized in discourses of application, the function of constitutional review can be located in a court.[138] Legal discourses can 'lay claim to a comparatively high presumption of rationality'.[139]

This idea seems naïve. A constitutional court will unavoidably have to further develop constitutional norms in a legislative manner because discourses

[134] ibid 274.
[135] ibid 276.
[136] Zurn, *Deliberative Democracy and the Institutions of Judicial Review* (n 15) 239.
[137] ibid 242–43.
[138] Habermas, *Between Facts and Norms* (n 69) 266; Zurn, *Deliberative Democracy and the Institutions of Judicial Review* (n 15) 245–46.
[139] Habermas, *Between Facts and Norms* (n 69) 266.

of justification and application cannot be wholly separated and because the abstract nature of many constitutional provisions certainly renders them subject to reasonable interpretive disagreement.[140] Habermas himself argues that the set of basic rights needs to be specified in an ongoing manner and in light of changing circumstances. The basis for this would be the democratic process itself. Yet, the constitutionalization of these rights, especially where coupled to judicial review, appears to hamper this ideal.

This concern also applies to judicial review on the basis of political rights, such as the right to vote and the right to free speech. As Habermas acknowledges, these 'basic rights to equal opportunities to participate in processes of opinion- and will-formation' apply reflexively to further development of the different categories of rights, including these political participation rights themselves.[141] Put more simply, by exercising their rights to political participation, citizens must also work out how to specify these rights to participation themselves. This makes sense, because reasonable disagreement does not just exist over liberal rights that protect private autonomy but also over rights that protect public autonomy, such as freedom of expression.[142] Process-based judicial review, as favoured by Ely, therefore does not do away entirely with democratic concerns about judicial review.[143]

For these reasons, the idea of co-originality entails that the best we can hope for is that every time a democratic majority adopts legislation, this is accompanied by good-faith deliberation on whether such legislation is compatible with the preconditions of democratic legitimacy. In any case, Habermas' account suggests that constitutional review should be an important part of legislating, where legislatures themselves assess whether legislation complies with the constitution.[144] The constitution must be part of an ongoing discourse, in which the constitution serves as a standard both to assess existing democratic practices, as an ideal to be further realized through legislation, but also as a standard that must be open to contestation itself.

Despite democratic concerns about letting electorally unaccountable judges decide on the fundamental constitutional questions of a political order, the institution of judicial review could be justified as second best. In this vein, judicial review could be justified if there are good reasons to suppose that legislatures by

[140] Zurn, *Deliberative Democracy and the Institutions of Judicial Review* (n 15) 256–62.

[141] Habermas, *Between Facts and Norms* (n 69) 123.

[142] See, for more elaborate criticisms on Ely's views, Bellamy, *Political Constitutionalism* (n 9) 107–18; Laurence Tribe, *The Puzzling Persistence of Process-Based Constitutional Theories* (1980) <http://hdl.handle.net/20.500.13051/15960> accessed 1 August 2022; Mark Tushnet, *Darkness on the Edge of Town: The Contributions of John Hart Ely to Constitutional Theory* (1980) <http://hdl.handle.net/20.500.13051/15958> accessed 1 August 2022.

[143] As Waldron puts it, '[d]emocracy is in part about democracy'. Waldron, *Law and Disagreement* (n 10) 296 and 282–312. Christoph Möllers and Richard Bellamy invoke the metaphor of a ship that one builds and repairs whilst at sea. Möllers, 'Legalität, Legitimität und Legitimation' (n 1) 336–38; Bellamy, *Political Constitutionalism* (n 9) 174.

[144] Zurn, *Deliberative Democracy and the Institutions of Judicial Review* (n 15) ch 9.

themselves do not adequately take into account the preconditions of democracy, because they are insufficiently deliberative.[145] Attaining the ideal of deliberative democracy could, for example, require a division of labour between representative institutions that aggregate preferences and constitutional courts that engage in the more deliberative and principled reasoning regarding fundamental questions of the political order.[146] This brings me to the viewpoint of political constitutionalists, who reject judicial review not only because it is undemocratic, but also because they doubt it leads to better decision-making on constitutional matters.

5. Political Constitutionalism and the Case Against Judicial Review

Political constitutionalists, such as Jeremy Waldron, Mark Tushnet, and Richard Bellamy, argue that in well-functioning democracies, legislatures are better placed, or at least equally well-placed as constitutional courts, to address rights issues.[147] The problem of reasonable disagreement about rights and the importance of democracy therefore leads them to reject rights-based judicial review. Yet, as I argue in this section, they offer limited evidence to back up their claim that legislatures take rights seriously and risk relying on an idealized view of the democratic process.

5.1 The Case Against Judicial Review

The political constitutionalists' argument against judicial review depends on a number of conditions. Waldron articulates these as part of his 'core case' against judicial review, distinguished from non-core cases in which 'judicial review might be deemed appropriate as an anomalous provision to deal with special pathologies'.[148] One condition on which the case against judicial review depends is that the society in question has 'democratic institutions in reasonably good working order, including a representative legislature elected on the basis of universal adult suffrage'.[149] This does not mean that these institutions work perfectly or that they cannot be improved, but that they function reasonably well. Waldron also assumes

[145] See also Zurn, *Deliberative Democracy and the Institutions of Judicial Review* (n 15) 245–47. Conrado Hübner Mendes argues for judicial review as a mechanism that leads to better deliberation about constitutional essentials. Conrado Hübner Mendes, 'Neither Dialogue Nor Last Word—Deliberative Separation of Powers 3' (2011) 5 Legisprudence 1.

[146] For a critical perspective on a number of such views, see Zurn, *Deliberative Democracy and the Institutions of Judicial Review* (n 15) 163–220.

[147] Waldron, 'The Core of the Case Against Judicial Review' (n 2); Bellamy, *Political Constitutionalism* (n 9); Tushnet, *Taking the Constitution Away from the Courts* (n 117).

[148] Waldron, 'The Core of the Case Against Judicial Review' (n 2) 1359.

[149] ibid 1360.

that the legislature has experience in dealing with difficult issues of justice and social policy; that the legislative process includes various safeguards, such as committee scrutiny and bicameralism; and that the legislative process connects to wider debates in society. In addition, there is 'a culture of democracy, valuing responsible deliberation and political equality'.[150] Moreover, 'the institutions, procedures, and practices of legislation are kept under constant review' from the perspective of political equality.[151]

A second condition is that there 'is a strong commitment on the part of most members of the society we are contemplating to the idea of individual and minority rights'.[152] This means that:

> [T]hey accept that individuals have certain interests and are entitled to certain liberties that should not be denied simply because it would be more convenient for most people to deny them. They believe that minorities are entitled to a degree of support, recognition, and insulation that is not necessarily guaranteed by their numbers or by their political weight.[153]

However, they reasonably and in good faith disagree about rights. Such rights disagreements do not just concern their outer ranges of application. They often concern central applications of the rights in question and raise major political and moral issues, such as the legality of abortion, the desirability of affirmative action, and what rights criminal suspects should be granted in a fair trial. Nor do Waldron and other political constitutionalists believe that this position amounts to rights scepticism or moral relativism. The recognition of disagreement does not exclude the option that one side is right, or that there is a true position about rights. It rather recognizes that disagreement is a feature of talk about rights and that such disagreement requires a solution.[154]

Under these conditions, Waldron and other political constitutionalists contend that legislatures can be expected to deliberate seriously about rights issues.[155] When a court is given the ability to strike down legislation incompatible with rights, it will take sides in good-faith disagreements among elected legislators that have settled their disagreement by majority decision. In this constellation, the

[150] ibid 1361.
[151] ibid 1362.
[152] ibid 1364.
[153] ibid 1364.
[154] See also Waldron, 'A Right-Based Critique of Constitutional Rights' (n 71). Waldron sees the problem of disagreement as an epistemic problem in the sense that we have no established method to determine right answers about moral questions, regardless of whether such right answers exist. Waldron, *Law and Disagreement* (n 10) 164–87; Bellamy, 'Political Constitutionalism and the Human Rights Act' (n 10) 93.
[155] Perhaps Bellamy is more careful in his assessment of the actual functioning of democracy in Bellamy, 'Democracy as Public Law' (n 97) 1032. There he acknowledges the potential shortcomings of democratic process also in established democracies.

legitimacy of the court's role can no longer be justified solely with the argument that the court protects rights. Given that courts do not allow for a better form of citizens' participation than the ordinary political process and are consequently less democratic, the key issue is whether courts are more likely to arrive at better judgments about rights than legislatures.[156] The case for judicial review thus depends on a comparative assessment of courts' and legislatures' abilities, with outcome-based considerations as the yardstick. Such a comparison should take into account that no mechanism for settling rights disagreements will be perfect. Any decision-making procedure may lead to errors. The comparison must also take into account reasonable disagreement. A decision-making procedure should not be favoured because it achieves particular controversial outcomes that are subject to reasonable disagreement.[157] The outcome-based case for or against judicial review must instead be based on a comparison of broader institutional features that influence the way legislatures and courts make decisions.[158]

Assessed along these lines, political constitutionalists doubt that courts will do better than legislatures. A key argument they reject is that constitutional courts focus on the protection of individuals, because courts consider individual cases and would therefore be better placed to protect rights. Waldron calls this argument 'mostly a myth'.[159] Cases before courts are often brought by advocacy groups that want a particular interpretation of rights to be implemented based on general considerations rather than on the basis of individual cases. Moreover, in systems with abstract forms of review, there often are no concrete cases at the source of a judgment. At the same time, within the legislative process individuals can direct the attention of legislators to the possible impact of legislation on their individual position. As a result, legislatures may be seen to be in a better position to weigh all the different interests affected by a particular legislative act.[160]

A second argument is that judges are oriented towards a written rights charter, which ensures that cases focus on the rights issues at stake. Yet, one problem with this view is that the text of a written rights charter usually does not provide a clear answer to rights disagreements. As Waldron submits, people on different sides of an argument will often consider that the text of a rights charter pleads in their favour:

> One lesson of American constitutional experience is that the words of each provision tend to take on a life of their own, becoming the obsessive catchphrase for expressing everything one might want to say about the right in question.[161]

156 Waldron, 'The Core of the Case Against Judicial Review' (n 2) 1372–73; Bellamy, 'Democracy as Public Law' (n 97) 1030.
157 Waldron, 'The Core of the Case Against Judicial Review' (n 2) 1373–74.
158 Kavanagh, 'Participation and Judicial Review' (n 109) 466.
159 Waldron, 'The Core of the Case Against Judicial Review' (n 2) 1379.
160 ibid 1379–80. Similarly: Bellamy, *Political Constitutionalism* (n 9) 29–34.
161 Waldron, 'The Core of the Case Against Judicial Review' (n 2) 1381.

The threat is rather that a written rights charter, interpreted by judges, will make disputes over rights focus on the precise wording of the legal provisions rather than on the actual issues at stake. Waldron argues that courts are likely to be worried about their legitimacy and therefore 'cling to their authorizing texts and debate their interpretation rather than venturing out to discuss moral reasons directly'.[162] The judicial treatment of rights is therefore likely to focus on the wrong issues.[163] The focus on a rights charter may also come at the expense of rights not included in the list, such as socioeconomic rights.

This problem also casts doubt on the idea that courts would be better at protecting rights because they give elaborate reasons for their judgments. As courts often do not approach the moral issues head-on, their reasoning has a partly technical character. Courts focus on the words of an authoritative text and often base themselves on previous decisions on the matter.[164]

Waldron argues that legislative debate, in comparison, is often very rich. He submits that in the United Kingdom (UK) House of Commons debate on the Medical Termination of Pregnancy Bill from 1966, politicians talked through and focused 'on all of the questions that need to be addressed when abortion is being debated' and that they 'debated the questions passionately, but also thoroughly and honourably, with attention to the rights, principles, and pragmatic issues on both sides'.[165]

On balance, it is therefore doubtful that the reasons offered by judges for particular rights interpretations are better than those offered by legislators. Legislators give reasons for the legislation they adopt in the political debates preceding the adoption of such laws. Waldron argues, however, that unlike courts, legislatures are better able to address the moral issues at stake head-on.[166] This provides the opposite picture of that offered by Dworkin, who maintained that courts are unlike legislatures precisely because courts will address the moral issues implicated in rights disputes. Waldron's point of view appears to be supported by empirical research on judicial review and constitutional courts, in the sense that judicial review is said to lead to the judicialization of politics. This process signifies an increasing influence of courts on political actors. On the basis of a comparative study of the

[162] ibid 1381. A similar point is made by Judith N Shklar, *Legalism* (Harvard University Press 1964) 10–12.

[163] Waldron, 'The Core of the Case Against Judicial Review' (n 2) 1381–82; Bellamy, *Political Constitutionalism* (n 9) 36–37; Tushnet, *Taking the Constitution Away from the Courts* (n 117) 60.

[164] Waldron, 'The Core of the Case Against Judicial Review' (n 2) 1382–84.

[165] ibid 1384. Note that Waldron's standard of assessment seems to be that of an observer with full knowledge of the relevant moral questions and issues who in light of this knowledge is able to assess that legislative debate is of high quality. This standard of evaluation seems inconsistent with his epistemic doubts about moral knowledge and hence the need to accommodate reasonable disagreement in a democratic process. Clearly, the standard of evaluation adopted by Waldron in the quoted phrase cannot be the normal standard for assessing the constitutional quality of legislative debate.

[166] ibid 1384; Jeremy Waldron, 'Judges as Moral Reasoners' (2009) 7 International Journal of Constitutional Law 2.

Italian, Spanish, French, and German constitutional courts, Alec Stone Sweet concludes that legislatures become more like judges themselves under the spectre of judicial review. The constitutional courts need to maintain their status as neutral arbiters between parties to a dispute and therefore depict their decision-making as merely 'judicial' rather than 'political'. They portray their reasoning as logically deriving correct outcomes from the provisions of higher constitutional law and provide partial victories to different parties to a dispute. Such review subsequently affects legislative action. Partisan political debate is partly displaced by a more formal legal discourse about the meaning of constitutional rules in which the different political stakes are no longer addressed directly. Within this discourse, the constitutional court's case law and its interpretation by legal scholars play a key role.[167]

5.2 Challenges

Despite the cogency of the political constitutionalists' case against judicial review, their arguments face at least three key difficulties. First, it is not clear how realistic their assumptions are about the functioning of legislatures.[168] Political constitutionalists offer compelling arguments why judges may not be best at deciding rights issues. They rightly point out that legal constitutionalists often paint an idealized picture of judicial decision-making.[169] Yet, political constitutionalists may in turn be criticized for idealizing the legislative process. They assume that legislatures, as well as citizens more generally, take rights seriously. For that reason, legislatures can be expected to seriously address the moral stakes in deciding rights issues and will be at least as well-positioned as courts to address questions about the protection of fundamental rights. This assumption about the quality of the

167 Sweet, *Governing with Judges* (n 11) 139–52 and 194–204. For similar concerns see also Yannis Papadopoulos, *Democracy in Crisis? Politics, Governance and Policy* (Palgrave Macmillan 2013) 191–213. Comparing the German and US context, Michaela Hailbronner has noted how the German Constitutional Court relies extensively on scholarly literature in its judgments. By contrast, the German Constitutional Court hardly recognizes the legislature or citizens as constitutional interpreters. In the US, on the other hand, she notes that judicial supremacy is more contested and that the Supreme Court more readily acknowledges the importance of public opinion in interpreting the constitution. The relevance of scholarly literature instead is much lower. Michaela Hailbronner, 'We the Experts. Die Geschlossene Gesellschaft Der Verfassungsinterpreten' (2014) 53 Der Staat 425.

168 Theunis Roux, 'In Defence of Empirical Entanglement: The Methodological Flaw in Waldron's Case against Judicial Review' in Graeme Orr and others (eds), *The Cambridge Handbook of Deliberative Constitutionalism* (Cambridge University Press 2018) <www.cambridge.org/core/books/cambridge-handbook-of-deliberative-constitutionalism/in-defence-of-empirical-entanglement-the-methodological-flaw-in-waldrons-case-against-judicial-review/BEC729510B3EAC60783287820BAF6DEE> accessed 1 August 2022; Guillaume Tusseau, 'A Plea for a Hint of Empiricism in Constitutional Theory: A Comment on Cesare Pinelli's Constitutional Reasoning and Political Deliberation' (2013) 14 German Law Journal 1184.

169 For Waldron's criticism on this idealization of judicial decision-making, see Jeremy Waldron, *The Dignity of Legislation* (Cambridge University Press 1999).

legislative process may be seen as over-optimistic. Waldron, for example, does not offer much evidence to back it up.[170] He mostly dwells on one legislative debate from one country to support this point, namely the UK House of Commons debates on the Medical Termination of Pregnancy Bill from 1966.[171] Furthermore, the rise and apparent popularity of authoritarian and illiberal politics, propagated by the likes of Viktor Orbán, Jarosław Kaczyński, and Donald Trump, raise further questions about the capacity of legislatures to adequately safeguard individual and minority rights. By now it is unfortunately no longer clear—if it ever was—that even in countries with a long democratic tradition, such as the US, constitutional rights and democracy itself are safe in the hands of elected politicians.[172] Better insights into the actual functioning and respective capabilities of legislatures and courts are consequently key in assessing how the function of constitutional review is best institutionalized and whether it justifies judicial review.[173]

That we do not really know whether legislatures take rights as seriously as Waldron and other judicial review critics suggest, allows for a different appreciation of the precommitment argument discussed in section 4.2.[174] Uncertainty about the ability of legislatures to address rights issues means that the drafting of a constitution is commonly made with incomplete information as to whether one can expect the legislature to take rights issues seriously. Given such uncertainty, it is possible for citizens to reasonably disagree about the desirability of including constitutional constraints and judicial review in a constitution. The decision by a constituent power to entrench constitutional constraints and/or authorize judicial

[170] In *Law and Disagreement* Waldron states this as an assumption, but he believes it to be 'true empirically that citizens and representatives often do vote on the basis of good faith and relatively impartial opinions about justice, rights, and the common good'. He also sees this part of his theory as 'an aspirational quality'. Waldron, *Law and Disagreement* (n 10) 14. In *The Dignity of Legislation*, however, this assumption appears less empirical, but is stated as an ideal. Waldron, *The Dignity of Legislation* (n 169) 2. Tushnet offers a more elaborate analysis on the role of the US Supreme Court within US politics; see, eg, Tushnet, *Taking the Constitution Away from the Courts* (n 117) 129–53.

[171] See also Andreas Follesdal, 'Why the European Court of Human Rights Might Be Democratically Legitimate—A Modest Defense' (2009) 27 Nordisk Tidsskrift for Menneskerettigheter 289, 299. In *Law and Disagreement* Waldron refers to his 'experience' with national debates in the UK and New Zealand, which he regards as equally 'robust and well-informed', as well as to debates in the UK about homosexual law reform. Waldron, *Law and Disagreement* (n 10) 290.

[172] Conor Gearty, 'The Courts in Europe Today: Subverting or Saving Democracy?—Cristina E. Parau, Transnational Networking and Elite Self-Empowerment. The Making of the Judiciary in Contemporary Europe and Beyond (Oxford University Press 2018) Pp. 350.' (2020) 16 European Constitutional Law Review 770.

[173] Bellamy considers this point in the following manner: 'It might be objected that democratic politics in the era of the USA (Trump), Turkey (Erdogan), and Hungary (Orban), to name but three countries, is in poor shape. Yet, so is judicial review in these countries. One cannot save democracy by non-democratic means: as the Conservative take-over of the US Supreme Court amply demonstrates, that merely compounds the problem.' Richard Bellamy, 'The Republican Core of the Case for Judicial Review: A Reply to Tom Hickey. Why Political Constitutionalism Requires Equality of Power and Weak Review' (2019) 17 International Journal of Constitutional Law 317, 328.

[174] Waldron argues against precommitment as a justification for judicial review based on the assumption that legislative deliberations ordinarily include deliberations over issues of moral principle, but are marked by reasonable disagreement over such issues. Waldron, *Law and Disagreement* (n 10) ch 12.

review may thus be seen as a reasonable response to historical circumstances. Most European constitutional courts were founded in states at a time when they had little or no experience with democracy and where a general commitment to the idea of rights or democracy among its population could not be taken for granted.[175] For example, when the German Constitutional Court was founded after the Second World War there was a reasonable expectation that the wider population did not yet take the rights of minorities seriously. As the historian Tony Judt reports, in the years 1945–49 'a consistent majority of Germans believed that "Nazism was a good idea, badly applied"'.[176] In 1952, three years after West Germany's new constitution had been adopted, 25 per cent of the West German population still stated that they had a good opinion of Adolf Hitler, while 37 per cent still thought it better for Germany not to have Jews on its territory.[177] In Spain and Portugal, constitutional courts were set up after the fall of authoritarian, non-democratic regimes. In Eastern European countries, they were founded after the fall of Communism. In such circumstances, there are grounds to expect that the democratic process may not be fully respectful of rights. For these reasons, it is difficult to maintain that the institution of judicial review is democratically illegitimate per se. Rather, it is pivotal to see how it functions in practice compared to a system without such review and to assess whether one of these systems is more legitimate in light of the available evidence. This is important as well because the historical circumstances that once justified setting up judicial review may no longer hold in the present.[178] Precommitment thus offers a qualified justification for establishing this institution.

The second type of difficulty for political constitutionalists is that their normative commitments cannot completely rule out the legitimacy of judicial review.[179] Waldron argues that citizens and legislatures take rights seriously, but that they reasonably and in good faith disagree about what their protection requires. This condition appears to require that the justification of political decisions must at least rest on public reasons, as discussed in section 3.2. On this basis, persons can only

175 Before the Second World War most European parliamentary systems embraced legislative supremacy, but the war's destruction and Europe's experience with totalitarianism led to a shift in thinking about state power. What emerged in Western Europe was a constrained form of democracy in which stability became a major goal and that was informed by a distrust of popular sovereignty and even distrust of parliamentary sovereignty. On the history related to this see Jan-Werner Müller, *Contesting Democracy* (Yale University Press 2011) 128–30 and 146–50.

176 Tony Judt, *Postwar: A History of Europe since 1945* (Penguin Books 2005) 58.

177 ibid 58.

178 In this sense, eg in relation to the German context, see Ulrich R Haltern, 'High Time for a Check-up: Progressivism, Populism and Constitutional Review in Germany' (1996) Jean Monnet Working Papers <http://jeanmonnetprogram.org/1996-jean-monnet-working-papers/> accessed 1 August 2022; Katja Gelinsky, 'Interview with Professor Dr. Christoph Möllers, Humboldt University, Berlin, Faculty of Law: On the Occasion of the 60th Anniversary of the German Federal Constitutional Court ("Bundesverfassungsgericht")' (2012) 13 German Law Journal 165; Matthias Jestaedt and others (eds), *Das entgrenzte Gericht. Eine kritische Bilanz nach Sechzig Jahren Bundesverfassungsgericht* (Suhrkamp 2011).

179 Similarly: Thomas Christiano, 'Waldron on Law and Disagreement' (2000) 19 Law and Philosophy 513, 530, and 538–42.

be seen to take rights seriously where they appeal in good faith to public reasons in justifying their claims to others. Yet, judicial review could then still be legitimate if it is simply aimed at correcting unreasonable democratic decision-making.[180] The deliberative quality of the legislative process could be the focus of judicial review, an option I further explore in section 6. Similarly, courts could supposedly safeguard that a society's democratic institutions remain in reasonably good working order, which is an assumption underpinning the political constitutionalists' case against judicial review. The key question is then no longer whether judicial review could be legitimate, but rather whether it is necessary and how likely it is that courts would accept a more minimalist theory of interpretation.[181]

A third and related issue is that political constitutionalists present the problem of judicial review in an all-or-nothing fashion. Waldron's comparative institutional analysis between courts and legislatures asks which institution is better at deciding rights issues. This overlooks the possibility that courts can take considerations about institutional capability into account when they review legislation. Where their review would be merely directed at examining whether the prior political process was sufficiently deliberative, they would not wholly supplant legislative choices on matters of rights, but rather assess their reasonableness. In this manner, the question about judicial review concerns not just whether courts or legislatures are better at deciding rights issues, but whether courts may correct for some of the legitimacy deficits in legislative processes without encroaching upon the priority of democracy.[182]

6. Carving Out a Limited Role for Judicial Review

The challenges to the political constitutionalists' arguments discussed in the previous section leave open a number of justifications for judicial review that take account of the political constitutionalists' objections.[183] One is that courts could still legitimately apply more minimal forms of review. Mark Tushnet, for example, reasons that it would be a good thing to have a restricted role for judicial review to protect the right to vote, to ensure that people can still criticize the government, to maintain that people have some private space to develop their ideas about

[180] In a similar sense: Rawls' introduction to the paperback edition of Rawls, *Political Liberalism* (n 8) xlix; Christiano, 'Waldron on Law and Disagreement' (n 179) 530.

[181] Mark Tushnet addresses this issue explicitly and still rejects judicial review. See Tushnet, *Taking the Constitution Away from the Courts* (n 117) 155–63.

[182] See eg the work of Kumm who argues that proportionality analysis amounts to a public reason test: Mattias Kumm, 'Institutionalising Socratic Contestation: The Rationalist Human Rights Paradigm, Legitimate Authority and the Point of Judicial Review' (2007) 1 European Journal of Legal Studies 1; Mattias Kumm, 'The Turn to Justification: On the Structure and Domain of Human Rights Practice' in Adam Etinson (ed), *Human Rights: Moral or Political?* (Oxford University Press 2018).

[183] See similarly Hickey, 'The Republican Core of the Case for Judicial Review' (n 97).

politics, and to deal with real constitutional crises.[184] Similarly, and drawing on the European context, Mattias Kumm has argued that rights-based judicial review institutionalizes a practice of Socratic contestation. In his view, proportionality review entails a check of whether the exercise of public authority conforms to public reason. Judicial review thus ensures that the exercise of public authority remains reasonable.[185] Rights should be understood as having a wide scope, but subject to a broad range of possible restrictions. Conceivably the scope of rights should be so wide that they allow citizens to challenge the justifiability of practically any government measure. However, rights infringements merely trigger a process in which courts assess their justification. In this vein, courts should assess the reasons supporting government decisions that infringe rights, by checking whether they have a legitimate aim, whether they are suitable to achieve this aim, whether they could have been reached by equally effective but less intrusive measures, and, finally, whether the extent to which the measures that further the legitimate aim outweighs the extent of the rights infringement. Kumm argues that in this way judicial review serves to address particular pathologies of the legislative process. It helps to weed out legislation that rests on traditions, conventions, or specific religious conceptions that cannot serve as a basis for public justification, or legislation that, as a result of legislative capture, gives unjustified special benefits to particular groups.

In principle, such more limited forms of review avoid the main democratic objections to judicial review. The political constitutionalists' case against judicial review rests on the general assumption that the democratic process is reasonable. As proportionality review aims to safeguard this reasonable quality, it looks largely immune to democratic objections against judicial review. Yet, such theories of interpretation face two key difficulties. First, there is no guarantee that judges will actually apply a particular interpretive theory. Once given the power to review legislation, judges may end up doing much more. Theories of interpretation therefore appear of limited help in addressing questions of institutional design. This problem relates to the second difficulty, namely that interpretive theories are themselves indeterminate and touch upon many issues that people reasonably disagree about. Proportionality review, for example, can be very intrusive, particularly where courts engage directly in balancing different interests. Tushnet acknowledges these problems and submits that, for such reasons, judicial review is best dispensed with in the US context.[186]

184 Tushnet, *Taking the Constitution Away from the Courts* (n 117) 157–63.

185 Kumm, 'Institutionalising Socratic Contestation' (n 182); Mattias Kumm, 'The Idea of Socratic Contestation and the Right to Justification: The Point of Rights-Based Proportionality Review' (2010) 4 Law & Ethics of Human Rights 142; Kumm, 'The Turn to Justification' (n 182).

186 Tushnet states: 'Arguments about what courts should do are not completely ineffective, but our nation's experience with judicial review gives little reason to believe that such arguments have a substantial impact on what the justices do.' Mark Tushnet, *Taking the Constitution Away from the Courts* (Princeton University Press 2000) 155 and see further 154–63.

A different idea to justify judicial review is to see it as the embodiment of a right to a hearing, as argued by Alon Harel, Tsvi Kahana, and Adam Shinar.[187] Given that a constitution embodies the preconditions for democratically legitimate law, law can claim legitimacy only where these preconditions are fulfilled. Although there is no unequivocal standard to establish when that is the case, there is good reason to give citizens the ability to contest legislation before an independent institution on constitutional grounds. Like proportionality review, the right to a hearing invokes the language of justification. It consists of 'the opportunity to voice a grievance, the opportunity to be provided with a justification for a decision that impinges (or may impinge) on one's rights, and the duty to reconsider the initial decision giving rise to the grievance'.[188] Harel, Kahana, and Shinar submit that the right to question and challenge legislative decisions provides an intrinsic reason for judicial review rather than one merely dependent on the outcomes reached, a claim also made by Kumm in relation to proportionality review.[189]

However, by itself the right to a hearing does not provide a conclusive argument for strong-form judicial review. Such a right requires that citizens are owed a justification and a reconsideration of the original decision when they deem that legislation violates their rights. It does not tell us how that reconsideration should take place, nor does it offer decisive grounds for holding that courts should make the ultimate decision, only that the original decision is reconsidered. Providing a right to a hearing is compatible with weak-form review, where courts are competent to hear constitutional challenges to legislation, but where legislatures retain the final say.[190]

This idea of weak-form review has gained currency in contemporary constitutional debates and is supported by political constitutionalists.[191] Such weak-form judicial review exists in a number of variations. One variant is that judges only have the power to interpret ordinary legislation in conformity with a list of constitutional rights insofar as this is possible without distorting the legislation's meaning. A second variant is that courts also have the power to declare that ordinary law and constitutional norms are incompatible, but do not have the power to give legal

[187] Alon Harel and Tsvi Kahana, 'The Easy Core Case for Judicial Review' (2010) 2 Journal of Legal Analysis 227; Alon Harel and Adam Shinar, 'Between Judicial and Legislative Supremacy: A Cautious Defense of Constrained Judicial Review' (2012) 10 International Journal of Constitutional Law 950; Alon Harel, *Why Law Matters* (Oxford University Press 2014) ch 6 <https://doi.org/10.1093/acprof:oso/9780199643271.001.0001> accessed 2 August 2022. For a similar view, see Cristina Lafont, 'Philosophical Foundations of Judicial Review' in David Dyzenhaus and Malcolm Thorburn (eds), *Philosophical Foundations of Constitutional Law* (Oxford University Press 2016) <https://doi.org/10.1093/acprof:oso/9780198754527.003.0014> accessed 2 August 2022.

[188] Harel and Kahana, 'The Easy Core Case for Judicial Review' (n 187) 238–39.

[189] ibid; Harel and Shinar, Between Judicial and Legislative Supremacy' (n 187); Kumm, 'The Idea of Socratic Contestation' (n 185) 170–71.

[190] I take Harel to essentially agree with this position. See Harel, *Why Law Matters* (n 187) 216–23; Harel and Shinar, 'Between Judicial and Legislative Supremacy' (n 187) 973–74.

[191] See eg Michelman, 'Why Not Just Say No?' (n 9); Bellamy, 'Democracy as Public Law' (n 97).

effect to such a declaration, although there may be provisions for a fast-track legislative amendment. A third variant is that the judicial interpretation of constitutional norms can be overridden in the ordinary legislative process.[192] Given that courts lack the final say on the meaning of constitutional norms, weak-form judicial review is not subject to the main democratic objections that face strong-form judicial review. Instead, it allows an ongoing discourse between various institutions about the constitution.[193] In addition, weak-form review in concrete cases can help address unintended or unanticipated consequences of legislation for individuals' rights, as well as counter different forms of inertia that potentially burden the legislative process.[194]

Still, any such institutional argument would benefit from a better understanding of why and how legislatures would be inadequately equipped to protect the constitution by themselves, as well as how judicial review has actually functioned in societies where it exists. Strong-form review could still be considered justified as a second-best option where in practice legislatures do not seriously deliberate constitutional matters, while weak-form review may be too weak to address this problem. A key issue is consequently whether a political system with judicial review somehow better ensures that deliberation on constitutional questions takes place, compared to a system without such review. Addressing this issue requires an answer to at least three questions that can be seen as more empirical in nature. The first question is how legislatures debate constitutional issues in the absence of judicial review and whether this can plausibly qualify as reasonable. Answering this question should contribute to the further understanding of whether legislatures take the protection of constitutional rights and other constitutional issues sufficiently seriously in their deliberations, although they disagree about their proper protection. The second is how these legislative deliberations

192 Tushnet, *Weak Courts, Strong Rights* (n 2) 24–33. New Zealand was an example of the first variant, but the New Zealand Supreme Court ruled in 2018 that it can issue declarations of incompatibility as well. The UK is an example of the second, where the British Human Rights Act 1998 instructs judges to interpret statutes in conformity with fundamental rights and also authorizes them to declare such statutes incompatible with fundamental rights. Such declarations of incompatibility, however, have no immediate legal effects. Canada is an example of the third variant. For a large part of the Canadian Charter of Rights and Freedoms, section 33 allows the Canadian parliament and legislatures of the provinces to override court judgments in which legislation is held to have violated the Charter.

193 This seems to fit well with Habermas' idea of co-originality. See also Baxter, *Habermas: The Discourse Theory* (n 28) 143–45.

194 Rosalind Dixon, 'The Core Case for Weak-Form Judicial Review' (2017) 38 Cardozo Law Review 2193. Dixon distinguishes between priority-driven burdens of inertia and coalition-driven burdens of inertia. Priority-driven burdens of inertia result from legislative capacity constraints. As a result, legislative majorities will focus on certain priorities, which may come at the expense of attending to rights-based claims that have a relatively low priority but are supported by a majority of the population. Coalition-driven burdens of inertia relate to the political dynamics of political parties. A party may want to keep particular rights claims off the legislative agenda because the party is internally divided on the issue, even if the rights claims in question have broad popular support. See similarly: Mark Tushnet, 'The Relation Between Political Constitutionalism and Weak-Form Judicial Review' (2013) 14 German Law Journal 2249, 2249; Bellamy, 'Democracy as Public Law' (n 97) 1036.

over constitutional issues compare to the assessment of constitutional courts on similar issues. The third is how judicial review impacts on subsequent legislative deliberations. For example, when the legislative process falls significantly short of the deliberative ideal, courts may adopt more intrusive forms of review to compensate for this problem, especially where it improves the subsequent deliberative quality of the legislative process. The proper judicial function must be tied to a better understanding of the role constitutional issues play in legislative deliberations.

The consequence is that any assessment of the democratic legitimacy of judicial review is likely to be dependent on specific political, historical, and social contexts. It must also be acknowledged that there is no unequivocal normative standard to assess the quality of legislative and judicial deliberations on constitutional issues. They require the researcher to make contextual assessments about the reasonable quality of political and judicial decision-making. Proportionality-type reasoning as proposed by Kumm can be a useful tool in this regard. Yet, evaluations of whether a legislative process was reasonable or whether its deliberative quality was improved by subsequent judicial review are likely to be subject to reasonable disagreement themselves. The only option seems to be to engage critically with legislative and judicial reasoning, to assess the different arguments offered, and ultimately to consider whether legislatures reasonably addressed the underlying constitutional concerns in relation to a particular constitutional controversy or that courts made up for deficits in this regard.[195] Such an assessment is in turn open to question. Nonetheless, focusing on the actual performance of legislatures and courts will hopefully foster a better understanding of the validity of the empirical presuppositions on which the debate between critics and proponents of judicial review partly depends.[196] Such enquiries are therefore of value even for those who reject the democratic objections against judicial review articulated in this chapter.

[195] A possible way to side-step this problem could be to come up with a particular set of constitutional standards—rights and other standards—including their required interpretation and argue that any political system should satisfy them. Although one could acknowledge that these rights will be controversial and subject to disagreement, one could simply claim that people with such beliefs are wrong. Subsequently the set of constitutional standards could be used to compare different political systems with and without judicial review, to enquire which systems achieve better outcomes as assessed by these constitutional standards, and research whether the difference in outcomes can be seen as caused by the existence of judicial review. This appears to be the approach followed in the David L Cingranelli and David L Richards, *The CIRI Human Rights Data Project* (2014) <www.humanrightsdata.com/> accessed 1 August 2022. Drawing on this dataset Arthur Dyevre concludes that 'the effect of judicial review on empowerment rights is robust against alternative explanations' (p 58). The empowerment rights include rights such as freedom of speech, workers' rights, freedom of movement, freedom of religion, and rights to political participation. However, he does stress the need for more and better empirical research. Arthur Dyevre, 'Technocracy and Distrust: Revisiting the Rationale for Constitutional Review' (2015) 13 International Journal of Constitutional Law 30.

[196] Tusseau, 'A Plea for a Hint of Empiricism' (n 168).

7. Conclusion

Judicial review poses a democratic challenge because it allows electorally unaccountable courts to override the decisions of democratically elected legislatures. As was argued in this chapter, the best justification for such review is that it safeguards the preconditions of democratic legitimacy, understood along the lines of Habermas' theory of deliberative democracy. On this approach, the constitution is understood as laying down the preconditions for a democratically legitimate lawmaking process, primarily by setting up a system of rights to private and public autonomy. The constitution, however, must be realized and specified in ongoing democratic discourses. This approach avoids the problem of the legal constitutionalists' justification of constitutionalism and judicial review, where the democratic process is subjected to the outcomes of a pre-political agreement on the requirements of justice. On the other hand, it also clarifies how the democratic legitimacy of legislation depends on the continued guarantee of persons' rights to private and public autonomy.

A crucial difficulty with Habermas' co-originality thesis is, however, that the precise relation between democracy and constitutionalism becomes unclear. Because constitutional norms are a precondition for a legitimate democratic process, but also require specification within the democratic process, constitutional norms can no longer serve as an uncontroversial standard to assess democratically adopted legislation. At the same time, in order to accept the legitimacy of such legislation it must also be ascertained whether legislation complies with constitutional norms.

In a democratic society, a constitution thus functions both as a standard to assess the legitimacy of law and as expressing an ideal to be further realized in law, but also as a set of norms that itself must be open to revision in light of new insights and arguments. Beyond certain minimal requirements, the best we can hope for in the domestic context is that there is ongoing deliberation about whether a country's laws remain compatible with the preconditions of democratic legitimacy. This entails that legislating must be accompanied by a check of whether such legislation complies with the norms and ideals laid down in the constitution, but not necessarily that this check should be exercised by a court. Whether the institution of judicial review is necessary, what type of review a constitutional court should exercise, and how this institution should be given shape all depend on an assessment of the comparative abilities of legislatures and constitutional courts to address the legislation's constitutional implications. Such comparative assessments must be empirically informed.

I argued in this chapter that judicial review in a weak form fits well with the deliberative conception of democracy. Weak-form review allows citizens to contest the outcomes of democratic procedures before an independent court on the grounds that the conditions for democratically legitimate legislation were not respected. At the same time, it leaves the ultimate decision on the constitutionality of legislation to the legislature. Thus, weak-form review prevents the courts from displacing the assessment of the legislature and ensures that an ongoing democratic discourse on the constitution can continue. Nonetheless, the case for weak-form review is contingent on the empirical assumption that legislatures can be expected to seriously consider the constitutional implications of the laws they enact.

3

National Constitutional Courts' Review of European Law and its Democratic Legitimacy

1. Introduction

The previous chapter discussed the normative justification for judicial review in the domestic context. The current chapter turns to the legitimacy of the national constitutional court's review of European law. As I argued in the last chapter, the best justification for judicial review of legislation in the domestic context is that it safeguards considered deliberation on whether legislation complies with the preconditions for democratically legitimate law-making. Yet, to understand whether judicial review better ensures that such deliberation takes place, further comparative institutional research is required. This research should shed more light on how legislatures and constitutional judges address the constitutional implications of legislation, as well as how judicial review affects subsequent deliberations in the legislative process.

The present chapter builds on this idea to assess the legitimacy of the national constitutional courts' review of European law. Recall that in this book I use the term European law as a broad notion. It includes EU-related legal instruments that strictly fall outside the scope of the EU Treaties but nonetheless clearly concern the EU. In addition, the term European law also refers to European treaties before their formal entry into force.[1]

Generally speaking, judicial review of European law by national constitutional courts raises a structurally similar democratic concern to that in the domestic context. As in the domestic context, judicial review of European law subjects the decision-making of political institutions to constitutional constraints as interpreted by democratically unaccountable constitutional courts. There is even reason to consider the democratic legitimacy of such review as more problematic in the EU context. In the national context, constitutional court judgments will mainly have repercussions for political decision-making within a single state. Yet, when national courts assess European law, their judgments have potential consequences

[1] See the Introduction (Chapter 1, section 2).

Judging European Democracy. Nik de Boer, Oxford University Press. © Nik de Boer 2023.
DOI: 10.1093/oso/9780192845238.003.0003

for the EU as a whole, affecting citizens across Europe.[2] In the national context, the democratic problem with judicial review is attenuated to some extent by the limited democratic qualities of courts. As discussed in the previous chapter, constitutional courts possess such limited democratic qualities, because their judges are commonly appointed by representative institutions and because they are likely to take account of public opinion. Yet, these democratic qualities have a mainly national source. They have less normative force when the courts' decisions have significant repercussions beyond a single state.

Despite raising a similar democratic concern, assessing the legitimacy of the national constitutional courts' review of European law must be sensitive to the relevant characteristics of the EU context. My aim in this chapter is to explain how three such features affect the legitimacy of the national constitutional courts' role in relation to the EU. First, there are several concerns about the democratic legitimacy of the EU. The case against judicial review in the national context is premised on the assumption that democratic institutions are in reasonably good working order. In the EU there are serious questions about whether that assumption holds. In this respect, the EU seems to be what Waldron would call a non-core case: a setting in which the arguments against judicial review do not fully apply. This consideration does not entail, however, that democratic objections to judicial review have no purchase in the EU context. Despite concerns about the democratic qualities of the EU's decision-making processes, the case against judicial review is at least partly comparative. Using such a comparative lens, the EU's political institutions still possess stronger democratic qualities than national constitutional courts.[3] However, one could argue that the national constitutional courts' review of European law is a justified response to the EU's democratic shortcomings.[4] One idea is that such review helps counter the undemocratic features of the EU's decision-making process. A related idea is that the EU's undemocratic features make the constitutional courts pivotal in ensuring that constitutional issues are duly considered. The EU's democratic legitimacy problems may negatively impact on how constitutional

[2] Although the extent of this problem will depend on the nature of the case and the power of the Member State where the constitutional court is based. For example, where a national constitutional court holds EU law inapplicable in the national legal order on constitutional grounds, this will have fewer consequences for the overall effectiveness of EU law where the court is, say, in Estonia rather than in Germany.

[3] Martijn van den Brink, 'Justice, Legitimacy and the Authority of Legislation within the European Union' (2019) 82 The Modern Law Review 293.

[4] For various views on how the supposed democratic shortcomings of the EU matter for the national constitutional courts' review of European law, see eg Dieter Grimm, 'Defending Sovereign Statehood Against Transforming the Union Into a State' (2009) 5 European Constitutional Law Review; European Constitutional Law Review 353; Dieter Grimm, 'The Role of National Constitutional Courts in European Democracy' in Dieter Grimm (ed), *The Constitution of European Democracy* (Oxford University Press 2017); Mattias Kumm, 'The Jurisprudence of Constitutional Conflict: Constitutional Supremacy in Europe before and after the Constitutional Treaty' (2005) 11 European Law Journal 262.

issues are addressed in the political process, making judicial review a necessary safeguard.

This first issue is explored in section 2 of this chapter, where I largely reject the view that national constitutional courts should address the EU's democratic legitimacy problems. How the EU should be made more democratic is a complex political question on which there exist multiple competing and reasonable viewpoints. Where national constitutional courts assess the EU on democratic grounds, they consequently risk constraining legitimate political decision-making on this issue. I argue that this leaves two options to justify the national courts' review. One is that they should employ more minimal forms of review if this allows them to address democratic legitimacy problems of the EU in a way that is beyond reasonable disagreement. Another is to argue that the courts' review better ensures ongoing deliberation on constitutional questions compared to a situation in which such review would not take place. As follows from Chapter 2, this second justification requires empirically informed comparative institutional assessments.

Section 3 discusses the second relevant characteristic of the EU context. This concerns how the institutional setting of the EU differs from that of the domestic context and how this aspect matters for the legitimacy of the national constitutional courts' review. Different institutions located at different levels of government are involved in EU decision-making and the institutional constellation differs depending on the type of measure under review. Normative assessments of the constitutional courts' role should be sensitive to these institutional settings. Their review may be considered more legitimate in some settings as compared to others. To offer the most prominent example: national constitutional review may provide a justified counterbalance to the power of the Court of Justice of the European Union (CJEU), but that rationale is much less convincing when the national courts' review limits the decision-making of national and EU legislatures. Section 3 sketches these different institutional constellations and shows why and how they matter for assessing the legitimacy of the constitutional courts' review of European law.

Section 4 discusses the third relevant aspect of the EU context, namely the grounds on which national courts review European law. The discussion in Chapter 2 focused on rights-based review, which is the main issue in the debate over the legitimacy of judicial review in the domestic setting. In the EU, fundamental rights are historically an important ground for national constitutional courts to resist the primacy of EU law. Yet, over the past three decades the focus of the national courts' review has turned to issues of constitutional identity and competence divisions between the EU and its Member States. In sections 4.2 and 4.3, I argue that democratic objections also apply to these other grounds of review. I also show how these objections are underappreciated in existing assessments of the national courts' role. The best justification for review on the basis of constitutional identity and competence divisions is that it better safeguards considered deliberation on constitutional questions related to the EU than when left to political institutions. Again, establishing whether the national constitutional courts' review can be justified in this manner requires empirically informed comparative institutional assessments. For that reason, the subsequent chapters contain a case study of the GFCC that offers such a comparative assessment. I note finally that the discussion in the present chapter is not meant to provide an exhaustive overview of the national courts' relevant case law.[5] Instead, it serves to understand the legitimacy of their review in light of the possible ways that such review is exercised.

2. Should Democracy be a Standard for Reviewing European Law?

To understand how the EU's democratic legitimacy problems matter for assessing the legitimacy of the national constitutional courts' review of European law, I first discuss what these problems are. In this respect, I focus on the problems of executive dominance, over-constitutionalization, and the EU's functional orientation as key concerns. Subsequently, I consider possible solutions and argue why national constitutional courts should have only a limited role in trying to bring these about.

2.1 The EU's Democratic Legitimacy Problems

2.1.1 Executive dominance

Although the Treaty on European Union (TEU) proclaims that the 'functioning of the Union shall be founded on representative democracy',[6] there are several reasons to believe that the EU suffers from democratic legitimacy problems. Key among these is the problem of executive dominance: executive actors rather than directly representative institutions dominate the EU's decision-making processes.

The formal mechanisms of ensuring democratic accountability and will-formation in the EU proceed in two ways: directly through elections for the European Parliament (EP) and more indirectly through national elections.[7] The EP is directly elected by the citizens of the Member States but does not have all the formal competences that national parliaments commonly have. The EP has formal

[5] Such overviews are provided elsewhere, see Anneli Albi and Samo Bardutzky (eds), *National Constitutions in European and Global Governance: Democracy, Rights, the Rule of Law* (TMC Asser Press 2019); Leonard FM Besselink and others, *National Constitutional Avenues for Further EU Integration* (Study requested by the European Parliament's Committee on Legal Affairs and Constitutional Affairs Committee of the European Parliament, DG for Internal Policies Study 2014) <www.europarl.europa.eu/RegData/etudes/etudes/join/2014/493046/IPOL-JURI_ET(2014)493046_EN.pdf> accessed 2 August 2022; Ana Bobić, *The Jurisprudence of Constitutional Conflict in the European Union* (Oxford University Press 2022).

[6] Art 10(1) TEU.

[7] See also art 10(2) TEU.

rights of co-decision in many competence areas of the EU, but some are still excluded. Also, the Commission retains the nearly exclusive right to initiate legislation in the EU. In addition, the EP has less influence on the composition of the European Commission than most national parliaments have on their respective national governments. The EP must approve the President of the Commission as well as its composition, but individual commissioners are proposed by the Member States. Moreover, the Parliament can only force the Commission to resign if it has a two-thirds majority.[8]

As a consequence, the EU's institutional set-up lacks what Hix and Føllesdal call an 'electoral contest for political leadership at the European level or the basic direction of the EU policy agenda'.[9] The EU decision-making process suffers from a lack of contestation over different policy alternatives and political positions, because 'there is no room to present a rival set of leadership candidates (a government "in waiting") and a rival policy agenda'.[10] Under such circumstances, it is difficult for citizens to distinguish between opposition to the EU as a whole, and opposition to current EU policies.[11]

These problems are not fully remedied by the involvement of national parliaments. In national elections, citizens can choose representatives in their national parliaments, who in turn are supposed to hold their governments acting in the Council and European Council accountable. This set-up, however, has democratic shortcomings. First, there is the problem of the collective. National parliaments can only hold their individual governments to account and not the Council as a whole.[12] This is a problem, particularly where decision-making in the Council proceeds by qualified majority rather than unanimity, as individual Member States can be outvoted, and national parliaments therefore cannot control the EU's exercise of legislative powers. Secondly, lack of information hinders democratic accountability and will-formation. Decisions taken in the Council are often the result of

[8] Yannis Papadopoulos, *Democracy in Crisis? Politics, Governance and Policy* (Palgrave Macmillan 2013) 102–03. See also art 17 TEU.

[9] Andreas Føllesdal and Simon Hix, 'Why There Is a Democratic Deficit in the EU: A Response to Majone and Moravscik' (2006) 44 Journal of Common Market Studies 533, 522.

[10] Føllesdal and Hix, 'Why There Is a Democratic Deficit in the EU' (n 9) 548.

[11] ibid 548–50. I leave open whether the *Spitzenkandidaten* process can satisfactorily address this problem. The process entails that the EP elections provide an indirect election of the Commission Presidency. Each of the main EP political groups proposes a candidate for the Presidency during the elections, and the candidate of the party with the relative majority is appointed Commission President. In 2014, this procedure was indeed followed when the candidate of the European People's Party, Jean-Claude Juncker, became Commission President. In 2019, however, the process was not repeated. See, on these issues, Jan-Herman Reestman and Leonard FM Besselink, 'Spitzenkandidaten and the European Union's System of Government' (2019) 15 European Constitutional Law Review 609. Even if successful, the Commission's composition would still not be subject to the same influence of the EP as most national governments are from their respective national parliaments. The success of the *Spitzenkandidaten* process was contested in any case. For a critical view, see Marco Goldoni, 'Politicising EU Lawmaking? The Spitzenkandidaten Experiment as a Cautionary Tale' (2016) 22 European Law Journal 279.

[12] Deirdre Curtin, 'Challenging Executive Dominance in European Democracy' (2014) 77 Modern Law Review 1, 31–32.

compromises, while a lack of transparency surrounds these negotiations.[13] Under these circumstances 'governments can claim credit for the positive aspects as they shift blame to negotiation partners for the negative aspects'.[14]

The problem of executive dominance increased with the response of the EU Member States' governments to the eurozone crisis. The European Council and the eurozone summits, composed of the representatives of the eurozone Member States, came to play a crucial role for new steps towards further European integration. Yet, these meetings were not public and often lack effective oversight by national parliaments or the EP.[15] In addition, this mode of decision-making has been said to follow a logic of international power, rather than respecting the equality of the Member States.[16] Finally, more technocratic institutions, such as the Commission and the European Central Bank (ECB), were given an enhanced role in supervising Member States' economic and financial policies, limiting national autonomy.[17] The resulting situation is one that Jürgen Habermas has called 'executive federalism': decision-making by political elites behind closed doors rather than through an 'argumentative conflict of opinions with the broad public'.[18]

2.1.2 Over-constitutionalization, depoliticization, and judicialization

A second and related democratic problem in the EU results from the skewed balance between law and politics compared to that of the Member States. It is not just the case that the EU's decision-making processes are dominated by executive actors, but also that the legal and institutional architecture of the EU appears to structurally privilege certain political considerations over others. This problem stems from two factors. The first is what has been called the EU's over-constitutionalization: much of EU law is resistant to change, limiting the freedom that political institutions have to consider different policy options, and resulting in excessive power of the CJEU. Secondly, the EU's functional institutional design is said to privilege certain political considerations over others.

The problem of over-constitutionalization exists because the adoption and amendment of most norms of EU law are subject to considerable consensus

[13] ibid 2–4 and 11–29. See also 2–4 and 11–29.

[14] Papadopoulos, *Democracy in Crisis?* (n 8) 104. On the issue of transparency, see also Maarten Hillebrandt, 'Living Transparency: The Development of Access to Documents in the Council of the EU and Its Democratic Implications' (PhD thesis, University of Amsterdam 2017).

[15] Wolfgang Wessels and others, 'Democratic Control in the Member States of the European Council and the Euro Zone Summits' (Study requested by the Constitutional Affairs Committee of the European Parliament, DG for Internal Policies Study 2013); Curtin, 'Challenging Executive Dominance in European Democracy' (n 12) 7–10 and 16–19.

[16] Ben Crum, 'Saving the Euro at the Cost of Democracy?' (2013) 51 Journal of Common Market Studies 614, 622.

[17] See eg Jukka Snell, 'The Trilemma of European Economic and Monetary Integration, and Its Consequences' (2016) 22 European Law Journal 157.

[18] Jürgen Habermas, *The Crisis of the European Union: A Response* (English edn, Polity 2012) 6; Mark Dawson, 'The Legal and Political Accountability Structure of 'Post-Crisis' EU Economic Governance' (2015) 53 JCMS: Journal of Common Market Studies 976, 988–90.

requirements, similarly to national constitutional law. This makes EU law difficult to change. Changing the primary law enshrined in the EU Treaties requires unanimity among the Member States and a burdensome ratification process.[19] However, and as noted by Dieter Grimm, the EU Treaties contain a great number of provisions that would be ordinary law in the Member States. They are not restricted to provisions that ordinarily fulfil the functions of a constitution.[20] The consensus requirements for secondary EU law are also considerable, although less demanding than for Treaty change.[21]

At the same time, EU law does have direct effect in the Member States' legal orders, and primacy over conflicting national law. This constellation has made the CJEU a highly powerful institution. The Court is able to further develop the law, whereas it is difficult for political institutions to correct their decisions.[22] The concern mirrors the problematic democratic legitimacy of constitutional courts in the domestic context, but in a heightened sense, as the EU Treaties are even more difficult to amend than most national constitutions. In turn, the CJEU's interpretations of EU law have negative effects on the democratic autonomy of the Member States, which has been noted as a problem, particularly in the area of internal market law.[23] Although the CJEU allows a wide range of possible justifications for national rules impeding free movement,[24] the Court still judges whether national rules satisfy both a legitimate purpose as well as the requirement of proportionality.[25]

According to Scharpf, the CJEU's case law has had important substantive effects on the course of European integration and its democratic legitimacy. First, there are defects in terms of participation, as the cases that come before the Court are likely to be 'an extremely skewed sample of all the interest constellations that are affected by European integration'.[26] For citizens and companies that compose the less

[19] See art 48 TEU.

[20] Dieter Grimm, 'The Democratic Costs of Constitutionalisation: The European Case' (2015) 21 European Law Journal 460, 470.

[21] Even under the ordinary legislative procedure the Member States acting in the Council still need to agree a qualified majority (arts 289 and 294 TFEU). Such a qualified majority requires 'at least 55 % of the members of the Council, comprising at least fifteen of them and representing Member States comprising at least 65 % of the population of the Union', art 16(4) TEU.

[22] Grimm, 'The Democratic Costs of Constitutionalisation' (n 20) 471; Fritz W Scharpf, 'Legitimacy in the Multi-Level European Polity' in Petra Dobner and Martin Loughlin (eds), *The Twilight of Constitutionalism?* (Oxford University Press 2010).

[23] The CJEU's broad interpretation of the EU's free movement rights subjects a very broad range of national rules to possible review, namely any national rule that potentially impedes transnational trade. The key case that marked this expansive interpretation is the CJEU's 1974 *Dassonville* case, Case 8/74 *Procureur du Roi v Benoît and Gustave Dassonville* [1974] ECR 837. On this issue, see Miguel Poiares Maduro, 'Europe and the Constitution: What If This Is as Good as It Gets?' in Joseph HH Weiler and Marlene Wind (eds), *European Constitutionalism Beyond the State* (Cambridge University Press 2003) 58–59 and 158–59.

[24] Case 120/78 *Rewe-Zentral AG v Bundesmonopolverwaltung für Branntwein* (*Cassis de Dijon*) [1979] ECR 649, especially para 8.

[25] Fritz W Scharpf, 'The Asymmetry of European Integration, or Why the EU Cannot Be a 'Social Market Economy'' (2010) 8 Socio-Economic Review 211, 220.

[26] ibid 221.

mobile majority in Europe, who often benefit from national regulations and policies, there is little interest in bringing a case before the CJEU. Secondly, the exercise of judicial power favours deregulation of national regimes. The CJEU can only disallow national regulations that impede free movement rules but cannot replace the national policy with a common European framework.[27] The development of such a common European framework by means of EU legislation is difficult, given the high consensus requirements in the EU legislative process and the wide differences between Member States' interests and preferences. The judicial enforcement of the Treaty freedoms thus makes it likely that there is 'a strong asymmetry between judicially imposed negative integration and legislative positive integration'.[28]

The second and related problem is that the EU's functional design means that EU legislation must be adopted pursuant to certain goals that are not open to full democratic discussion themselves. The EU has been set up to achieve a limited number of aims, which is reflected in a limited set of functional competences. The prime example of this functional design is that a significant number of the EU's competences are geared towards the creation of an internal market. As a result, the EU's laws and policies must often pursue specific aims determined in the Treaties. One concern is that this functional orientation limits political contestation over the underlying goals and that the EU cannot or does not take certain normative concerns adequately into account. For example, it has been noted that the EU's economic orientation limits its ability to fully take into account other non-economic normative concerns. At the same time, the goals underlying the EU's competences are broad enough to authorize legislation that affects a wide range of policy areas: they do not restrict the EU's legislative authority to specific sectors, and prohibitions of harmonization in specific fields do not work effectively to contain EU legislative action.[29]

2.1.3 Possible ways to democratize the EU

In a nutshell, the answer to the challenges of executive dominance, over-constitutionalization, judicialization, and functional design can be sought in a politicization of the EU's decision-making process. Various proposals to this effect have been made. One proposal is to increase the power of directly elected

[27] ibid 221 and 223.

[28] ibid 223. According to Scharpf, this has adverse effects, particularly for so-called social market economies with more extensive welfare states, which are more vulnerable to deregulation. The Court's case law that upholds mobility rights of individuals and firms, risks undermining the solidarity and reciprocity on which these social market economies are built. On these points see 233–38.

[29] For concerns along these lines with several remaining differences, see Gareth Davies, 'Democracy and Legitimacy in the Shadow of Purposive Competence' (2015) 21 European Law Journal 2; Sacha Garben, 'Confronting the Competence Conundrum: Democratising the European Union through an Expansion of Its Legislative Powers' [2014] Oxford Journal of Legal Studies 1, 20–22; Marija Bartl, 'The Way We Do Europe: Subsidiarity and the Substantive Democratic Deficit' (2015) 21 European Law Journal 23.

institutions, that is, the EP and national parliaments.[30] Another is to scale back the content of the Treaties to their constitutional elements and give other norms the status of secondary law, while possibly subjecting the latter to majoritarian voting procedures.[31] With respect to the functional design of the EU, some have argued that the EU's competences should be organized in a more sector-specific manner: defined in terms of a power over a specific field, rather than in terms of a particular goal to be achieved.[32] Others have argued for enlarging the EU's competences or even giving up strictly demarcating the EU and Member State competences altogether. This would reduce their current functional focus and put economic considerations on a par with other concerns.[33] Moreover, as the euro crisis has shown, demarcating the EU and Member States' competences does not prevent the Member States from cooperating outside the EU Treaty Framework in a manner that is arguably more questionable in terms of democratic legitimacy.[34]

It is not necessary to discuss the relative merits of these different proposals here. The key question here is rather whether national constitutional courts should aim to correct the EU's democratic shortcomings. Certainly, some authors and constitutional courts believe that democracy-based review is a good idea.[35] Yet, as I discuss next, there are grounds to be sceptical.

2.2 Democratizing the EU and the Role of Constitutional Courts

2.2.1 Democracy-based constitutional review and the challenge of disagreement

The idea that national constitutional courts should correct the democratic shortcomings of the EU runs into the following problem: it is likely to embroil these courts in many contested political issues. How the EU should be made more

[30] See eg Mark Dawson and Floris De Witte, 'From Balance to Conflict: A New Constitution for the EU' (2016) 22 European Law Journal 204. For an account focused more on the role of national parliaments, see Richard Bellamy, 'A European Republic of Sovereign States: Sovereignty, Republicanism and the European Union' (2016) 15 European Journal of Political Theory 1; Sandra Kröger and Richard Bellamy, 'Beyond a Constraining Dissensus: The Role of National Parliaments in Domesticating and Normalising the Politicization of European Integration' (2016) 14 Comparative European Politics 131.

[31] Grimm, 'The Democratic Costs of Constitutionalisation' (n 20) 473; Fritz W Scharpf, 'After the Crash: A Perspective on European Multilevel Democracy' (2015) 21 European Law Journal 384, 400–05. Another idea is to create a political override of the CJEU, eg by the European Council: Scharpf, 'Legitimacy in the Multi-Level European Polity' (n 22).

[32] Davies, 'Democracy and Legitimacy in the Shadow of Purposive Competence' (n 29) 2 and 14.

[33] According to Sacha Garben, '[i]t is in fact precisely because the current competence constellation does not effectively contain EU integration that we need to enhance the EU's formal powers, counterintuitive as it may sound.' Garben, 'Confronting the Competence Conundrum' (n 29) 2.

[34] Sacha Garben voices similar criticism against the Open Method of Coordination, Garben, 'Confronting the Competence Conundrum' (n 29) 11–15.

[35] Most of the GFCC's review revolves around the principle of democracy and has been supported by, eg, Grimm, 'The Role of National Constitutional Courts' (n 4).

democratic is subject to reasonable disagreement, as there are many competing perspectives on how the EU should be assessed in democratic terms.

One influential view is that the EU cannot become a fully democratic organization or cannot be understood as a political community similar to a nation-state. Rather than to try and democratize the EU at the European level, it would therefore be better to defend the decision-making autonomy of national democracies by protecting their essential competences and prevent the EU's power expansion.[36]

This view is informed by two key arguments. One is that transforming the EU into a real European democracy is impossible because there is no European people or *demos*. The 'no-*demos*' thesis holds that only where citizens identify with each other to a sufficient degree will they accept being outvoted in a majoritarian democratic process and accept redistributive policies. For that reason, democracy requires a shared national identity that involves a sense of shared history, culture, and common language. Supposedly the EU lacks such a shared identity. Consequently, the social bases for majoritarian democracy and redistributive policies are not present.[37] The second argument is that there is no European-wide public sphere: the mediation mechanism between formal political institutions on the one hand, and citizens and civil society on the other does not function as well on the European level as on the nation-state level. The reasons are that there is no Europeanized political party system, no well-developed European civil society, no sufficiently Europeanized media, and no common European language. European citizens thus lack the ability to effectively influence politics at the EU level.[38]

These arguments present a challenge to attempts at democratizing the EU. Strengthening the powers of the EP could not meaningfully make the EU more democratic, but risks making matters worse by diminishing the powers of the Member State governments in the Council.[39] Scaling back the content of the Treaties or enhancing the EU's legislative powers could likewise threaten the

[36] This is essentially the approach of the GFCC and supported to some extent by Grimm, 'Defending Sovereign Statehood' (n 4); Grimm, 'The Role of National Constitutional Courts' (n 4). Similar arguments are voiced by Scharpf, 'Legitimacy in the Multi-Level European Polity' (n 22). For an elaborate justification of an EU in which Member States would remain the main source of democratic legitimacy, see Richard Bellamy, *A Republican Europe of States: Cosmopolitanism, Intergovernmentalism and Democracy in the EU* (Cambridge University Press 2019).

[37] For a discussion of such arguments, see eg David Miller, *Citizenship and National Identity* (Polity Press 2000) 75–80; David Miller, *On Nationality* (Clarendon Press 1995) 99–108; Joseph HH Weiler, Ulrich R Haltern, and Franz Mayer, 'European Democracy and Its Critique' (1995) EUI Working Paper RSC No 95/11 <http://cadmus.eui.eu/bitstream/handle/1814/1386/95_11.pdf> accessed 1 August 2022; Bellamy, *A Republican Europe of States* (n 36). This line of thinking is of course reflected in the GFCC's *Maastricht* judgment and to some degree in its *Lisbon* judgment.

[38] Dieter Grimm, 'The Achievement of Constitutionalism and Its Prospects in a Changed World' in Petra Dobner and Martin Loughlin (eds), *The Twilight of Constitutionalism?* (Oxford University Press 2010) 21–22; Dieter Grimm, 'Does Europe Need a Constitution?' (1995) 1 European Law Journal 282, 292–99. Again, the argument is reflected in the case law of the GFCC, particularly its judgments on the Maastricht and Lisbon Treaties.

[39] On these points see Grimm, 'The Democratic Costs of Constitutionalisation' (n 20) 472; Weiler, Haltern, and Mayer, 'European Democracy and Its Critique' (n 37).

autonomy of the Member States and be ill-advised. Both arguments indicate that the democratization of the EU is by no means a straightforward task. Even if one rejects the no-*demos* thesis and the public sphere argument, a consideration is still that European institutions are more distant to citizens than national parliaments. It is thus harder for citizens to meaningfully participate in European-level politics. For example, in 2015 a national MP represented on average around 52,000 voters, whereas on average there was one Member of the EP for every 673,000 voters.[40]

In turn, the no-*demos* thesis and the public sphere argument are contested. For example, Habermas argues that civic solidarity is the result of political integration rather than vice versa. He also considers that the opening up of national public spheres would be sufficient to achieve the requisite Europe-wide communication.[41] These discussions raise complex empirical and moral issues, for which courts have no obvious expertise.

There is also the competing charge that the nation-state by itself suffers from democratic shortcomings.[42] A first argument is that democratic decision-making is based on the ideal that persons should have an equal right to participate in the decisions that affect them.[43] This ideal of political equality favours including all persons in the decision-making processes that affect them. Yet, in real life such a right is attached to being a citizen of a particular state. The formation of a political community implies a moment of closure where those who belong to the 'people' or '*demos*' are distinguished from those outside it.[44] To reconcile such exclusion with the underlying ideal of political equality, one requires a sufficient degree of congruence between those belonging to the 'people' and those affected by its decisions. It is doubtful whether such congruence can exist and whether convincing criteria can be given to distinguish those 'affected' from the 'non-affected' by collective decisions of a nation-state.[45] Yet, particularly in the present-day interconnected

[40] Olivier Rozenberg and Claudia Hefftler, 'Introduction' in Claudia Hefftler and others (eds), *The Palgrave Handbook of National Parliaments and the European Union* (Palgrave Macmillan 2015) 3.

[41] Jürgen Habermas, 'Democracy in Europe: Why the Development of the EU into a Transnational Democracy Is Necessary and How It Is Possible' (2015) 21 European Law Journal 546, 552–54. See, for similar lines of thought, Jürgen Habermas, 'Remarks on Dieter Grimm's 'Does Europe Need a Constitution?'' (1995) 1 European Law Journal 303, 307; Føllesdal and Hix, 'Why There Is a Democratic Deficit in the EU' (n 9) 550. For empirical evidence that a majority of Europeans consider themselves both national and European and that national public spheres have undergone a process of increased Europeanization, see Thomas Risse, 'No Demos? Identities and Public Spheres in the Euro Crisis' (2014) 52 Journal of Common Market Studies 1207. See also the work of Nancy Fraser, who offers an elaborate analysis of the problems with applying the concept of the public sphere beyond the nation-state and favours a rethinking of how public spheres could still perform their democratic function in this changed context. Nancy Fraser, *Scales of Justice, Reimagining Political Space in a Globalizing World* (Columbia University Press 2010) 67–99.

[42] For an elaborate discussion of such problems, see also Bellamy, *A Republican Europe of States* (n 36) ch 1.

[43] Jürgen Habermas, *Between Facts and Norms* (Polity Press 1996) 107–09.

[44] Chantal Mouffe, *The Democratic Paradox* (Verso 2000) 36–57.

[45] For such an attempt, see Mattias Kumm, 'The Cosmopolitan Turn in Constitutionalism: An Integrated Conception of Public Law' (2013) 20 Indiana Journal of Global Legal Studies 629.

world, the assumption of congruence between those affected by the collective decisions of a nation-state and those that have a right to participate in such decision-making no longer seems to hold. Decisions of one state now fundamentally affect the livelihoods of citizens in other states.[46]

This connects to a second idea, namely that a democratic polity is 'a community that rightly governs itself and determines its own future.'[47] Equally, in today's world, the assumptions at the basis of this ideal of collective self-determination no longer hold with equal force. Processes of globalization have undermined the capacity of nation-states to solve several pressing political problems.[48] Prominent examples are environmental problems and the effective regulation of global markets.[49] Furthermore, as the decisions of one state now fundamentally affect those of others, the capacity for self-determination of single states is consequently affected.

On this reading, the setting up and strengthening of supranational governance structures is a way to enhance the democratic legitimacy of existing governance structures: European integration presents both an opportunity for political decision-making to become more inclusive regarding the persons it affects, as well as an opportunity to take back control over policy areas over which nation-states no longer possess effective influence.[50]

These competing viewpoints on how European integration relates to democratic ideals make clear that the issue of how the EU should be democratized depends on complex moral and empirical assessments, subject to reasonable disagreement. For example, some may conclude that further European integration enhances democratic ideals on balance, even if they acknowledge problems with the lack of a shared identity and public sphere in the EU.

Such disagreement makes it difficult to argue that national constitutional courts should review European law in order to address the EU's democratic legitimacy

[46] Jürgen Habermas, *The Postnational Constellation* (The MIT Press 2001) 70; Fraser, *Scales of Justice* (n 41) 92. Fraser proposes a different standard than shared citizenship that she refers to as 'the all-subjected principle' (at 96).

[47] David Held, *Models of Democracy* (3rd edn, Stanford University Press 2006) 291–92. Similarly, Habermas, *The Postnational Constellation* (n 46) 60.

[48] For an influential contribution, see Dani Rodrik, *The Globalization Paradox: Democracy and the Future of the World Economy* (WW Norton & Company 2011) 184–206. According to Rodrik, economic globalization involves a political trilemma: one cannot have national sovereignty, democracy, and economic globalization at the same time. Instead, one must choose between any combination of two. National democracy and deep global economic integration are therefore incompatible.

[49] Held, *Models of Democracy* (n 47) 290–304. This argument about 'effectiveness' also plays an important role in Nancy Fraser's arguments about rethinking public sphere theory, see Fraser, *Scales of Justice* (n 41) 96–98.

[50] Habermas, *The Postnational Constellation* (n 46) 60–62. Some go even further and argue that the answer lies in a cosmopolitan democracy with political institutions that 'would coexist with the system of states but which would override states in clearly defined spheres of activity where those activities have demonstrable transnational and international consequences.' Held, *Models of Democracy* (n 47) 305. Such proposals have, however, been criticized as naive or too idealistic. Habermas, for example, argues that such a world community of citizens would lack the civil solidarity necessary to become fully democratic and achieve goals of social justice.

problems. Rather than straightforwardly enhancing the EU's democratic legitimacy, their review would risk constraining political debate over many fundamental questions about the EU. Particularly so, because existing political left–right divisions are likely to affect ideas about how the EU should be assessed democratically. To name a few examples: for parties that favour liberal economic policies, the loss of the political capacity to intervene in markets is likely to be less of a problem than for social-democratic parties that favour more extensive redistributive schemes; parties that attach greater political value to protecting the environment will see a greater need for transnational cooperation in the field of the environment, whereas parties that value local communities and identities are more likely to resist competence transfers to a transnational level.

2.2.2 Limited review and comparative institutional assessments

Two conclusions follow. First, the national constitutional courts' review could be considered as democracy-enhancing where it addresses problems concerning the EU's democratic legitimacy that are beyond reasonable disagreement. For example, it could be the case that courts help strengthen national parliamentary oversight of the executive and facilitate more transparency in EU decision-making. With such review, national courts do not seem to impose themselves on the contested relationship between the EU and its Member States but do counter executive dominance in European affairs.

In this vein, the GFCC has demanded improved rights of participation and access to information on EU affairs for its national parliament on a number of occasions.[51] These cases also provide an indication that parliaments may be reluctant to provide adequate oversight themselves. The main political cleavage in parliamentary systems commonly runs between the government-supporting parliamentary majority and the opposition, rather than between the executive and the legislature. For that reason, the government-supporting majority generally has an interest in sustaining and supporting the government.[52] Constitutional courts' review may then be instrumental in overcoming the unwillingness of parliamentary majorities

[51] See eg Bundesverfassungsgericht, judgment of 30 June 2009, 2 BvE 2/08 (*Lisbon* judgment). On this specific part of the judgment, see Philipp Kiiver, 'The Lisbon Judgment of the German Constitutional Court: A Court-Ordered Strengthening of the National Legislature in the EU' (2010) 16 European Law Journal 578. During the euro crisis the GFCC made similar demands in a number of cases: Bundesverfassungsgericht, judgment of 7 September 2011, 2 BvR 987/10 (*EFSF*); Bundesverfassungsgericht, judgment of 28 February 2012, 2 BvE 8/11 (*Neuner Gremium*); Bundesverfassungsgericht, judgment of 19 June 2012, 2 BvE 4/11 (Information on ESM and Euro Plus Pact Negotiations); Bundesverfassungsgericht, judgment of 12 September 2012, 2 BvR 1390/12 (*ESM* interim ruling).

[52] Thomas Winzen, 'Political Integration and National Parliaments in Europe' (2010) 2 Living Reviews in Democracy <https://ethz.ch/content/dam/ethz/special-interest/gess/cis/cis-dam/CIS_DAM_2015/WorkingPapers/Living_Reviews_Democracy/Winzen.pdf> accessed 2 August 2022. See also Thomas Winzen, 'European Integration and National Parliamentary Oversight Institutions' (2012) 14 European Union Politics 297, 301–06.

to create strong parliamentary oversight.[53] A caveat is that the desirable degree of parliamentary oversight is subject to political considerations, while court-ordered parliamentary oversight may be ineffective.[54] For example, tying the hands of government representatives too extensively could hamper the effectiveness of EU decision-making or have detrimental effects on the national interest.[55] These issues require further research. Where court-ordered parliamentary oversight proves ineffective and substitutes reasonable political assessments, its democratic legitimacy appears problematic. Yet, where courts do take into account competing considerations on the desirable level of parliamentary oversight, but counter unjustified executive dominance, their review is more difficult to oppose on democratic grounds.

A second conclusion is that, in other cases, an empirically informed comparative institutional assessment between constitutional courts and other institutions becomes more important. If such an assessment shows that the national courts are better placed to address constitutional questions on the EU or that their judgments improve democratic debate rather than constrain it, their review can be seen as positive from a democratic viewpoint even if their case law is not foolproof.[56] Such comparative assessments, however, must be made with reference to the specific institutional constellations in which review takes place. To this issue I now turn.

3. Making Institutional Comparisons in the EU Context

In the national context, the democratic legitimacy of judicial review depends on a comparative institutional assessment between a national constitutional court

[53] In a similar sense, Peter Lindseth, *Power and Legitimacy: Reconciling Europe and the Nation-State* (Oxford University Press 2010) 178; Eyal Benvenisti and George W Downs, 'The Democratizing Effects of Transjudicial Coordination' 8 Utrecht Law Review 158, 166–67.

[54] This is a reason to argue that national legislatures should decide for themselves how to organize oversight of their executives. For example, the Czech constitutional court explicitly left it to the legislature itself to determine how parliament should participate in EU decision-making, although it did recommend such provisions; see Constitutional Court of the Czech Republic (Ústavní soud), judgment of 26 November 2008, Pl ÚS 19/08 (*Treaty of Lisbon I*) paras 153 and 165–67. See also Mattias Wendel, 'Lisbon Before the Courts: Comparative Perspectives' (2011) 7 European Constitutional Law Review 96. The GFCC's case law on the oversight rights of its national parliament in EU affairs appears to be unique. For an overview, see Christina Fasone and Nicola Lupo, 'Constitutional Review and the Powers of National Parliaments in EU Affairs' in Davor Jancic (ed), *National Parliaments after the Lisbon Treaty and the Euro Crisis* (Oxford University Press 2017).

[55] Philipp Kiiver, 'The Lisbon Judgment of the German Constitutional Court: A Court-Ordered Strengthening of the National Legislature in the EU' (2010) 16 European Law Journal 578, 586. Kiiver notes this point but is critical of it. Parliamentary access to information can also result in information overload if a parliament does not introduce procedures to process such information. See Winzen, 'Political Integration and National Parliaments in Europe' (n 52).

[56] eg in this vein Mattias Kumm has suggested that the national constitutional courts can 'play a significant role as contributors to and facilitators of democratic deliberations in their respective political orders'. Kumm, 'The Jurisprudence of Constitutional Conflict' (n 4) 292. In addition, he argues along Dworkinian lines that courts could act as a 'forum of principle', at 280 in particular fn 54.

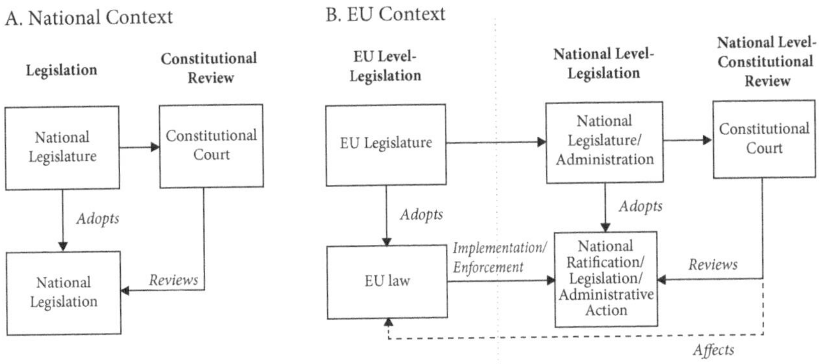

Figure 3.1 Constitutional review national and EU context compared
Source: Author's creation.

and legislature. In the EU context the institutional setting differs. A key difference is that several political institutions located at different governance levels can be involved in the making of European law. As a consequence, the comparative institutional assessment relevant for assessing the legitimacy of a national constitutional court's review changes. Figure 3.1 provides a general and simplified sketch of how judicial review in the national context thus differs from the EU context. This picture is further refined depending on the type of measure under review, which changes the institutional constellation. I distinguish between the review of EU Treaties and similar legal instruments in the context of ratification, and the review of EU primary and secondary law subsequent to ratification. The aim of Figures 3.1 to 3.4 is to clarify these different institutional constellations, although such figures necessarily provide a simplified picture.

3.1 Review of European Treaties and Similar Instruments

Several national constitutional courts engage in constitutional review of EU and related treaties in the context of ratification. Landmark cases such as the GFCC's *Maastricht-Urteil*, *Lissabon-Urteil*, and judgment on the European Stability Mechanism (ESM) concern the constitutionality of Germany's ratification of the respective treaties.[57] Such judgments usually address both the constitutionality of ratification as well as the constitutionality of the accompanying implementing

[57] Bundesverfassungsgericht, judgment of 12 October 1993, 2 BvR 2134/92 (*Maastricht* judgment) (translation in [1994] 1 CMLR 57); Bundesverfassungsgericht, judgment of 30 June 2009, 2 BvE 2/08 (*Lisbon* judgment); Bundesverfassungsgericht, judgment of 18 March 2014, 2 BvR 1390/12 (*ESM* final ruling).

legislation.[58] In several Member States, such review commonly takes place prior to ratification, for example in Germany, France, and Spain.[59] In other Member States, review of treaties takes place after ratification. For example, in Denmark the Danish Supreme Court has adopted a wide interpretation of the legal standing of individuals wishing to challenge European treaties after ratification.[60] A common characteristic of the review of treaties is its abstract nature: it does not take place in the context of a specific controversy, but rather concerns the constitutionality of a treaty as a whole.

Where a national constitutional court reviews a treaty, it subjects the decision-making by two political institutions to review: the treaty drafters and the national institution competent to ratify the treaty.[61] Under the current ordinary revision procedure of Article 48 TEU, EU Treaty amendments will be drafted by a Convention 'composed of representatives of the national Parliaments, of the Heads of State or Government of the Member States, of the European Parliament and of the Commission'.[62] Subsequently, a conference of representatives of the governments of the Member States determines the Treaty amendments by 'common accord'.[63] Treaties concluded outside the EU Treaty Framework are negotiated by the EU Member States,[64] not in a convention. To enter into force, EU Treaties and amendments have to be ratified by the Member States in accordance with their respective constitutional requirements.[65] The national institution competent to ratify EU Treaties is commonly the national legislature. The same holds for EU-related treaties that strictly fall outside the EU Treaty Framework. Figure 3.2 provides a simplified sketch of this constellation.

Consequently, where a national constitutional court reviews the ratification of an EU Treaty or related treaty, the court's constitutional assessment of the treaty will have been preceded by discussion and deliberation among the treaty drafters and the national legislature. The legitimacy of the national constitutional court's intervention therefore has to be assessed in comparison to these two institutions: it has to be considered how the national court's assessment of the treaty's constitutional implications compares to that of the treaty drafters and the national legislature, as well as how such judgments impact on subsequent political decision-making.

[58] In some Member States, such as Spain and France, the treaty itself is directly under review. In other Member States, such as Germany, it is the ratification Act that is subject to review. Nonetheless, the difference does not seem to have much practical effect. Monica Claes, 'The National Courts' Mandate in the European Constitution' (PhD thesis, Maastricht University 2004) 406.

[59] See further ibid 393–418.

[60] The Supreme Court of Denmark (*Højesteret*), case 272/1994, decision of 12 August 1996 (*Maastricht*—admissibility). See also Claes, 'The National Courts' Mandate' (n 58) 434–38.

[61] EU Treaty amendments are generally not subject to judicial review by the CJEU.

[62] Art 48(3) TEU.

[63] Art 48(4) TEU.

[64] Or a smaller group of Member States, as has been the case with several of the euro crisis legal instruments.

[65] See art 48(5) TEU.

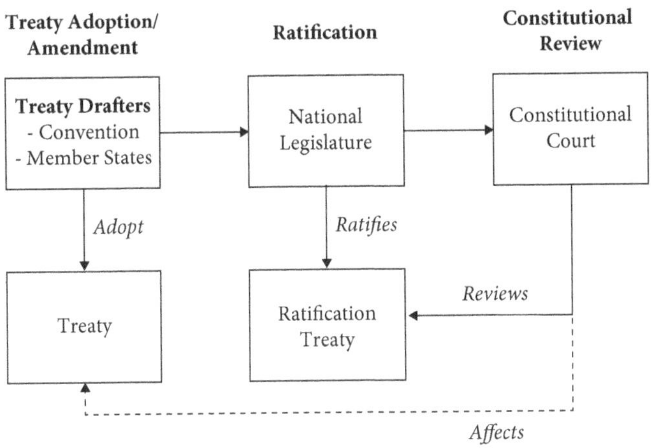

Figure 3.2 Constitutional review of treaties by a national constitutional court
Source: Author's creation.

3.2 Review of Primary and Secondary EU Law After Ratification

The assessment changes where a national constitutional court reviews EU law after ratification. After ratification, national constitutional courts can review provisions of EU law, their interpretation by the CJEU, or their implementation into national law. There are only a few cases in which a national constitutional court has explicitly judged EU law unconstitutional. Mostly, national constitutional courts have threatened to review EU law after ratification but have refrained from actually judging norms of EU law unconstitutional.[66]

Again, an evaluation of the legitimacy of a national constitutional court's review of EU law after ratification and its implementation requires an assessment of the institutional setting in each constellation. For this purpose, I sketch the institutional setting in the case of review of EU primary law and that of EU secondary law in the form of Directives and Regulations.

3.2.1 Primary EU law

Figure 3.3 first sketches the institutional constellation should a national court decide to review primary EU law on the basis of national constitutional law, after ratification. Examples are found in the area of free movement where national constitutional norms have conflicted on several occasions with the EU Treaty freedoms. In the case of *Omega*, for example, the protection of human dignity as protected by the German constitution conflicted with the freedom to provide

[66] For a number of exceptions, see subsection 4.3.1 below.

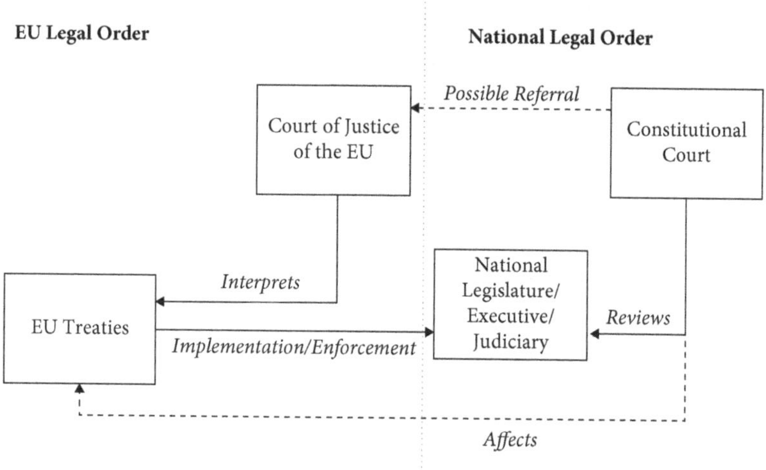

Figure 3.3 National constitutional review of primary EU law
Source: Author's creation.

services.[67] In the case of *Sayn-Wittgenstein*, the Austrian constitutional principle of equality and the prohibition on titles of nobility conflicted with EU citizens' right to move and reside freely in the territory of another Member State under Article 21 TFEU.[68] On the one hand, such constellations raise a similar concern to the review of Treaty norms in the context of ratification. Should a national court hold a norm of primary EU law inapplicable within the national legal order on constitutional grounds, the court can be seen to override a particular political choice laid down in the Treaty. In addition, the national court's review may have subsequent effects on the leeway of legislative institutions on both the EU and national levels.[69]

On the other hand, a case involving the review of primary EU law subsequent to ratification may highlight a constitutional problem not foreseen within the Treaty negotiations. This may provide a reason for a national court to raise a constitutional concern. A further difference within this constellation is that a national constitutional court could refer the issue to the CJEU for a preliminary ruling.

[67] Case C–36/02 *Omega Spielhallen- und Automatenaufstellungs-GmbH v Oberbürgermeisterin der Bundesstadt Bonn* [2004] ECR I–9609.

[68] Case C–208/09 *Ilonka Sayn-Wittgenstein v Landeshauptmann von Wien* [2010] ECR I–13693; see also Leonard FM Besselink, 'Case C-208/09, Ilonka Sayn-Wittgenstein v. Landeshauptmann von Wien, Judgment of the Court (Second Chamber) of 22 December, Nyr.' (2012) 49 Common Market Law Review 671. A more recent similar case was Case C–438/14 *Nabiel Peter Bogendorff von Woltersdorff v Standesamt der Stadt Karlsruhe and Zentraler Juristischer Dienst der Stadt Karlsruhe* [2016] EU:C:2016:401.

[69] Admittedly, whether this is also the case with *ultra vires* review, is a more complicated issue that I discuss elaborately in section 4.

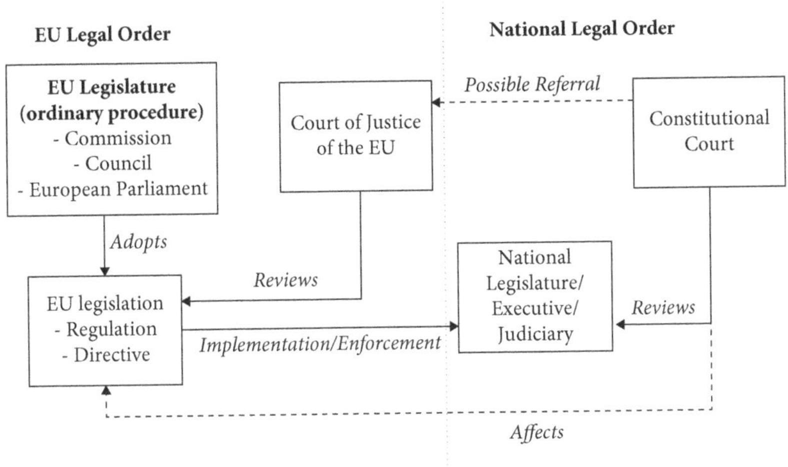

Figure 3.4 National constitutional review of secondary EU law
Source: Author's creation.

Another possibility is that the national court's review is actually directed at the interpretation of EU primary law by the CJEU. In this sense, the national court could function as a counterforce to expansive interpretations of EU law by the CJEU that are insufficiently subject to political correction, given the burdensome requirements for Treaty change.[70]

3.2.2 Secondary EU law

A second constellation is that a national constitutional court reviews a provision of secondary EU legislation, that is, a Regulation or a Directive, on constitutional grounds.[71] Figure 3.4 sketches this modality of review. This constellation involves several institutions: the EU legislature, the national legislature in case the legal instrument is a Directive, and finally the CJEU to which a national constitutional court could refer the question. Which institutions compose the EU legislature in turn depends on the legal basis in the Treaty. In the ordinary legislative procedure, the Council and the EP jointly adopt EU legislation, on a proposal by the Commission.[72] Assessing the legitimacy of the national constitutional court's review of secondary EU law would then require an assessment of how

[70] As Scharpf notes, one may grant that here the national constitutional courts' resistance could be seen to have a certain democratic effect, as 'judicial review exercised by national constitutional courts is embedded in national political cultures with taken-for-granted normative and cognitive understandings and shared discourses about appropriate policy choices'. Scharpf, 'Legitimacy in the Multi-Level European Polity' (n 22).

[71] I focus on legislation and consequently exclude 'decisions' as they lack general application but have to specify to whom they are addressed and 'shall be binding only on them'. See art 288 TFEU.

[72] See arts 289 and 294 TFEU.

the constitutional issue has been taken into account by these three legislative actors. Additional questions are whether the CJEU could address the issue, and how the national constitutional courts' review impacts on subsequent political decision-making.

A national court's review may also be directed only at the national implementing legislation, while leaving the underlying EU legal instrument intact.[73] In such a case the institutional comparison is more straightforward and largely the same as in the national context. A difference with the purely national context, however, is that the measure originates from the EU context. This may alter a national legislature's perception of its responsibilities and leeway compared to a purely national setting. For example, in the proceedings before the GFCC on the Framework Decision on the European Arrest Warrant (EAW) of April 2005, several *Bundestag* members gave the impression that they had not fully considered the constitutional implications in the parliamentary proceedings. Green party member Hans-Christian Ströbele even declared he had felt 'normatively unfree' to change the legislation because of its European pedigree.[74]

An assessment of the legitimacy of the national constitutional courts' review should take into account these different institutional constellations in which review takes place. In addition, the national courts' review should be assessed in relation to the specific grounds for such review. For each ground, it has to be asked whether a national constitutional court is better placed to address this specific constitutional issue and how its judgment will affect subsequent decision-making by other institutions. To these grounds I now turn, where I discuss the legitimacy of the national courts' review in light of these different institutional constellations.

4. Assessing the Grounds of Review

The grounds for the national constitutional courts' review of European law are commonly divided in three categories: fundamental rights, constitutional identity, and *ultra vires* review. Regarding fundamental rights I will be relatively brief. The now elaborate system for the protection of fundamental rights at the EU level makes a strong role for national constitutional courts largely unnecessary. I devote more attention to constitutional identity and *ultra vires* review. For both grounds, I discuss how they function in the national courts' case law. Subsequently, I show

[73] As was the case in various national judgments on the European Arrest Warrant. See, on this issue, Jan Komárek, 'European Constitutionalism and the European Arrest Warrant: In Search of the Limits of "Contrapunctual Principles"' (2007) 44 Common Market Law Review 9.

[74] Dietmar Hipp, 'Fehler im Denksystem' *Der Spiegel* (27 April 2005) <www.spiegel.de/spiegel/print/d-40077635.html> accessed 2 August 2022. Interview with Franz Mayer, Professor of Public Law at Universität Bielefeld and representative of the German Bundestag in the Lisbon and EFSF cases (Berlin, Germany, 28 May 2015).

that both types of review are liable to implicate constitutional courts in highly contested constitutional questions relating to the EU. Democratic grounds thus favour leaving these issues to the relevant political institutions of the EU and the Member States. On this basis, I criticize existing ideas on the national constitutional courts' role, such as the idea of settling constitutional conflicts through judicial dialogue. Yet, I accept that the national constitutional courts' review would be justified where it compensates for a lack of serious deliberation on constitutional issues by political institutions or where it catalyses further democratic deliberation.

4.1 Fundamental Rights

Fundamental rights are historically the first ground on which national courts have contested the primacy of EU law over conflicting national law. This story is familiar, and my discussion will therefore be relatively brief. Initially, the CJEU refused to recognize fundamental rights as part of the EU legal order.[75] This refusal, however, met with resistance by the German and Italian constitutional courts who threatened to constitutionally review EU law—at the time still Community law[76]—on the ground of constitutional rights.[77] The resulting threat to primacy is regarded as an important reason why the CJEU recognized fundamental rights as part of the general principles of EU law.[78] In its *Solange I* judgment of 1974, the GFCC nonetheless held that it still reserved the right to review EU law on the basis of national constitutional rights as long as there was no adequate protection of fundamental rights at the EU level. The GFCC changed this position in its *Solange II* decision of 1986. It held that it would no longer review EU law on its compatibility with national constitutional rights, because of the improved protection of fundamental rights in the EU, and so long as the protection of fundamental rights in the EU

[75] See Case 1/58 *Friedrich Stork & Cie v High Authority of the European Coal and Steel Community* [1959] EU:C:1959:4.

[76] To keep matters simple, I simply refer to the EU and EU law in the rest of my discussion.

[77] For the Italian position, see Constitutional Court of Italy (*Corte costituzionale*), judgment of 27 December 1973, no 183, 27 *Giurisprudenza Costituzionale* 1973, I, 2401 ss (*Frontini v Ministero delle Finanze*); Constitutional Court of Italy (*Corte costituzionale*), judgment of 21 April 1989, no 232, *Giurisprudenza Costituzionale* 1989, I, 1001 ss (*SpA Fragd v Amministrazione delle Finanze*); English translation in Andrew Oppenheimer (ed), *The Relationship between European Community Law and National Law: The Cases* (Cambridge University Press 2003) 629 and 653.

[78] See eg Alec Stone Sweet, *Governing with Judges: Constitutional Politics in Europe* (Oxford University Press 2000) 170–72; Allard Knook, 'The Court, the Charter, and the Vertical Division of Powers in the European Union' (2005) 42 Common Market Law Review 367, 368. Historically, see Bill Davies, *Resisting the European Court of Justice. West Germany Confrontation with European Law, 1949–1979* (Cambridge University Press 2012). For a different view see, however, Julio Baquero Cruz, 'The Legacy of the Maastricht-Urteil and the Pluralist Movement' (2008) 14(4) European Law Journal 389. Early cases in which the CJEU recognized fundamental rights as part of the EU legal order are Case 29/69 *Erich Stauder v City of Ulm—Sozialamt* [1969] ECR 419; Case 11/70 *Internationale Handelsgesellschaft mbH v Einfuhr- und Vorratsstelle für Getreide und Futtermittel* [1970] ECR 1125.

remained substantially similar.[79] The German Court essentially affirmed this position in later judgments.[80]

Because of these events, the protection of fundamental rights, as such, no longer seems an acute ground of constitutional conflict.[81] An elaborate system for the protection of fundamental rights now exists at the EU level, particularly since the EU Charter of Fundamental Rights has become formally binding.[82] To a very large extent, this has accommodated the national constitutional courts' concerns about the protection of fundamental rights at the EU level. Since the coming into force of the Charter there has been a significant rise in the number of preliminary references from ordinary courts on fundamental rights amounting to what some have called a 'rights revolution'.[83]

Under these circumstances, there appears little ground for national constitutional courts to review EU law on the basis of fundamental rights as such. It seems that judicial protection of fundamental rights can also be performed by the CJEU without risk to the uniformity and effectiveness of EU law.[84] Where national courts are of the opinion that EU law violates fundamental rights norms, they can refer the issue to the CJEU. Perhaps they should reserve a residual power to review EU law on the basis of rights, if the EU level of protection falls below a certain minimum standard.[85] By and large, this approach also appears to be the one adopted by

[79] Bundesverfassungsgericht, judgment of 22 October 1986, 2 BvR 197/83 *(Solange II)*.

[80] See eg Bundesverfassungsgericht, judgment of 30 June 2009, 2 BvE 2/08 (*Lisbon* judgment) para 337; see, in more detail, Mehrdad Payandeh, 'Constitutional Review of EU Law after Honeywell: Contextualizing the Relationship between the German Constitutional Court and the EU Court of Justice' (2011) 48 Common Market Law Review 9, 13–14.

[81] Fundamental rights are a possible ground of review of EU law for various other national constitutional courts such as the Czech Constitutional Court, the French Constitutional Council, and the Spanish Constitutional Court.

[82] See art 6(1) TEU.

[83] Jan Komárek, 'The Place of Constitutional Courts in the EU' (2013) 9 European Constitutional Law Review 420, 421.

[84] One could of course wonder whether the extent of rights protection at the EU level is a desirable outcome and whether the initial resistance of the German and Italian Constitutional Courts to the primacy of EU law was justified. An argument in favour of Germany's initial *Solange* case law is that, at the time, EU law was directly effective and had primacy over conflicting national law, but a clear democratic procedure at the EU level was not in place. Democratic concerns about rights-based review in the domestic context were therefore not as pressing in the EU context, nor could it be taken for granted that the implications of EU legislation for fundamental rights would be subjected to rigorous democratic deliberation. In this sense, see Joseph HH Weiler, 'Eurocracy and Distrust: Some Questions Concerning the Role of the European Court of Justice in the Protection of Fundamental Human Rights within the Legal Order of the European Communities' (1986) 61 Washington Law Review 1103. In Bundesverfassungsgericht, judgment of 29 May 1974, BvL 52/71 (*Solange I*) the GFCC invoked the democratic shortcomings of the Community as a justification for fundamental rights' review (see in particular para 23). The dissenting minority in turn criticized this part of the majority judgment, see in particular para 62. Whether the democratic shortcomings of the Community at the time really justified the position of the GFCC and Italian Constitutional Court, however, requires further empirical research.

[85] This was of course the approach of the GFCC in Bundesverfassungsgericht, judgment of 22 October 1986, 2 BvR 197/83 (*Solange II*); Bundesverfassungsgericht, order of 7 June 2000, 2 BvL 1/97 (*Bananas*).

national courts. Several of them, including the GFCC, now even accept EU fundamental rights as a standard for review.[86]

The problem under the current system is arguably rather that the CJEU's elaborate rights protection comes at the expense of reasonable choices made by both the EU and national legislatures. As the CJEU's judgment in *Åkerberg Fransson* confirms, the scope of the EU fundamental rights standard is broad.[87] It applies not just where Member States act as so-called agents of EU law and implement or enforce EU law provisions, but also where Member States derogate from EU law and where they adopt a national measure that preconditions the exercise of a right established by EU law. Beyond that, there still remains considerable uncertainty about the scope of the EU fundamental rights standards.[88] The consequence is that Member State courts will have to apply the EU rights standard in a great number of situations, even if under national law these courts have a more limited mandate to review legislation on the basis of fundamental rights. In many cases, the CJEU will be competent to review the compatibility of Member State action with the Charter, thus partly displacing national courts and other institutions as interpreters of rights obligations.

In this context, the CJEU's case law often fails to acknowledge the contested democratic legitimacy of judicial review, which for some EU Member States is still a key reason to reject such review or to concentrate this competence in specialized constitutional courts.[89] In *Åkerberg Fransson*, for example, the CJEU held that the Swedish judicial practice on the application of human rights was not compatible with EU law. This practice is that judges only disapply national legislation if the infringement with the EU Charter or ECHR followed clearly from the provision's text or related case law.[90] Arguably, and paradoxically, the role of the national constitutional courts could be to counter these expansive interpretations by the CJEU, thus reclaiming space for politics. I return to this idea in discussing identity review and *ultra vires* review and show how such review still raises democratic challenges.

[86] Mattias Wendel, 'The Two-Faced Guardian: Or How One Half of the German Federal Constitutional Court Became a European Fundamental Rights Court' (2020) 57 Common Market Law Review 1383. Bundesverfassungsgericht, order of 6 November 2019, 1 BvR 16/13 (*Right to be forgotten I*); Bundesverfassungsgericht, order of 6 November 2019, 1 BvR 276/17 (*Right to be forgotten II*).

[87] Case C-617/10 *Åklagaren v Hans Åkerberg Fransson* [2013] EU:C:2013:280.

[88] I rely on the distinctions drawn by Emily Hancox, 'The Meaning of "Implementing" EU Law under Article 51(1) of the Charter: Åkerberg Fransson' (2013) 50 Common Market Law Review 1411, 1418–27. The case affirms prior case law of the CJEU concerning the scope of application of EU law's general principles that include fundamental rights.

[89] Criticisms along similar lines are voiced by Komárek, 'The Place of Constitutional Courts in the EU' (n 83); Jan Komárek, 'National Constitutional Courts in the European Constitutional Democracy' (2014) 12 International Journal of Constitutional Law 525; Jan Komárek, 'Why National Constitutional Courts Should Not Embrace EU Fundamental Rights' (2014) LSE Law, Society and Economy Working Papers <https://papers.ssrn.com/sol3/papers.cfm?abstract_id=2510290> accessed 1 August 2022.

[90] Case C-617/10 *Åklagaren v Hans Åkerberg Fransson* [2013] EU:C:2013:280, at paras 43–48. Other cases to which such concerns may apply are Case C-409/06 *Winner Wetten GmbH v Bürgermeisterin der Stadt Bergheim* [2010] ECR I-8015 and Cases C-188/10 and 189/10 *Aziz Melki and Sélim Abdeli* [2010] EU:C:2010:363.

A further role for national courts may exist where EU fundamental rights protection is absent. This is an issue with some of the legal instruments adopted in response to the euro crisis, where the CJEU has been reluctant to apply the Charter. Instruments adopted under international law, such as the ESM, fall outside the scope of EU law.[91] Consequently, the fundamental rights protection offered by EU law does not fully apply. This is a problem, particularly in relation to the macroeconomic adjustment programmes that Member States have to adopt as part of receiving financial assistance under the ESM or European Financial Stability Facility (EFSF).[92] These programmes raised several concerns from the perspective of social rights.[93] Moreover, there are serious concerns about democratic deficiencies in the procedure by which these adjustment programmes were adopted.[94] As a result, rights-based review of such measures by national constitutional courts may be desirable.[95] In this vein, the Portuguese Constitutional Court struck down several measures implementing the Portuguese economic adjustment programme, finding that these measures violated constitutional principles akin to fundamental rights, such as equality, legal certainty, and the protection of legitimate expectations.[96] Still, a full assessment of the legitimacy of such review would require an analysis

[91] Case C-370/12 *Thomas Pringle v Government of Ireland* [2012] EU:C:2012:756.

[92] For a critical assessment, see Claire Kilpatrick, 'Are the Bailouts Immune to EU Social Challenge Because They Are Not EU Law?' (2014) 10 European Constitutional Law Review 393. In Joined Cases C-8/15 P-10/15 P *Ledra Advertising Ltd v European Commission and European Central Bank (ECB)* [2016] EU:C:2016:701 the CJEU held that the Charter is applicable to the EU institutions when they are engaged in making financial assistance conditionality agreements. In Joined Cases C-105/15 P-109/15 P *Konstantinos Mallis v European Commission and European Central Bank (ECB)* [2016] EU:C:2016:702, however, the Court concluded that the Charter does not apply to the euro group. For an assessment of the applicability of the Charter to the assistance programmes, see Anastasia Poulou, 'Financial Assistance Conditionality and Human Rights Protection: What Is the Role of the EU Charter of Fundamental Rights?' (2017) 54 Common Market Law Review 991; Menelaos Markakis, *Accountability in the Economic and Monetary Union: Foundations, Policy, and Governance* (Oxford University Press 2020) 234–42; Anastasia Karatzia and Menelaos Markakis, 'Court of Justice Financial Assistance Conditionality and Effective Judicial Protection: Chrysostomides' [2022] Common Market Law Review 501.

[93] See eg Claire Kilpatrick and Bruno De Witte (eds), *Social Rights in Times of Crisis in the Eurozone: The Role of Fundamental Rights' Challenges* (2014) EUI Working Paper LAW 2014/05 <cadmus.eui.eu> accessed 2 August 2022.

[94] These issues are discussed in more detail in Chapters 5 and 6.

[95] eg Anastasia Poulou states that this is the case because '[m]easuring financial assistance conditions against human rights standards would counterbalance the executive-expertise bias of the making of financial assistance conditionality to purely market-driven choices, which already dominate the post-crisis European governance framework. Reliance on the Charter would also induce actors preparing and enforcing lending conditions to more carefully assess the impact of their actions on human rights and to adopt more inclusive and responsive procedures, actively engaging civil society actors and social partners in the making of conditionality.' Poulou, 'Financial Assistance Conditionality and Human Rights Protection' (n 92) 1024–25. See similarly Kári Hólmar Ragnarsson, 'The Counter-Majoritarian Difficulty in a Neoliberal World: Socio-Economic Rights and Deference in Post-2008 Austerity Cases' (2019) 8 Global Constitutionalism 605; Teresa Violante, 'Bring Back the Politics: The PSPP Ruling in Its Institutional Context' (2020) 21 German Law Journal 1045, 1054–55.

[96] See Mariana Canotilho, Teresa Violante, and Rui Lanceiro, 'Austerity Measures under Judicial Scrutiny: The Portuguese Constitutional Case-Law' (2015) 11 European Constitutional Law Review 155.

of the process by which such adjustment programmes are adopted, the reasons on which they are based, and whether the courts' judgments are an effective way to address the underlying social concerns.[97]

Another remaining source of potential conflict between the EU constitutional order and that of the Member States exists where national standards and the EU standard for the protection of fundamental rights diverge. Despite an important degree of commonality, there is also considerable divergence between the Member States regarding the standards for rights protection. Some Member States constitutionally recognize particular fundamental rights not protected in other Member States, different Member States strike different balances between rights and competing interests, and national courts interpret similar rights provisions differently. In establishing a fundamental rights case law at the European level, the CJEU has always drawn on the common constitutional traditions of the Member States as well as international human rights treaties.[98] Yet, the CJEU has also maintained that the EU standard for the protection of fundamental rights is an autonomous standard. Furthermore, the CJEU has claimed the exclusive competence to determine this standard.[99] This raises the possibility that the EU standard of rights protection may conflict with national standards.[100] I treat this issue in the next section as part of the protection of national constitutional identity.

4.2 National Constitutional Identity

4.2.1 Constitutional identity in the national constitutional courts' case law

The issue of constitutional identity has become the more central source of constitutional conflict in the past few decades, although there is considerable overlap between constitutional identity and fundamental rights.[101] National constitutional

[97] See eg, in a different context, on some of the potential pitfalls of social rights enforcement by courts, David Landau, 'The Reality of Social Rights Enforcement' (2012) 53 Harvard International Law Journal 189.

[98] See Case 4/73 *Nold KG v Commission* [1974] ECR 491. On this issue see eg Paul Craig and Gráinne De Búrca, *EU Law: Text, Cases and Materials* (Oxford University Press 2015) 380ff.

[99] See also Case 4/73 *Nold KG v Commission* [1974] ECR 491; Case 44/79 *Liselotte Hauer v Land Rheinland-Pfalz* [1979] EU:C:1979:290, 1979-03727; Case 11/70 *Internationale Handelsgesellschaft mbH v Einfuhr- und Vorratsstelle für Getreide und Futtermittel* [1970] ECR 1125; Case C–399/11 *Stefano Melloni v Ministerio Fiscal* [2013] EU:C:2013:107.

[100] For classic treatments of this problem, see Leonard FM Besselink, 'Entrapped by the Maximum Standard: On Fundamental Rights, Pluralism and Subsidiarity in the European Union' (1998) 35 Common Market Law Review 629; Joseph HH Weiler, 'Fundamental Rights and Fundamental Boundaries: On the Conflict of Standards and Values in the Protection of Human Rights in the European Legal Space' in Joseph HH Weiler (ed) *The Constitution of Europe: 'Do the New Clothes Have an Emperor?' And Other Essays on European Integration* (Cambridge University Press 1999).

[101] In Germany, for example, the protection of human dignity enshrined in art 1(1) of the German Basic Law is part of constitutional identity, which requires safeguarding 'the core of human dignity in fundamental rights'. See eg Bundesverfassungsgericht, judgment of 21 June 2016, 2 BvR 2728/13 (*OMT* final) para 138; Bundesverfassungsgericht, judgment of 15 December 2015, 2 BvR 2735/14 (*European Arrest Warrant II*) paras 48–50. Another example is Italy, where the Italian Constitutional

identity or comparable grounds feature in the case law of several national constitutional courts.[102] Such identity review functions as a limit to further European integration and to the effects of EU law within the respective national legal orders. The notion of constitutional identity is relevant under EU law as well. Article 4(2) TEU states that the EU 'shall respect the equality of Member States before the Treaties as well as their national identities, inherent in their fundamental structures, political and constitutional, inclusive of regional and local self-government'. This provision is understood, by some at least, to put a legal obligation on the EU to respect national constitutional identity.[103]

Yet, there is considerable lack of clarity about the meaning of constitutional identity, and the Member States have different understandings of the notion. Comparative research shows also that the notion as such often does not feature in Member States' constitutions. Instead, it is 'a judicial construct drawn from states' constitutional law broadly conceived'.[104] Constitutional courts thus play a crucial role in determining and shaping the content of constitutional identity.[105]

To grasp what constitutional identity is, I distinguish between a broad and a narrow understanding.[106] On the broad understanding, constitutional identity

Court adopted a doctrine of counter-limits (*contro-limiti*) that it equates to constitutional identity, and which comprises the inalienable rights of man, next to the fundamental principles of the Italian constitution. See Constitutional Court of Italy (*Corte costituzionale*), judgment of 21 April 1989, no 232, *Giurisprudenza Costituzionale* 1989, I, 1001 ss (*SpA Fragd v Amministrazione delle Finanze*); see further Besselink and others, *National Constitutional Avenues* (n 5) 151–53. For its equivalence to constitutional identity, see Constitutional Court of Italy (*Corte costituzionale*), order of 23 November 2016, no 24 (*Taricco I*) paras 6 and 8. See also Federico Fabbrini and Oreste Pollicino, 'Constitutional Identity in Italy: Institutional Disagreements at a Time of Political Change' in Christian Calliess and Gerhard van der Schyff (eds), *Constitutional Identity in a Europe of Multilevel Constitutionalism* (Cambridge University Press 2019) 213–19 <www.cambridge.org/core/books/constitutional-identity-in-a-europe-of-multilevel-constitutionalism/constitutional-identity-in-italy/ABEAB8F8C2821CB333E779BE33B60830> accessed 1 August 2022; Clara Rauchegger, 'National Constitutional Rights and the Primacy of EU Law: M.A.S.' [2018] Common Market Law Review 1521.

[102] For recent overviews of several Member States' positions, see Besselink and others, *National Constitutional Avenues* (n 5); Gerhard van der Schyff, 'Member States of the European Union, Constitutions, and Identity: A Comparative Perspective' in Christian Calliess and Gerhard van der Schyff (eds), *Constitutional Identity in a Europe of Multilevel Constitutionalism* (Cambridge University Press 2019); Luke Dimitrios Spieker, 'Framing and Managing Constitutional Identity Conflicts: How to Stabilize the Modus Vivendi between the Court of Justice and National Constitutional Courts' [2020] Common Market Law Review 361. Spieker states that identity review has been established by constitutional courts in eight Member States: Germany, Italy, the Czech Republic, Poland, Hungary, Spain, and Belgium.

[103] See eg Leonard FM Besselink, 'National and Constitutional Identity before and after Lisbon' (2010) 6 Utrecht Law Review 36; Armin Von Bogdandy and Stephan Schill, 'Overcoming Absolute Primacy: Respect for National Identity under the Lisbon Treaty' (2011) 48 Common Market Law Review 1417; François-Xavier Millet, *L'Union européenne et l'identité constitutionnelle des États membres* (LGDJ, Lextenso éditions 2013) 1–21.

[104] Schyff, 'Member States of the European Union, Constitutions, and Identity' (n 102) 307–08.

[105] ibid 313–17.

[106] I find this distinction most useful for my purposes. Other distinctions are possible. Spieker for example, distinguishes between understanding constitutional identity as connected 'to principles of *universal* validity located *within* the constitution' and identity that derives from '*pre-*, *supra-* or

comprises the fundamental constitutional principles underlying the national constitutional order. Such principles are not necessarily peculiar to a specific Member State but can be shared by various constitutional orders. They can also overlap considerably with the core values of the EU as listed in Article 2 TEU and, to a significant extent, can be understood as underpinning constitutional democracy as such.[107] The GFCC's case law offers an example of this broader approach, where the notion of constitutional identity has also been most fully elaborated in case law. German constitutional identity consists of the principles declared unamendable by Article 79(3) of the German Basic Law (BL), its so-called 'eternity clause'. These include the principle of democracy, the rule of law, the principle of the social state, the principle of the federal state, as well as respect for human dignity and the core of fundamental rights guarantees.[108] Other examples are: Spain, where constitutional identity refers to 'the fundamental principles of the social and democratic State of Law established by the national Constitution';[109] Belgium, where constitutional identity includes the fundamental values of the constitution;[110] and the Czech Republic, where constitutional identity is understood as roughly equivalent to the substantive core of the Czech Constitution, which includes, at least, the principle of democracy and the rule of law.[111]

In connection to this broad reading of constitutional identity, several Member States relate the protection of independent statehood to constitutional identity.[112] In Germany, this idea is again most developed. In its judgment on the Lisbon Treaty, the GFCC identified five areas in which the German parliament should retain significant autonomous decision-making power: criminal law, the monopoly

extra-constitutional factors relating to an *idiosyncratic* history, culture or ethnicity'. Spieker, 'Framing and Managing Constitutional Identity Conflicts' (n 102) 368.

107 On the overlap between art 2 and constitutional principles making up constitutional identity, see Spieker, 'Framing and Managing Constitutional Identity Conflicts' (n 102).

108 Bundesverfassungsgericht, judgment of 30 June 2009, 2 BvE 2/08 (*Lisbon* judgment) para 217.

109 Spanish Constitutional Tribunal, Declaration 1/2004 in case no 6603–2004, available in English at <www.tribunalconstitucional.es/ResolucionesTraducidas/Declaration%201-2004.pdf> accessed 27 December 2017 (Constitutional Treaty). [*Tribunal Constitucional*, Opinion 1/2004 of 12 December 2004, para II, 2.] See also Camilo Schutte, 'Spain Tribunal Constitucional on the European Constitution. Declaration of 13 December 2004' (2005) 1 European Constitutional Law Review 281, 287.

110 Belgian Constitutional Court no 62/2016, 28 April 2016 (Fiscal Compact) para (B.8.7). See also Elke Cloots, 'Constitutional Identity in Belgium: A Thing of Mystery' in Christian Calliess and Gerhard van der Schyff (eds), *Constitutional Identity in a Europe of Multilevel Constitutionalism* (Cambridge University Press 2019).

111 David Kosař and Ladislav Vyhnánek, 'Constitutional Identity in the Czech Republic: A New Twist on an Old-Fashioned Idea?' in Christian Calliess and Gerhard van der Schyff (eds), *Constitutional Identity in a Europe of Multilevel Constitutionalism* (Cambridge University Press 2019).

112 Schyff, 'Member States of the European Union, Constitutions, and Identity' (n 102) 332; Spieker, 'Framing and Managing Constitutional Identity Conflicts' (n 102) 372–73. Examples include: Supreme Court of Denmark (Højesteret), Case 361/1997, Decision of 6 April 1998 (*Maastricht*) (summary translated in [1999] 3 CMLR 854); Polish Constitutional Tribunal, judgment of 11 May 2005, K 18/04 (*Accession Treaty*); Constitutional Court of the Czech Republic (Ústavní soud), judgment of 3 November 2009, Pl ÚS 29/09 (*Treaty of Lisbon II*). See further Besselink and others, *National Constitutional Avenues* (n 5).

on the use of force of both the military and the police, fundamental fiscal decisions, decisions relating to the principle of the social state, and decisions with particular cultural importance.[113] The list does not prohibit the transfer of any legislative authority in these areas, but underlines that the EU's engagement in these areas is prone to endanger constitutional identity.[114] During the euro crisis, the budgetary autonomy of the *Bundestag* became a key issue. The GFCC maintains that the *Bundestag* cannot transfer its overall budgetary responsibility to the EU or another international organization. Instead, the *Bundestag* must remain the place in which the autonomous decisions on revenue and expenditure are made.[115]

A second and narrower understanding of constitutional identity is that it only encompasses a core of constitutional norms specific to a Member State, such as those relating to its form of government, those expressing particular national values, or those containing particular fundamental rights.[116] The French Constitutional Council interprets constitutional identity in this way. Although the full content of French constitutional identity is unclear, the French Constitutional Council appears to understand it as referring to constitutional norms that are specifically French. Possible examples are: the constitutional norm determining the category of people entitled to vote in French elections; the criteria for access to public functions; the principle of *laïcité*; and the ban on granting specific rights to ethnic, linguistic, and other minorities.[117] Where a constitutional principle is part of both the EU and the French legal order, the CJEU must provide protection.[118]

A further feature of the French approach is that constitutional identity serves as a standard of review only in relation to secondary EU law. By contrast, German constitutional identity also functions as the standard for review when competences are conferred by means of a new Treaty. Commonality exists nonetheless, because the French Constitutional Council does review whether EU Treaty amendments and new treaties are in accordance with fundamental rights, and whether they transfer competences deemed fundamental for the exercise of national sovereignty.[119] The

[113] Bundesverfassungsgericht, judgment of 30 June 2009, 2 BvE 2/08 (*Lisbon* judgment) para 252.

[114] On this point, Grimm, 'Defending Sovereign Statehood' (n 4) 368.

[115] This case law is further discussed in Chapter 5.

[116] See eg Millet, *L'Union européenne et l'identité* (n 103) 11; and for similar ideas Bogdandy and Schill, 'Overcoming Absolute Primacy' (n 103) 1330–40.

[117] On these issues, see Jan-Herman Reestman, 'The Franco-German Constitutional Divide, Reflections on National and Constitutional Identity' (2009) 5 European Constitutional Law Review 374, 384–90; Besselink and others, *National Constitutional Avenues* (n 5) 25 and 102–03; François-Xavier Millet, 'Constitutional Identity in France: Vices and—Above All—Virtues' in Christian Calliess and Gerhard van der Schyff (eds), *Constitutional Identity in a Europe of Multilevel Constitutionalism* (Cambridge University Press 2019) 146–51. A key case is French Constitutional Council (*Conseil constitutionnel*), case no 2006–540 DC, decision of 27 July 2006 (*Copyright and Related Rights in the Information Society*).

[118] This is commonly inferred from French Constitutional Council (*Conseil constitutionnel*), case no 2004–498 DC, decision of 29 July 2004 (*Bioethics*). It was more recently confirmed in French Constitutional Council (*Conseil constitutionnel*), case no 2021–940 QPC, decision of 15 October 2021 (*Société Air France*).

[119] The French Constitutional Council submits that it will also review whether Treaty provisions run 'counter to the Constitution'. French Constitutional Council (*Conseil constitutionnel*), case no 2004–505

latter is the case when the competences historically belong to the core of national sovereignty, such as defence, foreign affairs, monetary policy, and justice and home affairs. In addition, Member States must lose their grip on the exercise of these competences.[120]

The two approaches to constitutional identity converge insofar as conflicts between the EU and Member States occur when constitutional norms are given different understandings in the different legal orders. In addition, on the first, broader understanding of constitutional identity, the constitutional principles of a Member State may still reflect specific national choices and historical experiences. The significance of human dignity in German constitutional law, for example, is clearly a reflection of that country's history.[121]

4.2.2 The political dimension of constitutional identity

Respect for national constitutional identities can be considered important both when understood in its broader and in its narrower sense as explained above. First, I take it largely for granted that respect for constitutional principles such as the rule of law, human dignity, and democracy is important. They are part of the EU's foundational values and are widely seen as fundamental to constitutional democracy as such. Secondly, where constitutional identity refers to a core of constitutional norms specific to a Member State, the protection of identity may be important to respect a Member State's basic democratic choices on fundamental values and its collective identity.[122] In this second sense, Member States' constitutional identities can be seen as context-dependent interpretations of the preconditions of a democratically legitimate political process reflecting specific historical and cultural circumstances. In addition, the idea that the Member States

DC, decision of 19 November 2004 (Treaty establishing a Constitution for Europe) para 7. Millet, however, maintains that in practice the Conseil limits its review to fundamental rights and respect for the exercise of national sovereignty. Millet, 'Constitutional Identity in France' (n 117) 138.

[120] eg because voting will be by qualified majority. See, on these issues, French Constitutional Council (*Conseil constitutionnel*), case no 92-308 DC, decision of 9 April 1992 (*Maastricht*); French Constitutional Council (*Conseil constitutionnel*), case no 2004-505 DC, decision of 19 November 2004 (Treaty establishing a Constitution for Europe); French Constitutional Council (*Conseil constitutionnel*), case no 2007-560 DC, decision of 20 December 2007 (*Lisbon*). See further Millet, 'Constitutional Identity in France' (n 117) 136–40; Besselink and others, *National Constitutional Avenues* (n 5) 104–05.

[121] Another example is Belgium, where constitutional identity comprises both the fundamental values of the Belgian constitution as well as constitutional norms that express its national identity, such as those on federalism and language protection. Cloots, 'Constitutional Identity in Belgium' (n 110) 72–82.

[122] See eg Weiler, 'Fundamental Rights and Fundamental Boundaries' (n 100) 102–07; Joseph HH Weiler, 'In Defence of the Status Quo: Europe's Constitutional Sonderweg' in Joseph HH Weiler and Marlene Wind (eds), *European Constitutionalism Beyond the State* (Cambridge University Press 2003) 15; Kumm, 'The Jurisprudence of Constitutional Conflict' (n 4) 296–98; Aida Torres Pérez, *Conflicts of Rights in the European Union, A Theory of Supranational Adjudication* (Oxford University Press 2009) 83–86.

should retain decision-making power in certain areas may reflect a justified concern that these areas are particularly important for the Member States' democratic self-government.

Yet, despite these reasons for respecting constitutional identity, there are strong democratic grounds against letting constitutional courts review European law on this basis. As with rights-based judicial review in the domestic context, such review allows courts to decide issues of significant political and moral importance on which there exists reasonable disagreement, while constraining political branches to decide these issues themselves. That is the case for three key reasons.

First, the notion of national constitutional identity itself leaves open a wide variety of possible interpretations. As already explained, constitutional courts themselves play a crucial role in constructing the content of constitutional identity in their respective legal orders. Even when one assumes that there exists agreement on the constitutional norms that make up constitutional identity in a particular Member State, these norms commonly still leave open a wide variety of possible interpretations. Constitutional courts invoking constitutional identity in EU-related case law are therefore likely to play a significant role in deciding what the identity of their respective constitutional order is, what this identity means, and how its content is to be understood in relation to the EU.

Secondly, like with constitutional rights, the interpretation of the norms that make up constitutional identity require judges to make evaluative judgments on issues over which there exists persistent and reasonable disagreement. In part, this objection is the same as against rights-based review because constitutional identity review overlaps considerably with rights-based review. Insofar as identity review comprises constitutional provisions that relate to the basic structure of government or competence divisions between different levels of government, similar objections apply.[123] In section 2.3, I discussed the complex normative questions that the issue of democracy raises in the EU context. Other aspects of constitutional identity raise similar challenges. Related to democracy, for example, is the idea that Member States should retain substantial decision-making power in key competence areas. Yet, the judicial determination of 'essential' Member State competences faces the problem that democratic politics is commonly about what the state or government should do: liberals, social democrats, libertarians, and Christian-democrats have widely different ideas about what essential state competences are.[124] In addition, if the asymmetrical nature of the EU's competences raises a democratic problem,

[123] Stone refers to such review as 'structural judicial review' and offers a democratic case against it. See Adrienne Stone, 'Judicial Review Without Rights: Some Problems for the Democratic Legitimacy of Structural Judicial Review' (2008) 28 Oxford Journal of Legal Studies 1; Adrienne Stone, 'Democratic Objections to Structural Judicial Review and the Judicial Role in Constitutional Law' (2010) 60 The University of Toronto Law Journal 109.

[124] On this point also Daniel Halberstam and Christoph Möllers, 'The German Constitutional Court Says "Ja Zu Deutschland!"' (2009) 10 German Law Journal 1241, 1249–51; Christoph Schönberger, 'Lisbon in Karlsruhe: Maastricht's Epigonies at Sea' (2009) 10 German Law Journal 1201, 1209–10.

retaining substantial decision-making powers at the national level and preventing the EU from exercising certain powers may only perpetuate this difficulty. Take fiscal decisions: these might be politically salient, but the Member States' ability to effectively raise taxes is also affected by tax competition between the Member States, arguably making EU-wide action crucial. Criminal law provides another example: the existence of open borders affects the ability of the national police to effectively tackle trans-border crime. This could be a key reason to increase the EU's competences in the field of criminal law. The idea that Member States should retain substantial competences in certain fields is consequently a position subject to reasonable disagreement.

Thirdly, when national constitutional courts review European law on the basis of constitutional identity, they risk imposing constitutional limits on decision-making by the political branches, thus curtailing their decision-making. That is a problem, in particular where constitutional identity is part of the unamendable provisions of the constitution.[125] In Germany, for example, constitutional identity cannot be amended through the ordinary procedure for constitutional amendments,[126] but only through a decision of the people who are the ultimate holders of all state authority.[127] This makes the constitutional hurdles especially difficult to overcome, amounting to a form of 'super counter-majoritarianism'.[128] In other Member States the hurdles may be less high, but they are still considerable. In France, for example, constitutional identity can be amended by a three-fifths majority in both Houses of Parliament or, alternatively, after approval in a referendum.[129]

For these reasons, there are strong democratic grounds to treat the protection of constitutional identity as a primarily political issue. Some national courts explicitly recognize this point and leave significant room to the political branches in determining constitutional identity. The case law of the Danish Supreme Court and Czech Constitutional Court provides an example.[130] These courts grant

125 Spieker, 'Framing and Managing Constitutional Identity Conflicts' (n 102) notes that this is the case in Germany and Italy, while the situation is not so clear in the Czech Republic, Hungary, Poland, and Spain. He notes that in France and Belgium identity limits can be overcome by means of a constitutional amendment.

126 A two-thirds majority in the *Bundestag* and *Bundesrat*, see art 79(1) and (2) BL.

127 Art 20(2) BL and its interpretation in para 216 of the *Lisbon* judgment.

128 Halberstam and Möllers, 'The German Constitutional Court Says "Ja"' (n 124) 1255–56; Mattias Wendel, 'The Fog of Identity and Judicial Contestation: Preventive and Defensive Constitutional Identity Review in Germany' (2021) 27 European Public Law 465

129 Art 89(5) of the French constitution declares that the 'republican form of government shall not be the object of any amendment'. Nonetheless, this is unlikely to make a practical difference because the Constitutional Council does not review the constitutionality of constitutional amendments. Reestman, 'The Franco-German Constitutional Divide' (n 117) 388–89. He refers to French Constitutional Council (*Conseil constitutionnel*), case no 2003–469 DC, decision of 26 March 2003, paras 2–3. See also Besselink and others, *National Constitutional Avenues* (n 5) 105–06.

130 Supreme Court of Denmark (Højesteret), case no 361/1997, decision of 6 April 1998 (*Maastricht*) (summary translated in [1999] 3 CMLR 854); Constitutional Court of the Czech Republic (Ústavní soud), judgment of 3 November 2009, Pl ÚS 29/09 (*Treaty of Lisbon II*), paras 110–11. A similar approach was taken by the Supreme Court of Estonia (*Riigikohus*) in judgment (*en banc*) of 12 July 2012, case no 3-4-1-6-12. See, on these points, also Monica Claes and Jan-Herman Reestman, 'The Protection

considerable leeway to its national legislature in determining when competence transfers to the EU would go so far that their respective countries could no longer be considered independent states.[131]

Yet, assessments as to whether courts should address issues of constitutional identity, or instead leave them to political actors, are hardly reflected in existing appraisals of the role of national constitutional courts. In the next subsections I discuss two ideas in more detail. The first is that constitutional differences between the EU and the Member States should be settled in a judicial dialogue between the national constitutional courts and the CJEU. Although this idea has gained considerable support, the legitimacy of such a dialogue is limited when considered in a comparative institutional setting. Secondly, on similar grounds, I criticize arguments that national constitutional courts should be allowed to invoke national constitutional identity as a limit to the primacy of EU law. Subsequently, I explain the importance of further comparative institutional research.

4.2.3 The limits of judicial dialogue

Various scholars support the idea that national courts and the CJEU should solve constitutional conflicts in a dialogue with national courts.[132] Such judicial dialogue does in fact take place. The construction of the European legal order has from the outset been a cooperative process between the CJEU and national legal actors.[133] Courts interact formally through the preliminary reference procedure of Article 267 TFEU, but they also meet on a more informal basis.[134] Beyond that, they take into account each other's decisions.[135] A key example of the latter is the response

of National Constitutional Identity and the Limits of European Integration at the Occasion of the Gauweiler Case' (2016) 16 German Law Journal 917.

[131] One could also point out that in several Member States the content of national constitutional identity remains vague and thus leaves significant leeway to the legislature. See eg Cloots, 'Constitutional Identity in Belgium' (n 110) 67; José Martín Y Pérez de Nanclares, 'Constitutional Identity in Spain: Commitment to European Integration without Giving Up the Essence of the Constitution' in Christian Calliess and Gerhard van der Schyff (eds), *Constitutional Identity in a Europe of Multilevel Constitutionalism* (Cambridge University Press 2019) 278–80.

[132] For views in favour of a form of dialogue or cooperation, see Miguel Poiares Maduro, 'Contrapunctual Law: Europe's Constitutional Pluralism in Action' in Neil Walker (ed), *Sovereignty in Transition* (Hart Publishing 2003) 525–30; Marta Cartabia, 'Europe and Rights: Taking Dialogue Seriously' [2009] European Constitutional Law Review 5; Bogdandy and Schill, 'Overcoming Absolute Primacy' (n 103) 1440; Andreas Voßkuhle, 'Multilevel Cooperation of the European Constitutional Courts: Der Europäische Verfassungsgerichtsverbund' (2010) 6 European Constitutional Law Review 175; Ana Bobić, 'Constitutional Pluralism Is Not Dead: An Analysis of Interactions between Constitutional Courts of Member States and the European Court of Justice' (2017) 18 German Law Journal 1395.

[133] Maduro, 'Contrapunctual Law' (n 132) 512–17.

[134] See eg the description of former CJEU Judge Timmermans on some of these more informal dialogues between the ECJ and the national courts, in Christiaan Timmermans, 'Voorrang van Het Unierecht Door Multilevel Rechterlijke Samenwerking' [2012] Sociaal-Economische Wetgeving 50.

[135] Wendel provides an overview of different types of engagement by national constitutional courts: Mattias Wendel, 'Comparative Reasoning and the Making of a Common Constitutional Law: EU-Related Decisions of National Constitutional Courts in a Transnational Perspective' (2013) 11 International Journal of Constitutional Law 981.

of the CJEU to the German *Solange I* judgment, which prompted the CJEU to strengthen the protection of fundamental rights at the EU level.[136]

The normative appeal of addressing constitutional conflicts through judicial dialogue is intertwined with the recognition of reasonable disagreement on constitutional norms, and the consequent need to take account of constitutional diversity. This idea is reflected in one of the most elaborate defences of judicial dialogue for solving constitutional conflicts, namely that brought forward by Aida Torres Pérez in the context of fundamental rights adjudication.[137] Her argument for judicial dialogue rests on a more general philosophical claim that the interpretation of fundamental rights is not about discovering universal truths. Instead, values are constituted and shaped inter-subjectively through an exchange of arguments. The advantage of judicial dialogue is that courts construct the constitutional norms of the EU in an argumentative fashion, that it stimulates participation in the practice of interpretation, and that it allows the courts to accommodate claims of different national constitutional orders in an open-ended way. In the view of Torres Pérez, this judicial dialogue should take place through the preliminary reference procedure of Article 267 TFEU. The dialogic ideal puts certain demands on the CJEU's reasoning: the European Court needs to take into account the various arguments brought forward and reflect on how these arguments are weighed in the judicial process.[138] The CJEU is to adopt a form of comparative constitutional reasoning, in which it reflects on and justifies its judgments in light of the different constitutional viewpoints of the Member States. Where national courts make references to the CJEU, they are to explain the reasons for particular constitutional provisions or interpretations.[139]

Much less convincing, however, is the idea that this dialogue should primarily take place between courts. Torres Pérez maintains that there are six prerequisites for a good, working judicial dialogue: (i) there must be competing viewpoints about the law; (ii) at the same time, there must be common ground for mutual understanding; (iii) none of the participants must have complete authority over the other; (iv) these participants must see themselves as engaged in a common enterprise in which they respect each other; (v) they should have an equal opportunity to participate; and (vi) the dialogue must extend over time.[140]

A key difficulty, however, lies with prerequisite (v): equal opportunity to participate. Certainly, a dialogue between national courts and the CJEU is more participatory than where the CJEU would be the sole interpreter of the constitutional

[136] For historical evidence on the importance of this judgment for EU fundamental rights protection, see Davies, *Resisting the European Court of Justice* (n 78).

[137] Pérez, *Conflicts of Rights in the European Union* (n 122) 97–140. The criticism discussed here is similar to my argument in Nik de Boer, 'The False Promise of Constitutional Pluralism' in Matej Avbelj, and Gareth Davies (eds), *A Research Handbook of Legal Pluralism and EU Law* (Edward Elgar 2018).

[138] Pérez, *Conflicts of Rights in the European Union* (n 122) 112–17.

[139] ibid 141–78.

[140] ibid 118ff.

norms applicable in the framework of EU law. Yet, in a judicial dialogue, the range of participants is in principle limited to the Member State courts and the CJEU. Torres Pérez submits, nonetheless, that these courts 'are far more accessible than EU legislative bodies'.[141] That is a dubious assertion, as discussed already in Chapter 2, because access to courts is costly. It is likely that parties with significant financial resources will find it easier to effectively pursue their interests by judicial means. In addition, and as noted in subsection 2.1.2, particularly mobile citizens, organizations, and companies are likely to have an interest in litigating on the basis of EU law. The cases that end up before the CJEU are therefore unlikely to be representative of all interests affected by European integration.

By comparison the EU's legislative bodies—the European Commission, the EP, and the Council—have a far better claim to represent the citizens' interests. European citizens directly elect the EP, and the Member States' government representatives in the Council are accountable to national parliaments. Despite democratic problems in the EU's political process, EU citizens thus have a right to participate in the EU's decision-making through their vote for the EP and in national elections. For national courts and the CJEU, such political accountability generally does not exist: once appointed, the judges are supposed to be independent. Further factors limit the ability of citizens to influence CJEU judgments. The EU Treaties declare that decisions in the Union should be taken 'as openly as possible',[142] that the EP shall meet in public, and the Council shall meet in public 'when considering and voting on a draft legislative act'.[143] Judges and Advocates General of the CJEU, however, must swear that they will 'preserve the secrecy of the deliberations of the Court'.[144] In addition, the parties' submissions in cases pending before the Court are not accessible until after the hearing. The Court claims that it has to protect itself from external pressure.[145] Also, a large part of the dialogue between European courts appears to take place in informal settings behind closed doors.[146]

[141] ibid 128.

[142] Art 1 TEU.

[143] Art 15(2) TFEU.

[144] Consolidated Version of the Rules of Procedure of the Court of Justice [2010] OJ C177/1, art 4.

[145] Deirdre Curtin and Päivi Leino-Sandberg, *Openness, Transparency and the Right of Access to Documents in the EU* (European Parliament 2016) PE 556.973 12–13 <www.europarl.europa.eu/thinktank/en/document.html?reference=IPOL_IDA%282016%29556973> accessed 2 August 2022; Deirdre Curtin, 'Judging EU Secrecy' [2012] Cahiers de droit européen 459. See also the Joined Cases C-514/07 P, 528/07 P and 532/07 P Association de la presse internationale ASBL (API) [2010] ECR II-03201. In April 2022, the CJEU did announce that it would start offering a livestream of hearings and handing down of judgments; see Court of Justice of the European Union Press Release 63/22, Broadcast by streaming of hearings and the handing down of judgments and opinions of the Court of Justice (22 April 2022).

[146] See the account of former CJEU Judge Timmermans, 'Voorrang van Het Unierecht' (n 134). For a discussion of judicial networks in Europe, see Maartje De Visser and Monica Claes, 'Are You Networked Yet? On Dialogues in European Judicial Networks' (2012) 8 Utrecht Law Review 100.

Even if the Member States' governments, the European institutions, as well as the parties to a particular legal dispute can submit observations before the CJEU, they are not the decision-makers in a judicial dispute.[147] Therefore, they cannot count as equal participants in this dialogue. Furthermore, between the class of real participants—the courts—there are likely to exist large power differentials. Constitutional courts from powerful Member States probably wield more power in such a dialogue.[148] Also, the ability of Member States' courts to engage in a judicial dialogue is likely to be uneven. Some courts have more limited jurisdiction than others and, in some Member States, courts have no or only a very restricted role in adjudicating constitutional matters.[149]

For all these reasons, the participatory qualities of a European judicial dialogue should not be overestimated. Steps could of course be taken to enhance the legitimating potential of the European judicial dialogue by furthering the transparency of the judicial process, allowing a wider range of relevant actors to make observations, and encouraging the deliberative quality of the judicial process by giving individual judges of the CJEU the option to deliver dissenting opinions.[150] Yet, the judicial dialogue concerns constitutional norms that bind the EU's legislative bodies and national legislatures when they act within the scope of EU law. Consequently, the justification for settling constitutional controversies between the EU and its Member States in a judicial dialogue cannot rest merely on its participatory qualities. Instead, it must be argued that the judges involved in this dialogue are better placed to consider constitutional questions than the political institutions, or that their judgments improve political debate. As I have argued before, substantiating this argument requires an empirically informed comparative institutional assessment in the various possible constellations outlined in section 3 of this chapter.

4.2.4 The problem with national constitutional identity as a limit to primacy

The same criticism can be voiced against those who see constitutional identity not just as a ground for judicial dialogue, but even as a limit to the primacy of EU law. Thus, for example, Armin von Bogdandy and Stephan Schill argue that Article 4(2)

[147] See arts 23 of the Statute of the Court of Justice of the European Union and 96 of the Rules of Procedure of the Court of Justice.

[148] On this point, see also Michael A Wilkinson, 'Economic Messianism and Constitutional Power in a "German Europe": All Courts Are Equal, but Some Courts Are More Equal than Others' [2014] LSE Law, Society and Economy Working Papers <https://papers.ssrn.com/sol3/papers.cfm?abstract_id=2522919> accessed 1 August 2022.

[149] See also Tomi Tuominen, 'Aspects of Constitutional Pluralism in Light of the Gauweiler Saga' (2018) 43 European Law Review 186; Tomi Tuominen, *The Euro Crisis and Constitutional Pluralism* (Edward Elgar 2021) especially ch 6. On such concerns in the Danish context, see Jens Elo Rytter and Marlene Wind, 'In Need of Juristocracy? The Silence of Denmark in the Development of European Legal Norms' (2011) 9 International Journal of Constitutional Law 470.

[150] For a number of proposals in the context of international courts, see Armin von Bogdandy and Ingo Venzke, 'In Whose Name? An Investigation of International Courts' Public Authority and Its Democratic Justification' (2012) 23(1) The European Journal of International Law 7.

TEU permits 'domestic constitutional courts to invoke, under certain limited circumstances, constitutional limits to the primacy of EU law'.[151] This requires that 'a proportional balance be found' between the uniform application of EU law and the national constitutional identity of a particular Member State.[152] Yet, that would allow national courts to make highly contested judgments about when the protection of constitutional identity is more important than the uniform application of EU law.

The more limited proposal of Mattias Kumm partly addresses this concern. In his view, there can be compelling democratic grounds for allowing Member States' constitutional courts to uphold specific national constitutional commitments against EU law. According to Kumm, conflicts between national constitutional law and EU law can be seen as clashes between competing underlying ideals. On the one hand, respecting the primacy of EU law upholds the rule of law at the EU level. On the other hand, allowing Member States to uphold important national constitutional commitments can amount to respecting these Member States' fundamental democratic choices.[153] Where such a constitutional commitment is clear and specific, and reflects 'a constitutional essential', Kumm submits that 'concerns related to democratic legitimacy override considerations relating to the uniform and effective enforcement of EU law'.[154] That result is justified in the light of the democratic shortcomings of the EU, such as the lack of electoral competition over the EU's policy direction and the missing sociological prerequisites for a European democracy—a shared European identity, public sphere, and civil society. The requirement that a national constitutional commitment is 'clear and specific' is intended to ensure that the commitment has in fact been adopted by the constitutional legislature and therefore reflects an important democratic choice.[155] The demand that these clear and specific commitments are constitutionally essential means to ensure that not every specific constitutional commitment would justify derogation from EU law.[156]

[151] Bogdandy and Schill, 'Overcoming Absolute Primacy' (n 103) 1419.

[152] ibid 1441.

[153] Mattias Kumm and Victor Ferreres Comella, 'The Primacy Clause of the Constitutional Treaty and the Future of Constitutional Conflict in the European Union' (2005) 3 International Journal of Constitutional Law 473; Mattias Kumm, 'Rethinking Constitutional Authority: On the Structure and Limits of Constitutional Pluralism' in Matej Avbelj and Jan Komárek (eds), *Constitutional Pluralism in the European Union and Beyond* (Hart Publishing 2012); Mattias Kumm, 'The Moral Point of Constitutional Pluralism' in Julie Dickson and Pavlos Eleftheriadis (eds), *Philosophical Foundations of European Union Law* (Oxford University Press 2012) 216–46.

[154] Kumm, 'The Jurisprudence of Constitutional Conflict' (n 4) 298.

[155] Note that Kumm also acknowledges that constitutional conflicts are driven by courts, and he argues that the power of Member States to change the constitution in order to prevent the application of EC rules 'has not been of any relevance in the process of European integration whatsoever. No state has ever reacted to losing a political legislative battle on the European level by entrenching a specific provision constitutionally to prevent the application of the unwanted EC rules. It is not surprising, therefore, that it is not the *political actors* that are most concerned with the issue of constitutional conflict.' Kumm, 'The Jurisprudence of Constitutional Conflict' (n 4) 280, also 281.

[156] ibid 296–98.

The democratic grounds for Kumm's identity-based exception to the primacy of EU law, however, stand in tension with the court-centric focus of his position. In fact, these democratic reasons present a powerful argument why the protection of constitutional identity should be left primarily to the political branches. That is the case firstly because Kumm's conflict rule does not remove judicial discretion. Whether a commitment is 'clear and specific' in a particular situation probably requires interpretation and cannot be settled in advance. The distinction between open-ended principles and 'clear and specific' commitments is also not clear-cut.[157] In addition, national constitutional courts would still have to determine whether the national constitutional norm is constitutionally essential. Secondly, and despite democratic problems in the EU, democratic arguments do not unequivocally favour Kumm's proposed solution. Constitutional norms are commonly entrenched against ordinary legislative change. Changing them usually requires a supermajority of some kind. Therefore, if the adoption of a particular constitutional norm proves to be a bad idea, if circumstances change, or political parties change their ideas about the desirability of the norm, the norm will still remain in place as long as a political minority supports it.[158] The fact that a constitutional provision is clear and specific, and is considered constitutionally essential by the courts, therefore does not necessarily indicate its strong democratic support.[159] At the same time, the EU's law-making process may be more responsive to the interests of the persons affected in a specific policy area than national political processes. Democratic reasons, therefore, do not clearly favour upholding national constitutional commitments against EU law.

In light of these arguments, it is not clear that the burden of protecting constitutional commitments should fall to the national constitutional courts. Kumm's proposal is most convincing in the event that the constitutional concerns were not taken into account in the law-making process. This could be the case if a national legislature was not able to bring these constitutional concerns to the fore or the constitutional conflict was not foreseen. Another possibility is that political institutions involved in making EU law are less well-positioned than constitutional courts in addressing the constitutional implications of EU legislation, or that the

[157] See, on this point more generally, Stone, 'Judicial Review Without Rights' (n 123) 8–10.

One example is the previously existing Irish constitutional protection for the life of the unborn. The text of art 40(3) of the Irish constitution merely stated: 'The state acknowledges the right to life of the unborn and, with due regard to the equal right to life of the mother, guarantees in its laws to respect, and, as far as practicable, by its laws to defend and vindicate that right.' The text itself appears to leave open various interpretations. Also, it was unclear whether this constitutional provision could justify restrictions on the right to travel in order to obtain an abortion. An additional question was how the constitutional provision related to the freedom to provide information on abortions abroad. These issues were the subject of further litigation before the Irish Supreme Court and ultimately clarified by constitutional amendment. On these events, see Claes, 'The National Courts' Mandate' (n 58) 443–50.

[158] Scharpf, 'Legitimacy in the Multi-Level European Polity' (n 22) 100.

[159] A similar point is made by Cruz, 'The Legacy of the Maastricht-Urteil and the Pluralist Movement' (n 78).

courts' review improves subsequent political debate. However, answering these questions requires a comparative institutional assessment.

4.2.5 Courts or politics? Assessing the legitimacy of identity review in a comparative institutional perspective

In order to evaluate the legitimacy of the national constitutional courts' identity review, it is consequently crucial to take account of the different constellations in which such review takes place. First, where the review concerns a treaty or secondary EU law, the Member States are heavily involved in negotiating these measures through their national governments.[160] They possess a veto over EU Treaty change and the conclusion of other treaties. For the adoption of secondary law, the Council is a co-legislator or in some cases even the only legislative institution operating at the EU level. The Council thus possesses a veto over virtually all EU legislation. If a Member State regards a particular national constitutional concern as crucially important, the Member State government could raise the problem during the Treaty negotiations or the legislative proceedings on the EU level.[161] In addition, the national legislature could raise the issue in the case of Treaty ratification or in the implementation of a Directive. Examples that constitutional concerns are accommodated within these political processes do exist.[162] Upon request of the Irish government, a protocol was annexed to the Treaty of Maastricht stipulating that nothing in the Treaty would affect the application of—the then still applicable—Irish constitutional law on abortion.[163] Differentiated integration provides another example. Several Member States have opted out of European cooperation in certain policy areas. Such opting-out may represent a Member State's choice to retain political autonomy in policy areas they consider especially important.[164]

There are also examples, however, where political institutions appear not to have taken constitutional concerns sufficiently into account. The adoption of the Framework Decision on the European Arrest Warrant (EAW) may have been such a case.[165] The EAW created constitutional problems in several Member States,

[160] Fritz Scharpf has even argued that the 'consensus requirements of the EU's "Community Method" are so high that it appears most unlikely that EU legislation would ever override the politically salient interests of even a small group of Member States'. Scharpf, 'After the Crash' (n 31) 395.

[161] And the national legislature could force the government to ensure consideration of the issue if it has put in place adequate parliamentary scrutiny of EU affairs. See, in a similar fashion, on the virtues of the legislative procedure in this sense, Scharpf, 'Legitimacy in the Multi-Level European Polity' (n 22).

[162] See, in detail, Pietro Faraguna, 'Taking Constitutional Identities Away from the Courts' (2016) 41 Brooklyn Journal of International Law 491.

[163] See the Protocol annexed to the Treaty on European Union and to the Treaties establishing the European Communities. Currently a protocol is attached to the Treaty of Lisbon 'on the concerns of the Irish people' that contains a similar provision in art 1, see <http://eur-lex.europa.eu/LexUriServ/LexUriServ.do?uri=OJ:L:2013:060:0131:0139:EN:PDF> accessed 2 August 2022.

[164] Frank Schimmelfennig, Dirk Leuffen, and Berthold Rittberger, 'The European Union as a System of Differentiated Integration: Interdependence, Politicization and Differentiation' (2015) 22 Journal of European Public Policy 764.

[165] Council Framework Decision 2002/584/JHA of 13 June 2002 on the European arrest warrant and the surrender procedures between Member States [2002] OJ L190/1.

particularly because it conflicted with national constitutional prohibitions on the extradition of nationals.[166] Yet, the instrument was hastily adopted on the European level in the aftermath of 11 September 2001.[167] Moreover, the lack of parliamentary involvement may have prevented constitutional concerns from being adequately addressed: the Council adopted the framework decision and the EP only had to be consulted.[168] There are also indications that some national parliaments did not fully consider the EAW's constitutional implications in the national legislative procedures.[169] In such cases, national identity review by the constitutional courts could be a way to ensure that constitutional issues are given due consideration.[170]

Still, such shortcomings in the political process leave open various ways for national courts to respond: different types of review may have different consequences for the role of political institutions. For example, the Polish Constitutional Court held the EAW implementing legislation to be unconstitutional, but temporarily left in place the contested legislation and required the constitutional legislature to amend the Polish constitution within eighteen months.[171] The Polish Court thus left it to the constitutional legislature to correct the incompatibility. By contrast, the GFCC not only declared the implementing legislation void in its entirety, but also appeared to reject part of the approach in the EAW as incompatible with the unamendable parts of the German constitution.[172] The Polish Court's approach

[166] See, on these issues, Elspeth Guild, 'Introduction' in Elspeth Guild (ed), *Constitutional Challenges to the European Arrest Warrant* (Wolf Legal Publishers 2006); Komárek, 'European Constitutionalism and the European Arrest Warrant' (n 73).

[167] Daniel Halberstam, 'Constitutional Heterarchy: The Centrality of Conflict in the European Union and the United States' [2008] *U of Michigan Public Law Working Paper No 111* <http://ssrn.com/abstract=1147769> accessed 1 August 2022; Elspeth Guild, 'Introduction' in Elspeth Guild (ed), *Constitutional Challenges to the European Arrest Warrant* (Wolf Legal Publishers 2006).

[168] See former arts 34(2) and 39 TEU at <http://eur-lex.europa.eu/legal-content/EN/TXT/PDF/?uri=CELEX:C2002/325/01&from=EN> accessed 2 August 2022.

[169] See subsection 3.2.2. On the German adoption, see also Florian Geyer, 'The European Arrest Warrant in Germany—Constitutional Mistrust toward the Concept of Mutual Trust' in Elspeth Guild (ed), *Constitutional Challenges to the European Arrest Warrant* (Wolf Legal Publishers 2006) 101–10.

[170] The case of *Melloni* (Case C-399/11 *Stefano Melloni v Ministerio Fiscal* [2013] EU:C:2013:107) also concerned the EAW but seems to merit a different assessment. In this case the EAW conflicted with the case law of the Spanish Constitutional Court on trials *in absentia*. The case law from the Spanish Constitutional Court had established that persons convicted for serious offences *in absentia* could not be surrendered if the judgment was not subject to review. The EAW itself, however, specifically provided for a different standard that did not allow the Spanish authorities to refuse surrender in the specific case. The Council had thus struck a different balance between the protection of fundamental rights and judicial cooperation in criminal matters. The EAW provision, moreover, complied with the case law of the European Court of Human Rights. In this case it is less clear that the Council had not properly considered the constitutional implications of its decision. See further, on these issues, Nik de Boer, 'Addressing Rights Divergences under the Charter: Melloni' (2013) 50 Common Market Law Review 1083.

[171] Polish Constitutional Tribunal, judgment of 27 April 2005, P 1/05, available in English at <https://trybunal.gov.pl/fileadmin/content/omowienia/P_1_05_full_GB.pdf> accessed 2 August 2022 (*European Arrest Warrant*). The Czech Constitutional Court chose to construe the EAW as consistent with the constitution: Constitutional Court of the Czech Republic (Ústavní soud), judgment of 3 May 2006, Pl ÚS 66/04 (*European Arrest Warrant*).

[172] Bundesverfassungsgericht, judgment of 18 July 2005, 2 BvR 2236/04 (*European Arrest Warrant I*). See also the dissenting opinion of Judge Lübbe-Wolff, arguing that the EAW's deficiencies did 'not justify the nullification of the entire Act'. In addition, she criticized the majority's

may be preferable from a democratic point of view, but it could also be the case that the GFCC's approach ensured better consideration of all the relevant constitutional questions. Close study of the political process and the impact of constitutional court judgments on this process should help in clarifying the legitimacy of the national constitutional interventions.

The case for review by national constitutional courts is stronger in institutional constellations where the constitutional conflict results from non-political decision-making. Most commonly, this will be the case where the conflict between national constitutional law results from an interpretation by the CJEU of EU primary law. In such a constellation, the CJEU's interpretation can only be reversed if the Member States agree to change the EU Treaties by unanimity. The difficulty of doing this gives the CJEU extensive leeway to further develop the norms of EU primary law without legislative control. Review by national constitutional courts may then help to curb excessive judicial power on the EU level and safeguard interpretive pluralism that is sensitive to national constitutional considerations.[173] A similar consideration could apply to the CJEU's interpretations of secondary EU law. In this constellation, the national constitutional courts could ensure that the CJEU interprets the law in such a manner that it does not encroach upon national constitutional concerns. Yet, at the same time, the national courts should ensure that they do not foreclose the leeway for political actors to interpret national constitutional identity in a different manner.

4.3. *Ultra Vires* Review

4.3.1 *Ultra vires* review in the case law of national constitutional courts

A further ground that some national constitutional courts have put forward to review EU law is *ultra vires* review. *Ultra vires* acts are those EU acts that exceed the EU's competences.[174] This type of review emerged in the GFCC's *Maastricht-Urteil* of 1993, where the German Court judged itself competent to review whether secondary EU law and other EU decisions remained within the scope of the EU's competences laid down in the Treaties.[175] The GFCC reasoned that the German

approach to the ban on the extradition of Germans: 'The attempt to anchor it in higher spheres (of natural law, as it were), deeper (historical) ones and broader ones (under natural law), leads astray' (para 1). On these issues, see Komárek, 'European Constitutionalism and the European Arrest Warrant' (n 73) 19–25.

[173] Which is a way to justify cases such as Case C-36/02 *Omega Spielhallen- und Automatenaufstellungs-GmbH v Oberbürgermeisterin der Bundesstadt Bonn* [2004] ECR I-09609; Case C-208/09 *Ilonka Sayn-Wittgenstein v Landeshauptmann von Wien* [2010] ECR I-13693.

[174] For further elaboration on the notion, see Franz Mayer, 'Kompetenzüberschreitung und Letzentscheidung' (PhD thesis, Munich University 2000) 24–30.

[175] Bundesverfassungsgericht, judgment of 12 October 1993, 2 BvR 2134/92 (Maastricht) (translation in [1994] 1 CMLR 57) para 49.

parliament had an essential role in providing the EU's public authority with democratic legitimacy. For this reason, the powers conferred on the EU would have to be limited and sufficiently certain, as otherwise the EU's exercise of authority would fall outside the powers to which the national legislature had assented. EU law adopted outside this framework would be inapplicable in the German legal order and the GFCC could review whether this was the case. Effectively, the GFCC's *ultra vires* review entails that the German Court can independently interpret EU law, through the lens of national constitutional law.[176] This idea contradicts the CJEU's understanding of the principle of primacy. The CJEU holds that it has the sole competence to review whether EU law has been validly adopted under the EU Treaties.[177]

In its *Lisbon* judgment, the GFCC reaffirmed its position with some qualifications. *Ultra vires* review would be a last resort, it could only be exercised by the GFCC and not by other German courts, and it would have to be exercised in accordance with the Basic Law's openness towards European law (*Europarechtsfreundlichkeit*). The German Court would also review whether the EU's legal acts adhered to the principle of subsidiarity.[178] In the subsequent *Honeywell* case, however, the GFCC adopted a more restrictive approach. It would only conduct *ultra vires* review of manifest competence violations with structural significance for the competence division between the Member States and the EU.[179] Furthermore, the GFCC would first give the CJEU the opportunity to rule on the matter in the context of a preliminary ruling.[180] In this respect, the CJEU would have 'a right to tolerance of error'.[181]

Despite these strict conditions, the GFCC ruled in May 2020 that the ECB's Public Sector Purchasing Programme (PSPP) was *ultra vires*, and, with that, also the prior CJEU judgment that upheld the programme's legality.[182] Having previously set the bar for *ultra vires* review so high, the GFCC now had to declare the CJEU's ruling as 'simply not comprehensible' and 'objectively arbitrary'.[183] This

[176] Franz Mayer, 'Rebel Without a Cause? A Critical Analysis of the German Constitutional Court's OMT Reference' (2014) 15 German Law Journal 111, 116–17.

[177] As can be inferred from Case C–314/85 *Foto Frost v Hauptzollamt Lübeck-Ost* [1987] ECR 4199; Court of Justice of the European Union Press Release 58/20, Press release following the judgment of the German Constitutional Court of 5 May 2020 (8 May 2020).

[178] Bundesverfassungsgericht, judgment of 30 June 2009, 2 BvE 2/08 (*Lisbon* judgment) para 240–41. See also the discussion in Payandeh, 'Constitutional Review of EU Law after Honeywell' (n 80) 15–16. Mehrdad Payandeh, Constitutional Review of EU Law after *Honeywell*: Contextualizing the Relationship between the German Constitutional Court and the EU Court of Justice (2011) 48(1) Common Market Law Review 15–16.

[179] Bundesverfassungsgericht, judgment of 6 July 2010, 2 BvR 2661/06 (*Honeywell*) para 61.

[180] ibid para 60.

[181] ibid para 66.

[182] In a comment on the Honeywell decision, Christoph Möllers noted that there was 'almost no chance' that the strict conditions for the activation of *ultra vires* would 'ever be met'. Christoph Möllers, 'Constitutional Ultra Vires Review of European Acts Only Under Exceptional Circumstances; Decision of 6 July 2010, 2 BvR 2661/06, Honeywell' (2011) 7 European Constitutional Law Review 161, 166.

[183] Bundesverfassungsgericht, judgment of 5 May 2020, 2 BvR 859/15 (*PSPP*) para 118.

assessment led to significant criticism. Commentators stressed that the high hurdles for an *ultra vires* finding, as developed by the GFCC, were not actually met.[184] Prior, to the *PSPP* judgment, the GFCC had fired noticeable warning shots. In its decision on the anti-terrorism database, the Court stated that the CJEU's judgment in *Åkerberg Fransson* would be *ultra vires* if interpreted in an expansive manner.[185] In 2014, the GFCC came close to concluding that the ECB's policy of Outright Monetary Transactions (OMT) fell outside the ECB's mandate, but ultimately backed down after the CJEU held that the policy was not contrary to EU law.[186]

Ultra vires review has found resonance with some constitutional courts in other Member States.[187] In 2012, the Czech Constitutional Court declared a decision of the CJEU to be an *ultra vires* EU act.[188] The Czech judgment is probably best regarded as an anomaly to be explained against the backdrop of the Constitutional Court's clash with the Czech Supreme Administrative Court on the specific subject matter of the case.[189] In its decisions on the Lisbon Treaty, the Czech Constitutional Court had stated that *ultra vires* would be an *ultima ratio*.[190] In Denmark, the Supreme Court also acknowledges the possibility of *ultra vires* review, but likewise only in extraordinary circumstances and after the CJEU has been given the possibility of ruling on the matter.[191] In the *Ajos* judgment from 2016, however, the

[184] See eg Franz Mayer, 'The Ultra Vires Ruling: Deconstructing the German Federal Constitutional Court's PSPP Decision of 5 May 2020' (2021) 16 European Constitutional Law Review 733, 751–57; Wendel, 'The Two-Faced Guardian' (n 86) 1418–19.

[185] Bundesverfassungsgericht, judgment of 24 April 2013, 1 BvR 1215/07 (*Counter-terrorism database*). However, the Åkerberg Fransson case did not provide this expansive reading of the Charter's scope. See Editorial Comments, 'Ultra Vires—Has the Bundesverfassungsgericht Shown Its Teeth?' (2013) 50 Common Market Law Review 925.

[186] See Bundesverfassungsgericht, order of 14 January 2014 2 BvR 2728/13 (*OMT* referral); Case C-62/14 Peter Gauweiler v Deutscher Bundestag [2015] EU:C:2015:555; and Bundesverfassungsgericht, judgment of 21 June 2016, 2 BvR 2728/13 (*OMT* final ruling). See further Chapters 5 and 7. The reference of the GFCC was also criticized for not sticking to the *Honeywell* requirements. See eg Mayer, 'Rebel Without a Cause?' (n 176) 118–19 and 137–39; Jürgen Bast, 'Don't Act Beyond Your Powers: The Perils and Pitfalls of the German Constitutional Court's Ultra Vires Review' (2014) 15 German Law Journal 147, 178–79.

[187] For a recent overview of eight Member States, see Niels Petersen and Konstantin Chatziathanasiou, 'Primacy's Twilight?' (European Parliament 2021) PE 692.276 27–45 <www.europarl.europa.eu/thinktank/en/document/IPOL_STU(2021)692276> accessed 1 August 2022. Arguably the Cohn-Bendit case of the French *Conseil d'État* can qualify as a further instance of *ultra vires* review (French Conseil d'État, judgment of 22 December 1978 (*Ministre de l'intérieur* c *Cohn-Bendit*)). Yet the *Conseil d'État* departed from this line of case law in 2009. See Chloé Charpy, 'France. The Conseil d'État Abandons Its Cohn Bendit Case-Law; Conseil d'État, 30 October 2009, Mme Perreux' (2010) 6 European Constitutional Law Review 123.

[188] Constitutional Court of the Czech Republic (Ústavní soud), judgment of 31 January 2012, Pl ÚS 5/12 (Holubec); handed down in response to Case C-399/09 *Landtová* [2011] ECR I-5573.

[189] Michal Bobek, 'Landtová, Holubec, and the Problem of an Uncooperative Court: Implications for the Preliminary Rulings Procedure' (2014) 10 European Constitutional Law Review 54.

[190] Constitutional Court of the Czech Republic (Ústavní soud), judgment of 26 November 2008, Pl ÚS 19/08 (*Treaty of Lisbon I*); Constitutional Court of the Czech Republic (Ústavní soud), judgment of 3 November 2009, Pl ÚS 29/09 (*Treaty of Lisbon II*).

[191] Supreme Court of Denmark (Højesteret), Case 361/1997, decision of 6 April 1998 (Maastricht) (summary translated in [1999] 3 CMLR 854); Supreme Court of Denmark (Højesteret), Case 199/2012, decision of 20 February 2013 (*Lisbon*) (translation on <https://domstol.dk/media/0xebqufh/199-12-english.pdf> accessed 2 August 2022); Helle Krunke, 'The Danish Lisbon Judgment—Danish Supreme

Danish Supreme Court refused to comply with the guidelines laid down by the CJEU on the principle of non-discrimination on grounds of age. The Danish Court thus effectively declared the CJEU's interpretation *ultra vires*.[192] More recently, the Polish Constitutional Tribunal has held on several occasions that the CJEU's case law on judicial independence is outside the EU's competences.[193] However, the Polish situation presents a rather special case. Since 2015, the Polish Constitutional Tribunal has lost its independence amidst a more general decay of democratic institutions in Poland.[194]

4.3.2 Democracy and *ultra vires* review

The national courts' insistence on the limited nature of the EU's competences finds support in the overall EU legal framework. The principle of conferral is a basic constitutional principle of the EU. It establishes that 'the Union shall act only within the limits of the competences conferred upon it by the Member States in the Treaties to attain the objectives set out therein'.[195] Conversely, competences not conferred on the Union remain with the Member States.[196] In addition, the principle of subsidiarity states that in areas where the EU does not have exclusive competence it 'shall act only if and in so far as the objectives of the proposed action cannot be sufficiently achieved by the Member States, either at the central level or at regional and local level, but can rather by reason of the scale or effects of the proposed action be better achieved at Union level'.[197]

Yet the legitimacy of *ultra vires* review by national courts is fiercely contested. Competence review in the EU is already provided for by the CJEU. The national constitutional courts' review thus comes on top of an already existing judicial safeguard. A reason to concentrate such competence review in the CJEU is that this promotes the uniform interpretation of EU law and legal certainty. These values

Court, Case 199/2012, Judgment of 20 February 2013' (2014) 10 European Constitutional Law Review 542, 548–49 and 561.

[192] Supreme Court of Denmark (Højesteret), Case 15/2014, decision of 6 December 2016 (*Ajos*) (translation on <https://domstol.dk/media/2udgvvvb/judgment-15-2014.pdf> accessed 2 August 2022). Although the Danish Court possibly already adopted a stricter standard in its judgment on the Lisbon Treaty: Supreme Court of Denmark (Højesteret), Case 199/2012, decision of 20 February 2013 (*Lisbon*) (translation on <https://domstol.dk/media/0xebqufh/199-12-english.pdf> accessed 2 August 2022). See also Mikael Rask Madsen, Henrik Palmer Olsen, and Urška Šadl, 'Competing Supremacies and Clashing Institutional Rationalities: The Danish Supreme Court's Decision in the Ajos Case and the National Limits of Judicial Cooperation' (2017) 23 European Law Journal 140, 147.

[193] Polish Constitutional Tribunal, judgment of 21 April 2020, Kpt 1/20; Polish Constitutional Tribunal, judgment of 14 July 2021, P 7/20; Polish Constitutional Tribunal, judgment, 7 October 2021, K 3/21.

[194] On these issues, see eg Stanislaw Biernat, 'How Far Is It from Warsaw to Luxembourg and Karlsruhe: The Impact of the PSPP Judgment on Poland' (2020) 21 German Law Journal 1104; Wojciech Sadurski, *Poland's Constitutional Breakdown* (Oxford University Press 2019).

[195] Art 5(2) TEU.

[196] ibid.

[197] Art 5(3) TEU.

would be harmed where national constitutional courts adopt their own versions of EU law and, according to some, even risk undermining the foundations of the EU legal order.[198]

The countervailing consideration is that *ultra vires* review by national courts is justified for democratic reasons. The idea is that such review offers necessary protection for the democratic autonomy of the Member States against encroachment by the EU. An overstepping by the EU of its competences would curtail the legislative competences left to national legislatures, without prior authorization by these national legislatures. Given the EU's democratic shortcomings, this loss in Member State autonomy results in a loss in democratic legitimacy. The GFCC's viewpoint in this respect seems particularly strong, as it is informed by the idea that there is no European identity or European public sphere to buttress a European democracy. In this constellation, the EU derives its democratic legitimacy primarily from the Member States.[199] The act by which a national parliament confers authority on the EU is consequently a crucial basis for the EU's legitimacy.

A further argument for *ultra vires* review by national courts is that the CJEU is not a sufficiently neutral arbiter between the EU and its Member States. Instead, it is seen to favour an expansive interpretation of the EU's competences to the Member States' detriment.[200] In this respect, it has been argued that the threat of *ultra vires* review by national constitutional courts has induced the CJEU to take the issue of competences more seriously.[201] Some authors have proposed to remedy the CJEU's supposed lack of neutrality in competence disputes by setting up a new judicial chamber or court with jurisdiction to rule on the competence division between the EU and its Member States.[202] The idea is that such a court should be composed of

[198] See, for such concerns, Mayer, 'Rebel Without a Cause?' (n 176) 115 and 133; R Daniel Kelemen, 'On the Unsustainability of Constitutional Pluralism' (2016) 23 Maastricht Journal of European and Comparative Law 136; Julio Baquero Cruz, 'Another Look at Constitutional Pluralism in the European Union' (2016) 22 European Law Journal 356; R Daniel Kelemen and others, 'National Courts Cannot Override CJEU Judgments: A Joint Statement in Defense of the EU Legal Order' (*VerfBlog*, 26 May 2020) <https://verfassungsblog.de/national-courts-cannot-override-cjeu-judgments/.

[199] This reasoning is especially present in Bundesverfassungsgericht, judgment of 12 October 1993, 2 BvR 2134/92 (Maastricht) (translation in [1994] 1 CMLR 57).

[200] See eg Udo di Fabio, 'Karlsruhe Makes a Referral' (2014) 15 German Law Journal 107, 109; Kumm, 'The Jurisprudence of Constitutional Conflict' (n 4). Interview with Peter Huber, Judge at the German Federal Constitutional Court and judge rapporteur in most EU-related cases (Karlsruhe, Germany, 23 April 2015). For a historical assessment, see Joseph HH Weiler, 'The Transformation of Europe' (1991) 100 The Yale Law Journal 2403; Joseph HH Weiler, *The Constitution of Europe: 'Do the New Clothes Have an Emperor?' And Other Essays on European Integration* (Cambridge University Press 1999) ch 9.

[201] The CJEU's *Tobacco Advertising* judgment is seen by some as a response to this threat: Case C–376/98 Federal Republic of Germany v European Parliament and Council of the European Union [2000] ECR I–8419. See Halberstam, 'Constitutional Heterarchy' (n 167); Voßkuhle, 'Multilevel Cooperation of the European Constitutional Courts' (n 132) 195; Kumm, 'The Jurisprudence of Constitutional Conflict' (n 4) 295–96.

[202] Lindseth, *Power and Legitimacy* (n 53) 273–77; Daniel Sarmiento and Joseph HH Weiler, 'The EU Judiciary After Weiss' (*Verfassungsblog: On Matters Constitutional*, 2020) <https://verfassungsblog.de/the-eu-judiciary-after-weiss/> accessed 1 August 2022; Weiler, *The Constitution of Europe* (n 200) 321–23.

both CJEU judges and judges from national constitutional or equivalent supreme courts. As a result, this new court would provide a more balanced assessment of competence issues and institutionalize deliberation between national and CJEU judges without harming the uniform interpretation of EU law.

However, such proposals skip over the question as to whether and to what extent competence disputes should be decided by courts in the first place. The challenge in this respect is that democratic objections also apply to *ultra vires* review by courts, a problem pointed out in the context of judicial review on the basis of competence divisions in federal states.[203] Just like constitutional rights, provisions on the division of powers often also suffer from a lack of specificity and require interpretation. In the EU, this is the case in particular for the legal bases that allow the adoption of legislation pursuant to broad goals.[204] As a result, their interpretation is subject to reasonable disagreement, requiring judges to make contested evaluative choices.[205] For example, where the EU legislature chooses to adopt legislative measures on the basis of Article 114(1) TFEU, it can only do so if such measures 'have as their object the establishment and functioning of the internal market'. What the establishment and functioning of the internal market requires defies an easy answer and is subject to many different possible political interpretations.[206]

What is more, when interpreting competence provisions, judges will have to make evaluative judgments on the underlying values safeguarded by the division of competences. The Australian scholar Adrienne Stone powerfully explains this dilemma in a federal context. She notes that the idea of federalism is in itself a contested theory of government and that there is disagreement about how it is best realized even between those committed to the idea.[207] Federalism is commonly understood as a system of government that balances the value of centralized government with that of greater local control. Centralization allows for coordination of activities across an entire nation. Local control, on the other hand, is thought to prevent too great a concentration of power, to better achieve proximity of the governed to the governors, to foster experimentation and innovation, and to facilitate the living together of diverse cultural groups. The balance between these values, however, is a matter for debate.[208] Consequently, just as a political process may

[203] Stone, 'Judicial Review Without Rights' (n 123); Stone, 'Democratic Objections' (n 123).

[204] In similar sense, Joseph HH Weiler, Anne-Marie Slaughter, and Alec Stone Sweet, 'Prologue—The European Court of Justice' in Joseph HH Weiler, Anne-Marie Slaughter, and Alec Stone Sweet (eds), *The European Courts and National Courts* (Hart 1998) vii; Payandeh, 'Constitutional Review of EU Law after Honeywell' (n 80) 24–25; Paul Craig, 'The ECJ and Ultra Vires Action: A Conceptual Analysis' (2011) 48 Common Market Law Review 395.

[205] Bast, 'Don't Act Beyond Your Powers' (n 186) 181.

[206] Gareth Davies, 'Does the Court of Justice Own the Treaties? Interpretative Pluralism as a Solution to Over-constitutionalisation' (2018) 24 European Law Journal 358, 368.

[207] Stone, 'Judicial Review Without Rights' (n 123) 12–14. In a different sense, Schertzer speaks of the 'inherently contested nature of diverse federations'. Robert Schertzer, 'Federal Arbiters as Facilitators: Towards an Integrated Federal and Judicial Theory for Diverse States' (2017) 15 International Journal of Constitutional Law 110, 112.

[208] Stone, 'Judicial Review Without Rights' (n 123) 14.

concern principled and good faith disagreement over rights, it may also concern principled and good faith disagreement over the proper competence divisions between constituent parts of government.[209] Judicial review on the basis of competences gives courts discretion to decide these issues against majoritarian decisions under circumstances of reasonable disagreement, while judges possess no special capacity to decide these issues.[210]

Contestation over competence boundaries in the EU between national courts and the CJEU shows that similar normative disagreements exist about the appropriate balance between centralization at the EU level and leaving issues under national control. The GFCC's justification for *ultra vires* review is informed by a contested interpretation of democracy. The nationally oriented view of the Karlsruhe Court favours a limited interpretation of the EU's competences. That position discounts that a key reason to adopt legislation on the EU level may be that similar measures on the national level would have limited or no effect, or greatly impact on the interests of outsiders.[211] In this manner, European integration may even be seen as a way to overcome democratic deficits of the nation-state. Also, a strict enforcement of the EU's competence limits may actually exacerbate undemocratic features of the EU's political system. If a key democratic problem of the EU lies in its functional orientation and lack of politicization over the underlying goals that EU legislation may pursue, the solution is not to ensure stricter scrutiny of whether EU legislation pursues such narrow goals. Rather, democratic grounds would favour an interpretation of these competences that leaves room for competing perspectives. In addition, the GFCC's *ultra vires* review appears, at times, to extend to all Treaty norms.[212] If the over-constitutionalization of the EU is a problem, however, the additional enforcement of constitutional limits on the EU's political action will only aggravate this problem.

It is also not the case that judicial review on the basis of competences has no countermajoritarian effects. The democratic objection to rights-based review stems from the fact that it allows judges to override legislative majoritarian decision-making. Some argue, however, that disputes about competences do not concern *whether* a legislative body should decide, but rather *which* legislative institution should decide an issue.[213] In the EU, the argument would then be that an *ultra vires*

[209] ibid 24–27.

[210] ibid 8–10. See similarly Christoph Möllers, *The Three Branches: A Comparative Model of Separation of Powers* (Oxford University Press 2013) 132–33.

[211] For similar concerns, Cruz, 'The Legacy of the Maastricht-Urteil and the Pluralist Movement' (n 78) 17–18.

[212] See the discussion by Franz Mayer that the GFCC's *ultra vires* sometimes appears to be a 'comprehensive general judicial review of EU law'. Franz C Mayer, 'The Ultra Vires Ruling: Deconstructing the German Federal Constitutional Court's PSPP Decision of 5 May 2020' (2020) 16 European Constitutional Law Review 733, 15 and 23.

[213] For this argument in a context of federal states, see Nicholas Aroney, 'Reasonable Disagreement, Democracy and the Judicial Safeguards of Federalism' (2008) 27 The University of Queensland Law Journal 129, especially 140–41.

ruling would still leave the Member State legislatures free to enact the same law at the national level. The court would be merely deciding whether the EU legislature or the Member States' legislatures are competent to decide. The problem with this argument is that Member State legislatures may not be able to re-enact the same legislation at the national level, because its limited territorial scope significantly alters its effect.[214] In federal states, it is well known that the question of whether a particular issue should be regulated at the federal or state level often cannot be separated from the political question of how the issue should be regulated.[215] A further problem in the EU results from the difficulties in amending the EU Treaties. Treaty change requires unanimity while, in several Member States, such amendments require ratification by a qualified majority of some sort.[216] If a Member State legislature would disagree with an *ultra vires* ruling, it cannot override such a judgment by itself. For these reasons, also *ultra vires* review can be countermajoritarian.

Reasonable disagreement over the interpretation of competence divisions consequently provides a reason to leave competence questions to legislatures rather than courts.[217] Still, a complication is that it is not immediately clear which legislature at which level of government should then decide the matter. To argue that the legislature on the EU level should decide competence conflicts—or the federal legislature in federal states—would privilege the views of the EU legislature on the competence division over those of the Member State legislatures. That outcome could be considered question-begging, because in competence disputes the issue at stake is which legislature should have decision-making power.[218] Leaving the settlement of competence conflicts to a court that is independent of both legislatures avoids this objection of 'question-begging'.

A more democratic alternative that also addresses this concern is to settle competence conflicts through a political mechanism in which both levels of government are equally included.[219] This could be done by providing political safeguards for the Member States' competences in the legislative process. In the context of

[214] Stone, 'Democratic Objections' (n 123) 117–18.

[215] Möllers refers in particular to examples from the US, such as gun control and health care; see Christoph Möllers, 'Legalität, Legitimität und Legitimation des Bundesverfassungsgerichts' in Matthias Jestaedt and others (eds), *Das entgrenzte Gericht* (Suhrkamp 2011) 339–40.

[216] In some Member States, ratification of a new EU Treaty merely requires an ordinary majority. This is the case for example in the Netherlands, Belgium, Spain, and Italy. See Besselink and others, *National Constitutional Avenues* (n 5) 31. In most Member States, however, Treaty amendments require ratification by a special majority. For example, in Germany, the conclusion of EU Treaty amendments requires a two-thirds majority in the *Bundestag* and *Bundesrat* (art 23 BL); in Ireland, significant competence transfers require constitutional amendment by referendum as determined by the Supreme Court of Ireland, decision of 18 February and 9 April 1987, Crotty v An Taoiseach [1987] ILRM 400. In Denmark, certain Treaty changes would require a three-fifths majority in parliament or approval in a popular referendum.

[217] See similarly Dawson and Witte, 'From Balance to Conflict' (n 30) 222–23.

[218] Jeffrey Goldsworthy, 'Structural Judicial Review and the Objection from Democracy' (2010) 60 The University of Toronto Law Journal 137.

[219] See, by analogy, ibid 141.

federal states, various authors have in fact argued that federalism is best maintained through such political safeguards. In the US context, Herbert Wechsler reasoned that the great extent of the states' involvement in the national government offers considerable safeguards to the states' competences, for example because two senators represent each state in the US Senate.[220] Consequently, where the national parliament can be seen to represent both the national and local levels of government, judges have good reason to adopt a deferential standard of review where they scrutinize competence boundaries.[221] This is particularly so where constitutional competence divisions are hard to change by constitutional amendment.[222] As I discuss in the next subsection, the EU's legislative process offers various such political safeguards, providing grounds for leaving competence issues to the EU legislature.

4.3.3 Comparing political and judicial safeguards

The institutional structure of the EU provides various political safeguards. First, the Member States are heavily involved in negotiating any piece of secondary EU legislation through their representation in the Council. In principle, the national governments that sit in the Council are democratically accountable to their national parliaments. Therefore, if these national parliaments believe that the EU encroaches upon their legislative competences, they could voice their concerns and ensure that they are taken into account by their respective governments.

Secondly, since the coming into force of the Treaty of Lisbon, national parliaments have the opportunity to directly object to legislative proposals on subsidiarity grounds.[223] When a third of the national parliaments object to a legislative proposal on grounds of subsidiarity, the proposal has to be reviewed and the institution that submitted the proposal—usually the Commission—will have to justify its decision to maintain, amend, or withdraw its proposal.[224] If a majority of parliaments holds that a legislative proposal is incompatible with the principle of subsidiarity, the Commission must review its proposal.[225] If the Commission subsequently maintains its proposal, it must justify in a reasoned opinion why it deems the proposal compatible with the subsidiarity principle and submit this opinion to the Union legislature.[226] This political safeguard provides national parliaments

[220] Herbert Wechsler, 'The Political Safeguards of Federalism: The Role of the States in the Composition and Selection of the National Government' (1954) 54 Columbia Law Review 543. Larry Kramer argues that political safeguards indeed do the job in the US context, but for different reasons than Wechsler maintained: Larry D Kramer, 'Putting the Politics Back into the Political Safeguards of Federalism' (2000) 100 Columbia Law Review 215.

[221] Goldsworthy, 'Structural Judicial Review' (n 218).

[222] Möllers, 'Legalität, Legitimität und Legitimation' (n 215) 340–41; Möllers, *The Three Branches* (n 210) 134.

[223] Protocol (no 2) on the application of the principles of subsidiarity and proportionality. See, in this sense, also Kumm, 'The Jurisprudence of Constitutional Conflict' (n 4).

[224] Each Member State has two votes, whereas each parliamentary chamber has one vote in bicameral systems. See art 7(1) protocol 2.

[225] This procedure applies to the ordinary legislative procedure, see art 7(3) protocol 2.

[226] See art 7 of the protocol on the application of the principles of subsidiarity and proportionality.

a further way of preventing the hollowing out of their legislative competence as a result of EU legislative action.

For these reasons, it is not clear that national constitutional courts should engage in *ultra vires* review of EU legislative action. The political safeguards present a justification for the considerable leeway that the CJEU gives to the European legislature in interpreting the competence boundaries between the EU and its Member States. It could be the case, however, that these political safeguards do not function adequately in practice, making an additional role of the national courts desirable. The assumption is that political institutions give competence issues serious consideration. This is an issue that has to be the subject of further research that compares the ability of different institutions to address questions about the EU's competences.[227]

The best case for national courts' *ultra vires* review lies where it concerns decision-making that is not legislative in nature. In particular, the national constitutional courts could possibly provide a counterweight to the expansive interpretations of EU primary law by the CJEU.[228] Yet, even in such constellations, the risk is that national courts take a contested position on underlying constitutional principles and pose limits to political decision-making.

The *Ajos* judgment by the Danish Supreme Court provides an example.[229] The case concerned a conflict between Danish law and the general principle prohibiting age discrimination developed in the CJEU's case law. In its preliminary ruling, the CJEU required the Danish Court to also apply this principle in situations between private parties. However, the CJEU's solution conflicted with the Danish Court's long-standing interpretation of the applicable Danish legislation. The Supreme Court reasoned that changing this interpretation would be *contra legem* and violate the principles of legal certainty and legitimate expectations. Moreover, the Danish Supreme Court has an interpretive tradition of judicial restraint that is rooted in democratic considerations.

Against this backdrop, the Danish Court refused to comply with the CJEU's guidelines. Yet, in reaching that conclusion, the Danish Court did not simply criticize the CJEU's expansive case law on democratic grounds. Instead, it felt the need to dwell on the relation between EU and national constitutional law more generally. The Danish judges determined that the Danish accession law served as the basis for the applicability of EU law in Denmark and accorded key importance to the Danish parliamentary proceedings in determining the limits of the EU's legal

227 One such study by Jacob Öberg notes that 'the general assessment of national parliaments' role in countering "competence creep" is positive'. Jacob Öberg, 'National Parliaments and Political Control of EU Competences: A Sufficient Safeguard of Federalism?' (2018) 24 European Public Law 965, 731.

228 In this sense particularly, Grimm, 'The Role of National Constitutional Courts' (n 4).

229 Supreme Court of Denmark (Højesteret), Case 15/2014, decision of 6 December 2016 (*Ajos*) (translation on <https://domstol.dk/media/2udgvvvb/judgment-15-2014.pdf> accessed 2 August 2022).

authority. On this basis, the Danish Court concluded that it would overstep its judicial mandate by applying the principle of non-discrimination on grounds of age to the case at hand.[230] However, the Court's reasoning overshot its target: the narrow interpretation of the EU's competences restricts not just the CJEU, but also poses potential limits to EU legislative acts.[231]

The same problem arises with *ultra vires* review of decision-making by EU executive institutions that has a direct legal basis in the EU Treaties. Here the lack of political safeguards similarly makes *ultra vires* review more easily justifiable. However, the GFCC's review of the ECB's OMT policy illustrates its complications. Even though the democratic legitimacy of the ECB's role is contested, given its high degree of independence from political institutions, the ECB's OMT policy has also been widely credited as crucial in preventing the further escalation of the eurozone debt crisis.[232] Declaring this policy *ultra vires* would probably have significant and irreversible political ramifications, while based on a contested understanding of democracy. This problem was aptly described by dissenting Judge Lübbe-Wolff:

> That some few independent German judges—invoking the German interpretation of the principle of democracy, the limits of admissible competences of the ECB following from this interpretation, and our reading of Art. 123 et seq. TFEU—make a decision with incalculable consequences for the operating currency of the euro zone and the national economies depending on it appears as an anomaly of questionable democratic character.[233]

In the same case, Judge Gerhardt stated in a dissent that the competence scrutiny should, also in this case, have been left to Germany's political institutions. The federal government had approved the OMT policy and the German *Bundestag* had accepted this 'with open eyes—against the backdrop of an intensive public debate, after having heard the President of the European Central Bank, and [. . .] on the basis of the Bundestag's observation and assessment of the acts of the European Central Bank'.[234] In addition, the *Bundestag* could have criticized the OMT

[230] On the case see also Urška Šadl and Sabine Mair, 'Mutual Disempowerment: Case C-441/14 Dansk Industri, Acting on Behalf of Ajos A/S v Estate of Karsten Eigil Rasmussen and Case No. 15/2014 Dansk Industri (DI) Acting for Ajos A/S v The Estate Left by A' (2017) 13 European Constitutional Law Review 347; Madsen, Olsen and Šadl, 'Competing Supremacies and Clashing Institutional Rationalities' (n 192).

[231] For similar considerations, see Helle Krunke and Sune Klinge, 'The Danish Ajos Case: The Missing Case from Maastricht and Lisbon' (2018) 3 European Papers 157. They qualify the Danish Court on the one hand as signalling 'respect of the political institutions' and 'as more passive' itself, while on the other hand also as 'active and self-confident' (167–68).

[232] See eg Paul de Grauwe, *Economics of Monetary Union* (Oxford University Press 2014) 120–21; Vestert Borger, 'Outright Monetary Transactions and the Stability Mandate of the ECB: Gauweiler' (2016) 53 Common Market Law Review 139, 143–48.

[233] Bundesverfassungsgericht, order of 14 January 2014 2 BvR 2728/13 (*OMT* referral), Dissent by Judge Lübbe-Wolff, para 28.

[234] ibid Dissent by Judge Gerhardt, para 23.

programme and brought actions for annulment before the CJEU: 'The fact that it did none of this does not indicate a democratic deficit, but is an expression of its majority decision for a certain policy when handling the sovereign debt crisis in the euro currency area.'[235]

Whether such implicit consent provides sufficient democratic authorization for the ECB's actions can be doubted.[236] Nonetheless, the considerations by Judge Gerhardt reveal a fundamental point: if *ultra vires* review is about protecting the space for democratic politics and the power of national parliaments in particular, there is good reason to leave it primarily to political institutions to prevent *ultra vires* acts. Rather than focusing on the role of courts, efforts should then be directed at strengthening political safeguards, such as a political override of CJEU decisions, de-constitutionalization of the Treaties, and a further strengthening of the position of national parliaments in the EU legislative process. A solution that does involve national courts but avoids the democratic problems discussed above is weak-form judicial review. Where a national court signals that it considers an act of EU institutions *ultra vires* but refrains from giving such a finding legal effect, it would leave it to political institutions to address the problem. That said, whether these solutions are fully adequate also remains an issue in need of further research. Such research should consider whether and how political institutions consider questions about the EU's competences and their relation to democratic government.

5. Conclusion

The EU-related case law of national constitutional courts has been justified for various reasons: as protecting the democratic autonomy of the Member States, as putting pressure on the EU to democratize, as allowing contestation and dialogue over constitutional issues, or as a way to ensure respect for national constitutional identities. Such justifications do not fully address, however, that the courts' review of European law also raises democratic concerns. Despite the EU's democratic legitimacy problems, it is still more democratic to leave it to political institutions to address constitutional issues in the context of European integration. This institutional consideration also applies where the national courts' review is directly justified on democratic grounds. The question of how the EU should be further democratized is itself a complex political issue subject to a variety of diverging reasonable viewpoints.

235 ibid Dissent by Judge Gerhardt, para 23.

236 For a more elaborate analysis, see Nik de Boer and Jens van 't Klooster, 'The ECB, the Courts and the Issue of Democratic Legitimacy after Weiss' (2020) 57 Common Market Law Review 1689, 1723–24.

Instead, I have argued in this chapter that the legitimacy of the constitutional courts' review depends on a comparative institutional assessment between constitutional courts and political institutions. The constitutional courts' review could be a way to better ensure that constitutional issues are given due consideration in the making of European law, such as questions relating to constitutional identity or competence issues. Yet, to understand whether that is the case, further comparative institutional research is required. That research should take into account the institutional constellation in which review takes place, how the constitutional issues that a national court raises played a role in the prior decision-making process, as well as how the constitutional court judgments impact on subsequent political deliberations.

The case study of the GFCC—the protagonist in the debate on the role of national constitutional courts in relation to the EU—in the following chapters explores these questions in more depth. The subsequent chapters focus on three pivotal constitutional episodes: the adoption and the ratification process of the Maastricht Treaty, the euro crisis, and the Covid-19 crisis, including the aftermath of the GFCC's *PSPP* ruling. These chapters consider how the constitutional issues raised by the GFCC in its judgment on the Maastricht Treaty, as well as its euro crisis case law, were treated by the German legislature and the relevant European institutions. They also assess how the GFCC's case law impacted on subsequent decision-making within these political institutions. Chapter 7 assesses the political consequences of the GFCC's EU-related case law during the Covid-19 pandemic. More specifically, the chapter analyses the repercussions of the GFCC's *PSPP* ruling on political debates concerning the role of the ECB, as well as the impact of the GFCC's case law more broadly on the EU's response to the economic consequences of the pandemic. The selected episodes do not exhaust the different possible institutional constellations in which review of European law by national constitutional courts takes place. Nonetheless, they offer several novel insights on the legitimacy of identity review, *ultra vires* review, and the role that national constitutional courts may play in enhancing national parliamentary oversight.

4
The Rise of Judicial Euroscepticism: Maastricht

1. Introduction

The current chapter turns the focus to the GFCC's *Maastricht-Urteil* of 12 October 1993, in which the German Court reviewed the Treaty of Maastricht on its compatibility with the German constitution. The adoption of the Maastricht Treaty stands out as a key moment in the history of European integration. The Treaty considerably expanded the EU's competences, and the agreement on a timetable and conditions for the Economic and Monetary Union (EMU) presented a sweeping change. This increase in powers made questions about the EU's legitimacy more pressing than before.[1]

The GFCC's *Maastricht-Urteil*, in turn, is a landmark case. The judgment focused on the EU's democratic legitimacy but, in contrast to previous case law, the Court raised doubts about the possibility of achieving democracy at the European level. This approach laid the basis for the Court's future evaluation of European integration and has had a lasting impact on EU constitutional discourse as well as the EU-related case law of constitutional courts in other Member States.[2]

In line with the purpose of this book, the current chapter considers how the key constitutional issues raised in the *Maastricht-Urteil* were considered in the prior political deliberations by the Treaty drafters and by the German *Bundestag*. In addition, the chapter analyses how the judgment impacted on political debate in its immediate aftermath.

This discussion serves to assess three possible justifications for the *Maastricht* judgment. The first justification is that, despite the judgment's shortcomings, the GFCC compensated for a lack of serious consideration of the constitutional implications of the Treaty in the prior political process. The main shortcoming of the *Maastricht-Urteil* itself is that Karlsruhe chose to construe the constitutional principle of democracy as at odds with the process of European integration: it held that the democratic legitimation of the EU derived primarily from the *Bundestag* and

[1] See also Claudia Schrag Sternberg, *The Struggle for EU Legitimacy: Public Contestation, 1950–2005* (Palgrave Macmillan 2013) 104.
[2] See, on both points, Julio Baquero Cruz, 'The Legacy of the Maastricht-Urteil and the Pluralist Movement' (2008) 14(4) European Law Journal 389–422.

Judging European Democracy. Nik de Boer, Oxford University Press. © Nik de Boer 2023.
DOI: 10.1093/oso/9780192845238.003.0004

that the societal preconditions for democracy on the European level—a European public sphere and *demos*—were not yet present. In light of the EU's democratic shortcomings, the German *Bundestag* would have to retain substantial competences. In addition, the German Court would review whether Union acts, including CJEU judgments, remained within the boundaries of the EU's conferred competences. This interpretation of the principle of democracy, however, raises a democratic problem itself. It rests on a contested understanding of the relation between national sovereignty and democracy. Consequently, Karlsruhe's interpretation of democracy is liable to restrict political contestation over the form that democracy should take in the EU. The approach of tying democracy to national sovereignty dismisses democratic reasons for European integration.

Nonetheless, one could argue that the Court at least addressed the constitutional implications of the Treaty where the political institutions failed to do so. In this vein Justin Collings has argued:

> The judgment's enduring significance lay in the Court's willingness to identify democratic deficiencies in the Union treaty about which few politicians in any major party were willing to speak. There had been little discussion or debate among the country's uniformly Europhile parties about the best or most democratically-legitimate paths towards further integration. It was the contribution of the Maastricht complainants, and of the justices of the Second Senate, to get the conversation going.[3]

[3] Justin Collings, *Democracy's Guardians: A History of the German Federal Constitutional Court, 1951–2001* (Oxford University Press, 2015) 280. Various authors have offered similar justifications for the judgment. Matthias Herdegen argued that '[t]he large consensus within Parliament did not allow for a profound discussion of Maastricht's implications, of the quality the political class of France and of other Member States has offered to its citizens'. Mattias Herdegen, 'Maastricht and the German Constitutional Court—Constitutional Restraints for an Ever Closer Union' (1994) 31(2) *Common Market Law Review* 235, 249. Juliane Kokott said of the judgment: 'It is also partly a compensation for the lack of a proper political debate on the implications of the Maastricht Treaty and the monetary union. Such a discussion took place too late and too superficially in Germany. This factor furthers ambiguous feelings in the population. The *Maastricht* decision takes away the basis for some of these ambiguous feelings and fears. This way, European integration is better accepted in the country.' Juliane Kokott, 'Report on Germany' in Joseph HH Weiler, Anne-Marie Slaughter, and Alec Stone Sweet (eds), *The European Court and National Courts—Doctrine and Jurisprudence* (Hart 1998) 131. Monica Claes has submitted that in the context of European integration '[t]here may be a need to re-think democracy and constitutional foundations *tout court*, not only from a European perspective, but also in the context of the national Constitutions. The need to take these fundamental constitutional principles—shared throughout Western Europe—seriously may well be the most important message of the *Bundesverfassungsgericht* sent out in the *Maastricht Urteil*.' Monica Claes, *The National Courts' Mandate in the European Constitution* (PhD thesis, Maastricht University 2004) 10–11. Mattias Kumm has characterized the *Maastricht-Urteil* as the best-known instance where a national court played 'an important role legitimating political actors as well as addressing the concerns raised by those opposing ratification in a principled fashion'. Mattias Kumm, 'The Jurisprudence of Constitutional Conflict: Constitutional Supremacy in Europe Before and After the Constitutional Treaty' (2005) 11(3) European Law Journal 262, 280, fn 54.

As the chapter shows, this argument cannot be sustained. The constitutional implications of the Maastricht Treaty and the EU's democratic shortcomings had been amply discussed in the prior ratification debates. In the *Bundestag*, there was widespread agreement that the Maastricht Treaty had significant democratic shortcomings and that these should be resolved in the future. In fact, the German legislature even amended the Basic Law to ensure that the EU would further develop in accordance with the fundamental principles of the Basic Law, democracy included. In the context of monetary union, the story is somewhat different. There, neither the political institutions nor the Court fully addressed the implications of monetary union, in particular the possibility of a crisis.

A second justification for the judgment is that the Maastricht ratification debates only devoted such significant attention to constitutional issues because of the GFCC's prior *Solange* case law, as well as the possibility of subsequent constitutional review. The idea is that without the GFCC's prior case law on the EU, constitutional issues would have played a far less prominent role in the ratification debates. This defence is more difficult to assess, but probably does not stand either, because the desire to strengthen the EU's democratic legitimacy was a long-held wish of German political elites that already preceded the *Solange* case law.

A third justification is that the Court catalysed further debate by raising issues not fully addressed within the prior political process. Along these lines, it has been argued that the GFCC played an important democratic role, because it provided a substitute for public debate: in Germany the GFCC provided a forum for resistance to the Treaty, which in other Member States took a political form.[4] This view is not without merit. In the strong pro-integration climate of German politics, it could be difficult for parliamentarians to make arguments critical of European integration. There was no opposition to the idea of European integration as such in the German ratification debates. The GFCC eventually provided a more critical viewpoint and through an expansive interpretation of the Basic Law gave those critical of European integration an additional forum to voice their concerns.

Still, for a constitutional court to play this part entails a strange reversal of roles. Apparently German politics was not political enough, whereas the GFCC's more Euro-critical stance sought to 'politicize' a debate which was too apolitical. This role does not suit the position of a constitutional court: it is not merely an influential voice within public debate, but acts as the guardian of a constitutional framework

[4] See Herdegen, 'Maastricht and the German Constitutional Court' (n 3) 249. More recently, Peter Huber, a member of the GFCC's Second Senate, described the function of the Karlsruhe courtroom as a 'democratic compensation or valve' in Peter M Huber, 'Art 19 IV GG', in Hermann von Mangoldt and others (eds), *GG Kommentar* (6th edn, 2010), para 350. Wolfgang Kahl has argued that the Karlsruhe proceedings compensate for the lack of direct democracy at the federal level in Germany, see Wolfgang Kahl, 'Bewältigung der Staatsschuldenkrise unter Kontrolle des Bundesverfassungsgerichts' [2013] Deutsches Verwaltungsblatt 197, 207. I have taken both citations from Mattias Wendel, 'Exceeding Judicial Competence in the Name of Democracy: The German Federal Constitutional Court's OMT Reference' (2014) 10 European Constitutional Law Review 263, 283.

that is supposed to bind democratic politics. In the context of Maastricht, the Court could still play the role of facilitating opposition, because the judgment was sufficiently open to various interpretations. German politicians could frame the ruling as perfectly compatible with their previously held political viewpoints, while outside parliament the judgment did lead to debate on new issues. Over the longer term, however, the Court's case law has proved more problematic, as the subsequent chapter on the euro crisis underlines.

The remainder of the current chapter substantiates these arguments and is structured along the two main themes of the *Maastricht-Urteil* and the judgment's political reception. Section 2 first considers the general topic of democracy and the related theme of competences. In this section, I contrast the Court's assessment with how these issues were dealt with in the prior political deliberations at both the EU level and in Germany. Section 3 similarly considers the EMU, a key part of the Maastricht Treaty and the GFCC's judgment, yet one that until the crisis hardly featured in EU constitutional scholarship and assessments of the *Maastricht-Urteil.* Section 4 assesses the reception of the judgment by the German government and *Bundestag* in the immediate aftermath of the *Maastricht* judgment and dwells on its reception at the European level. The conclusion draws together the main findings.

2. Comparing Judicial and Political Assessments of European Democracy

2.1 Connecting Statehood and Democracy: The GFCC's *Maastricht-Urteil*

The key legal issue in the *Maastricht-Urteil* was whether the German Act of Accession to the Treaty on European Union violated the right to vote of Article 38 BL and the democratic principle of Article 20 BL. The judgment stands out because it connected democracy to the protection of sovereign statehood. This idea is reminiscent of the writings of judge rapporteur Paul Kirchhoff and a particular strand of German constitutional thought.[5]

An important novelty in the judgment was the Court's interpretation of the right to vote of Article 38 BL. Article 38(1) BL states that '[m]embers of the German

[5] Christoph Möllers, *Der vermisste Leviathan—Staatstheorie in der Bundesrepublik* (Suhrkamp 2008) 72–75; Christophe Majastre, 'Penser l'état contre l'europe: la genèse d'une orthodoxie juridique dans la République Fédérale d'Allemagne De 1949 à l'arrêt Maastricht' (2019) 69 Revue française de science politique 117; Jo Eric Kushal Murkens, 'The Future of Staatsrecht: Dominance, Demise or Demystification?' (2007) 70 Modern Law Review 731; Monika Polzin, 'Constitutional Identity, Unconstitutional Amendments and the Idea of Constituent Power: The Development of the Doctrine of Constitutional Identity in German Constitutional Law' (2016) 14 International Journal of Constitutional Law 411. The Court's ruling appears to be a watered-down version of the arguments spelled out in Paul Kirchhof, 'Deutsches Verfassungsrecht und Europäisches Gemeinschaftsrecht' [1991] Europarecht-Beiheft 1 11.

Bundestag shall be elected in general, direct, free, equal and secret elections'. In addition, Article 38(2) BL holds that '[a]ny person who has attained the age of eighteen shall be entitled to vote'.[6] In its *Maastricht* judgment, the Court ruled that this right has substantive content: it guarantees German citizens not just a formal right to elect the German *Bundestag*, but also 'the fundamental democratic content of that right' by which citizens legitimate and influence the exercise of public authority.[7] Competence transfers by the *Bundestag* to the EU affect this democratic content.[8] They would be permissible unless such transfers reduced the *Bundestag*'s powers to such an extent that the democratic principle of Article 20(1) and (2) BL and the eternity clause of Article 79(3) BL would be breached.[9] The Court considered that for the question of admissibility, the complainant Manfred Brunner had sufficiently substantiated that this could be the case, as the Treaty enhanced the powers of the Union and European Communities in several respects.[10]

The Court's interpretation of Article 38 BL was controversial and a departure from earlier case law.[11] The consequence of understanding the right to vote in this substantive manner, is that all German citizens gain the possibility to challenge transfers of German sovereign powers to the EU before the GFCC, without the need to show specific injury.[12] This allowed the Court to engage in 'abstract' review of the Treaty on the basis of a constitutional complaint, whereas the Basic Law reserves this function to the federal government, a *Land* government, or, still at the time, a third of the Members of the *Bundestag*.[13] The overwhelming political support for the Maastricht Treaty, however, had prevented a constitutional challenge in abstract review proceedings.[14]

[6] As translated by Christian Tomuschat, David P Currie, and Donald P Kommers in cooperation with the Language Service of the German Bundestag. Available at <www.bundestag.de/en/documents/legal> accessed 1 August 2022.

[7] Bundesverfassungsgericht, judgment of 12 October 1993, 2 BvR 2134/92 (Maastricht) (translation in [1994] 1 CMLR 57) para 4 (hereafter BVerfG, *Maastricht*).

[8] I decided to speak of 'transfers' as the GFCC uses this wording, even though art 5 TEU speaks of 'conferral'.

[9] BVerfG, *Maastricht* (n 7) paras 5–6.

[10] ibid paras 7–9.

[11] Reportedly, it was also the subject of significant discussion among the GFCC's judges, see Ingo Winkelmann (ed), *Das Maastricht-Urteil des Bundesverfassungsgerichts vom 12. Oktober 1993, Dokumentation des Verfahrens mit Einführung* (Dunckler & Humblot 1994) 36–37. Even a current judge of the Second Senate, Doris König, held a very critical view of this case law in her habilitation: Doris König, *Die Übertragung von Hoheitsrechten im Rahmen des Europäischen Integrationsprozesses—Anwendungsbereich und Schranken des Art. 23 Des Grundgesetzes* (Duncker & Humblot 2000) 476–80 in particular.

[12] Tomuschat qualified this as an '*actio popularis*' that logically should also apply any time competences would be removed from the Bundestag to the executive or Bundesrat, but especially to every Act approving an international treaty that concerned the setting-up of an international organization. Christian Tomuschat, 'Die Europaïsche Union unter der Aufsicht des Bundesverfassungsgerichts' (1993) 20 Europäische Grundrechte-Zeitschrift 489, 491. See also Jo Eric Murkens, *From Empire to Union: Conceptions of German Constitutional Law since 1871* (Oxford University Press 2013) 181–83.

[13] Art 93(1) and (2) BL.

[14] Winkelmann, *Das Maastricht-Urteil* (n 11) 21.

The connection between sovereign statehood and democracy shines through in how the Court subsequently spelled out the content of the democratic principle: it voiced scepticism about the possibility of achieving democracy at the European level, pointed to outer limits of German participation in European integration, and determined that the democratic legitimacy of the EU depended foremost on national parliaments.[15]

First, the Court did accept that Germany could transfer sovereign rights to a supranational community even though this would change the democratic legitimation of public authority. Although such transfers would diminish the *Bundestag*'s powers and consequently the citizens' influence on public authority, the Court held that the form of democratic legitimation on the European level could be different from that on the German level. The judges also acknowledged that such power transfers could indirectly enhance the citizens' powers by increasing the Member States' potential for influencing the political will of the community. In addition, the Court pointed to the provisions in the Basic Law allowing European integration. It was therefore acceptable that executives in the Council could adopt legislation on the basis of majority decisions rather than unanimity.[16] However, the Court also noted that 'the majority principle [...] finds its limits in the constitutional principles and basic interests of the member-States'.[17]

Secondly, the Court held that the democratic legitimation of the European Communities depended primarily on the national parliaments. Crucial here was the legislation by which the *Bundestag* would authorize a conferral of sovereign powers to the EU: 'in the statute assenting to accession to a community of States is found the democratic legitimation of both the existence of the community of States itself and of its powers to take majority decisions which are binding on the member-States.'[18] In addition, the German people should have a continued influence on the supranational community. Such legitimation had to come in the first place from the national parliaments.[19] The European Parliament was judged important as well, but only as 'the source of a supplementary democratic support'.[20] In this context, the Court did not discuss the actual powers of the European Parliament, such as the introduction of the co-decision procedure. Nonetheless, it confidently proclaimed that the Treaty confers new competences on the European organs, but that these 'are not yet supported by a corresponding strengthening and extension of the democratic bases'.[21]

[15] Volkmar Götz argued, however, that the judgment was 'Europe-friendly' (*integrationsfreundlich*): Volkmar Götz, 'Das Maastricht-Urteil des BVerfG' (1993) 48(22) Juristenzeitung 1081, 1086.

[16] BVerfG, *Maastricht* (n 7) paras 36–37. The Court noted that, on the European level, legislative competence could lie with executives to a greater degree than at the national level.

[17] ibid para 37. This statement is an allusion to the so-called Luxembourg compromise.

[18] ibid para 37.

[19] ibid paras 38–39.

[20] ibid para 40.

[21] ibid para 106; Tomuschat, 'Die Europaïsche Union unter der Aufsicht (n 12) 493.

Thirdly, the Court held that democracy depends on 'certain pre-legal conditions',[22] namely the existence of a European public sphere that could develop in the future but did not at that time exist. Elements of such a shared public sphere would be common political parties, media, and civil society organizations. The Court, moreover, stressed that citizens should be entitled to communicate in their own language with the sovereign authority and noted the importance of openness and transparency.[23] The fact that a shared European public sphere did not yet exist entailed 'that functions and powers of substantial importance must remain for the German Bundestag'.[24] In justifying that proposition, the Court also alluded to the need for a stronger form of national identity that has been the source of considerable criticism:[25]

> The States need sufficiently important spheres of activity of their own in which the people of each can develop and articulate itself in a process of political will-formation which it legitimates and controls, in order thus to give legal expression to what binds the people together (to a greater or lesser degree of homogeneity) spiritually, socially and politically.[26]

This more sceptical statement on the possibility of realizing democracy beyond the state can, however, be contrasted with the Court's more conciliatory statement at the end of its judgment 'that the democratic bases of the Union will be built in step with the integration process, and a living democracy will also be maintained in the member-States as integration progresses'.[27]

Fourthly, and given the *Bundestag*'s importance in providing the EU's democratic legitimacy, the GFCC reasoned that the *Bundestag* would have to 'decide on German membership of the European Union and on its continuation and development'.[28] For this reason, the statute containing the conferral of powers to the Union has to specify the powers and functions of the supranational community with sufficient certainty. Otherwise, the transfer would amount to a general authorization incompatible with Article 38 and the core of the principle of democracy as protected by Article 79(3) of the constitution. The deciding factor, in the view of the Court, was that the Union's powers (as laid down in the Treaty and accepted in the national accession law) would be sufficiently 'predictable' for the German

22 BVerfG, *Maastricht* (n 7) para 41.

23 ibid paras 41–42.

24 ibid para 44.

25 See, in particular, Joseph HH Weiler, 'Does Europe Need a Constitution? Demos, Telos and the German Maastricht Decision' (1995) 1(3) European Law Journal 219. See also Murkens, *From Empire to Union* (n 12); Tomuschat, 'Die Europaïsche Union unter der Aufsicht (n 12) 496.

26 BVerfG, *Maastricht* (n 7) para 44. In this context the Court referred to the work of Herman Heller, but commentators have argued that the work of Carl Schmitt is probably the true origin of the reference to homogeneity. See Murkens, *From Empire to Union* (n 12) 195.

27 BVerfG, *Maastricht* (n 7) para 107 and similarly para 43.

28 ibid para 47.

legislature. If the Union developed powers no longer covered by the Treaty provisions, the legislative instruments adopted would have to be considered as not legally binding in Germany. The GFCC itself would be competent to review whether Community law would still fall within the bounds of these competences.[29]

For several reasons, the Court held that the Treaty satisfied these criteria. The EU was a federation of states or '*Staatenverbund*', not a European state based on the people of one European nation. There was hence no need to review whether Germany could become part of a European state. Sovereignty remained with the Member States as 'Masters of the Treaties'. Germany could revoke its adherence to the EU and thus retained its sovereignty.[30] In addition, the new Article 23 of the Basic Law safeguarded the continued influence of the *Bundestag*.[31] The competences in the Treaty were sufficiently specific: the Community could only act within its limited competences, which the principles of proportionality and subsidiarity further restricted.[32] The Court also warned that in the future it would no longer accept a dynamic interpretation of the Treaty by the Union institutions, including the CJEU. Interpretations equivalent to 'an extension of the Treaty' would 'not produce binding effects for Germany'.[33]

2.2 Intergovernmentalism versus Supranationalism: Democracy in the Treaty Negotiations

The GFCC was not the first institution to raise the topic of democracy, and the way in which the Court linked national sovereignty and democracy was politically contested. During the Treaty negotiations, democratic legitimacy was explicitly named as one of the five topics discussed in the Intergovernmental Conference (IGC) on Political Union.[34] The Member States nevertheless disagreed on whether the future organization of Europe should be more supranational or intergovernmental in nature and held different viewpoints on whether the European Parliament's competences should be enhanced.

In the course of the negotiations, Germany put strong emphasis on the creation of federal structures and considered alleviating the democratic deficit to be a top

[29] ibid paras 48–49.

[30] ibid paras 51–55. The judgment, however, was ambiguous as to whether Germany could do so unilaterally or jointly with the other Member States.

[31] ibid para 56.

[32] See ibid paras 59–105.

[33] ibid para 99.

[34] The IGC dealt with the following five areas: democratic legitimacy through enhanced powers of the European Parliament; Common Foreign and Security Policy; European citizenship; extension of Community competences in areas such as social policy, health, and the environment; and the strengthening of the Union's effectiveness and efficiency. Conclusions of the European Council of 14 and 15 December 1990 at <www.consilium.europa.eu/media/20537/1990_december_-_rome__eng__part_i.pdf> accessed 1 August 2022.

priority. Chancellor Helmut Kohl went so far as to make extending the powers of the European Parliament a condition for approving EMU.[35] Italy, Belgium, the Netherlands, and Luxembourg took a similar position, favouring a supranational Europe as well as an extension of the European Parliament's powers. Spain and Greece also favoured a stronger position of the Parliament, while Spain took the initiative to introduce European citizenship.

France, Portugal, Denmark, and the UK, however, favoured European cooperation along intergovernmental lines. France in particular preferred a strong position of the European Council and the Council. It opposed granting more powers to the European Parliament and Commission. In June 1991, French President Mitterrand expressed this position in clear terms during a lunch with Dutch Foreign Minister Van Den Broek and Prime Minister Lubbers: '*Le Parlement Européen est zéro. La Commission Européenne est zéro. Zéro plus zero fait zéro.*'[36]

The result was a compromise. Germany accommodated France to a degree, because of the importance it attached to maintaining Franco-German relations. This led to a strengthening of the European Council. France made concessions by accepting more rights for the European Parliament on which Germany insisted.[37] An attempt by the Netherlands to forge agreement on a Treaty with a more supranational orientation failed dramatically. During the Luxembourg Presidency in the first half of 1991, a draft Treaty was negotiated that was more intergovernmental than supranational in inspiration and that introduced the so-called three-pillar structure.[38] Due to the limited administrative capacity of the Luxembourg Presidency, the drafting of the Treaty had been largely left to the Member States' permanent representatives in Brussels and the Council secretariat. The result favoured the position of the Council, and France had a strong influence.[39] Unhappy with this outcome, the Netherlands presented a new draft Treaty during its subsequent Council Presidency in the second half of 1991. This design replaced the pillar structure with a unified Community structure and extended the powers of the European Parliament considerably.[40] However, on 30 September 1991, ten of the twelve EEC Member States rejected these proposals. Among them was Germany,

35 Rita Beuter, 'Germany and the Ratification of the Maastricht Treaty' in Finn Laursen and Sophie Vanhoonacker (eds), *The Ratification of the Maastricht Treaty: Issues, Debates and Future Implications* (European Institute of Public Administration Maastricht 1994) 87, 87–88; Finn Laursen, Sophie Vanhoonacker, and Robert Wester, 'Overview of the Negotiations' in Finn Laursen and Sophie Vanhoonacker (eds), *The Intergovernmental Conference on Political Union* (European Institute of Public Administration Maastricht 1992) 3, 14; Christa van Wijnbergen, 'The Federal Republic of Germany' in Finn Laursen and Sophie Vanhoonacker (eds), *The Intergovernmental Conference on Political Union* (European Institute of Public Administration Maastricht 1992) 49, 58–59.

36 See Bob van den Bos, *Mirakel en Debacle* (PhD thesis, Universiteit Leiden 2008) 322; see also the interview with Van den Broek in Roel Janssen, *De Euro* (De Bezige Bij 2012) 170.

37 The overview of the countries' position is based on Van den Bos, *Mirakel en Debacle* (n 36) 87–98.

38 Consisting of the European Communities, the Common Foreign and Security Policy, and Justice and Home Affairs. The latter two policy areas would be organized along intergovernmental lines.

39 Van den Bos, *Mirakel en Debacle* (n 36) 88, 169–70, and 217.

40 ibid 217–19, 174–77, and 364.

which had chosen to align itself with France, despite its earlier position on political union.[41] Thereupon the Dutch returned to the Luxembourg draft as the basis for further negotiations in which the pillar structure was maintained, although the Member States later decided that the procedure of co-decision would apply to a much wider range of areas.[42] At the final Maastricht summit on 9–10 December 1991, an agreement on political union was reached. Significant opposition to the supranational views of some Member States thus resulted in a Treaty with a comparatively strong intergovernmental orientation.[43]

2.3 Coming to Terms with a Disappointing Result: Ratification

Given the outcomes on political union, German parliamentarians generally perceived the Maastricht Treaty to be a disappointing result.[44] Despite their disappointment, a very large parliamentary majority accepted the Treaty as a compromise. Opposition to the Maastricht Treaty as such was fairly limited. A significant pro-European consensus existed within the political branches: the *Bundestag* approved the Treaty with 543 votes, 8 votes against, and 17 abstentions; the *Bundesrat* adopted it unanimously.[45] The main political parties supported the Treaty: the German government coalition of the Christian Democratic Union (CDU), its smaller Bavarian sister party the Christian Social Union (CSU), and the liberal Free Democratic Party (FDP), as well as the main opposition party, the Social Democratic Party of Germany (SPD). Of the two smaller opposition groups from the former East Germany, the Party of Democratic Socialism (PDS/Linke Liste) opposed the Maastricht Treaty, whereas Bündnis 90/Die Grünen was split.[46]

[41] See ibid 137–47 and 213–16. The decision was possibly influenced by the negative personal feelings of Genscher stemming from Dutch opposition to the German wishes for the recognition of Croatia and Slovenia, as well as the response of Dutch Prime Minister Lubbers to German reunification.

[42] Laursen, 'Overview of the Negotiations' (n 35) 17–19; Van den Bos, *Mirakel en Debacle* (n 36) 149–50.

[43] Laursen, 'Overview of the Negotiations' (n 35) 21–23; Van den Bos, *Mirakel en Debacle* (n 36) 150–52.

[44] See, in this sense, also Heidemarie Wieczorek-Zeul, 'Der Vertrag von Maastricht im Deutschen Bundestag' (1993) 48(13–14) Europa-Archiv 405.

[45] See Plenarprotokoll 12/126, Stenografischer Bericht der 126. Sitzung des Deutschen Bundestages am 2. Dezember 1992 (hereafter Plenarprotokoll 12/126), 10879–82; and Plenarprotokoll 650, Stenografischer Bericht der 650. Sitzung des Deutschen Bundesrates am 18. Dezember 1992 (Maastricht final debate), 653.

[46] In the first all-German elections of 1990, the 5 per cent threshold for parties to obtain seats in the *Bundestag* was applied separately to the former East and West German territories. The PDS/Linke Liste and Bündnis 90/Die Grünen thus entered the *Bundestag*, although they did not meet the 5 per cent nationwide threshold. The Party of Democratic Socialism (PDS/Linke Liste) was the successor of the Socialist Unity Party (SED) that had ruled East Germany. In 2007 it merged with the Electoral Alternative for Labour and Social Justice (WASG) into Die Linke. Bündnis 90/Die Grünen entered the *Bundestag* as a coalition of the East German Greens and Alliance '90, a union of opposition groups from the GDR In May 1993 these groups merged with the West German Greens into the party Bündnis 90/ Die Grünen.

The significant political support for the Treaty did not mean that the parliamentarians failed to address the constitutional implications of this further step in European integration. Rather, they discussed these extensively; the Treaty's democratic shortcomings, in particular, were a key concern. The parliamentary debates show, moreover, that most parliamentarians had a different vision than the GFCC on the link between national sovereignty and democracy. A majority emphasized the importance of the European Parliament rather than that of national parliaments (sub-s 2.3.1). The constitution was amended to ensure that the EU would develop in accordance with the core constitutional principles of the German constitution, but these principles were not regarded as opposed to European integration (sub-s 2.3.2). Furthermore, the idea that democracy would require a homogeneous *demos* (sub-s 2.3.3) or that the EU should have limited competences (sub-s 2.3.4) were clearly contested. Finally, there is limited evidence to suggest that the constitutional quality of these debates was the result of prior GFCC case law (sub-s 2.3.5).

2.3.1 The democratic shortcomings of Maastricht as a central concern

Notwithstanding the pro-European stance of Germany's main political parties, the democratic shortcomings of the Maastricht architecture were a central, if not *the* central, concern in the German parliamentary debate. In this sense, the report of the *Bundestag*'s Special Committee on the EU generally welcomed the Maastricht Treaty as an important step in the process of European integration and as the basis 'for a peaceful, secure, social and economically stable Europe'.[47] The committee, however, noted the Union's democratic shortcomings and deemed further control and decision-making powers for the European Parliament necessary.[48] The Parliament's position needed to be strengthened in the revision conference of 1996. For the SPD and Bündnis 90/Die Grünen this would not suffice: they called on the government to move the planned revision conference of 1996 forward to 1994 in order to strengthen and democratize the political union.[49] The SPD also demanded that the German *Bundestag* should only consent to further competence transfers in the future if the European Parliament would obtain an equal right of co-decision over European legislation.[50]

The issue of democracy also featured prominently in the *Bundestag* plenary debates. Most parliamentarians and government members accepted the Treaty as a compromise that strengthened the EU in democratic terms, but still had

47 Beschlußempfehlung und Bericht des Sonderausschusses 'Europäische Union (Vertrag von Maastricht)', BT-Dr 12/3895 of 01.12.1992, 15 (hereafter BT-Dr 12/3895).

48 BT-Dr 12/3895 (n 47) 16.

49 BT-Dr 12/3366 of 7.10.1992: Antrag der Fraktion SPD, 2 and 5 (hereafter BT-Dr 12/3366); Antrag der Abgeordneten Gerd Poppe, Werner Schulz (Berlin), Dr Wolfgang Ullmann, Konrad Weiß (Berlin), Vera Wollenberger und der Gruppe Bündnis 90/Die Grünen, BT-Dr 12/3367 of 07.10.1992, 3 (hereafter BT-Dr 12/3367); BT-Dr 12/3895 (n 47) 16.

50 It also coupled this demand to a plea for further transparency in the Council. See BT-Dr 12/3366 (n 49) 2 and 5; and BT-Dr 12/3895 (n 47) 16.

many democratic shortcomings. They noted in particular the limited role of the European Parliament and the dominant role of the executive, and put forward that, in the future, the European Parliament should develop into a fully-fledged parliament with powers comparable to those of national parliaments, and as an equal to the Council of Ministers.[51] Some combined such concerns with pleas for greater transparency[52] or a strengthened role for national parliaments.[53] There were also politicians who voiced explicit scepticism about the ability of national parliaments to control the Council appropriately and hence stressed the need to strengthen the European Parliament's powers.[54] Others instead expressed concerns about the distance between European politics and the citizens of the Member States and emphasized the need to improve the rights of national parliaments and sub-state entities.[55] Yet, overall the democratic shortcomings of the Treaty were clearly a key concern for Germany's politicians.

2.3.2 Constitutionalizing future aspirations: the new Article 23 in the Basic Law

The aspiration to improve the democratic character of the EU was even laid down in the German Basic Law with the new European integration clause of Article 23.[56] This provision not only made Germany's participation in the further development of European integration a constitutional objective, but also

[51] See eg the following statements in Plenarprotokoll 12/110, Stenografischer Bericht der 110. Sitzung des Deutschen Bundestages am 8. Oktober 1992 (hereafter Plenarprotokoll 12/110): Kinkel, 9319; Waigel, 9323; Wieczorek-Zeul (SPD), 9328–30; Graf Lambsdorff (FDP), 9338; Gysi (Linke Liste), 9341; Werner Schulz (Bündnis 90/Die Grüne), 9342–43; Renate Hellwig (CDU/CSU), 9345–46; Verheugen (SPD), 9348 and 9351; Staatsminister Gerster, 9358–59; Staatsminister Goppel, 9361; Gerd Poppe (Bündnis 90/Die Grüne), 9370–71; Irmer (FDP), 9389. See also eg the statements by Wieczorek-Zeul (SPD), 10815 and Kohl, 10827 in Plenarprotokoll 12/126 (n 45).

[52] See eg the statements of Kinkel, 9318–19 and Michael Stübgen (CDU/CSU), 9372 in Plenarprotokoll 12/110 (n 51); Wieczorek-Zeul (SPD), 10815.

[53] eg Graf Lambsdorff (FDP), 9338 and Christian Schmidt (CDU/CSU), 9357; Staatsminister Helmrich, 9359–60; and Staatsminister Goppel, 9361 in Plenarprotokoll 12/110 (n 51).

[54] See, in this sense, eg Renate Hellwig (CDU/CSU), 9346 in Plenarprotokoll 12/110 (n 51).

[55] See eg the statement of Minister Herbert Helmrich in *Bundestag* Plenarprotokoll 12/110 (n 51) 9360–61. Bündnis 90/Die Grüne stressed both an enhanced role for the European Parliament as well as stronger involvement of the regions in EU decision-making, see BT-Dr 12/3367 (n 49) 2.

[56] The change was based on the recommendations of a Joint Constitutional Committee of the *Bundestag* and *Bundesrat* (hereafter the JCC) constituted in November 1991 to deal with the constitutional issues relating to German reunification. A considerable part of the discussions by this committee was devoted to European integration and subsequently taken up by the special committee on EU Affairs that dealt with the ratification of the Maastricht Treaty. Consequently, many constitutional issues were discussed elaborately during the German ratification process and long before the GFCC considered them. In addition to the insertion of art 23, a new art 44 was inserted into the Basic Law and changes were made to arts 24, 28, 50, 52, 88, and 115 of the Basic Law. Beyond the issues discussed in this chapter, several other issues regarding art 23 BL were intensively discussed, such as the exact requirements for a two-thirds majority under art 23(1). On the deliberations of the JCC, see Bericht der Gemeinsamen Verfassungskommission gemäß Beschluß des Deutschen Bundestages—Drucksachen 12/1590, 12/1670—und Beschluß des Bundesrates—Drucksache 741/91 (Beschluß), BT-Dr 12/6000 of 05.11.1993 (hereafter BT-Dr 12/6000). On these discussions, see also König, *Die Übertragung von Hoheitsrechten* (n 11) 138–88.

specified the conditions under which such development had to take place. Through a '*Struktursicherungsklausel*' the European Union would have to be committed to 'democratic, social and federal principles, to the rule of law, and to the principle of subsidiarity' and should guarantee 'a level of protection of basic rights essentially comparable to that afforded by this Basic Law'.[57] The clause mirrored the eternity clause of Article 79(3) of the Basic Law with the addition of the subsidiarity principle.[58]

Article 23 also clarified that sovereign powers could be transferred by the German Federation by statute and with consent of the *Bundesrat*. Accession to the EU, changes in the EU's Treaty foundations, 'and comparable regulations that amend or supplement this Basic law' would require a constitutional majority of two-thirds of the Members in the *Bundestag* and *Bundesrat*[59] and be subject to the 'eternity clause' of Article 79(3) BL. Finally, the new Article 23 provided that the German *Bundestag* and *Bundesrat* would participate in matters concerning the EU.[60] Article 23(2) BL required the federal government to 'keep the Bundestag and the Bundesrat informed, comprehensively and at the earliest possible time'.[61] Article 23(3) BL laid down that the federal government must allow the *Bundestag* to take position before the government cooperates in European legislation and that the federal government must take this position into account in the negotiations.[62] These rights were further specified in the Act on Cooperation between the Federal Government and the German Bundestag in European Union Matters (EUZBBG).[63]

57 Art 23 BL. Formally, art 23 BL only binds German state institutions. It is thus up to German state institutions to ensure that the development of the EU is based on the principles listed in that provision.

58 BT-Dr 12/6000 (n 56) 20; BT-Dr 12/3338 of 02.10.1992 Gesetzentwurf der Bundesregierung Entwurf eines Gesetzes zur Änderung des Grundgesetzes, 4 (hereafter BT-Dr 12/3338).

59 In accordance with art 79(2) BL.

60 BT-Dr 12/3338 (n 58) 6; some parts of the original proposal were changed in the subsequent deliberations. See also BT-Dr 12/6000 (n 56) 20–24; and BT-Dr 12/3896 of 01.12.1992: Beschlußempfehlung und Bericht des Sonderausschusses 'Europäische Union (Vertrag von Maastricht)', 16–17 (hereafter BT-Dr 12/3896). The latter report also mentions how experts agreed that a new 'Europa-Artikel' should be included in the Basic Law, 16–17.

61 Art 23(2) BL; see also BT-Dr 12/3896 (n 60) 5.

62 A more far-reaching proposal by the SPD was not accepted. On the basis of this proposal the *Bundestag*'s positions would have to be the basis for the federal government's negotiations. An underlying reason appeared to be that this alternative would have been at odds with the equality of the *Bundestag* and *Bundesrat*'s positions. See BT-Dr 12/6000 (n 56) 22.

63 Gesetz über die Zusammenarbeit von Bundesregierung und Deutschem Bundestag in Angelegenheiten der Europaïschen Union vom 12. März 1993, *Bundesgesetzblatt* I 1993, 311 (version Maastricht). The Act specified that the government would have to inform the *Bundestag* about all plans that could be of interest for the Federal Republic of Germany (see art 3 and p 23 of BT-Dr 12/3896 (n 60)). The *Bundestag* would be sent the proposals for Directives and Regulations and be informed about their essential content and purpose as well as the decision-making process (art 4). The government would also need to give the *Bundestag* ample time to state its position before consenting to the adoption of legal acts (art 5). In addition, art 45 was inserted into the Basic Law, which provided that the *Bundestag* could set up a committee for EU Affairs. The *Bundestag* plenary could authorize the committee to exercise its rights in art 23 BL. See BT-Dr 12/6000 (n 56) 24.

The importance of ensuring adequate democratic legitimation of the EU's decision-making procedures, as well as the need to respect the unamendable principles of the German Basic Law, thus featured prominently within the German parliamentary ratification debates. According to the Joint Constitutional Committee of the *Bundestag* and *Bundesrat* (hereinafter the JCC) that prepared the constitutional changes, the main reason for the new Article 23 BL was that European integration had developed from cooperation of a primarily economic nature to a more political one. Therefore, the EU could no longer be satisfactorily characterized as an international organization in the sense of Article 24(1) BL, the prior constitutional basis for European integration. Instead, the EU had become a supranational body more similar to a state.[64] Article 23 sought to provide a sound constitutional basis for this qualitative change.[65]

Whereas the GFCC would relate the issue of democracy to the problem of an absent European public sphere and shared identity, the parliamentarians generally did not point to an inherent opposition between the Basic Law and European integration. The *Bundestag*'s Special Committee on the European Union declared instead that the new Article 23(1) BL expressed the openness of the German constitutional order towards Europe.[66] Rupert Scholz (CDU/CSU)—one of the two chairpersons of the JCC[67]—held that the more competences that were transferred to the EU, the more persistent the demand would become to ensure an equivalent democratic legitimation and control of the supranational competences. Concretely, this would mean above all that the European Parliament should develop into a real and effective authority for democratic legitimation, control, and legislation.[68] A similar position was expressed by Günther Verheugen (SPD), the chairperson of the *Bundestag*'s Special Committee on the European Union.[69] His pro-European stance was far-reaching:

> We all thought that the unity of our fatherland could be realized first in a unified Europe. It turned out differently. National unity came before European unity. Therefore it is necessary to enshrine in the Basic Law our will for Europe.[70]

[64] Scholz used the notion 'eigenstaatlich' in Rupert Scholz, 'Grundgesetz und Europäische Einigung—Zu den reformpolitischen Empfehlungen der gemeinsamen Verfassungskommission' [1992] Die Neue Juristische Wochenschrift 2593, 2594; see also BT-Dr 12/6000 (n 56) 20.

[65] Although it was not clear whether the move towards a European Union would go beyond what art 24 BL still allowed, see Winkelmann, *Das Maastricht-Urteil* (n 11) 20.

[66] BT-Dr 12/3896 (n 60) 18. Rupert Scholz stated that the provision was meant not just to complete the general commitment to 'a united Europe' in the Basic Law's preamble, but that it also provided an explicit authorization to create European unity in the form of the EU. Scholz, 'Grundgesetz und Europäische Einigung' (n 64) 2598.

[67] The other chairperson was Dr Henning Voscherau (SPD).

[68] Scholz, 'Grundgesetz und Europäische Einigung' (n 64) 2598; see in a similar vein, Verheugen (SPD), 9348 in in Plenarprotokoll 12/110 (n 51).

[69] Verheugen (SPD), Plenarprotokoll 12/110 (n 51) 9348.

[70] ibid 9348, author's translation.

That the new Article 23 took the place of the former provision on German unification had symbolic significance. According to Verheugen it showed that after German unification, the unity of Europe was the next big task for the German people.[71]

For certain *Bundestag* members the democratic shortcomings of the EU were a reason to withhold their consent to the Treaty. For example, Peter Conradi, one of the only two SPD members that opposed the Treaty, expressed doubts that Article 79(3) BL would be compatible with power transfers to the European level without sufficient democratic safeguards.[72] Yet, he still expressed a pro-European stance:

> I want the political Union of Europe. However, the United States of Europe will only come about when wanted and supported by the peoples of Europe. The Maastricht Treaty, however, does not accomplish this.[73]

The PDS/Linke Liste also opposed the Maastricht Treaty, but likewise did not disagree with European integration as such. The party was against the Treaty rather because it would prevent Europe from being 'open to the world, democratic, socially just, peaceful and in the long run non-military, in which the political fundamental rights and democratic principles are fully realised'.[74]

2.3.3 Contested connections: democracy, the people, and the state

The legal nature of the EU and the demands that Article 23 would impose on the EU's organization were nonetheless subject to some debate. Politicians held competing visions on the relation between European integration, democracy, the state, and its people. Unlike the GFCC, the political deliberations showed more appreciation of how the sovereignty of the newly unified Germany connected to the Treaty and European integration. For example, the Government's *Denkschrift* on the Treaty noted how European integration and German unification were 'two sides of the same coin'.[75] Nonetheless, the government held that the EU was not yet a state,

[71] ibid 9348.

[72] Peter Conradi (SPD), Plenarprotokoll 12/110 (n 51) note 51, 9385–86. He expected that the GFCC would find the Treaty problematic and doubted the ability of the European Parliament to adequately represent the people. Modrow (PDS/Linke Liste) also argued the Maastricht Treaty's democratic deficit was unconstitutional, see Plenarprotokoll 12/126 (n 45) 10820.

[73] Peter Conradi (SPD), Plenarprotokoll 12/110 (n 51) 9386.

[74] BT-Dr 12/3322 of 30.09.1992: Antrag der Gruppe der PDS/Linke Liste—Maastrichter Vertrag über die Europäische Union, 4 (hereafter BT-Dr 12/332; see also Hans Modrow, Plenarprotokoll 12/126 (n 45) 10819. The group supported a stronger position for the European Parliament but was also more open to direct forms of democracy, such as referenda (BT-Dr 12/3322, 2). The Greens similarly supported other forms of democracy in the EU, such as the participation of NGOs and new hearing rights in the decision-making process for specifically affected persons. See BT-Dr 12/3367 (n 49) 2.

[75] BT-Dr 12/3334 of 01.10.1992 Gesetzentwurf der Bundesregierung Entwurf eines Gesetzes zum Vertrag vom 7. Februar 1992 über die Europäische Union, 82: 'Die deutsche Einigung war von Anfang an eng mit dem europäischen Einigungsprozeß verbunden. Für die Bundesregierung stellen die europäische und die deutsche Einigung zwei Seiten derselben Medaille dar.'

but a 'compound of states' ('*Staatenverbindung*') based on an international treaty. The demand that the EU should be democratic therefore could not entail that identical requirements would be placed on parliamentary representation and parliamentary legislative competences as within the Member States.[76] The government also noted that the factual prerequisites for the existence of a European state were lacking, such as a state people ('*Staatsvolk*'). Most problematic in the government's eyes was that furnishing the European Parliament with the competences of a state-like parliament would alter the legal nature of the EU. It would turn into a federal state ('*Bundesstaat*') because this parliament would be elected on the basis of democratic equality and would have to decide according to the democratic majority principle. Given that this degree of integration had not yet been reached, the role of the European Parliament envisaged in the Maastricht Treaty complied with democratic requirements, although further integration could require additional steps.[77] The government also indicated that the constitutional objective of European integration did not entail an inevitable path towards a European federal state. It left open whether such a transition would require a special act of the constituent power or whether a further constitutional change would be sufficient.[78]

Some *Bundestag* members expressly embraced the prospect of establishing a European federal state.[79] Others were more cautious. Foreign Minister Kinkel of the FDP as well as Finance Minister Waigel of the CSU took care to stress that the EU would not entail the loss of national identity, or cause centralization.[80] Chancellor Kohl also argued that the EU should not turn into a super-state, but a unified Europe that would respect national identity and unity in diversity.[81] A few *Bundestag* members voiced a more Eurosceptical position. Most critical was probably Jürgen Augustinowitz (CDU/CSU), who supported the Maastricht Treaty only on the condition that the political union would not turn into a federal state ('*Bundesstaat*'). His goal was a 'united Europe of the fatherlands ["*Vaterländer*"]',

[76] BT-Dr 12/3338 (n 58) 6.

[77] The government referred to a meeting with experts of the joint constitutional committee of 22 May 1992. See BT-Dr 12/3338 (n 58) 6.

[78] In this respect, the government referred to differing opinions on the matter by constitutional experts. BT-Dr 12/3338 (n 58) 7.

[79] eg Günter Verheugen of the SPD held that the new art 23 BL would allow Germany to establish a European federal state ('*Bundesstaat*'). Plenarprotokoll 12/110 (n 51) 9348. In the last plenary on the Treaty, however, he expressed caution against defining final goals for the EU, because notions such as a European federal state could 'cause anxiety and mistrust elsewhere'. He noted in particular the smaller Member States' fear that they might perish in a superstructure and could imagine a Europe 'in which the nation-state would still perform meaningful tasks for a long time'. He also held that probably the time was not ripe to determine 'in which form the unification will one day be completed'. Plenarprotokoll 12/126 (n 45) 10832–33. Andreas Schockenhoff of the CDU/CSU also explicitly embraced Maastricht as an important step towards a European federal state ('*europaïschen Bundesstaat*') in Plenarprotokoll 12/110 (n 51) 9383.

[80] Kinkel, Plenarprotokoll 12/110 (n 51) 9317 and 9318; Waigel, Plenarprotokoll 12/110 (n 51) 9322–23.

[81] Although this did not seem to exclude a federal Europe, see Kohl, Plenarprotokoll 12/126 (n 45) 10828.

a Europe in which the national identity of the respective citizens was to be 'strictly respected'.[82]

Disagreements about the relation between the people and state authority also surfaced in discussions on the amendment of Article 28 BL. The amendment granted Union citizens the right to vote in German municipal elections as required by the EU citizenship provisions. This change led to a wider discussion on the right to vote, reflecting different understandings of democracy and the relation between a people and the exercise of public authority. Whereas the GFCC had alluded to a notion of the people as a pre-political homogeneous entity, the political parties on the left instead relied on a reading of democracy that favoured including all persons in the decision-making processes that were permanently subjected to them. In the JCC, the SPD and the City of Hamburg proposed to extend the right to vote in municipal elections to all foreigners with permanent residence in Germany:[83]

> It is in accordance with the democratic idea, in particular the idea of freedom contained in it, to establish congruence between the holders of democratic political rights and those permanently subjected to rule.[84]

Bündnis 90/Die Grünen and the PDS/Linke Liste supported such an extension of the right to vote in the ratification debates. Furthermore, the SPD, FDP, and Bündnis 90/Die Grünen agreed that it lay 'in the logic of the further development of the European Union' to make the place of residence determinative also for votes to the *Landtag* and the *Bundestag*, as well as similar elections.[85]

Yet, the proposal to extend the right to vote to non-Union citizens in municipal elections did not carry the required two-thirds majority. Its opponents expressed an understanding of popular sovereignty explicitly tied to the German people, more akin to that of the GFCC's *Maastricht-Urteil*. In their view, the Basic Law attached the right to vote to German citizens because Article 20(2) BL determined

[82] Plenarprotokoll 12/126 (n 45) 10904; Peter Paziorek of the CDU/CSU similarly argued that Europe should not become a centralized state ('*Zentralstaat*') or a federal state ('*Bundesstaat*'): Europe should respect the national identity, culture, and way of life of each of its Member States. Dr Peter Paziorek (CDU/CSU), Plenarprotokoll 12/126 (n 45) 10907.

[83] They also argued that this would further the integration of foreigners with long-term residence in Germany and submitted that this would prevent the existence of two classes of foreigners—EU citizens and others permanently living in Germany. BT-Dr 12/6000 (n 56) 98; see also Wieczorek-Zeul, Plenarprotokoll 12/126 (n 45) 10813–14.

[84] BT-Dr 12/6000 (n 56) 98. The *Bundesverfassungsgericht*'s case law was mustered in support of this view, namely Bundesverfassungsgericht, judgment of 31 October 1990, 2 BvF 2, 6/89 (*Ausländerwahlrecht I*).

[85] BT-Dr 12/3896 (n 60) 21. In the plenary debates Hans Eichel, the SPD prime minister of the state of Hessen, explicitly argued that the notion of a state's people ('*Staatsvolk*') should be freed from the idea of the nation: all persons that legally and permanently resided in Germany should be regarded as equal citizens. See Ministerpräsident Hans Eichel (Hessen), Plenarprotokoll 12/126 (n 45) 10850. Ulrich Irmer of the FDP expressed similar ideas, see ibid 10818.

the people of the German Federal Republic as the subject and bearer of state authority.[86]

2.3.4 Democratic self-determination and the scope of EU competences: too wide or too limited?

The logic of the GFCC's reasoning was that the *Bundestag* should remain the primary source of the EU's democratic legitimacy and that, as a derived order, the EU's competences should be specific and certain. The Court thus judged the limited nature of the EU's competences as favourable from a democratic viewpoint and approvingly noted the principles of proportionality and subsidiarity as limits on the EU's powers. However, this perspective misses the point that the limitation of the EU's competence may be seen as democratically problematic itself, because it limits the range of possible policies that the EU can pursue. Such limits are liable to restrict the available political choice on the EU level and may affect various political positions differently. In particular, it has been argued that the economic orientation of the EU's competences has adverse consequences for the treatment of other non-economic considerations.[87] In this respect, the competence division between the EU and its Member States is not democratically neutral per se.

The parliamentary discussions on the subsidiarity principle raised this problem. Generally, the subsidiarity principle was welcomed and even elevated to the level of constitutional law with its inclusion in Article 23(1) BL. Still, the principle could not mask political disagreements about the areas in which further European integration would be desirable. Unlike the GFCC's appreciation of the limited nature of the EU's competences, the left-wing parties actually argued that integration in the area of social and environmental affairs had not gone far enough. The SPD, for example, contended that necessary steps should be taken to create a social and environmental union next to, and of equal rank to, the economic union, a call mirrored by the PDS/Linke Liste and Bündnis 90/Die Grüne.[88] In this context, the SPD warned that the subsidiarity principle should not be used as an excuse for deregulation, to stop necessary harmonization, or to call into question social and environmental standards.[89]

[86] BT-Dr 12/6000 (n 56) 98. In their view, giving the right to vote in municipal elections to all permanently residing foreigners could therefore affect arts 20(2) and 79(3) BL. In addition, they held that giving the right to vote to foreigners should be the outcome of a process of integration: 'Who[ever] wants to participate in the political will-formation must commit him or herself to the respective community.'

[87] As was discussed in Chapter 3.

[88] BT-Dr 12/3366 (n 49) 3; see in this direction eg also Fritz Gautier, Plenarprotokoll 12/110 (n 51) 9374. The PDS/Linke Liste also called for steps towards a 'genuine social union', BT-Dr 12/3322 (n 74) 1. Bündnis 90/Die Grüne similarly called for a social and ecological Union, see eg Werner Schulz, Plenarprotokoll 12/110 (n 51) 9342; BT-Dr 12/3367 (n 49).

[89] BT-Dr 12/3366 (n 49) 3. See also Heidemarie Wieczorek-Zeul's criticism of the principle, Plenarprotokoll 12/110 (n 51) 9328. Gysi of the PDS also criticized the principle as vague, see Plenarprotokoll 12/110 (n 51) 9341–42.

Such considerations, however, had no place in the GFCC's sovereignty-based understanding of democracy on the basis of which the subsidiarity was simply welcomed as 'a strict limit on Community action'.[90]

2.3.5 Did the GFCC's prior EU case law enhance the quality of parliamentary debate?

The German parliamentary debates on the Maastricht Treaty thus devoted considerable attention to the constitutional implications of the Treaty and, more specifically, to the issue of democracy. Also, the *Bundestag*'s assessment of these issues was not clearly unreasonable or of lesser quality than the GFCC's subsequent assessment. Both the *Bundestag* and the GFCC approved the Treaty, despite raising concerns about the EU's democratic legitimacy. The main difference between the assessments of the two institutions was that a majority of the *Bundestag* favoured a pro-European understanding of democracy, whereas the GFCC adopted a more national conception. Compared to the GFCC's assessment, the *Bundestag*'s debate was also more open to different understandings of democracy. For these reasons, I submit that the GFCC's *Maastricht-Urteil* cannot be justified as a remedy for the political institutions' failure to discuss the constitutional implications of the Treaty.

One could of course counter that these constitutional discussions took place only because of the GFCC's prior case law and the possibility of subsequent constitutional review. This challenge is difficult to fully answer because it asks about a counterfactual situation that is impossible to completely assess, that is, how the political deliberations in Germany would have taken place if the GFCC had not existed or had never ruled on European integration.

A way to approximate an answer is to try to assess the influence of the Court's prior case law on the political discussions. In this respect, there is support for the claim that the Court's prior EU-related judgments had an influence. The insertion of Article 23 BL can be seen as the reflection of German academic and public debates, dating back to the 1950s, 1960s, and 1970s, which in turn influenced the *Solange* case law. Article 23 BL expresses the idea that there would have to exist a homogeneity of value orientations between the German constitution and the EU's structures. As a result, the EU would have to respect basic principles of the German constitution, although not with exactly the same scope or meaning as at the national level.[91]

[90] BVerfG, *Maastricht* (n 7) para 63.

[91] On these issues, see König, *Die Übertragung von Hoheitsrechten* (n 11) 279–92. Bill Davies offers a historical study of the intellectual debates surrounding on this theme in Bill Davies, 'Resistance to European Law and Constitutional Identity in Germany: Herbert Kraus and Solange in Its Intellectual Context' (2015) 21 European Law Journal 434 (hereafter Davies, 'Herbert Kraus and Solange'). Davies focuses on Herbert Kraus and the idea of structural congruence. König notes, however, that the idea of structural congruence was later generally rejected in favour of the less demanding homogeneity of value orientations, see König, *Die Übertragung von Hoheitsrechten* (n 11) 281.

Still, the quality of the constitutional discussions in Germany cannot be wholly attributed to the prior case law of the GFCC. The parliamentary documents on the changes to the Basic Law mention the GFCC's judgments explicitly in only a few cases.[92] The *Solange* case law played a role in discussions on when competence transfers would require a constitutional majority.[93] The new Article 23(1) BL also followed the *Solange* case law insofar as it demanded that the EU guarantee 'a level of protection of basic rights essentially comparable to that afforded by this Basic Law'.[94] But beyond these specific references, the parliamentary documents do not mention the GFCC's case law explicitly as a basis for the constitutional changes. Also, Germany's political institutions had already favoured strengthening the European Parliament, before the Court's *Solange* case law.[95] Furthermore, the primary impetus for setting up the JCC had been to deal with the constitutional implications of the Treaty of Reunification between the former East and West Germany. The constitutional committee eventually defined its task as broader than this, and also considered other constitutional questions that had become relevant in the political debate.[96] The concerns of the German *Länder* were another driver for setting up the committee. They had made their consent to the Treaty conditional upon change of the Basic Law and a strengthening of their participation rights in EU affairs.[97]

[92] eg it was clear that the amendment of art 28 was prompted by the GFCC's case law, as the GFCC's interpretation of the existing art 28 was judged incompatible with expanding the right to vote to EU citizens. See BT-Dr 12/3338 (n 58) 11; BT-Dr 12/6000 (n 56) 19; Bundesverfassungsgericht, judgment of 31 October 1990, 2 BvF 3/89 (*Ausländerwahlrecht Hamburg*).

[93] The issue was subject to disagreement between the *Bundesrat* and the federal government. See BT-Dr 12/6000 (n 56) 28; BT-Dr 12/3338 (n 58) 12 and 14; BT-Dr 12/3896 (n 60) 18–19. Another case that played a role in these discussions was Bundesverfassungsgericht, decision of 23 June 1981, 2 BvR 1107, 1124/77 und 195/79 (*Eurocontrol I*); see further on these issues: König, *Die Übertragung von Hoheitsrechten* (n 11) 163–64, 182, 303–13; Mattias Wendel, *Permeabilität im Europäischen Verfassungsrecht* (Mohr Siebeck 2011) 241–46.

[94] Scholz, 'Grundgesetz und europäische Einigung' (n 64) 2598; BT-Dr 12/6000 (n 56) 21. There was some discussion on the exact wording, see BT-Dr 12/3896 (n 60) 19, yet a proposal for amendment was rejected because the wording had been extensively discussed in the joint constitutional committee.

[95] Bill Davies, *Resisting the European Court of Justice. West Germany confrontation with European Law, 1949–1979* (Cambridge University Press 2012) 138–79, in particular 171.

[96] See BT-Dr 12/6000 (n 56) 5 and 10. The basis for the constitutional committee lay in art 5 of the *Einigungsvertrag*.

[97] See Winkelmann, *Das Maastricht-Urteil* (n 11) 20; Beuter, 'Germany and the Ratification of the Maastricht Treaty' (n 35) 95–96; Beuter notes that the *Länder* supported the ratification of Maastricht upon the condition that the Basic Law would be amended. In March 1992, the *Länder* prime ministers had decided unanimously that the Basic Law should be changed. The Bundesrat had previously set up its own constitutional committee to strengthen federalism in Germany and Europe. Its conclusions formed a basis for the subsequent discussions of the JCC, see BT-Dr 12/6000 (n 56) 6.

3. Monetary Union: Political and Judicial Mistakes

3.1 The GFCC: Constitutionalizing EMU's Asymmetries

The second part of the story in this chapter concerns the agreement on the EMU. This agreement was the most important change introduced by the Maastricht Treaty and a key element in the GFCC's judgment. Yet, prior to the euro crisis, the part relating to the EMU in the *Maastricht-Urteil* often played a marginal role in scholarly discussions.[98] That part is nonetheless of key importance and has played a crucial role in the euro crisis. In a nutshell, the Court accepted Germany's participation in a future EMU, because it could be considered a '*Stabilitätsgemeinschaft*', a 'community based on stability' geared towards price stability and sound public finances.[99] In hindsight, this assessment appears problematic, because it turned the EMU's stability focus into a constitutional requirement for Germany's participation. At the same time, the Court's national reading of democracy cast doubt on the possibility of moving towards a political union, which, according to many commentators, is necessary for a democratic and socially just monetary union. To understand this problem with the judgment, it is first necessary to outline the Maastricht EMU legal architecture.

3.1.1 Asymmetric union: Maastricht's EMU architecture

Two principal and related considerations informed the original EMU framework: price stability and national fiscal responsibility, that is, the idea that the eurozone Member States would remain responsible for their own fiscal and economic policies, including their own debts.[100] In line with the idea of national fiscal responsibility, the Maastricht framework made monetary policy an exclusive EU competence,[101] but left fiscal and economic policy largely to the Member States.[102] Monetary policy generally refers to the policy of a monetary authority to control

[98] eg in the important contributions of Kumm and Baquero Cruz to the pluralism literature, the monetary union is not discussed. See Kumm, 'The Jurisprudence of Constitutional Conflict' (n 3); Julio Baquero Cruz, 'The Legacy of the Maastricht-Urteil and the Pluralist Movement' (2007) EUI Working Papers RSCAS 2007/13 < https://cadmus.eui.eu/handle/1814/6760> accessed 2 August 2022. On this same point, see Christian Joerges, 'Where the Law Ends' (*Verfassungsblog*, 2014) <http://verfassungsblog.de/where-the-law-ends/> accessed 1 August 2022.

[99] BVerfG, *Maastricht* (n 7) para 78.

[100] On price stability as a goal in the EMU, see also Matthias Herdegen, 'Price Stability and Budgetary Restraints in the Economic and Monetary Union: The Law as Guardian of Economic Wisdom' (1998) 35 Common Market Law Review 9. The ECB regards price stability as the prevention of continued inflation and deflation. It defined price stability in 1998 as 'a year-on-year increase in the Harmonised Index of Consumer Prices (HICP) for the euro area of below 2%'. In 2003 it reformulated this target as an inflation rate of 'below, but close to 2 %'. See Kaarlo Tuori and Klaus Tuori, *The Eurozone Crisis. A Constitutional Analysis* (Cambridge University Press 2014) 59 and also <www.ecb.europa.eu/mopo/strategy/pricestab/html/index.en.html> accessed 1 August 2022.

[101] See art 3(1) TFEU.

[102] Tuori and Tuori, *The Eurozone Crisis* (n 100) 27–34.

the supply of money. Fiscal policy refers to the state's acquirement of public funds through taxation and debt, as well as the assignment of those funds through public expenditure. Economic policy is commonly understood as a broader notion. It captures both monetary and fiscal policy and may be understood to include other public interventions in the economy, such as regulation of the labour market.[103] Ordinarily, states control both monetary policy and fiscal policy and can use both as instruments of economic policy.

The two considerations—price stability and national fiscal responsibility—are reflected in the EMU provisions in several ways. Price stability constitutes the primary objective of EU monetary policy.[104] Its importance is reflected in the independence of the ECB and the national central banks that together form the European System of Central Banks (ESCB).[105] The objective of price stability also informs the legal constraints on national fiscal and economic policies. These national policies are to pursue the objective of sound public finances in order to prevent the unsustainable fiscal policies of one Member State from providing the ECB with an incentive to adopt a more expansive monetary policy.[106] Article 104c TEC (currently Article 126 TFEU), and the protocol on the excessive deficit procedure, laid down the procedure to prevent excessive Member State budget deficits and government debts, which the protocol put at 3 per cent and 60 per cent of gross domestic product respectively.[107] The prohibition on monetary financing of Article 123(1) TFEU[108] similarly disciplines Member States' fiscal policies and prevents the ECB from being forced to print money to finance a Member State's budget deficits.[109]

The constraints on national fiscal policies and the prohibition of monetary financing also reflect the idea of national fiscal responsibility.[110] Preventing one Member State's fiscal policies from becoming unsustainable was additionally meant to ensure that the Member States would not be forced to aid each other.

[103] Alicia Hinarejos, *The Euro Area Crisis in Constitutional Perspective* (Oxford University Press 2015) 3–5; Tuori and Tuori, *The Eurozone Crisis* (n 100) 31.

[104] See the current art 119(1) TFEU and art 105 TEC at the time of Maastricht. It is also the primary goal of the European System of Central Banks (art 127(1) TFEU). At Maastricht the commitment to price stability was also laid down in art 3A TEC. Currently, it is stated as a general goal of the EU in art 3(3) TFEU.

[105] Art 106 TEC and the current art 282 TFEU. Its independence was ensured in particular by art 107 TEC, and currently by art 130 TFEU.

[106] See the current art 119(3) TFEU (art 3a TEC) and the excessive deficit procedure of art 126 TFEU (art 104c TEC).

[107] In its Maastricht form, this procedure also relied heavily on legally non-binding measures, although as an ultimate recourse the Council could impose sanctions on Member States in the form of non-interest-bearing deposits or fines. See art 104c(11) TEC. See also Jörn Pipkorn, 'Legal Arrangements in the Treaty of Maastricht for the Effectiveness of the Economic and Monetary Union' (1994) 31 Common Market Law Review 263, 277–80.

[108] Previously art 104 TEC.

[109] Paul de Grauwe, *Economics of Monetary Union* (Oxford University Press 2014) 148–52 and 215–16.

[110] Hinarejos, *The Euro Area Crisis in Constitutional Perspective* (n 103) 5–6.

The prohibition of financial bailouts in the so-called 'no-bailout clause'[111] can be understood in this light and subjects the Member States to the discipline of the markets. The expectation was that financial markets would charge higher interest to those states with unsustainable budgetary policies, thus forcing them to adjust.[112] Similar reasons informed the prohibition on monetary financing, as this prohibition reduces the incentive for Member States to run deficits.[113]

This stability-oriented EMU architecture raises various democratic concerns. First, as noted by Matthias Herdegen, the legal framework entrenches certain economic priorities in the Treaty and 'limits political choices between conflicting objectives'.[114] The overriding importance of price stability limits the consideration of other economic and social considerations, such as high employment.[115] In particular, the Treaty norms on excessive deficits and government debt limit democratic choice in national economic policy.[116] Assigning monetary policy to a politically independent central bank with the objective of ensuring price stability presents a departure from Keynesian thought in which expansionary monetary and fiscal policies are seen as means to ensure high employment and high economic growth.[117]

Secondly, the separation of economic and monetary competences also raises a potentially bigger problem.[118] A key argument is that the transfer of monetary competence also restricts national autonomy in economic and fiscal policy. Economists contend that a monetary union without a budgetary union is inherently fragile and vulnerable to asymmetric shocks, that is, shocks that affect the eurozone Member States unevenly. Within the EMU, the eurozone states have given up control over their national currencies and lost the ability to conduct an independent monetary policy. When hit by an asymmetric shock, a Member State can therefore no longer devalue its currency or use its domestic interest rate to increase its competitiveness

[111] In the Maastricht Treaty this was art 104b TEC, currently it is art 125 TFEU.

[112] Pipkorn, 'Legal Arrangements in the Treaty of Maastricht' (n 107) 275; Michael Ioannidis, 'Europe's New Transformations: How the EU Economic Constitution Changed During the Eurozone Crisis' (2016) 53 Common Market Law Review 1237, 1249–52.

[113] De Grauwe, *Economics of Monetary Union* (n 109) 218–23. Considerations of price stability and national fiscal responsibility likewise informed the criteria that the Member States had to fulfil for entering the single currency. These convergence criteria required the EMU participants to have stable inflation rates, low government deficits and government debt levels, no devaluation for the previous two years, and a stable interest rate. See arts 104c and 109j TEC, the Protocol on the Excessive Deficit Procedure, as well as the Protocol on the Convergence Criteria Referred to in Article 109j of the Treaty Establishing the European Community.

[114] Herdegen, 'Price Stability' (n 100) 10.

[115] ibid 15.

[116] Although a flexible interpretation of these norms could arguably prevent significant encroachment on the policy space of political institutions. For this argument, even after the euro crisis, see Clemens Kaupa, 'Has (Downturn-)Austerity Really Been "Constitutionalized" in Europe? On the Ideological Dimension of Such a Claim' (2017) 44(1) Journal of Law and Society 32.

[117] De Grauwe, *Economics of Monetary Union* (n 109) 150–51.

[118] It must be noted that these arguments are contested; see, in particular, Martin Sandbu, *Europe's Orphan: The Future of the Euro and the Politics of Debt* (Princeton University Press 2016).

to address higher unemployment. Instead, it can try to push down wages to regain competitiveness. This option, however, is normally more difficult and depends on the organization of the labour market.[119]

An additional problem is that financial markets can force EMU Member States into default. When a Member State faces an asymmetric economic shock, it will typically run a higher budget deficit: economic decline leads to loss in tax income, and higher unemployment will lead to higher tax expenditure. Distrust by the financial markets may, however, trigger a liquidity crisis. Fear that a Member State will be unable to repay its debts can lead investors to sell the Member State's government bonds. Within the monetary union the exchange rate no longer plays a stabilizing role, and the Member State can no longer finance its government debts with the help of central banks. In this scenario, the Member State can be faced with an outflow of capital, a deeper recession, and a consequent further growth in government debt, forcing the Member State to adopt budgetary austerity or default. Allowing the central bank to act as a lender of last resort and centralizing substantial parts of national budgets and debts in a budgetary union would protect the Member States from being forced into default. Budgetary centralization also allows the setting up of a transfer mechanism that would work as a stabilizer and reduce the negative impact of asymmetric shocks.[120] The centralization of national budgets, however, would require a significant transfer of sovereignty over taxation and spending from the Member States to the European level. It would require a political union.[121]

3.1.2 The GFCC's assessment: stability as a constitutional requirement

Based on these considerations, the shortcomings of the GFCC's assessment of the EMU architecture in its *Maastricht* judgment are twofold. First, in the Court's sovereignty-based understanding of democracy, the stability focus of the EMU is turned into a constitutional requirement, rather than criticized from a democratic

[119] See eg de Grauwe, *Economics of Monetary Union* (n 109) 3–10; Barry Eichengreen, 'Should the Maastricht Treaty be Saved?' (1992) 74 Princeton Studies in International Finance 12–25. The seminal work on optimum currency areas is Robert Mundell, 'A Theory of Optimum Currency Areas' (1961) 51(4) The American Economic Review 657.

[120] An alternative mechanism would be to increase labour flexibility by enhancing wage flexibility or labour mobility. Workers could move from depressed regions to regions that experience an economic boom. Cultural and linguistic barriers between European countries, however, inhibit labour mobility, and labour mobility in Europe is lower than in the United States, see Barry Eichengreen, 'Should the Maastricht Treaty be Saved?' (n 119) 22–23; de Grauwe, *Economics of Monetary Union* (n 109) 74–79. Achieving wage flexibility would supposedly require the reform of labour market institutions.

[121] On the economics of monetary unions generally see de Grauwe, *Economics of Monetary Union* (n 109), particularly 3–69, 70–98, and 109–33. The idea that monetary union requires some form of budgetary union had been articulated long before the crisis, see Martin Feldstein. 'Europe's Monetary Union: The Case Against EMU' *The Economist* (13 June 1992); Eichengreen, 'Should the Maastricht Treaty be Saved?' (n 119); Donald Macdougall, 'Report of the Study Group on the Role of Public Finance in European Integration, Volume I: General Report (The MacDougall Report)' (Brussels, April 1977); Wynne Godley, 'Maastricht and All That' (1992) 14(19) London Review of Books 3.

perspective. The logic of the Court's reasoning dictates that the conferral of powers to the EU has to be sufficiently specific. On the basis of this logic, the Court judged the development of the monetary union sufficiently predictable after entry into the third stage, because it would be geared specifically to maintaining stability, in particular price stability. The Court thus positively evaluated the provisions and institutional arrangements that contributed to price stability, such as the prohibition on monetary financing, the no-bailout clause, and the Member States' duty to avoid excessive deficits.[122] Changes to this 'community based on stability' would require Treaty change or justify withdrawal:

> This conception of the currency union as a community based on stability is the basis and subject-matter of the German Act of Accession. If the monetary union should not be able to develop on a continuing basis the stability present at the beginning of the third stage within the meaning of the agreed mandate for stabilisation, it would be abandoning the Treaty conception.[123]

However, the Court hardly considered that the focus on price stability limits the political consideration of other objectives and affects national autonomy in economic policy. For the Court, these requirements were simply limitations on the EU's authority and positively evaluated from a democratic point of view.[124] One could defend the Court's assessment of the EMU as merely showing deference to political actors, who, after all, decided the EMU legal architecture.[125] Yet, the Court went further by actively turning the notion of the '*Stabilitätsgemeinschaft*' into a democratic requirement. The condition is comprehensible as a political demand stemming from German stability anxieties, but as a democratic requirement it is at least one-sided.[126]

At one point, the Court did consider democratic concerns about the focus on price stability, namely in its discussion of the ECB's independence. According to the Court, the transfer of monetary policy to the ECB did affect the principle of democracy: monetary policy was an 'essential political area', as maintaining the value of the currency supports individual freedom and 'through the money supply, the state of public finances and the political spheres dependent thereon are

[122] BVerfG, *Maastricht* (n 7) para 89.

[123] ibid para 90. In a similar vein, the Court held that entry into EMU's third stage would be sufficiently predictable or subject to sufficient parliamentary responsibility in its development. The convergence criteria, the right of the *Bundestag* to assess compliance with the convergence criteria, as well as the need for preparatory work by the Member States before entry into the third stage, all ensured sufficient predictability. Therefore, by ratifying the EU Treaty, Germany would be moving into a monetary union in which guarantees for stability were in place. See paras 80–88.

[124] Similarly, Joerges, 'Where the Law Ends' (n 98).

[125] Götz, 'Das Maastricht-Urteil des BVerfG' (n 15) 1085.

[126] Similarly, Juliane Kokott explains the paragraphs on EMU in the *Maastricht* judgment as stemming from concerns about the loss of the D-Mark. Kokott, 'Report on Germany' (n 3) 110–11.

determined'.[127] However, the Court held this to be an acceptable modification of the democratic principle:

> [I]t takes account of the special characteristic of (tested and proven—in scientific terms as well—in the German legal system) that an independent central bank is a better guarantee of the value of the currency, and thus of a generally sound economic basis for the state's budgetary policies and for private planning and transactions in the exercise of rights of economic freedom, than state bodies, which as regards their opportunities and means for action are essentially dependent on the supply and value of the currency, and rely on the short-term consent of political forces.[128]

The transfer of monetary competences to the ECB was thus considered acceptable because its mandate focused on price stability. By implication, though, the ECB's independence would become more problematic if the ECB moved beyond this narrow mandate. This problem lies at the basis of the GFCC's more recent challenges to the ECB's decision on Outright Monetary Transactions (OMT) and its decision to declare the ECB's Public Sector Purchasing Programme *ultra vires*.[129]

The second problem is that the Court hardly addressed the fragility of the monetary union. The argument had been made before the Court that the viability of the monetary union would depend on being supplemented by an economic union and that otherwise the monetary union's development would be factually unpredictable. The GFCC rejected this argument. It argued that such an extension would simply require a Treaty amendment or abandonment of the common currency. The Court also considered the argument that the EMU would require a political union 'embracing all essential economic functions',[130] as had been argued by *Bundesbank* President Schlesinger in the oral hearings at the Court. According to the Court this was not a question 'of constitutional law, however, but of politics' that would similarly require future Treaty amendment and the assent of the German *Bundestag*.[131]

Writing in 2010, Ernst-Wolfgang Böckenförde—one of the judges who handed down the *Maastricht-Urteil*—argued that the instability of the EMU's original architecture had been foreseen at the time of the judgment. He reaffirmed, however, that its solution lay in political responsibility. Different options for Europe's future now had to be discussed and weighed, including whether political union should be completed with a system of financial transfers or whether the EMU

[127] BVerfG, *Maastricht* (n 7) para 95.
[128] ibid para 96.
[129] Bundesverfassungsgericht, order of 14 January 2014, 2 BvR 2728/13 (*OMT* referral); Bundesverfassungsgericht, judgment of 5 May 2020, 2 BvR 859/15 etc. (*PSPP*). Although the approach of the GFCC in both cases is more restrictive towards the ECB than that of its *Maastricht* decision, see Wendel, 'Exceeding Judicial Competence' (n 4) 301.
[130] BVerfG, *Maastricht* (n 7) para 92.
[131] ibid para 93.

should be limited to a smaller circle of stronger economies. In this sense, he contended that the crisis presented Europe with a chance to finally decide on the future of Europe and impart it with renewed popular legitimacy.[132]

These arguments overlook two issues. First, the significant difficulties of Treaty change mean that far-reaching Treaty changes could well be near-impossible in the context of an economic crisis. Secondly, the Court's separation of constitutional law and politics ignores that the Court itself had expressed doubts on the possible attainment of a political union. After all, it had held that the factual preconditions for a democratic EU—a European public sphere and a European *demos*—were not in place and that sufficient sovereign powers would have to remain with the *Bundestag*. By stressing the dependence of the EU's democratic legitimacy on the *Bundestag*, the Court itself seemed to indicate that the development of the EU into a European state-like order would not be compatible with the Basic Law, although it refrained from saying this in so many words.

The Court's 2009 judgment on the Lisbon Treaty appears to have made the achievement of such a political union all the more problematic by determining 'fundamental fiscal decisions on public revenue and public expenditure' as an area that is especially 'sensitive for the ability of a constitutional state to democratically shape itself'.[133] The puzzle of the *Maastricht-Urteil* and its subsequent further development in the *Lisbon* judgment is that the entry into the EMU was accepted under conditions that have not worked in practice, and yet that the Court simultaneously seemed to bar the route to overcome these obstacles.

3.2 The Treaty Negotiations: Incomplete Deliberations and Incomplete Monetary Union

If the GFCC did not fully address the shortcomings of the Maastricht EMU framework, the same can probably be said about the Treaty negotiations: the EMU negotiations have been noted for their failure to adequately consider EMU's impact on national sovereignty and its relation to democracy.

The fact that agreement on EMU was possible at Maastricht without a transfer of economic and budgetary competence meant a break with previous political discussions.[134] German Chancellor Kohl and his Foreign Minister Genscher had

132 Ernst-Wolfgang Böckenförde, 'Kennt die europäische Not kein Gebot?' *Neue Zürcher Zeitung* (21 June 2010).

133 Bundesverfassungsgericht, judgment of 30 June 2009, 2 BvE 2/08 (*Lisbon* judgment), para 252.

134 Early discussions on European monetary integration dating back to the 1960s already showed a split between the 'economist' and 'monetarist' way of thinking about monetary integration. The 'economists' held that economic integration should accompany monetary integration or even that monetary union should stand at the end of a process of economic integration. The latter is the so-called coronation theory. The 'monetarists' instead held that monetary integration should come first and would lead to broader economic convergence. See André Szász, *The Road to European Monetary Union* (Macmillan & St Martin's Press 1999) 7–14 and 154–58; and Harold James, *Making the European Monetary Union*

stated repeatedly that EMU had to be linked to political union. For them, as well as for French President Mitterrand, EMU was an instrument to achieve some sort of political union. Yet, there were different understandings about what political union entailed.[135] France preferred the idea of an 'economic government', in which decision-making by economic and monetary experts would ultimately be subordinated to politics. Germany, on the other hand, preferred a 'community of stability', as its historical experience with hyperinflation favoured depoliticization of monetary policy in an independent central bank. Ideas about political union were also not fully developed, and mutual suspicion between France and Germany prevented an agreement. Germany, in particular, feared that French proposals for an 'economic government' would undermine the ECB's independence.[136]

Four factors appear to have been of particular importance for why an agreement on EMU was possible and why it took the specific form it did.[137] First, German unification led to renewed fears of German dominance. The agreement on EMU was intended to safeguard future peace and stability by committing Germany to Europe.[138]

Secondly, underlying the negotiations was a so-called paradigm about sound money and sound public finances. The economic shocks of the 1970s had discredited Keynesian policies, and from the mid-1970s a new consensus emerged among EC central bankers and policymakers around the belief that monetary policy was neutral towards unemployment and growth in the long run.[139] The new paradigm favoured 'disinflation, budgetary discipline, and currency stability' and stressed 'the vital importance of credibility of policies within the financial markets'.[140] Key importance was attached to central bank independence and the

(Harvard University Press 2012) 93. On coronation theory and the German position in the Werner Report, see Kenneth Dyson and Kevin Featherstone, *The Road to Maastricht: Negotiating Economic and Monetary Union* (Oxford University Press 1999) 289–92. The 1970 Werner Report's programme on how EMU could be achieved in a ten-year period put great emphasis on the need for economic convergence. It also stated that political union should accompany monetary and economic union in the final stage. Pierre Werner and others, 'Report to the Council and the Commission on the realisation by stages of Economic and Monetary Union in the Community, "Werner Report"' Council—Commission of the European Communities (Luxembourg 1970).

[135] See, on this point, eg Van den Bos, *Mirakel en Debacle* (n 36) 169 and 251–54; the interview with Cees Maas in Janssen, *De Euro* (n 36) 105–35. On different conceptions of EPU and its linkage with EMU offered by Genscher, Mitterrand, and Kohl, see Dyson and Featherstone, *The Road to Maastricht* (n 134) 31–32.

[136] See also Jean Pisani-Ferry, *The Euro Crisis and its Aftermath* (Oxford University Press 2013) 33–37; Szász, The Road to European Monetary Union (n 134) 155–58.

[137] Although opinions diverge on why EMU happened. For a review of the literature, see Tal Sadeh and Amy Verdun, 'Explaining Europe's Monetary Union: A Survey of the Literature' (2009) 11 International Studies Review 277.

[138] Dyson and Featherstone, *The Road to Maastricht* (n 134) 756–58.

[139] An elaborate treatment of the underlying economic policy beliefs is offered by Kathleen R McNamara, *The Currency of Ideas* (Cornell University Press 1998). She refers to a 'neoliberal policy consensus'.

[140] Dyson and Featherstone, *The Road to Maastricht* (n 134) 2 and 28–33.

German central bank became the leading model. This set of beliefs forged an EC-wide epistemic community that helped bring about unanimous agreement in the Delors Committee, which in turn formed a crucial basis for the IGC.[141] In addition, it ensured that the monetary element had primacy over the fiscal element in EMU.

Thirdly, within the previously existing European Monetary System (EMS), Germany and its *Bundesbank* had the most powerful position. For France, in particular, the agreement on EMU was a way to address this asymmetry. However, Germany's strategic position within the EMS meant it had a strong bargaining position in the EMU negotiations and was able to steer the EMU agreement in line with its strong anti-inflationary preferences.[142]

Fourthly, EMU was negotiated in a small circle and had a depoliticized character.[143] It was a deliberate strategy of Kohl and Delors to bind the central bankers by creating the Delors Committee. By asking the Committee how EMU could be realized and not whether it should, the agenda was limited and depoliticized. The Delors Report itself reflected the prevailing norms of central bankers and set the terms for much of the remaining debate on EMU.[144] The subsequent EMU negotiations were conducted largely in a small executive circle. Dyson and Featherstone note that the 'basic substantive content of EMU negotiations was resolved in and around two intimate and relatively isolated institutional venues—the EC Monetary Committee and the Committee of EC Central Banks'.[145] This privileged a very small number of finance ministry and central bank officials in determining the outcome of the EMU negotiations. The result was that several contentious issues were kept off the agenda, in particular the relationship between political union and EMU.[146] However, this restriction was also a condition for successful negotiation, because the 'EMU agreement probably represented the maximum sacrifice of national political autonomy that could be reached voluntarily'.[147] In this respect, democratic reasons informed the decision to leave economic competences with the Member

[141] Committee for the Study of Economic and Monetary Union, 'Report on Economic and Monetary Union in the European Community (Delors Report)' (Office for Official Publications of the EC, Luxembourg 1989). On the role of the committee, see also Amy Verdun, 'The Role of the Delors Committee in the Creation of EMU: An Epistemic Community?' (1999) 6(2) Journal of European Public Policy 308.

[142] Andrew Moravcsik, *The Choice for Europe: Social Purpose and State Power from Messina to Maastricht* (Routledge 1998) 379–417, 430–47, and 461–67. See also de Grauwe, *Economics of Monetary Union* (n 109) 150–52.

[143] Dyson and Featherstone, *The Road to Maastricht* (n 134) 748.

[144] ibid 773–74.

[145] ibid 755.

[146] ibid 755. See also the interview with Cees Maas in Janssen, *De Euro* (n 36) 105–35; for most sectoral interest groups the implications of EMU were difficult to oversee. The only sectoral interest the negotiators really had to deal with was that of the central bankers. See Dyson and Featherstone, *The Road to Maastricht* (n 134) 746 and 755.

[147] Dyson and Featherstone, *The Road to Maastricht* (n 134) 783.

States, as these were thought to require democratic legitimation that could only be provided at the Member State level.[148]

3.3 German Stability Anxieties

Within the subsequent German ratification debates, the link between monetary union on the one hand, and economic and budgetary competences on the other, played a limited role. German debate instead focused on concerns about the future currency's stability. The agreement on EMU was not without controversy in Germany. The currency union touched on the important symbolic nature of the D-Mark for German economic success and stability. 'D-mark patriotism' therefore emerged as one strand of opposition to EMU and was voiced primarily in the popular press as well as within the CSU by Peter Gauweiler, then a Bavarian State Minister. The *Bundesbank* and academic economists expressed criticism along the lines of coronation theory, which stressed the need for a comprehensive political union in order to make the monetary union successful.[149]

German Chancellor Kohl responded to these challenges by associating opposition to EMU with nationalist politics and by invoking the Basic Law's preamble for a united and peaceful Europe.[150] The justification for EMU by the *Bundestag*'s financial committee was likewise embedded in the view that European integration was necessary to maintain peace and prevent nationalism.[151] In addition, Kohl argued that further progress in the area of political union would have to be achieved in the future.[152]

Opposition to EMU was reflected and partly accommodated in the German parliamentary debates but focused on German stability anxieties.[153] The relationship

[148] Tuori and Tuori, *The Eurozone Crisis* (n 100) 209; Hinarejos, *The Euro Area Crisis in Constitutional Perspective* (n 103) 15.

[149] Dyson and Featherstone, *The Road to Maastricht* (n 134) 448–51. On D-Mark patriotism see also Schrag Sternberg, *The Struggle for EU Legitimacy* (n 1) 107–09. On the position of the *Bundesbank*, see also Beuter, 'Germany and the Ratification of the Maastricht Treaty' (n 35) 97. In the *Frankfurter Allgemeine Zeitung* of 11 June 1992, sixty economists published a manifesto against Maastricht. They noted that the economically weaker countries would face more competition in a monetary union, resulting in higher unemployment and requiring transfers. A political union that could legitimate such transfers democratically, however, did not yet exist. For this manifesto and various other manifestos on Maastricht, see Rudolf Hrbek, 'Kontroversen und Manifeste zum Vertrag von Maastricht' (1992) 4 Integration 225.

[150] Dyson and Featherstone, *The Road to Maastricht* (n 134) 448–51; Kohl, Plenarprotokoll 12/126 (n 45) 10823–24; see also Helmut Kohl, *Erinnerungen 1990–1994* (Droemer 2007) 390.

[151] Further reasons were the economic benefits for both Germany and the Community as a whole. In addition, EMU was presented as an important step in the closer integration of the Community, as a logical completion of the internal market, but also as the logical arrangement towards a political union. BT-Dr 12/3895 (n 47) 20–21.

[152] Dyson and Featherstone, *The Road to Maastricht* (n 134) 450–51.

[153] Wieczorek-Zeul also notes that the public discussion on the Maastricht Treaty mainly concerned worries about currency stability: Wieczorek-Zeul, 'Der Vertrag von Maastricht im Deutschen Bundestag' (n 44) 410. In a vote declaration Wolfgang Schulhoff (CDU/CSU) did raise concerns about leaving the path of coronation theory and stressed the need for stronger coordination of financial and

between political and monetary union and the possibility of a crisis played a limited role. The *Bundestag*'s financial committee discussed various concerns about EMU, such as the fear that the new currency would lack stability, that the convergence criteria would not be strictly enforced, or that EMU would turn into a transfer union for which Germany would be its main paymaster.[154] The committee sought to allay such fears by emphasizing that the convergence criteria would have to be interpreted strictly: 'The future European currency must be and must stay as stable as the German Mark.'[155] In addition, the committee stressed the importance of price stability in the ECB's mandate, as well as the ECB's political independence. It underlined how the institution was based on the *Bundesbank* model.[156] The committee also acknowledged the D-Mark's importance as a 'symbol not just for a successful economic policy after the Second World War, but also for the retrieval of democratic, successful statehood'.[157] In this respect, it was considered crucial for 'the consent of the German people' to designate Frankfurt as the seat of the future ECB, as this would be a 'symbol and agenda for a stability oriented politics of the European Central Bank'.[158] Finance Minister Waigel of the CSU and Chancellor Kohl similarly underscored the importance of price stability. Waigel declared that he would not have signed the Treaty if he had had worries about the stability of the future currency.[159]

Most of these issues found their way into a parliamentary declaration adopted by a large parliamentary majority after the final plenary debate.[160] Article 88 BL was amended to further safeguard price stability in EMU by elevating price stability and central bank independence to the level of German constitutional law.[161]

economic policies. Schulhoff, Plenarprotokoll 12/126 (n 45) 10905–06. Also concerned about not following the path of coronation theory was Jürgen Augustinowitz (CDU/CSU), 10904.

[154] See the report of the *Bundestag*'s finance committee in BT-Dr 12/3895 (n 47) 21.

[155] BT-Dr 12/3895 (n 47) 22. See, in a similar sense, about the entry conditions for EMU, Waigel, Plenarprotokoll 12/110 (n 51) 9321–22.

[156] Finance Minister Waigel also stressed that the European currency would be based on the German model and that the currency union would not abolish the strong D-Mark, but that the stability of the future European currency would be 'even better protected by the Treaty of Maastricht under international law than the German mark by the German monetary constitution' (Waigel, Plenarprotokoll 12/110 (n 51) 9321).

[157] BT-Dr 12/3895 (n 47) 25.

[158] In addition, the finance committee expressed hesitation at creating a single currency given the symbolic importance of the D-Mark. On both points, see BT-Dr 12/3895 (n 47) 25.

[159] Waigel, Plenarprotokoll 12/110 (n 51) 9320–21; Kohl, Plenarprotokoll 12/126 (n 45) 10826.

[160] Such as the need for parliamentary consent before the entry into the EMU's third phase, the desire for Frankfurt as the ECB's seat, the need for a strict interpretation of the convergence criteria, and the overriding importance of safeguarding the stability of the future currency, see Entschließungsantrag der Fraktionen der CDU/CSU, SPD und FDP zu dem Gesetzentwurf der Bundesregierung—Drucksachen 12/3334, 12/3895—Entwurf eines Gesetzes zum Vertrag vom 7. Februar 1992 über die Europäische Union, BT-Dr 12/3906 of 02.12.1992 (hereafter BT-Dr 12/3906). For the vote, see Plenarprotokoll 12/126 (n 45) 10879 and 10885–87.

[161] Art 88 BL; BT-Dr 12/3895 (n 47) 18; Wieczorek-Zeul, 'Der Vertrag von Maastricht im Deutschen Bundestag' (n 44) 409.

As a further safeguard for the currency's future stability, the *Bundestag* reserved the right to assess the fulfilment of the convergence criteria before EMU's third phase, an assessment that the government would have to respect in its decision-making on the European level.[162]

The possibility of a crisis was debated only partly. In the parliamentary deliberations, it was acknowledged that giving up the exchange rate instrument and the power over monetary policy would have important consequences for the Member States' economic and financial policies. The financial committee accepted that significant economic difficulties affecting one Member State could put political pressure on the other Member States to help out, despite the prohibition on bailouts.[163] In this respect, the committee noted that there was no historical precedent for a sustainable currency union without it being coupled with an economic, financial, and general political bond (*'Zusammenhalt'*). Consequently, this part of the Treaty would have to be reconsidered in the intergovernmental revision conference of 1996: the existing sanction mechanisms were considered insufficient, and new instruments would have to be developed.[164] Yet, the report did not give further details.

The asymmetry of economic and monetary competences in the Treaty was defended as fitting with the principle of subsidiarity.[165] The *Bundestag* financial committee argued that the Member States' economic competences should not be transferred to the EU because this would actually make coping with regional and national problems more difficult.[166] It was in any case clear that a parliamentary majority opposed the idea that EMU would become a transfer union. The cohesion funds were not to be used for general budgetary support.[167] Of all parties, only the PDS/Linke Liste clearly rejected the stability-oriented currency and favoured a Community financial policy 'that steers transfer payments to economically disadvantaged regions'.[168] The party also noted the importance of coordinated economic and financial politics, and harmonization in the field of taxation.[169]

In sum, both in the Treaty negotiations, as well as in the German parliamentary debates, the implications of monetary union were not fully addressed. Nor was this

[162] BT-Dr 12/3906 (n 160); the *Bundesrat* adopted an almost identical resolution: Beschluß des Bundesrates—Gesetz zum Vertrag vom 7. Februar 1992 über die Europäische Union, BR-Drucksache 810/92 of 18.12.1992, 6–7.

[163] See also the concerns of the German Greens, who argued that, in case of external macroeconomic shocks affecting individual Member States, it would be difficult especially for the economically weaker Member States to still conduct independent macroeconomic stability policies. They submitted that additional mechanisms would be necessary. BT-Dr 12/3895 (n 47) 18.

[164] BT-Dr 12/3895 (n 47) 25–26. Similarly, stressing the need for progress on political union, Dr Norbert Wieczorek (SPD), Plenarprotokoll 12/126 (n 45) 10842–43.

[165] BT-Dr 12/3895 (n 47) 21.

[166] ibid 21.

[167] ibid 26; see also Waigel, Plenarprotokoll 12/126 (n 45) 10841.

[168] BT-Dr 12/3322 (n 74) 1.

[169] ibid 3; Uwe Jens (SPD) also criticized the stability focus, which he qualified as an unsustainable political straitjacket: Jens, Plenarprotokoll 12/126 (n 45) 10902–03.

shortcoming addressed by the GFCC. Instead, the German Court turned the stability focus of EMU into a constitutional requirement and cast doubt on the possibility of moving towards a full political union.

4. Did the *Maastricht* Judgment Facilitate Democratic Deliberation?

In the previous sections, I have argued that the GFCC's *Maastricht-Urteil* cannot be justified as a remedy for the political institutions' failure to adequately consider the constitutional implications of the Maastricht Treaty. Regarding the general topic of democracy, the Court partly reiterated democratic concerns already raised at the political level, but also linked the notions of statehood and democracy, thus raising doubts about the potential of enhancing the EU's democratic legitimacy. In addition, that these political discussions took place in the way they did cannot be wholly attributed to the Court's prior case law. In relation to EMU, the story is different: both in the Treaty negotiations, the *Bundestag*, and in the Karlsruhe Court proceedings the implications of EMU were not fully assessed. The Court's ruling, nonetheless, appeared to make matters worse by rendering modifications of the EMU legal framework more challenging.

Notwithstanding these arguments, a different justification for the *Maastricht* judgment is that it led to further democratic debate on issues that were not raised within the political institutions, but nonetheless had popular support. This justification fits with a broader diagnosis surrounding the Maastricht Treaty, namely that the difficulties in the ratification process marked a breakdown of the so-called permissive consensus by the public towards European integration.[170] The rejection of the Treaty by the Danes in a referendum and its acceptance by only a narrow majority in the French referendum exposed the fact that the broader population had more preoccupations about European integration than political elites. In Germany, the process that led to the constitutional challenge of the Treaty has been typified as a belated response to the political implications of the Treaty, which in other countries were discussed in the context of a referendum.[171] The judgment also fits with analyses on the politicization of European integration in post-Maastricht

[170] Andreas Føllesdal, 'Survey Article: The Legitimacy Deficits of the European Union' (2006) 14 (4) Journal of Political Philosophy 441; Liesbet Hooghe and Gary Marks, 'A Postfunctionalist Theory of European Integration: From Permissive Consensus to Constraining Dissensus' (2009) 39(1) British Journal of Political Science 1; Finn Laursen, 'The Not-So-Permissive Consensus: Thoughts on the Maastricht Treaty and the Future of European Integration' in Finn Laursen and Sophie Vanhoonacker (eds), *The Ratification of the Maastricht Treaty: Issues, Debates and Future Implications* (European Institute of Public Administration Maastricht 1994) 295.

[171] Beuter, 'Germany and the Ratification of the Maastricht Treaty' (n 35) 104–06. Claudia Schrag Sternberg notes that during the French referendum campaign the supposed absence of a European nation and shared identity were important grounds on which the Treaty was opposed: Schrag Sternberg, *The Struggle for EU Legitimacy* (n 1) 118–22.

Europe: political debates on Europe have become increasingly politicized over issues of identity, as, in many countries, Eurosceptical parties have come to reject European integration as a threat to national sovereignty and identity.[172] Within the German context of Maastricht, it was the GFCC that raised similar concerns, thus providing the Euroscepticism that was lacking from the debate within the political branches.

This justification of the *Maastricht* judgment rests on two key elements. First, that the debates within the German parliament on the Maastricht Treaty did not fully reflect public opinion on the Treaty and that more Eurosceptical viewpoints were hardly discussed. Secondly, that the Court proceedings ensured that these viewpoints could be considered further. I discuss both elements in turn in the following subsections.

4.1 German Public Debate before the *Maastricht* Judgment

Public opinion surveys on the Treaty of Maastricht from 1992 did indicate that the German population had more preoccupations about the Treaty than the overwhelming support in the political branches suggested. According to an opinion poll of August 1992, 44 per cent of the German population would vote in favour of the Treaty if a referendum were held, but 30 per cent said they would vote against, and 26 per cent were undecided. A poll from October of the same year found that 41 per cent of the German population would vote against the Treaty.[173] Public opinion polls also indicated that the German population had limited knowledge of the Treaty.[174] Furthermore, the Treaty had not been the object of intense public debate. Debate on the Maastricht Treaty remained mostly confined to academia and institutions such as the *Bundesbank*. Public concerns arose over the loss of the D-Mark after critical articles appeared in popular newspapers.[175] The parliamentary proceedings also took place under considerable time pressure, as the government wanted to conclude them before the special European Council in Edinburgh on 10 December 1992, but only introduced the Treaty after the summer break in 1992.[176]

The lack of popular debate on Maastricht has been attributed to the country's preoccupation with German reunification, the economic recession,

[172] See Hooghe and Marks, 'A Postfunctionalist Theory' (n 170) 17 and 21.

[173] Beuter, 'Germany and the Ratification of the Maastricht Treaty' (n 35) 104.

[174] See Roger Knoben, 'Public Opinion in the European Union' in Finn Laursen and Sophie Vanhoonacker (eds), *The Ratification of the Maastricht Treaty: Issues, Debates and Future Implications* (European Institute of Public Administration Maastricht 1994) 319.

[175] See the various opinion polls in Beuter, 'Germany and the Ratification of the Maastricht Treaty' (n 35) 104–05; and Roger Knoben, 'Public Opinion in the European Union' in Finn Laursen and Sophie Vanhoonacker (eds), *The Ratification of the Maastricht Treaty: Issues, Debates and Future Implications* (European Institute of Public Administration Maastricht 1994) 319.

[176] Winkelmann, *Das Maastricht-Urteil* (n 11) 19.

and a general disinterest. The year of ratification, 1992, was a difficult year for the newly unified Germany. Unification proved costly: rising inflation and high interest rates led to diminishing economic growth and increasing unemployment. In addition, there was an increase in racism, xenophobia, and anti-Semitism. A number of violent attacks against foreigners led to fears of a resurgent German nationalism.[177]

Within this context, politicians stressed how Germany needed to show its commitment to a unified Europe to stem fears about revived German nationalism. There was a widespread belief that the Treaty could not fail in Germany. German interest and European integration were construed as compatible, because European integration aimed to protect Germany from itself.[178]

The downside of this overall justificatory frame was that the choice between approving the Maastricht Treaty and rejecting it was put as a choice between preserving stability and peace in Europe on the one hand, and disorder and disunity on the other.[179] Finance Minister Waigel, for example, argued that the alternative to European integration would be 'a return to the selfish national fragmentation of Europe' and 'instability'.[180] Peter Kittelman of the CDU/CSU bluntly stated that a rejection of Maastricht would take Europe in the direction 'of the thirty years' war' rather than towards 'a human, peaceful coexistence'.[181]

These arguments, however, also delegitimized more critical positions on the Treaty, a concern reflected in the statement of Peter Conradi (SPD):[182]

> I do not speak for my party ['*Fraktion*'], but for some in my party. I speak for those people who feel doubts about the Treaty and who have fears. I take it as wrong to put these people in the corner of the extreme right, to denounce them, as some MEP's ['*Europaabgeordnete*' in the original] do.[183]

This feature of the German debate made opposition to European integration challenging. As Jan-Werner Müller still commented in 2010: 'Euroscepticism as a

[177] Mary Fulbrook, *A History of Germany 1918–2014: The Divided Nation* (Wiley-Blackwell 2014) 279–80 and 285; Beuter, 'Germany and the Ratification of the Maastricht Treaty' (n 35) 87–89.

[178] See eg BT-Dr 12/3366 (n 49) 1; the statement by Foreign Minister Kinkel, Plenarprotokoll 12/110 (n 51) 9316–17; and the statements in Plenarprotokoll 12/126 (n 45) by Wieczorek Zeul (SPD), 10813; Verheugen (SPD), 10834; Ulrich Briefs, 10876; Chancellor Kohl (CDU/CSU), 10824–25.

[179] See also Schrag Sternberg, *The Struggle for EU Legitimacy* (n 1) 113.

[180] Plenarprotokoll 12/110 (n 51) 9323. The full quote is 'Für uns Deutsche wie für unsere Nachbarn liegt die Zukunft in Europa; denn die Alternative lautet: Zurück zur national-egoistischen Aufsplitterung Europas, zurück zu Koalitionen, wechselnden Partnerschaften und zur Instabilität. Wer den Vertrag ablehnt, wird auf den untauglichen Versuch beschränkt, mit den Antworten von gestern die Fragen von morgen zu beantworten.'

[181] Peter Kittelmann, Plenarprotokoll 12/110 (n 51) 9387.

[182] Schrag Sternberg makes a similar point about discourse in the German press. Schrag Sternberg, *The Struggle for EU Legitimacy* (n 1) 113.

[183] Peter Conradi (SPD), Plenarprotokoll 12/110 (n 51) 9385.

principled suspicion of integration (and as a set of nationalist feelings) remains almost a political taboo.'[184]

Nonetheless, concerns about broader popular discontent with European integration did play a role in the political debates, particularly in light of the French and Danish referenda and, as discussed, concerns about losing the D-Mark. They were not ignored, but ideas about their cause and solution diverged.[185]

The *Bundestag* also debated holding a referendum on Germany's accession to the EU and the Treaty, as had been proposed by the PDS/Linke Liste. The PDS justified this proposal as a means to safeguard popular consent for a decision that would change the constitutional nature of Germany and would affect German sovereignty.[186] For such a decision the parliament itself could not replace the people.[187]

The CDU/CSU and FDP resisted this call for a referendum and preferred what Otto Graf Lambsdorff (FDP) called an '*Aufklärungskampagne*': a campaign in which politicians better explained the benefits and importance of European

[184] Jan-Werner Müller, 'In the Shadows of Statism: Peculiarities of the German Debates on European Integration' in Justine Lacroix and Kalypso Nicolaïdis (eds), *European Stories* (Oxford University Press 2010) 88. On the historical reasons for broad German support for European integration, see Davies, 'Herbert Kraus and Solange' (n 91) 95. The political situation has now changed.

[185] Politicians translated fears about the Treaty as fears about centralization, bureaucracy, a loss of national identity, as well as fears about the future stability of the common currency. In this sense, see eg the contributions in Plenarprotokoll 12/110 (n 51) of: Kinkel, 9318; Waigel, 9322–23; Michael Stübgen (CDU/CSU), 9372; Wieczorek-Zeul (SPD), 9329; Graf Lambsdorf (FDP), 9333; Dr Helmut Haussmann (FDP), 9353. See also Ulrich Irmer (FDP), Plenarprotokoll 12/126 (n 45) 10817. The SPD and Bündnis 90/Die Grünen held that part of the answer had to be sought in strengthening the social and environmental components of the internal market to keep the lasting support of citizens, see eg BT-Dr 12/3366 (n 49) 3. Some argued that popular discontent stemmed from the EU's democratic shortcomings. See in Plenarprotokoll 12/110 (n 51) eg Heidemarie Wieczorek-Zeul (SPD), 9328; Rita Süssmuth (CDU/CSU), 9332; Otto Graf Lambsdorff (FDP), 9334; Verheugen (SPD), 9349; Staatsminister Herbert Helmrich, 9359–60; Wolfgang Roth (SPD), 9365; Michael Stübgen (CDU/CSU), 9372; and see also for example Ulrich Irmer (FDP), Plenarprotokoll 12/126 (n 45) 10817. Yet, voices were also heard that seemed to go in the opposite direction. Rita Süssmuth of the CDU/CSU called for enthusiasm for Europe ('*Europabegeisterung*') and recalled a lesson of Monnet: '[T]he closer this Europe comes, the greater the resistance, the more the dream comes true, the greater the danger that it loses energy and strength.' See Plenarprotokoll 12/110 (n 51) 9330. In a somewhat similar vein, Renate Hellwig (CDU/CSU) stated that politicians needed to persuade the citizens. What was needed was '*Überzeugungsarbeit*'. See Plenarprotokoll 12/110 (n 51) 9345.

[186] Gesetzentwurf der Abgeordneten Dr Gregor Gysi, Andrea Lederer und der Gruppe der PDS/Linke Liste—Entwurf eines Gesetzes zur Durchführung eines Volksentscheids über die Mitgliedschaft der Bundesrepublik Deutschland in einer Europäischen Union und die Ratifizierung des Maastrichter Vertrages über eine Europäische Union (Europa-Abstimmungsgesetz), BT-Dr 12/3353 of 06.10.1992 (hereafter BT-Dr 12/3353). The original says, at 3: 'Die Bundesrepublik Deutschland hat die Absicht, Mitglied einer Europäischen Union zu werden. Dies zieht eine veränderte Verfaßtheit in grundsätzlichen Fragen nach sich. Eine solche Frage, die die Souveränität der Bundesrepublik Deutschland betrifft, sollte nicht ohne die Zustimmung des Volkes entschieden werden.' See also BT-Dr 12/3322 (n 74) 3.

[187] The call for a referendum was explicitly based on art 20(2) BL, which states that all state authority is derived from the people. See, in particular, BT-Dr 12/3353 (n 186) 1–3; and the statement of Gysi (PDS/Linke Liste), Plenarprotokoll 12/110 (n 51) 9339–40. On arguments for a referendum, see also the contributions of Andrea Lederer (PDS/Linke Liste), 9353–54 and Gerd Poppe (Bündnis 90/Die Grünen) 9370–71. In the final plenary (Plenarprotokoll 12/126 (n 45)) support was expressed also by Modrow, 10820; Ingrid Köppe (Bündnis 90/Die Grünen), 10856; Renate Schmidt (Nürnberg) (SPD), 10908; and Konrad Weiß (Bündnis 90/Die Grünen), 10884–85.

integration.[188] Some politicians delegitimized the referendum proposal by undermining the credibility of the PDS/Linke Liste as the successor of the German Democratic Republic's (GDR) governing party. Andreas Schockenhoff of the CDU/CSU, for example, pointed out that the party's predecessors in the GDR had suppressed and silenced the people.[189]

Yet, the idea of holding a referendum did receive serious consideration. An important reason against was constitutional in nature: it would not sit well with Germany's constitutional ordering as a representative democracy.[190] The introduction of referenda and other forms of direct democracy had previously been discussed in the Joint Constitutional Committee. In that context, most of the familiar reasons for and against referenda seem to have been considered.[191] The SPD and Bündnis 90/Die Grünen had proposed to supplement the parliamentary system with elements of direct democracy such as referenda and popular initiatives as a way to strengthen German democracy.[192] The CDU/CSU and FDP opposed this

188 Otto Graf Lambsdorff (FDP), Plenarprotokoll 12/110 (n 51) 9337. Similar pleas were made by, eg, Renate Hellwig (CDU/CSU), 9345–47; Helmut Haussmann (CDU/CSU), 9352 and 9353; Wolfgang Roth (SPD), 9364–65; Hans Stercken (CDU/CSU), 9366–67; Cornelia von Teichman (FDP), 9368; Wilfried Seibel (CDU/CSU), 9376; Andreas Schockenhoff (CDU/CSU), 9384; Peter Kittelmann (CDU/CSU), 9387–88.

189 Plenarprotokoll 12/110 (n 51) 9384. See also the statement of Michael Stübgen (CDU/CSU), 9372, who described the party as being far removed from the other parties in its basic beliefs and stances.

190 Foreign Minister Kinkel stated that the Basic Law made a basic choice for representative democracy: Plenarprotokoll 12/110 (n 51) 9319. In this vein, the *Bundestag*'s financial committee had stated that, on the basis of the German constitution, a referendum was 'neither required nor possible' (BT-Dr 12/3895 (n 47) 23). The PDS/Linke Liste explicitly tried to repudiate such arguments by invoking the views of constitutional experts that the Basic Law did not prohibit referenda. Gysi (PDS/Linke Liste), Plenarprotokoll 12/110 (n 51) 9339–40.

191 The issue was discussed on 14 May 1992 in the committee's sixth meeting. A further hearing with experts was held on 17 June 1992. In the final meeting of the committee on 11 February 1993 it turned out that no proposal could carry the required two-thirds majority. BT-Dr 12/6000 (n 56) 83.

192 They named the alienation of parts of the population from the political parties as an important reason, evinced by increasing numbers of non-voters and the turn of many to radical parties. In addition, they argued that experiences with direct democracy had shown a willingness of the wider population to actively contribute to the community. The introduction of participatory elements would strengthen the people's position as the bearers of sovereignty by increasing influence on its exercise. They also argued it would strengthen Germany's democratic nature, because a democracy rests on active, interested, and responsible citizens. In this respect, they contended that the situation had changed in relation to the years in which the German Basic Law was concluded. Unlike then, one could now build on a firm democratic self-understanding of the German people built up over forty years and a peaceful popular revolution in the former GDR The German people could be considered 'mature' ('*reif*'), 'responsible' ('*verantwortlich*'), and 'rational'. BT-Dr 12/6000 (n 56) 84. The opponents offered a host of reasons against introducing forms of direct democracy. These would only allow for a yes or no decision and therefore not allow for the necessary finding of compromises needed in a pluralistic society; endanger the protection of minorities, because neither the groups initiating referenda nor the voters would be committed to the common good; ask ordinary citizens to decide political decisions that would often be too complex for them to decide in an objective manner and would raise problems of populism; benefit well-organized particular interests and give non-democratically legitimated associations instruments to enhance their power; and lead to a weakening of Germany's federal structure, as it would disrupt the legislative power balance between the *Bundestag* and *Bundesrat*. Finally, in their view, it would be illusory to expect that the introduction of plebiscitary elements of democracy would help in overcoming the alienation of people from politics. Political parties would simply use them to their advantage and would hence be able to escape their parliamentary responsibility. BT-Dr 12/6000 (n 56) 85–86.

proposal largely on constitutional grounds: the breakdown of the Weimar Republic had led the Parliamentary Council in 1949 to deliberately choose a system of parliamentary representative democracy in the Basic Law. Weimar's parliamentary democracy had stood under permanent pressure of plebiscitary decision-making possibilities, even though in practice few such decisions were taken and '[p]recisely on the basis of this historical experience did the Parliamentary Council for the *Grundgesetz* deliberately not include forms of direct democracy'.[193]

The proposals of the SPD and Bündnis 90/Die Grünen consequently did not carry the required two-thirds majority. In the subsequent deliberations on the Maastricht Treaty, the SPD submitted that if the possibility of referenda had been introduced in the constitution, the Maastricht Treaty would have been an occasion for holding a referendum. However, the party did not support the demand for a referendum only on the Maastricht Treaty.[194] In sum, the political branches were not deaf towards public concerns about the Treaty, but for various reasons they rejected directly involving the people, while politicians themselves voiced little opposition to the idea of European integration as such.

4.2 Facilitating Euroscepticism: Debate in the Context of, and after, the *Maastricht* Judgment

Within this context, the Court can be seen to have facilitated further democratic debate in two ways. First, the Court proceedings provided an additional forum for certain voices to make their concerns heard. The expansive interpretation of Article 38 BL, moreover, provided that in the future, German citizens would have an additional forum to voice their misgivings about European integration.[195] Secondly, by incorporating more Euro-critical elements into its judgment, the Court itself provided a form of counter-politics to the strong pro-European consensus. In its *Maastricht* judgment, the Court put forward arguments raised in other countries by Euro-critics.[196] In an analysis of German public debate surrounding the judgment, Claudia Schrag Sternberg notes how the Court proceedings impacted on public discourse:

[193] With the exception in the area of municipal self-determination (art 28 BL) and in the area of the 'Neugliederung' (art 29) [the revision of the Länder territories, NdB]. BT-Dr 12/6000 (n 56) 85. The proponents of introducing forms of direct democracy into the Basic Law contested this reading. In their view, the Weimar republic did not collapse due to popular referenda. See BT-Dr 12/6000 (n 56) 84.

[194] Wieczorek-Zeul (SPD), Plenarprotokoll 12/110 (n 51) 9329; BT-Dr 12/3895 (n 47) 45.

[195] On this issue in the context of the later euro crisis, see Wendel, 'Exceeding Judicial Competence' (n 4) 282–84.

[196] eg similar arguments were raised in the French referendum debates: Schrag Sternberg, *The Struggle for EU Legitimacy* (n 1) 116–22.

> In the German public sphere, the court's decision and the claimants' arguments boosted discourses that linked concepts of demos (people as in body politic) and ethnos (people as in ethno-cultural community). The possibility of a European *Staatsvolk* began to be discussed widely—and often in terms of the lack of shared European language, history, and culture.[197]

Manfred Brunner, the only complainant whose claim was held admissible, used the significant public attention surrounding the proceedings to launch a book with his vision on Europe.[198]

The *Maastricht-Urteil* itself was a partial victory for the various sides to the dispute.[199] For this reason, it bolstered the position of Euro-critics to some extent. Following the Court's ruling, Manfred Brunner declared the single currency 'dead and buried'.[200] Likewise his lawyer Karl-Albrecht Schachtschneider—the '*Euro-Fighter*'[201] who has attacked almost all the important steps in European integration since the Treaty of Maastricht—maintains that 'the Federal Constitutional Court has made the counterpolitics, not the government, not the Parliament'.[202] Schachtschneider's quote reflects how the German Court provided an avenue for Euro-critics to voice their dissent about European integration.[203] However, this potentially gives certain political viewpoints an elevated status not matched by their actual political support.[204] The mismatch between a more Euro-sceptical public and the strong pro-European stance of political elites nonetheless may be seen as a justification.

A second concern is more pressing, namely that the GFCC interprets a constitutional framework that is supposed to bind democratic politics. The Court therefore

[197] ibid 123.

[198] Roger Morgan and Thomas Christiansen, 'The New Germany and European Union after Maastricht: The Difficult Way Ahead' in Stephen Martin (ed), *The Construction of Europe: Essays in Honour of Emile Noël* (Kluwer 1994) 113, 124.

[199] Stone Sweet argues that this is a common tactic employed by constitutional courts: Alec Stone Sweet, *Governing with Judges: Constitutional Politics in Europe* (Oxford University Press 2000) 148 and 200.

[200] Morgan and Christiansen, 'The New Germany and European Union after Maastricht' (n 198) 124.

[201] 'Karl-Albrecht Schachtschneider: "Ich bin Euro-Gegner. Voll und ganz"' *Frankfurter Allgemeine Zeitung* (4 April 2011).

[202] Interview with Karl-Albrecht Schachtschneider, legal representative of Manfred Brunner in the *Maastricht* case and complainant in multiple other EU-related cases before the GFCC (Berlin, 29 May 2015).

[203] In addition, the judgment seemed to coincide with a change in the political climate, where resistance to European integration seemed more acceptable. On 1 November 1993, the day at which the Treaty entered into force, the Bavarian Prime Minister of the CSU, Edmund Stoiber, gave a critical interview in which he rejected the idea of a federal European state. This interview, however, was not explicitly related to the judgment, although indirectly the Court's ruling may have contributed to a climate in which such critical views were more acceptable. Morgan and Christiansen, 'The New Germany and European Union after Maastricht' (n 198) 124–26; Winkelmann, *Das Maastricht-Urteil* (n 11) 62.

[204] On this point, see also Christoph Möllers, 'Legalität, Legitimität und Legitimation des Bundesverfassungsgerichts' in Matthias Jestaedt and others (eds), *Das entgrenzte Gericht. Eine kritische Bilanz nach sechzig Jahren Bundesverfassungsgericht* (Suhrkamp 2011) 281, 377–78.

seems badly placed to allow political opposition, as it rules on the legal framework in which the political contest takes place. Nonetheless, the *Maastricht* judgment did not really constrain subsequent debate within the political branches because it was sufficiently open to different interpretations. However, neither did the judgment lead to much further debate. Only a few politicians contested the judgment and generally there is little evidence that it altered political positions or views on the future of European integration in the immediate aftermath of the judgment.[205] The political reception of the *Maastricht* judgment by both the German government and the *Bundestag* showed that politicians predominantly framed the judgment as if it coincided fully with their previous political viewpoints and positions on the Treaty, and on European integration more generally.

In a brief press conference devoted to the *Maastricht* judgment, Chancellor Helmut Kohl focused on the fact that the Maastricht Treaty had been confirmed as compatible with the Constitution:

> For the Federal Government, the decision from Karlsruhe provides an important milestone for the European integration process and its continuation. With this decision the road is free to bring into force the Treaty of Maastricht by 1 November 1993.[206]

In a further assessment of the judgment, the government noted that the judgment had confirmed and encouraged the government's politics directed at European unification.[207] The more Eurosceptical elements in the Court's judgment did not leave a clear mark. The government saw the openness of the Basic Law towards Europe affirmed, as well as its position that the gradual expansion of the Community would have to result in a more transparent decision-making process and in further powers of the European Parliament being developed.[208] The government did note that substantial competences would have to remain with the *Bundestag*, but

[205] Criticism was voiced by Hans Modrow (PDS/Linke Liste), 15615; Wolfgang Ullman (Bündnis 90/Die Grünen), 15616; and the independent MP Ulrich Briefs, 15627 in a *Bundestag* debate on the judgment: Plenarprotokoll 12/181, Stenografischer Bericht der 181. Sitzung des Deutschen Bundestages am 20. Oktober 1993 (hereafter Plenarprotokoll 12/181). See also BT-Dr 12/6520 of 29.12.1993: Antwort der Bundesregierung auf eine Kleine Anfrage aus dem Deutschen Bundestag zu den Konsequenzen aus dem Urteil des Zweiten Senats des Bundesverfassungsgericht vom 12. Oktober 1993 (Maastricht-Urteil) (hereafter BT-Dr 12/6520).

[206] Author's translation of Presseerklärung des Bundeskanzlers, Nr 386/93 v 12. Oktober 1993, a Abgedr in BullBReg Nr 87 v 16. Oktober 1993, S 990 f, reprinted in Winkelmann, *Das Maastricht-Urteil* (n 11) 636.

[207] Bewerting des Urteils durch die Bundesregierung, Runderlaβ des Auswärtigen Amts vom 30.11.1993 reprinted in Winkelmann, *Das Maastricht-Urteil* (n 11) 682–83.

[208] ibid 687. Such an assessment is also given by Kohl in his autobiography, see Kohl, *Erinnerungen* (n 150) 613–18.

declared that the GFCC had not determined whether the Basic Law would allow or exclude Germany's participation in a European state.[209]

On 20 October 1993, a *Bundestag* debate was devoted to the implications of the *Maastricht-Urteil*. There, both the coalition parties CDU/CSU and FDP, as well as the SPD, framed the decision to their political advantage. Wilfried Seibel (CDU/CSU) perhaps best summed up the discussion by declaring that the Court's judgment must have been good, given 'that every side has declared itself winner'.[210] In this vein, Klaus Kinkel, Minister of Foreign Affairs, declared the decision 'a success for the politics of the German government and also a success for Europe'.[211] In a similar manner, Finance Minister Waigel proclaimed that the judgment was a milestone for 'our European politics'. Following the GFCC's judgment, fundamental criticism on the Maastricht Treaty could no longer be justified.[212] The SPD instead used the ruling to criticize Chancellor Helmut Kohl and his government. Heidemarie Wieczorek-Zeul claimed that:

> The Federal Constitutional Court has agreed with all issues that the SPD anchored in the ratification procedure in the Bundestag and the Bundesrat, with the German Bundestag and with the SPD's appeals in the ratification debate. One can say: if the Federal Government had gone forward in the way it had planned for the ratification, it would have definitely run against the wall, and the Constitutional Court's judgment would have run fully against it.[213]

The political responses to the judgment do indicate that the judgment was perceived as supporting previous political claims to enhance the democratic nature of the EU. Several *Bundestag* members invoked the *Maastricht* judgment to stress the need for sufficient parliamentary oversight of the executive acting in EU affairs.[214] The *Bundestag* did not obviously take up the GFCC's scepticism towards

209 Winkelmann, *Das Maastricht-Urteil* (n 11) 687–89. König comments that the *Maastricht-Urteil* in its fundamental conception speaks against German participation in a European federal state, although this is not explicitly ruled out. See König, *Die Übertragung von Hoheitsrechten* (n 11) 507.

210 Plenarprotokoll 12/181 (n 205) 15625.

211 ibid statement of Klaus Kinkel, 15616.

212 ibid statement by Waigel, 15622. *Bundestag* members of the CDU/CSU and FDP governing coalition made similar statements. Burkhard Zurheide of the FDP held, for example, that the judgment had established 'nothing new', but merely confirmed what the parliament and government had planned to do and had done in the past anyway: Burkhard Zurheide, 15618. A similar statement was made by Helmut Haussmann (FDP), 15612. Peter Kittelmann (CDU/CSU) rejected claims that the GFCC had cast doubts on the government's previous European politics, at 15614; Michael Stübgen (CDU/CSU), 15627, also declared that the Maastricht Treaty in no way went against the German constitution.

213 Wieczorek-Zeul, Plenarprotokoll 12/181 (n 205) 15613.

214 ibid 15613; and, in the same debate, Kittelman (CDU/CSU), 15614; Stübgen (CDU/CSU), 15628; Verheugen (SPD), 15619; Hellwig (CDU/CSU), 15620–21. Members of parliament from the FDP, the CDU/CSU, and the SPD, as well as Foreign Minister Kinkel on behalf of the government, stressed that there could be no automatic passage into the third stage of the EMU. See Dr Helmut Haussmann (FDP), 15612; Wieczorek-Zeul (SPD), 15613; Kinkel, 15617; Zurheide (FDP), 15619; Wilfried Seibel (CDU/CSU), 15624. The SPD also contended that the judgment would help end the secret nature of European decision-making, see Wieczorek-Zeul (SPD), 15613–14; Verheugen (SPD), 15619.

the establishment of democracy on the European level. For example, Peter Kittelman (CDU/CSU) merely noted how the judgment had confirmed the democratic importance of both the *Bundestag* and the European Parliament.[215] Foreign Minister Kinkel stated that the government would continue to strive for a stronger European Parliament and noted positively that the GFCC had explicitly emphasized the European Parliament's complementary role.[216]

Likewise, there were few signs that politicians had altered their political positions regarding the future development of European integration. According to Foreign Minister Kinkel, the judgment entailed no alteration of German European politics and did not exclude future integration: the democratic foundations of the Union could be built up in step with proceeding integration, as 'a commitment to proceeding European integration'.[217] A united Europe remained the goal.[218] Verheugen of the SPD argued that the judgment left the future of European integration fully open, including to a United States of Europe.[219] Nonetheless, Finance Minister Waigel adopted a more cautious tone, pointing out that the CSU was committed to a Europe of the nation-states: 'More than a *Staatenverbund*, but certainly not a Federal State (*Bundesstaat*).'[220]

Thus, despite its Euro-critical tone, the GFCC's judgment could be interpreted as support for efforts to further democratize the EU, although the political impact of the judgment appears to have been limited.[221] The special European Council of 29 October 1993 was devoted to the implementation of the Maastricht Treaty and paid special attention to the democratic deficit. The Conclusions asked 'all the Institutions and political bodies to combine their efforts for the purpose of effectively promoting—in the letter and in the spirit—the democratic dimension of the Union'.[222] Whether the GFCC's *Maastricht* judgment helped bring about this conclusion is an issue for further research. Still, in light of the prior political deliberations, it is clear that strong support for enhancing the EU's democratic features existed within Germany's political institutions well before the Court's ruling.

[215] The key issue, in his view, was that European unification had to be better democratically legitimated, more transparent, close to its citizens, and predictable. Kittelman, Plenarprotokoll 12/181 (n 205) 15614.

[216] Kinkel, Plenarprotokoll 12/181 (n 205) 15617 See, in a similar vein, BT-Dr 12/6520 (n 205) 692.

[217] Kinkel, Plenarprotokoll 12/181 (n 205) 15617.

[218] He did admit that the citizens did not want a European '*Zentralstaat*' and that the EU would not replace the nation-states. It would develop into a union of its own sort. Kinkel, Plenarprotokoll 12/181 (n 205) 15617–18.

[219] Verheugen, Plenarprotokoll 12/181 (n 205) 15620.

[220] Waigel, Plenarprotokoll 12/181 (n 205) 15622.

[221] Interview with Jean-Paul Jacqué, former Director in the Legal Service of the Council of the European Union (Brussels, Belgium, 8 December 2015); see, similarly, Franz Mayer, 'Kompetenzüberschreitung und Letzentscheidung' (PhD thesis, Ludwig-Maximillians-Universität München 2000) 134. Mayer notes that political reactions were hardly visible, and that the judgment did not play a significant role in the revision conference that led to the Treaty of Amsterdam.

[222] Conclusions of the Extraordinary European Council of 29 October 1993 <www.europarl.europa.eu/summits/brussels2/default_en.htm> accessed 1 August 2022, 7.

5. Conclusion

At Maastricht, the GFCC did not function as a 'forum of principle' compared to a political process that did not take into account the constitutional implications of the Maastricht Treaty. Despite a strong pro-European political consensus, the *Bundestag* extensively discussed the Treaty's constitutional implications and noted the democratic shortcomings of the EU as a particular concern. In addition, it is not clear that the GFCC's prior case law or the possibility of constitutional review decisively impacted on the German parliamentary deliberations.

The political deliberations on monetary union tell a different story. In retrospect, the shortcomings of the stability-oriented framework were not fully addressed, either in the Treaty negotiations, or in the subsequent German ratification debates. The focus on price stability as a goal of overriding importance in the EMU architecture was hardly seen as raising a democratic concern. That a monetary union without an economic and budgetary union would be highly fragile—as the euro crisis has exposed—was likewise not the subject of extensive political debate. Yet, in this respect the GFCC fared no better. First, because the Court turned the stability orientation of EMU into a constitutional condition for German participation. Secondly, because its judgment raised doubts about the possibility of achieving a political union that could help in overcoming EMU's shortcomings.

Ultimately, the main difference between the GFCC's assessment of the Treaty and that of the *Bundestag* was that the GFCC offered a state-centred view of democracy, while the parliamentary majority adopted a more pro-European understanding. Whereas the political branches had stressed the importance and the potential of European integration, the GFCC focused on its limitations. By connecting the theme of democracy to sovereign statehood, a shared national identity and public sphere, the GFCC raised concerns that, in the wake of Maastricht, have often been voiced by Eurosceptics. The Court provided an additional forum to those critical of European integration to raise their concerns about European integration and partly reflected that concern within its judgment.[223] In the context of Maastricht, the Court's role in allowing further debate on the Treaty still seemed to work: public debate on the Treaty had been limited and started late; opinion polls indicated that the political branches were more favourable to the Treaty than the wider public; Euroscepticism was still a taboo within German political debate; the *Maastricht-Urteil* did lead to the consideration of new issues, particularly that of national identity; and at the same time, the constitutional limits of European integration articulated by the Court still allowed several interpretations and therefore did not really constrain political debate.

[223] See, for a similar assessment of the *Maastricht* judgment, Christoph Schönberger, '*Lisbon* in Karlsruhe: *Maastricht's* Epigonies at Sea' (2009) 10(8) German Law Journal 1201, 1217.

Following Maastricht, the GFCC adopted a stance more accommodating of European integration and left room for politics.[224] In this spirit, the GFCC rejected as 'manifestly unfounded' the constitutional complaints against Germany's participation in EMU's third stage, even though the convergence criteria had been interpreted flexibly.[225]

In the longer term, however, the outlook has proved to be more problematic, particularly after the Court returned to the themes of Maastricht in its 2009 *Lisbon* judgment. Within the context of the euro crisis, the constitutional constraints imposed on European integration became troublesome: by casting doubt on the realization of democracy at the European level, but at the same time approving Maastricht, the Court turned the failure of Maastricht into a potentially larger constitutional problem. If the failure of Maastricht was the absence of a political and democratic structure that would make EMU viable as a democratic project, the GFCC put into question the idea that such a union could ever be achieved. In the context of the euro crisis around twenty years later, this became a pressing concern that calls into question the democratic justification of the GFCC's EU-related case law.

[224] Such as the Bundesverfassungsgericht, judgment of 22 March 1995, 2 BvG 1/89 (*TV Broadcasting Directive*) and Bundesverfassungsgericht, order of 7 June 2000, 2 BvL 1/97 (*Bananas III*). On these points see Claes, *The National Courts' Mandate* (n 3) 406–07; Kokott, 'Report on Germany' (n 3) 129; Donald Kommers and Russel Miller, *The Constitutional Jurisprudence of the Federal Republic of Germany* (Duke University Press 2012) 339–40.

[225] Bundesverfassungsgericht, order of 31 March 1998, 2 BvR 1877/97 and 2 BvR 50/98.

5
The Euro Crisis and the Judicialization of Euro-Politics

1. Introduction

The GFCC returned to the core tenets of its *Maastricht* judgment with its ruling on the Lisbon Treaty in June 2009.[1] The controversial ruling approved the Treaty but imposed several constraints on European integration that appeared much more restrictive than at Maastricht. The Karlsruhe judges now ruled out the possibility that Germany could accede to a European federal state under the Basic Law and were highly critical of the EU's democratic credentials. At the same time, the Court did not seem to allow a solution to the EU's democratic deficit, because resolving that deficit would turn the EU into a state. Moreover, the German judges held that extensive competence transfers were not permitted in five areas: criminal law; the monopoly on the use of force; fundamental fiscal decisions; decisions on the social state; and decisions with particular cultural importance, such as family law and education.[2] As a result, the judgment was widely interpreted as limiting the prospects for further European integration.[3] An analysis by the Commission legal service concluded that 'Karlsruhe appears to leave (at best) limited room for any future treaties seeking to transfer further competencies to the EU'.[4]

Yet, just a few months later, it emerged that the euro area could face a major crisis, as problems concerning Greece's sovereign debt position became apparent.

[1] Bundesverfassungsgericht, judgment of 30 June 2009, 2 BvE 2/08 (*Lisbon* judgment).

[2] See, on these points, also the analyses of the judgment by Daniel Thym, 'In the Name of Sovereign Statehood: A Critical Introduction to the *Lisbon* Judgment of the German Constitutional Court' (2009) 46 Common Market Law Review 1795, 1812–17; Christian Wohlfahrt, 'The *Lisbon Case*: A Critical Summary' (2009) 10(8) German Law Journal 1277, 1277–86; Editorial Comments, 'On the *Lissabon-Urteil*: Democracy and a Democratic Paradox' (2009) 5 European Constitutional Law Review 341; Daniel Halberstam and Christoph Möllers, 'The German Constitutional Court says "*Ja zu Deutschland!*"' (2009) 10(8) German Law Journal 1241.

[3] The judgment was widely criticized from various angles and by numerous scholars from different schools of thought. See eg Matthias Jestaedt, 'Warum in die Ferne schweifen wenn der Masstab liegt so nah?' (2009) 48 Der Staat 497; Christoph Schönberger, 'Lisbon in Karlsruhe: Maastricht's Epigonies At Sea' (2009) 10 German Law Journal 1201. There were a number of judgments on the Lisbon Treaty in other Member States, none of which was so restrictive as that of the GFCC in terms of constitutional identity, see Mattias Wendel, 'Lisbon Before the Courts: Comparative Perspectives' (2011) 7 European Constitutional Law Review 96.

[4] European Commission Legal Service, 'Analysis of the judgment of the German Constitutional Court of 30 June 2009 on the Treaty of Lisbon, and of the German legislation adopted thereupon' (Brussels, 18 September 2009) JUR(2009) 55096 LRR/CL/FH/bds 2.

Judging European Democracy. Nik de Boer, Oxford University Press. © Nik de Boer 2023.
DOI: 10.1093/oso/9780192845238.003.0005

In the spring of 2010, problems had started to spread to other countries.[5] By May 2010, the financial stability of the euro area as a whole had come under threat, with potentially disastrous consequences for the global economy.[6] In response, the euro area Member States and the EU institutions adopted an array of measures that changed the face of the monetary union: mechanisms of financial assistance to aid euro area Member States in financial difficulties, more extensive supervision on national budgets, and strengthened economic governance, as well as an EU banking union.[7] The crisis led to a significant expansion of the EU's powers, which affects politically sensitive areas, such as the budgetary powers of national parliaments. A discussion about substantial further changes to the EMU still continues, most recently in the wake of the Covid-19 pandemic and its economic consequences.[8]

The far-reaching changes in the EU's powers raised various constitutional concerns and a great deal of constitutional litigation before the GFCC, as well as other national constitutional courts.[9] In multiple crisis-related judgments, the GFCC has held that the German *Bundestag* must retain control of fundamental budgetary decisions. Because decisions on taxation and public spending are key political choices that often go to the core of what democratic politics seems to be all about, the GFCC has a point. Yet, the Court's insistence on the *Bundestag*'s budgetary powers hardly takes account of the significant interdependencies that already exist between the EMU Member States. In fact, the Member States' decision-making on economic policy is restricted, and the euro crisis exposed how Member States can be faced with adverse economic developments that they no longer control. Within debates over the monetary union, several commentators therefore argue that budgetary powers should be transferred to the EU in order to make the monetary union viable and ensure political control over economic policy.[10]

As I aim to show in this chapter, the GFCC's rulings constrained political debate over various alternatives for the EMU's future. During the crisis several signs emerged that room within the Basic Law for further European integration was

[5] Jean Pisani-Ferry, *The Euro Crisis and its Aftermath* (Oxford University Press 2013) 8–9; Thomas Mayer, *Europe's Unfinished Currency* (Anthem Press 2012) 108–09.

[6] 'No Going Back' *The Economist* (London, 13 May 2010).

[7] See eg Michael Ioannidis, 'Europe's New Transformations: How the EU Economic Constitution Changed During the Eurozone Crisis' (2016) 53 Common Market Law Review 1237, 1237–82.

[8] See eg European Commission, 'A Blueprint for a Deep and Genuine Economic and Monetary Union' (Brussels, 28 November) COM(2012) 777 final/2; European Commission, 'Reflection Paper on the Deepening of the Economic and Monetary Union' (Brussels, 31 May) COM(2017) 291; Herman Van Rompuy, 'Towards a Genuine Economic and Monetary Union (Four Presidents' Report)' (2012) EUCO <https://www.consilium.europa.eu/media/23818/134069.pdf> accessed 2 August 2022; Jean-Claude Juncker, 'Completing Europe's Economic and Monetary Union (Five Presidents' Report)' (European Commission 2015) <https://ec.europa.eu/info/publications/five-presidents-report-completing-europes-economic-and-monetary-union_en> accessed 2 August 2022. On the post-Covid developments, see Chapter 7.

[9] For an overview of several constitutional concerns raised in the legal debate, see Thomas Beukers, 'Legal Writing(s) on the Eurozone Crisis' (2015) 11 EUI Working Papers < https://cadmus.eui.eu/handle/1814/35418> accessed 2 August 2022.

[10] See section 4.2 below.

largely exhausted: it seems that virtually every significant new step in the European integration process will now be challenged before the Karlsruhe Court, and the GFCC's case law has had notable effects on the political process in Germany and at the European level. The Court's insistence on German budgetary sovereignty reinforced a type of politics in which financial assistance was given under strict conditionality. It helped to discredit ideas that the EU should have more competences in economic and fiscal policy, or that the Member States should jointly issue debt. A more positive development of the GFCC's crisis case law was that the Court strengthened the *Bundestag*'s position in EU affairs, contributing to better parliamentary control of the executive operating at the EU level. I discuss this development in the next chapter, which focuses specifically on parliamentary oversight.

This chapter focuses on the role of the GFCC in the euro crisis and, in particular, on the political consequences of the Court's national interpretation of the principle of democracy. The chapter concentrates on events between 2010 and 2014. My argument consists of the following steps. Section 2 first gives a brief outline of the EU's response to the crisis as necessary context to the role of the GFCC during the crisis. Section 3 subsequently discusses the main elements of the GFCC's euro crisis case law. In section 4, I argue why the GFCC's national understanding of democracy offers only a partial perspective on the democratic concerns that arose out of the crisis and why it privileges particular political viewpoints. Section 5 discusses the role of the GFCC case law in the German political debates on the euro crisis and shows how this case law restricted political deliberation over the EMU's future. In section 6, I discuss how the GFCC's case law impacted on decision-making at the EU level in relation to financial assistance and the banking union. The Conclusion finally sums up the argument.

2. Fixing the Monetary Union? The EU's Euro Crisis Response

The announcement of 16 October 2009 by Greek Prime Minister George Papandreou is generally seen as the starting point of the euro crisis. His declaration that the previous Greek debt and deficit figures had been fundamentally wrong led investors to distrust Greek government bonds and set off a sharp rise in the borrowing costs for Greece.[11] In the spring of 2010, problems spread to other countries culminating in a European-wide sovereign debt crisis. The EU's response to that

[11] The initially communicated deficit figure for 2009 of 6.7 per cent of GDP had to be revised to 12.7 per cent and ultimately proved to be beyond 15 per cent of GDP. See, on these events, 'Papandreou Tries to Prop up the Pillars' *The Economist* (London, 17 December 2009); Andrew Willis, 'Revised Greek deficit figures cause outrage' *EU Observer* (20 October 2009) <https://euobserver.com/economic/28853> accessed 2 August 2022; the Eurostat report on Greek debt: European Commission, 'Report on Greek Government Deficit and Debt Statistics' (Brussels, 8 January) COM(2010) 1 final; Pisani-Ferry, *The Euro Crisis* (n 5) 8–9; Mayer, *Europe's Unfinished Currency* (n 5) 107–08.

crisis can be divided into three categories: the establishment of financial assistance mechanisms, more extensive supervision on national budgets and strengthened economic governance, and new financial market regulation, primarily in the form of a banking union.

2.1 Providing Financial Assistance

The first of the assistance mechanisms was the Greek loan facility agreement, agreed upon on 25 March 2010 by the euro area heads of state or government, and adopted after much initial hesitation.[12] The facility consisted of coordinated bilateral loans from the euro area Member States to Greece.[13] In May 2010, two further assistance mechanisms were set up, as the loan facility to Greece proved insufficient to halt the crisis.[14] The first was the European Financial Stabilisation Mechanism (EFSM): an assistance mechanism adopted under EU law allowing the Council to grant financial assistance of up to €60 billion, if necessary, to preserve the stability of the euro area.[15] The second was the European Financial Stability Facility (EFSF): a special purpose vehicle (SPV) registered as a company under Luxembourg law with the euro area Member States as its shareholders, established outside the EU Treaties' framework and with the capacity to grant financial assistance up to a total of €440 billion.[16] The EFSF was subsequently changed twice. In

[12] On 11 February 2010, they first declared their intention to take 'determined and coordinated action, if needed, to safeguard the financial stability of the euro area as a whole'. Statement by the Heads of State or Government of the European Union of 11 February 2010 <www.consilium.europa.eu/media/20485/112856.pdf> accessed 2 August 2022. On 25 March 2010, the euro area heads of state or government indicated their readiness to 'contribute to coordinated bilateral loans', still to be considered an 'ultima ratio' and subject to 'unanimity' and 'strong conditionality'. See Statement by the Heads of State and Government of the Euro Area of 25 March 2010 <www.consilium.europa.eu/media/21429/20100325-statement-of-the-heads-of-state-or-government-of-the-euro-area-en.pdf> accessed 2 August 2022. On 23 April 2010, Greece formally requested financial assistance and on 2 May 2010, the Eurogroup announced that such assistance would be provided in the form of coordinated bilateral loans totalling €80 billion together with €30 billion of assistance provided by the International Monetary Fund (IMF). See Statement by the Eurogroup of 2 May 2010 and Joint statement on financial support programme for Greece by Commissioner Olli Rehn and IMF Managing Director Dominique Strauss-Kahn of 2 May 2010 <http://ec.europa.eu/economy_finance/articles/eu_economic_situation/2010-05-03-statement-commissioner-rehn-imf-on-greece_en.htm> accessed 2 August 2022.

[13] It was based on an inter-creditor agreement between the lenders and an agreement between the lender Member States and Greece. See also Alberto De Gregorio Merino, 'Legal Developments in the Economic and Monetary Union During the Debt Crisis: the Mechanisms of Financial Assistance' (2012) 49 Common Market Law Review 1614, 1616–18.

[14] By then the financial stability of the euro area as a whole had come under threat. See 'No Going Back' (n 6).

[15] Council Regulation (EU) 407/2010 of 11 May 2010 establishing a European Financial Stabilisation Mechanism [2010] OJ L118/1 (EFSM Regulation). It was adopted on the basis of art 122(2) TFEU. Decision-making proceeded by qualified majority. See art 3 of the Regulation. The EFSM could provide financial assistance on the basis of the Union budget and was therefore limited in size. See Merino 'Legal Developments in the Economic and Monetary Union' (n 13) 1618–19.

[16] The EFSF provided assistance with the proceeds of the bonds that it issued on the basis of the Member States' financial guarantees. The framework agreement between the Member States and the

March 2011, the heads of state or government of the euro area agreed to increase their guarantee commitments to the EFSF from €440 billion to €780 billion to make the lending capacity fully effective. In July 2011, they provided the EFSF with additional powers.[17]

The European Stability Mechanism (ESM) is the successor to the EFSF: a permanent assistance mechanism based on a treaty under public international law capable of providing up to €700 billion in financial assistance.[18] It is backed up by capital from the euro area Member States and finances its activities through the proceeds of the bonds it issues.[19] The EU heads of state or government decided to establish the ESM at the European Council of 28–29 October 2010.[20] The Member States signed the Treaty on 2 February 2012. The ESM's establishment was accompanied by an amendment of Article 136 TFEU that inserted a new paragraph (3) confirming the ability of the Member States to set up a stability mechanism. Assistance under all four mechanisms—the Greek loan facility, the EFSM, EFSF, and ESM—is tied to conditionality: Member States receiving assistance had to agree to extensive economic adjustment programmes as a condition for funds.[21]

EFSF on the arrangements for the guarantees and the procedure for giving of financial assistance was concluded on 7 June 2010. The EFSF's last assistance programme expired on 30 June 2015. See further <www.esm.europa.eu/about-us/efsf/before-the-esm> accessed 2 August 2022.

[17] These were: the power to intervene in secondary markets to avoid contagion, to finance and recapitalize financial institutions through governments, and to provide precautionary credit lines to countries under pressure from the financial markets. Statement by the Heads of State or Government of the Euro Area and EU Institutions, of 21 July 2011 <www.consilium.europa.eu/media/21426/20110721-statement-by-the-heads-of-state-or-government-of-the-euro-area-and-eu-institutions-en.pdf> accessed 2 August 2022; see Merino 'Legal Developments in the Economic and Monetary Union' (n 13) 1620.

[18] Treaty establishing the European Stability Mechanism, 27 September 2012 <https://eur-lex.europa.eu/legal-content/EN/TXT/PDF/?uri=CELEX:42012A0202(01)&from=EN> accessed 2 August 2022.

[19] The types of assistance that can be granted are the same as those under the EFSF, except that the ESM also has the competence to recapitalize banks directly. See ESM, 'ESM direct bank recapitalisation instrument adopted', Press Release, 8 December 2014 <https://www.esm.europa.eu/press-releases/esm-direct-bank-recapitalisation-instrument-adopted> accessed 2 August 2022. The capital is divided into paid-in shares and callable shares. The Member States' capital shares are based on their capital subscription key to the ECB.

[20] See Conclusions of the European Council of 28–29 October 2010, doc no EUCO 25/1/10, REV 1 <www.consilium.europa.eu/uedocs/cms_data/docs/pressdata/en/ec/117496.pdf> accessed 2 August 2022.

[21] See eg Council of the European Union, Press release 9596/10, 9–10 May 2010 <www.consilium.europa.eu/uedocs/cms_data/docs/pressdata/en/ecofin/114324.pdf> accessed 2 August 2022; art 3 of the EFSM Regulation (n 15); and consideration 2 preamble, EFSF Framework Agreement and art 2(1) of the EFSF Framework Agreement. These conditions are laid down in memoranda of understanding negotiated between the Member State concerned and the Troika of the Commission, ECB, and IMF. The Commission signs the agreement on behalf of the Council or euro area Member States respectively, with the Member State concerned. The Troika is also tasked with monitoring compliance with the conditionality attached to assistance programmes. See arts 3 and 4(2) EFSM Regulation (n 15) and arts 2 and 3 of the EFSF Framework Agreement. See also art 13 of the ESM Treaty.

In addition to these mechanisms, the ECB took on an expanded role.[22] Most noteworthy is the ECB's policy of Outright Monetary Transactions (OMT), announced at the height of the crisis in August 2012.[23] With OMT the Bank committed to buy unlimited amounts of sovereign bonds on the secondary markets.[24] The policy has been widely credited with calming sovereign debt markets and bringing the euro crisis under control.[25] The mere announcement of the programme caused euro area government bond spreads to drop, and the programme never had to be put into practice. Yet, the policy was also controversial, leading to constitutional challenge in Germany.

2.2 Tightening Budget Rules and Enhancing Economic Governance

The second pillar of the EU's crisis response consisted of measures to enhance budgetary and economic surveillance. Several of these measures aimed to address the weaknesses of the Stability and Growth Pact (SGP) adopted in 1997.[26] The SGP was meant to further strengthen the achievement of sound national budgetary policies after entry into the third stage of the EMU. The Pact consisted of two arms. The first arm—also known as the preventive arm— aimed to prevent Member States from running excessive budgetary deficits. The second arm—known as the corrective arm— provided a procedure and the possibility of imposing sanctions in case such deficits existed.[27] However, in 2003 the SGP was effectively

[22] Following Alicia Hinarejos, *The Euro Area Crisis in Constitutional Perspective* (Oxford University Press 2015) 19–24. Through its enhanced liquidity support the ECB has essentially made it easier for banks to obtain liquidity at the ECB. Although it threatened to deny liquidity to banks in Ireland, Portugal, and Spain, thereby inducing these Member States to accept financial assistance and adopt reforms. See Hinarejos, *The Euro Area Crisis* (n 22) 20–21.

[23] A prior scheme was the 2010 Securities Market Programme (SMP). This programme, however, was not fully successful, partly because the modalities were unclear, the programme was limited in size, and the ECB had no effective way of imposing reforms on those Member States it helped. See Thomas Beukers, 'The New ECB and its Relationship with the Eurozone Member States: Between Central Bank Independence and Central Bank Intervention' (2013) 50 Common Market Law Review 1579, 1598–601; Zsolt Darvas, 'The ECB's Magic Wand' (2012) 47 Intereconomics 266.

[24] On its technical features, see ECB, 'Technical features of Outright Monetary Transactions', Press release, 6 September 2012
<https://www.ecb.europa.eu/press/pr/date/2012/html/pr120906_1.en.html> accessed 2 August 2022

[25] See eg Niamh Moloney, 'European Banking Union: Assessing its Risks and Resilience' (2014) 51 Common Market Law Review 1609, 1622–23; Darvas, 'The ECB's Magic Wand' (n 23); Paul de Grauwe, *Economics of Monetary Union* (Oxford University Press 2014) 120–24.

[26] The Pact consisted of a legally non-binding European Council Resolution and two Council Regulations: Resolution of the European Council on the Stability and Growth Pact of 17 June 1997 [1997] OJ C236/1; Council Regulation (EC) 1466/97/EC of 7 July 1997 on the strengthening of the surveillance and coordination of budgetary positions [1997] OJ L209/1; and Council Regulation (EC) 1467/97/EC of 7 July 1997 on speeding up and clarifying the implementation of the excessive deficit procedure [1997] OJ L209/6.

[27] De Grauwe, *Economics of Monetary Union* (n 25) 214–15; Hinarejos, *The Euro Area Crisis* (n 22) 7–8.

suspended.[28] During the crisis, several measures were adopted to reinstate respect for budgetary discipline by reinforcing the system of sanctions in the SGP. Key were the so-called 'Six-pack' and 'Two-pack' legislative packages.[29]

Another key measure was the Treaty on Stability, Coordination and Governance, also known as the Fiscal Compact.[30] The Fiscal Compact is an international Treaty concluded between the EU Member States, excluding the UK and the Czech Republic. The Pact requires the parties to implement a balanced budget rule in national law and a correction mechanism 'through provisions of binding force and permanent character, preferably constitutional, or otherwise guaranteed to be fully respected and adhered to throughout the national budgetary processes'.[31] The inclusion of strict budgetary requirements in the form of a treaty was meant to reduce the risk that they would be softened in the future, as had happened with the SGP.[32]

2.3 Regulating Financial Markets and Establishing a Banking Union

The third pillar of the EU's crisis response concerned financial regulation, and the banking union in particular.[33] The EU banking union is an EU-level system

[28] On these events, see 'Deficits and Finance' *The Economist* (2 September 2003); Editorial Comments, 'Whither the Stability and Growth Pact?' (2004) 41 Common Market Law Review 1193; Jean-Victor Louis, 'The Review of the Stability and Growth Pact' (2006) 43 Common Market Law Review 85; and also the introduction in Martin Heipertz and Amy Verdun, *Ruling Europe: The Politics of the Stability and Growth Pact* (Cambridge University Press 2010). See also Case C-27/04 *Commission v Council* [2004] EU:C:2004:436. The SGP was changed by Council Regulation (EC) 1055/2005 of 27 June 2005 and amending Regulation (EC) No 1466/97 on the strengthening of the surveillance of budgetary positions and the surveillance and coordination of economic policies [2005] OJ L174/1; and Council Regulation (EC) 1056/2005 of 27 June 2005 amending Regulation (EC) No 1467/97 of 27 June 2005 on speeding up and clarifying the implementation of the excessive deficit procedure [2005] OJ L174/5.

[29] The so-called Six-Pack was the first of the series of measures, a package of five Regulations and one Directive adopted in November 2011 aiming to improve the surveillance of budgetary and economic policies. The Two-Pack are two additional Regulations, to further strengthen surveillance of eurozone Member State budgets. See further Hinarejos, *The Euro Area Crisis* (n 22) 30–31 and 34–35; and Kenneth Armstrong, 'The New Governance of EU Fiscal Discipline' (2013) 38(5) European Law Review 601, 601–17.

[30] Treaty on Stability, Coordination and Governance <www.consilium.europa.eu/media/20399/st00tscg26_en12.pdf> accessed 2 August 2022.

[31] Art 3(2) TSCG. Art 3(1)(b) of the Treaty states that this balanced budget rule 'shall be deemed to be respected if the annual structural balance of the general government is at its country-specific medium-term objective, as defined in the revised Stability and Growth Pact, with a lower limit of a structural deficit of 0,5 % of the gross domestic product at market prices'. A previous draft even made mandatory the implementation of these rules into constitutional norms. See Valentin Kreilinger, 'The Making of a New Treaty: Six Rounds of Political Bargaining' (2012) 32 Notre Europe Policy Brief V, 3.

[32] Interview with EU official # 3 (Brussels, Belgium, 4 November 2015); Paul Craig, 'The Stability, Coordination and Governance Treaty: Principle, Politics and Pragmatism' (2012) 37(3) European Law Review 231, 232–33.

[33] On the initial EU response to the financial crisis, see Niamh Moloney, 'EU Financial Market Regulation after the Global Financial Crisis: "More Europe" or More Risks?' (2010) 47 Common Market Law Review 1317, 1317–83; Moloney, 'European Banking Union' (n 25) 1619–22; and the recommendations in the De Larosière Group, 'The High-Level Group on Financial Supervision in the EU' (Brussels, 25 February 2009).

for both the supervision and resolution of euro area banks.[34] It consists of two pillars: the Single Supervisory Mechanism (SSM) and the Single Resolution Mechanism (SRM). The proposed third pillar of the banking union is a common European Deposit Insurance Scheme.[35] However, at the time of writing, negotiations on this scheme still appeared to be in a deadlock.[36] The SSM brings the supervision of credit institutions of the euro area Member States under a common supervisory system.[37] The SRM is the mechanism for the resolution of failing banks. It consists of an EU-level authority that decides on the schemes for the resolution of banks—the Single Resolution Board—and a common resolution fund—the Single Resolution Fund. The Single Resolution Fund is a fund for the resolution of failing banks and is financed by contributions from banks. It is partly based on an intergovernmental agreement concluded between the EU Member States except the UK and Sweden, concluded on 21 May 2014.[38]

3. The GFCC's Assessment: Protecting Budgetary Sovereignty

3.1 Main Elements of the Case Law

The GFCC addressed constitutional concerns about Germany's participation in the crisis measures in multiple judgments. It ruled on the constitutionality of the Greek loan facility and the EFSF,[39] the delegation of the parliament's budgetary responsibility to a special committee of nine *Bundestag* members,[40] the information

[34] Banks from non-euro-area Member States can fall under the Single Supervision Mechanism if these Member States join the mechanism.

[35] See European Commission, 'Banking Union' <http://ec.europa.eu/finance/general-policy/banking-union/european-deposit-insurance-scheme/index_en.htm> accessed 8 August 2022 and European Commission, 'Proposal for a regulation of the European Parliament and of the Council amending Regulation (EU) 806/2014 in order to establish a European Deposit Insurance Scheme', COM(2015) 586 final.

[36] Martin Arnold, 'EU Recovery Fund Deal Revives Hopes for Eurozone Banking Union' *Financial Times* (Frankfurt, 24 July 2020).

[37] The SSM does not apply to all supervisory tasks and does not directly supervise all banks, see Moloney, 'European Banking Union' (n 25) 1631–38; and Council Regulation (EU) 1024/2013 of 15 October 2013 conferring specific tasks on the European Central Bank concerning policies relating to the prudential supervision of credit institutions [2013] OJ L287/63 (SSM Regulation).

[38] The fund consists of national compartments that are gradually merged over the course of eight years (2016–23). During the initial build-up of the Single Resolution Fund, bridging finance is provided by each participating Member State in the form of 'a harmonised Loan Facility Agreement' with the Single Resolution Board. The maximum aggregate amount of these loans amounts to €55 billion. Yet, these are to be used as a last resort. See Statement on Banking Union and bridge financing arrangements for the Single Resolution Fund adopted by Ministers of the 28 Member States meeting in the margins of the Council (ECOFIN) of 8 December 2015 <www.consilium.europa.eu/nl/press/press-releases/2015/12/08/statement-by-28-ministers-on-banking-union-and-bridge-financing-arrangements-to-srf/pdf> accessed 2 August 2022.

[39] Bundesverfassungsgericht, judgment of 7 September 2011, 2 BvR 987/10 (*Greek loan facility and EFSF*).

[40] Bundesverfassungsgericht, judgment of 28 February 2012, 2 BvE 8/11 (*Neuner Gremium*).

rights of the *Bundestag* on EU affairs,[41] the ESM and the Fiscal Compact,[42] the ECB's policy of OMT,[43] the banking union[44] and most recently the ECB's Public Sector Purchase Programme (PSPP).[45] All of these cases focused on the democratic nature of the euro crisis measures and their implementation in Germany. However, until the GFCC declared the PSPP *ultra vires* in May 2020, the Court did not find that any of these crisis measures in themselves violated the German Basic Law.[46] It did, nonetheless, accompany the ratification of the ESM Treaty with conditions in its interim judgment of 12 September 2012.

Most of the GFCC's rulings have two main elements. First, at various points the GFCC demanded enhanced participation and information rights for the German *Bundestag*. In this sense, the Court empowered its national parliament, an issue discussed in the next chapter. Secondly, the GFCC insisted that the *Bundestag* must retain its budgetary powers. This requirement also subjects the *Bundestag*'s powers to constitutional limits and raises a democratic concern.

The Court's case law builds on its interpretation of Article 38(1) BL adopted at Maastricht: the transfer of too many *Bundestag* powers to the EU would hollow out the substance of the right to vote in a manner incompatible with the democracy principle of Article 20(1) and (2) BL, which is part of the unamendable core of German constitutional identity of Article 79(3) BL.[47]

A key question in the Court's crisis case law was whether the euro crisis measures eroded the *Bundestag*'s budgetary powers in a manner contrary to the right to vote and would thus violate German constitutional identity. The GFCC had held in its *Lisbon* judgment that the *Bundestag* should retain significant decision-making power with regard to 'fundamental fiscal decisions on public revenue and public expenditure'.[48] Following this tenet, the German Court has consistently ruled that 'fundamental decisions on public revenue and public expenditure are part of the core of parliamentary rights in democracy'.[49] If this competence were transferred to the European level or otherwise seriously curtailed, the right to vote would be

41 Bundesverfassungsgericht, judgment of 19 June 2012, 2 BvE 4/11 (*Information on ESM and Euro Plus Pact Negotiations*).

42 Bundesverfassungsgericht, judgment of 12 September 2012, 2 BvR 1390/12 (*ESM* interim ruling). Bundesverfassungsgericht, judgment of 18 March 2014, 2 BvR 1390/12 (*ESM* final ruling).

43 Bundesverfassungsgericht, order of 14 January 2014 2 BvR 2728/13 (*OMT* referral). Bundesverfassungsgericht, judgment of 21 June 2016, 2 BvR 2728/13 (*OMT* final ruling).

44 Bundesverfassungsgericht, judgment of 30 July 2019, 2 BvR 1685/14 (*Banking union*).

45 Bundesverfassungsgericht, order of 18 July 2017, 2 BvR 859/15 (*PSPP* referral); Bundesverfassungsgericht, judgment of 5 May 2020, 2 BvR 859/15 (*PSPP*). See also the constitutional complaint Dietrich Murswiek 'Eurokrise—Materialien zu den Prozessen <www.dietrich-murswiek.de/materialien.html> accessed 2 August 2022.

46 This does not hold, however, for all aspects of the implementation of these obligations in German law.

47 BVerfG, *Greek loan facility and EFSF* (n 39) para 120; BVerfG, *ESM* final ruling (n 42) para 159.

48 BVerfG, *Lisbon* judgment (n 1) para 252.

49 BVerfG, *Greek loan facility and EFSF* (n 39) para 104; see also para 161 of BVerfG, *ESM* final ruling (n 42), although worded in a different way.

infringed.[50] The *Bundestag* cannot therefore 'transfer its budgetary responsibility to other actors by means of imprecise budgetary authorisations'[51] or authorize Germany's participation in a financial mechanism that could lead to 'incalculable burdens'.[52]

Similarly, these constitutional limits rule out 'an intergovernmentally or supranationally agreed automatic guarantee or performance which is not subject to strict requirements and whose effects are not limited, which—once it has been set in motion—is removed from the Bundestag's control and influence'.[53] Rather, the *Bundestag* must individually approve each large-scale aid measure.[54] In addition, the *Bundestag* must have access to the information it needs to assess the consequences and background of the decisions with budgetary implications.[55] Also, if the magnitude of the supranational agreements is 'of structural significance for Parliament's right to decide on the budget', then the *Bundestag* must have sufficient influence on the way the funds are used.[56] The Court has held that there could be an ultimate limit to the financial commitments that Germany can constitutionally accede to.[57] The GFCC, nonetheless, only rules out manifest violations of the *Bundestag*'s budgetary responsibility and gives the *Bundestag* a wide margin of discretion.[58]

Next to identity review, *ultra vires* review also played a role in the Court's crisis case law. Manifest and structurally significant competence violations by EU institutions are *ultra vires*. Where EU institutions manifestly exceed their competences, they move beyond the conferral of competences democratically authorized by the *Bundestag* in the act approving the Treaties, the so-called European integration agenda. The Court considers such a transgression of competences by EU institutions as contrary to the right to vote and the constitutional principle of democracy. *Ultra vires* review is a hybrid standard of review, as it is based on German constitutional law but requires the GFCC to independently interpret EU law

[50] See eg BVerfG, *Greek loan facility and EFSF* (n 39) para 121: 'There is a violation of the right to vote if the German *Bundestag* relinquishes its parliamentary budget responsibility with the effect that it or a future *Bundestag* can no longer exercise the right to decide on the budget on its own responsibility.'

[51] ibid para 125.

[52] ibid para 125 and BVerfG, *ESM* final ruling (n 42) para 163.

[53] BVerfG, *Greek loan facility and EFSF* (n 39) para 127; BVerfG, *ESM* final ruling (n 42) para 164.

[54] BVerfG, *Greek loan facility and EFSF* (n 39) para 128.

[55] BVerfG, *ESM* final ruling (n 42) para 166.

[56] BVerfG, *Greek loan facility and EFSF* (n 39) para 128; BVerfG, *ESM* final ruling (n 42) para 165. Or, as the Court stated it in the latter judgment: 'The larger the financial amount of the liability commitments or of commitment appropriations, the more effectively structured the German *Bundestag*'s rights to approve and to refuse and its right to monitor must be' (para 163).

[57] This would be the case 'if payment obligations and liability commitments took effect in such a way that the budget autonomy was not merely restricted but suspended for at least a considerable period of time'. BVerfG, *ESM* final ruling (n 42) para 174.

[58] See eg BVerfG, *ESM* interim ruling (n 42) paras 216–17; BVerfG, *ESM* final ruling (n 42) para 175. See also Mattias Wendel, 'Judicial Restraint and the Return to Openness: The Decision of the German Federal Constitutional Court on the ESM and the Fiscal Treaty of 12 September 2012' (2013) 14 German Law Journal 21, 41–44.

through the lens of national constitutional law.[59] In this way, EU law itself becomes a standard of review for the GFCC. During the euro crisis, opponents of the EU's crisis response argued that several of the crisis measures constituted a departure from the '*Stabilitätsgemeinschaft*' envisaged at Maastricht, which the Court had determined as a constitutional requirement for Germany's participation in the EMU. Nonetheless, most cases revolved around constitutional identity. Only in the cases on the ECB's OMT policy and the PSPP did the *ultra vires* question take centre stage.

3.2 Judging Financial Assistance and Budget Rules

The principles described in the previous section formed the basis for the GFCC's assessment of German participation in the various crisis measures. The GFCC first considered German participation in the Greek loan facility, the EFSM, and the EFSF in a judgment of 7 September 2011 (the *EFSF* case), and upheld German participation in all three instruments. German participation in the Greek loan facility was constitutional because the amount and purpose of German financial liabilities were restricted, and the loans were conditional on agreements with Greece.[60] The Court came to the same conclusion regarding the EFSF and on the basis of similar reasons. Nonetheless, in relation to the EFSF, the GFCC did rule that the German government would have to obtain the consent of the *Bundestag*'s budget committee prior to giving a guarantee: the implementing legislation had to be interpreted in this manner, as the wording of the relevant provision had left open a different possible reading.[61]

The Court adopted similar reasoning in its assessment of the ESM and Fiscal Compact: first in an interim judgment of 12 September 2012,[62] and finally in a judgment in the principal proceedings of 18 March 2014.[63] Again, the Court rejected the challenge that these instruments impaired the *Bundestag*'s budgetary responsibility, although it did make ratification of the ESM dependent on certain conditions.

In relation to the Fiscal Compact, the Court held that the principle of democracy of Article 20(1) and (2) BL allows the *Bundestag* to commit itself to a particular

59 See also Chapter 3, subsection 4.3.1; Chapter 4, section 2.1. On the relation between *ultra vires* and identity review, see Christian Calliess, 'Constitutional Identity in Germany: One for Three or Three in One?' in Christian Calliess and Gerhard van der Schyff (eds), *Constitutional Identity in a Europe of Multilevel Constitutionalism* (Cambridge University Press 2019). See also BVerfG, *OMT* final ruling (n 43) especially para 153; BVerfG, *Banking union* (n 44) paras 204–05.

60 BVerfG, *Greek loan facility and EFSF* (n 39) para 139.

61 ibid para 141. It required the federal government only to 'endeavour to reach agreement with the German *Bundestag* budget committee' prior to giving guarantees.

62 BVerfG, *ESM* interim ruling (n 42).

63 BVerfG, *ESM* final ruling (n 42).

budget and fiscal policy, even if made under international or European law. The Karlsruhe Court deemed that such a commitment might in fact be necessary to avoid problematic levels of debt in the long run, and prevent a de facto restriction of the *Bundestag*'s budgetary powers.[64] The Court thus explicitly left it to the legislature to determine whether restrictions on democratic decision-making concerning the budget should be made in the present.[65] The lack of an explicit right to terminate the Treaty was also not considered a problem, because the general rules of international law on the termination of treaties provide sufficient safeguards.[66]

The GFCC allowed German participation in the ESM because German payments to the ESM were limited and did not exceed the ultimate permissible limits still compatible with the principle of democracy.[67] A specific reason why the Court upheld the ESM was that the German representative could veto decisions affecting the overall budgetary responsibility of the *Bundestag*. Hence, German implementation legislation could ensure the democratic legitimation of ESM decisions if the German representative would be bound by clear parliamentary instructions. Under normal circumstances, the ESM Board of Governors decides on the grant of financial assistance by unanimity. In case of urgency, however, decisions can be adopted by a super-qualified majority of 85 per cent of the votes cast.[68] A German veto right also exists under this emergency voting procedure, because Germany's high share in the ESM's capital gives it 27.1464 per cent of the voting rights. The same holds for ESM decisions taken by qualified majority, which require at least 80 per cent of the votes.[69]

Nonetheless, in its interim judgment of 12 September 2012 the Court expressed hesitation on two points. First, it considered that the provisions on revised and increased capital calls could be interpreted as giving rise to unlimited German payment obligations. Such an interpretation had to be precluded.[70] Secondly, the

[64] ibid paras 168–69.

[65] ibid para 173. In the eyes of the Court, the Fiscal Compact also did not give the EU institutions 'powers which affect the overall budgetary responsibility of the German *Bundestag* and does not force the Federal Republic of Germany to make a permanent commitment regarding its economic policy that can no longer be reversed'. In the view of the Court, the Treaty does not give 'the European Commission authority to impose specific substantive requirements for the structuring of the budgets'. Important in this respect was the consideration that the correction mechanism laid down in art 3(2) of the Treaty is subject to 'the reservation that the parliamentary prerogatives shall be respected' (para 244).

[66] BVerfG, *ESM* final ruling (n 42) paras 243–45. See also BVerfG, *ESM* interim ruling (n 42) paras 300–19.

[67] BVerfG, *ESM* final ruling (n 42) paras 183–89. The EU heads of state or government decided to establish a permanent assistance mechanism at the European Council of 28–29 October 2010: Conclusions of the European Council of 28–29 October 2010, doc no EUCO 25/1/10, REV 1 <www.consilium.europa.eu/uedocs/cms_data/docs/pressdata/en/ec/117496.pdf> accessed 2 August 2022. The Treaty was signed by the Member States on 2 February 2012.

[68] Art 4(4) TESM; see also Merino 'Legal Developments in the Economic and Monetary Union' (n 13) 1621–24.

[69] BVerfG, *ESM* final ruling (n 42) paras 190–93. The Court did stress, however, that Germany would have to prevent the suspension of its voting rights under the procedures of the ESM, paras 194–212.

[70] BVerfG, *ESM* interim ruling (n 42) paras 240–53.

GFCC was critical of the provisions on the basis of which ESM documents were held inviolable and the members and staff of the ESM bodies were subject to professional secrecy.[71] Information necessary to assess the decisions of the ESM could not be withheld from the *Bundestag*. The Court held that:

> a ratification of the Treaty establishing the European Stability Mechanism is only permissible if the Federal Republic of Germany ensures an interpretation of the Treaty which guarantees that with regard to their decisions, *Bundestag* and *Bundesrat* will receive the information which they need to be able to develop an informed opinion.[72]

In response, the ESM Treaty parties adopted a joint interpretive declaration, in addition to a unilateral declaration by Germany. These declarations state that the ESM Members' payment liabilities are limited and that 'no provision of the Treaty may be interpreted as leading to payment obligations higher than the portion of the authorised capital stock corresponding to each ESM Member, as specified in Annex II of the Treaty, without prior agreement of each Member's representative and due regard to national procedures'.[73] In addition, they declare that 'Article 32(5), Article 34 and Article 35(1) of the Treaty do not prevent providing comprehensive information to the national parliaments, as foreseen by national regulation'.[74] These declarations satisfied the Court that the German payment obligations under the ESM would be limited and that the *Bundestag* would receive the required information, because they effectively precluded contrary interpretations.[75]

3.3 'Stabilitätsgemeinschaft' and Review of the ECB's Policies

Most of the GFCC's crisis case law focused on the *Bundestag*'s budgetary autonomy. Opponents of the crisis measures, however, also voiced the related but different concern that the measures were *ultra vires*, because they entailed a departure from the EMU's original design as a '*Stabilitätsgemeinschaft*'. A key question in this respect was whether the financial assistance mechanisms violated the TFEU's no-bailout clause.[76]

71 Art 32(1) and art 34 ESM Treaty.

72 BVerfG, *ESM* interim ruling (n 42) para 259.

73 Declaration by all parties on the Treaty establishing the European Stability Mechanism, 27 September 2012 <https://verdragenbank.overheid.nl/en/Treaty/Details/012706_b.html> accessed 2 August 2022.

74 ibid.

75 BVerfG, *ESM* final ruling (n 42) paras 186–89 and 213–14.

76 For a legal discussion of such concerns, see Matthias Ruffert, 'The European Debt Crisis and European Union Law' (2011) 48 Common Market Law Review 1777, 1785–86; Dariusz Adamski, 'National Power Games and Structural Failures in the European Macroeconomic Governance' (2012) 49 Common Market Law Review 1319, 1329–31; Rainer Palmstorfer, 'To Bail Out or Not to Bail Out?

Initially the Court was reluctant to engage with these challenges. In the *EFSF* case, the Court declared them inadmissible.[77] In its assessment of the ESM and Fiscal Compact, the Court only reflected to a limited extent on the notion of a '*Stabilitätsgemeinschaft*'. The Court appeared to accept that the introduction of Article 136(3) TFEU and the ESM had changed the nature of the EMU to some extent but considered that essential parts of 'the stability architecture' were still in place.[78] The establishment of a permanent assistance mechanism affirmed the wish of the Member States and the EU to restrict the ECB to its limited mandate. In addition, the Court considered it important that Article 136(3) TFEU would not release Member States from the obligation to pursue budgetary discipline and that assistance would be given only if indispensable to the stability of the euro area as a whole.[79]

Ultra vires review, however, re-emerged in the Court's assessment of the ECB's OMT programme, of which the GFCC proved extremely critical. The Court doubted that the policy lay within the ECB's legal mandate and questioned whether the policy violated the prohibition on monetary financing enshrined in Article 123 TFEU.[80] The Court also stated that the policy could infringe on German constitutional identity, if the programme had negative repercussions for the budgetary responsibility of the German parliament. This would happen if the programme's implementation created losses for the *Bundesbank* with ultimately negative consequences for the German federal budget.[81] The GFCC referred the *ultra vires* question to the CJEU, but already expressed that it was much inclined to consider the OMT programme *ultra vires*.[82]

The judgment was highly controversial given the widely acknowledged role of the OMT programme in defusing the crisis.[83] Within the Court, the decision elicited two powerful dissents. Justice Lübbe-Wolff said that the ruling went 'beyond the limits of judicial competence under the principles of democracy and separation of powers'.[84] Justice Gerhardt held that the ordinary democratic avenues provided sufficient safeguards for respecting the division of powers between the

The Current Framework of Financial Assistance for Euro Area Member States Measured against the Requirements of EU Primary Law' (2012) 6 European Law Review 771, 775–80; Jean-Victor Louis, 'Guest Editorial: The No-Bailout Clause and Rescue packages' (2010) 47 Common Market Law Review 971, 983–85.

[77] BVerfG, *Greek loan facility and EFSF* (n 39). The Court offered limited reflections on the EU Treaty framework in para 129 of the judgment and hinted that the measures attacked were compatible with that framework in para 137.

[78] BVerfG, *ESM* interim ruling (n 42) para 233.

[79] ibid para 233; BVerfG, *ESM* final ruling (n 42) paras 180–82.

[80] BVerfG, *OMT* referral (n 43), paras 56–94.

[81] ibid paras 102–03.

[82] ibid paras 55, 69, and 84.

[83] See eg the contributions to the special issue in the *German Law Journal* on the *OMT* judgment in (2014)15(2) *German Law Journal*.

[84] BVerfG, *OMT* referral (n 43), Dissenting Opinion of Justice Lübbe-Wolff, para 3.

EU and its Member States.[85] The fact that the *Bundestag* had not taken steps against the programme did 'not indicate a democratic deficit', but was 'an expression of its majority decision for a certain policy when handling the sovereign debt crisis in the euro currency area'.[86]

The CJEU likewise held that OMT lay within the confines of the ECB's powers. The European judges ruled that the policy's objective of 'safeguarding an appropriate transmission of monetary policy' contributed to the ECB's primary objective of maintaining price stability.[87] The CJEU further considered that the policy complied with the principle of proportionality and granted the ECB a broad discretion.[88] It also dismissed claims that the policy violated Article 123 TFEU, judging that the ECB was not prohibited from purchasing government bonds on the secondary markets. Various safeguards in the programme would ensure that the programme did not have an effect equivalent to primary market purchases or 'lessen the impetus of the Member States concerned to follow a sound budgetary policy'.[89]

The GFCC accepted this finding and, despite 'significant concerns', declined to declare the ECB's policy *ultra vires*.[90] The Court similarly rejected that Germany's constitutional identity had been infringed.[91] In a statement that hardly seemed to reflect reality, the GFCC's President Andreas Voßkuhle declared: 'The European legal community has emerged from this process in a strengthened manner.'[92]

Four years later, on 5 May 2020, the outcome was different when, to the shock of many, the German judges did declare the ECB's *PSPP* judgment *ultra vires*. The policy had again been the object of a preliminary reference procedure when the German Court had referred questions to the CJEU in July 2017. While the European Court upheld the legality of the PSPP,[93] the German judges deemed that both the ECB and CJEU had insufficiently assessed the proportionality of the PSPP.[94]

Finally, as Europe started to face a new crisis as result of the Covid-19 pandemic in the spring of 2020, new constitutional challenges emerged that were still the subject of litigation at the time of writing. These new constitutional challenges, as well as the *PSPP* ruling, will be discussed in Chapter 7.

85 ibid Dissenting Opinion of Justice Gerhardt, para 8.

86 ibid Dissenting Opinion of Justice Gerhardt, para 23.

87 Case C-62/14 *Peter Gauweiler v Deutscher Bundestag* [2015] EU:C:2015:555, paras 46–52 (hereafter CJEU, *Gauweiler*).

88 ibid paras 66–92.

89 The quote is from para 109; for the rest, see CJEU, *Gauweiler* (n 87) paras 93–127.

90 BVerfG, *OMT* final ruling (n 43); see, in particular, para 175.

91 ibid paras 210–19.

92 Alexander Armbruster, 'Verfassungsgericht erlaubt EZB-Programm unter Auflagen' *Frankfurter Allgemeine Zeitung* (Frankfurt, 21 June 2016) <www.faz.net/aktuell/wirtschaft/konjunktur/euro-krise-verfassungsgericht-erlaubt-ezb-programm-unter-auflagen-14299519.html> accessed 2 August 2022. The original quote is: 'Die Europäische Rechtsgemeinschaft ist aus diesem Verfahren gestärkt hervor gegangen.'

93 Case C-493/17 *Weiss and Others* [2018] ECLI:EU:C:2018:1000.

94 BVerfG, *PSPP* (n 45).

4. Challenging the Court's Assessment: Protecting Sovereignty at the Expense of Democracy?

That the GFCC sees budgetary decisions as belonging to the core of democratic politics is understandable. Budgetary decisions commonly involve key political choices with significant distributive implications. They are ordinarily the source of significant disagreement between different political parties and reflect different visions about what a just society is. Historically, the parliamentary right to adopt the budget is closely connected to the emergence of representative democracy.[95] Were citizens to lose the possibility of influencing budgetary decisions, their democratic rights would certainly be impaired.

Yet, the GFCC's case law tells only part of the story. It overlooks the fact that the budgetary decisions of one state may have significant effects on those of others, particularly within a monetary union. In addition, a monetary union factually restricts the ability of its Member States to determine economic policy. Transferring budgetary competences to the EU level may therefore be a way to gain political control over economic policy in line with the ideal of democratic, collective self-determination.

In this context, it is helpful to understand that different political ideas have been articulated about the causes of the euro crisis and its proper solution. These readings are politically loaded: they reflect different visions on the main political concerns that the crisis has raised and about the proper response to them. Crucially, they echo different understandings of why and how the euro crisis raises a democratic problem. Simplifying matters a little, I distinguish between two such readings.

4.1 A Crisis of Excessive Debt?

On the first reading, the crisis was caused by the failure of certain Member States to abide by the rules of fiscal discipline necessary for the monetary union to work.[96] In this view, a key problem is that the Maastricht architecture, as supplemented by the SGP in 1997, failed to achieve the desired fiscal discipline.[97] According to

[95] Christoph Gröpl, 'Schritte zur Europäisierung des Haushaltsrechts' (2013) 52(1) Der Staat 1, 24.

[96] Reflecting on this narrative, see also Matthias Matthijs and Kathleen McNamara, 'The Euro Crisis' Theory Effect: Northern Saints, Southern Sinners, and the Demise of the Eurobond' (2015) 37(2) Journal of European Integration 229.

[97] The Pact consisted of a legally non-binding European Council Resolution and two Council Regulations adopted in 1997 on the basis of the current arts 121 and 126 TFEU (see above n 26). The expectation was that the Stability and Growth Pact would ensure that, in practice, the budgetary norms would be complied with, see Hugo J Hahn, 'The Stability Pact for European Monetary Union: Compliance with Deficit Limit as a Constant Legal Duty' (1998) 35 Common Market Law Review 77.

critics, the failure of the SGP opened the door to fiscal profligacy, resulting in the euro crisis when certain Member States' government debts proved unsustainable. An additional problem is that financial markets did not force the Member States to pursue sound budgetary policies either. Between the introduction of the euro in 1999 and the financial crisis in 2008, financial markets priced the default risk of different euro area Member States as essentially the same, despite their widely diverging economic and budgetary performances.[98]

The main threat to democracy on this reading comes from the possibility that one Member State ends up paying for the other, and thus partly loses its budgetary sovereignty.[99] The chief method of addressing the crisis should then be to tackle the problem of debt by strengthening the rules and enforcement mechanisms on fiscal discipline.[100] A further argument for retaining national budgetary sovereignty is that only the national political spheres are sufficiently democratic to legitimize these important political choices.

The GFCC's case law is compatible with this reading of the crisis. The Court demands that the German *Bundestag* retain its budgetary sovereignty and interprets Member States' obligations to pursue budgetary discipline mostly as protecting their budgetary sovereignty.

4.2 Or a Crisis of the Markets?

The second reading, however, conflicts with the GFCC's insistence on national budgetary sovereignty. On this reading, the financial markets, free movement of capital, and the incompleteness of the monetary union were the main causes of the crisis. This view connects to concerns raised by some economists, as discussed in the previous chapter, that a monetary union without a budgetary union is highly fragile and significantly reduces national autonomy in economic policy.[101] On this reading, the influx of capital from banks in northern Member States prior to the crisis caused a credit bubble in other, mostly southern, Member States. The process was aided by the uniform interest rate policy of the ECB, which was too low to stop the excessive demand for credit in southern Member States. After the financial crisis hit with the fall of Lehman Brothers in 2008, credit lines between the north and south dried up. Creditors started to withdraw their capital from these states, ultimately leading to severe difficulties for those southern Member States

[98] De Grauwe, *Economics of Monetary Union* (n 25) 216–18; Michael Ioannidis, 'Europe's New Transformations: How the EU Economic Constitution Changed During the Eurozone Crisis' (2016) 53 Common Market Law Review 1237, 1253.

[99] See Dietrich Murswiek, 'ECB, ECJ, Democracy, and the Federal Constitutional Court: Notes on the Federal Constitutional Court's Referral from 14 January 2014' (2014) 15(2) German Law Journal 147.

[100] Pisani-Ferry, *The Euro Crisis* (n 5) xi. See also Miguel Poiares Maduro, 'A New Governance for the European Union and the Euro: Democracy and Justice' (2012) 11 RCSAS Policy Papers 3.

[101] See, on this issue, Chapter 4, section 3.1.

in financing their sovereign debt.[102] In connection with these concerns, some have pointed to the high costs that Member States have incurred in order to save financially troubled banks, leading to increased government debt and pressure on their abilities to borrow.[103] Moreover, some economists have pointed out that German social policies prior to the crisis had negative externalities for other Member States in the eurozone. For example, the decision by Germany to lower social security contributions in 2008 and increase VAT is said to have decreased demand for imports and increased Germany's exports. Such imbalances within the eurozone have been perceived as a contributing factor to the crisis.[104]

This view stresses that individual Member States can be faced with the negative consequences of free capital movement in a monetary union, without having democratic control.[105] The deep interdependence created by European integration has not been met by the development of adequate political institutions at the EU level. National democracies are unable to effectively address transnational issues, nor do they have a say in the decisions of other nations that affect them.[106]

A solution to this problem could be to further European integration in areas of economic and fiscal policy. The centralization of considerable parts of national budgets and the joint issue of debt would protect the Member States from default, as discussed in the previous chapter. In addition, the setting-up of a transfer mechanism would reduce the negative impact of asymmetric economic shocks on the Member States.[107] This solution, however, would require a far-reaching transfer of competences to the European level. Centralizing substantial parts of national budgets into a common European budget would entail that key political choices about economic policy would have to take place at the European level: it would require a political union. Yet, this solution conflicts with the GFCC's insistence on budgetary sovereignty.

An alternative is to dissolve the EMU in order to make room for national democracy.[108] Yet, dissolution of the eurozone would come with massive costs.[109] The

[102] See eg Pisani-Ferry, *The Euro Crisis* (n 5) 47–73; Fritz W Scharpf, 'Monetary Union, Fiscal Crisis and the Disabling of Democratic Accountability' in Armin Schäfer and Wolfgang Streeck (eds), *Politics in the Age of Austerity* (Polity Press 2013) 114–29.

[103] Mattias Kumm, 'What Kind of a Constitutional Crisis Is Europe in and What Should Be Done About It?' [2013] WZB Discussion Paper SP IV <https://bibliothek.wzb.eu/pdf/2013/iv13-801.pdf> accessed 2 August 2022; Jens van 't Klooster, 'Democracy and the European Central Bank's Emergency Powers' (2018) 42 Midwest Studies in Philosophy 270, 275–76.

[104] See Sebastian Dullien and Ulrike Guerot, 'The Long Shadow of Ordoliberalism: Germany's Approach to the Euro Crisis' (2012) European Council of Foreign Relations Policy Brief <www.ecfr.eu/publications/summary/the_long_shadow_of_ordoliberalism_germanys_approach_to_the_euro_crisis> accessed 2 August 2022; Bill Lucarelli, *Endgame for the Euro: A Critical History* (Palgrave Pivot 2013) 104–18; Scharpf, 'Monetary Union' (n 102) 114–20.

[105] Maduro, 'New Governance' (n 100) 3–5.

[106] ibid 5–6.

[107] See also the discussion in Chapter 4, section 3.1.

[108] Wolfgang Streeck, *Buying Time: The Delayed Crisis of Democratic Capitalism* (Verso 2014) 165–89.

[109] On these dilemmas, see also Claus Offe, 'Europe Entrapped: Does the EU Have the Political Capacity to Overcome its Current Crisis?' (2013) 19(5) European Law Journal 595.

criticism voiced by many is that the EU instead chose a third option in the form of 'executive federalism': it saved the EMU and national sovereignty at the expense of democracy. In essence, the EU and its Member States chose to tighten the parameters in which national economic policy can take place and strengthened the co-ordination of economic and fiscal policies.[110] The result is that economic policy remains a national competence in name, but national policy space is limited to a great extent.[111] Particularly for debtor states receiving financial assistance under the ESM or EFSF, the conditionality programmes have severely curtailed national policy autonomy, although formally these Member States have remained sovereign.[112]

On this understanding, the GFCC's case law protects German sovereignty at the expense of democracy. This problem is further aggravated by the fact that the constitutional provisions at the basis of the Court's scrutiny are part of the eternity clause: they cannot be changed through an ordinary revision procedure of the constitution but require authorization by the German people acting as the original constituent power.[113]

The GFCC's case law can also be criticized for adopting a specifically German perspective. For example, only France and Italy have similar decision-making powers within the ESM and are able to veto emergency decisions.[114] The GFCC

110 On the notion, see Ben Crum, 'Saving the Euro at the Cost of Democracy?' (2013) 51(4) Journal of Common Market Studies 614; Alicia Hinarejos, 'Fiscal Federalism in the European Union. Evolution and Future Choices for EMU' (2013) 50 Common Market Law Review 1621.

111 Such concerns have also been raised about the original Maastricht Treaty framework, see Matthias J Herdegen, 'Price Stability and Budgetary Restraints in the Economic and Monetary Union: The Law as Guardian of Economic Wisdom' (1998) 35 Common Market Law Review 9.

112 For such concerns, see Mark Dawson and Floris De Witte, 'From Balance to Conflict: A New Constitution for the EU' (2016) 22 European Law Journal 204, 217–21. Crum 'Saving the Euro' (n 110); Jukka Snell, 'The Trilemma of European Economic and Monetary Integration, and its Consequences' (2016) 22 European Law Journal 157, 166–67.

113 This, at least, is the position adopted by the GFCC in its *Lisbon* ruling, BVerfG, *Lisbon* judgment (n 1).

114 See Annex I of the ESM Treaty. When the Estonian Supreme Court judged the constitutionality of the ESM, it had to face the fact that Estonia can be overruled in the ESM's emergency procedure. The Estonian Court accepted this in order to preserve the stability of the eurozone and with it the 'economic and financial stability of Estonia'. Supreme Court of Estonia (*Riigikohus*), judgment (*en banc*) of 12 July 2012, Case no 3–4-1–6-12. See, on these points, Jan-Herman Reestman, 'Legitimacy through Adjudication: The ESM Treaty and the Fiscal Compact before the National Courts' in Thomas Beukers, Bruno De Witte, and Claire Kilpatrick (eds), *Constitutional Change Through Euro-Crisis Law* (Cambridge University Press 2017); Carri Ginter, 'Constitutionality of the European Stability Mechanism in Estonia: Applying Proportionality to Sovereignty' (2013) 9(2) European Constitutional Law Review 335. More extensive discussions of the national courts' case law have been provided elsewhere, see Federico Fabbrini, 'The Euro-Crisis and the Courts: Judicial Review and the Political Process in Comparative Perspective' (2014) 32(1) Berkeley Journal of International Law 64; as well as the chapter by Jan-Herman Reestman already referred to above. The Austrian Constitutional Court also acknowledged the need to counter 'potential unpredictable economic and social losses' and deferred to the decision of the Austrian *Nationalrat* in this respect: Verfassungsgerichtshof, Decision SV 2/12–18 of 16 March 2013 (ESM), para B.3.5.3, point 57. The GFCC's focus on the limits to the EU's competences likewise finds its contrast in the advisory opinions of the Council of State in the Netherlands. For example,

also does not consider the possibly negative repercussions of German decisions for other Member States. The effects of the conditionality agreements on the debtor states' self-determination do not feature in the judgments. On the contrary, the Court appreciated the limited nature of financial assistance and its concomitant conditionality as positive from a democratic perspective. Its requirement that the EMU remain a 'community based on stability' supports policies that ensure budgetary discipline. In several debtor states, nonetheless, national courts have grappled with the negative repercussions of austerity measures on social rights.[115] On such grounds the Portuguese Constitutional Court repeatedly struck down parts of the State Budget Law.[116]

For all these reasons, the GFCC's crisis case law raises a democratic problem. Its case law rests on a particular national understanding of democracy that is liable to restrict political debate over how democratic ideals are best realized in the EU post-crisis. Still, one could contend that, despite these deficiencies, the GFCC ensured that constitutional issues and democratic requirements were taken seriously during the crisis and that its case law catalysed further political debate on these important issues. The available evidence, however, indicates that the GFCC restricts political debate over different solutions to the crisis both in German politics as well as at the EU level.

the Dutch Council criticized the fact that the ESM was not subject to control by the EP and CJEU. In the eyes of the Council, national parliaments could only partially replace democratic control by the EP, because they could not hold the ESM as a whole democratically accountable. See *Kamerstukken II*, 2011/2012, 33 221, nr 4 (Advies Raad van State en Nader Rapport), 2, 4–6; see also the Council's criticism on the Fiscal Compact in *Kamerstukken II*, 2011/2012, 33 319, nr 4 (Advies Raad van State en Nader Rapport), 2–4.

[115] Although constitutional challenges have often been based on broader constitutional norms like equal treatment. See, for discussions of such case law and concerns about social rights, Claire Kilpatrick and Bruno De Witte, 'A Comparative Framing of Fundamental Rights Challenges to Social Crisis Measures in the Eurozone' (2014) 7 Sieps European Policy Analysis <www.sieps.se/en/publications/2014/a-comparative-framing-of-fundamental-rights-challenges-to-social-crisis-measures-in-the-eurozone-20147epa/> accessed 2 August 2022; Claire Kilpatrick and Bruno De Witte (eds), *Social Rights in Times of Crisis in the Eurozone: The Role of Fundamental Rights' Challenges* (2014) EUI Working Paper LAW 2014/05 Florence 2014/5) <https://cadmus.eui.eu/handle/1814/31247> accessed 2 August 2022; Kaarlo Tuori and Klaus Tuori, *The Eurozone Crisis. A Constitutional Analysis* (Cambridge University Press 2014) 231–41.

[116] See Portuguese Constitutional Court, Decision 353/2012 (State Budget 2012); Portuguese Constitutional Court, Decision 187/2013 (State Budget 2013); Portuguese Constitutional Court, Decision 413/2014 (State Budget 2014); and the more elaborate discussion in Mariana Canotilho, Teresa Violante, and Rui Lanceiro, 'Austerity Measures under Judicial Scrutiny: The Portuguese Constitutional Case-law' (2015) 11(1) European Constitutional Law Review 155.

5. Distorting Democratic Debate: The GFCC and the German Political Process

5.1 Positions within German Political Debate

To understand the impact of the GFCC's case law on the political process, I first explain the different positions within German political debate during the crisis. Subsequently, I situate the role of the GFCC case law within these debates. The crisis debates took place against the background of a strong pro-European consensus in German politics, limiting political conflict between political parties over European integration. Still, the centre-right governing coalition and the left-wing opposition offered conflicting visions of the causes of the crisis and different ideas about how it should be addressed. The GFCC's case law was more compatible with the political stance of the governing coalition at the time and limited the possibility to successfully argue for political alternatives.

5.1.1 Debt as the problem: the position of the government coalition

In the debates on the EFSF in May 2010, the coalition parties of the liberal FDP and the Christian democratic CDU/CSU put forward an approach to handling the crisis that consisted of three main elements. First, they argued that the assistance measures were necessary as a last resort. The survival of the currency union was now at stake and if nothing were done this would have disastrous consequences for the European project. As Chancellor Merkel famously expressed, 'if the Euro fails, then Europe fails.'[117] The proposed course of action was presented as without any alternative.[118]

Secondly, both governing parties argued that the main cause of the crisis lay in excessive debt: too many Member States had lived beyond their means.[119] The answer to the crisis thus lay primarily in creating a true European 'culture of stability' that would ensure debt consolidation and currency stability. The change and weakening of the Stability and Growth Pact prior to the crisis had been a terrible

[117] 'Das ist unsere historische Aufgabe; denn scheitert der Euro, dann scheitert Europa. Wenden wir diese Gefahr aber ab, dann werden der Euro und Europa stärker als zuvor sein.' Merkel, Plenarprotokoll 17/42, Stenografischer Bericht der 42. Sitzung des Deutschen Bundestages am 19. Mai 2010 (hereafter Plenarprotokoll 17/42 EFSF first plenary), 4126; Foreign Minister Westerwelle also stated that Europe was at stake ('Es geht darum: Finden Sie, dass Europa stehen soll, oder finden Sie, dass es fallen soll? Darum geht es heute'), Plenarprotokoll 17/44, Stenografischer Bericht der 44. Sitzung des Deutschen Bundestages am 21. Mai 2010 (hereafter Plenarprotokoll 17/44 EFSF second plenary), 4435. Similar concerns were expressed by: Homburger (FDP), (EFSF first plenary), 4135; Kauder (CDU/CSU), (EFSF first plenary), 4142; Barthle (CDU/CSU), (EFSF first plenary), 4155; Otto Fricke (FDP) (EFSF second plenary), 4417.

[118] See eg Plenarprotokoll 17/42 EFSF first plenary (n 117) 4126; Fricke (FDP) Plenarprotokoll 17/44 EFSF second plenary (n 115) 4417.

[119] See Plenarprotokoll 17/42 EFSF first plenary (n 117) and the contributions of: Merkel, 4128; FDP Homburger (FDP), 4138; Kauder (CDU/CSU), 4143.

mistake. A new stability culture should include better and more automatic sanctions against euro Member States with excessive deficits, more efforts towards debt reduction, withholding voting rights of Member States that violated the rules, and orderly state insolvency procedures.[120] The FDP and CDU/CSU opposed the creation of a transfer union in which joint liability would be created for individual Member States. This would remove the incentives for Member States to ensure budgetary consolidation and structural reforms.[121] Financial assistance could be given to Member States in financial trouble, but only as a last resort, under strict conditions that would ensure a path towards budgetary stability and only under the condition that Germany itself would decide about the deployment of assistance. In this design, the budget rights of the *Bundestag* would be fully respected.[122]

Thirdly, both governing parties acknowledged that the financial markets had played an additional role and that better financial regulation was needed. Chancellor Merkel stressed that, as a matter of justice, financial market actors should take on a bigger share of the costs of the crisis.[123] Nonetheless, Merkel and her coalition partners held that the financial markets had not caused the euro crisis, but merely aggravated it.[124]

5.1.2 A crisis of the markets: the position of the opposition parties

By contrast, the opposition parties of the SPD, Bündnis 90/Die Grünen, and Die Linke pointed to different causes: the financial markets and the 2008 banking crisis, the incompleteness of the monetary union, and German policies prior to the crisis. The opposition parties also expressed concerns about the negative social and economic consequences of the coalition's crisis politics. Of these three opposition parties, Die Linke was the most critical: it rejected the financial assistance package to Greece, the EFSF, the ESM, and the Fiscal Compact, which it associated with

[120] See Plenarprotokoll 17/42 EFSF first plenary (n 117) and the statements of Merkel, 4129; Homburger (FDP), 4137 and 4139; Hans-Peter Friedrich (CDU/CSU), 4150–51. For complaints about the Stability and Growth Pact, see Plenarprotokoll 17/44 EFSF second plenary (n 115) and the contributions of: Fricke (FDP), 4418; also Schäuble (CDU/CSU), 4426; Westerwelle (FDP), 4436.

[121] See Merkel in Plenarprotokoll 17/42 EFSF first plenary (n 117), 4127; Homburger (FDP), 4139; Barthle (CDU/CSU), 4156. In the same sense see also Plenarprotokoll 17/44 EFSF second plenary (n 117) and the contributions by Meister (CDU/CSU), 4414 and Bartholomäus Kalb (CDU/CSU), 4440.

[122] Merkel, Plenarprotokoll 17/42 EFSF first plenary (n 117) 4127; Barthle (CDU/CSU) also stressed a German veto-right, 4156; for the conditions, see also Schäuble, Plenarprotokoll 17/44 EFSF second plenary (n 117) 4426.

[123] Merkel, Plenarprotokoll 17/42 EFSF first plenary (n 117) 4129–413. Merkel accepted a tax on financial markets, either through a financial activity tax or a financial transaction tax. See also Schäuble supporting the idea of a worldwide, European, or even eurozone financial transaction tax, Plenarprotokoll 17/44 EFSF second plenary (n 117) 4427–28.

[124] Plenarprotokoll 17/42 EFSF first plenary (n 117), 4128–29. See, in similar vein, Hans-Peter Friedrich (CDU/CSU), 4151; Homburger (FDP), 4136; and Dautzenberg (CDU/CSU), 4153–54. See also Fricke (FDP), Plenarprotokoll 17/44 EFSF second plenary (n 117) 4417–18; Michael Meister (CDU/CSU) argued that both excessive debt as well as the financial crisis had caused the euro crisis, 4413; Finance Minister Schäuble argued that excessive deficits were the cause of speculation, see 4426; Foreign Minister Westerwelle argued in a similar vein, 4435.

socially unjust and economically unsound austerity politics. The SPD and Bündnis 90/Die Grünen, however, less strongly opposed policies of debt reduction, but favoured more space for socially and ecologically balanced reform.[125]

In the debates on the EFSF, the SPD's parliamentary leader, Frank-Walter Steinmeier, demanded that the financial sector make a bigger contribution towards solving the problems.[126] He strongly criticized the government's position that 'we had lived beyond our means', but argued that 'those who had lived beyond their means no longer knew what the means of the majority of Germans are'.[127] Sigmar Gabriel of the SPD contended that another central cause of the crisis was the lack of common European economic and financial politics. These 'birth defects' of the EMU had to be corrected.[128] This would also make clear how Germany had contributed to the crisis by having pushed down wages and facilitating tax competition. Further European integration was required in order to achieve a 'social Europe' that was 'more than the internal market'.[129] The SPD linked this narrative to concerns about democracy, as Steinmeier declared:

> Much is at stake. Either we are able to reconcile the situation, reorder the markets and distribute the burden fairly, or we can undermine confidence in Europe and its Member States, as well as confidence in politics and democracy.[130]

The Greens raised similar concerns. They acknowledged that debt consolidation was necessary but stressed the need to do this in a socially balanced manner. Party leader Jürgen Trittin argued that there was a more fundamental point: a currency union required a common economic policy.[131] The debt-financed German export

[125] See Daniela Kietz, *Politisierung trotz Parteienkonsens: Bundestag, Bundesrat und die Euro-Krise* (Bertelsmann Stiftung 2013) 39–42. See also Entschließungsantrag der Fraktion der SPD zu der dritten Beratung des Gesetzentwurfs der Fraktionen der CDU/CSU und FDP—Drucksachen 17/1544, 17/1561, 17/1562—Entwurf eines Gesetzes zur Übernahme von Gewährleistungen zum Erhalt der für die Finanzstabilität in der Währungsunion erforderlichen Zahlungsfähigkeit der Hellenischen Republik (Währungsunion-Finanzstabilitätsgesetz—WFStG), BT-Dr 17/1639 of 06.05.2010.

[126] Plenarprotokoll 17/42 EFSF first plenary (n 117) 4131. The SPD ultimately abstained in the vote on the EFSF, because it demanded more action by the government in regulating financial markets and the introduction of a financial transaction tax. See Plenarprotokoll 17/42 EFSF first plenary (n 117) note 113, 4134; and also Schneider (SPD), 4148. Kressel (SPD), Plenarprotokoll 17/44 EFSF second plenary (n 117) 4415–17 offered a similar criticism of the government.

[127] 'Die Wahrheit ist: Diejenigen, die über die Verhältnisse gelebt haben, wissen nicht einmal, wie die Verhältnisse für die Mehrzahl der Menschen in Deutschland sind.' Plenarprotokoll 17/42 EFSF first plenary (n 117) 4133. See similar statement, Sigmar Gabriel (SPD), Plenarprotokoll 17/44 EFSF second plenary (n 117) 4432–33.

[128] Sigmar Gabriel (SPD), Plenarprotokoll 17/44 EFSF second plenary (n 117) 4432–33.

[129] ibid 4432–33.

[130] Plenarprotokoll 17/42 EFSF first plenary (n 117) 4134.

[131] See Trittin (Bündnis 90/Die Grünen), Plenarprotokoll 17/39, Stenografischer Bericht der 39. Sitzung des Deutschen Bundestages am 5. Mai 2010 (hereafter Plenarprotokoll 17/39 Greek loan facility first plenary), 3740.

surpluses were unsustainable, and demand in Germany had to be stimulated.[132] The Greens similarly demanded better financial market supervision and a financial transaction tax. They stressed that the primacy of politics over the markets had to be restored.[133] In addition, they supported a 'Green New Deal' that would come with investment, education, and social justice.[134]

Die Linke likewise called for stronger regulation of the financial markets to restore the primacy of politics.[135] In the EFSF debates, party leader Gregor Gysi stated:

> Today we are dealing with a fundamental question for our society and Europe. Today we are deciding whether there is a rule of politics again, whether democracy rules again, or whether it remains with the rule of speculators and banks, so that there is hardly any democracy.[136]

The party also pointed to the problem that debtor states within the eurozone were no longer able to devalue their currencies.[137] Like the SPD, Die Linke argued that Germany's own policies had contributed to the crisis: Germany's policy of wage restraint had contributed to a high export surplus for Germany, but also to significant trade imbalances within the eurozone, and a worsened competitive position for countries such as Greece.[138] The party strongly opposed the austerity policy of the government that led to social cuts both in Germany as well as the rest of Europe, particularly in debtor states. Such austerity was both socially unjust as well as economically unsound, because it would only aggravate the crisis.[139] The party rejected the idea that people had lived beyond their means: Germany's debt burden

[132] Trittin (Bündnis 90/Die Grünen), Plenarprotokoll 17/42 EFSF first plenary (n 117) 4147–48. See also Trittin (Bündnis 90/Die Grünen), Plenarprotokoll 17/39 Greek loan facility first plenary (n 131) 3740–41.

[133] Fritz Kuhn (Bündnis 90/Die Grünen), Plenarprotokoll 17/44 EFSF second plenary (n 117) 4424.

[134] See BT-Dr 17/1808 of 20.05.2010: Entschließungsantrag der Abgeordneten Jürgen Trittin, Renate Künast, Fritz Kuhn, Dr Frithjof Schmidt, Dr Gerhard Schick, Kerstin Andreae, Lisa Paus und der Fraktion Bündnis 90/Die Grünen zu der dritten Beratung des Gesetzentwurfs der Fraktionen der CDU/CSU und FDP—Drucksachen 17/1685, 17/1740, 17/1741—Entwurf eines Gesetzes zur Übernahme von Gewährleistungen im Rahmen eines europäischen Stabilisierungsmechanismus.

[135] See in Plenarprotokoll 17/42 EFSF first plenary (n 117) the contributions by Ernst (Die Linke), 4152 and Loetschz (Die Linke), 4142.

[136] 'Es geht heute um eine Schicksalsfrage für unsere Gesellschaft und für Europa. Sie entscheiden heute mit darüber, ob es wieder eine Herrschaft der Politik gibt, ob wieder Demokratie herrscht oder ob es bei der Herrschaft der Spekulanten und Banken bleibt, sodass es kaum Demokratie gibt' (Gysi, Plenarprotokoll 17/44 EFSF second plenary (n 117) 4422). For similar remarks by Gysi see 4420 and 4422.

[137] Gysi, Plenarprotokoll 17/44 EFSF second plenary (n 117) 4419–20.

[138] Ernst (Die Linke), Plenarprotokoll 17/42 EFSF first plenary (n 117) 4152–53.

[139] Plenarprotokoll 17/42 EFSF first plenary (n 117) 4141; also Ernst (Die Linke), 4153. In Plenarprotokoll 17/44 EFSF second plenary (n 117), see the remarks of Gysi, 4419–20. Gysi stated: 'Das ist die Art von Politik, die Sie betreiben, und das kann nicht gut gehen; denn der Sozialabbau ist nicht nur ungerecht, sondern dadurch wird auch die Wirtschaft gedrosselt' (4420).

had instead risen as a result of tax cuts for the rich.[140] Rather than the coalition's austerity politics, Die Linke argued for a European investment programme; debt relief for the debtor countries; a financial transaction tax; a harmonization of taxes, social, and environmental standards; as well as harmonization in the area of wages.[141]

5.2 The GFCC as a Chamber for the Euro-critics

Despite political conflict between the German opposition and coalition over the best approach to the crisis, a strong pro-European consensus among the major political parties remained in place during the crisis. This context helps to explain why the Karlsruhe Court was used as a forum for opposition to European integration and the crisis measures more specifically. Large majorities in the German *Bundestag* supported the Greek loan facility, the EFSF, the ESM, and Fiscal Compact.[142] Die Linke opposed these measures, as its predecessor the PDS had opposed the Maastricht Treaty, but the party did not oppose European integration as such. It was only in 2013 that a German Eurosceptical party was founded at the federal level with the Alternative für Deutschland (AfD), and not until September 2017 did this party obtain seats in the *Bundestag*. The barrier for new parties to enter the *Bundestag* is also significant, as they must obtain a minimum of 5 per cent of the national vote in order to gain seats there.[143]

There were, nonetheless, several politicians with a more Eurosceptical political position, as minorities within the different *Bundestag* political groups. Particularly within the FDP and, to a lesser extent, within the CDU/CSU, there was strong opposition to taking over any liability risk for the sovereign debt of other states. Over the course of the crisis, the number of dissenters within the governing coalition grew. In May 2010, only six members of the coalition parties rejected the EFSF,

140 Plenarprotokoll 17/42 EFSF first plenary (n 117) 4141; Gysi, Plenarprotokoll 17/44 EFSF second plenary (n 117) 4420–21.

141 Plenarprotokoll 17/42 EFSF first plenary (n 117) 4141; Gysi, Plenarprotokoll 17/44 EFSF second plenary (n 117) 4420–21.

142 The Greek loan facility was supported by 391 votes, 72 votes against, and 139 abstentions. See Drucksache 17/41, 4019; the EFSF was supported by 319 votes, 73 against, and 195 abstentions, Plenarprotokoll 17/44 EFSF second plenary (n 117) 4443; later changes to the EFSF were supported by 523 votes, 85 against, and 3 abstentions, Plenarprotokoll 17/130, Stenografischer Bericht der 130. Sitzung des Deutschen Bundestages am 29. September 2011 (hereafter Plenarprotokoll 17/130 EFSF extension second plenary), 15236; the ESM was supported by 493 votes, 106 against, and 5 abstentions, Plenarprotokoll 17/188, Stenografischer Bericht der 188. Sitzung des Deutschen Bundestages am 29. Juni 2012 (hereafter Plenarprotokoll 17/188 ESM and Fiscal Compact second plenary), 22740; the Fiscal Compact was supported by 491 votes, 111 votes against, and 6 abstentions, see also Plenarprotokoll 17/188, 22736.

143 Art 6(3) of the Bundeswahlgesetz in der Fassung der Bekanntmachung vom 23. Juli 1993 (BGBl. I S. 1288, 1594), das zuletzt durch Artikel 2 des Gesetzes vom 3. Juni 2021 (BGBl. I S. 1482) geändert worden ist.

whereas four abstained. By September 2011, however, thirteen members voted against changes to the EFSF and two abstained. In June 2012, twenty-six *Bundestag* members of the coalition groups rejected the ESM.[144] Within the FDP, moreover, significant debate ensued over the ESM, after *Bundestag* member Frank Schäffler and former FDP politician Burkhard Hirsch called for a vote on the ESM by the party members in September 2011.[145] Although the internal party vote ultimately did not meet the requisite quorum, 44.2 per cent of the votes within the FDP were cast against the ESM.[146]

In the spring of 2012, ten *Bundestag* members of the CDU/CSU and the FDP formed an alliance against the ESM, arguing that every Member State in the eurozone should be responsible for its own financial obligations.[147] Several civil society organizations and associations of undertakings publicly supported this opposition, such as the *Bünd der Steuerzahler* (union of taxpayers), the *Verbund der Familienunternhemer* (association of family entrepreneurs), the '*Bündnis Bürgerwille*' group and the *Verband der Jungen Unternehmer* (association of young entrepreneurs). Prominent public figures that opposed the EU's crisis response included economist Hans Werner Sinn, the former director of the Ifo Institute for economic studies, and Hans-Olaf Henkel, former head of the *Bundesverband der Deutschen Industrie* (Federation of German Industries).[148]

German parliamentary debate did not at all times fully reflect these public controversies. As a result of the *Bundestag*'s procedures, critical voices within the parties were not always represented in the parliamentary debates. Speakers in plenary debates are usually those that stick to the party line. Plenary speaking time is limited and normally determined on the basis of the parties' relative strength in the *Bundestag*, while the groups themselves distribute the limited allotted speaking time to different speakers. However, in order to better reflect the controversial nature of the euro crisis measures, *Bundestag* President Norbert Lammert granted two dissenters the right to speak in the plenary debates on the EFSF changes in September 2011, independently of the time allotted to the different parties. The move was controversial and heavily criticized by several *Bundestag* party leaders, as it deviated from the usual arrangements on the allotment of speaking time.[149]

[144] See also Kietz, 'Politisierung trotz Parteienkonsens' (n 125) 35–37.

[145] See Peter Müller, 'FDP Mitgliederentscheid soll Rettungsschirm stoppen' *Spiegel Online* (Hamburg, 9 September 2011). Schäffler and Hirsch opposed the ESM as a move into a transfer union, as a violation of the EU Treaty, and as a violation of the Basic Law, because it would hollow out the *Bundestag*'s budgetary sovereignty.

[146] The quorum was narrowly missed. It required that 33.3 per cent of the FDP party members vote, which only 31.6 per cent did. Of the votes, 54.5 per cent were in favour of the ESM. See Peter Carstens, 'Knapper Sieg über Euro-Skeptiker' *Frankfurter Allgemeine Zeitung* (Frankfurt, 16 December 2011). On these events, see also Kietz, 'Politisierung trotz Parteienkonsens' (n 125) 34–38.

[147] See Klaus-Peter Willsch and others, 'Allianz gegen den ESM' (23 May 2012) on file with the author.

[148] See 'Wutbürger sammeln sich zum Euro-Angriff' *Handelsblatt* (Düsseldorf, 29 May 2012); and also Kietz, 'Politisierung trotz Parteienkonsens' (n 125) 36–39.

[149] 'Streit um Rederecht für Euro-Rettungskritiker' *Handelsblatt* (Düsseldorf, 30 September 2011); '"Mein Widerstand war grundsätzlich"' *Frankfurter Allgemeine Zeitung* (Frankfurt, 21 April

Within this context, the GFCC has served as 'a chamber for Euro-critics': a forum for critical *Bundestag* members, and an extra-parliamentary opposition to contest the euro crisis measures.[150] By turning to Karlsruhe, this opposition was able to ensure public attention for their viewpoint that the crisis measures constituted a dangerous departure from a stability-oriented monetary union, and a threat to German welfare and democracy.[151]

In turn, the German Court has not been unwilling to serve as a forum for such dissent. Not only does the Court's broad interpretation of Article 38 BL make such review possible, but judges have also suggested that the lack of criticism on the EU in German political debate is a problem.[152] Justice Huber, the judge rapporteur in several of the crisis cases, has contended that the Court is an 'opposition to the mainstream'.[153]

Yet, by taking up this role, the Court ultimately limits the scope for political decision-making, both within the *Bundestag* as well as on the European level. Although the Court upheld the core elements of the EU's crisis response, its focus on the *Bundestag*'s budgetary sovereignty lends support to claims that the Member States should remain responsible for their own debts in a stability-oriented EMU.

2012); Jasper von Altenbockum, 'Schwache Chefs' *Frankfurter Allgemeine Zeitung* (Frankfurt, 17 April 2012);Günter Bannas, 'Auch Abweichler dürfen lange reden' *Frankfurter Allgemeine Zeitung* (Frankfurt, 16 April 2012);Thorsten Denker, 'Lammert gegen alle' *Süddeutsche Zeitung* (Munich, 29 September 2011).

150 The phrase 'chamber for Euro-critics' comes from Interview with Christoph Mollers, Professor of Public Law and Jurisprudence, Faculty of Law, Humboldt-University Berlin and representative of the German *Bundestag* in the ESM case (Berlin, Germany, 20 April 2015) (hereafter Interview Möllers).

151 Kietz, 'Politisierung trotz Parteienkonsens' (n 125) 44. For example, in May 2010 Peter Gauweiler opposed the EFSF, together with two other dissenting CDU/CSU members, in language that resembled the GFCC's *Maastricht* judgment: 'They argued that the assistance measures entailed a break with an EMU based on the pillars of sound budgetary policies and price stability contrary to the articles, but in any case against the spirit of the existing European Treaties'. Plenarprotokoll 17/44 EFSF second plenary (n 117) 4500. Similar concerns were expressed by *Bundestag* members that either abstained or voted against the legislation, see eg Frank Schäffler of the FDP, Plenarprotokoll 17/44 EFSF second plenary (n 117) 4496; Alexander Funk (CDU/CSU), 4493–94; Veronika Bellman (CDU/CSU), 4491–93; and Hermann Otto Solms (FDP), 4498–99. Gauweiler subsequently filed a constitutional complaint against the aid to Greece, the EFSM, and the EFSF arguing that 'the concept of the stability union provided for by the Treaty is permanently destroyed and replaced by the completely different concept of a liability and transfer union'. BVerfG, *Greek loan facility and EFSF* (n 39) para 42.

152 Interview with former judge at the German Federal Constitutional Court (Berlin, Germany 20 April 2015); Interview with Peter Huber, Judge at the German Federal Constitutional Court and judge rapporteur in most EU-related cases (Karlsruhe, Germany, 23 April 2015) (hereafter Interview Huber). Another former judge was more cautious and rejects this as a constitutionally relevant ground: Interview with former judge at the German Federal Constitutional Court (Bonn, Germany, 29 June 2015). Christoph Möllers as an observer also sees this as a reason for the Court's role: Interview Möllers (n 150).

153 Franz Mayer, 'Rebel Without a Cause? A Critical Analysis of the German Constitutional Court's OMT Reference' (2014) 15 German Law Journal 111, 142; Mattias Wendel, 'Exceeding Judicial Competence in the Name of Democracy: The German Federal Constitutional Court's OMT Reference' (2014) 10 European Constitutional Law Review 263, 283 and the references on that page. Similar remarks were made by Huber in a personal interview: Interview Huber (n 152). There he argued that in his view there was a big gap between the ideas on Europe of the political elites and the wider population.

More difficult to square with the GFCC's reading of the constitution is the position that the EU should have more competences in economic and fiscal policy, and that Member States should jointly issue debt in order to make the monetary union more viable and democratic.

5.3 Constraining Political Debate: The Constitutional Disqualification of Eurobonds

The German political discussions on introducing Eurobonds offer the clearest example of how the GFCC's case law constrained political debate.[154] Eurobonds are commonly defined as bonds issued by all the eurozone Member States together or by the EU at a uniform interest rate. For these bonds, the eurozone Member States would have joint and several liability.[155] The idea is that the introduction of such bonds would lower the cost of borrowing for financially troubled eurozone states, because the interest rate on Eurobonds would be the same or possibly even lower than the weighted average of the national bonds' interest rates. Yet, the introduction of Eurobonds creates a moral hazard, as it could reduce the Member States' incentives to maintain budgetary discipline. In addition, the common liability that such bonds would entail raises a democratic concern, because it makes one Member State liable for the budgetary policy choices of others. To remedy this problem, the introduction of Eurobonds would probably have to be accompanied by further competence transfers in the sphere of economic policy, with requisite democratic legitimation at the European level. Eurobonds would probably also be incompatible with the no-bailout provision of Article 125 TFEU, insofar as the euro area Member States would be liable for the commitments of each other.[156]

On 5 December 2010, while negotiations on the ESM were already considerably advanced, Luxembourg's Treasury Minister, Jean-Claude Juncker, and Italy's

[154] The discussion on Eurobonds is crucial. As Matthijs and McNamara have noted: 'Eurobonds were a plausible functional response to the ills that plagued Europe's monetary union, yet they were set aside in favor of policies of austerity and structural reform, even as they arguably made the problem worse. Telling the story of the rise and fall of Eurobonds allows us to understand the entanglement of economic policymaking around the euro, a project at the heart of European integration and critical to its future path.' Matthijs and McNamara 'Northern Saints, Southern Sinners' (n 96) 232.

[155] For early proposal, see Paul de Grauwe and Wim Moesen, 'Gains for All: A Proposal for a Common Euro Bond' (2009) 3 Intereconomics 132. One of the best-known proposals is the Blue Bond proposal: Jacques Della and Jakob von Weizsäcker, 'The Blue Bond Proposal' (2010) 3 Bruegel Policy Brief <http://bruegel.org/wp-content/uploads/imported/publications/1005-PB-Blue_Bonds.pdf> accessed 2 August 2022; Franz Mayer and Christian Heidfeld, 'Verfassungs- und europarechtliche Aspekte der Einführung von Eurobonds' (2012) Neue Juristische Wochenschrift 422, 422–27 (hereafter Mayer and Heidfeld, 'Einführung von Eurobonds'); also Pisani-Ferry, *The Euro Crisis* (n 5) 147–48.

[156] See Merino, 'Legal Developments in the Economic and Monetary Union' (n 13) 1630–32. See, on these issues, also Expert Group on Debt Redemption Fund and Eurobills, 'Final Report' (2014) <http://ec.europa.eu/economy_finance/articles/governance/2014-03-31-redemption_fund_and_eurobills_en.htm> accessed 2 August 2022.

Minister of Economy and Finance, Giulio Tremonti, published an article in the *Financial Times* arguing for the introduction of Eurobonds as a more lasting solution to the crisis.[157] The German government swiftly rejected this proposal, because it would make Germany responsible for the debts of other states, lead to higher interest rates on German government bonds, and would also remove the incentives for Member States to have budgetary discipline.[158] The SPD, however, expressed cautious support. On 14 December 2010, SPD party leader Frank-Walter Steinmeier and former Finance Minister Peer Steinbrück wrote in the *Financial Times* that a better approach to the euro crisis was needed. They called for 'a combination of a haircut for debt holders, debt guarantees for stable countries and the limited introduction of European-wide bonds in the medium term, accompanied by more aligned fiscal policies'.[159] Eurobonds would have to be accompanied by 'political reforms' that would allow 'European institutions to establish tighter controls over fiscal and economic stability, alongside common minimum standards on wage and welfare policies, as well as capital and corporate taxation'.[160]

In the *Bundestag* debate of the following day, Steinmeier called for the introduction of Eurobonds within a fully-fledged political union. This political union aimed to remove the EMU's birth defects and put in place clear rules for sound budgetary policies, combined with harmonization in the fields of labour policy, social policy, and tax law.[161] The Greens had already expressed support for Eurobonds as a short-term measure in March 2010. Like the SPD, they had then already called for more EU action in the area of labour, social, and tax policy, and more generally for a democratically legitimated European economic government.[162] Party leader Trittin articulated similar ideas in the *Bundestag* debate of 15 December 2010 and criticized Merkel as a 'teutonic savings monster' ('*teutonisches Sparmonster*').[163] Die Linke also expressed support for Eurobonds, and even for bond buying by the ECB as a transitional solution, before a 'fundamental revision of the Lisbon Treaty' could be realized.[164] The opposition parties thus proposed significant competence transfers to the EU level in areas that the GFCC had determined as 'sovereignty sensitive' in its *Lisbon* ruling. Yet, for these parties the aim was precisely to prevent

157 Jean-Claude Juncker and Giulio Tremonti, 'E-bonds Would End the Crisis' *Financial Times* (London, 6 December 2010).

158 'Merkel bleibt bei Euro-Bonds hart' *ZEIT ONLINE* (Berlin,15 December 2010); 'Merkel wehrt sich gegen Arroganz-Vorwürfe' *ZEIT ONLINE* (Berlin, 16 December 2010).

159 Frank-Walter Steinmeier and Peer Steinbrück, 'Germany Must Lead Fightback' *Financial Times* (London, 14 December 2010).

160 ibid. Peter Ludlow, 'Doing Whatever is Required? The European Council of 16–17 December 2010' 8(4) Eurocomment Briefing Note (Brussels, 2011) 12–14.

161 Plenarprotokoll 17/80, Stenografischer Bericht der 80. Sitzung des Deutschen Bundestages am 15. Dezember 2010 (hereafter Plenarprotokoll 17/80 debate on European Council), 8820–23.

162 Bündnis 90/Die Grünen, Zukunft der Währungsunion—Zukunft Europas, Konsequenzen aus der Schuldenkrise in Griechenland, Fraktionsbeschluss of 15 March 2010.

163 Trittin, Plenarprotokoll 17/80 debate on European Council (n 161) 8829.

164 Lötschz, Plenarprotokoll 17/80 debate on European Council (n 161) 8826.

harmful competition between Member States, that in their view effectively undermined national democratic choices. As a proposed SPD resolution put it: 'The European Union is and remains our chance to shape globalisation.'[165]

The GFCC's judgment on the EFSF of September 2011, however, raised constitutional doubts about the opposition's proposals, the idea of Eurobonds in particular. In that case, the Court declared complaints about the no-bailout clause inadmissible, but did hold as constitutionally impermissible 'an intergovernmentally or supranationally agreed automatic guarantee or performance which is not subject to strict requirements and whose effects are not limited, which—once it has been set in motion—is removed from the Bundestag's control and influence'.[166] On this basis, some German scholars have concluded that Eurobonds and similar instruments for the mutualization of debt were constitutionally impermissible.[167] An additional constitutional hurdle for Eurobonds is that, according to the GFCC, there is a quantitative limit to the liabilities that the German *Bundestag* can constitutionally agree to.[168]

The Court's ruling shifted the terms of the political debate, as the governing parties invoked the judgment to disqualify the opposition's support for Eurobonds. In addition, the coalition parties used the judgment to underline that their handling of the crisis had been the right approach. In a debate on budgetary matters held on the day of the judgment, Chancellor Merkel argued that the Court had confirmed the government's approach of 'self-responsibility and solidarity'. By this she meant that Member States would remain responsible for their own budgetary policies and that assistance would be conditional on debtor states' steps towards sound budgetary policies.[169] In the subsequent parliamentary debates on changes to the EFSF, spokespersons of the governing parties used the GFCC's judgment to criticize the opposition's stance on Eurobonds. Norbert Barthle of the CDU/CSU stated, for example:

> Dear colleagues of red and green, the Federal Constitutional Court opinion is unambiguous: under the given conditions Euro-Bonds are unconstitutional. Therefore, it is astonishing, how the SPD and Greens now difficultly distance themselves from these Euro-Bonds, while for weeks and months they

[165] Entschließungsantrag der Fraktion der SPD zu der Abgabe einer Regierungserklärung durch die Bundeskanzlerin zum Europäischen Rat am 16./17. Dezember 2010 in Brüssel, BT-Dr 17/4183 of 14.12.2010, 6.

[166] BVerfG, *Greek loan facility and EFSF* (n 39) para 127; BVerfG, *ESM* final ruling (n 42) para 164.

[167] See eg Christoph Gröpl, 'Schritte zur Europäisierung des Haushaltsrechts' (2013) 52 Der Staat 1, 15.

[168] Not all modalities of Eurobonds may raise constitutional problems to the same extent. See also Mayer and Heidfeld, 'Einführung von Eurobonds' (n 155) 428; and see Annex 7 of Expert Group on Debt Redemption Fund and Eurobills, Final Report (Brussels 2014).

[169] Merkel, Plenarprotokoll 17/123, Stenografischer Bericht der 123. Sitzung des Deutschen Bundestages am 7. September 2011 (debate on 2012 budget), 14471.

> have previously demanded the Federal Government to introduce Euro-Bonds immediately.[170]

Rainer Brüderle of the FDP referred to the GFCC's pronouncement as 'a slap in the face for the basic idea' of Eurobonds.[171] In a newspaper article, Peter Gauweiler likewise claimed the judgment as a victory, despite the fact that his constitutional complaints had been rejected: the ruling was a victory for 'parliamentary democracy' and had put constitutional barriers in place against 'the march into a liability and debt union'.[172]

The Greens and the SPD nonetheless framed the judgment in the opposite way, arguing that Eurobonds were perfectly compatible with the *EFSF* judgment, and that the GFCC had left the road to further European integration fully open. Jürgen Trittin called the judgment a 'crushing defeat' for 'D-Mark chauvinists' within the ranks of the coalition parties.[173] He argued that 'the message from Karlsruhe' was instead that the European institutions had to be strengthened.[174] Similarly, his fellow party member Manuel Sarazzin declared that the GFCC had pointed towards the limits of the EU Treaties rather than to constitutional limits: the Court had left leeway for a pro-European line in German European politics and had in no way foreclosed the introduction of Eurobonds.[175] Axel Schäfer of the SPD declared that the GFCC 'opened the way for further European integration and thus obliges us to go this way'.[176]

Public statements by constitutional judges, however, cast doubts on this reading. In an interview with the *Frankfurter Allgemeine Zeitung* of 25 September 2011, the GFCC's President, Andreas Voßkuhle, stated that the space within the German Basic Law for further European integration was 'probably largely exhausted'.[177] The constitutionality of Eurobonds would depend on its precise modalities. Nonetheless, for the transfer of further core competences to the EU level,

170 Statement by Norbert Barthle (CDU/CSU), Plenarprotokoll 17/124, Stenografischer Bericht der 124. Sitzung des Deutschen Bundestages am 8. September 2011 (hereafter Plenarprotokoll 17/124 EFSF extension first plenary), 14573.

171 Statement by Rainer Brüderle (FDP), Plenarprotokoll 17/130 EFSF extension second plenary (n 142) 15211; Fricke of the FDP had stated the previous day in *Handelsblatt* that the GFCC had prohibited Eurobonds: "Urteil ist klare Absage an Euro-Bonds' *Handelsblatt* (Düsseldorf, 7 September 2011).

172 Peter Gauweiler and Dietrich Murswiek. 'Sieg durch Niederlage' *Focus Magazin* (19 September 2011) <www.focus.de/politik/deutschland/sieg-durch-niederlage-politik_id_2278453.html> accessed 2 August 2022.

173 Trittin (Bündnis 90/Die Grüne), Plenarprotokoll 17/124 EFSF extension first plenary (n 170) 14565.

174 ibid 14565.

175 Sarrazin (Bündnis 90/Die Grüne), Plenarprotokoll 17/124 EFSF extension first plenary (n 170) 14573.

176 Schäfer (SPD), Plenarprotokoll 17/124 EFSF extension first plenary (n 170) 14569. 'Das Bundesverfassungsgericht hat den Weg zur weiteren europäischen Integration geöffnet und uns damit verpflichtet, ihn zu gehen.'

177 Melanie Mann and Inge Kloepfer, '"Mehr Europa lässt das Grundgesetz kaum zu"' *Frankfurter Allgemeine Zeitung* (Frankfurt, 25 September 2011) (interview with Justice Andreas Vosskuhle).

a referendum for a new German constitution would be necessary.[178] A few days earlier, Justice Huber had likewise declared in the *Süddeutsche Zeitung* that the introduction of a supranational European economic government would be difficult to reconcile with the Basic Law. It would require a referendum. Huber did leave room for the introduction of Eurobonds under certain modalities, namely if the *Bundestag* plenary were to approve every tranche of bonds.[179] Yet, overall, these statements seemed to leave little doubt that the opposition's far-reaching proposals for further European integration would require a constitutional referendum.[180]

In this light, it is surprising that the opposition parties did not contest the merits of the GFCC's ruling. The opposition parties' arguments about Eurobonds fitted within a broader political narrative that gave democratic concerns a key place. However, these parties did not contrast their more pro-European interpretation of democracy with the more national sovereignty-focused conception of the Court.

The absence of contestation over the merits of GFCC judgments is consistent with the general treatment of the Court's rulings in German political debate. There is a high degree of respect for the Court's judgments, and explicit contestation by politicians is uncommon.[181] Where it happens, politicians generally do not engage with the judgments' merits, but rather criticize them as too political in nature.[182]

[178] ibid.

[179] Wolfgang Janisch and Heribert Prallt, '"Keine europaïsche Wirtschaftsregierung ohne Änderung des Grundgesetzes"' *Süddeutsche Zeitung* (München, 19 September 2011) (interview with Justice Peter Huber).

[180] In an interview with *Der Spiegel* of 23 December 2011, departing Justice Udo di Fabio and judge rapporteur for the GFCC's *Lisbon* judgment qualified Eurobonds as a mechanism that 'in principle' would raise problems with the German principle of democracy. Nonetheless, he maintained that the Karlsruhe Court had not obstructed further European integration but had instead strengthened Germany's position. He qualified Voßkuhle's remarks on the constitutional limits for further European integration as concerning 'far-reaching competence transfers, which currently are not under discussion' (34). More generally, he referred to the possible decision of the German sovereign people to enter a European federal state as 'a completely theoretical question' (36). Moreover, one of his answers betrayed a politically contested reading of the crisis, as he asked rhetorically: 'Imagine that all Member States had far underbid the stability criteria, had made their economies more competitive and had conceptually worked better together: what problem would the EU then have had at all?' ('Stellen Sie sich vor, alle Mitgliedstaaten hätten die Stabilitätskriterien weit unterboten, ihre Wirtschaft wettbewerbsfähig gemacht und konzeptionell weit besser zusammengearbeitet: Welches Problem hätte die EU heute überhaupt?') (38). See Dietmar Hipp and Thomas Darnstädt, '"Der Bundesstaat ist ein Irrtum"' *Der Spiegel* (22 December 2011) <www.spiegel.de/politik/der-bundesstaat-ist-ein-irrtum-a-205029f4-0002-0001-0000-000083328883> accessed 2 August 2022.

[181] Interview with Otto Fricke, former *Bundestag* member for the FDP and chair of the *Bundestag*'s budget committee between 2005 and 2009 (Berlin, Germany, 6 May 2015); Interview Huber (n 152); Interview with Franz Mayer, Professor of Public Law at Universität Bielefeld and representative of the German *Bundestag* in the *Lisbon* and *EFSF* cases (Berlin, Germany, 28 May 2015) (hereafter Interview Franz Mayer); Interview with former judge at the German Federal Constitutional Court (Bonn, Germany, 29 June 2015); Interview Möllers (n 150); Interview with Ingolf Pernice, Professor of Public Law, European Law and Public International Law at Humboldt-Universität zu Berlin and representative of the German *Bundestag* in the *Lisbon* case (Berlin, Germany, 16 April 2015); Gesine Lötzsch did indicate that there is more criticism of the Court than in the past, although it remained rare (Interview with Gesine Lötzsch, *Bundestag* member for Die Linke and chair of the *Bundestag*'s budget committee (Berlin, Germany, 27 May 2015)).

[182] Interview with Gesine Lötzsch, *Bundestag* member for Die Linke and chair of the *Bundestag*'s budget committee (Berlin, Germany, 27 May 2015); Interview with former judge at the German Federal

Three reasons probably explain the absence of such contestation. First, the GFCC's crisis judgments have all been 'partial victories'. For example, the SPD and the Greens were happy with the enhanced rights of the *Bundestag* in the EFSF and used this part of the judgment to criticize the governing coalition.[183] Had they criticized the GFCC, they probably would have also undermined their own reliance on the Court's authority.[184] Secondly, the GFCC enjoys broad popular support. It is therefore not in the interest of politicians to take issue with the Court's rulings.[185] Instead, it is in their interest to try and construe the judgments as perfectly compatible with their own political viewpoints or to ignore the judgment altogether. The third reason is that respect for the Court is probably informed by a belief in the separation of powers, on the basis of which the GFCC should be recognized as the ultimate authority in constitutional matters.[186] In this vein, *Bundestag* President Lammert declared in the debates on the ESM and Fiscal Compact:

> I would like to clarify that it is not the parliamentary groups that are competent for determining the constitutionality of legislation, not even the constitutional body of the German Bundestag, but the Federal Constitutional Court. I believe it is a minimum requirement of respect towards our colleagues [fellow *Bundestag* members] as well as towards this competence in our constitutional order not to claim exclusive authority in this respect.[187]

The *Bundestag* therefore does not consider itself an interpreter of the constitution equal to the GFCC. For this reason, it is difficult to maintain that the Court's judgments add to German political debate without constraining it. In the case of Eurobonds, its advantages and disadvantages had already been discussed in the prior political debates and in light of competing visions on their relation to democracy. The effect of the GFCC's ruling was that a debate on the merits of Eurobonds

Constitutional Court (Bonn, Germany, 29 June 2015); Interview Franz Mayer (n 181). See also Michaela Hailbronner, 'We the Experts. Die geschlossene Gesellschaft der Verfassungsinterpreten' (2014) 53(3) Der Staat 425.

[183] See Sarrazin (Bündnis 90/Die Grüne), Plenarprotokoll 17/124 EFSF extension first plenary (n 170) 14572 and Schäfer (SPD), 14569. For more details, see the next chapter.

[184] Gesine Lötzsch of Die Linke, and chair of the *Bundestag*'s budget committee declared, for example, that Die Linke 'felt always partly supported by the judgments'. Interview with Gesine Lötzsch, *Bundestag* member for Die Linke and chair of the *Bundestag*'s budget committee (Berlin, Germany, 27 May 2015).

[185] Interview with Otto Fricke, former *Bundestag* member for the FDP and chair of the *Bundestag*'s budget committee between 2005 and 2009 (Berlin, Germany, 6 May 2015); Interview Franz Mayer (n 181); Interview with former judge at the German Federal Constitutional Court (Bonn, Germany, 29 June 2015).

[186] This was a view expressed by Lothar Binding (SPD), *Bundestag* member for the SPD, in an interview held in Berlin, Germany, 29 April 2015.

[187] Lammert, Plenarprotokoll 17/188 ESM and Fiscal Compact second plenary (n 142) 22735. Similar points were made by Lothar Binding, Plenarprotokoll 17/188, 22757 and Otto Fricke, Plenarprotokoll 17/188, 22726.

was partly replaced by an interpretive debate over the Court's ruling. In addition, the governing coalition tried to use the judgment to simply move the topic off the parliamentary agenda.

Nonetheless, the GFCC's judgment did not push Eurobonds off the agenda entirely.[188] In the final debate on the ESM and the TSCG of June 2012, Sigmar Gabriel of the SPD still expressed some cautious support: the introduction of Eurobonds would require a 'real fiscal union' and a 'European finance minister'.[189] In the 2013 *Bundestag* elections, the Greens also still supported the introduction of Eurobonds in the medium term. Both the SPD and the Greens favoured a debt redemption fund as a more lasting solution, in which debts above 60 per cent would be mutualized.[190] Yet, on 29 October 2013, the German newspaper *Die Zeit* reported that the SPD no longer supported the introduction of Eurobonds within the coalition talks with the CDU/CSU. The newspaper quoted SPD negotiator Martin Schulz as stating that their introduction would not be constitutionally possible and reported that the idea had in any case been controversial within the party.[191]

5.4 Exploring the Constitutional Limits: Debating a Constitutional Referendum

The GFCC's *EFSF* judgment and the newspaper interviews of Justices Voßkuhle and Huber sparked a debate about whether Germany should have a constitutional referendum on further European integration.[192] In November 2011, the SPD's Michael Roth pleaded for a constitutional referendum on further European integration.[193] By the summer of 2012, various high-profile politicians supported the idea. By

[188] 'Rot-Grün distanziert sich von Hollandes Euro-Bonds' *Die Welt* (Hamburg, 24 May 2012); 'SPD und Grüne schlagen Alternative zu Euro-Bonds vor' *ZEIT ONLINE* (Berlin, 24 May 2012).

[189] Plenarprotokoll 17/188 ESM and Fiscal Compact second plenary (n 142) 22702.

[190] Othmara Glas, 'Grüne: Für Eurobonds und europäischen Mindestlohn' *Euractiv* (31 July 2013) <www.euractiv.de/section/wahlen-und-macht/news/grune-fur-eurobonds-und-europaischen-mindestlohn/> accessed 2 August 2022; Othmara Glas, 'SPD: Für Euro-Haftung und Rückübertragung von EU-Kompetenzen' *Euractiv* (23 July 2013) <www.euractiv.de/section/wahlen-und-macht/news/spd-fur-euro-haftung-und-ruckubertragung-von-eu-kompetenzen/> accessed 2 August 2022; SPD, 'Das wir entscheidet, das Regierungsprogramm 2013–2017' <www.spd.de/fileadmin/Dokumente/Beschluesse/Bundesparteitag/20130415_regierungsprogramm_2013_2017.pdf> accessed 2 August 2022. The debt redemption fund was proposed by the German Council of Economic Experts in 2011 and subsequently endorsed by the SPD and Greens. See Sachverständigenrat zur Begutachtung der gesamtwirtschaftlichen Entwicklung, 'Jahresgutachten 2011/12 "Verantwortung für Europa wahrnehmen"' Bonifatius GmbH Buch-Druck-Verlag (Paderborn); see also Mayer, *Europe's Unfinished Currency* (n 5) 114–15.

[191] Lisa Caspari, 'Teambuilding-Maßnahme Europa' *ZEIT ONLINE* (Berlin, 29 October 2013).

[192] See eg the article by Horst Dreier who argued that a constitutional assembly could also be an option. Horst Dreier, 'Verfassungsreform: Ein neues Deutschland' *ZEIT ONLINE* (Berlin, 20 October 2011).

[193] Michael Roth, 'Für eine Volksabstimmung über Europa' *Euractiv* (14 November 2011) <www.euractiv.de/section/prioritaten-der-eu-fur-2020/opinion/fur-eine-volksabstimmung-uber-europa/> accessed 2 August 2022; *Der Spiegel* reported in November 2011 that Merkel and Schäuble supported holding a referendum: 'Merkel Eyes Constitution Revamp to Boost EU Powers' *Spiegel Online* (Hamburg, 14 November 2011).

this time, the GFCC had ruled on issues related to the crisis in two further judgments.[194] In June, newspapers reported that Finance Minister Schäuble supported a referendum for an extensive reform of the European institutions. This would include common budgetary policies, an EU finance minister, and a banking union, as well as a strengthened European Parliament and a directly chosen Commission President.[195] Peer Steinbrück of the SPD similarly supported a referendum: 'Who has listened attentively to the constitutional judges knows that things cannot be done differently.'[196] The chairman of the CSU, Horst Seehofer, had already supported introducing referenda on European issues in February 2012[197] and now supported Schäuble's plea.[198] Merkel, however, was much more hesitant.[199]

The issue played a role in the *Bundestag*'s final plenary debate on the ESM and Fiscal Compact of 29 June 2012. The SPD and the Greens again argued that a real political union should be developed with further power transfer to the EU. This was to be coupled to a democratization of the European decision-making process, primarily through a strengthening of the European Parliament. The SPD accompanied this proposal by calls for a referendum, as Sigmar Gabriel declared:

> For a real political Union we need new democratic structures and also the transfer of national sovereign rights to the European level. Many of these can be made without a change in the Basic Law, others require changes in the Basic Law, for which one definitely should also get the agreement of our citizens through referenda. At the end certainly stands a referendum on our Constitution.[200]

The call for a referendum fitted the SPD's long-standing support for direct democracy. Gabriel also justified his proposal in order to prevent the EU from staying an 'elite project'.[201] The preceding events, however, do indicate that the GFCC's case law played a role. The discussion on holding a constitutional referendum only really started after Huber and Voßkuhle had pointed in this direction.[202]

194 BVerfG, *Neuner Gremium* (n 40). BVerfG, *Information on ESM and Euro Plus Pact Negotiations* (n 41).

195 'Schäuble erwartet Volksabstimmung über neue Verfassung' *Handelsblatt* (24 June 2012); 'Spitzenpolitiker rechnen mit Volksabstimmung in Deutschland' *Spiegel Online* (Hamburg, 24 June 2012).

196 Quoted in 'Schäuble erwartet Volksabstimmung über neue Verfassung' (n 195).

197 Jochen Gaugele, Claus Christian Malzahn, and Daniel Friedrich Sturm, 'Seehofer fordert Volksabstimmung über Euro-Rettung' *Die Welt* (Hamburg, 12 February 2012).

198 'Seehofer unterstützt Schäubles Vorstoß' *Frankfurter Allgemeine Zeitung* (Frankfurt, 26 June 2012).

199 'Merkel rechnet nicht mit baldiger Volksabstimmung' *Frankfurter Allgemeine Zeitung* (Frankfurt, 25 June 2012).

200 Gabriel (SPD), Plenarprotokoll 17/188 ESM and Fiscal Compact second plenary (n 142) 22706.

201 Gabriel (SPD), Plenarprotokoll 17/188 ESM and Fiscal Compact second plenary (n 142) 22707.

202 The Greens, however, did not support the calls for a referendum, although they did call for a fundamental change in Europe's political constitution. Trittin (Bündis 90/Die Grünen), Plenarprotokoll 17/188 ESM and Fiscal Compact second plenary (n 142) 22714. They supported a constitutional assembly that would deal with constitutional questions after a comprehensive reform of the European treaties had been adopted by a European convention. The party supported Europe-wide referenda after

Support for a referendum could also be found at the other end of the political spectrum, namely by dissenters in the FDP and CSU that opposed the ESM and TSCG, as well as further European integration. Frank Schäffler of the FDP and Peter Gauweiler of the CSU contended that the Fiscal Compact and ESM presented a step towards a European state and that a referendum was necessary.[203] Perhaps surprisingly, Die Linke made the same argument during the first plenary on the ESM and Fiscal Compact, because it heavily opposed both instruments. The party, however, did not oppose a federal Europe 'if it concerned a social, free, democratic and ecological Europe of the peoples'.[204]

In August 2012, newspapers reported that the FDP's parliamentary leader, Rainer Brüderle, supported holding a referendum on further steps in tackling the euro crisis.[205] Opposing reasons motivated the different parties. Gabriel of the SPD and CDU Finance Minister Schäuble wanted a referendum to achieve further steps in European integration. Seehofer of the CSU and Brüderle of the FDP, on the other hand, favoured a referendum precisely to prevent this result and particularly to prevent further money flowing to debtor countries.[206]

The debate appeared to have come to an end in the coalition negotiations of 2013 between the CDU, CSU, and SPD. The CSU and SPD initially agreed on a proposal to introduce referenda at the federal level that would give German citizens a say on European issues.[207] Nonetheless, the CDU opposed the idea and moved the proposal off the table.[208]

a change to the European Treaties. In April 2016, the leader of the German Greens in the European Parliament, Rebecca Harms, spoke out against referenda in single Member States that affected the EU as a whole: 'Grünen-Abgeordnete lehnt EU-Volksabstimmungen ab' *Spiegel Online* (8 April 2016) <www.spiegel.de/politik/ausland/referendum-in-den-niederlanden-harms-ist-gegen-volksabstimmungen-a-1086067.html> accessed 2 August 2022.

[203] Gauweiler (CDU/CSU), Plenarprotokoll 17/188 ESM and Fiscal Compact second plenary (n 142) 22724–25.

[204] Gysi (Die Linke), Plenarprotokoll 17/172, Stenografischer Bericht der 172. Sitzung des Deutschen Bundestages am 29. März 2012 (hereafter Plenarprotokoll 17/172 ESM and Fiscal Compact first plenary), 20220.

[205] 'Brüderle hält Volksabstimmung über EU-Zukunft für möglich' *Frankfurter Allgemeine Zeitung* (Frankfurt, 10 August 2012); Ludwig Greven, 'Das Volk fragen—aber verantwortungsvoll' *ZEIT ONLINE* (Berlin, 14 August 2012) (hereafter Greven, 'Volk fragen'). For the viewpoint of *Bundestag* President Lammert, see 'Lammert hält verfassungsgebende Versammlung für vorstellbar' *Süddeutsche Zeitung* (München, 1 July 2012).

[206] Greven, 'Volk fragen' (n 205).

[207] 'Volksabstimmungen bundesweit geplant' *Die Welt* (Hamburg, 12 November 2013); Robert Roßmann, 'Union und SPD wollen bundesweite Volksabstimmungen' *Süddeutsche Zeitung* (München, 12 November 2013)

[208] 'CDU will keine Volksabstimmungen auf Bundesebene' *Handelsblatt* (Düsseldorf, 12 November 2013); Philipp Wittrock, 'CDU beerdigt Pläne für Volksabstimmungen' *Spiegel Online* (Hamburg, 12 November 2013).

5.5 The Increasing Importance of Constitutional Arguments: The Fiscal Compact and ESM Debates

Besides the discussion on the referendum, arguments about constitutional limits to European integration came to play a more important role in the German crisis debates over time. In the parliamentary debates on the ESM and the Fiscal Compact of March and June 2012, a whole range of arguments were made with reference to the Basic Law. This can also be explained by the fact that the proposed measures were simply very far-reaching: all parties regarded the discussions as fundamental in nature.[209] Still, the GFCC's rulings left their mark. First, in light of a GFCC judgment of 19 June 2012,[210] the coalition parties considered that both the ESM Treaty and the Fiscal Compact qualified as 'matters concerning the EU' within the meaning of Article 23(1) and (2) BL.[211] To remove any constitutional doubts, the coalition parties decided that a two-thirds constitutional majority should adopt the Treaties.[212] In return for their support for the measures, the SPD and Greens obtained agreement on a 'Pact for sustainable growth and employment'. In the Pact, the four parliamentary groups agreed to introduce a financial transaction tax, even if not all EU Member States would participate. In addition, the Pact provided for initiatives on growth and employment and action against youth unemployment.[213] Nonetheless, the *Frankfurter Allgemeine Zeitung* reported that the governing coalition had rejected any mention of a 'debt redemption fund' by pointing to constitutional objections from Karlsruhe.[214]

209 Volker Kauder of the CDU/CSU called the decisions 'existential' for Europe. Plenarprotokoll 17/188 ESM and Fiscal Compact second plenary (n 142) 22711. In the same debate, Brüderle of the FDP spoke of 'constitutionally uncharted territory' (22707). Gabriel of the SPD stated Europe had arrived at 'a crossroads' (22706). Trittin of the Greens spoke of the 'challenge to re-establish this Europe' (22714). Sahra Wagenknecht of Die Linke spoke of a 'coup against the Basic Law' (22710).

210 BVerfG, *Information on ESM and Euro Plus Pact Negotiations* (n 41). The case is discussed in more detail in the next chapter.

211 For the Fiscal Compact, however, the coalition parties had already decided in March 2012 that ratification required a constitutional majority. See legal proposal: Gesetzentwurf der Fraktionen der CDU/CSU und FDP, Entwurf eines Gesetzes zu dem Vertrag vom 2. März 2012 über Stabilität, Koordinierung und Steuerung in der Wirtschafts- und Währungsunion, BT-Dr 17/9046 of 20.03.2012, 18; Finance Minister Schäuble, Plenarprotokoll 17/172 ESM and Fiscal Compact first plenary (n 204) 20213.

212 Bericht des Haushaltsausschusses (8. Ausschuss)—a) zu dem Gesetzentwurf der Fraktionen der CDU/CSU und FDP—Drucksache 17/9045—Entwurf eines Gesetzes zu dem Vertrag vom 2. Februar 2012 zur Einrichtung des Europäischen Stabilitätsmechanismus (and other matters), BT-Dr 17/10172 of 28.06.2012, 5–6 and 8; Bericht des Haushaltsausschusses (8. Ausschuss) a) zu dem Gesetzentwurf der Fraktionen der CDU/CSU und FDP—Drucksache 17/9046 –Entwurf eines Gesetzes zu dem Vertrag vom 2. März 2012 über Stabilität, Koordinierung und Steuerung in der Wirtschafts- und Währungsunion (and other matters), BT-Dr 17/10171 of 28.06.2012, 3.

213 Gemeinsames Papier der Bundesregierung und der Fraktionen CDU/CSU, FDP, SPD und Bündnis 90/Die Grünen im Deutschen Bundestag vom 21. Juni 2012, 'Pakt für nachhaltiges Wachstum und Beschäftigung' <https://archiv.bundesregierung.de/ContentArchiv/DE/Archiv17/_Anlagen/2012/06/2012-06-21-wachstum-pakt.pdf?__blob=publicationFile&v=3> accessed 2 August 2022; see also Jasper von Altenbockum, 'Donnerkeil und Sänfte' *Frankfurter Allgemeine Zeitung* (Frankfurt, 28 June 2012).

214 'Gauck unterzeichnet Fiskalpakt vorerst nicht' *Frankfurter Allgemeine Zeitung* (Frankfurt, 21 June 2012); on this proposal and its constitutionality, see Frank Schorkopf, 'Verfassungsrechtliche Grenzen und Möglichkeitenfür eine Umsetzung des Schuldentilgungspaktes des Sachverständigenrates'

Secondly, Die Linke invoked the GFCC's case law to attack the measures. The party fiercely opposed both the ESM and the Fiscal Compact. Die Linke's concerns were mostly directed at the Fiscal Compact. Party leader Gysi argued that the Compact violated the democracy principle and the eternity clause of the Basic Law.[215] Laying down debt brakes in an international treaty without the possibility for change would force the Member States into permanent austerity politics. This would be a significant violation of the *Bundestag*'s budgetary powers, as the GFCC had determined in its *Lisbon* judgment.[216] The party also argued against the ESM on constitutional grounds, which in its view would impair the budgetary rights of the *Bundestag*, as the extent of liabilities was potentially unrestricted.[217] The party's resistance to the ESM was perhaps more surprising, given that Die Linke had consistently favoured more solidarity in the EU. Still, the party opposed the ESM because, in its view, the risk of state insolvencies and debt cuts would be transferred to the ordinary taxpayer rather than to the banks and the wealthy. Die Linke instead favoured setting up a European bank for public loans with the ability to refinance itself at the ECB. This would decouple state finances from the financial markets.[218] In a resolution, Die Linke also called for a fundamental reform of the EU Treaties to be negotiated in a European Convention, and to be subjected to a referendum afterwards. Among other things, the Treaty reform should make the social state a founding principle of the EU, introduce EU-wide minimum wages, cancel free movement of capital, provide a basis for the coordination of tax policies, delete or change the provisions on excessive deficits, as well as do away with the ECB's mandate focused on price stability.[219] Following the conclusion of the parliamentary debates, Die Linke took its constitutional concerns to the GFCC.

Sachverständigenrat zur Begutachtung der gesamtwirtschaftlichen Entwicklung, Gutachten of 20 July 2012 <www.sachverstaendigenrat-wirtschaft.de/fileadmin/dateiablage/download/publikationen/rechtsgutachten_schuldentilgungspakt.pdf> accessed 2 August 2022.

[215] Arts 20 and 79(3) BL.

[216] Plenarprotokoll 17/172 ESM and Fiscal Compact first plenary (n 204) 20219–20; and 22720. See also Antrag der Abgeordneten Alexander Ulrich, Wolfgang Gehrcke, Jan van Aken, Christine Buchholz, Sevim Dağdelen, Dr Diether Dehm, Werner Dreibus, Annette Groth, Heike Hänsel, Inge Höger, Dr Barbara Höll, Andrej Hunko, Harald Koch, Niema Movassat, Thomas Nord, Paul Schäfer (Köln), Michael Schlecht, Kathrin Vogler, Sahra Wagenknecht, Katrin Werner, und der Fraktion Die Linke, BT-Dr 17/9147 of 27.03.2012. Similar arguments against the Fiscal Compact can be found in Plenarprotokoll 17/188 ESM and Fiscal Compact second plenary (n 142) and the declarations of (all Die Linke): Matthias Birkwald, 22757–58; Wolfgang Gehrcke, 22736; Heike Hänsel, 22734–35; Christine Bucholz, 22759–60; Dagmar Enkelmann, 22762–63; Nicole Gohlke, 22765; Annette Groth, 22766–67; Harald Koch, 22770; Kathrin Vogler, 22784–85; Inge Höger, Andrej Hunko, Ulla Jelpke, Alexander Süßmair, and Katrin Werner, 22794–95.

[217] BT-Dr 17/10172 (n 212) 7.

[218] ibid 7–8. See also Antrag der Abgeordneten Dr Gesine Lötzsch, Dr Kirsten Tackmann, Dr Dietmar Bartsch, Herbert Behrens, Karin Binder, Heidrun Bluhm, Steffen Bockhahn, Roland Claus, Katrin Kunert, Caren Lay, Sabine Leidig, Michael Leutert, Thomas Lutze, Kornelia Möller, Wolfgang Neskovic, Jens Petermann, Ingrid Remmers, Dr Ilia Seifert, Kersten Steinke, Sabine Stüber, Alexander Süßmair, und der Fraktion Die Linke, BT-Dr 17/9146 of 27.03.2012.

[219] BT-Dr 17/9148 of 27.03.2012: Antrag der Abgeordneten Dr Diether Dehm, Andrej Hunko, Thomas Nord, Alexander Ulrich, Wolfgang Gehrcke, Jan van Aken, Christine Buchholz, Sevim

Thirdly, several *Bundestag* members within the SPD and the Greens raised similar arguments against the Fiscal Compact as Die Linke. The Fiscal Compact would lead to permanent austerity politics with troubling social consequences. They also argued that the Treaty violated the Basic Law, or at least raised serious democratic concerns, because it significantly restricted the *Bundestag*'s budgetary powers. In their view, an alternative approach was required with more solidarity, competence transfers to the European level in economic and fiscal policy, as well as enhancing structures for democratic legitimation at the EU level.[220]

Fourthly, within the CDU/CSU and FDP, German liabilities under the ESM raised more concerns. The coalition parties qualified the Fiscal Compact as an essential element of a sustainable stability union ('*dauernhaften Stabilitätsunion*'). For them, the ESM and the Fiscal Compact presented two sides of the same coin, a nexus between 'solidarity and solidity'.[221] A number of parliamentarians from the CDU/CSU and FDP, however, argued that the ESM went too far: it made Germany liable for the debts of other states, turned the eurozone into a transfer union, and effectively transformed the EU into a federal state. They considered this result to be not only economically unsound, but also contrary to Article 38 BL and the GFCC's case law. The main problem, in their view, had not been the absence of a political union tied to EMU, but the violation of the no-bailout clause in 2010. Rather than criticizing the Fiscal Compact from a democratic perspective, they named it a 'toothless tiger': an inadequate means to ensure sound budgetary policies.[222]

By June 2012, the GFCC's case law was thus invoked from different ends of the political spectrum to oppose the ESM and Fiscal Compact. The GFCC's rulings on the ESM and Fiscal Compact nonetheless appear to have affected the various

Dagˇdelen, Werner Dreibus, Annette Groth, Heike Hänsel, Inge Höger, Harald Koch, Niema Movassat, Wolfgang Neskovic, Paul Schäfer (Köln), Michael Schlecht, Kathrin Vogler, Sahra Wagenknecht, Katrin Werner, und der Fraktion Die Linke.

220 See, for such concerns, Plenarprotokoll 17/188 ESM and Fiscal Compact second plenary (n 142) and the vote declarations of: Marco Bulow (SPD), 22760–61; Dr Matthias Miersch (SPD), 2272–73; Beate Müller-Gemmeke (Bündnis 90/Die Grünen), 22774–75; Swen Schulz (Spandau) (SPD), 22778; Wolfgang Strengmann-Kuhn (Bündnis 90/Die Grünen), 22781–83; Hans-Christian Ströbele (Bündnis 90/Die Grünen), 22783–84; joint declaration of Lisa Paus, Katja Dörner, and Sven-Christian Kindler (Bündnis 90/Diegrünen), 22789–90; Gerhard Schick, Maria Klein-Schmeink, and Sylvia Kotting-Uhl (Bündnis 90/Die Grünen), 22791–93; Anton Hofreiter, Ulrich Schneider, and Beate Walter-Rosenheimer (all Bündnis 90/Die Grünen), 22793–94; joint declaration of Werner Schieder (Weiden), Klaus Barthel, Wolfgang Gunkel, Gabriele Hiller-Ohm, Daniela Kolbe (Leipzig), Hilde Mattheis, Ottmar Schreiner, Rüdiger Veit, und Waltraud Wolff (Wolmirstedt) (SPD), 22797.

221 Merkel, Plenarprotokoll 17/188 ESM and Fiscal Compact second plenary (n 142) 22699. Finance Minister Schäuble, Plenarprotokoll 17/172 ESM and Fiscal Compact first plenary (n 204) 20210–13.

222 Bellmann (CDU/CSU), Plenarprotokoll 17/188 ESM and Fiscal Compact second plenary (n 142) 22752, 22751–53; Frank Schäffler, Sylvia Canel, and Dr Lutz Knopek (all FDP), Manfred Kolbe und Klaus-Peter Willsch (CDU/CSU), 22795–97. In between these different positions Peter Danckert and Rolf Schwanitz of the SPD took a middle position. They argued both that the possible German liabilities under the ESM exceeded the permissible constitutional limits, as well as that the Fiscal Compact limited the *Bundestag*'s budgetary sovereignty to a constitutionally impermissible extent. For these reasons, they announced a challenge to the measures before the GFCC. Peter Danckert (SPD), 22723–24; Rolf Schwanitz (SPD), 22779–81.

concerns differently. The Court upheld the ESM Treaty, but also ruled that German liabilities should be clearly limited, following the logic of the Euro-critics on the political right. The Fiscal Compact appeared to cause less concern as the Court had always attached key importance to budgetary discipline by qualifying the EMU as a community of stability. Moreover, the Court held that the Fiscal Compact could be justified to avoid problematic levels of debt in the long run that would limit the *Bundestag*'s budgetary powers. Yet, this argument could probably have been made for all of the crisis measures, as their introduction always aimed at securing the eurozone's financial stability. Another crisis would surely have had negative repercussions for the Member States' debt positions. The one-sidedness of the GFCC's views is reflected in the extra-judicial writing of Andreas Voßkuhle, President of the GFCC at the time, as he claimed that the Court's case law was a reason for the adoption of the Fiscal Compact in the first place:

> The obligation of the Member States, laid down in the Fiscal Compact, to submit a balanced budget and to introduce a national debt brake also borrows from the case-law of the Federal Constitutional Court. It aims at maintaining budgetary discipline and therefore takes account of the constitutional requirement to safeguard the parliaments' budgetary sovereignty.[223]

5.6 A Constitutional Referendum as a Way Out?

With its case law, the GFCC put in place constitutional hurdles against steps towards mutualization of debts and more integration in economic and fiscal policy, even though calls for such steps were rooted in democratic arguments. The available evidence shows that in this manner the Court's case law constrained political debate about different visions of the monetary union's future. Yet the justices themselves provided a possible way out by arguing that a popular referendum would be sufficient to overcome these constitutional hurdles. Ultimately, Karlsruhe's case law may therefore not be as undemocratic as it appears. Although there are many arguments against referenda, it seems hard to argue that they are undemocratic.

The idea that German constitutional hurdles to European integration could be overcome through a popular referendum rests on the doctrinal position that only the German people as the constituent power are able to give themselves a new constitution.[224] This position is based on Article 146 BL, which states that the Basic Law 'shall cease to apply on the day on which a constitution freely adopted by the German people takes effect'.

[223] Andreas Voßkuhle, '"European Integration Through Law": The Contribution of the Federal Constitutional Court' (2017) 58 European Journal of Sociology 145, 160.

[224] See BVerfG, *Lisbon* judgment (n 1) paras 179–80; Interview Huber (n 152).

According to Justice Huber, such a constitutional referendum would not necessarily have to result in an entirely different constitution but could also make an exception to Article 79(3) BL for European affairs.[225]

Nonetheless, the idea that a referendum would be necessary for steps in European integration beyond the limits of Article 79(3) is not merely a doctrinal position. A number of constitutional judges appear to share the idea that such a step would require a higher degree of legitimation that only the German people themselves can provide.[226] According to Justice Huber, a constitutional majority of two-thirds would not suffice, because such a majority can be obtained relatively easily. He also argues that there is 'a clear discrepancy between the political elite [. . .] and the population, not just in questions concerning Europe'.[227] More generally, Huber has a favourable view of direct democracy.[228]

Still, this idea of a constitutional referendum raises a number of questions. Firstly, the reading of Article 146 BL on which it rests is highly contested.[229] Tobias Herbst, for example, argues that Article 146 BL has lost its value since German reunification: the Article only meant to ensure that the Basic Law would not stand in the way of German reunification. To interpret Article 146 BL as an independent ground to move beyond Article 79(3) BL would disregard the purpose of Article 79(3), which, in light of the Weimar experience, aims to prevent Germany from falling into a dictatorship.[230] Moreover, the German Basic Law contains very few provisions on direct democracy.[231] As was discussed in the previous chapter, the idea of introducing more elements of direct democracy was debated by the Joint Constitutional Committee at the time of the Maastricht Treaty. A key reason why the JCC rejected the option was that it would entail a break with the clear decision of the constitution's founders, namely, that in light of the Weimar experience, Germany should have a system of representative government. In order to protect the stability of the German constitutional order, even the introduction of some elements of direct democracy was thus wholly rejected. This makes it difficult to comprehend why a referendum would then be able to legitimate an abrogation of

225 Interview Huber (n 152).

226 ibid; Interview with former judge at the German Federal Constitutional Court (Bonn, Germany, 29 June 2015).

227 Interview Huber (n 152).

228 Reinhard Müller, 'Wie demokratisch ist direkte Demokratie?' *Frankfurter Allgemeine Zeitung* (Frankfurt, 7 November 2011) <www.faz.net/aktuell/politik/volksentscheide-wie-demokratisch-ist-direkte-demokratie-11520785.html> accessed 2 August 2022.

229 Interview Franz Mayer (n 181); Interview Möllers (n 150).

230 Tobias Herbst, 'Legale Abschaffung des Grundgesetzes nach Art. 146 GG?' [2012] Zeitschrift für Rechtspolitik 33, 33–35. Similarly critical on the Court's use of art 79(3) BL as the GFCC's standard for assessing European integration were: Daniel Halberstam and Christoph Möllers, 'The German Constitutional Court Says "Ja Zu Deutschland!"' (2009) 10 German Law Journal 1241, 1254; Schönberger, 'Lisbon in Karlsruhe' (n 3) 1208; Mattias Wendel, 'The Fog of Identity and Judicial Contestation: Preventive and Defensive Constitutional Identity Review in Germany' (2021) 27 European Public Law 465.

231 In a similar vein, Interview Möllers (n 150).

the Basic Law altogether, including the guarantees of Article 79(3) that aim to preserve the integrity of Germany's constitutional order.

Secondly, from the viewpoint of the GFCC's case law, the idea is paradoxical, given that the Court has always attached so much importance to the *Bundestag*'s position as an exemplar of democratic politics. Apparently, fundamental questions on the future of Europe require a type of democratic debate that the German *Bundestag* cannot sufficiently provide.

Yet, the most difficult aspect of a constitutional referendum on European integration is that the arguments already seem highly tilted towards rejection of further European integration. Opponents of further integration could muster all the GFCC's arguments against such a move: logically, further European integration would require Germans to give up their cherished Basic Law and constitute a violation of the democratic principle.

6. Effects of the GFCC Case Law on European Decision-making

The effects of the GFCC's case law were not restricted to German politics, but also influenced decision-making at the European level. The Karlsruhe rulings contributed to a crisis politics in which financial assistance would only be given as a last resort, subject to conditionality that would bring debtor states on a path towards budgetary discipline, and in which German liability would be limited and subject to a German veto. A sign of the growing importance of the GFCC's case law for European integration was that, in April 2013, several GFCC judges visited Commission President Barroso to discuss 'how to best ensure the respect of democracy and the rule of law in the EU and its Member States'.[232]

6.1 Making Financial Assistance a Last Resort: The EFSF and ESM

German constitutional concerns already played a role in the spring of 2010, when the euro area Member States discussed various alternatives to deal with the spreading crisis. A particular concern for Germany was that a rescue mechanism could not violate the no-bailout clause of Article 125 TFEU, because the GFCC's *Maastricht* judgment considered this clause an essential part of the '*Stabilitätsgemeinschaft*' that the EMU was meant to be. Consequently, any crisis

[232] This text was taken from <http://ec.europa.eu/avservices/photo/photoDetails.cfm?sitelang=en&ref=023108#1> accessed 27 December 2017. The link, however, is no longer available and I was unable to relocate details of this visit elsewhere on the internet.

mechanism that would violate this clause risked being defeated in proceedings before the Court in Karlsruhe, particularly after the Court's critical *Lisbon* ruling of 2009.[233] Already in February 2010, the four academics that had challenged Germany's entry into the EMU in 1998 threatened to bring another case before the GFCC if assistance were to be provided to Greece.[234]

6.1.1 Moving outside the Treaty framework: the EFSF

One of the ideas discussed in the spring of 2010 was to set up a European Monetary Fund (EMF) with features similar to the IMF.[235] The German government had a positive stance towards the idea of an EMF, but it deemed the proposal incompatible with the TFEU's no-bailout clause. The setting-up of an EMF would therefore require Treaty change.[236] Germany liked the option of providing bilateral loans because it seemed a good way to get around the no-bailout clause. However, the provision of bilateral loans was ultimately deemed insufficient to deal with the extent of the problems and seen as unable to provide a credible solution in the eyes of the markets.[237]

Ultimately, the idea to create a special purpose vehicle (SPV) in the form of the EFSF was a last minute one. On 7 May 2010, the heads of state or government of the euro area declared that the Commission would 'propose a European stabilization mechanism to preserve financial stability in Europe'.[238] The details of this

233 Interview with EU official #1 (Brussels, Belgium, 3 November 2015). See also the statements of interior Minister Thomas de Maizière quoted in Charlemagne, 'Germany: Europe's Fed-up Sugar Daddy' *Economist* (20 May 2010) <www.economist.com/blogs/charlemagne/2010/05/euro_crisis_6> accessed 2 August 2022. See also Peter Ludlow, 'In the Last Resort: The European Council and the Euro Crisis' (2010) 7(7/8) Eurocomment Briefing Note 10 and 14–15; and 'Now Comes the Pain' *The Economist* (London, 1 May 2010).

234 See Michael Brackmann and Jens Münchrath, 'Finanzhilfe für Griechenland: "Wir ziehen wieder nach Karlsruhe"' *Handelsblatt* (Düsseldorf, 22 February 2010) <www.handelsblatt.com/politik/konjunktur/oekonomie/nachrichten/finanzhilfe-fuer-griechenland-wir-ziehen-wieder-nach-karlsruhe/3374780.html> accessed 2 August 2022.

235 For various proposals, see Thomas Mayer, 'The Case for a European Monetary Fund' (2009) 3 Intereconomics 138, 138–41; Daniel Gros and Thomas Mayer, 'How to Deal with the Threat of Sovereign Default in Europe: Towards a Euro(pean) Monetary Fund' (2010) 2 Intereconomics 64, 64–68.

236 'Schäuble fordert Europäischen Währungsfonds' *Spiegel Online* (Hamburg, 6 March 2010) <www.spiegel.de/politik/ausland/krise-in-griechenland-schaeuble-fordert-europaeischen-waehrungsfonds-a-682167.html> accessed 2 August 2022; Quentin Peel, 'Merkel Warns of Hurdles in EMF Plan' *Financial Times* (London, 8 March 2010) <www.ft.com/content/6fdeed16-2ad9-11df-886b-00144feabdc0> accessed 2 August 2022. See also, on these events, Ledina Gocaj and Sophie Meunier, 'Time Will Tell: The EFSF, the ESM, and the Euro Crisis' (2013) 35(3) Journal of European Integration 239, 242.

237 Gocaj and Meunier, 'Time Will Tell' (n 236) 242; Yves Leterme, Prime Minister of Belgium at the time, proposed setting up a European debt agency that would issue common euro area debt instruments and mirrored proposals for Eurobonds. This proposal, however, would have also required Treaty change. See Yves Leterme, 'Pour une agence européenne de la dette' *Le Monde* (Paris 5 March 2010) <www.lemonde.fr/idees/article/2010/03/05/pour-une-agence-europeenne-de-la-dette-par-yves-leterme_1314894_3232.html> accessed 2 August 2022.

238 Statement by the Heads of State or Government of the Euro Area of 7 May 2010 <www.consilium.europa.eu/media/21430/20100507-statement-of-the-heads-of-state-or-government-of-the-euro-area-en.pdf> accessed 2 August 2022.

mechanism were worked out by the Commission over the weekend of 8 and 9 May 2010 and submitted to a special meeting of the Economic and Financial Affairs Council (Ecofin) on 9 May 2010.[239] The original Commission proposals, however, were unacceptable to Germany. The Commission proposed a eurozone rescue fund of €500 billion, operating under Commission authority to be adopted on the basis of Article 122 TFEU.[240] The German government raised concerns about budgetary sovereignty and objected that the proposal would be difficult to pass review by the GFCC. The proposed fund required the euro area Member States to provide financial guarantees above the ceiling of the EU's own resources in the EU budget. The proposal would therefore also violate the decision on own resources, which requires approval by the Member States 'in accordance with their respective constitutional requirements'.[241] From these discussions the EFSF emerged as a compromise.[242] The original Commission proposal was adopted in the form of the much smaller EFSM, where the total amount of financial assistance was limited to the funds available within the EU budget. This meant that the EFSM had a maximum lending capacity of €60 billion.[243]

In the aftermath of the infamous weekend of 8 and 9 May 2010, German Chancellor Merkel was criticized from various sides for her lack of decisive action on solving the growing crisis.[244] This behaviour was partly explained by her reluctance to support assistance measures prior to the important regional elections of 9 May in Nord Rhine-Westphalia.[245] Assistance to troubled euro Member States was unpopular among voters, and the coalition allegedly wanted to postpone the

[239] Council of the European Union, Press release 9596/10 <www.consilium.europa.eu/uedocs/cms_data/docs/pressdata/en/ecofin/114324.pdf> accessed 2 August 2022.

[240] European Commission, Proposal for a Council Regulation establishing a European financial stabilization, (Brussels, 9 May 2010) COM(2010) 2010 final.

[241] See art 311 TFEU and Council Decision no 2007/436/EC, Euratom of 7 June 2007 on the system of the European Communities' own resources [2007] OJ L163/17.

[242] The description of these events is based on Tony Barber, 'Saving the Euro: Dinner on the Edge of the Abyss' *Financial Times* (London 10 October 2010) <https://www.ft.com/content/190b32ae-d49a-11df-b230-00144feabdc0> accessed 2 August 2022; Ludlow, 'In the Last Resort' (n 233) 30ff; Interview with EU official #1 (Brussels, Belgium, 3 November 2015); Interview with EU official #2 (Brussels, Belgium, 3 November 2015); Interview with EU official # 3 (Brussels, Belgium, 4 November 2015). There is disagreement as to whether the concerns under EU law or those under German constitutional law were decisive. The *Financial Times* article by Barber quotes former EU commissioner Rehn in the following manner: 'If Germany had endorsed the Commission's proposals, they would have flown. But the Germans made the point that there might be problems getting the proposals past their constitutional court.' In addition, and according to Ludlow, Merkel had already referred to possible troubles with the GFCC during the working dinner of the euro area head of state on 7 May 2010, see Ludlow, 'In the Last Resort' (n 233) 32–34.

[243] See art 2(2) of the EFSM Regulation (n 15), which explicitly limits the 'outstanding loans or credit lines' to 'the margin available under the own resources ceiling for payment appropriations'.

[244] See Wolfgang Proissl, 'Why Germany Fell out of Love with Europe' (2010) Bruegel Essay and Lecture Series <http://bruegel.org/2010/06/why-germany-fell-out-of-love-with-europe/> accessed 2 August 2022, 27–28.

[245] See eg Katinka Barysch, 'Germany, the Euro and the Politics of the Bail-Out' (2010) Centre for European Reform Briefing Note <www.cer.org.uk> accessed 2 August 2022.

decision on financial assistance until after the election. This failed, because the situation in the eurozone proved to be so pressing that it was necessary to find a solution before the elections took place. Political ideology was another factor, as the giving of financial assistance was controversial within the ranks of the FDP and CDU/CSU. Nonetheless, the threat that assistance measures could be successfully challenged before the GFCC has been noted as a contributing factor. The fear was that elaborate assistance mechanisms would not survive a constitutional challenge, unless it could be shown that aid to Greece was a last resort to save the EMU.[246] Germany could ultimately accept the compatibility of financial assistance with Article 125 TFEU if such assistance were to be a last resort granted under strict conditionality that would bring debtor countries on a path towards budgetary stability. It accepted a purposive reading of Article 125 TFEU: the giving of assistance, subject to strict conditionality that replaced market logic, could be accepted because the no-bailout rule was meant to ensure Member States' budgetary discipline by subjecting their fiscal policies to the discipline of financial markets.[247]

The specific contribution of the GFCC's case law, compared to the role of electoral politics and political ideology, is difficult to disentangle. Different factors overlapped and probably reinforced each other.[248] Yet, overall it seems fair to say that the GFCC's case law had three effects. First, it contributed to a relatively strict interpretation of Article 125 TFEU that supported austerity policies in debtor states, policies that would later be heavily criticized by the German opposition. Secondly,

[246] Proissl, 'Why Germany Fell out of Love with Europe' (n 244) 27–29; Ludlow, 'In the Last Resort' (n 233) 48–50.

[247] Interview with EU official #1 (Brussels, Belgium, 3 November 2015); the German Minister for Interior Affairs, Thomas De Maizière, who acted as the German representative in the negotiations over the EFSF, declared on the conditions for bailouts: 'One is if the euro is in danger. A second precondition is that countries being helped must do everything to help themselves. Those two preconditions have now been met, and [the eurozone defence fund] is in line with German law: we are providing loan guarantees under strict conditions, including conditions set by the International Monetary Fund.' In the same interview he declared: 'And we have a very strong federal constitutional court, as became clear with respect to its ruling on the Lisbon Treaty. The idea that German law can be interpreted strictly on the one hand, but that EU law can somehow be more political than legal, on the other, is not acceptable to Germany. It is not Euroscepticism when a German chancellor has to check that a new EU law is compatible with German law. It serves the cause of building law and justice in Europe. You cannot just say the law does not matter, and we have to take a decision quickly.' Charlemagne, 'Germany: Europe's Fed-up Sugar Daddy' (n 233). See also, in a similar vein, Gocaj and Meunier, 'Time Will Tell' (n 236) 246–47; Ludlow, 'In the Last Resort' (n 233) 14–16 and 19. For further assessments in a similar direction, see Deutscher Bundestag Wissenschaftliche Dienste, sind Finanzhilfen der EU an Griechenland durch deutsche Zustimmungsakte zu den Europäischen Verträgen gedeckt und könnte dies vom Bundesverfassungsgericht überprüft werden?, no. 3—3000—143/10, 4 May 2010 <www.bundestag.de/resource/blob/407314/6ffb62a01ca31240bc1a3a66f56d92ed/WD-3-143-10-pdf-data.pdf> accessed 2 August 2022; as well as Merino 'Legal Developments in the Economic and Monetary Union' (n 13) 1625–27.

[248] The former Permanent Representative for the Netherlands at the EU, Tom de Bruijn, recalls that Germany was generally reticent in putting forward that its hesitations stemmed from constitutional concerns. In his perception, German negotiators experienced the Court's case law as a constraint. Interview with Tom de Bruijn, former Permanent Representative of the Netherlands at the European Union (The Hague, the Netherlands, 18 November 2015).

the strict interpretation contributed to the German government's stance that assistance would really have to be given as an *ultima ratio*. That position ultimately contributed to the fact that the assistance mechanisms had to be designed in a crisis atmosphere over the weekend of 8 and 9 May. As a further result, the national parliaments were, to a large extent, excluded.[249] Thirdly, the GFCC's case law contributed to the EFSF's adoption outside the EU Treaty framework. That decision ensured a German veto on the assistance mechanism and thus safeguarded the *Bundestag*'s budgetary sovereignty.

6.1.2 Inducing Treaty change: the ESM

Both the EFSF and EFSM were intended as temporary measures.[250] Over the course of 2010, however, it transpired that a permanent assistance mechanism was required.[251] Germany insisted that a permanent mechanism would require a Treaty change in order to remove legal uncertainties about its compatibility with the Treaties, particularly as, in the meantime, the EFSF and EFSM had been challenged in Karlsruhe.[252] Other Member States, however, were reluctant to engage in the complex exercise of revising the Treaties, given the possibly burdensome parliamentary ratification process or the need for referenda.[253] The solution was ultimately found in a minor amendment to Article 136(3) TFEU using the simplified Treaty revision procedure of Article 48(6) TEU:

> The Member States whose currency is the euro may establish a stability mechanism to be activated if indispensable to safeguard the stability of the euro area as a whole. The granting of any required financial assistance under the mechanism will be made subject to strict conditionality.

[249] Which in turn led to accusations by the German opposition that the government had violated its constitutional obligations. See the next chapter on this point.

[250] See art 9a (Review clause) of the EFSM Regulation (n 15). The EFSF was meant to expire in 2013.

[251] The decision to set up such a permanent mechanism was made at the European Council of 28 and 29 October 2010, where agreement was also reached on a limited Treaty change: Conclusions of the European Council of 28–29 October 2010, doc no EUCO 25/1/10, REV 1 <www.consilium.europa.eu/uedocs/cms_data/docs/pressdata/en/ec/117496.pdf> accessed 2 August 2022. See further also Conclusions of the European Council of 16–17 December 2010, doc no EUCO 30/1/10 <www.consilium.europa.eu/uedocs/cms_data/docs/pressdata/en/ec/118578.pdf> accessed 2 August 2022.

[252] Peter Ludlow, 'The Euro Crisis Once Again' (2010) 8(3) Eurocomment Briefing Note 10; Barysch, 'Germany, the Euro and the Politics of the Bail-Out' (n 245); Bruno de Witte, 'Using International Law in the Euro Crisis' (2013) No 4 ARENA Working Paper 20 December 2016 <www.arena.uio.no> accessed 2 August 2022, 6–7; Merino 'Legal Developments in the Economic and Monetary Union' (n 13) 1641. See also the remarks of Dutch Prime Minister Rutte, who confirms that the Treaty change was a German demand stemming from constitutional concerns: *Handelingen II*, 2010/2011, no 64, item 5, 30.

[253] Ludlow, 'The Euro Crisis Once Again' (n 252) 16–17 and 19–22; Interview with Tom de Bruijn, former Permanent Representative of the Netherlands at the European Union (The Hague, the Netherlands, 18 November 2015).

This provision effectively laid down the purposive interpretation of the no-bailout clause in the TFEU. The Article states that financial assistance is a last resort to 'safeguard the stability of the euro area as a whole' and can only be granted under 'strict conditionality'. The Article thus meant to guarantee the compatibility of a permanent assistance mechanism with Article 125 TFEU.[254] In *Pringle*, this interpretation was eventually also accepted by the CJEU.[255] Nonetheless, the CJEU's interpretation of the no-bailout clause seems to have translated the austerity measures imposed on debtor states into a constitutional requirement.[256]

Finally, German constitutional concerns influenced the design of the ESM. The fact that Germany retains a veto power under the ESM's emergency voting procedure is apparently no coincidence but relates to constitutional concerns about budgetary sovereignty.[257] As discussed, such a veto position is not available to several smaller Member States.

6.2 Banking Union: Making the Single Resolution Fund Intergovernmental

Another episode in which German constitutional concerns played a significant role was the EU negotiations of the Single Resolution Mechanism (SRM), a key component of the European banking union.[258] As discussed, the SRM is a mechanism

[254] Interview with EU official #1 (Brussels, Belgium, 3 November 2015); Interview with EU official # 3 (Brussels, Belgium, 4 November 2015); support that art 136(3) TFEU was prompted by German constitutional concerns comes from an interview with Luuk van Middelaar, Professor of Foundations and Practice of the European Union and its Institutions and former speechwriter and advisor of the first permanent President of the European Council, Herman Van Rompuy (2010–14) (Leiden, the Netherlands, 10 November 2015). For further support for the idea that Germany insisted on wording that ensured assistance would be a last resort, see also Ludlow, 'Doing Whatever is Required?' (n 160) 14 and 18. See also, on the reading of this provision, Merino 'Legal Developments in the Economic and Monetary Union' (n 13) 1628–30.

[255] Case C 370/12 *Thomas Pringle v Government of Ireland* [2012] EU:C:2012:756. A further condition of the assistance is that the recipient Member State remain 'responsible to its creditors for its financial commitments' (at para 138ff of the judgment). On the interpretation of the no-bailout provision, see also Vestert Borger, 'The ESM and the European Court's Predicament in *Pringle*' (2013) 14 German Law Journal 113, 131–32; Chris Koedooder, 'The *Pringle* Judgment: Economic and/or Monetary Union' (2013) 37(1) Fordham International Law Journal 112, 121–24; Tuori and Tuori, *The Eurozone Crisis* (n115) 120–34; Pieter-Augustijn Van Malleghem, '*Pringle*: A Paradigm Shift in the European Union's Monetary Constitution' (2013) 14 (1) German Law Journal 141.

[256] Tuori and Tuori, *The Eurozone Crisis* (n 115) 133–34; Van Malleghem, '*Pringle*' (n 255) 162–64. Highly critical on this aspect is Harm Schepel, 'The Bank, the Bond, and the Bail-out: On the Legal Construction of Market Discipline in the Eurozone' (2017) 44(1) Journal of Law and Society 79.

[257] Interview with EU official #2 (Brussels, Belgium, 3 November 2015). Voßkuhle, who was the President of the GFCC at the time, claims a similar link, writing extra-judicially in Voßkuhle, 'European Integration Through Law' (n 223) 160.

[258] Important information on the negotiations and the constitutional concerns was obtained through interviews with EU officials: Interview with EU official #1 (Brussels, Belgium, 3 November 2015); Interview with EU official #2 (Brussels, Belgium, 3 November 2015); Interview with EU official # 3 (Brussels, Belgium, 4 November 2015); Interview with former member of the Eurogroup Working Group and of the Economic and Financial Committee (Zoom interview, 29 July 2021).

for the resolution of failing banks in the euro area. The SRM includes a Single Resolution Fund (SRF) that serves to fund the costs associated with the resolution of banks. It is financed by contributions raised at the national level through levies on banks.[259] These contributions are transferred by the Member States into national compartments that are progressively mutualized into a common European fund over the course of eight years (2016–2023).[260] An important reason for a euro-area-wide fund was that it would provide a more effective way to deal with banking crises. Such crises are often asymmetrical in nature, as they are concentrated in some Member States. A common fund could contribute to breaking the vicious cycle between national fiscal positions and their banking sector.[261]

The German government, however, raised both political and legal objections to the initial Commission proposal for an SRM introduced in July 2013.[262] The Commission proposed to establish a common European fund without national compartments, and with Article 114 TFEU as the legal basis. Politically, Germany and other northern Member States raised concerns over moral hazard.[263] If banks were to be resolved through a common European fund, then the Member States could lose their incentive to effectively supervise and regulate their banking sectors. For this reason, Germany favoured a network of national funds rather than a common European fund. A compromise was ultimately found, in that the SRF would be divided into different national compartments. These would be gradually merged over the course of eight years. In the first year, the costs for bank resolution would be borne primarily by the national compartment corresponding to the Member State where the respective bank is established. In the following years, this share would gradually decrease, and the share of other compartments increase.

[259] See arts 67–71 in conjunction with art 2 of Regulation (EU) 806/2014 of the European Parliament and of the Council of 15 July 2014 establishing uniform rules and a uniform procedure for the resolution of credit institutions and certain investment firms in the framework of a Single Resolution Mechanism and a Single Resolution Fund and amending Regulation (EU) 1093/2010 [2014] OJ L225/1 (SRM Regulation).

[260] See arts 1, 4, and 5 of the Agreement on the transfer and mutualisation of contributions to the Single Resolution Fund, see Council of the European Union of 14 May 2014, 8457/14 <http://register.consilium.europa.eu/doc/srv?l=EN&f=ST%208457%202014%20INIT> accessed 2 August 2022 (hereafter SRF IGA).

[261] European Commission, 'Proposal for a Regulation of the European Parliament and of the Council establishing uniform rules and a uniform procedure for the resolution of credit institutions and certain investment firms in the framework of a Single Resolution Mechanism and a Single Bank Resolution Fund and amending Regulation (EU) 1093/2010 of the European Parliament and of the Council', COM(2013) 520 final, 14–15 (hereafter Commission SRM Proposal).

[262] Commission SRM Proposal (n 261). The German concerns predated the Commission proposal and were already voiced in the spring of 2013. See eg Alex Barker, 'Berlin Demands Treaty Change for Bank Reforms' *Financial Times* (Brussels, 14 April 2013) <www.ft.com/content/eea3918c-a51b-11e2-8777-00144feabdc0> accessed 2 August 2022.

[263] On these negotiations generally, see the account of former Eurogroup President Dijsselbloem in Jeroen Dijsselbloem, *De Eurocrisis* (Prometheus 2018) 146–57. See also David Howarth and Lucia Quaglia, 'The Steep Road to European Banking Union: Constructing the Single Resolution Mechanism' (2014) 52 Journal of Common Market Studies 125.

After eight years, the separate national compartments would cease to exist and would have merged into a common fund.[264]

Besides this political issue of moral hazard, the German government also voiced legal concerns.[265] Initially the German government argued that the Commission proposal required a Treaty change, because there was no proper legal basis.[266] In the subsequent negotiations, the German government moderated its stance and argued that the proposal could not be adopted on the basis of Article 114 TFEU but should instead be adopted on the basis of Article 352 TFEU. The Council legal service, in turn, felt confident that the legal basis of Article 114 TFEU was appropriate, which undermined the German position.[267] It subsequently transpired that the problem for Germany was constitutional in nature. One of the German government's concerns was that a mutualization of financial risks would be incompatible with the *Bundestag*'s budgetary sovereignty. The German government feared that the setting-up of a European resolution scheme could put German taxpayers on the hook for bank resolutions without prior approval by the *Bundestag*.[268] The German government also held that Article 114 TFEU could not be used to impose a European levy on banks. Nor could this legal basis be used to impose an obligation on the Member States to transfer the contributions raised at the national level to the fund, or to mutualize national contributions into a common fund.[269] A key concern of the German government was again that such EU-imposed requirements would violate the *Bundestag*'s budgetary sovereignty. Decision-making under Article 114 TFEU would not be subject to a German veto and, as result, could not guarantee the *Bundestag*'s budgetary sovereignty. The GFCC had already accepted the various previous crisis mechanisms, but representatives of the Court apparently pointed out to the German government that the SRM could be the last straw for Karlsruhe, finally provoking it into revolt against Brussels.[270]

264 See art 5 of SRF IGA (n 260).

265 Former Eurogroup President Dijsselbloem notes that Germany was rather alone in voicing legal concerns relating to the SRM, see Dijsselbloem, *De Eurocrisis* (n 263) 147–48 and 151.

266 Schäuble voiced such arguments already in May 2013 in an op-ed the *Financial Times*: Wolfgang Schäuble, 'Banking Union Must Be Built on Firm Foundations' *Financial Times* (London, 12 May 2013). Initial German responses to the Commission SRM proposal are also described in 'Commission banking union plans met with scepticism' (11 July 2013) <http://openeuropeblog.blogspot.nl/2013/07/commission-banking-union-plans-met-with.html> accessed 2 August 2022. See also Benjamin Fox, 'Brussels on Collision Course with Germany on Banking Union' *EU Observer* (Brussels, 10 July 2013).

267 The Commission's firm opinion that art 114 was the correct legal basis apparently also helped to disarm German opposition, see Rachel A Epstein and Martin Rhodes, 'The Political Dynamics Behind Europe's New Banking Union' (2016) 39(3) West European Politics 415, 427.

268 See on this Howarth and Quaglia, 'The Steep Road to European Banking Union' (n 263) 129–30 and 133–35.

269 See, on this point, Schriftliche Fragen mit den in der Woche vom 13. Januar 2014 eingegangenen Antworten der Bundesregierung, BT-Dr 18/298 of 17.01.2014, 16–17.

270 The Council press release announcing the ultimate agreement on the IGA does not specify any details on the constitutional concerns, but merely notes: 'Using an intergovernmental agreement to establish rules on the transfer and mutualisation of contributions is intended to provide maximum legal certainty. The Council decided on this approach in December, given legal and constitutional concerns

Prompted by high-level political actors in Brussels and Berlin, members of the Council legal service reportedly met informally with staff of the GFCC to discuss the constitutional concerns. These meetings allegedly contributed to easing the pressure and helped bring about a compromise: the German government accepted Article 114 TFEU as the basis for the SRM, except for the obligation to transfer and mutualize the contributions raised at the national level into a common fund.[271] The latter obligations were put in a separate intergovernmental agreement (IGA).[272] This set-up entails that the commitment to transfer and mutualize funds in the SRF requires ratification in the national legal orders, which in turn ensures that the German *Bundestag* has a veto over the agreement and its budgetary sovereignty is guaranteed.[273] The Council compromise of December 2013 also clarified that, '[t]o guarantee member states' budgetary sovereignty, the draft regulation would prohibit decisions requiring a member state to provide extraordinary public support without its prior approval under national budgetary procedures'.[274]

The European Parliament strongly objected to the IGA, however, not least because it was initially excluded from the intergovernmental negotiations.[275] In a letter of 20 January 2013, written to Commission President Barroso at the request of the Parliament's Conference of Presidents,[276] EP President Schulz wrote

in certain member states.' Council of the European Union, 'Member states sign agreement on bank resolution fund', Brussels, 21 May 2014 <http://register.consilium.europa.eu/doc/srv?l=EN&f=ST%2010088%202014%20INIT> accessed 2 August 2022.

[271] See also Council Decision of the representatives of the euro area Member States meeting within the Council of the European Union and Terms of reference concerning the intergovernmental agreement on the Single Resolution Fund, 20 December 2013, 18134/13 <https://data.consilium.europa.eu/doc/document/ST%2018134%202013%20INIT/EN/pdf> accessed 2 August 2022

[272] SRF IGA (n 260).

[273] As is confirmed by recital 7 of the SRF IGA (n 260): 'Nonetheless, the participating Member States who raise the contributions on the institutions located in their respective territories according to the BRR Directive and the SRM Regulation, remain competent to transfer those contributions towards the Fund. The obligation to transfer the contributions raised at national level towards the Fund does not derive from the law of the Union. Such obligation will be established by this Agreement which lays down the conditions upon which the Contracting Parties, in accordance with their respective constitutional requirements, jointly agree to transfer the contributions that they raise at national level to the Fund.' See also recital 9. Recital 20 of the SRM Regulation (n 259) contains similar language and art 67(1) of the SRM Regulation confirms that the Fund 'shall be filled in accordance with the rules on transferring the funds raised at national level towards the Fund as laid down in the Agreement'.

[274] Council of the European Union, 'Council agrees general approach on Single Resolution Mechanism', Brussels, 18 December 2013 <www.consilium.europa.eu/uedocs/cms_data/docs/pressdata/en/ecofin/140190.pdf> accessed 2 August 2022. See also European Commission, 'Commissioner Michel Barnier's remarks at the ECOFIN Council press conference' (Brussels, 19 December 2013) MEMO/13/1186 <https://ec.europa.eu/commission/presscorner/detail/en/MEMO_13_1186> accessed 2 August 2022.

[275] See also Dave Keating, 'MEPs Cry Foul over Council Plans for Banking Union that Bypass EU' *Politico* (Brussels, 12 November 2013).

[276] The conference of Presidents of the European Parliament consists of the President of Parliament and the chairmen of the political groups, see <www.europarl.europa.eu/about-parliament/en/organisation-and-rules/organisation/political-bodies> accessed 2 August 2022. Similar concerns were voiced in the German *Bundestag* by Bündnis 90/Die Grünen in Antrag der Abgeordneten Dr Gerhard

that the decision to exclude certain issues from the Commission proposal constituted an 'unacceptable precedent' because it infringed 'the right of initiative of the Commission' and 'the legislative powers of the Parliament as co-legislator' and it 'undermined the Community method'.[277] In a letter of 15 January 2014 to the Council Presidency, the EP's Committee on Economic and Monetary Affairs had expressed its disagreement in similar terms. It noted that the move violated core EU constitutional principles, namely 'the principle of sincere cooperation (Article 4(3) TEU), the principle of institutional balance and the principle of democracy'.[278] Eventually, the EP's concerns were allayed to some extent after the Council invited the Parliament to participate in the intergovernmental negotiations on the SRF.[279] A compromise between the EP and Council was ultimately reached on 20 March 2014, which ensured that the deal could be finalized in April 2014 during the last plenary session of the 7th parliamentary term.[280]

The exclusion of the European Parliament from an important part of the SRM negotiations underlines that the GFCC's interpretation of democracy comes at the expense of efforts to strengthen democratic structures at the EU level. There is an irony in this turn of events: in the name of democracy, the case law of the GFCC contributes to a particular policy outcome that is apparently even negotiated with the help of the GFCC itself; yet initially leads to the exclusion of Europe's directly elected parliament from the negotiations, which then invokes the principle of democracy to protest against this course of events.[281]

Schick, Manuel Sarrazin, Kerstin Andreae, Dieter Janecek, Uwe Kekeritz, Sven-Christian Kindler, Dr Tobias Lindner, Beate Müller-Gemmeke, Claudia Roth (Augsburg), Dr Frithjof Schmidt, Dr Wolfgang Strengmann-Kuhn, Jürgen Trittin, und der Fraktion Bündnis 90/Die Grünen, BT-Dr 18/1340 of 07.05.2014.

[277] Martin Schulz, Letter to Mr José Manuel Barroso, President of the European Commission, of 20 January 2014, no 301049.

[278] Sharon Bowles and others, Letter to the Greek Presidency of the EU of 15 January 2014, no 200209. Further concerns are also noted in Council of the European Union, Report on Single Resolution Mechanism, 7 February 2014, no 6187/14. At the beginning of March 2014, the European Parliament still voiced concerns. A press release of 5 March 2014 states as part of the EP's position: 'The need for an intergovernmental chapter remains dubious and legal justifications have yet to be provided by member states.' See European Parliament, Press Release of 5 March 2014, 'MEPs lay out final offer on bank single resolution mechanism'<www.europarl.europa.eu/news/en/press-room/20140305IPR37601/meps-lay-out-final-offer-on-bank-single-resolution-mechanism> accessed 2 August 2022.

[279] Moloney, 'European Banking Union' (n 25) 1658–59.

[280] European Parliament Press Release of 20 March 2014, 'Parliament negotiators rescue seriously damaged bank resolution system' <www.europarl.europa.eu/news/en/news-room/20140319IPR39310/parliament-negotiators-rescue-seriously-damaged-bank-resolution-system> accessed 2 August 2022.

[281] It also has been argued that the intergovernmental agreement is more vulnerable to judicial review by national constitutional courts because such courts are often competent to review international treaties. See Federico Fabbrini, 'On Banks, Courts and International Law' (2014) 21(3) Maastricht Journal of European and Comparative Law 444, 456–62. See, more generally, Fabbrini, 'The Euro-Crisis and the Courts' (n 114). In the context of the SRM, this critique seems unjustified, as the relation appears to have been exactly the opposite: the SRF negotiations show that the adoption of an intergovernmental agreement meant to prevent successful constitutional challenges in Germany against the SRM.

Finally, in its ruling on the banking union of 30 July 2019, the GFCC affirmed that the IGA was a key reason why the SRM was compatible with the German constitution. The Court held that 'Art. 114 (1) TFEU does, in principle, not authorize the European Union to impose levies on individuals or companies'.[282] Yet, the Court considered that the obligation to impose the bank levy derived from national law, not EU law. The obligation to transfer the revenue from these levies to the SRF, in turn, was based on the IGA. For those reasons, the GFCC held that the imposition of the levy could not be *ultra vires*.[283] In a similar vein, the GFCC found that the SRM Regulation did not encroach on the overall budgetary responsibility of the *Bundestag*. The Court did hold that '[a]n independent right of the European Union to impose levies would indeed encroach on the overall budgetary responsibility' of the *Bundestag*, because 'it falls to the *Bundestag* to determine the overall financial burden imposed on citizens'.[284] Yet precisely because 'the imposition of the bank levy and the transfer of its revenue to the Single Resolution Fund is not based on the SRM Regulation, but on *Bundestag* decisions, an encroachment on the overall budgetary responsibility of the *Bundestag* cannot be found'.[285]

7. Conclusion

A positive way of looking at the GFCC's role during the euro crisis is that it contributed to the democratic legitimacy of the German political process by providing an additional avenue for Euro-critics to voice their dissent. As discussed, such voices were not always fully represented within the *Bundestag*. Politicians with a Eurosceptical viewpoint were often minorities within the different parties, and the *Bundestag* debates did not fully reflect the controversial nature of the crisis measures. The GFCC itself raised a Euro-critical viewpoint that for a long time remained largely absent in German parliamentary debate. More provocatively, one could even say that the GFCC employed similar strategies to populist political parties: it put itself forward as the real voice of the people, legitimated its own position on the basis of distrust of political elites, and appeared to share a preference for direct democracy.

Yet, it is highly doubtful that a constitutional court can legitimately provide an avenue for opposition to European integration. Despite a strong pro-European consensus in German politics, there was also significant inter-party contestation

Given that the GFCC is the most assertive court in relation to European integration, successful constitutional challenges against the SRF agreement in other jurisdictions are unlikely.

282 BVerfG, *Banking union* (n 44) para 299.
283 ibid paras 300–07.
284 ibid para 308.
285 ibid para 309.

about the best approach to handle the euro crisis. German political parties adopted different narratives about the crisis, informed by different sets of values and beliefs, leading to different views on the EU's future. The centre-right governing coalition of the CDU/CSU and FDP at the time generally aimed at creating a true European 'stability culture' to replace the failed Maastricht architecture. These parties favoured a handling of the crisis that focused on debt consolidation, limited financial assistance under strict conditionality, as well as a rejection of more extensive debt sharing. The left-wing opposition parties, however, put forward a narrative that focused less on debt, but more on the role of the financial markets and the lack of a shared European economic policy. These parties expressed support for more solidarity and sharing of liabilities, opposed austerity politics, and argued for further Europeanization of Member States' economic and fiscal policies. Their proposals were rooted in the idea that further European integration would better ensure citizens' collective self-determination and would make a more social Europe possible.

The key problem is that the GFCC's case law affected these different positions unevenly. The Court's case law reinforced a particular type of politics: a politics in which budgetary discipline and retaining German budgetary sovereignty is of overriding importance. The Court made the achievement of political alternatives more burdensome and, in the name of democracy, constitutionalized a type of politics that several commentators see as the antithesis of democratic government. It became doubtful that the left wing's alternatives were still achievable within the framework of the Basic Law.

The idea that the GFCC's interventions simply enriched German political debate on the EU's future is difficult to maintain. The Court's judgments are rarely contested in German politics. Instead, the Court was accorded the final authority in interpreting the German constitution. The available evidence is rather that the GFCC's case law limited the room for political contestation over different possible interpretations of the constitution and on how constitutional ideals should be realized within the EU.

The GFCC's case law is also at odds with strengthening democratic legitimacy at the European level. The European negotiations on the SRM illustrate how the Court's insistence on budgetary sovereignty came at the expense of the European Parliament. From a European perspective this appears problematic. For example, within the ESM a veto position is certainly not available to all Member States. Yet, at the same time, the GFCC's approach stands in the way of a democratic solution at the European level.

In the end, Karlsruhe itself may have provided a way out of this conundrum: apparently the constitutional limits on European integration could be amended through a vote of the German people in a referendum. This position affirms that fundamental constitutional questions on European integration cannot be answered outside democratic debate. In a way, the GFCC's case law therefore brings us back to a choice between representative democracy and direct democracy in deciding Europe's future. From a purely democratic perspective it is difficult to make a choice between the two. However, from a constitutional point of view the position is paradoxical, given the very limited provisions in the Basic Law for direct democracy, and the explicit constitutional choice for a representative system. Moreover, the GFCC's case law already seems to have steered the debate towards the rejection of further European integration. An even-handed debate on Europe's future will only ensue if German politicians start contesting the GFCC's EU-related case law. Germans should treat the Court's pronouncements on democracy for what they are: a particular and contested position on the issue, yet by no means the only legitimate one.

6
Court-Ordered Parliamentary Oversight and the Euro Crisis

1. Introduction

Although the German Federal Constitutional Court's (GFCC) euro crisis case law had negative repercussions for democratic politics, there is also a more positive side to this case law. The reason is that the Court requires the *Bundestag* to have a say in decisions affecting its budgetary responsibility. In this manner, the Court has contributed to a progressive strengthening of the *Bundestag*'s participation and information rights during the crisis, both in EU affairs generally, as well as regarding decisions of the European Financial Stability Facility (EFSF) and European Stability Mechanism (ESM) more specifically. By doing so, the GFCC has created space for democratic politics rather than constraining it and contributed to democratic control of the executive.

As this chapter explains, the *Bundestag*'s information and participation rights in EU affairs were the source of a pronounced conflict between the *Bundestag* and German government over the course of the crisis.[1] At several points, the GFCC played a crucial role in strengthening the *Bundestag*'s position. Two issues regarding the *Bundestag*'s position were disputed. One was its involvement in decisions by the EFSF and ESM, which the government preferred to restrict. Another issue concerned the *Bundestag*'s participation and information rights in the design of most of the euro crisis measures. Here the German government only provided limited information on the European negotiations and restricted the ability of the *Bundestag* to influence these negotiations.

For both issues, the GFCC played an important role in ensuring better participation and information rights for the *Bundestag*.[2] There is considerable evidence that this strengthening of the *Bundestag*'s position would not have occurred without the GFCC's interventions. The GFCC thus helped to counter the growing dominance of the executive during the crisis and to reclaim territory for national democracy. Comparative research even indicates that the resulting overhaul of the *Bundestag*'s

[1] Similar concerns arose for the *Bundesrat*, which are not discussed here. See, on this issue, Daniela Kietz, *Politisierung trotz Parteienkonsens: Bundestag, Bundesrat und die Euro-Krise* (Bertelsmann Stiftung 2013) 31–33.

[2] On the *Bundesrat*, see ibid 21–33.

Judging European Democracy. Nik de Boer, Oxford University Press. © Nik de Boer 2023.
DOI: 10.1093/oso/9780192845238.003.0006

rights in EU affairs turned the German parliament into one of the most powerful in Europe.[3]

The current chapter details how the GFCC helped enhance the *Bundestag*'s powers in EU affairs. Section 2 first discusses how the GFCC contributed to enhancing the *Bundestag*'s position within the EFSF and ESM. Section 3 then explains the role of the Court in enhancing the *Bundestag*'s information rights regarding negotiations at the EU level. Section 4 concludes and discusses the chapter's findings in a broader context.

2. The GFCC and the Rights of the *Bundestag* in the Rescue Mechanisms

The initial legislative framework on the EFSF provided only limited decision-making rights to the *Bundestag*. Yet, two key interventions by the GFCC helped strengthen the *Bundestag*'s participation and information rights regarding decisions of the EFSF and the ESM.

2.1 The EFSF: From Limited to More Extensive Oversight

At the start of the euro crisis, the German government proved reluctant to give the *Bundestag* extensive decision-making rights within the EFSF. The government preferred limiting the *Bundestag*'s role to a single approval of the mechanism rather than providing it with a veto on specific decisions to give financial assistance. In the government's view, such a parliamentary veto would undermine the instrument's credibility in the eyes of the capital markets.[4] The government's initial legislative proposal on the EFSF—the Act on the Assumption of Guarantees in Connection with a European Stabilisation Mechanism (StabMechG)—thus provided little in the form of parliamentary participation or information rights. Article 1(4) merely provided that the *Bundestag*'s budget committee would be informed if German guarantees were used to finance assistance, unless there were compelling reasons to make an exception. In addition, the proposed Article 1(4) stipulated that the

[3] Katrin Auel, Olivier Rozenberg, and Angela Tacea, 'Fighting Back? And, If So, How? Measuring Parliamentary Strength and Activity in EU Affairs' in Claudia Hefftler and others (eds), *The Palgrave Handbook of National Parliaments and the European Union* (Palgrave Macmillan 2015) 60; Oliver Höing, 'Differentation of Parliamentary Powers: The German Constitutional Court and the German Bundestag within the financial crisis' (2012) 9 OPAL Online Paper Series.

[4] See Schäuble, Plenarprotokoll 17/44, Stenografischer Bericht der 44. Sitzung des Deutschen Bundestages am 21. Mai 2010 (EFSF second plenary) 4427 (hereafter Plenarprotokoll 17/44 (EFSF second plenary)); See also 'Bundestagspräsident blockiert Schäubles Blankoscheck-Pläne' *Handelsblatt* (Berlin/Brussels, 24 August 2011) <www.handelsblatt.com/politik/international/euro-rettungsschirm-bundestagspraesident-blockiert-schaeubles-blankoscheck-plaene/4533824.html> accessed 2 August 2022.

budget committee would be informed quarterly about the financial guarantees already given and how they were used.[5]

The parliamentary groups of the Christian democratic CDU/CSU, the liberal FDP, and the Greens (Bündnis 90/Die Grüne) subsequently changed this provision in order to strengthen the *Bundestag*'s rights, a move supported by the SPD.[6] In the new version, Article 1(4) stated that the government should endeavour to reach an agreement with the budget committee prior to agreeing to financial assistance, instead of merely providing information. An exception was possible if there were compelling reasons to give financial guarantees before an agreement was reached. In that case, the budget committee would have to be informed immediately afterwards. Still, the government would have to justify in detail the absolute necessity of taking up these guarantees prior to an agreement.[7]

The *Bundestag*'s rights became the topic of debate again in the spring and summer of 2011 when changes to the EFSF and the establishment of the ESM were debated. At that time, parliamentarians from both the coalition and opposition parties argued that significant parliamentary involvement within the EFSF and ESM was needed.[8] There were also visible disagreements between the government and the parliamentary coalition groups. *Bundestag* President Norbert Lammert (CDU/CSU), the parliamentary leader of the CDU/CSU Volker Kauder, as well as the FDP's secretary-general Christian Lindner publicly called for adequate decision-making rights for the *Bundestag* on rescue operations.[9]

The GFCC judgment of 7 September 2011 on Germany's participation in the EFSF, and the financial aid to Greece, helped bring about a strengthening of the *Bundestag*'s rights.[10] The Court upheld the constitutionality of the two acts

[5] BT-Dr 17/1685 of 11.05.2010: Gesetzentwurf der Fraktionen der CDU/CSU und FDP Entwurf eines Gesetzes zur Übernahme von Gewährleistungen im Rahmen eines europäischen Stabilisierungsmechanismus.

[6] See BT-Dr 17/1741 of 20.05.2010: Bericht des Haushaltsausschusses (8. Ausschuss) zu dem Gesetzentwurf der Fraktionen der CDU/CSU und FDP—Drucksache 17/1685—Entwurf eines Gesetzes zur Übernahme von Gewährleistungen im Rahmen eines europäischen Stabilisierungsmechanismus, 6 (hereafter BT-Dr 17/1741).

[7] ibid 3; BT-Dr 17/1740 of 19.05.2010: Beschlussempfehlung des Haushaltsausschusses (8. Ausschuss) zu dem Gesetzentwurf der Fraktionen der CDU/CSU und FDP—Drucksache 17/1685—Entwurf eines Gesetzes zur Übernahme von Gewährleistungen im Rahmen eines europäischen Stabilisierungsmechanismus, 3; Gesetz zur Übernahme von Gewährleistungen im Rahmen eines europäischen Stabilisierungsmechanismus vom 22. Mai 2010, Bundesgesetzblatt I 2010, 627 (StabMechG).

[8] Kietz, 'Politisierung trotz Parteienkonsens' (n 1) 29. See eg Deutscher Bundestag, 'Kanzleramt soll "parlamentsfreundlicher" arbeiten' <www.bundestag.de/dokumente/textarchiv/2011/33702982_kw11_pa_europa/204826> accessed 2 August 2022.

[9] Kietz, 'Politisierung trotz Parteienkonsens' (n 1) 29. See also 'Bundestagspräsident blockiert Schäubles Blankoscheck-Pläne' (n 4); 'Lammert fürchtet Entmündigung des Bundestags bei Euro-Rettung' *ZEIT ONLINE* (24 August 2011) <www.zeit.de/zustimmung?url=https%3A%2F%2Fwww.zeit.de%2Fpolitik%2Fdeutschland%2F2011-08%2Feuro-rettung-lammert-schaeuble> accessed 2 August 2022.

[10] See also the expectation of the Bundestag President Lammert in 'Bundestagspräsident blockiert Schäubles Blankoscheck-Pläne' (n 4).

authorizing the financial support. Yet, for the legislation that authorized German participation in the EFSF, the Court concluded that its provisions did not ensure the 'continuing influence of the *Bundestag* on the guarantee decisions' and 'would not prevent parliamentary budget autonomy being affected in a manner which would adversely affect the right to vote'.[11] The GFCC demanded that Article 1(4) of the StabMechG was to be interpreted in a specific manner: the government would have to obtain the consent of the *Bundestag*'s budget committee before new guarantees could be given. Nonetheless, the Court upheld the exception that no such consent was needed if there were compelling reasons.[12]

The judgment subsequently played an important role in the parliamentary debates of September 2011 on the changes to the EFSF and the required modifications to the StabMechG. On the same day as the GFCC's judgment, the parliamentary groups of the CDU/CSU and FDP introduced a proposal to strengthen the participation and information rights of the *Bundestag* in the framework of the EFSF.[13] The original legislative proposal of 5 September 2011 had left the issue open in anticipation of the GFCC's judgment.[14] The Court's ruling inspired the proposed changes, although the coalition parties argued that the new provisions went beyond what the Court had required.[15] In contrast to the initial debates on the EFSF, the government now seemed to affirm the involvement of the *Bundestag* as essential. For example, in his opening speech to the *Bundestag* plenary Finance Minister Schäuble declared that the 'budget right of the Bundestag is the basic principle of our parliamentary democracy'.[16]

[11] Bundesverfassungsgericht, judgment of 7 September 2011, 2 BvR 987/10 (*Greek loan facility and EFSF*) (hereafter BVerfG, *Greek loan facility and EFSF*) para 141.

[12] ibid para 141.

[13] BT-Dr 17/6945 of 07.09.2011: Antrag der Fraktionen der CDU/CSU und FDP Parlamentsrechte im Rahmen zukünftiger europäischer Stabilisierungsmaßnahmen sichern und stärken.

[14] BT-Dr 17/6916 of 05.09.2011: Gesetzentwurf der Fraktionen der CDU/CSU und FDP Entwurf eines Gesetzes zur Änderung des Gesetzes zur Übernahme von Gewährleistungen im Rahmen eines europäischen Stabilisierungsmechanismus, see especially 6.

[15] See BT-Dr 17/7130 of 26.09.2011: Bericht des Haushaltsausschusses (8. Ausschuss) a) zu dem Gesetzentwurf der Fraktionen der CDU/CSU und FDP—Drucksache 17/6916—Entwurf eines Gesetzes zur Änderung des Gesetzes zur Übernahme von Gewährleistungen im Rahmen eines europäischen Stabilisierungsmechanismus b) zu dem Antrag der Fraktionen der CDU/CSU und FDP—Drucksache 17/6945—Parlamentsrechte im Rahmen zukünftiger europäischer Stabilisierungsmaßnahmen sichern und stärken, 4 (hereafter BT-Dr 17/7130). The Greens were also of the view that the provisions went beyond what the GFCC had required, 7.

[16] Plenarprotokoll 17/124, Stenografischer Bericht der 124. Sitzung des Deutschen Bundestages am 8 September 2011 (EFSF extension first plenary) 14551 (hereafter Plenarprotokoll 17/124 (EFSF extension first plenary)). In the second plenary debate on the EFSF changes, Volker Kauder (CDU/CSU) stated that the legislative bill represented a paradigm change from a Europe of national governments that decide matters in the Councils to a Europe of the parliaments ('Von einem Europa der nationalen Regierungen, die in den Räten beieinandersitzen, sind wir auf dem Weg zu einem Europa der Parlamente'), Plenarprotokoll 17/130, Stenografischer Bericht der 130. Sitzung des Deutschen Bundestages am 29. September 2011 (EFSF extension second plenary) 15204 (hereafter Plenarprotokoll 17/130 (EFSF extension second plenary)). Rainer Brüderle of the FDP explicitly stated support for this part of Kauder's statement and spoke of Germany as an example for the rest of Europe, Plenarprotokoll 17/130 (EFSF extension second plenary) 15211.

The modified legislation provided for more extensive parliamentary participation and information rights on several fronts. Decisions affecting the *Bundestag*'s overall budgetary responsibility would be subject to the prior consent of the *Bundestag* as a whole.[17] Without such consent, the German representative on the EFSF could not vote in favour of or abstain from a decision in these areas. Consent of the *Bundestag* plenary would be required in at least four situations: for agreements on financial assistance by the EFSF, for essential changes to such agreements,[18] for changes to the EFSF Framework Agreement, and in case rights and obligations under the EFSF were to be transferred to the ESM.[19] The budget committee would participate in the EFSF's decision-making in all other matters affecting the budgetary responsibility of the *Bundestag*.[20] Furthermore, the government would have to inform the German *Bundestag* 'comprehensively, at the earliest possible date, continuously and as a general rule in writing'.[21]

2.2 The Lure of Confidentiality: The '*Neuner Gremium*' and its Demise

Despite these changes, a major shortcoming remained. A special committee, the so-called '*Neuner Gremium*', could take over the participation rights of the plenary in cases of particular urgency and confidentiality.[22] The *Bundestag* plenary would elect this committee from the ranks of the budget committee. The government could assert such urgency and confidentiality, which in turn could be rebutted by a majority of the special committee's members.[23] In case of particular confidentiality,

17 Art 3 Gesetz zur Änderung des Gesetzes zur Übernahme von Gewährleistungen im Rahmen eines europaïschen Stabilisierungsmechanismus vom 9. Oktober 2011, *Bundesgesetzblatt* I 2011, 1992 (amended StabMechG).

18 And more specifically for changes that would have effects on the amount of financial guarantees.

19 See art 3(2) of the amended StabMechG.

20 See art 4 of the amended StabMechG. Art 4(2) of the Act determined that two specific areas required prior consent of the budget committee, namely the adoption or amendment of EFSF's Board of Directors' guidelines, as well as decisions by the EFSF to employ further instruments in the context of an existing assistance agreement or the alteration of the conditions attached to such assistance. Again, in these situations the German representative on the EFSF could not vote in favour of or abstain from a decision with this content absent prior approval of the budget committee.

21 Art 5 of the amended StabMechG. The Article also required the German government to communicate all available documents that the budget committee and plenary would need to exercise its rights within the scope of the Act. In addition, the government was obliged to communicate an assessment of a new application for financial aid within seven days (art 5(4)) and needed to give information on the use of the guarantees quarterly (art 5(5)).

22 See art 3(1) of the of the amended StabMechG.

23 Art 3(4) and (5) of the amended StabMechG. In case of precautionary measures, loans to recapitalize financial institutions and the purchase of government bonds on the secondary market in order to prevent the dangers of contagion, there would be a presumption of 'particular urgency or confidentiality'. The translation comes from Bundesverfassungsgericht, judgment of 28 February 2012, 2 BvE 8/11 (*Neuner Gremium*) paras 24 and 40 (hereafter BVerfG, *Neuner Gremium*).

the information rights of the *Bundestag* could also be restricted to the special committee.[24]

The provisions for the special committee were the source of disagreement. The coalition parties[25] and the Greens[26] saw no constitutional problems but Die Linke[27] and particularly the SPD[28] voiced doubts. The establishment of the committee was also the subject of a heated exchange during an expert meeting. Franz Mayer, a constitutional scholar and the *Bundestag*'s legal representative in the *EFSF* case, argued that the special committee did not comply with constitutional requirements. However, the CDU/CSU and FDP strongly defended the committee.[29] A proposal of the SPD to limit the committee's competences and room for confidentiality was rejected.[30] Despite these concerns, the SPD ultimately voted in favour of the changed legislation together with all other parties except Die Linke.[31]

The *Bundestag*'s approval, however, did not conclude the matter, as Peter Danckert and Swen Schulz of the SPD challenged the Act before the GFCC. They did so against the wishes of their own party and initially at their own expense.[32] Danckert and Schulz argued that the provisions on the special committee violated their rights as *Bundestag* members.

The two SPD parliamentarians ultimately won their case before the GFCC. On 26 October 2011, the *Bundestag*'s plenary unanimously elected the special committee for the duration of one legislature.[33] However, in an interim decision one day later, the GFCC banned it from being used.[34] Subsequently, on 28 February 2012, the GFCC delivered its judgment in the principal proceedings and held that the extensive delegation of powers to the committee was unconstitutional.[35] The provisions on the special committee excluded *Bundestag* members that were not part of the committee from participating in essential decisions affecting the *Bundestag*'s budgetary responsibility. This exclusion violated Article 38(1) of the Basic Law

24 Art 5(7) of the amended StabMechG, translation from BVerfG, *Neuner Gremium* (n 23) para 58.

25 See BT-Dr 17/7130 (n 15) 4.

26 BT-Dr 17/7130 (n 15) 7.

27 Gysi (Die Linke), Plenarprotokoll 17/130 (EFSF extension second plenary) (n 16) 15213.

28 BT-Dr 17/7130 (n 15) 5.

29 Interview with Franz Mayer, Professor of Public Law at Universität Bielefeld and representative of the German Bundestag in the *Lisbon* and *EFSF* cases (Berlin, Germany, 28 May 2015).

30 BT-Dr 17/7130 (n 15) 5.

31 Plenarprotokoll 17/130 (EFSF extension second plenary) (n 16) 15236–39.

32 Danckert has indicated that the legal fees amounted to €15,000, by no means a negligible sum. Other parties also exerted significant pressure on Danckert. When the Court decided to uphold his complaint in an interim ruling, Danckert was told in the budget committee that all international consequences would be his fault. The GFCC ultimately ordered the German government to pay Danckert and Schulz's legal fees. Interview with Peter Danckert, former member of the *Bundestag* for the SPD (Berlin, Germany, 12 May 2015).

33 See Bundesverfassungsgericht, judgment of 27 October 2011, 2 BvE 8/11 (*Neuner Gremium* interim ruling) para 61 (hereafter BVerfG, *Neuner Gremium* interim ruling).

34 ibid; see also Sabine Mair and Malte Kröge, 'Constitutional Change through Euro Crisis Law: Germany' (28 December 2015) <http://eurocrisislaw.eui.eu/germany/> accessed 2 August 2022, 24.

35 BVerfG, *Neuner Gremium* (n 23).

(BL), because it could not be fully justified in order to maintain parliament's capability to function. The Court considered that, in principle, the *Bundestag* must exercise its function of representing the people 'as a body of representation in its entirety and through the participation of all its members […] not through individual members, a group of members or the parliamentary majority'.[36] Therefore, the *Bundestag* members all have the same rights of participation, such as the right to speak, the right to vote, the right of initiative, the right to ask questions, and the right to information.[37] Moreover, the Court underlined once more that the *Bundestag* also has a particularly important role in relation to the adoption of the budget, 'in a system of intergovernmental governing'.[38] A general authorization for the government to give guarantees would not be sufficient if this were to leave the risk 'of a serious reduction of the latitude for future budgetary decisions'.[39] In such a case, the legislature must also lay down 'flanking framework conditions',[40] which, for example, mean that crucial decisions concerning guarantee authorizations are subject to the *Bundestag*'s participation.[41]

Legal interests of 'constitutional status' could justify limitations on the *Bundestag* members' rights, such as the parliament's ability to function. The *Bundestag* could therefore organize itself to enable a better handling of the complexities of its legislative task.[42] Nonetheless, this competence is subject to the principle of proportionality, and restrictions on its members' rights could not go beyond what is 'absolutely necessary'.[43] The *Bundestag*'s delegation of tasks to a subsidiary body must therefore comply with the principle of mirror image: each committee must be a 'microcosm of the plenary session in its political weighting'.[44] In addition, restrictions on the provision of information to members not belonging to the subsidiary body must be absolutely necessary.[45]

The Court deemed that the extensive power delegations to the special committee did not satisfy these requirements. Only for decisions to buy government bonds on the secondary market could the delegation be justified. For such decisions, confidentiality was necessary. The Court was convinced by Finance Minister Schäuble and *Bundestag* member Peter Altmaier that 'if even the mere planning of such an emergency measure were to become known, this would be sufficient to defeat its success'.[46] This did not apply, however, to other decisions of the EFSF, which all required a number of preparatory measures that would be public. Keeping the

36 ibid para 102.
37 ibid paras 103 and 104.
38 ibid para 109; and further at paras 105–08.
39 ibid para 112.
40 ibid para 112.
41 ibid para 112.
42 ibid para 114; and further at paras 115–17.
43 ibid paras 125 and 119–24.
44 ibid para 127.
45 ibid paras 125–31.
46 ibid para 150.

subsequent decisions secret could therefore not be justified.[47] The Court was also not convinced that requirements of urgency could justify delegation to the special committee. Such reasons could at best justify the delegation of some decisions to the budget committee. Again, a reason for this finding was that all the EFSF assistance measures would require a large number of preparatory measures. There was hence no convincing need to delegate decision-making powers to the special committee for reasons of urgency.[48]

2.3 Parliamentary Oversight Coming of Age: The ESM

The judgment on the *Neuner Gremium* led the *Bundestag* to adapt the StabMechG again in order to comply with GFCC's requirements: the special committee would now only be able to decide on secondary market interventions, and only in the case of special confidentiality being required.[49] The regulation for urgent cases was entirely taken out of the legislation.[50] The legislative changes also provided a further extension of the plenary's powers.[51] The parliamentary debates on these changes were again marked by a change in language among the *Bundestag* members and the GFCC was credited with enhancing the parliament's role.[52] Norbert Barthle of the CDU/CSU stated that an urgent crisis politics could not jeopardize the fundamental constitutional rights of single members of parliament.[53] Rolf Schwanitz of the SPD spoke of an 'emancipation process of the parliament' that lasted over two years and had now ended well .[54] Otto Fricke of the FDP named it 'a good day for the separation of powers and for democracy'.[55] The FDP and SPD also explicitly

[47] ibid para 151.

[48] ibid paras 145–47.

[49] See BT-Dr 17/9145 of 27.03.2012: Gesetzentwurf der Fraktionen CDU/CSU, SPD, FDP und Bündnis 90/Die Grünen Entwurf eines Gesetzes zur Änderung des Stabilisierungsmechanismusge setzes (hereafter BT-Dr 17/9145). The final amended Act is: Zweites Gesetz zur Änderung des Stabi lisierungsmechanismusgesetzes vom 23. Mai 2012, *Bundesgesetzblatt* I 2012, 1166 (second amended StabMechG).

[50] See, on this point and the reasons, Prizka Hinz, Plenarprotokoll 17/176, Stenografischer Bericht der 176. Sitzung des Deutschen Bundestages am 27. April 2012 (Neuner Gremium second plenary), 20931 (hereafter Plenarprotokoll 17/176 (Neuner Gremium second plenary)).

[51] In addition, on the basis of Art 4(5) StabMechG the budget committee could now organize public hearings on governmental proposals and submissions where a quarter of the budget committee's members, consisting of minimally two parliamentary groups, so requested. BT-Dr 17/9435 of 25.04.2012: Beschlussempfehlung und Bericht des Haushaltsausschusses (8. Ausschuss) zu dem Gesetzentwurf der Fraktionen CDU/CSU, SPD, FDP und Bündnis 90/Die Grünen—Drucksache 17/ 9145—Entwurf eines Gesetzes zur Änderung des Stabilisierungsmechanismusgesetzes; BT-Dr 17/9145 (n 49).

[52] Plenarprotokoll 17/176 (Neuner Gremium second plenary) (n 50): Schwanitz (SPD), 20927; Barthle (CDU/CSU) spoke of expressing respect for the Court, 20926; Fricke (FDP), 20928–29; Hinz (Bündnis 90/Die Grünen), 20931; Kalb (CDU/CSU), 20932.

[53] Barthle (CDU/CSU), Plenarprotokoll 17/176 (Neuner Gremium second plenary) (n 50) 20926.

[54] Rolf Schwanitz (SPD), Plenarprotokoll 17/176 (Neuner Gremium second plenary) (n 50) 20927.

[55] Fricke (FDP), Plenarprotokoll 17/176 (Neuner Gremium second plenary) (n 50) 20929–30.

acknowledged that the judgment did not fully accord with their previous stances and that they had come to new insights.[56] A further result was that the legislation accompanying Germany's ratification of the ESM adopted on 29 June 2012—the Act for Financial Participation in the European Stability Mechanism (ESMFinG)—provided participation and information rights for the *Bundestag* similar to those of the amended StabMechG.[57]

Finally, the GFCC's interim judgment on the ESM of 12 September 2012 further strengthened the *Bundestag*'s position and even that of other national parliaments. As discussed in the previous chapter, the judgment clarified that the ESM Treaty provisions could not be invoked to prevent the provision of information to the *Bundestag* and *Bundesrat*. The adoption of a declaration by the Treaty's contracting parties to this effect was a direct result of the judgment.

In sum, the GFCC helped to bring about significant extensions of the *Bundestag*'s participation and information rights in the framework of the EFSF and later the ESM. Whereas the initial legislation on the EFSF contained only limited provisions on the *Bundestag*'s involvement, two years and two judgments later the legislation contained several provisions to safeguard the *Bundestag*'s involvement in both the EFSF and ESM.

It is unlikely that the changes described would have come about fully without the GFCC's interventions. On the one hand, the time pressure under which the

[56] Fricke (FDP), Plenarprotokoll 17/176 (Neuner Gremium second plenary) (n 50) 20929; Schwanitz (SPD), 20927.

[57] Art 4 ESMFinG requires the approval of the *Bundestag*'s plenary for decisions to grant stability support, decisions to start negotiations on conditionality and on the ultimate approval of a Memorandum of Understanding, as well as decisions to change the authorized capital stock. See art 4 of Gesetz zur finanziellen Beteiligung am Europäischen Stabilitätsmechanismus vom 13. September 2012, *Bundesgesetzblatt* I, 1918 (ESMFinG); art 5 of the ESMFinG lays down that the *Bundestag*'s budget committee shall be involved in all other matters of the ESM affecting the *Bundestag*'s budgetary responsibility. Decisions that require prior approval by the budget committee include: decisions on the provision of additional instruments within existing financial assistance agreements and changes in the conditionality requirements, decisions on calling in capital, changes in the guidelines on the modalities for implementing financial assistance, decisions about the detailed terms and conditions that apply to capital changes made under art 10(1) of the ESM Treaty, and interpretations or decisions concerning professional secrecy under art 34 of the ESM Treaty. For other issues, the German federal government must 'involve the budget committee and take account of its opinions'. See art 5(3) ESMFinG. The Act permits a special committee to exercise the *Bundestag*'s rights, but only where the purchase of government bonds on the secondary market is intended and special confidentiality is required. (See art 6(1) ESMFinG; translation from Bundesverfassungsgericht, judgment of 18 March 2014, 2 BvR 1390/12 (*ESM* final ruling), para 14). Art 7 of the Act provides that the federal government has the obligation to inform the German *Bundestag* and *Bundesrat* 'comprehensively, at the earliest possible date, continuously and as a general rule in writing'. In addition, the federal government has the obligation to communicate to the *Bundestag* all documents available to it so that the *Bundestag* can exercise its participation rights. See art 7(2) ESMFinG. The explanations of the *Bundestag*'s budget committee show that these provisions of the ESMFinG were substantially influenced by the GFCC judgments on the EFSF and on the special committee. See BT-Dr 17/10172 of 28. 06. 2012: Bericht des Haushaltsausschusses (8. Ausschuss)—a) zu dem Gesetzentwurf der Fraktionen der CDU/CSU und FDP—Drucksache 17/9045—Entwurf eines Gesetzes zu dem Vertrag vom 2. Februar 2012 zur Einrichtung des Europäischen Stabilitätsmechanismus (and other matters), 10–15.

Bundestag first decided on the EFSF in May 2010 did not help. The initial agreement to establish the EFSF was made in an extremely tense context. The details of the EFSF and EFSM had to be worked out over the weekend of 8 and 9 May and were only made public in the early morning of 10 May, just before the markets in Asia opened.[58] The legislative proposal for the StabMechG was subsequently introduced on 11 May and adopted by the *Bundestag* already on 21 May. The German governing parties clearly wanted to adopt the legislation quickly in order to calm the markets and offer a good example to other Member States.[59] Consequently, there was very little time to fully address the issue of parliamentary participation in the EFSF. By the time the changes to the EFSF were debated in 2011, a year had passed and there was cross-party pressure to ensure adequate involvement of the *Bundestag* within the EFSF and future ESM. In some respects, the strengthening of the *Bundestag*'s rights also went beyond what the GFCC had required.[60] On the other hand, the *Bundestag* was aware of the constitutional objections to the establishment of the *Neuner Gremium* in 2011 but failed to take action. The German parliament changed its approach only after two of its members had successfully challenged the establishment of this committee before the GFCC, while these two parliamentarians had initiated the lawsuit against the wishes of even their own party. Based on these considerations, I conclude that it is unlikely that the *Bundestag* would have fully strengthened its position without the GFCC's intervention.[61] The case on the *Neuner Gremium* also indicates that the Court was able to consider reasons in favour of confidentiality, thus accommodating possible political justifications for the formation of the special committee. The GFCC's case law helped to strengthen the democratic legitimacy of decision-making within the EFSF and ESM, while leaving room for the legislature to put in place special arrangements for effective decision-making.

[58] Jean Pisani-Ferry, *The Euro Crisis and its Aftermath* (Oxford University Press 2013) 78–79.

[59] See eg the statement of Finance Minister Schäuble to his effect, Plenarprotokoll 17/44 (EFSF second plenary) (n 4) 4426–27.

[60] This was stressed several times by parliamentarians, see eg the position of the CDU in BT-Dr 17/7130 (n 15); Buschmann (FDP), Plenarprotokoll 17/124 (EFSF extension first plenary) (n 16) 14574.

[61] The influence of the GFCC is acknowledged by those within the *Bundestag* as well as by close observers of the Court. See Interview with Gesine Lötzsch, *Bundestag* member for Die Linke and chair of the *Bundestag*'s budget committee (Berlin, Germany, 27 May 2015); Interview with Christian Hirte, *Bundestag* member for the CDU (Berlin, Germany, 24 April 2015); Interview with Peter Danckert, former member of the *Bundestag* for the SPD (Berlin, Germany, 12 May 2015); Interview with Christoph Möllers, Professor of Public Law and Jurisprudence, Faculty of Law, Humboldt-University Berlin and representative of the German *Bundestag* in the *ESM* case (Berlin, Germany, 20 April 2015); Interview with Franz Mayer, Professor of Public Law at Universität Bielefeld and representative of the German *Bundestag* in the *Lisbon* and *EFSF* cases (Berlin, Germany, 28 May 2015).

3. Parliamentary Oversight of Acts Outside the EU Framework

A second controversy concerned the *Bundestag*'s information and participation rights in relation to the adoption of legal measures strictly falling outside the EU legal framework. Article 23(2) BL gives the *Bundesrat* and *Bundestag* the right to participate and be informed 'in matters concerning the European Union', while Article 23(3) BL states that the *Bundestag* shall have an opportunity to state its position before the federal government participates in 'legislative acts of the European Union'.[62] Because several of the crisis measures were adopted outside the EU Treaty framework, the government argued that these issues were not 'matters concerning the European Union' and that Article 23(2) and (3) did not apply. Accordingly, the government provided little information on the EU-level crisis negotiations to the *Bundestag*, limiting the parliament's influence on the EU negotiations. Again, it was the GFCC that settled the conflict between the *Bundestag* and the government in the *Bundestag*'s favour.

3.1 Cloaked Negotiations: The EFSF

Problems started in the spring of 2010 when the German government provided little information on the EU-level crisis negotiations. As a result, the *Bundestag* had limited influence on the design of the Greek loan facility, the EFSF, or the EFSM. As discussed, these initial rescue mechanisms were also decided under considerable time pressure. The *Bundestag* had to decide on the Greek loan facility in expedited proceedings of four days from 3 May 2010 until 7 May 2010. In the final *Bundestag* debate on 7 May, the *Bundestag* had no information on a further rescue package. Nonetheless, already on the same evening, the heads of state or government of the euro area announced a European stabilization mechanism that was to be worked out over the weekend and agreed as the EFSF and EFSM.[63]

When the German government introduced the StabMechG to authorize Germany's participation in the EFSF, a dispute arose as to whether the government had violated its obligations under the Basic Law and the more specific legislation on parliamentary participation. The opposition parties heavily criticized the government's failure to adequately involve the *Bundestag* in its decision-making, as well as its failure to provide adequate information on the assistance mechanisms prior to, during, and after the decisions were taken at the European level.[64]

[62] Art 23(2) Basic Law.

[63] Statement by the Heads of State or Government of the Euro Area of 7 May 2010, <www.consilium.europa.eu/media/21430/20100507-statement-of-the-heads-of-state-or-government-of-the-euro-area-en.pdf> accessed 2 August 2022; Kietz, 'Politisierung trotz Parteienkonsens' (n 1) 21–22.

[64] BT-Dr 17/1741 (n 6) 5–6 (Bündnis 90/Die Grünen); 5 (Die Linke); 4 (SPD). See also Steinmeier (SPD Plenarprotokoll 17/42, Stenografischer Bericht der 42. Sitzung des Deutschen Bundestages am

A repeated criticism was that the government had delayed the decision on the assistance mechanism because its establishment would have harmed the governing parties in the important regional elections of 9 May 2010, in North Rhine-Westphalia.[65] In legal terms, the three opposition parties of Bündnis 90/Die Grünen, SDP, and Die Linke held that the government had breached Article 23(2) BL by failing to provide adequate information.[66] They also argued that the government had violated Article 23(3) BL because it had not allowed the *Bundestag* to take a position before agreeing to the measures in the Council.[67] Finance Minister Schäuble argued, however, that the government had not violated Article 23 BL. In his view the Article did not apply to the EFSF, because the instrument was concluded outside the EU legal framework.[68]

The opposition parties also protested that they had limited information on the EFSF's design. When the *Bundestag* debated the StabMechG, the precise details of the EFSF framework agreement had not yet been communicated to the *Bundestag*. The German legislature ultimately approved the StabMechG on 21 May 2010, thus authorizing German participation in the EFSF, but the EFSF framework agreement

19. Mai 2010 (EFSF first plenary), 4132–33 (hereafter Plenarprotokoll 17/42 (EFSF first plenary)). See also the statements by Carsten Schneider of the SDP in the first plenary debate, 4148. Some members of the CDU/CSU also voiced criticism, see 'Die Angst der Abnicker' *Focus Magazin* (21 May 2010) <www.focus.de/politik/deutschland/die-angst-der-abnicker-euro-rettungspaket_id_1767164.html> accessed 2 August 2022.

[65] The opposition parties severely criticized the government's indecisiveness and its failure to provide adequate information about the possible rescue measures prior to the establishment of the EFSF. See Steinmeier (SPD), Plenarprotokoll 17/42 (EFSF first plenary) (n 64) 4132; Lötzsch (Die Linke), 4141; Trittin (Bündnis 90/Die Grünen), 4144; Volker Beck (Köln) (Bündnis 90/Die Grünen), Plenarprotokoll 17/44 (EFSF second plenary) (n 4) 4411; Sigmar Gabriel (SDP), Plenarprotokoll 17/44 (EFSF second plenary) (n 4) 4434.

[66] See Volker Beck (Köln) (Bündnis 90/Die Grünen), Plenarprotokoll 17/44 (EFSF second plenary) (n 4) 4411; BT-Dr. 17/1810 of 20.05.2010: Entschließungsantrag der Fraktion der SPD zu der dritten Beratung des Gesetzentwurfs der Fraktionen der CDU/CSU und FDP—Drucksachen 17/1685, 17/1740, 17/1741—Entwurf eines Gesetzes zur Übernahme von Gewährleistungen im Rahmen eines europäischen Stabilisierungsmechanismus (hereafter BT-Dr 17/1810); BT-Dr. 17/1808 of 20.05.2010: Entschließungsantrag der Abgeordneten Jürgen Trittin, Renate Künast, Fritz Kuhn, Dr Frithjof Schmidt, Dr Gerhard Schick, Kerstin Andreae, Lisa Paus und der Fraktion Bündnis 90/Die Grünen zu der dritten Beratung des Gesetzentwurfs der Fraktionen der CDU/CSU und FDP—Drucksachen 17/1685, 17/1740, 17/1741—Entwurf eines Gesetzes zur Übernahme von Gewährleistungen im Rahmen eines europäischen Stabilisierungsmechanismus; and further BT-Dr. 17/1811 of 20.05.2010: Entschließungsantrag der Abgeordneten Michael Schlecht, Sahra Wagenknecht, Dr. Axel Troost und der Fraktion DIE LINKE zu der dritten Beratung des Gesetzentwurfs der Fraktionen der CDU/CSU und FDP—Drucksachen 17/1685, 17/1740, 17/1741—Entwurf eines Gesetzes zur Übernahme von Gewährleistungen im Rahmen eines europäischen Stabilisierungsmechanismus.

[67] See Trittin (Bündnis 90/Die Grünen), Plenarprotokoll 17/42 (EFSF first plenary) (n 64) 4145–46; Fritz Kuhn (Bündnis 90/Die Grünen), Plenarprotokoll 17/44 (EFSF second plenary) (n 4) 4423; Hans-Christian Ströbele (Bündnis 90/Die Grünen), 4498; BT-Dr 17/1741 (n 6) 5 (Die Linke); The SPD argued that there had been too little time to properly take a position on the EFSM Regulation, see also BT-Dr 17/1810 (n 66), 3.

[68] Schäuble argued the Article only applied to the establishment of the EFSM, but he contended that in this respect the government had done nothing wrong: the Council formally adopted the EFSM on Tuesday 11 May, whereas the parliamentary leaders of all parties had been informed about this mechanism on Monday 10 May. Schäuble, Plenarprotokoll 17/44 (EFSF second plenary) (n 4) 4425.

was only concluded on 7 June 2010, well after the German parliamentary debates on the EFSF were concluded. Initially, the government had merely provided a one-page paper, laying down the core points of the EFSF's design.[69] At the time of the final parliamentary debate on the StabMechG of 21 May 2010, the details of the EFSF agreement were still not known to the *Bundestag*, despite promises by Chancellor Merkel to give the agreement before the vote. For this reason, the opposition parties of Die Linke and the Greens requested to postpone the vote until the details of the agreement were known, while the SPD also voiced strong criticism of the government's dealings with the *Bundestag*.[70] The coalition parties rejected such postponement, but did include the provision in the StabMechG that the Finance Ministry would have to present the EFSF framework agreement to the budget committee before financial guarantees could be given.[71]

3.2 Repeated Failure and Constitutional Challenge: Secrecy in the ESM and Euro Plus Pact Negotiations

Problems with the *Bundestag*'s access to information arose again in the spring of 2011 concerning the negotiations of the ESM and the Euro Plus Pact. Despite repeated complaints and requests for more information by *Bundestag* members, the German government failed to adequately inform the *Bundestag* about the ongoing negotiations. Often, the government only informed the *Bundestag* orally, but would not provide key documents on the negotiations. For example, the government had not provided the *Bundestag* with a Commission text on the ESM already in its possession on 21 February 2011. Nor did the government provide a draft of the ESM Treaty of 6 April 2011. Instead the *Bundestag* ended up requesting various drafts of the Treaty from the Austrian National Council, the lower house of the Austrian parliament.[72] Concerns about the government's information provision were not just voiced by the opposition but also by the President of the *Bundestag*, Norbert Lammert (CDU/CSU), and by Gunther Krichbaum (CDU/CSU), chairperson of the *Bundestag*'s EU affairs committee.[73] On 12 May 2011, the EU affairs committee

[69] See eg Trittin, Plenarprotokoll 17/42 (EFSF first plenary) (n 64) 4145–46.

[70] See Plenarprotokoll 17/44 (EFSF second plenary) (n 4) 4407–12 and 4422–23. The SPD abstained in this vote on postponement.

[71] Art 1(5) of the amended StabMechG; BT-Dr 17/1741 (n 6) 3.

[72] See, on these events, Bundesverfassungsgericht, judgment of 19 June 2012, 2 BvE 4/11 (*Information on ESM and Euro Plus Pact Negotiations*) para 2–42 (hereafter BVerfG, *Information on ESM and Euro Plus Pact Negotiations*).

[73] See Kietz, 'Politisierung trotz Parteienkonsens' (n 1) 23. See also BT-Dr 17/4881 of 22.02.2011: Antrag der Fraktion der SPD zum Entwurf eines Beschlusses des Europäischen Rates zur Änderung des Vertrags über die Arbeitsweise der Europäischen Union hinsichtlich eines Stabilitätsmechanismus für die Mitgliedstaaten, deren Währung der Euro ist—Ratsdok. 17620/10 (EUCO 30/10) Anlage I.

protested across party lines against the government's failure to forward a draft of the ESM Treaty.[74]

The Greens ultimately took the issue to the GFCC, arguing that the government had violated its constitutional duty to provide information to the *Bundestag* on EU matters. The GFCC upheld these claims and laid down key standards on the government's duty to inform the *Bundestag* on EU matters. The Court rejected the government's argument that Article 23 BL did not apply to the ESM and the Euro Plus Pact negotiations because they had been concluded outside the EU legal framework.[75] Instead, the Court adopted a broad reading of the *Bundestag*'s constitutional right to participate 'in matters concerning the European Union'. The Karlsruhe judges granted that the German government has primary responsibility in the area of foreign affairs and security policy for functional reasons. Nonetheless, the insertion of Article 23 into the Basic Law had been a reaction to significant power shifts in favour of the executive associated with European integration. The constitutional provision was intended to compensate for the *Bundestag*'s loss of power and ensure sufficient democratic legitimation of EU decision-making.[76] Consequently, the *Bundestag*'s Article 23(2) BL right to participate 'in matters concerning the European Union' had to be understood in a broad sense. It applies not just to EU legislation or amendments of EU primary law, but also to other issues that stand in particular proximity to EU law, or that supplement EU law, including agreements under international law.[77] Both the ESM and the Euro Plus Pact qualified as EU matters, given their close connection to EU objectives and the involvement of EU bodies in their operation.[78]

The GFCC also laid down important requirements on the scope, timing, and form of the government's information provision to the *Bundestag*. Article 23(2) BL was intended to enable an effective *Bundestag* influence on the government's positions at the EU level and serve the public nature of the parliamentary process, a key aspect of the principle of democracy.[79] The government, therefore, must inform the *Bundestag* comprehensively on EU affairs. This means that the information provision has to be more intensive where the matter is more complex, or where the matter is more intrusive with regard to the legislature's competences. The government's duty to provide information extends to informal meetings as well as the government's position. Furthermore, confidentiality cannot bar the

[74] See BVerfG, *Information on ESM and Euro Plus Pact Negotiations* (n 72) para 28; Kietz, 'Politisierung trotz Parteienkonsens' (n 1) 24.

[75] See the government's position in BVerfG, *Information on ESM and Euro Plus Pact Negotiations* (n 72) paras 56–70.

[76] ibid paras 96–98.

[77] ibid paras 99–100) Whether an issue qualifies as an EU matter depends on various factors including its contents, objectives, and effects (para 100) and see the further considerations in paras 101–05.

[78] ibid paras 134–44 and 154–58.

[79] ibid paras 107–14.

information provision to the *Bundestag* because information can be sent confidentially. The duty to provide information is moreover a continuing one. The government must actively prevent information asymmetries between itself and the *Bundestag* as negotiations proceed and the amount of information available to the government increases.[80]

The Court also considered the early provision of information to the *Bundestag* as essential. Otherwise, the *Bundestag* could be confronted with *faits accomplis*. The *Bundestag* should receive the information 'at the latest at a time which enables the *Bundestag* to consider the matter in depth and to prepare an opinion before the Federal Government makes declarations with outward effect, in particular binding declarations on legislative acts of the European Union and intergovernmental agreements'.[81] Information must therefore be provided as soon as it enters 'the sphere of influence of the Federal Government'.[82] In principle, the government should provide the information in writing to the *Bundestag* as a whole. Information to individual *Bundestag* members does not satisfy the demands of Article 23(2) BL. The requirement that the information be written serves its 'clarity, consolidation and reproducibility'.[83] Exceptions can be made if this is the only way to provide the information at the earliest possible date.[84]

Finally, the Court held that limits to the government's duty to provide information flow from the principle of the separation of powers. The government has 'a core area of specifically executive responsibility which includes an area of initiative, consultation and action which is fundamentally confidential'.[85] As long 'as the internal development of informed opinion of the Federal Government has not been completed', the parliament has no right to information.[86]

According to the Court, the German government had failed to respect these standards. The ESM related to the *Bundestag*'s overall budgetary responsibility and the provision of 'particularly comprehensive and detailed information'[87] had therefore been necessary. In a similar vein, the Court found that the Euro Plus Pact touched on the legislative competences of the *Bundestag*. The government should have informed the *Bundestag* 'in full of the initiatives and early stages of the negotiations'.[88] The government had failed to do so. In the case of the ESM, the government had not forwarded specific documents to the *Bundestag* that had been in its possession. Regarding the Euro Plus Pact, the government had failed to share its intention with the *Bundestag* to draft such a Pact.[89]

80 ibid paras 117–23.
81 ibid para 127.
82 ibid para 128.
83 ibid para 131.
84 ibid para 132.
85 ibid para 115.
86 ibid para 115; also para 124.
87 ibid para 145.
88 ibid para 159.
89 ibid para 160–64.

3.3 General Overhaul of Parliamentary Oversight Rights

The GFCC's judgment of 19 June 2012 proved to be crucial in the further development of the *Bundestag*'s participation and information rights: it led to a complete overhaul of those rights in the Act on Cooperation between the Federal Government and the German *Bundestag* in European Union Matters (EUZBBG). On 27 June 2012 the CDU/CSU, SPD, FDP, and Bündnis 90/Die Grünen filed a resolution that called for a revision of the EUZBBG in order to implement the Court's judgment.[90] After its adoption in the Maastricht ratification process, the EUZBBG had been last amended in 2009. The 2009 version specified the government's information duties to the *Bundestag*,[91] laid down which documents had to be forwarded to the *Bundestag*,[92] and identified those EU projects for which the government had to provide the *Bundestag* with the opportunity to state its position.[93] Yet, after the GFCC's judgment of 19 June 2012, a large parliamentary majority agreed that these provisions no longer sufficed to safeguard sufficient parliamentary involvement in EU affairs.

Initial changes to the EUZBBG were made in the context of the ratification of the Fiscal Compact.[94] These changes clarified first that the *Bundestag*'s participation and information rights of the EUZBBG would also apply to proposals for international treaties and other arrangements closely related to EU law, as well as matters falling within the scope of the Fiscal Compact and other international treaties or agreements concerning the EMU.[95] Secondly, the changes clarified that the government's duty to inform the *Bundestag* also applied to these intergovernmental settings, as well as to meetings of the Eurogroup and Euro-summits, including to all preparatory working groups and committees.[96] Thirdly, the changes made clear that information on Eurogroup meetings and information on meetings

[90] BT-Dr 17/10152 of 27.06.2012: Entschließungsantrag der Fraktionen CDU/CSU, SPD, FDP und Bündnis 90/Die Grünen zu der dritten Beratung des Gesetzentwurfs der Fraktionen der CDU/CSU und FDP—Drucksachen 17/9046, 17/10125—Entwurf eines Gesetzes zu dem Vertrag vom 2. März 2012 über Stabilität, Koordinierung und Steuerung in der Wirtschafts- und Währungsunion; BT-Dr 17/10171 of 28.06.2012: Bericht des Haushaltsausschusses (8. Ausschuss), 4 (hereafter BT-Dr 17/10171); accepted on 29 June 2012, see Plenarprotokoll 17/188, Stenografischer Bericht der 188. Sitzung des Deutschen Bundestages am 29. Juni 2012 (ESM and Fiscal Compact second plenary), 22739.

[91] Arts 3 and 4 Gesetz zur Änderung des Gesetzes über die Zusammenarbeit von Bundesregierung und Deutschem Bundestag in Angelegenheiten der Europaïschen Union vom 22. September 2009 *Bundesgesetzblatt* I 2009, 3026 (EUZBBG version 2009).

[92] Arts 3 and 5 EUZBBG 2009 version.

[93] Arts 3 and 9 EUZBBG 2009 version. See also Oliver Höing, 'With a Little Help of the Constitutional Court: The Bundestag on Its Way to an Active Policy Shaper' in Claudia Hefftler and others (eds), *The Palgrave Handbook of National Parliaments and the European Union* (Palgrave Macmillan 2015) 191, 193.

[94] See BT-Dr 17/10171 (n 90) in particular 7; BT-Dr 17/10125 of 27.06.2012: Beschlussempfehlung des Haushaltsausschusses (8. Ausschuss), in particular 5.

[95] Art 3(1) EUZBBG as amended by Gesetz zu dem Vertrag vom 2. März 2012 über Stabilität, Koordinierung und Steuerung in der Wirtschafts- und Währungsunion vom 13. September 2012 *Bundesgesetzblatt* II 2012, 1006 (EUZBBG September 2012 version).

[96] Art 3(3) EUZBBG September 2012 version.

of the Economic and Financial Committee of Article 134 TFEU should in principle be provided in writing.[97]

In March and April 2013, the *Bundestag* fully revised the EUZBBG on the basis of a legislative proposal supported by all parties. An important reason was the need to clarify the application of the EUZBBG to several of the crisis measures adopted outside the EU legal framework.[98] The revision made clear that the EUZBBG also applies to activities that formally fall outside the EU legal framework but are nonetheless closely related to EU law.[99] Important further changes were that the government must inform the *Bundestag* about the negotiation process on the EU level in writing and that oral information only has a supplementary role;[100] that the legislation specifies in much greater detail the documents that should be transmitted to the *Bundestag*;[101] that the *Bundestag* can also request all 'unofficial documents';[102] and that a quarter of the *Bundestag* members can demand that the government explain, in a plenary debate, why it has deviated from the *Bundestag*'s position.[103]

The events leading up to the revision of the EUZBBG, as well as the parliamentary deliberations on that revision, reveal that the changes were a response to the GFCC's judgment of 19 June 2012.[104] The German government repeatedly failed to adequately inform the *Bundestag* on the adoption of several of the euro crisis measures between 2010 and 2012, but the *Bundestag* only moved to address this

[97] Which is why Art 5(4) EUZBBG was changed. The Economic and Financial Committee is an advisory body set up to promote the coordination of 'the policies of Member States to the full extent needed for the functioning of the internal market' (art 134 TFEU). The Committee is composed 'of senior officials from national administrations and central banks, the European Central Bank and the Commission'. See European Council and Council of the European Union, 'Economic and Financial Committee' <www.consilium.europa.eu/en/council-eu/preparatory-bodies/economic-financial-committee/> accessed 2 August 2022.

[98] BT-Dr 17/12816 of 19.03.2013: Gesetzentwurf der Fraktionen CDU/CSU, SPD, FDP, Die Linke und Bündnis 90/Die Grünen Entwurf eines Gesetzes über die Zusammenarbeit von Bundesregierung und Deutschem Bundestag in Angelegenheiten der Europäischen Union (EUZBBG), 8 (hereafter BT-Dr 17/12816).

[99] Arts 1(2), 3(3), and 5(1) Gesetz über die Zusammenarbeit von Bundesregierung und Deutschem Bundestag in Angelegenheiten der Europaïschen Union vom 4. Juli 2013 *Bundesgesetzblatt* I 2013, 2170 (EUZBBG 2013 version).

[100] Art 3(1) EUZBBG 2013 version.

[101] Art 4 EUZBBG 2013 version.

[102] Art 4(3) EUZBBG 2013 version.

[103] Art 8(5) EUZBBG 2013 version; see also the Gesetzentwurf BT-Dr 17/12816 (n 98) and Höing, 'With a Little Help of the Constitutional Court' (n 93) 193–95.

[104] See eg the repeated references to the case in BT-Dr 17/12816 (n 98); BT-Dr 17/13142 of 17.04.2013: Beschlussempfehlung und Bericht des Ausschusses für die Angelegenheiten der Europäischen Union (21. Ausschuss) a) zu dem Gesetzentwurf der Fraktionen CDU/CSU, SPD, FDP, Die Linke und Bündnis 90/Die Grünen—Drucksache 17/12816—Entwurf eines Gesetzes über die Zusammenarbeit von Bundesregierung und Deutschem Bundestag in Angelegenheiten der Europäischen Union (EUZBBG) b) zu dem Antrag der Fraktionen der CDU/CSU und FDP—Drucksache 17/8137—Begleitgesetzgebung zum Vertrag von Lissabon konsequent anwenden—Mitwirkungsrechte des Bundestages in Angelegenheiten der Europäischen Union weiter stärken; Plenarprotokoll 17/232, Stenografischer Bericht der 232. Sitzung des Deutschen Bundestages am 22. März 2013 (EUZBBG revision first plenary); Plenarprotokoll 17/234, Stenografischer Bericht der 234. Sitzung des Deutschen Bundestages am 18. April 2013 (EUZBBG revision second plenary).

problem after the GFCC had so demanded. This sequence of events makes it unlikely that the revision of the EUZBBG would have come about in the same way without the GFCC's intervention. Although the coalition parties protested against the government's information provision during the crisis, they would have had to engage in an open conflict with the government to change the situation. It has been noted that, politically, such an open conflict would have been almost impossible, making intervention by the GFCC indispensable for change.[105]

The full practical implications of these changes are to be explored elsewhere. Nonetheless, there are signs that the legal changes have not been mere paper tigers. Although parliamentary majorities will almost always support their government, a number of parliamentarians indicated that it is an advantage that assistance decisions were subject to a prior parliamentary discussion.[106] In addition, the *Bundestag*'s improved access to information enables better scrutiny, particularly of intergovernmental decision-making fora. A reported downside of the system is the possibility for information overload, especially because the materials are often complex and decisions may need to be made in a short time span.[107] The fact that European negotiations often proceed quickly has more generally been noted as a remaining problem for effective parliamentary oversight.[108]

4. Conclusion

This chapter discussed the positive democratic effects of several interventions by the GFCC during the euro crisis. There is considerable evidence that the GFCC contributed to a strengthening of the *Bundestag*'s position in EU affairs. In parliamentary systems where a parliamentary majority supports the government, open conflict between the government and parliament may be unlikely. In Germany, this factor appears to have been an important reason why the GFCC was ultimately needed to strengthen the *Bundestag*'s position during the euro crisis. As a result of the Court's interventions, the *Bundestag* has a significantly stronger information position as well as stronger participation rights in EU affairs. It is also unlikely that the *Bundestag* would have obtained an equally strong position without the Court's rulings. From a democratic perspective this result is positive, especially as the

[105] Kietz, 'Politisierung trotz Parteienkonsens' (n 1) 27.

[106] Interview with Gesine Lötzsch, *Bundestag* member for Die Linke and chair of the *Bundestag*'s budget committee (Berlin, Germany, 27 May 2015); Interview with Christian Hirte, *Bundestag* member for the CDU (Berlin, Germany, 24 April 2015); Interview with Otto Fricke, former *Bundestag* member for the FDP and chair of the *Bundestag*'s budget committee between 2005 and 2009 (Berlin, Germany, 6 May 2015).

[107] Gesine Lötzsch, *Bundestag* member for Die Linke and chair of the *Bundestag*'s budget committee (Berlin, Germany, 27 May 2015); Interview with Lothar Binding, *Bundestag* member for the SPD (Berlin, Germany, 29 April 2015); Interview with Peter Danckert, former member of the *Bundestag* for the SPD (Berlin, Germany, 12 May 2015).

[108] Interview with Christian Hirte, *Bundestag* member for the CDU (Berlin, Germany, 24 April 2015).

Court was also able to consider and address countervailing concerns. In its judgment on the *Neuner Gremium*, it admitted that even in a democracy there can be a legitimate need for secrecy. Yet, the Court was also able to distinguish the cases in which confidentiality was justified from those in which the grounds were weak. In this respect, the GFCC was thus able to address specific shortcomings in the political process without rejecting the *Bundestag*'s approach as wholly unconstitutional.

A full assessment of the GFCC's role during the crisis nuances the positive picture. As discussed in the previous chapter, the threat that any assistance mechanisms would be struck down by the Court contributed to an escalation of the crisis in the spring of 2010. Yet, this escalation initially also marginalized the *Bundestag*'s role. Also, the decision to adopt the EFSF outside the EU Treaty framework was partly prompted by German constitutional considerations. Ironically, it was also this move that gave the German government an argument not to provide the *Bundestag* with essential information about negotiations on the ESM and Euro Plus Pact. These events illustrate how the threat of *ultra vires* review does not obviously benefit democratic legitimacy. The threat did not prevent European measures from eventually being adopted, merely that these were agreed outside the EU framework. Although this move ensured a German veto, there was no involvement of the European Parliament, and transparency concerns remained.

Finally, and as I argued in the previous chapter, the GFCC's case law had broader problematic consequences for democratic politics. And although national parliaments may be key in strengthening the EU's democratic legitimacy, there are limitations: significant asymmetries between national parliaments exist, and some national parliaments are able to take decisions that fundamentally affect citizens in other Member States, without those citizens being included in the process.[109] During the crisis, the debtor states' de facto sovereignty appears to have been severely curtailed, with negative repercussions for the position of their parliaments. For example, in 2011 the ECB addressed secret letters to Spain and Italy containing detailed instructions on reforms to be implemented in exchange for assistance through the ECB's bond-buying schemes.[110] In Ireland, a draft budget was leaked in November 2011 from the German budget committee, which had obtained the document for the approval of releasing assistance funds. The draft budget had been sent to all EU finance ministers, but not yet to Irish parliamentarians. The leak was consequently seen as evidence of extensive foreign intrusion in Irish affairs.[111]

[109] An initial overview of such asymmetries has been provided by Höing, 'Differentation of Parliamentary Powers' (n 3).

[110] Similar allegations about the ECB have been made in the context of Ireland. On all these events see Claire Kilpatrick, 'On the Rule of Law and Economic Emergency: The Degradation of Basic Legal Values in Europe's Bailouts' (2015) 35 Oxford Journal of Legal Studies 325, 344–45.

[111] Arthur Beesley, 'Our Loss of Economic Sovereignty May Be Just the Beginning' *The Irish Times* (22 November 2011); Stephen Coutts, 'Constitutional Change through Euro Crisis Law: Ireland' (2 March 2014) <http://eurocrisislaw.eui.eu/ireland> accessed 2 August 2022; Siobhán Dowling, 'Ireland's Budget Leak to Germany Brings Home Some Harsh Realities' *The Guardian* (18 November 2011) <www.theguardian.com/commentisfree/2011/nov/18/ireland-budget-germany-leak> accessed 2

In the GFCC's interpretation of democracy, the potential repercussions for other Member States of German budgetary decision-making play no role. Although the GFCC's strengthening of the *Bundestag*'s position is positive from a democratic perspective, the *Bundestag* alone can hardly legitimize decisions with significant effects on citizens outside Germany.[112]

August 2022; Jamie Smyth and Peter Spiegel, 'Irish Angry Over Budget Leak to Germany' *Financial Times* (Dublin/Brussels, 18 November 2011) <www.ft.com/content/bd9ab93a-11fb-11e1-a114-00144feabdc0> accessed 2 August 2022.

[112] Mark Dawson and Floris De Witte, 'From Balance to Conflict: A New Constitution for the EU' (2016) 22(2) European Law Journal 204, 220.

7

The *PSPP* Ruling and the Pandemic: A Move to Weak Review?

1. Introduction

This chapter considers the German Federal Constitutional Court's (GFCC) *PSPP* ruling and its aftermath, as well as the role of the German Constitutional Court in the EU's response to the Covid-19 pandemic. In the spring of 2020, Europe found itself in the midst of both combating the pandemic and dealing with its economic fallout. As the public health emergency unfolded, Member States imposed strict lockdowns. An unprecedented economic contraction followed, and fears of a new euro crisis emerged, leading to renewed discussions over the EMU's future.[1] Ultimately, the EU responded with various measures, the most ground-breaking of which was Next Generation EU (NGEU), a massive recovery plan of €750 billion. The plan meant that Germany departed from its long-held taboo on joint EU borrowing and fiscal transfers, making NGEU a considerable change in the architecture of the Economic and Monetary Union (EMU).

Amidst these events, the GFCC found itself in the limelight again. On 5 May 2020, Germany's constitutional judges ruled that both the ECB and the CJEU had acted *ultra vires*. The German Court held that the European Central Bank's (ECB) Public Sector Purchasing Programme (PSPP) exceeded the Central Bank's competences under the EU Treaties, because the ECB had failed to properly substantiate the programme's proportionality.[2] In doing so, the German judges cast aside as *ultra vires* the CJEU's *Weiss* judgment, which had previously upheld the PSPP.[3] According to the GFCC, its European counterpart had failed to properly review the proportionality of the ECB's actions. That failure, the judges in Karlsruhe reasoned, made the CJEU's interpretation of the Treaties 'simply not comprehensible and thus objectively arbitrary'.[4]

[1] See eg Adam Tooze, *Shutdown: How Covid Shook the World's Economy* (Penguin 2021) chs 4, 5, and 9.

[2] Bundesverfassungsgericht, judgment of 5 May 2020, 2 BvR 859/15 (*PSPP*) (hereafter BVerfG, *PSPP*).

[3] Case C-493/17 *Weiss*, EU:C:2018:1000 (hereafter CJEU, *Weiss*).

[4] BVerfG, *PSPP* (n 2) para 118; The qualification followed from the GFCC's self-imposed standards in the *Honeywell* case for finding EU acts *ultra vires*, Bundesverfassungsgericht, judgment of 6 July 2010, 2 BvR 2661/06 (*Honeywell*). For criticism on this part of the judgment see, among others, Franz Mayer, 'The Ultra Vires Ruling: Deconstructing the German Federal Constitutional Court's PSPP Decision of 5 May 2020' (2021) 16 European Constitutional Law Review 733.

Judging European Democracy. Nik de Boer, Oxford University Press.
DOI: 10.1093/oso/9780192845238.003.0007

The GFCC's first ever *ultra vires* ruling presented a significant escalation in the Court's treatment of EU law and its dealings with the CJEU. It was also a further sign that the trajectory of European integration and the GFCC's understanding of the German constitution had become increasingly at odds.[5] The *PSPP* ruling was widely criticized by legal commentators as well as in the broader media, especially for its attack on the primacy of EU law and the CJEU's authority.[6] Others feared its negative consequences for the ECB's role and the stability of the eurozone.[7] The CJEU responded with an exceptional press release, while the European Commission eventually decided to launch infringement proceedings against Germany.[8]

After the dust settled, the consequences of the ruling were less drastic than some had predicted, at least in the short term. Despite the harsh tone of its judgment, the Karlsruhe Court applied a weak remedy, allowing political institutions to find a solution, which was how the conflict was solved. Still, the GFCC's reasoning on the monetary financing prohibition put into question whether the ECB's newly launched Pandemic Emergency Purchase Programme (PEPP) would survive scrutiny by the German judges.[9] It was not long until fresh constitutional complaints were filed against this new ECB programme before the Karlsruhe Court.[10] A further question was whether the NGEU package was compatible with the *Bundestag*'s budgetary sovereignty and the EU Treaty framework.[11] The GFCC dismissed a legal challenge in summary proceedings on 15 April 2021, granting the *Bundestag*

5 In this direction, see also Dieter Grimm, 'A Long Time Coming' (2020) 21 German Law Journal 944.

6 See eg Niels Petersen and Konstantin Chatziathanasiou, 'Primacy's Twilight?' (European Parliament 2021) PE 692.276 60–61 <www.europarl.europa.eu/thinktank/en/document/IPOL_STU(2021)692276> accessed 1 August 2022; Jürgen Basedow and others, 'European Integration: Quo Vadis? A Critical Commentary on the PSPP Judgment of the German Federal Constitutional Court of May 5, 2020' (2021) 19 International Journal of Constitutional Law 188, 192. The judgment led to a flood of legal commentary, especially on Verfassungsblog, and was the subject of special issues in the *German Law Journal* and *ICON*. For an overview of the commentaries, see Mayer, 'The Ultra Vires Ruling' (n 4) fns 3–12.

7 Willem H Buiter, 'Germany's Judges Declare War on the ECB' (*Project Syndicate*, 6 May 2020) <www.project-syndicate.org/commentary/german-constitution-court-ecb-pspp-ruling-by-willem-h-buiter-2020-05> accessed 1 August 2022.

8 Court of Justice of the European Union Press Release 58/20, Press release following the judgment of the German Constitutional Court of 5 May 2020 (8 May 2020); European Commission, 'June Infringements Package: Key Decisions', Brussels, 9 June 2021 <https://ec.europa.eu/commission/presscorner/detail/en/inf_21_2743> accessed 2 August 2022 (hereafter Commission, 'June Infringements Package').

9 For an analysis, see Ana Bobić and Mark Dawson, 'Making Sense of the "Incomprehensible": The PSPP Judgment of the German Federal Constitutional Court' (2020) 57 Common Market Law Review 1953, 1989–94.

10 David Marsh, 'Fresh German Legal Battle over ECB Easing' (*OMFIF*, 17 June 2020) <www.omfif.org/2020/06/fresh-german-legal-battle-over-ecb-easing/> accessed 2 August 2022; Holger Zschäpitz, '"Krasser Fall von Staatsfinanzierung"—EZB Wird an Grenzen Ihres Mandats Erinnert' *Die Welt* (11 March 2021) <www.welt.de/wirtschaft/article228033723/EZB-Notfallprogramm-PEPP-Klaeger-ziehen-vor-Bundesverfassungsgericht.html> accessed 2 August 2022.

11 See also Mattias Wendel, 'The Fog of Identity and Judicial Contestation: Preventive and Defensive Constitutional Identity Review in Germany' (2021) 27 European Public Law 465, 477–79.

a wide margin of assessment, although—at the time of writing—the issue still awaited a ruling in the main proceedings and may well be referred to the CJEU.

The aim of this chapter is to understand the political consequences of the GFCC's EU-related case law during the Covid-19 crisis. More specifically, the chapter analyses the impact of the *PSPP* ruling on political debates concerning the role of the ECB, as well as the impact on NGEU of the GFCC's case law more broadly. As these events were still unfolding at the time of writing, the analysis is partly preliminary. The story has several sides. On the one hand, the *PSPP* ruling was an escalation that potentially endangered the role of the ECB and the stability of the EU legal order. Yet, the GFCC ultimately applied a weak remedy. The German Court pointed to democratic problems with the ECB but left it to political institutions to address them. As the chapter shows, this helped foster further political debate in Germany about the legitimacy of the ECB and contributed to greater openness on the justification of monetary policy. What is more, by taking the bold step of declaring both an ECB and a CJEU programme *ultra vires*, the GFCC probably overplayed its hand. The judgment led to significant criticism of the GFCC. This included German politicians, several of whom (unlike during the euro crisis) were willing to contest the GFCC's case law and its interpretation of the German constitution. Such contestation of the GFCC's interpretation of the German constitution is a welcome democratic development.

A somewhat similar picture emerges from the study of NGEU. Although the GFCC has long expressed doubts about the constitutionality of further European fiscal integration, the Court had so far—at time of writing—proved unwilling to stand in the way of this new recovery plan.[12] Some even argued that the *PSPP* ruling provided an impetus for further fiscal integration, because the judgment put into question the ECB's crisis-fighting role. As the analysis below reveals, however, it is unclear whether the *PSPP* ruling was an important cause for NGEU. Other factors played a key role. Moreover, legal features of NGEU show that concerns about constitutional identity and *ultra vires* review were still an influence on the design of the recovery plan. Nonetheless, for several German politicians, the GFCC's case law did not present an impediment to publicly calling for fiscal union. Equally remarkable is that politicians of the Christian-democratic CDU/CSU and centre-right liberal Free Democratic Party (FDP) continued to oppose such fiscal union but appeared unwilling to rely on the authority of the GFCC in this regard. In the German parliamentary debates on NGEU, the GFCC's case law looked like a fringe argument that was primarily invoked by the Eurosceptic Alternative für Deutschland (AfD) to oppose the new recovery plan.

Taken together, the *PSPP* judgment and its aftermath may entail that, compared to the euro crisis, the GFCC will be more inclined to leave the development of the

12 Bundesverfassungsgericht, decision of 15 April 2021, 2 BvR 547/21 (*NGEU decision on preliminary injunction*) (hereafter BVerfG, *NGEU decision on preliminary injunction*).

EU to political institutions and Germany's elected politicians themselves are more willing to treat this issue as a political matter. Both developments are welcome, because it is more democratically legitimate when key constitutional questions about European integration are left to political institutions rather than decided by courts. Future developments, however, will have to be awaited to assess whether this reading is correct. The remainder of this chapter proceeds as follows. Section 2 first provides a brief overview of the main developments in the EMU since the euro crisis and especially of the new measures agreed in response to the Covid-19 pandemic. Section 3 discusses the *PSPP* judgment in relation to democratic concerns about the role of the ECB. Section 4 subsequently focuses on the role of the GFCC in relation to NGEU.

2. EMU Developments since the Euro Crisis

While many far-reaching reforms of the EMU had been proposed both during and in the aftermath of the euro crisis, reform of Europe's monetary union largely ground to a halt when the urgency receded.[13] The election of Emmanuel Macron as President of France in 2017 did give renewed impetus to political debates over eurozone reform. He launched ambitious proposals for a substantial eurozone budget, a European finance minister, and eurozone parliament.[14] Yet, the most that the Member States could agree on in 2018 was a significantly watered down version of Macron's initiatives, while political divisions blocked further changes. France and other southern Member States favoured more extensive risk sharing, such as fiscal transfers or the joint issue of debt. Germany and other northern Member States preferred risk reduction, by ensuring better prevention of economic crises and letting Member States take action themselves to resolve economic problems.[15] On balance, the extensive changes in the EMU agreed upon during the euro crisis were heavily focused on risk reduction. Instruments for risk sharing that were agreed upon, such as the ESM, remained largely under control of the Member States.[16]

[13] See eg Herman van Rompuy, 'Towards a Genuine Economic and Monetary Union (Four Presidents' Report)' (European Council 2012) 120/12 <www.consilium.europa.eu/media/23818/134069.pdf> accessed 2 August 2022; Jean-Claude Juncker, 'Completing Europe's Economic and Monetary Union (Five Presidents' Report) (European Commission 2015) <https://ec.europa.eu/info/publications/five-presidents-report-completing-europes-economic-and-monetary-union_en> accessed 2 August 2022.

[14] Emmanuel Macron, 'Sorbonne Speech' (26 September 2017) <http://international.blogs.ouest-france.fr/archive/2017/09/29/macron-sorbonne-verbatim-europe-18583.html> accessed 2 August 2022.

[15] See eg Thomas Gutschker and Eckart Lohse, 'Europa muss handlungsfähig sein—nach außen und innen' *Frankfurter Allgemeine Zeitung* (Berlin, 3 June 2018).

[16] Daniel Seikel and Achim Truger, 'The Blocked Completion of the European Monetary Union' (WSI Institute of Economic and Social Research 2019) WSI Report 52 <www.boeckler.de/en/faust-detail.htm?sync_id=8520> accessed 1 June 2022; Lucas Guttenberg and Eulalia Rubio, 'The Future of the Eurozone: Cross-Perspective from France and Germany' (Jacques Delors Institute 2018) Policy Brief <https://institutdelors.eu/wp-content/uploads/2020/08/RencontresdEvian-EMU-GuttenbergRubio-Sept2018-3.pdf> accessed 1 June 2022; Lucas Guttenberg, 'Un nouveau départ pour la Zone

As discussed in Chapter 5, this outcome was in line with, and influenced by, the GFCC's insistence on maintaining the budgetary autonomy of the *Bundestag*.

In 2020, significant change became possible as a result of the Covid-19 pandemic. The spread of the Covid-19 virus to Europe led to fears of a new euro crisis, especially as Italy was hit hard.[17] In March 2020, Italy's government debt already amounted to 136 per cent of Italian GDP. It was expected to rise further to 155 per cent over the course of the year, as a result of the Covid-19 crisis.[18] France and Spain, Member States with more limited but still relatively high debt to GDP ratios, were also affected significantly. Given their already high level of public indebtedness, southern Member States had less financial ability than northern Member States to deal with the economic consequences of the pandemic or support a later recovery. The consequent risk was that the Covid-19 crisis would deepen economic differences in the EU.[19] As a result, the debate over risk sharing in the eurozone gained new momentum.

Still, initial discussions among European governments showed familiar fault lines. Germany and other northern states remained opposed to joint bonds.[20] On 23 March 2020, the Council did activate the general escape clause in the Stability and Growth Pact.[21] This allowed Member States to temporarily deviate from the

Euro?' (Jacques Delors Institute 2019) <https://institutdelors.eu/publications/a-new-approach-to-eurozone-reform-2/> accessed 1 August 2022; David Howarth and Joachim Schild, 'Nein to "Transfer Union": The German Brake on the Construction of a European Union Fiscal Capacity' (2021) 43 Journal of European Integration 209.

[17] Tony Barber, 'Italy's Struggle with Coronavirus Threatens All of the Eurozone' *Financial Times* (13 March 2020) <www.ft.com/content/6d3b5ff4-646c-11ea-b3f3-fe4680ea68b5> accessed 2 August 2022; Wolfgang Münchau, 'Eurozone Stability is under Threat Again' *Financial Times* (15 March 2020) <www.ft.com/content/d8086302-6545-11ea-a6cd-df28cc3c6a68> accessed 2 August 2022; Tommy Stubbington, 'Rise in Italian Yields Has Echoes of Eurozone Debt Crisis' *Financial Times* (17 March 2020) <www.ft.com/content/3e372b66-684a-11ea-800d-da70cff6e4d3> accessed 2 August 2022.

[18] Tooze, *Shutdown* (n 1) 177.

[19] Ulrich Krotz and Lucas Schramm, 'Embedded Bilateralism, Integration Theory, and European Crisis Politics: France, Germany, and the Birth of the EU Corona Recovery Fund' (2022) 60 Journal of Common Market Studies 526, 531–32.

[20] FT Reporters, 'EU Leaders Clash over Coronavirus Response' (26 March 2020) <www.ft.com/content/c3e4db7e-c45a-4113-9bf6-d5d5580fa0ba> accessed 2 August 2022. See also Howarth and Schild, 'Nein to "Transfer Union"' (n 16) 218–19; Amandine Crespy and Lucas Schramm, 'Breaking the Budgetary Taboo: German Preference Formation in the EU's Response to the Covid-19 Crisis' [2021] German Politics 1, 2; Krotz and Schramm, 'Embedded Bilateralism' (n 19) 531–33.

[21] See Statement of EU ministers of finance on the Stability and Growth Pact in light of the COVID-19 crisis of 23 March 2020 <www.consilium.europa.eu/en/press/press-releases/2020/03/23/statement-of-eu-ministers-of-finance-on-the-stability-and-growth-pact-in-light-of-the-covid-19-crisis/> accessed 2 August 2022; European Commission, 'Communication from the Commission to the Council on the activation of the general escape clause of the Stability and Growth Pact', COM(2020) 123 final <https://ec.europa.eu/info/sites/default/files/economy-finance/2_en_act_part1_v3-adopted_text.pdf> accessed 2 August 2022. The clause is contained in arts 5(1), 6(3), 9(1), and 10(3) of Council Regulation (EC) 1466/97 on the strengthening of the surveillance of budgetary positions and the surveillance and coordination of economic policies [1997] OJ L209/1 and arts 3(5) and 5(2) of Council Regulation (EC) 1467/97 on speeding up and clarifying the implementation of the excessive deficit procedure [1997] OJ L209/6.

EU's fiscal rules in order to combat the Covid-19 economic shock. Shortly before this, the Commission had also decided to offer substantial exemptions to state aid rules.[22] Further measures included the European instrument for temporary Support to mitigate Unemployment Risks in an Emergency, abbreviated as SURE.[23] The instrument was based on Article 122 TFEU and could provide financial assistance of up to €100 billion in the form of loans 'to address sudden increases in public expenditure for the preservation of employment'.[24] Alongside this, discussions focused on the use of the ESM to support troubled Member States. On 9 April 2020, the Eurogroup agreed to establish a 'Pandemic Crisis Support'. This meant that the ESM could provide credit lines to euro area Member States 'to support domestic financing of direct and indirect healthcare, cure and prevention related costs due to the COVID 19 crisis'.[25] Unlike previous ESM programmes, the money came without macroeconomic conditions attached. Yet, Member States proved unwilling to draw on the fund, as the ESM was tainted with the traumatic austerity policies of the euro crisis.[26] The Eurogroup of 9 April, and the European Council of 23 April 2020, did also agree to work towards a new 'Recovery Fund'.

[22] European Commission, 'State aid: Commission adopts Temporary Framework to enable Member States to further support the economy in the COVID-19 outbreak', Press release, Brussels, 19 March 2020 <https://ec.europa.eu/commission/presscorner/detail/en/IP_20_496> accessed 2 August 2022; European Commission, 'Temporary Framework for State aid measures to support the economy in the current COVID-19 outbreak (Communication)', (Brussels, 19 March 2020) COM(2020) 1863 final <https://ec.europa.eu/competition/state_aid/what_is_new/sa_covid19_temporary-framework.pdf> accessed 2 August 2022.

[23] European Commission 'Proposal for a COUNCIL REGULATION on the establishment of a European instrument for temporary support to mitigate unemployment risks in an emergency (SURE) following the COVID-19 outbreak', (Brussels 2 April 2020) COM(2020) 139 final <https://eur-lex.europa.eu/legal-content/EN/TXT/?uri=COM%3A2020%3A0139%3AFIN> accessed 2 August 2022. The Council adopted the instrument on 19 May 2020: Council Regulation (EU) 2020/672 on the establishment of a European instrument for temporary support to mitigate unemployment risks in an emergency (SURE) following the COVID-19 outbreak [2020] OJ L159/1.

[24] European Commission, 'SURE' <https://ec.europa.eu/info/business-economy-euro/economic-and-fiscal-policy-coordination/financial-assistance-eu/funding-mechanisms-and-facilities/sure_en> accessed 2 August 2022.

[25] Eurogroup, 'Report on the comprehensive economic policy response to the COVID-19 pandemic', Press release, 9 April 2020 <www.consilium.europa.eu/en/press/press-releases/2020/04/09/report-on-the-comprehensive-economic-policy-response-to-the-covid-19-pandemic/> accessed 2 August 2022, para 16; Eurogroup, 'Eurogroup Statement on the Pandemic Crisis Support', Press release, 8 May 2020 <www.consilium.europa.eu/nl/press/press-releases/2020/05/08/eurogroup-statement-on-the-pandemic-crisis-support/> accessed 2 August 2022. It was endorsed by the ESM Governing Board on 15 May 2020: ESM, 'ESM Board of Governors backs Pandemic Crisis Support', Press release, 15 May 2020 <www.esm.europa.eu/press-releases/esm-board-governors-backs-pandemic-crisis-support> accessed 2 August 2022.

[26] Sam Fleming and Miles Johnson, 'Giuseppe Conte Prepares for Toxic Choice on Eurozone Rescue Fund' *Financial Times* (Brussels and Rome, 21 April 2020) <www.ft.com/content/e5bc46a8-8317-4876-acb9-0bcc5b67dedd> accessed 2 August 2022; Martin Sandbu, 'The Eurozone's Bailout Fund Remains Unfairly Toxic' *Financial Times* (20 May 2020) <www.ft.com/content/2741caf1-5758-4a26-ac88-0cab6cf63500> accessed 2 August 2022; Tobias Tesche, 'Pandemic Politics: The European Union in Times of the Coronavirus Emergency' (2022) 60 Journal of Common Market Studies 480; Lucas Guttenberg, 'Time to Come Home if the ESM is to Stay Relevant, it Should Be Reinvented inside the EU' (Jacques Delors Institute & Bertelsmann Stiftung 2020) Policy Brief <www.delorscentre.eu/en/publications/detail/publication/time-to-come-home> accessed 1 August 2022.

Significant differences between northern and southern Member States remained, however, over the issue of common debt and on whether assistance should take the form of loans or grants.[27]

Meanwhile the ECB had taken the most decisive action. After some initial hesitation, the Central Bank announced its PEPP on 18 March 2020.[28] This new, massive bond-buying programme had an initial envelope of €750 billion, further increased to €1,350 billion in June 2020 and to €1,850 billion in December 2020.[29] Its stated aim was 'to counter the serious risks to price stability, the monetary policy transmission mechanism and the economic outlook in the euro area, which are posed by the outbreak and escalating diffusion of COVID-19'.[30] Unlike previous bond-buying programmes, the PEPP now included Greek government debt, and the ECB would be allowed to buy up much larger quantities of public debt issued by specific Member States. The Governing Council qualified the remaining limits on the programme as 'self-imposed', standing ready to revise them 'to the extent necessary to make its action proportionate to the risks that we face'.[31] This was the case even though both the CJEU and GFCC had previously deemed such limits important for the legality of ECB action, in particular regarding its compliance with the principle of proportionality and the monetary financing prohibition.

The key political shift came on 18 May 2020, when Germany gave up opposition to joint EU borrowing through a common call with France for a €500 billion EU recovery fund. This fund was to be distributed in the form of grants and financed 'by borrowing on markets on behalf of the EU'.[32] On 27 May 2020, the European Commission fleshed out those ideas with its proposal of NGEU, a huge new recovery plan of €750 billion, of which €500 billion were to be spent as subsidies

[27] Sam Fleming and Mehreen Khan, 'Eurozone Strikes Emergency Deal on Coronavirus Rescue' *Financial Times* (Brussels, 10 April 2020) <www.ft.com/content/b984101a-42b8-40db-9a92-6786aec2ba5c> accessed 2 August 2022; Sam Fleming and Mehreen Khan, 'EU Fails to Settle Rifts over Size and Shape of "Recovery Fund"' *Financial Times* (24 April 2020) <www.ft.com/content/cee2c14a-fa59-4684-a335-27cef1260fa6> accessed 2 August 2022.

[28] Decision (EU) 2020/440 of the European Central Bank on a temporary pandemic emergency purchase programme (ECB/2020/17) [2020] OJ L91/1 (hereafter PEPP).

[29] ECB, 'Monetary policy decisions', Press release 4 June 2020 <www.ecb.europa.eu/press/pr/date/2020/html/ecb.mp200604~a307d3429c.en.html> accessed 2 August 2022; ECB, 'Monetary policy decisions', Press release 10 December 2020 <www.ecb.europa.eu/press/pr/date/2020/html/ecb.mp201210~8c2778b843.en.html> accessed 2 August 2022; Decision (EU) 2021/174 of the European Central Bank amending Decision (EU) 2020/440 on a temporary pandemic emergency purchase programme (ECB/2021/6) [2021] OJ L50/29; Decision (EU) 2020/1143 of the European Central Bank of 28 July 2020 amending Decision (EU) 2020/440 on a temporary pandemic emergency purchase programme (ECB/2020/36) [2020] OJ L248/24.

[30] PEPP (n 28) para 4.

[31] ECB, 'ECB announces €750 billion Pandemic Emergency Purchase Programme (PEPP)', Press release, 18 March 2020 <www.ecb.europa.eu/press/pr/date/2020/html/ecb.pr200318_1~3949d6f266.en.html> accessed 2 August 2020; PEPP (n 28) para 6.

[32] German government, 'A French-German Initiative for the European Recovery from the Coronavirus Crisis', Press release, 18 May 2020 <www.bundeskanzler.de/resource/blob/1830100/1753772/414a4b5a1ca91d4f7146eeb2b39ee72b/2020-05-18-deutsch-franzoesischer-erklaerung-eng-data.pdf?download=1> accessed 2 August 2022.

rather than loans.[33] An amendment to the Own Resources Decision (ORD) would allow the EU to borrow the total sum on financial markets.[34] After a marathon session of the European Council, government leaders reached an agreement on the package and the new Multiannual Financial Framework (MFF) in the early morning of 21 July 2020. This deal retained the key elements of the Commission's proposal, but changes were made to the size, the ratio of loans versus subsidies, and the conditionality of the funds.[35] Agreement with the European Parliament and on further details in the Council was reached in the remaining months of 2020.[36] The main elements of the package were adopted in December 2020 and February 2021, although the ORD was subject to national ratification, a process only to be completed on 31 May 2021.

3. *Ultra Vires*: The *PSPP* Ruling and its Consequences

The GFCC's ruling on the PSPP came in the middle of the Covid-19 crisis and had been postponed by three weeks because of Covid-related restrictions.[37] The case reflected longer-standing democratic concerns about the ECB's unconventional post-crisis operations. The ECB's actions had been the subject of Karlsruhe Court proceedings before, culminating in the judicial saga on the ECB's OMT policy between 2014 and 2016, briefly discussed in Chapter 5. The present section first explains the dispute about the PSPP and the different legal assessments by the CJEU and GFCC.[38] Secondly, I explain why the GFCC did raise justified democratic objections about the ECB's role. Thirdly, I discuss the political reception of the judgment. On the one hand, the judgment's consequences were addressed politically, and the ruling did contribute to further political debate about, and openness of, the ECB's monetary policy. On the other hand, the GFCC's judgment was perceived by European institutions as an attack on the primacy of EU law and the CJEU. As a result, these institutions focused on defending the EU legal order without addressing democratic concerns about the ECB's role. Fourthly, I show that the GFCC was

[33] European Commission, 'The EU budget powering the recovery plan for Europe', COM(2020) 442 final <https://eur-lex.europa.eu/resource.html?uri=cellar:4524c01c-a0e6-11ea-9d2d-01aa75ed71a1.0003.02/DOC_1&format=PDF> accessed 2 August 2022.

[34] European Commission, 'Amended proposal for a Council decision on the system of Own Resources of the European Union', COM(2020) 445 final <https://ec.europa.eu/info/sites/default/files/about_the_european_commission/eu_budget/com_2020_445_en_act_v8.pdf> accessed 2 August 2022.

[35] Bruno de Witte, 'The European Union's Covid-19 Recovery Plan: The Legal Engineering of an Economic Policy Shift' (2021) 58 Common Market Law Review 635, 642.

[36] ibid 642.

[37] Franz Mayer, 'Auf dem Weg zum Richterfaustrecht?' (*Verfassungsblog*, 7 May 2020) <https://verfassungsblog.de/auf-dem-weg-zum-richterfaustrecht/> accessed 2 August 2022.

[38] Sections 3.1 and 3.2 follow the argument developed in Nik de Boer and Jens van 't Klooster, 'The ECB, the Courts and the Issue of Democratic Legitimacy after Weiss' (2020) 57 Common Market Law Review 1689. I thank Jens van 't Klooster for permission to restate these ideas here.

unwilling to stand in the way of the political solution to the *PSPP* ruling, and, fifthly, that subsequent political debate also brought about welcome political contestation of the GFCC's case law.

3.1 The Dispute

The PSPP is a programme of the ECB by which the Central Bank buys government bonds on a very large scale in order to fulfil its price stability objective.[39] It is part of the ECB's Asset Purchasing Programme (APP) launched in 2014 because the Central Bank had reached the technical limits of its interest rate policy.[40] For that reason, the ECB introduced a quantitative easing policy (QE), which entails the large-scale buying of financial assets with a longer maturity in order to boost economic activity through the financial system.

The ECB's QE policy was controversial, however, especially in Germany.[41] A major criticism was that the programme had limited positive effects on economic growth and actually served to protect highly indebted Member States. Consequently, the PSPP would, in practice, violate the prohibition of monetary financing of sovereign debt (Article 123 TFEU) and stand in the way of necessary reforms in some Member States. In addition, QE has alleged negative side effects, such as redistributive consequences in favour of owners of financial assets and real estate. Moreover, very low interest rates were considered to artificially prop up non-viable banks and businesses.[42] Informed by such concerns, opponents of the PSPP challenged its legality before the German Court, claiming among other things that the programme exceeded the ECB's legal mandate and, as a result, the competences conferred on the EU. The GFCC subsequently referred these issues to the CJEU in Luxembourg.[43]

The CJEU rejected these claims. It considered that the PSPP did fall within the scope of the ECB's legal mandate and thus within the competences of the EU.[44] The CJEU based that conclusion on two main considerations.[45] In a first step, the CJEU

[39] Decision (EU) 2015/774 of the European Central Bank on a secondary markets public sector asset purchase programme (ECB/2015/10) [2015] OJ L121/20.

[40] See <www.ecb.europa.eu/mopo/implement/app/html/index.en.html> accessed 2 August 2022.

[41] See eg Claire Jones and Stefan Wagstyl, 'The Eurozone: A Strained Bond' *Financial Times* (18 January 2015).

[42] Martin Arnold, 'Splits at the ECB Top Table over Mario Draghi's Last Big Stimulus' *Financial Times* (27 September 2019); Martin Arnold, 'Former Central Bankers Attack ECB's Monetary Policy' *Financial Times* (27 September 2019); Hervé Hannoun and others, 'Memorandum on the ECB's Monetary Policy' (2019) <www.hanswernersinn.de/en/memorand-ecb-monetary-policy-04102019> accessed 2 August 2022.

[43] Bundesverfassungsgericht, order of 18 July 2017, 2 BvR 859/15 (*PSPP* reference) (hereafter BVerfG, *PSPP* reference).

[44] CJEU, *Weiss* (n 3).

[45] See also Case C-62/14 *Peter Gauweiler v Deutscher Bundestag* [2015] EU:C:2015:555 (hereafter CJEU, *Gauweiler*); Case C-370/12 *Thomas Pringle v Government of Ireland* [2012] EU:C:2012:756 (hereafter CJEU, *Pringle*).

reasoned that the measure did constitute monetary policy. Monetary policy is an exclusive competence of the Union and the responsibility of the ECB.[46] To determine whether an ECB measure falls under its monetary policy competence, the CJEU looks primarily at the objectives of the respective measure, namely whether it pursues price stability.[47] Here, the CJEU largely follows how the ECB defines the objectives of the policy itself. In addition, the CJEU checks whether the instruments used are permitted by the Statute of the ESCB and of the ECB. If the measures can be characterized as monetary policy on these grounds, the second step is a proportionality test based on Article 5(4) of the Treaty on European Union (TEU). In this respect the CJEU gives the ECB a wide margin of discretion because the Central Bank has to make 'to make choices of a technical nature and to undertake complex forecasts and assessments'.[48] The CJEU consequently limits itself to analysing whether the Central Bank made manifest errors of assessment.

The GFCC took a very different approach. According to Karlsruhe, the ECB's mandate has to be interpreted restrictively for democratic reasons.[49] More specifically, the German Court did so on two grounds. First, if the ECB oversteps its competences, this impairs the economic policy competences of the Member States and, as a result, the democratic right of self-determination of German citizens.[50] Secondly, the ECB's high degree of independence from political institutions entails that it operates 'on the basis of a diminished level of democratic legitimation.'[51] For both reasons, Karlsruhe deemed that the ECB's mandate must be interpreted strictly and be subject to full judicial review.[52]

Concretely, the GFCC disagreed with the CJEU on how the economic policy effects should have been taken into account when assessing the PSPP. The German Court submitted that these effects are relevant for ascertaining whether a measure still qualifies as economic or monetary policy. According to the German judges, the economic policy effects of monetary policy can be so significant that they outweigh the monetary policy objective.[53] In that case, the ECB's measures should be

[46] Strictly speaking, arts 127 and 282 TFEU, read in conjunction with art 139(2)(c) TFEU, assign the monetary policy of the Union to the Eurosystem, which comprises the ECB and the national central banks of the euro area. However, for ease of reading and because the national central banks are hierarchically subordinated to the ECB's decision-making bodies, I refer simply to the ECB.

[47] CJEU, *Gauweiler* (n 45) paras 34–45; CJEU, *Weiss* (n 3) paras 40–70; CJEU, *Pringle* (n 45) paras 46–70.

[48] CJEU, *Weiss* (n 3) para 73; CJEU, *Gauweiler* (n 45) para 68.

[49] BVerfG, *PSPP* (n 2) paras 136, 142, and 143.

[50] BVerfG, *PSPP* (n 2) paras 142, 158–60; BVerfG, *PSPP* reference (n 43) para 65 and paras 102–03. See also Bundesverfassungsgericht, order of 14 January 2014, 2 BvR 2728/13 (*OMT* reference) paras 39–40 and 63–68 (hereafter BVerfG, *OMT* reference); Bundesverfassungsgericht, judgment of 21 June 2016, 2 BvR 2728/13 (*OMT* final) paras 183–86 (hereafter BVerfG, *OMT* final).

[51] BVerfG, *PSPP* (n 2) paras 143 and 159. See also BVerfG, *PSPP* reference (n 43) para 103; BVerfG, *OMT* reference (n 50) paras 58–59; BVerfG, *OMT* final (n 50) paras 187–89.

[52] BVerfG, *PSPP* (n 2) paras 143 and 159; see also BVerfG, *PSPP* reference (n 43) para 103; BVerfG, *OMT* reference (n 50) paras 58–59; BVerfG, *OMT* final (n 50) paras 187–89.

[53] See BVerfG, *PSPP* reference (n 43) para 121; BVerfG, *PSPP* (n 2) paras 139–43.

considered economic policy, not monetary policy, with the consequence that they are beyond the competence of the ECB and the Union. Put more simply, if an ECB programme has a merely limited impact on the inflation target, but results in large economic policy effects, then the programme actually constitutes economic policy, for which the ECB has no competence. The CJEU rejected this interpretation. The European Court distinguishes between monetary and economic policy solely on the basis of objectives and instruments, and it rejects a sharp delineation between monetary and economic policy.[54]

In its *PSPP* judgment, the German Court disagreed with its European counterpart mainly on the issue of proportionality.[55] The German judges stated that the CJEU should have considered whether the economic policy effects of the PSPP outweighed the monetary objectives. This assessment should have been part of the proportionality test under Article 5(4) TEU. In the eyes of the German judges, the CJEU's failure to conduct such an assessment rendered the proportionality test meaningless for the delineation of competences between the Member States and the Union: more specifically, the distinction between economic and monetary policy. The EU Court had therefore 'manifestly' exceeded its judicial mandate laid down in Article 19(1) TEU. This also led to a 'structurally significant shift in the division of competences to the detriment of the Member States'.[56] On this basis, the German Court concluded that the CJEU's judgment was *ultra vires* and without binding force in Germany.

Because the GFCC overruled the CJEU's ruling as *ultra vires*, it assessed itself whether the PSPP had been adopted within the scope of the ECB's competences. In this respect, the German Court voiced the same objection. The ECB had failed to publicly assess the programme's proportionality. Instead, it should have explained how it had balanced the economic effects against the monetary objective when developing and implementing the PSPP. The German Court listed a number of effects it deemed problematic. The PSPP would improve the financing conditions for Member States and thereby prevent them from carrying out necessary reforms. In addition, the Court pointed to the negative effect on savings and pensions and considered that very low interest rates would keep unprofitable companies afloat.[57] Because the ECB had failed to conduct the required proportionality test, the proportionality of the PSPP could not be established. The German Court therefore concluded that the PSPP exceeded the ECB's mandate: *ultra vires*.[58]

As a result, the PSPP could not, in principle, be applied in the German legal order. German state institutions, administrative bodies, and judges were no longer allowed to participate in the programme, a finding with specific relevance for the

[54] CJEU, *Weiss* (n 3) paras 60–67.
[55] BVerfG, *PSPP* (n 2) para 139.
[56] ibid paras 154–63.
[57] ibid paras 177–78.
[58] ibid para 179.

Bundesbank. Nevertheless, the GFCC offered a way out. The *Bundesbank* was allowed to continue participating in the PSPP for a transitional period of three months. Within that period, the ECB Governing Council should take a new decision that would demonstrate 'in a comprehensible and substantiated manner that the monetary policy objectives pursued by the ECB are not disproportionate to the economic and fiscal policy effects resulting from the programme'.[59] The judgment was formally addressed to the German government and the *Bundestag*. It fell upon these institutions to 'take steps seeking to ensure that the European Central Bank conducts a proportionality assessment'.[60] In this way the German judges refrained from immediately stopping German participation in the PSPP. The outcome left room for a political solution and, ultimately, the judgment contributed to more openness and debate about the political choices involved in monetary policy, which will be discussed in the next two subsections.

3.2 Democracy, the ECB, and Judicial Review

The GFCC's *PSPP* ruling can be seen as a reflection of heightened democratic concerns about the ECB's role since the 2007–2008 global financial crisis and the 2010–2012 eurozone crisis. The key democratic problem is that the original justification for the ECB's independence is increasingly difficult to sustain in light of the profoundly changed economic circumstances.[61]

The original justification for the ECB's independence, as discussed in Chapter 4, reflected a specific set of economic ideas that became dominant in the 1980s.[62] Economists, central bankers, and policymakers converged on the view that monetary policy should focus primarily on ensuring price stability. Stable prices would best support long-term economic growth and employment.[63] Central banks would best achieve price stability when independent.[64] In addition, the prevailing idea

[59] ibid para 235.

[60] ibid para 232.

[61] This argument is a shortened and restated version of de Boer and van 't Klooster, 'The ECB, the Courts and the Issue of Democratic Legitimacy' (n 38).

[62] See Kenneth Dyson and Kevin Featherstone, *The Road to Maastricht: Negotiating Economic and Monetary Union* (Oxford University Press 1999); Harold James, *Making the European Monetary Union* (Harvard University Press 2012); Kathleen McNamara, *The Currency of Ideas: Monetary Politics in the European Union* (Cornell University Press 1999).

[63] Inspired by the ideas of Milton Friedman, 'The Role of Monetary Policy' (1968) 58 American Economic Review 1.

[64] Finn E Kydland and Edward C Prescott, 'Rules Rather than Discretion: The Inconsistency of Optimal Plans' (1977) 85 Journal of Political Economy 473; Alan S Blinder, *Central Banking in Theory and Practice, The Lionel Robbins Lectures* (MIT Press 1999); Michael Emerson, Daniel Gros, and Alexander Italianer, *One Market, One Money: An Evaluation of the Potential Benefits and Costs of Forming an Economic and Monetary Union* (Oxford University Press 1992); Alberto Alesina and Lawrence H Summers, 'Central Bank Independence and Macroeconomic Performance: Some Comparative Evidence' (1993) 25 Journal of Money, Credit and Banking 151.

was that central banks should implement monetary policy by influencing interest rates in money markets.[65] Determining the right interest rate was meant to be a complex, but essentially technical, task because, in theory, there is one interest rate that corresponds to the long-term potential of the economy.

The legal architecture of the EMU conceived at Maastricht reflected these economic beliefs.[66] Under Article 127 TFEU, maintaining price stability is the primary objective of the ECB, while Article 130 TFEU gives the ECB a strong degree of independence from political institutions.[67] National governments, Union institutions, and all other bodies may not give the ECB or national central banks instructions on how they are to perform the tasks assigned to it.

In this constellation, the ECB's democratic legitimacy rests on its legal mandate as defined by the Member States in the Treaties. That mandate was established according to democratic procedures and should give the Central Bank a clearly defined set of tasks and objectives. For the proper implementation of the policy, the Central Bank is held accountable by explaining how its policy fits with the mandate.[68] A quantitative inflation target should provide a clear standard by which the ECB's monetary policy can be evaluated retrospectively. Because political institutions have no ability to sanction the actions of the ECB, judicial review theoretically plays an important role. The CJEU should be able to ensure that the ECB continues to operate within the limits of its mandate.[69]

This democratic justification for the ECB's independence has come under strain since the euro crisis. Since then, the ECB has faced difficult and politically controversial choices, even where it pursues the goal of price stability. The Treaty mandate gives the ECB little guidance in making these choices. The consequence is that,

[65] Claudio Borio, 'A Hundred Ways to Skin a Cat: Comparing Monetary Policy Operating Procedures in the United States, Japan and the Euro Area' (2001) BIS Working Papers No. 9 <www.bis.org/publ/bppdf/bispap09a.pdf> accessed 2 August 2022; Ulrich Bindseil, *Monetary Policy Operations and the Financial System* (Oxford University Press 2014).

[66] See Chapter 4.

[67] On the objective of price stability in the EMU legal framework, see Vestert Borger, 'Outright Monetary Transactions and the Stability Mandate of the ECB: Gauweiler' (2016) 53 Common Market Law Review 139; Matthias J Herdegen, 'Price Stability and Budgetary Restraints in the Economic and Monetary Union: The Law as Guardian of Economic Wisdom' (1998) 35 Common Market Law Review 9.

[68] ECB, 'The Accountability of the ECB' [2002] Monthly Bulletin 45; Diane Fromage and others, 'ECB Independence and Accountability Today: Towards a (Necessary) Redefinition?' (2019) 26 Maastricht Journal of European and Comparative Law 3; Rosa Lastra, 'The Independence of the European System of Central Banks' (1992) 33 Harvard International Law Journal 475; Rosa Lastra, *International Financial and Monetary Law* (Oxford University Press 2015); Paul Magnette, 'Towards "Accountable Independence"? Parliamentary Controls of the European Central Bank and the Rise of a New Democratic Model' (2000) 6 European Law Journal 326; René Smits, 'Accountability of the European Central Bank' [2019] Ars Aequi 27.

[69] Fabian Amtenbrink, 'Economic and Monetary Union' in Pieter Jan Kuijper and others (eds), *The Law of the European Union* (Kluwer Law International 2018) 940; Lastra, 'The Independence of the European System of Central Banks' (n 68) 500; Hanspeter K Scheller, *The European Central Bank: History, Role and Functions* (2nd edn, European Central Bank 2006).

in crucial cases, Europe's Central Bank no longer operates with clear democratic authorization.

The ECB thus faces 'democratic authorisation gaps'.[70] It is confronted with choices that have far-reaching consequences but for which its mandate offers limited guidance at best. One key example of such an authorization gap is the question of whether the ECB should intervene in response to a crisis in government bond markets. An assumption of the Maastricht EMU architecture was that the rules on excessive budget deficits and public debts, together with the no-bailout provision, would prevent such crises.[71] This assumption proved false in the spring of 2010, when panic took hold in European government bond markets. At the same time, the functioning of sovereign debt markets has implications for the implementation of monetary policy. The ECB's mandate, however, does not provide clarity on how the ECB should deal with this situation. The ECB chose to intervene by using its Securities Markets Programme (SMP) to buy up government bonds in 2010.[72] Then in 2012, the ECB launched the programme of Outright Monetary Transactions (OMT), in which it announced that it would purchase government bonds from Member States that could no longer finance themselves on the capital markets.[73] The ECB justified these interventions by invoking the monetary transmission mechanism. The crisis in the government bond market hindered the implementation of monetary policy and the achievement of price stability.[74] Yet, this interpretation of the mandate was contested. *Bundesbank* President Jens Weidmann, for example, argued that the OMT programme undermined the disciplining role of financial markets and was at odds with the Member States' own fiscal responsibility. In his view, there was a high risk that the OMT programme would eventually weaken the ECB's role in ensuring price stability.[75]

[70] This notion was coined in de Boer and van 't Klooster, 'The ECB, the Courts and the Issue of Democratic Legitimacy' (n 38). Recent work that uses the concept of an authorization gap to analyse the ECB's constitutional conundrum includes: Jens van 't Klooster, 'The Politics of the ECB's Market-Based Approach to Government Debt' [2022] Socio-economic review; Jens van 't Klooster and Nik de Boer, 'What to Do with the ECB's Secondary Mandate' (2022) Journal of Common Market Studies <https://doi.org/10.1111/jcms.13406>; Adam Tooze, 'Debating Central Bank Mandates' (2022) Forum for a New Economy, Working Papers 01 <www.newforum.org> accessed 2 August 2022; Laurence Scialom, Gaëtan Le Quang, and Jérôme Deyris, 'Shaky Foundations Central Bank Independence in the 21st Century' (2022) University of Paris Nanterre, EconomiX Working Papers 2022-16 <https://ideas.repec.org/p/drm/wpaper/2022-16.html> accessed 2 August 2022.

[71] Economic Committee for the Study of Economic and Monetary Union, 'Report on Economic and Monetary Union in the European Community (Delors Report)' (Office for Official Publications of the EC 1989); Kaarlo Tuori and Klaus Tuori, *The Eurozone Crisis. A Constitutional Analysis* (Cambridge University Press 2014).

[72] ECB, 'ECB decides on measures to address severe tensions in financial markets', Press release, 10 May 2010 <www.ecb.europa.eu/press/pr/date/2010/html/pr100510.en.html> accessed 2 August 2022.

[73] ECB, 'Technical features of Outright Monetary Transactions', Press release, 6 September 2012 <www.ecb.europa.eu/press/pr/date/2012/html/pr120906_1.en.html> accessed 2 August 2022.

[74] See on this, among other sources, ibid. <www.ecb.europa.eu/press/pr/date/2012/html/pr120906_1.en.html> accessed 2 August 2022; BVerfG, *OMT* reference (n 50) paras 7–12; CJEU, *Gauweiler* (n 45) paras 46–56 and Opinion of AG Cruz-Villalón, paras 209–12.

[75] Jens Weidmann, 'Eingangserklärung anlässlich der mündlichen Verhandlung im Hauptsacheverfahren ESM/EZB' 11 June 2013 <www.bundesbank.de/de/presse/stellungnahmen/

Similar concerns about the earlier SMP had prompted the resignation of former *Bundesbank* President Axel Weber and German ECB Executive Board member Jürgen Stark in 2011. These debates over the ECB's mandate were central to the judicial proceedings on the OMT before the GFCC and CJEU between 2014 and 2016.[76]

The legal dispute over the PSPP involved a similar authorization gap: namely what the ECB should do when it could not lower short-term interest rates any further to achieve its inflation target. After the crisis, the ECB lowered interest rates ever closer to 0 per cent. As a result, the ECB ran up against the technical limits of the interest rate instrument. In this case the ECB could choose to adjust the inflation target downwards, below the self-imposed 2 per cent inflation target. The other option was to introduce new instruments, which the ECB did with its QE programme. As discussed, this choice was controversial, even among central bankers themselves, given, among other things, the far-reaching consequences for public finances and alleged redistributive effects.

In these and other cases, it has fallen to the independent central bankers of the ECB's Governing Council to make far-reaching choices for which the legal mandate provides limited guidance at best. This democratic problem forms the backdrop to increased legal contestation about the ECB's role, culminating in both the judicial saga of the OMT as well as the PSPP.[77] The ECB's more recent actions in the context of the Covid-19 pandemic are a further example of the ECB acting without clear democratic authorization in the face of an economic shock.[78] The CJEU largely skips over this problem, as it accepts the ECB's contested policies as part of its monetary policy mandate without further addressing the democratic concern.[79] The Karlsruhe judges, on the other hand, make this democratic concern a key issue. The focus on proportionality helps to highlight the fact that the pursuit of price stability can have significant economic costs.

The GFCC's standard of review implies, however, that courts must review whether achieving the price stability objective outweighs the economic costs. This lands judges in uncomfortable territory. For one, it is not clear that judges possess

eingangserklaerung-anlaesslich-der-muendlichenverhandlung-im-hauptsacheverfahren-esm-ezb-662878> accessed 2 August 2022; Deutsche Bundesbank, 'Stellungnahme gegenüber dem Bundesverfassungsgericht zu den Verfahren mit den Az. 2 BvR 1390/12, 2 BvR 1421/12, 2 BvR 1439/12, 2 BvR 1824/12, 2 BvE 6/12' <www.bundesbank.de/de/startseite/stellungnahme-gegenueber-dem-bundesverfassungsgericht-zu-den-verfahren-mit-den-az-2-bvr-1390-12-2-bvr-1421-12-2-bvr-1439-12-2-bvr-1824-12-2-bve-6-12-799684> accessed 2 August 2022.

[76] Peter Spiegel, 'If the Euro Falls, Europe Falls' *Financial Times* (15 May 2020) <www.ft.com/content/b4e2e140-d9c3-11e3-920f-00144feabdc0> accessed 2 August 2022.

[77] For a more elaborate analysis of this democratic challenge, see de Boer and van 't Klooster, 'The ECB, the Courts and the Issue of Democratic Legitimacy' (n 38).

[78] PEPP (n 28).

[79] See the discussion by the CJEU of the ECB's institutional position in CJEU, *Weiss* (n 3) paras 48–52; CJEU, *Gauweiler* (n 45) Opinion of AG Cruz Villalón, paras 107–11.

the expertise to assess the content of monetary policy decisions.[80] This is reflected in the GFCC's *PSPP* judgment. The Court only identifies a limited set of negative economic effects of the PSPP and does not address the positive effects. In doing so, the German judges also ignored that the causal relationship between the PSPP and the effects mentioned is contested.[81]

Secondly, judicial review cannot compensate for the lack of democratic authorization. The ECB's Treaty mandate does not determine how the economic effects of monetary policy are to be evaluated. If the problem is that the ECB lacks the democratic authorization to make contested choices about the interpretation of its mandate, then the judges of the CJEU and the GFCC are in a structurally comparable position. Just like the central bankers, these judges are not democratically accountable to the electorate or to politically elected institutions. Furthermore, court proceedings usually only give a skewed picture of the positions and the interests involved in a particular issue.[82] The latter issue has been a recurrent problem in the proceedings before the Karlsruhe Constitutional Court. The core group of plaintiffs in the PSPP case shared a conservative political view. They included the original founders of the right-wing AfD, Joachim Starbatty and Bernd Lucke, the CSU politician Peter Gauweiler, the former president of the Federation of German Industries (BDI) Heinrich Weiss, as well as conservative legal scholars such as Karl Albrecht Schachtschneider and Markus Kerber.[83] Some explicitly stated that their aim was for the end of the euro.[84] The expert evidence consulted by the German Court also appeared one-sided.[85] It comprised mainly of German economists with conservative backgrounds and representatives of the German financial sector, such as the German Insurance Association and the Association of German Banks. The ruling reflected this limited view: the Constitutional Court only pointed to a

[80] Charles Goodhart and Rosa Lastra, 'Populism and Central Bank Independence' (2018) 29 Open Economies Review 49; Adam Tooze, 'The Death of the Central Bank Myth' *Foreign Policy* (13 May 2020) <https://foreignpolicy.com/2020/05/13/european-central-bank-myth-monetary-policy-german-court-ruling/> accessed 2 August 2022; Will Bateman, *Public Finance and Parliamentary Constitutionalism* (Cambridge University Press 2020) ch 8.

[81] This can also be read in the unofficial response by the ECB to the German *PSPP* ruling: ECB, 'Account of the monetary policy meeting of the Governing Council of the European Central Bank held in Frankfurt am Main on Wednesday and Thursday, 3–4 June 2020' <www.ecb.europa.eu/press/accounts/2022/html/ecb.mg220519~c9200dba08.en.html> accessed 2 August 2022.

[82] As discussed in Chapters 2 and 3 and noted by Richard Bellamy, 'The Democratic Qualities of Courts: A Critical Analysis of Three Arguments' (2013) 49(3) Representation 343; Fritz W Scharpf, 'The Asymmetry of European Integration, or Why the EU Cannot Be a "Social Market Economy"' (2010) 8 Socio-Economic Review 211; Jeremy Waldron, 'The Core of the Case Against Judicial Review' (2006) 115 The Yale Law Journal 1346.

[83] See Clément Fontan and Antoine de Cabanes, 'La Cour de Justice face à Gauweiler. La mise en récit de l'indépendance de la BCE' in Antoine Bailleux, Elsa Bernard, and Sophie Jacquot (eds), *Les récits judiciaires de l'Europe: concepts et typologie* (Bruylant 2019); Antoine De Cabanes and Clément Fontan, 'Why Germany's Far Right Wants Judges to Rule Europe's Monetary Policy' (*Jacobin*, 24 May 2020) <https://jacobin.com/2020/05/germany-europe-judges-afd-banks> accessed 2 August 2022.

[84] Markus C Kerber, 'Letter: Those Challenging the ECB's Rescue Measures Are Not Mad' *Financial Times* (27 April 2020).

[85] Tooze, 'The Death of the Central Bank Myth' (n 80).

specific set of affected interests that happened to be mostly those of German savers and pensioners.

The GFCC itself seemed to recognize the limits of its approach, as it did not want to go so far as to actually assess the proportionality of the PSPP. Instead, it indirectly demanded that the ECB better explain how the Central Bank balances the various interests. This weaker standard of review has the benefit that it requires the Central Bank to justify its operations more comprehensively. It demands more openness about how the Central Bank assessed the economic costs associated with monetary policy, possibly making alternative courses of action visible. Moreover, the judgment also led the *Bundestag* to explicitly affirm the proportionality of the ECB's programme, which can be understood as a form of *ex post* democratic authorization of the PSPP.[86] In this manner the GFCC fostered further political debate in Germany on the ECB's democratic legitimacy, as the next subsection will discuss.

3.3 Political Debate on the ECB After the *PSPP* Ruling

The GFCC's verdict that it fell on the *Bundestag* and German government to take steps to ensure that the ECB would conduct a proportionality review of the PSPP left room for a political solution to the constitutional conflict. It was through political channels that the issue was ultimately settled. On 24 June 2020, the ECB Governing Council decided to allow the *Bundesbank* to share a number of confidential documents with the German government and the *Bundestag*.[87] These documents meant to show that the ECB had in fact made the required proportionality assessment.[88] The ECB also published a report of its Governing Council meeting in which the economic effects of the PSPP were explicitly discussed.[89] On the basis of these documents, the German government and *Bundestag* declared that the ECB had fulfilled the GFCC's requirements.[90]

[86] See also Teresa Violante, 'Bring Back the Politics: The PSPP Ruling in Its Institutional Context' (2020) 21 German Law Journal 1045. See similarly, but more critically, Isabel Feichtner, 'The German Constitutional Court's PSPP Judgment: Impediment and Impetus for the Democratization of Europe' (2020) 21 German Law Journal 1090.

[87] See, on these events, Bundesverfassungsgericht, decision of 29 April 2021, 2 BvR 1651/15 (*PSPP Vollstreckungsanordnung*) (hereafter BVerfG, *PSPP Vollstreckungsanordnung*) paras 97–107.

[88] See Manfred Schäfers and Christian Seidenbiedel, 'Bundesregierung: EZB hat Urteil aus Karlsruhe erfüllt' *Frankfurter Allgemeine Zeitung* (29 June 2020) <www.faz.net/aktuell/wirtschaft/bundesregierung-ezb-hat-urteil-aus-karlsruhe-erfuellt-16837926.html> accessed 2 August 2022; Guy Chazan and Martin Arnold, 'German Finance Minister Moves to Resolve Court Stand-off with ECB' *Financial Times* (Berlin and Frankfurt, 29 June 2020) <www.ft.com/content/443a14d9-b631-4609-9ad1-7ee98b8249c5> accessed 2 August 2022; Yves Mersch, 'In the Spirit of European Cooperation' <www.ecb.europa.eu/press/key/date/2020/html/ecb.sp200702~87ce377373.en.html> accessed 2 August 2022.

[89] ECB, 'Account of the monetary policy meeting of the Governing Council of the European Central Bank' (n 81).

[90] See BVerfG, *PSPP Vollstreckungsanordnung* (n 87) paras 6–11 and paras 97–107; Antrag der Fraktionen CDU/CSU, SPD, FDP und Bündnis 90/Die Grünen—Urteil des Bundesverfassungsgerichts

There is little indication that the *PSPP* ruling led to a political discussion at the EU level regarding the ECB's independence and the legitimacy of its policies. The ECB itself was hesitant to respond to the GFCC at all, as this could set a precedent for scrutiny by other national courts and harm the Central Bank's independence.[91] Instead the ECB declared that it was subject to the jurisdiction of the CJEU.[92] Shortly after the ruling, Christine Lagarde, President of the ECB, asserted that the ECB remained 'undeterred in delivering on our price stability objective' and would do 'everything necessary within our mandate to support the recovery'.[93] A few weeks later, Isabel Schnabel, member of the ECB's executive board, told the *Financial Times*: 'We are not adjusting our monetary policy in any way in response to this ruling.'[94]

The CJEU issued an exceptional press release in which it reasserted its sole 'jurisdiction to rule that an act of an EU institution is contrary to EU law' in order to uphold the 'unity of the EU legal order', 'legal certainty', and 'the equality of Member States'.[95] The European Commission likewise asserted the primacy of EU law, stating in a press release that '[t]he final word on EU law is always spoken in Luxembourg'.[96] The Commission also made clear that it considered starting infringement proceedings against Germany, which it would actually begin on 9 June 2021. In the European Parliament, several MEPs expressed similar views on primacy, while some explicitly called for the start of infringement proceedings.[97] The Eurogroup discussed the *PSPP* ruling on 8 May 2020, where, according to the

zum Anleihekaufprogramm PSPP der Europäischen Zentralbank, BT-Dr 19/20621 of 01.07.2020 (hereafter BT-Dr 19/20621); Plenarprotokoll 19/170, Stenografischer Bericht der 170. Sitzung des Deutschen Bundestages am 2 Juli 2020 (hereafter Plenarprotokoll 19/170).

[91] Martin Arnold, 'Christine Lagarde Says ECB Is "Undeterred" by German Court Challenge' *Financial Times* (Frankfurt, 7 May 2020) <www.ft.com/content/d93008c5-2b3c-4b2e-9499-5eabaaa959db> accessed 2 August 2022.

[92] ECB, 'Press Conference Christine Lagarde, President of the ECB, Luis de Guindos, Vice-President of the ECB, Frankfurt am Main, 4 June 2020' <www.ecb.europa.eu/press/pressconf/2020/html/ecb.is200604~b479b8cfff.en.html> accessed 2 August 2022.

[93] Arnold, 'Christine Lagarde Says ECB Is "Undeterred"' (n 91).

[94] Martin Arnold, 'German ECB Executive Shrugs off Court Ruling against Bond Buying' *Financial Times* (Frankfurt, 27 May 2020) <www.ft.com/content/a48b8982-3e75-4a35-8fb5-a66f4fb0fedc> accessed 2 August 2022.

[95] Court of Justice of the European Union Press Release 58/20, Press release following the judgment of the German Constitutional Court of 5 May 2020 (8 May 2020).

[96] European Commission, 'Statement by President Von der Leyen' Brussels, 10 May 2020 <https://ec.europa.eu/commission/presscorner/detail/en/statement_20_846> accessed 2 August 2022.

[97] See Question for written answer E-004215/20 to the Commission Jean-Paul Garraud (ID), Gilles Lebreton (ID) (15 July 2020); Priority question for written answer P-004295/20 to the Commission Domènec Ruiz Devesa (S&D), Juan Fernando López Aguilar (S&D), Charles Goerens (Renew), Guy Verhofstadt (Renew), Sandro Gozi (Renew), Damian Boeselager (Verts/ALE) (20 July 2020); Question for written answer E-002887/20 to the Commission Vangelis Meimarakis (PPE) (11 May 2020); Question for written answer Z-035/2020 to the European Central Bank Rule 140 Nuno Melo (PPE) (29 May 2020); Question for written answer E-003385/20 to the Council Hélène Laporte (ID) (5 June 2020); European Parliament, 'Committee on Economic and Monetary Affairs Monetary Dialogue with Christine Lagarde, President of the European Central Bank', Brussels, 8 June 2020, Giegold (Verts/ALE) 11 and Schuster (S&D) 20.

Financial Times, German Finance Minister Scholz 'insisted that a solution would be found to keep the Bundesbank involved in ECB bond-buying' and that it was 'a matter to be dealt with in Germany rather than by the ECB'.[98]

Despite this unwillingness of European institutions to address the GFCC's ruling substantively, the judgment did contribute to more openness about the justification of monetary policy. This was evident from the report of the Governing Council meeting of 3 and 4 June 2020, which presented the ECB's unofficial reaction to the judgment. The report explicitly addressed the proportionality of the purchase programmes and noted 'broad agreement among members' that 'the negative side effects had so far been clearly outweighed by the positive effects of asset purchases on the economy in the pursuit of price stability'.[99] The ECB's 2021 monetary policy strategy also specifically affirms the importance of proportionality assessments for monetary policy decision-making.[100] Arguably, this reference to proportionality is also a result of the *PSPP* ruling.

In the German parliament, a substantive discussion of the ECB's role did take place. The *PSPP* ruling meant that the *Bundestag* explicitly grappled with the permissibility and desirability of the ECB's asset purchases. The parliament's plenary debated the *PSPP* judgment on 7 May 2020, two days after the judgment, as well as on 2 July 2020. In addition, the plenary discussed the PEPP on 28 May 2020, following a motion of the right-wing Eurosceptic AfD that called on the *Bundesbank* to immediately stop buying bonds under this new programme.[101] Regarding the PSPP, the Christian-democrats (CDU/CSU), the Social Democratic Party (SPD), the centre-right liberal Free Democratic Party (FDP), and the Greens (Bündnis 90/Die Grünen) openly confirmed on 2 July 2020 that, in their view, the ECB had fulfilled the required proportionality assessment.[102]

During these parliamentary debates, a variety of views on the ECB's role were expressed. Members of the social-democratic SPD expressly supported the role that the ECB had taken, noting that the central bankers had delivered a crucial contribution to stabilizing the European economies.[103] Parliamentarians of the SPD

[98] Sam Fleming and Martin Arnold, 'EU's Top Court Reasserts Primacy after German Challenge' *Financial Times* (Brussels and Frankfurt, 8 May 2020) <www.ft.com/content/894369cd-9631-43cc-8844-d6cd515e874b> accessed 2 August 2022; Eurogroup, 'Videoconference of 8 May 2020', Brussels, 14 May 2020 <www.consilium.europa.eu/media/43992/2020-05-08-summing-up-letter-rev01.pdf> accessed 2 August 2022.

[99] ECB, 'Account of the monetary policy meeting of the Governing Council of the European Central Bank' (n 81).

[100] ECB, 'The ECB's monetary policy strategy statement', 8 July 2021 <www.ecb.europa.eu/home/search/review/html/ecb.strategyreview_monpol_strategy_statement.en.html> accessed 2 August 2022.

[101] Antrag der Abgeordneten Peter Boehringer et al und der Fraktion der AfD—Rechtskonforme Zustände herstellen—PEPP-Anleihekäufe sofort beenden, BT-Dr 19/19516 of 27.05.2020, 2 (hereafter BT-Dr 19/19516).

[102] BT-Dr 19/20621 (n 90).

[103] Petry (SPD) Plenarprotokoll 19/170 (n 90) 21274–75; the contributions in Plenarprotokoll 19/158, Stenografischer Bericht der 158. Sitzung des Deutschen Bundestages am 7. Mai 2020 (hereafter Plenarprotokoll 19/158) by: Schneider (SPD) 190607; Petry (SPD) 19612; Schwarz (SPD) 19614; also

and the CDU/CSU also affirmed the importance of the ECB's independence.[104] Unsurprisingly, the AfD, a long-time critic of the ECB's policies, welcomed the *PSPP* judgment. Spokesperson Boehringer stated that the Constitutional Court had finally said 'what it should have said about the ECB's bond purchases in 2016 at the latest'.[105] The AfD called, among other things, for the 'establishment of a reporting body at the European Central Bank' which would submit summaries of monetary policy decisions to the German *Bundestag* every six months.[106] These should highlight constitutional considerations, especially 'proportionality and possible ultra vires actions'.[107] In turn, these reports and other current monetary policy decisions should be the object of plenary debates in the *Bundestag*.[108] Parliamentarians of the FDP were also critical of the ECB's role and stressed the dangers of the Central Bank's government debt buying.[109] The liberal FDP put forward a motion calling for the *Bundestag* to 'continuously monitor the ECB's compliance with its mandate'.[110] This included a call for a regular plenary debate on the ECB's annual report, a quarterly hearing with the *Bundesbank*, and the establishment of a subcommittee of the budget committee to review compliance with the monetary financing prohibition. The party also called for a 'fundamental discussion' on specifying the ECB's mandate.[111] The Left Party (Die Linke) also pleaded for a change of the EU Treaties, but with the very different aim of repealing the ban on monetary financing. Instead, the party favoured expanding the ECB's mandate to ensure that 'the ECB guarantees the solvency of national governments'.[112]

Hakverdi (SPD), Plenarprotokoll 19/163, Stenografischer Bericht der 163. Sitzung des Deutschen Bundestages am 28. Mai 2020 (hereafter Plenarprotokoll 19/163) 20273.

[104] Frieser (CDU/CSU), Plenarprotokoll 19/170 (n 90) 21282; Jung (CDU/CSU), Plenarprotokoll 19/170 (n 90) 21278; Schneider (SPD), Plenarprotokoll 19/158 (n 103) 19607; Rehberg (CDU/CSU), Plenarprotokoll 19/158 (n 103) 19610; Hakverdi (SPD), Plenarprotokoll 19/163 (n 103) 20273.

[105] Plenarprotokoll 19/158 (n 103) 19604. See similarly Albrecht Glaser (AfD), Plenarprotokoll 19/158 (n 103) 19611–12.

[106] Antrag der Abgeordneten Tobias Matthias Peterka et al und der Fraktion der AfD—Kritische und effektive Ausübung der sogenannten Integrationsverantwortung des Deutschen Bundestages im Zusammenhang mit Entscheidungen des Rates der Europäischen Zentralbank, BT-Dr 19/20616 of 01.07.2020, 2 (hereafter BT-Dr 19/20616).

[107] BT-Dr 19/20616 (n 106) 2.

[108] ibid 2.

[109] Toncar (FDP), Plenarprotokoll 19/170 (n 90) 21279–80; see also the vote declarations of Frank Schäffler, Christian Sauter, and Alexander Müller (FDP) who actually considered that the requirements of the GFCC's ruling had not been fulfilled, Plenarprotokoll 19/170 (n 90) 21356–57.

[110] Antrag der Abgeordneten Christian Dürr et al und der Fraktion der FDP—Verhältnismäßigkeitsprüfung fristgerecht dargelegt—Kontrolle der Grenzen der Geldpolitik als Daueraufgabe ernstnehmen, BT-Dr 19/20553 of 01.07.2020, 2 (hereafter BT-Dr 19/20553).

[111] ibid 2; see also Durr (FDP) Plenarprotokoll 19/158 (n 103) 19606; Toncar (FDP), Plenarprotokoll 19/170 (n 90) 21280; Toncar (FDP) Plenarprotokoll 19/163 (n 103) 20266.

[112] Antrag der Abgeordneten Fabio De Masi et al und der Fraktion DIE LINKE—Konflikt um die Geldpolitik der Europäischen Zentralbank politisch lösen—EU-Verträge ändern und geldpolitischen Dialog mit der Bundesbank verankern, BT-Dr 19/20552 of 30.06.2020, 3; see also De Masi (Die Linke), Plenarprotokoll 19/170 (n 90) 21280.

Although these proposals were rejected, the *Bundestag* did agree to establish a new dialogue between the *Bundesbank* president and the parliament's finance committee. The *Bundesbank* president would explain, and answer questions related to, the ECB's monetary policy decisions every three months.[113] The Greens and the Social Democrats also expressed their openness to consider a change in the ECB's mandate.[114]

Nonetheless, the plenary debate on the ECB's new programme (PEPP), adopted in response to the pandemic, made clear that a large majority of the *Bundestag* supported this programme. All other parties rejected the motion by the AfD that the *Bundesbank* should no longer participate in the PEPP.[115] The AfD reasoned that the PEPP violated the monetary financing prohibition as it did not comply with the requirements set out by the GFCC in its *PSPP* ruling.[116] Even the liberal FDP was unwilling to go along with this argument. Its spokesperson, Florian Toncar, stressed the critically different nature of the PEPP as an extraordinary response to the Covid-19 crisis.[117] In fact, Toncar accused the AfD of trying to use the GFCC in their quest to 'destroy our common currency'.[118] Parliamentarians of the CDU/CSU, SPD, and Bündnis 90/Die Grünen argued that the motion itself went against the ECB's independence, as constitutionally protected by Article 88 of the Basic Law.[119]

The GFCC's *PSPP* ruling thus contributed to further openness and political debate about the constitutional position of the ECB, as well as the desirability of its policies. The parliamentary proceedings on the PSPP and PEPP also provided explicit political backing for these programmes and thus constituted a form of *ex post* democratic authorization. Nonetheless, it has to be noted that the ECB's policies had already been the subject of increased political debate in the *Bundestag* for many years. During the euro crisis, the number of plenary debates on the ECB's policies in the *Bundestag* rose, where particular attention was given to issues of legality and side-effects. These debates were characterized by an increased overall critical stance towards the ECB. As a result of the AfD's entry in the *Bundestag*

[113] Jan Mallien 'Weidmann soll den Bundestag regelmäßig über EZB-Beschlüsse informieren' *Handelsblatt* (Frankfurt, 19 June 2020) < www.handelsblatt.com/finanzen/geldpolitik/bundesbank-president-weidmann-soll-den-bundestag-regelmaessig-ueber-ezb-beschluesse-informieren/25932334.html> accessed 2 August 2022.

[114] Petry (SPD) Plenarprotokoll 19/170 (n 90) 21276; Brantner (Bündnis 90/Die Grünen), Plenarprotokoll 19/158 (n 103) 19610.

[115] Beschlussempfehlung und Bericht des Haushaltsausschusses zu dem Antrag der Abgeordneten Peter Boehringer, Marcus Bühl, Martin Hohmann, weiterer Abgeordneter und der Fraktion der AfD—Drucksache 19/19516 –, BT-Dr 19/22587 of 16.09.2020.

[116] BT-Dr 19/19516 (n 101); Boehringer (AfD), Plenarprotokoll 19/163 (n 103) 20263–64; Plenarprotokoll 19/158 (n 103) 19604.

[117] Toncar (FDP), Plenarprotokoll 19/163 (n 103) 20265–66.

[118] ibid 20266.

[119] Rehberg (CDU/CSU), Plenarprotokoll 19/163 (n 103) 20264–65; Steffen (SPD), Plenarprotokoll 19/163 (n 103) 20267; Paus (Bündnis 90/Die Grünen), Plenarprotokoll 19/163 (n 103) 20270; Haase (CDU/CSU), Plenarprotokoll 19/163 (n 103) 20276.

in 2017 and its scepticism about the ECB's policies, the plenary again repeatedly debated the role of the ECB. Since then, in particular the AfD, the FDP, and, for different reasons, Die Linke have been highly critical of the ECB's policies.[120] The events following the *PSPP* ruling are therefore best understood as part of longer-standing political contestation of the ECB's policies, while the ongoing litigation before the Karlsruhe Court is itself a part of this broader debate.

3.4 The GFCC Accepts the Political Solution

Despite the actions taken by the ECB, German government, and the *Bundestag*, a number of the original litigants in the *PSPP* case held that the GFCC's requirements had not been fulfilled. In follow-up proceedings for a so-called order of execution, one group of litigants demanded access to the ECB's non-public documents. Another litigant claimed that the *Bundestag* and German government were still obliged to ensure that the ECB Governing Council 'takes a decision that entails a substantiated and comprehensible proportionality assessment'.[121] This applicant further sought to ensure that the *Bundesbank* would no longer participate in the implementation and execution of the PSPP.

The German Court dismissed these claims as inadmissible, because they exceeded the scope of possible review in proceedings for an order of execution.[122] The action sought by the applicants would require 'constitutional review of the measures taken after the judgment was rendered', which was not possible in this specific procedure for an order of execution.[123] Despite their inadmissibility, the GFCC ruled that the claims were unfounded even if they had been framed in a way that made them admissible.[124] It is likely that the Court took this step to prevent new constitutional challenges to the PSPP.[125] In so doing, the GFCC confirmed that the *Bundestag* and the government had complied with the requirements flowing from the original *PSPP* ruling.[126] The federal government and the *Bundestag*'s endeavours did lead the ECB's Governing Council to address the proportionality of the PSPP. The Court also considered that the *Bundestag* had 'substantially and genuinely' dealt with this issue, as 'a real debate, including an exchange of differing views, took place in Parliament to address the requirements arising from the judgment of 5 May 2020'.[127]

[120] Anna-Lena Högenauer, 'The Politicisation of the European Central Bank and the Bundestag' (2019) 7 Politics and Governance 291, 295–300.

[121] BVerfG, *PSPP Vollstreckungsanordnung* (n 87).

[122] ibid paras 71–88.

[123] ibid para 83.

[124] ibid para 89.

[125] Martin Nettesheim, 'Das Ende eines epochalen Verfassungsstreits' (*Verfassungsblog*, 18 May 2021) <https://verfassungsblog.de/das-ende-eines-epochalen-verfassungsstreits/> accessed 1 August 2022.

[126] BVerfG, *PSPP Vollstreckungsanordnung* (n 87) paras 95–111.

[127] ibid para 111.

Some passages in the judgment suggest that, ultimately, *ultra vires* review only entails a weak form of review in that it leaves the German government and the *Bundestag* 'a broad margin of appreciation, assessment and manoeuvre' in how to respond.[128] However, it is difficult to generalize from this specific case, because the limited review conducted by the GFCC is also a specific feature of proceedings for an order of execution.

3.5 Contestation and Infringement Proceedings

Despite the GFCC's weak remedy in the original PSPP proceedings, Karlsruhe's decision to declare the PSPP and the CJEU's *Weiss* ruling as *ultra vires* still presented a significant escalation. The GFCC had probably employed the weak remedy to minimize the negative consequences of its ruling.[129] Nonetheless, negative reactions to the *PSPP* judgment were vast, and included those of the Italian Prime Minister, the French Finance Minister, and a judge at the *Bundesgerichtshof*, Germany's highest civil and criminal court.[130] In an apparent exercise of damage control, the GFCC's departing President, Andreas Voßkuhle, as well as judge rapporteur Peter Huber gave several newspaper interviews to defend the ruling.[131]

That the Karlsruhe judges had crossed a line was also evident in the *Bundestag*, where a number of parliamentarians now voiced explicit criticism of the GFCC, in contrast to the reaction to key judgments on the euro crisis discussed in Chapter 5.[132] This criticism introduced welcome democratic contestation of the

[128] ibid para 90.

[129] Niels Petersen, 'Karlsruhe's Lochner Moment? A Rational Choice Perspective on the German Federal Constitutional Court's Relationship to the CJEU After the PSPP Decision' (2020) 21 German Law Journal 995.

[130] For the former, see Ben Hall and Martin Arnold, 'German Court Ruling Casts Doubt on European Monetary Policy' *Financial Times* (London and Frankfurt, 6 May 2020) <www.ft.com/content/07f19a1b-7494-439d-9765-7fd7ddf09860> accessed 2 August 2022. For the latter, see Peter Meier-Beck, 'Ultra Vires?' (*D'Kart*, 11 May 2020) <www.d-kart.de/en/blog/2020/05/11/ultra-vires/> accessed 2 August 2022.

[131] Reinhard Müller, '"Das EZB-Urteil war zwingend"' *Frankfurter Allgemeine Zeitung* (12 May 2020) <www.faz.net/aktuell/politik/inland/peter-huber-im-gespraech-das-ezb-urteil-war-zwingend-16766682.html> accessed 2 August 2022; Wolfgang Janisch and Stefan Kornelius, '"Wir haben Applaus von der falschen Seite bekommen" (Interview with Peter Huber)' *Süddeutsche Zeitung* (Karlsruhe, 12 May 2020) <www.sueddeutsche.de/politik/ezb-urteil-bundesverfassungsgericht-anleihenkaeufe-peter-michael-huber-1.4905311?reduced=true> accessed 2 August 2022; Giovanni di Lorenzo and Heinrich Wefing, '"Erfolg ist eher Kalt" (Interview with Andreas Voßkuhle)' *Die Zeit* (13 May 2020) <www.zeit.de/2020/21/andreas-vosskuhle-ezb-anleihenkaeufe-corona-krise> accessed 2 August 2022.

[132] Overall, reactions to the judgment were mixed. The governing parties of the CDU/CSU and SPD seemed mostly concerned with playing down the judgment's consequences. See eg Jung (CDU/CSU), Plenarprotokoll 19/158 (n 103) 19605; Rehberg (CDU/CSU), Plenarprotokoll 19/158 (n 103) 19610; Hirte (CDU/CSU), Plenarprotokoll 19/158 (n 103) 19615; Schneider (SPD), Plenarprotokoll 19/158 (n 103) 19607; Schwarz (SPD), Plenarprotokoll 19/158 (n 103) 19614–15; Petry (SPD), Plenarprotokoll 19/158 (n 103) 19612. The AfD welcomed the judgment, see eg Boehringer (AfD), Plenarprotokoll 19/158 (n 103) 19604; Glaser (AfD), Plenarprotokoll 19/158 (n 103) 19611–12. Positive notes were also voiced by others. Christian Dürr of the FDP explicitly welcomed the GFCC's judgment, qualifying it as 'pro-European' and strengthening the European Treaties (Plenarprotokoll 19/158 (n 103) 19606).

GFCC's interpretation of the German constitution in relation to European integration. Franziska Brantner of Bündnis 90/Die Grüne, for example, noted the judgment's negative consequences for the EU legal order.[133] The ruling had been received enthusiastically in Poland and Hungary and there were fears that these Member States would use the judgment to ignore the CJEU in their quarrels over the rule of law.[134] Brantner also qualified the judgment as a threat to the ECB's independence, which would cease to exist if other national courts were to claim similar powers to judge the ECB's actions and come up with conditions.[135] Fabio De Masi of Die Linke stated that economically 'the ruling made little sense',[136] while Heribert Hirte of the CDU/CSU held that the ruling did not reflect the full economic dimension of the case, as the Court had only discussed the disadvantages, and not the advantages of the PSPP.[137] Christian Petry of the SPD implicitly criticized the Constitutional Court by citing the pro-European preamble of the German Basic Law.[138] He also noted that the concept of 'national competence' did not feature in the constitution.[139]

The launch of infringement proceedings by the Commission in response to the *PSPP* ruling can be seen as a further opportunity for political contestation of the GFCC's case law. The question of whether the European Commission should launch such proceedings had divided legal minds. Some pointed to the issue of principle: Member States should not get away with subverting the primacy of EU law, especially given the possibility that Poland and Hungary would do the same.[140] This fear was realized when, on 7 October 2021, the Polish Constitutional Tribunal decided essentially that the CJEU's case law on judicial independence was unconstitutional. The judgment followed an application by the Prime Minister of Poland that had relied heavily on the case law of other constitutional courts on primacy, especially that of its German counterpart and its ruling on the PSPP.[141] Others,

Michelbach of the CDU/CSU similarly called the ruling 'profoundly pro-European' and held that it strengthened 'the rights of our citizens, the rights of savers, insurance holders, tenants, homeowners and investors' (Michelbach (CDU/CSU), Plenarprotokoll 19/158 (n 103) 19613).

[133] Plenarprotokoll 19/158 (n 103) 19609; the same concern was reflected in the speeches of Petry (SPD), Plenarprotokoll 19/158 (n 103) 19612 and Hirte (CDU/CSU), Plenarprotokoll 19/158 (n 103) 19616.

[134] Sam Fleming, James Shotter, and Valerie Hopkins, 'Eastern European States Sense Opportunity in German Court Ruling' *Financial Times* (10 May 2020).

[135] Plenarprotokoll 19/158 (n 103) 19609.

[136] ibid 19608; see also Plenarprotokoll 19/170 (n 90) 21280.

[137] Hirte (CDU/CSU), Plenarprotokoll 19/158 (n 103) 19615.

[138] This preamble states: 'Conscious of their responsibility before God and man, Inspired by the determination to promote world peace as an equal partner in a united Europe, the German people, in the exercise of their constituent power, have adopted this Basic Law.'

[139] Petry (SPD), Plenarprotokoll 19/158 (n 103) 19612; also Petry (SPD), Plenarprotokoll 19/170 (n 90) 21275.

[140] Thu Nguyen, 'A Matter of Principle' (*Verfassungsblog*, 11 June 2021) <https://verfassungsblog.de/a-matter-of-principle/> accessed 2 August 2022.

[141] Polish Constitutional Tribunal, judgment, 7 October 2021, K 3/21; Jakub Jaraczewski, 'Gazing into the Abyss: The K 3/21 Decision of the Polish Constitutional Tribunal' (*Verfassungsblog*, 12 October

however, opposed launching infringement proceedings. Judge rapporteur in the *PSPP* case, Peter Huber, warned that such a procedure would present a problematic escalation.[142] A further argument was that the issue of principle was not straightforward. In Poland and Hungary, the concern was that their governments were subverting the structures of constitutional democracy, using the undermining of judicial independence as a key component. The GFCC's *PSPP* ruling had instead called for stronger judicial control of an executive body, namely the ECB.[143] Moreover, a successful infringement procedure would require the German government to induce its independent constitutional court to change track, an outcome that could sit uneasily with the separation of powers.[144]

Yet, it is precisely the fact that an infringement procedure would require the German government to articulate its position on the GFCC's EU-related case law that should be seen as its main advantage. The Commission launched infringement proceedings in June 2021 by sending a letter of formal notice to the German government.[145] The Commission noted that the GFCC's *PSPP* judgment entailed a 'violation of fundamental principles of EU law, in particular the principles of autonomy, primacy, effectiveness and uniform application of Union law, as well as the respect of the jurisdiction of the European Court of Justice under Article 267 TFEU'.[146] It also considered that the judgment constituted 'a serious precedent, both for the future practice of the German Constitutional court itself, and for the supreme and constitutional courts and tribunals of other Member States'.[147]

By December 2021, however, the Commission had already closed the infringement procedure indicating that Germany had given 'very strong commitments' in its reply to the Commission's letter of formal notice.[148] These included a formal declaration that Germany 'affirms and recognises the principles of autonomy, primacy, effectiveness and uniform application of Union law as well as the values laid down in Article 2 TEU, including in particular the rule of law', as well as 'the

2021) <https://verfassungsblog.de/gazing-into-the-abyss/> accessed 2 August 2022; Marta Lasek-Markey, 'Poland's Constitutional Tribunal on the Status of EU Law: The Polish Government Got all the Answers it Needed from a Court it Controls' (*European Law Blog*, 21 October 2021) <https://europeanlawblog.eu/2021/10/21/polands-constitutional-tribunal-on-the-status-of-eu-law-the-polish-government-got-all-the-answers-it-needed-from-a-court-it-controls/> accessed 2 August 2022.

142 Janisch and Kornelius, '"Wir haben Applaus"' (n 131).

143 See eg 'Verfassungsrichter Dr. Ulrich Maidowski erklärt: Anders als die polnische Regierung will das Bundesverfassungsgericht mehr Kontrolle durch den Europäischen Gerichtshof' (27 May 2020) <www.iustitia.pl/en/activity/informations/3856-verfassungsrichter-dr-ulrich-maidowski-erklaert-anders-als-die-polnische-regierung-will-das-bundesverfassungsgericht-mehr-kontrolle-durch-den-europaeischen-gerichtshof> accessed 2 August 2022.

144 Bobić and Dawson, 'Making Sense of the "Incomprehensible"' (n 9) 1995.

145 Commission, 'June Infringements Package' (n 8) 14–15; Mehreen Khan and Guy Chazan, 'Brussels Takes Legal Action against German Constitutional Court' *Financial Times* (Brussels and Berlin, 9 June 2021) <www.ft.com/content/76aabe45-883f-4e3a-80d8-95928db47063> accessed 2 August 2022.

146 Commission, 'June Infringements Package' (n 8) 14–15.

147 ibid 15.

148 ibid 9.

authority of the Court of Justice of the European Union'.[149] The Commission also noted that the German government 'commits to use all the means at its disposal to avoid, in the future, a repetition of an "ultra vires" finding, and take an active role in that regard'.[150] Yet, a closer look at the German government's reply letter revealed only limited critical engagement with the GFCC's case law. Instead, the German government focused on the Europe-friendly elements of the GFCC's case law, providing a rosy picture of the Court's approach to European integration. To improve the relations between the CJEU and national courts, the German government also suggested establishing 'a structured judicial dialogue' between the CJEU and the highest and constitutional courts of the Member States 'in order to promote and strengthen the exchange and common understanding within the European judicial network'.[151] For this purpose, it proposed the creation of a 'platform for European judges' as a forum of regular exchange. The German government would seek a dialogue on this matter with the GFCC, while safeguarding its judicial independence. The emphasis by the German government on the Europe-friendliness of the German constitution could be seen as an implicit criticism of the GFCC. However, overall, the German government's letter hardly challenged the GFCC's case law, thus missing an opportunity to offer a political counterweight to the Court's disputable interpretations of the German Basic Law.

4. Next Generation EU

Another major constitutional question that arose in 2020 was whether the GFCC would consider the new recovery fund, NGEU, to be compatible with the German constitution. Germany's support for NGEU entailed a break with its previous taboo on joint EU borrowing and financial transfers between Member States.[152] Commentators consequently cast the establishment of the fund as a historic breakthrough. German Finance Minister Scholz even justified the move as Europe's Hamiltonian moment, referring to the occasion when the US federal government assumed the war debts of the states in 1790, based on a plan by Alexander

[149] ibid 9.

[150] ibid 9.

[151] German government, 'Mitteilung der Regierung der Bundesrepublik Deutschland an die Europäische Kommission vom 3. August 2021', 3 August 2021 <www.asktheeu.org/en/request/10318/response/35463/attach/2/doc%202%20DE%20reply%20to%20LFN%20de.pdf?cookie_passthrough=1> accessed 2 August 2022, 4; Martin Greive and Jan Hildebrand, 'Karlsruher Urteil zu EZB-Anleihekäufen: Bundesregierung hält EU-Vorwürfe für unbegründet' *Handelsblatt* (Berlin, 10 August 2021) <www.handelsblatt.com/politik/deutschland/streit-ueber-geldpolitik-karlsruher-urteil-zu-ezb-anleihekaeufen-bundesregierung-haelt-eu-vorwuerfe-fuer-unbegruendet/27498622.html> accessed 2 August 2022.

[152] Howarth and Schild, 'Nein to "Transfer Union"' (n 16) 219; Crespy and Schramm, 'Breaking the Budgetary Taboo' (n 20).

Hamilton, the first US Secretary of the Treasury.[153] Yet, given the GFCC's insistence that the *Bundestag* should retain its budgetary powers, questions naturally arose as to whether such a significant move could still be reconciled with the German constitution as interpreted by its Constitutional Court. There were also questions about the compatibility of NGEU with the EU Treaties, especially the principle of budgetary balance in Article 310 TFEU, the system of own resources in Article 311 TFEU, and the no-bailout provision in Article 125 TFEU.[154] It was unsurprising, therefore, that litigants challenged NGEU before the GFCC in fresh judicial proceedings. Paradoxically, it has also been argued that the GFCC's *PSPP* ruling had in fact been a key reason for the German government to throw its weight behind NGEU. Rather than being a bar to further European integration in economic and fiscal matters, the German Court supposedly provided an impetus for it.[155] I discuss this aspect in the following subsection and conclude that it is unclear whether the *PSSP* ruling was an important factor in the agreement on NGEU, while other factors were also likely to have played a major role. Subsequently, I discuss how constitutional concerns about budgetary sovereignty and a possible *ultra vires* ruling had not disappeared, how they probably impacted the design of NGEU, as well as how they were evaluated by the GFCC.

4.1 Did the *PSPP* Ruling Lead to NGEU?

The idea that the *PSPP* ruling played a major role in motivating Germany to support joint EU borrowing and financial transfers was based on the potential repercussions that the ruling could have for the ECB's policies. In the absence of a strong economic and fiscal dimension in the EMU, the ECB is crucial for responding to

[153] Ben Hall, Sam Fleming, and Guy Chazan, 'Is the Franco-German Plan Europe's "Hamiltonian" Moment?' *Financial Times* (London, Brussels and Berlin, 21 May 2020) <www.ft.com/content/2735a3f1-bc58-477c-9315-c98129d12852> accessed 2 August 2022; C Randall Henning and Martin Kessler, 'Fiscal Federalism: US History for Architects of Europe's Fiscal Union' (2012) Breugel Working Paper Series WP12-1 <www.bruegel.org/comment/fiscal-federalism-us-history-architects-europes-fiscal-union> accessed 2 August 2022.

[154] On a number of these issues, see Päivi Leino-Sandberg, 'Who Is Ultra Vires Now? The EU's Legal U-Turn in Interpreting Article 310 TFEU' (*Verfassungsblog: On Matters Constitutional*, 18 June 2020) <https://verfassungsblog.de/who-is-ultra-vires-now-the-eus-legal-u-turn-in-interpreting-article-310-tfeu/> accessed 1 August 2022; Päivi Leino-Sandberg and Matthias Ruffert, 'Next Generation EU and Its Constitutional Ramifications: A Critical Assessment' [2022] Common Market Law Review 433. See also Council of the European Union, 'Opinion of the Legal Service' (Brussels, 24 June 2020) 9062/20 <https://data.consilium.europa.eu/doc/document/ST-9062-2020-INIT/en/pdf> accessed 2 August 2022; Alberto de Gregorio Merino, 'The Recovery Plan: Solidarity and the Living Constitution' (*EU Law Live*, 6 March 2021) <https://eulawlive.com/long-read-the-recovery-plan-solidarity-and-the-living-constitution-by-alberto-de-gregorio-merino/> accessed 2 August 2022.

[155] For discussions in this direction, see Bobić and Dawson, 'Making Sense of the "Incomprehensible"' (n 9); Marco Dani and others, '"It's the Political Economy . . . !" A Moment of Truth for the Eurozone and the EU' (2021) 19 International Journal of Constitutional Law 309; Paul Dermine, 'The Ruling of the Bundesverfassungsgericht in PSPP—An Inquiry into Its Repercussions on the Economic and Monetary Union' (2020) 16 European Constitutional Law Review 525.

economic shocks and holding the euro together. The *PSPP* judgment cast doubt over the compatibility of this role with German constitutional law. According to an analysis by the *Financial Times*, '[f]ear was spreading in the German government that the constitutional court could go even further, and issue a similar challenge to the ECB's recently launched €750 billion pandemic emergency purchase programme (PEPP), the centrepiece of its crisis-fighting strategy'.[156] The article stated that, according to officials in Berlin and Paris, the *PSPP* ruling therefore 'tipped the balance for Ms. Merkel' in favour of the new recovery fund.[157] Chancellor Merkel herself had also linked the judgment to the need for further integration in the area of economic policy when she answered questions about the consequences of the *PSPP* judgment in the *Bundestag* on 13 May 2020.[158] Germany's left-wing political parties likewise made this connection when discussing the *PSPP* ruling. Franziska Brantner of the Greens held that a eurozone without common fiscal politics could not exist if the GFCC would not allow the ECB's unconventional policies. Taking Karlsruhe seriously would consequently entail taking seriously the idea of common European debt.[159] Fabio De Masi of Die Linke similarly declared that without the financing of states by the ECB, one could no longer refuse a common financial policy.[160] Christian Petry of the SPD thanked the GFCC for 'the wake-up call' and called the ruling an 'opportunity' to deepen European economic integration.[161] In this manner, the *PSPP* ruling could be seen as having a further democratic effect, spurring political institutions to address problems in the EMU, rather than allowing them to rely on the ECB's unelected central bankers.[162]

Nonetheless, it is contested that the *PSPP* ruling played a major causal role in bringing about German support for joint borrowing and transfers. In a reconstruction of the negotiations, Schramm indicates instead that other factors played a key role and that German plans were already well developed by the time of the *PSPP* ruling.[163] The timeline supports this interpretation of events, as only thirteen days separated the *PSPP* ruling of 5 May 2020 and the presentation of the

[156] Victor Mallet, Guy Chazan, and Sam Fleming, 'The Chain of Events That Led to Germany's Change over Europe's Recovery Fund' *Financial Times* (Brussels, 22 May 2020) <www.ft.com/content/1d8853f4-726d-4c06-a905-ed2f37d25eee> accessed 2 August 2022. This reading is supported by De Gregorio Merino, 'The Recovery Plan' (n 154); Tesche, 'Pandemic Politics' (n 26) 9.

[157] Mallet, Chazan, and Fleming, 'The Chain of Events That Led to Germany's Change' (n 156).

[158] Plenarprotokoll 19/159, Stenografischer Bericht der 159. Sitzung des Deutschen Bundestages am 13. Mai 2020, 19707.

[159] Plenarprotokoll 19/158 (n 103) 19609–10); also Brantner (Bündnis 90/Die Grünen), Plenarprotokoll 19/170 (n 90) 21281.

[160] Plenarprotokoll 19/158 (n 103) 19608.

[161] ibid 19613; also Petry (SPD), Plenarprotokoll 19/170 (n 90) 21276.

[162] De Gregorio Merino, 'The Recovery Plan' (n 154).

[163] On this aspect, see especially Lucas Schramm, 'Economic Ideas, Party Politics, or Material Interests? Explaining Germany's Support for the EU Corona Recovery Plan' [2021] Journal of European Public Policy 1, 17. See also Mattias Wendel, 'Paradoxes of Ultra-Vires Review: A Critical Review of the PSPP-Decision and Its Initial Reception' (2020) 21 German Law Journal 979, 991–92. Yet, Wendel does not back up this claim with further evidence.

Franco-German recovery plan on 18 May 2020, probably too short a time period to have made a decisive impact.

One factor that was likely to have played a significant role in Germany's policy shift is that the Covid-19 crisis was understood to be of a very different nature than the euro crisis. The dominant political narrative of the euro crisis had been that Member States in trouble owed their position to irresponsible fiscal behaviour. The pandemic instead came to be understood as a public health emergency and external shock that affected all and was no one's fault.[164] The different framing was evident when, on 25 March 2020, the government leaders of nine Member States—Belgium, France, Italy, Luxembourg, Spain, Portugal, Greece, Slovenia, and Ireland—addressed a letter to European Council President Charles Michel, calling for the introduction of 'a common debt instrument issued by a European institution'.[165] The letter stressed that the Covid-19 crisis created a shock 'for which no country bears responsibility'.[166] When Dutch Finance Minister Hoekstra had instead suggested earlier in the week that an enquiry should be conducted into why certain Member States had failed to build up financial buffers, this caused outrage among southern European Member States. Not long after, Hoekstra apologized for his lack of empathy.[167] Yet, at the same time, the German government and other northern Member States still opposed the call for joint bonds.[168] Over the course of April 2020, however, German political discourse shifted towards increased calls for greater European solidarity.[169] For example, when Chancellor Merkel addressed the *Bundestag* on 23 April 2020, she stated that the pandemic was no one's fault and justified 'significantly higher contributions to the European budget'.[170] In the

[164] Crespy and Schramm, 'Breaking the Budgetary Taboo' (n 20); Howarth and Schild, 'Nein to "Transfer Union"' (n 16); Luuk van Middelaar, *Een Europees Pandemonium* (Historische Uitgeverij 2021) 88–101 and 122–36 (translated in English as *Pandemonium: Saving Europe* (Agenda Publishing 2021)); Tesche, 'Pandemic Politics' (n 26) 2.

[165] Sarantis Michalopoulos, 'Nine Member States Ask for Eurobonds to Face Coronavirus Crisis' *Euractiv* (25 March 2020) <www.euractiv.com/section/economy-jobs/news/nine-member-states-ask-for-eurobonds-to-face-coronavirus-crisis/> accessed 2 August 2022.

[166] Sophie Wilmès and others, 'Letter to President of the European Council, Charles Michel' (25 March 2020) <https://twitter.com/Shahinvallee/status/1242790458926993409/photo/1> accessed 2 August 2022.

[167] Mehreen Khan, 'Straining the Ties That Bind the Eurozone' *Financial Times* (Brussels, 26 March 2020) <www.ft.com/content/f54d21cf-0701-492e-8516-8f60d000d68f> accessed 2 August 2022; Hans Von der Burchard, Ivo Oliveira, and Eline Schaart, 'Dutch Try to Calm North-South Economic Storm over Coronavirus' *Politico* (27 March 2020) <www.politico.eu/article/netherlands-try-to-calm-storm-over-repugnant-finance-ministers-comments/> accessed 2 August 2022; Marc Peeperkorn, 'Hoekstra Stribbelt Tegen Bij Steunpakket EU: "Een Nederlandse Middelvinger Naar Het Zuiden"' *de Volkskrant* (24 March 2020); Eline Schaart, 'Dutch Finance Minister Acknowledges Lack of Empathy on Corona Bonds' *Politico* (31 March 2020) <www.politico.eu/article/dutch-finance-minister-acknowledges-lack-of-empathy-on-corona-bonds/> accessed 2 August 2022.

[168] Crespy and Schramm, 'Breaking the Budgetary Taboo' (n 20) 10–12; Middelaar, *Een Europees Pandemonium* (n 164) 94.

[169] Crespy and Schramm, 'Breaking the Budgetary Taboo' (n 20) 13–14; Krotz and Schramm, 'Embedded Bilateralism' (n 19) 534.

[170] Plenarprotokoll 19/156, Stenografischer Bericht der 156. Sitzung des Deutschen Bundestages am 23. April 2020, 19300 (hereafter Plenarprotokoll 19/156).

meantime, Germany and France had intensified bilateral consultations, bringing their respective positions closer together.[171] These efforts resulted in the announcement by Macron and Merkel of their recovery plan on 18 May 2020. Presenting the plan, Merkel stressed that the EU was facing the 'gravest crisis in its history, and such a crisis demands appropriate answers'.[172] The Commission subsequently proposed NGEU, the recovery fund, on 27 May 2020. The close resemblance with the Franco-German plan was no coincidence, as Merkel, Macron, and Commission President Von der Leyen had repeatedly discussed the plans.[173]

Germany's material interests are a further explanation for its policy shift.[174] Although Covid-19 affected all Member States, southern EU Member States were hit particularly severely. Given their already high public debt to GDP ratios, these Member States lacked the financial power to fully combat the negative economic consequences of the Covid-19 crisis. The uneven financial leeway of Member States risked harming the economic recovery, while Italy's high government debt in particular raised fears of a new sovereign debt crisis. The pandemic also underlined the vulnerability and interdependence of the German economy. The lockdowns across Europe deeply affected German businesses as they significantly disrupted both demand and supply. As Chancellor Merkel stressed on 23 April 2020, 'Germany can only do well in the long run when Europe does well too.'[175]

In sum, it is uncertain that the *PSPP* ruling was a key reason why the German government chose to support NGEU.[176] The GFCC's case law is, in any case, difficult to see as an impetus for further European integration in the field of economic and fiscal policy. The GFCC has long stressed constitutional limits in this area

[171] Krotz and Schramm, 'Embedded Bilateralism' (n 19) 533.

[172] Sam Fleming, Victor Mallet, and Guy Chazan, 'Germany and France Unite in Call for €500bn Europe Recovery Fund' *Financial Times* (Brussels, Paris, and Berlin, 18 May 2020) <www.ft.com/content/c23ebc5e-cbf3-4ad8-85aa-032b574d0562> accessed 2 August 2022.

[173] Krotz and Schramm, 'Embedded Bilateralism' (n 19) 536; Middelaar, *Een Europees Pandemonium* (n 164) 96–98; Schramm, 'Economic Ideas, Party Politics, or Material Interests?' (n 163) 10–11.

[174] Howarth and Schild, 'Nein to "Transfer Union"' (n 16); Magnus G Schoeller and Olof Karlsson, 'Championing the "German Model"? Germany's Consistent Preferences on the Integration of Fiscal Constraints' (2021) 43 Journal of European Integration 191, 201–02; Schramm, 'Economic Ideas, Party Politics, or Material Interests?' (n 163); Tesche, 'Pandemic Politics' (n 26) 9–10.

[175] Plenarprotokoll 19/156 (n 170) 19299.

[176] Other explanatory factors for Germany's change in position are also contested. One such factor is that the SPD's participation in the government as junior coalition partner at the time made an important difference, given the SPD's more favourable stance on fiscal risk sharing. However, this idea is disputed because the push for the recovery plan was led by Chancellor Merkel, while the SPD Finance Minister apparently played no significant role in the preparations. Schramm, 'Economic Ideas, Party Politics, or Material Interests?' (n 163) 13–14. Another idea is that a shift in economic thinking among German decision-makers from an ordoliberal towards a more Keynesian approach was a key factor, see Matthias Matthijs, 'Hegemonic Leadership Is What States Make of It: Reading Kindleberger in Washington and Berlin' (2022) 29 Review of International Political Economy 371, 374–75, and 391–92; Guy Chazan, 'The Minds behind Germany's Shifting Fiscal Stance' *Financial Times* (Berlin, 9 June 2020) <www.ft.com/content/2503ce9c-cde9-4301-bba0-8301f7deaf3b> accessed 2 August 2022. There is, however, limited evidence that new economic ideas had become widespread among German policy-makers and the recovery fund was not a radical break with Germany's past policies. See, in detail, on this Schramm, 'Economic Ideas, Party Politics, or Material Interests?' (n 163) 13.

to protect the *Bundestag*'s budgetary autonomy and is sceptical of the European Parliament's capacity to provide democratic legitimacy for European decisions.[177] An analysis of NGEU, as well as a new constitutional challenge against NGEU before the GFCC reveal, moreover, that the threat of constitutional identity and *ultra vires* review had by no means disappeared. I discuss these issues in the next subsection.

4.2 The Spectre of Budgetary Sovereignty and *Ultra Vires* Review

Despite the high-minded rhetoric that some used to accompany the launch of NGEU, the plan was still a compromise. Schramm and Krotz note that Germany had opposed the joint liability of corona bonds, for both legal and political reasons.[178] Germany saw joint liability as contrary to the EU Treaties and opposed risking ultimate liability for the entire debt, a concern that may have also reflected constitutional worries about the *Bundestag*'s budget rights. It now agreed to large-scale EU borrowing and disbursing the money as grants, because the recovery fund was to be an exceptional and one-off fund, tied to the regular EU budget and for which the financial liability of individual Member States was limited.[179] These features were also crucial to ensure the domestic support of the conservatives of the CDU and CSU.[180]

Several legal characteristics of NGEU can be seen to protect the budget rights of national parliaments. The NGEU package consists of three components.[181] The first is the Regulation establishing the European Union Recovery Instrument, which determines the measures to be supported and the allocation of funds.[182] The second consists of various specific spending programmes to which the Recovery Instrument assigns the funds.[183] Key among these is the Recovery and Resilience Facility with a budget of around 90 per cent of the total NGEU resources.[184] Third

[177] Wendel, 'Paradoxes of Ultra-Vires Review' (n 163) 991–92.

[178] Krotz and Schramm, 'Embedded Bilateralism' (n 19) 533–36.

[179] ibid 535; Schramm, 'Economic Ideas, Party Politics, or Material Interests?' (n 163) 11–12; Howarth and Schild, 'Nein to "Transfer Union"' (n 16) 218–20.

[180] Crespy and Schramm, 'Breaking the Budgetary Taboo' (n 20) 16; Schramm, 'Economic Ideas, Party Politics, or Material Interests?' (n 163) 13–14. CDU/CSU, 'Starker Beitrag für europäische Solidarität', Press release of 18 May 2020 <www.cducsu.de/presse/pressemitteilungen/starker-beitrag-fuer-europaeische-solidaritaet> accessed 2 August 2022.

[181] See Witte, 'The European Union's Covid-19 Recovery Plan' (n 35) 636–37.

[182] Council Regulation (EU) 2020/2094 establishing a European Union Recovery Instrument to support the recovery in the aftermath of the COVID-19 crisis [2020] OJ L433I/23 (hereafter Recovery Instrument).

[183] ibid art 1(3).

[184] Regulation (EU) 2021/241 of the European Parliament and of the Council establishing the Recovery and Resilience Facility [2021] OJ L57/17.

is the amended ORD, which empowers the Commission to borrow €750 billion on capital markets.[185]

The ORD, in particular, provides a number of safeguards for the budgetary rights of national parliaments. Key to this is that the authorization for the Commission to borrow the sum is included in the ORD. This means that it had to be approved unanimously in the Council and ratified 'by the Member States in accordance with their respective constitutional requirements'.[186] Consequently, the Commission's borrowing was subject to ratification by the *Bundestag*, while additional borrowing would require a further amendment of the ORD and, thus, unanimous approval of the Member States. The ORD also makes clear that the Commission's empowerment to borrow is 'exceptional, temporary and limited'.[187] Exceptional, because the funds are to be used 'for the sole purpose of addressing the consequences of the COVID-19 crisis'.[188] Temporary, because no new net borrowing should take place after 2026, while the increase in the own resources ceiling would expire by 31 December 2058 at the latest.[189] Limited, because the sum that the Commission can borrow is capped at €750 billion at 2018 prices.[190]

The ORD also includes detailed provisions that limit the potential liability of individual Member States. This is visible in two ways. First, the Commission's borrowing does not create direct financial liabilities for Member States' budgets. Instead, repayment of the borrowed sums falls on the Union budget.[191] This means that they will have to be repaid by the creation of new own resources in the future, by increasing the payments of Member States or by reducing expenditure on other items in the EU budget.[192] The ORD itself still leaves open this repayment issue, although plans exist to introduce new own resources.[193] Secondly, the Commission is able to call on Member States only if the EU budget provides insufficient funds to cover repayment. For this purpose, Article 6 of the ORD provides an exceptional and temporary increase in the own resources ceiling of 0.6 per cent of the gross national income (GNI) of all the Member States. The own resources ceiling sets a maximum on the Member States' possible direct contributions to the EU budget. The exceptional increase in this ceiling is to be used solely for covering the

185 Council Decision (EU, Euratom) 2020/2053 on the system of own resources of the European Union and repealing Decision 2014/335/EU, Euratom [2020] OJ L424/1 (hereafter ORD); see especially arts 5 and 6.

186 Art 311 TFEU.

187 Recital 22 and art 5 ORD (n 185).

188 Art 5(1) ORD (n 185).

189 Recital 17 and art 6 ORD (n 185).

190 Art 5(1) ORD (n 185).

191 Art 5(2) ORD (n 185).

192 Witte, 'The European Union's Covid-19 Recovery Plan' (n 35) 680.

193 See ibid 665–67; recital 8 ORD (n 185); Interinstitutional Agreement between the European Parliament, the Council of the European Union, and the European Commission on budgetary discipline, on cooperation in budgetary matters and on sound financial management, as well as on new own resources, including a roadmap towards the introduction of new own resources [2020] OJ L433I/28.

EU's liabilities that result from the NGEU borrowing.[194] Yet, Article 9 ORD qualifies the option of calling on the Member States as 'a last resort', while the liability of individual Member States is limited.[195] In such a scenario the Commission is first required to 'generate the necessary liquidity by activating other measures', such as 'short-term financing on capital markets'.[196] If that proves impossible, the Commission can call on the Member States to provide the required funding shortfall, but only in proportion to their relative contributions to the EU budget.[197] Should a Member State fail to fulfil this call, the Commission can then call on the other Member States to supply the required funds. Yet such additional calls are also in proportion to their relative budget contributions, while the Member State that failed to honour the initial call remains liable.[198] Finally, Article 9(6) ORD limits the maximum amount of funds that can be called upon from a Member State to 'its GNI-based relative share in the extraordinary and temporary increase in the own resources ceiling'.

For the GFCC, it was precisely these features limiting the Member States' financial liabilities that were a key consideration for upholding the constitutionality of Germany's ratification of the ORD. A group of litigants led by Bernd Lucke (the original founder of the AfD, but who broke with the party in 2015), had filed a new lawsuit against German participation in NGEU.[199] They claimed that German liabilities impaired the *Bundestag*'s overall budgetary responsibility contrary to the principle of democracy, and thus violated German constitutional identity. In addition, they argued that the ORD was *ultra vires* by reason of violating the no-bailout provision of Article 125 TFEU, as well as Article 311 TFEU.[200] Yet, in proceedings for a preliminary injunction, the GFCC rejected the allegation that NGEU infringed the *Bundestag*'s budgetary autonomy, because the ORD limited German financial liabilities.[201] In this respect the GFCC also granted the legislature a wide

[194] See, on these issues, also Witte, 'The European Union's Covid-19 Recovery Plan' (n 35) 660–61 and 665.

[195] Art 9(4)–(6) ORD (n 185).

[196] ibid art 9(4).

[197] ibid art 9(5).

[198] ibid art 9(5).

[199] David Marsh and Andreas Meyer-Schwickerath, 'German Litigation May Trap ECB in Pincer' (*OMFIF*, 31 March 2021) <www.omfif.org/2021/03/german-litigation-may-trap-ecb-in-pincer/> accessed 2 August 2022.

[200] Hans-Detlef Horn, 'Antrag Auf Erlass Einer Einstweiligen Anordnung' <www.uni-marburg.de/de/fb01/professuren/oeffrecht/prof-dr-hans-detlef-horn/vb-gg-eratg-ea_publ.pdf> accessed 2 August 2022. See also BVerfG, *NGEU decision on preliminary injunction* (n 12) paras 88–91.

[201] BVerfG, *NGEU decision on preliminary injunction* (n 12) paras 98–102. The GFCC conducted a summary review. This does not mean that the legal evaluation is superficial, but rather that the analysis of the facts is cursory. Wendel concludes that 'although a violation of German constitutional identity is still considered possible in theory, the identity claim is in fact largely off the table'. Mattias Wendel, 'Next Generation EU and the German Federal Constitutional Court—The Decision on Preliminary Injunctions of 15 April 2021' (*BRIDGE Network Blog*, 17 May 2021) <https://bridgenetwork.eu/2021/05/17/next-generation-eu-and-the-german-federal-constitutional-court-the-decision-on-preliminary-injunctions-of-15-april-2021/> accessed 2 August 2022.

margin of assessment '[w]hen examining whether the scale of payment obligations and commitments to accept liability will result in the *Bundestag* relinquishing its budgetary autonomy'.[202] The *ultra vires* claims were not dealt with in substance, but left to the main proceedings and may well be referred to the CJEU.[203]

The safeguards for the national parliaments' budget rights contained in the ORD, as well as the importance that the GFCC later attached to these safeguards, indicate that constitutional concerns still played an important role in the legal design of NGEU.[204] It is also well documented that the Constitutional Law Committee of the Finnish parliament had strong reservations about the potential impact on Finnish budgetary sovereignty of the initial Commission proposal for NGEU.[205] This proposal did not yet include the detailed provisions of Article 9, which removed doubts that the Member States would have joint and several liability for the Commission's borrowing. Instead, the original proposal had stated merely that where 'the authorised appropriations entered in the budget are not sufficient for the Union to comply with its obligations resulting from borrowing […] the Member States shall make the resources necessary for that purpose available to the Commission'.[206] Concerns by the Constitutional Law Committee of the Finnish parliament played an important role in making explicit that the financial liabilities of individual Member States would be limited.

Nonetheless, in the *Bundestag* debates on the ORD of February and March 2021, constitutional constraints stemming from the GFCC's case law considerations had faded from view. On the left side of the political spectrum, the SPD Finance Minister, Olaf Scholz, and the SPD Minister of State for Europe, Michael Roth, both proclaimed NGEU as a step towards 'fiscal union'.[207] The idea that such a step would present constitutional difficulties was absent, in contrast to the SPD's position during the euro crisis.[208] Die Linke also declared itself 'prepared to enter into

[202] BVerfG, *NGEU decision on preliminary injunction* (n 12) para 97.

[203] See also Wendel, 'Next Generation EU and the German Federal Constitutional Court' (n 201).

[204] Chancellor Merkel also declared that respecting the national parliament's budget rights had been an important issue for the German government in the design of NGEU: Plenarprotokoll 19/166, Stenografischer Bericht der 166. Sitzung des Deutschen Bundestages am 18. Juni 2020, 20640.

[205] Leino-Sandberg, 'Who Is Ultra Vires Now?' (n 154); Päivi Leino-Sandberg, 'Between European Commitment and "Taking the Law Seriously"' (*Verfassungsblog: On Matters Constitutional*, 29 April 2021) <https://verfassungsblog.de/between-european-commitment-and-taking-the-law-seriously/> accessed 1 August 2022. The Finnish constitutional law committee also had objected to the interpretation of arts 310 and 125 TFEU.

[206] European Commission, 'Amended proposal for a Council decision on the system of Own Resources of the European Union', COM(2020) 445 final <https://ec.europa.eu/info/sites/default/files/about_the_european_commission/eu_budget/com_2020_445_en_act_v8.pdf> accessed 2 August 2022.

[207] Finance Minister Scholz, Plenarprotokoll 19/212, Stenografischer Bericht der 212. Sitzung des Deutschen Bundestages am 25 Februar 2021 (hereafter Plenarprotokoll 19/212) 26680; Minister of State for Europe Michael Roth, Plenarprotokoll 19/218 (n 208) 27480.

[208] Töns (SPD), Plenarprotokoll 19/218, Stenografischer Bericht der 218. Sitzung des Deutschen Bundestages am 25 März 2021 (hereafter Plenarprotokoll 19/218) 27489 did say that fiscal union would require a constitutional, two-thirds parliamentary majority.

the fiscal union'.[209] The Greens argued in a similar vein that the recovery instrument 'should be made permanent in order to finally solve the central problem of the Economic and Monetary Union—the lack of a budgetary complement to the common monetary policy'.[210] Franziska Brantner recalled that the GFCC's *PSPP* judgment had made clear that there was a need for fiscal policy at the European level.[211] In a *Bundestag* debate of 2 July 2020 on the repercussions of the *PSPP* ruling, she had even stated that the GFCC would act against the Europe-friendly nature of the German constitution should it block the road to a common European fiscal policy.[212]

The CDU/CSU and FDP, on the other hand, both made clear that, in their view, NGEU was not a step towards fiscal union. Instead, they stressed the exceptional and temporary nature of the rescue fund.[213] Yet, strikingly, neither party explicitly related their opposition to fiscal union to constitutional arguments about Germany's budgetary sovereignty. Eckhart Rehberg of the CDU/CSU indicated that the march to fiscal union would require a change of the EU Treaties, but not that this would necessitate an overhaul of the German constitution.[214] The FDP merely stated that the current ORD was not a 'legal precedent' for a more general competence of the EU to incur debt.[215]

[209] Ulrich (Die Linke), Plenarprotokoll 19/212 (n 207) 26693; Nonetheless, the party abstained from supporting NGEU, noting that it was 'too small', while demanding more taxes on the wealthy and corporations. See Plenarprotokoll 19/218 (n 208) 27485; Plenarprotokoll 19/212 (n 207) 26685–86 and 26692–93; Beschlussempfehlung und Bericht des Haushaltsausschusses zu dem Gesetzentwurf der Bundesregierung—Drucksache 19/26821—Entwurf eines Gesetzes zum Beschluss des Rates vom 14. Dezember 2020 über das Eigenmittelsystem der Europäischen Union und zur Aufhebung des Beschlusses 2014/335/EU, Euratom (Eigenmittelbeschluss-Ratifizierungsgesetz—ERatG), BT-Dr 19/27901 of 24.03.2021, 11 (hereafter BT-Dr 19/27901).

[210] BT-Dr 19/27901 (n 209) 12; Similarly Kindler (Bündnis 90/Die Grünen), Plenarprotokoll 19/212 (n 207) 26686–88. See also Antrag der Abgeordneten Dr Franziska Brantner et al und der Fraktion Bündnis 90/Die Grünen zu dem Beschluss (EU, Euratom) 2020/2053 des Rates vom 14. Dezember 2020 über das Eigenmittelsystem der Europäischen Union und zur Aufhebung des Beschlusses 2014/335/EU, Euratom, BT-Dr 19/27824 of 23.03.2021, 3, where the Greens state that a fiscal union is needed.

[211] Brantner (Bündnis 90/Die Grünen), Plenarprotokoll 19/218 (n 208) 27486.

[212] Brantner (Bündnis 90/Die Grünen), Plenarprotokoll 19/170 (n 90) 21281.

[213] Rehberg (CDU/CSU), Plenarprotokoll 19/212 (n 207) 26683–84; Berghegger (CDU/CSU), Plenarprotokoll 19/212 (n 207) 26691; Florian Oßner (CDU/CSU), Plenarprotokoll 19/212 (n 207) 26694; Rehberg (CDU/CSU), Plenarprotokoll 19/218 (n 208) 27482; Dürr (FDP), Plenarprotokoll 19/218 (n 208) 27483–84; Kuhle (FDP), Plenarprotokoll 19/212 (n 207) 26690; BT-Dr 19/27901 (n 209) 9–11. Florian Hahn (CDU/CSU) did engage with the legal arguments against the NGEU package but maintained that the package was compatible with the EU Treaties, as well as the Basic Law, see Plenarprotokoll 19/218 (n 208) 27487.

[214] He also stated that this would require a two-thirds majority in the *Bundestag*, but not that it would require a referendum. See Plenarprotokoll 19/218 (n 208) 27483.

[215] BT-Dr 19/27901 (n 209) 11; Antrag der Abgeordneten Otto Fricke et al und der Fraktion der FDP zu der dritten Beratung des Gesetzentwurfs der Bundesregierung—Drucksachen 19/26821, 19/27901—Entwurf eines Gesetzes zum Beschluss des Rates vom 14. Dezember 2020 über das Eigenmittelsystem der Europäischen Union und zur Aufhebung des Beschlusses 2014/335/EU, Euratom (Eigenmittelbeschluss-Ratifizierungsgesetz—ERatG), BT-Dr 19/2793 of 24.03.2021, 3 (hereafter BT-Dr 19/2793). The FDP proposed to change the Act on Cooperation between the Federal Government and the German Bundestag in European Union Matters (EUZBBG). In their view, the financial liabilities under NGEU affected the *Bundestag*'s overall budgetary responsibility, which required an enhanced role for the *Bundestag*'s budgetary committee (see Gesetzentwurf der Abgeordneten Otto Fricke et al

The only party that made questions about the legality and constitutionality of NGEU a primary concern was the AfD. It was also the only party that opposed the NGEU package.[216] Its spokesperson, Peter Boehringer, characterized NGEU as the last step into an 'illegal EU fiscal union'.[217] With explicit reference to the case law of the GFCC, the party considered the move both contrary to the EU Treaties as well as contrary to the budget right of the *Bundestag*.[218] Given the vast sums of money involved, Boehringer claimed that it was 'absurd' for the German government to claim that 'the budgetary sovereignty of future German parliaments is not affected'.[219] Next Generation EU constituted the illegal transformation of the EU into a state with which 'the ground of the free democratic basic order is clearly being abandoned'.[220]

Yet the AfD's constitutional arguments did not resonate with the other parties. The parliamentary debates on the ORD instead suggest that Germany's politicians had become less willing to invoke the GFCC's EU-related case law as an impediment to further European integration and more prepared to treat the future of the EMU as a political issue.

5. Conclusion

Although the GFCC's *ultra vires* ruling in the *PSPP* case presented a significant escalation in the GFCC's dealings with the EU, the weak remedy employed by the Court finally left it to political institutions to find a solution. A constructive reading of the ruling is that the German Court raised justified concerns about the democratic legitimacy of the ECB's policies, while leaving their resolution to political bodies and spurring further political debate on the ECB's constitutional position.

und der Fraktion der FDP—Entwurf eines Gesetzes zur Änderung Gesetzes über die Zusammenarbeit von Bundesregierung und Deutschem Bundestag in Angelegenheiten der Europäischen Union zur Stärkung der Beteiligungsrechte des Bundestages in Angelegenheiten des Aufbauinstruments Next Generation EU (Next-Generation-EUZBBG—NG-EUZBBG), BT-Dr 19/26877 of 23.02.2021). However, this proposal was rejected. In addition, the FDP claimed that the ratifying Act required adoption by a two-thirds majority in the *Bundestag* and *Bundesrat*. The party invoked the GFCC's case law on art 23 BL to support its point (BT-Dr 19/2793 (n 215) 4); see also Fricke (FDP) in Plenarprotokoll 19/212 (n 207) 26685. This idea was also rejected, even though a two-thirds majority did in practice adopt the law. The GFCC later refuted that a two-thirds majority would have been required, as this was not a case of 'a transfer of sovereign powers' (BVerfG, *NGEU decision on preliminary injunction* (n 12) paras 79, 78, and 80).

[216] See the voting records in Plenarprotokoll 19/218 (n 208) 27489.

[217] Plenarprotokoll 19/212 (n 207) 26681; also Plenarprotokoll 19/218 (n 208) 27481.

[218] Plenarprotokoll 19/212 (n 207) 26681–82; Plenarprotokoll 19/218 (n 208) 27481; BT-Dr 19/27901 (n 209) 9. In relation to the EU Treaties, the party specifically pointed to the incompatibility of NGEU with arts 310 and 311 TFEU, as well as the no-bailout clause of art 125 TFEU and the broader spirit of the Maastricht Treaty.

[219] Plenarprotokoll 19/212 (n 207) 26682; Plenarprotokoll 19/218 (n 208) 27482.

[220] Plenarprotokoll 19/218 (n 208) 27482; similarly Plenarprotokoll 19/212 (n 207) 26683.

Such weak review offers a way to reap the benefits of judicial review of European law while not obstructing democratic decision-making. It allows national constitutional courts to point out constitutional problems relating to European integration but leaves their resolution to political branches. As such, it is in line with the possibility of reasonable disagreement on how constitutional principles apply to the EU. In addition, the increased willingness of German politicians to dispute the constitutional interpretations of the GFCC offers welcome democratic contestation over the interpretation of constitutional principles about which reasonable disagreement is possible. Such contestation is in turn likely to have an effect on the GFCC's rulings, making it more hesitant to review European law or even induce it to significantly alter its approach to European integration.[221]

It remains to be seen whether the *PSPP* ruling, and the significant backlash it engendered, mark a turning point in the GFCC's EU-related case law. Formal proposals to alter the powers of the GFCC seem to have led nowhere.[222] Also, as this chapter analysed, the spectre of *ultra vires* and constitutional identity review continued to hover over the adoption and design of the NGEU, while various litigants mounted a new constitutional challenge to the ECB's PEPP. Nonetheless, by the time the cases on the PEPP and NGEU are finally decided—they are still pending at the time of writing—the composition of the GFCC's second senate may well have changed significantly. One of the key shapers of the GFCC's approach to the EU and President of the Court, Andreas Voβkuhle, left the bench in June 2020, and was replaced by Astrid Wallrabenstein, a nominee of the Greens. At the time of writing, Peter Huber, the judge rapporteur in the major EU-related cases, including the *PSPP* case, was set to depart the Court in November 2022. German political actors may opt to choose a successor with a different stance on European integration. These changes in personnel may lead to an alteration in the GFCC's approach to European integration, but the outcome in future cases will have to be awaited to draw more definitive conclusions.

[221] Petersen, 'Karlsruhe's Lochner Moment?' (n 129).

[222] For such proposals, see Ulrich Karpenstein and Maximilian Steinbeis, 'Die Stunde des Gesetzgebers' (*Verfassungsblog: On Matters Constitutional*, 19 July 2021) <https://verfassungsblog.de/die-stunde-des-gesetzgebers/> accessed 1 August 2022.

8
Conclusion

In *The Nine*, Jeffrey Toobin's bestseller on the United States Supreme Court, the author starts with a description of the building that houses the country's highest court: a grand building meant to inspire awe and respect for the Court's judges. Built on a small plot of land, its architect chose to give the building an impressive stairway. The Court could only be entered by ascending a series of steep steps, an experience that few visitors would forget and that emphasized how 'the justices would operate, literally, on a higher plane'.[1]

Having read the GFCC's judgments on European integration and how the Karlsruhe judges have often challenged key principles of EU law, seemingly claiming a higher legitimacy than its Luxembourg counterpart—the CJEU—I always imagined that the German Court's building would look similar to the one Toobin described in his account of the US Supreme Court.

Things turned out differently than I expected. When I visited the Karlsruhe Court in April 2015, I initially simply walked straight past the building. The Court building is interesting, but unimpressive, and not necessarily beautiful. Rather than steep steps, it offers concrete and a lot of glass. Later, when I was given a tour by one of the Court officials, I realized how much its architecture had been inspired and influenced by a different time, and different ideals, than its US counterpart. The gigantic windows that form the sides of the pleading room illuminate the chamber and symbolize the importance of transparency. The room where the judges put on their robes can be seen from the outside, demystifying their transition from ordinary citizens into the spokespersons of Germany's highest law. Finally, the Court's pleading room sits in the highest part of the building, showing that the citizens' interests are of the highest importance, and remain the source of the Court's legitimacy. During that visit, the Court really seemed to be a people's court and a guardian of democracy.

Yet, when it comes to the Court's EU-related case law, it appears that the Court's architects have better understood the inevitable tension at the basis of constitutional democracies than the judges themselves. Constitutions can be seen as laying down the preconditions for democratically legitimate government. However, what these preconditions require is unavoidably subject to reasonable disagreement in a democratic society. The ideal of having a democratic constitution is an enduring

[1] Jeffrey Toobin, *The Nine: Inside the Secret World of the Supreme Court* (Anchor Books 2008) 1–2.

Judging European Democracy. Nik de Boer, Oxford University Press. © Nik de Boer 2023.
DOI: 10.1093/oso/9780192845238.003.0008

project of constant rediscovery and elaboration rather than an ideal whose content can be comprehensively determined in the abstract. Allowing courts to review legislation on the basis of constitutional norms may be a wise strategy if it helps promote ongoing democratic deliberation about constitutional issues, or if it ensures that such issues are taken into account at all. Yet it may also obstruct this task if it takes the power to decide on fundamental societal questions away from the democratically elected branches of government. These considerations also apply to the way in which constitutional ideals should be realized in the European Union. And even if the EU has several democratic legitimacy problems, a fundamental difficulty is that there is no clear consensus on how the EU's democratic credentials should be improved.

This book set out to answer how we should assess the democratic legitimacy of the national constitutional court's review of European law and did so with three main aims. First, and primarily, to better understand the national constitutional courts' legitimate role in relation to the EU in a way that takes into account concerns about the democratic legitimacy of these courts. Secondly, to inform accounts of how national constitutional courts should use their review powers when they deal with European law. Thirdly, to provide ideas for institutional design. The current chapter sums up the book's main findings and discusses how they contribute to fulfilling these three aims. Section 1 first reiterates the main theoretical arguments of Chapters 2 and 3 on the democratic legitimacy of judicial review and the national constitutional courts' review of European law. This section reaffirms why it is important to compare legislative and judicial practice in evaluating the legitimacy of judicial review, and why it is pivotal to take into account the impact of such review on subsequent political decision-making. Section 2 then discusses the main findings of the case study and how they provide insights into the comparative institutional legitimacy of constitutional courts and political institutions in the EU context. Section 3 zooms out from the specific findings of the case study to consider what they teach about the legitimate role of national constitutional courts in the EU more generally. Section 4 offers a number of concluding thoughts.

1. On the Importance of Studying Political Processes and Institutions

In Chapters 2 and 3 of this book I argued that a critical engagement with judicial and legislative practice is pivotal in assessing the legitimacy of the constitutional courts' role. This is so both where it concerns the constitutional courts' review of legislation in the domestic context, as well as where it concerns their review of European law.

Chapter 2 discussed the dilemma involved in addressing the legitimacy of judicial review in the domestic context. Legal constitutionalists commonly justify constitutional constraints on democratic majority government as necessary to protect fundamental rights against the possible aberrations of oppressive majorities. The protection of these rights is considered a necessary precondition for the law's legitimacy, and legal constitutionalists defend judicial review as the best mechanism to ensure the protection of these rights. This defence is based on an idealized picture of courts as 'forums of principle', which are supposedly very well placed to address fundamental moral questions. The democratic process is instead regarded in a negative light: political majorities are seen as basing their positions on the preferences of self-interested persons, not on the basis of moral arguments.

Critics of this position have rightly pointed to two major problems with legal constitutionalism. Legal constitutionalists place the constitution outside the realm of ordinary democratic politics because the constitution establishes the legitimacy conditions for democratic politics. The first problem with this view is that it largely ignores that people can reasonably disagree about rights. They can disagree about which rights should be protected as a matter of basic justice, how these should be weighed against other normative considerations in case they conflict, and how these rights should be interpreted in concrete cases. Habermas, for example, points out that understandings of how to best protect fundamental rights have historically evolved in light of changing circumstances and in light of the different arguments, viewpoints, and experiences articulated by affected persons. Political constitutionalists argue that the democratic process offers a fairer way to resolve moral disagreements about rights than decision-making by courts. The democratic process gives citizens an equal right to participate, and decisions are taken after the exchange of reasons. In connection with this point, political constitutionalists also note a second problem with legal constitutionalism: it rests on an idealized picture of the way courts operate and sketches a picture of democratic politics that is too negative. Instead, political constitutionalists maintain that elected legislatures are forums in which the people's representatives deliberate in a responsible manner on matters of justice and rights. Judicial review of legislation is democratically problematic: by giving courts the ability to strike down legislation on constitutional grounds, these courts will often end up taking sides in good faith disagreements among elected legislators that have settled their disagreement by majority decision.

Although political constitutionalists point to important deficiencies in the legal constitutionalist's defence of judicial review, it must be acknowledged that mere majoritarian democratic decision-making cannot be regarded as sufficient to understand the legitimacy of law. Democratic majority decisions to abolish the democratic process, or decisions that do away with political rights, such as the right to freedom of expression or freedom of assembly, take away essential elements of a legitimate democratic process. Beyond that, majorities that do not take into account the views of those in the minority can hardly claim that such minorities should accept their decisions as legitimate. In this respect, Chapter 2 discussed Habermas' idea of the co-originality of constitutional rights and democracy, according to which the constitution lays down the institutional conditions for democratic will-formation. This idea of co-originality expresses the intuition that citizens can only participate as free and equal in a democratic process when they have a sufficient degree of independence to begin with. At the same time, co-originality also entails that the preconditions for a legitimate democratic process are themselves subject to reasonable disagreement. Therefore, one cannot legitimately place the constitution fully outside the realm of democratic politics. Instead, the preconditions for a legitimate democratic process embodied in a constitution must be specified within the democratic process itself in an ongoing manner and in light of changing circumstances. As I argued in Chapter 2, a democratic constitution should thus function as both a standard to assess the legitimacy of law, as expressing an ideal to be further realized in law, but also as a set of norms that itself must be open to revision in light of new insights and arguments.

In this vein, the ideal of deliberative democracy demands that there is ongoing deliberation on whether a country's laws remain compatible with the preconditions of democratic legitimacy. Yet Habermas' notion of co-originality emphasizes the limits of political philosophy in determining the relationship between constitutionalism and democracy: it is impossible to fully articulate in the abstract what the preconditions are for a legitimate democratic process. Deliberative democracy requires that legislating also involves good faith deliberation on whether such legislation is compatible with the preconditions for a legitimate democratic process. Judicial review can be a better means to ensure that such deliberation takes place, because it may be that, in practice, courts are better situated than legislatures to address constitutional questions. While proponents of judicial review often sketch an idealized picture of courts, judicial review critics instead may be seen to rely on an idealized picture of legislative politics. Key to assessing the democratic legitimacy of judicial review, therefore, is an assessment of the comparative abilities of legislatures and courts to address the constitutional implications of legislation. That is to say, one should take into account how legislatures and constitutional courts deliberate on constitutional matters in practice, as well as how the courts' review affects subsequent political decision-making.

Of course, better insights into the comparative functioning of courts and legislatures cannot by themselves answer how the legitimacy of judicial review should be assessed. It must also be granted that there is no unequivocal normative standard to address the deliberative quality of judicial and political decision-making. Still, a critical engagement with legislative and judicial practice has the potential to advance the debate over the democratic legitimacy of judicial review in at least three ways. First, it helps to show whether the empirical assumptions on the functioning of institutions that inform normative accounts on the democratic legitimacy of review stand up to reality. Secondly, in line with the main tenets of deliberative democratic theory, such enquiries connect to, and engage with, the arguments and reasons already offered within actual political debate. Thirdly, and closely connected to the previous point, bringing in a critical comparison of legislative and judicial practice probably helps to dispel a false sense of necessity that accompanies court judgments once these are handed down.[2] Understanding how aspects of court judgments were politically contested in prior political debate helps to grasp how the choices of courts are politically loaded and how they come at the expense of alternatives.

Chapter 3 drew out the implications of these arguments for assessing the democratic legitimacy of the national constitutional courts' review of European law. In a nutshell, the chapter argued that the role of constitutional courts in the EU should also be assessed in relation to political institutions. Much has been written about the national constitutional courts' EU-related case law over the past thirty years. Yet, too little attention has been paid to the courts' legitimacy compared to political institutions in deciding issues of constitutional importance for the EU. Not enough consideration has been given to how the national constitutional courts' review risks taking certain constitutional issues outside the realm of politics, whereas the comparative legitimacy of political institutions in addressing these issues may be greater. Existing scholarship on the constitutional courts' role in relation to the EU can sometimes give one the false impression that courts are the only institutions that address constitutional questions. Scholars that favour the dialogue and contestation that supposedly emanates from the national constitutional courts' review have insufficiently considered these courts' legitimacy in relation to other institutions. Similarly, one should not equate the notion of constitutional identity with what the courts say it is, as courts may construct such notions at the expense of other possible reasonable interpretations. The idea of constitutional pluralism more generally (which has become so influential following the GFCC's *Maastricht* judgment) is easily connected to fine-sounding notions of heterarchy, diversity, and openness, and opposed to seemingly less attractive notions of hierarchy and uniformity.

However, the focus on courts to the neglect of political institutions remains an important deficiency in current scholarship on the role of national constitutional courts and can only lead to incomplete assessments of the legitimacy of these courts' position. As the introduction of this book emphasized, when one asserts that constitutional identities should be respected, it is also important to address who determines what this identity consists of. And when one wishes to promote contestation or dialogue, it is important to consider who should do the contesting or the talking. For these reasons, and despite democratic legitimacy problems in the EU's decision-making processes, assessments of the constitutional courts' role should take into account the institutional constellation in which such review takes

[2] In this sense Duncan Kennedy speaks of a legitimation effect, which denotes that people associate the development of law through adjudication as 'natural, necessary, just' rather than as political. Duncan Kennedy, *A Critique of Adjudication* (Harvard University Press 1997) 241.

place, how the constitutional issues were considered in the prior political decision-making process, as well as how the constitutional court judgments impact subsequent political deliberations.

2. A Cautionary Tale: The GFCC and European Integration

What then can be learned from the case study on the GFCC's EU-related case law? In this book I have argued that two main conclusions follow. On the one hand, a key problem is that the GFCC's rulings on European integration ultimately raise several democratic problems. That is essentially the case because the Court has adopted a contested understanding of democracy according to which democracy is tied to the nation-state. This conception limits the ability of political actors to put forward different visions on the future of European integration and on the way in which democratic ideals within this process should be realized. That is not to say that politics is always perfect by itself. Yet portraying constitutional courts as 'forums of principle' or as necessarily better placed to deliberate on constitutional matters in the context of European integration is not accurate either. Instead, the case study showed how, in Germany, constitutional questions often formed a considerable part of political debate and how such political debates showed more openness to a variety of possible understandings of constitutional principles. Moreover, the idea that the GFCC's judgments have contributed to an improvement of democratic debate on constitutional matters in this context has limited support.

On the other hand, the case study also discussed how the GFCC strengthened the position of the German parliament in EU affairs and thus helped counter the dominance of the executive in this area of decision-making. Such review, which is more limited in nature and focuses more on the relationship between the executive and national parliaments, promotes democratic politics rather than constraining it. Zooming in on the case study, the next subsections point out that the GFCC has played three main roles in relation to European integration, each of which should be assessed differently from a democratic perspective.

2.1 'A Chamber for Euro-critics': Facilitating Dissent?

A first finding is that the German Court has provided an avenue for Euro-critics to voice their dissent about European integration, starting with its *Maastricht* judgment. For a long time, a strong pro-European consensus proved to be a key feature of German political discourse. This consensus meant that the Euro-critical position was not very well represented within the German *Bundestag*. The entry of the Eurosceptic party, Alternative for Germany (AfD), in the *Bundestag* in September 2017 has changed this situation. Yet, before the AfD's entry, Euro-critics remained minorities within the different *Bundestag* parties. The analysis of German parliamentary debates showed that it was not always easy for such critics to voice their concerns within the *Bundestag* debates. In the debates on the Maastricht Treaty, critical viewpoints on European integration were cast as anti-peace and associated with failed nationalist politics of the past. Although Euroscepticism is no longer as controversial in Germany as it was when the Maastricht Treaty was adopted, the pro-European parliamentary consensus endured during the euro crisis, despite significant opposition to the crisis measures outside parliament.

In this pro-European climate, the GFCC has provided a place for a more Euro-critical viewpoint. First, it has done so by admitting challenges to European Treaties and EU law through a wide and substantive interpretation of the right to vote in Article 38 BL. Thus, the courtroom has served as a forum for Euro-critics to attack European law in a manner that is also widely covered in the German media. Secondly, the GFCC itself has articulated such a critical perspective. It has done so by opting for a national interpretation of the principle of democracy and by putting down several constitutional limits to European integration. In this sense, the GFCC has served as 'a chamber for Euro-critics'.[3]

Still, it is highly questionable that the GFCC should provide an avenue for such dissent. As the trajectory of the GFCC's case law from Maastricht to the euro crisis underlines, the Court can provide such an avenue as long as its own judgments produce few concrete effects. For the GFCC's review of the Maastricht Treaty that may still have been the case. However, ultimately the Court's position as a guardian of a constitutional framework that is supposed to bind democratic politics is at odds with merely providing an additional road for political contestation. By adopting a particular and nationally oriented interpretation of the German principle of democracy, the Court ultimately ends up constraining the room for political debate in the *Bundestag*. The GFCC has elevated the Euro-critical viewpoint to the level of unamendable constitutional law.

2.2 Stifling European Democracy: Limiting Political Deliberation

Over time, the GFCC has not just provided a forum for dissent or a Euro-critical viewpoint in German political debate, but the Court's rulings eventually constrain the *Bundestag*'s ability to decide on Europe's future itself. In addition, the Court's rulings limit the space for political deliberation at the EU level. For several reasons,

[3] The phrase comes from Christoph Möllers: Interview with Christoph Möllers, Professor of Public Law and Jurisprudence, Faculty of Law, Humboldt-University Berlin and representative of the German Bundestag in the ESM case (Berlin, Germany, 20 April 2015).

this consequence of the GFCC's EU-related case law is of questionable democratic legitimacy.

First, the study of the German political debates showed that constitutional issues often featured prominently in these debates. When the *Bundestag* debated the Maastricht Treaty in 1992, the democratic shortcomings of this Treaty were probably the most pressing concern. Yet, most German politicians did not construe this as a problem of European integration as such but advocated a strengthening of the European Parliament. In addition, most parties did not share the idea that competence transfers to the EU would be somehow democratically problematic by themselves. Social-democratic and green parties feared in fact that the principle of subsidiarity would prevent a Europeanization of social and environmental policies and entrench the asymmetry of European integration. In addition, the GFCC's apparent position that a viable democracy requires one *demos*—a people with a sufficient common identity—was contested. For example, several German parties instead favoured granting all permanent residents the right to vote in order to 'restore a congruence between the holders of democratic political rights and those durably subject to an authority'.[4]

For these reasons, it is inappropriate to qualify the GFCC as 'a forum of principle', opposed to an unprincipled political process in which the Maastricht Treaty was justified on the basis of the narrow interests of particular constituencies and in which constitutional issues were not seriously discussed. Instead, the paradox of the German political debates on the Maastricht Treaty is that these debates arguably were not political enough and that the Court's judgment apparently served to make the debates more political. At the time of Maastricht, the Court may still have successfully played this role of politicizing the German European integration debate, because the *Maastricht-Urteil* was sufficiently vague to allow for widely divergent interpretations by several affected parties. The ruling could be interpreted as support for the German government and even for Europe as a whole, given the Court's approval of the Treaty; alternatively, it could be interpreted as a victory for democracy, given the Court's insistence on the role of the *Bundestag* and the supplementary role of the European Parliament; but, at the same time, the Court's constraints on further European integration could also be cast a victory for the Euro-critics.

The GFCC's 2009 judgment on the Lisbon Treaty as well as its subsequent judgments on the euro crisis, however, have resulted in a situation that is democratically more problematic. Despite the strong pro-European consensus in German politics, the *Bundestag* parties did offer competing visions on the EU's future that reflect fundamental political differences and competing ideas of social justice. The

[4] BT-Drucksache 12/6000 of 05.11.1993: Bericht der Gemeinsamen Verfassungskommission gemäß Beschluß des Deutschen Bundestages—Drucksachen 12/1590, 12/1670—und Beschluß des Bundesrates—Drucksache 741/91 (Beschluß), 98.

GFCC's case law ultimately affects these different positions unevenly. The Court's national interpretation of the principle of democracy means that several competences must remain to a significant degree with the German *Bundestag*. These areas include 'fundamental fiscal decisions' as well as 'decisions on the social state'.[5] In addition, the European Parliament is not seen as a democratic alternative to the *Bundestag*. Such an understanding of democracy was more readily compatible with the political position put forward by Germany's centre-right governing coalition during the crisis. As explained in Chapter 5, this coalition favoured promoting budgetary discipline, the creation of a genuine 'stability culture', and only limited financial assistance to debtor states given under strict conditionality in order not to reduce incentives for budgetary discipline. This approach limited the liability of Member States for each other's debts and preserved the national parliaments' budgetary sovereignty to a significant degree. Yet, at the same time, it has not prevented the Member States' budgetary policies from becoming increasingly subject to norms on budgetary discipline, and a great degree of coordination of economic policies within the EU now takes place.

The left-wing opposition, which at that time consisted of the Social Democratic Party (SPD), the Left Party (Die Linke), and the Greens (Bündnis 90/Die Grünen), instead focused more on the role of financial markets, the original design faults of the Economic and Monetary Union (EMU), as well as the negative effects of German economic policies on other European Member States. In addition, these parties were much more critical of Germany's and Europe's austerity politics. Instead, they generally favoured more European integration in tax, economic, and social policy, as well as increased debt sharing between the Member States. In several ways these proposals reflected a concern about democratic self-determination, although not equated with budgetary sovereignty. They felt the need to better regulate the financial markets in order to ensure political power above the markets. Further European integration in sensitive areas such as tax, social, and economic policy sought to overcome harmful competition between Member States that, in these parties' view, undermined the German social model and citizens' abilities for collective self-determination. The left-wing political parties in Germany favoured competence transfers in these areas precisely in order to restore the citizens' capacity for self-determination and make alternatives to austerity politics possible. Yet these competence transfers are more difficult to square with the GFCC's case law.

At the European level, the available evidence is that, during the euro crisis, the GFCC's case law also constrained European decision-making. On the one hand, it must be granted that without the GFCC's case law, the EU probably would not look radically different. On the other hand, however, it seems that in several respects the GFCC's case law has not helped to make things better. When the crisis

[5] Bundesverfassungsgericht, judgment of 30 June 2009, 2 BvE 2/08 (*Lisbon* judgment) para 252.

showed that the assumptions underlying the Maastricht stability architecture had proven to be false, there was a threat that any departure from the Treaty's provisions would be struck down in Karlsruhe. This threat probably exacerbated the crisis, because it put an additional obstacle in the way of a quick political response. Ironically, this turn of events also sidelined national parliaments, including the *Bundestag*. Furthermore, the Court's rulings favoured an intergovernmental approach to the crisis that has helped to retain a German veto on decisions affecting the *Bundestag*'s budget right. At the same time, this intergovernmental approach led to further concerns about executive dominance and a lack of transparency. In addition, the Court's case law appears consistent with the strict austerity policies imposed on debtor states that have led to serious concerns about the rule of law, democracy, and social rights in those Member States. Finally, the available insights on the impact of the Court's case law on the negotiations of the banking union indicate that the Court's insistence on budgetary sovereignty came at the expense of the European Parliament's position and the possibility that democratic solutions to Europe's legitimacy problems can be found at the European level.

The idea that the Court's interventions have merely contributed to a more informed democratic debate on these fundamental constitutional questions is difficult to uphold. During the euro crisis, the Court's judgments remained uncontested in German politics. Where the Court ruled, it replaced the *Bundestag* as the authoritative interpreter of the German Basic Law. The Court therefore limited the room for political contestation over European integration. And although the Court's rulings remain abstract and subject to multiple possible interpretations, several signs emerged that the room for further European integration within the Basic Law had become largely exhausted.[6]

As discussed in Chapter 7, the GFCC's *PSPP* judgment of 5 May 2020 presents in some ways a continuation of this problematic story but offers in other ways an idea of how things might change for the better. The decision of the German judges to declare both a CJEU judgment, as well as actions by the European Central Bank (ECB), to be *ultra vires* presented an escalation of the GFCC's dealings with EU law. In particular, the GFCC's attack on the primacy of EU law and the CJEU were severely criticized. Many condemned the German Constitutional Court for unjustifiably risking undermining the achievements of European legal integration. Yet, in other ways the case offered glimpses of a possible better future. The escalation by the GFCC made elected politicians willing to challenge the Karlsruhe judges, introducing welcome democratic contestation of the Court's reading of the German constitution. In addition, the GFCC did raise legitimate democratic

[6] As stated by the GFCC's President Voßkuhle at the time: Melanie Mann and Inge Kloepfer, 'Mehr Europa lässt das Grundgesetz kaum zu' (2011) *Frankfurter Allgemeine Zeitung* (25 September 2011) <www.faz.net/aktuell/wirtschaft/eurokrise/im-gespraech-andreas-vosskuhle-mehr-europa-laesst-das-grundgesetz-kaum-zu-11369184.html> accessed 1 August 2022.

concerns about the ECB's role and, most importantly, left it to Germany's elected politicians to resolve the issue. For that reason, the GFCC's *PSPP* ruling can ultimately be qualified as a form of weak review. In this manner, the ruling contributed to political debate on the democratic legitimacy of the ECB without the German Court itself deciding the matter. The discussion of Next Generation EU, the EU's new major step in the EMU, showed that the GFCC has so far—at least at the time of writing—been unwilling to stand in the way of this programme, but also that its case law still had an effect on the design of this new recovery programme. It remains to be seen whether the *PSPP* case and its aftermath mark a turning point in the GFCC's approach to European integration.

2.3 A Stronger Parliament: Enhancing Oversight

Despite significant concerns about the GFCC's EU-related case law, a more positive effect is that the Court strengthened the position of the German parliament. In this manner it countered the dominance of the executive in EU affairs. Particularly during the euro crisis, the Court repeatedly intervened to strengthen the *Bundestag*'s participation and information position in EU affairs. It is also clear that during the crisis, the German government repeatedly failed to adequately inform the *Bundestag* about ongoing European negotiations, and that the *Bundestag* itself took insufficient action to address this concern. At several points, the *Bundestag* failed to provide for extensive parliamentary oversight over the European Financial Stability Facility.

Thanks largely to the GFCC's interventions, the *Bundestag* obtained sufficiently strong information and participation rights in EU affairs. The events described in Chapter 6 also showed that it is unlikely that the *Bundestag* would have strengthened its position by itself. Ultimately, the *Bundestag* failed to do so when it had a chance, and it repeatedly only took decisive action after the Court intervened. As a result, the German *Bundestag* is now regarded as one of the strongest Member State parliaments in European affairs. There are also indications that these legal changes have made a positive difference in practice. Moreover, the Court has been able to take into account countervailing considerations, such as a legitimate need for executive confidentiality.

3. Weakening Review, Strengthening Democracy

What lessons do these findings provide for the legitimate role of national constitutional courts in the EU more generally? The case study of the GFCC, widely considered to be Europe's most influential and authoritative constitutional court, provides grounds to question the idea that constitutional courts have a better competence to deal with constitutional questions than legislatures in relation to the EU. That is the case for two main reasons. First, how the principles and ideals of national constitutions matter for European integration is a complex issue of significant political and moral importance, on which there are widely differing reasonable views. Secondly, the case study indicates that constitutional courts are neither clearly better than legislatures at considering the constitutional implications of European integration, nor does their review evidently improve subsequent political debate. Instead, constitutional courts risk constraining legitimate political decision-making in an undemocratic fashion. This holds for both types of review that now feature most prominently in the case law of national constitutional courts, namely constitutional identity review and *ultra vires* review.

In this section, I first discuss this legitimacy problem with the national constitutional courts' review of European law while also elaborating on the limitations of the study and issues that further research should address. Subsequently, I consider whether and how constitutional courts can play a role in relation to European integration that avoids this problem. I suggest that more deferential and weak review by constitutional courts would be more legitimate and could potentially help promote, rather than limit, democratic deliberation on constitutional questions relating to European integration. Nonetheless, the development of a fully-fledged account of the legitimate role of constitutional courts in relation to the EU requires more elaborate treatment elsewhere.

3.1 The Legitimacy Problem of the National Constitutional Courts' Review

To understand the legitimacy problem with the national constitutional courts' review of European law, I start with the issue of constitutional identity. As I argued in Chapter 3, respect for national constitutional identity may be important to honour the fundamental principles underlying a Member State's constitutional order. In part, such a constitutional identity will reflect a Member State's basic democratic choices on fundamental values and its collective identity. In that sense, constitutional identities can be seen as context-dependent interpretations of the preconditions for a democratically legitimate process. In addition, the idea that Member States should retain decision-making power in certain fields may reflect a legitimate concern about democratic self-government. Yet, the notion of constitutional identity leaves open a wide variety of possible interpretations and is subject to considerable reasonable disagreement. Consequently, constitutional courts that review European law on grounds of constitutional identity risk limiting the room for legitimate political disagreement on significant constitutional questions relating to European integration.

The case study of the GFCC confirms this problem. At the time of ratification of the Maastricht Treaty, the German legislature defined the German Basic Law as open to European integration. Elected parliamentarians perceived the constitution's structural principles not as obstacles to European integration, but as fundamental demands on the organization of the EU. The GFCC departed from this perspective by interpreting German constitutional identity as a protection of sovereign statehood. And although the GFCC's case law is sophisticated, it is also one-sided. In its review of the Maastricht Treaty, the Court gave limited attention to the possible importance of European integration, to the possible connection between Germany's emergence as a successful democracy and European integration, or to conceptions of democracy that give a more prominent place to the interests of outsiders. The idea that constitutional identity review would protect a Member State's most cherished constitutional values thus requires revision. In Germany, the GFCC's interpretation of constitutional identity by no means reflects the only possible interpretation of that identity. The available evidence indicates rather that the Court's review restricts political contestation over what this identity consists of amidst a variety of reasonable understandings.

The German example also indicates that different political parties disagree on what the EU should do, in a similar manner to the way they can disagree about the role of the state. Such disagreements are often difficult to separate entirely from conflicting conceptions of justice brought forward by different political groups. The political struggles over the EMU perhaps best illustrate this. Within this context there are good arguments to maintain that a monetary union without a budgetary union is highly fragile and significantly reduces national autonomy in economic policy. That might not be a problem for those political parties that favoured austerity policies and limited government intervention in markets. Yet, by casting doubt on the constitutional permissibility of transferring budgetary competences to the EU level, the GFCC constitutionalizes what, according to many, is a fundamental flaw in the set-up of the EMU with detrimental consequences for European democracy.

Ultra vires review by national constitutional courts raises similar democratic concerns. Such review is commonly justified to protect the democratic autonomy of the Member States. As I argued in Chapter 3, however, there are several counterarguments to this perspective. Not only does decentralized *ultra vires* review by national courts risk harming the uniform interpretation of EU law and legal certainty, but its democratic benefits are not obvious. The interpretation of competence boundaries between the EU and the Member States is also subject to reasonable disagreement. When interpreting competence provisions, courts will have to make evaluative judgments on the underlying values safeguarded by the competence division.

The GFCC's justification for *ultra vires* review offers a powerful illustration, as it rests on a contested interpretation of democracy and maintains that the EU's competences should be interpreted in a limited way for democratic reasons. A counterargument is that the adoption of legislation at the EU level can be informed by the conviction that this legislation is highly desirable for political reasons, but that similar legislation would be ineffective if adopted at the national level. The significant difficulties in amending the Treaties, moreover, favour an interpretation of the EU's competences that allows for different political viewpoints. A further problem is that strict *ultra vires* review may deepen rather than address the democratic concern about the EU's functional orientation that limits political contestation over the underlying goals of EU policies and legislation. Strict *ultra vires* review may also exacerbate the democratic problem that stems from the over-constitutionalization of the EU legal order.

The GFCC's review of the Maastricht Treaty, its judgments in the context of the euro crisis, as well as the more recent PSPP ruling, underline the downsides of *ultra vires* review in this respect. In its review of the Maastricht Treaty, the GFCC first determined the stability-orientation of the EMU as a constitutional requirement for Germany's participation in the EMU, subject to judicial review. This interpretation is at least one-sided, because the stability-orientation of the EMU can be seen as imposing significant restrictions on political decision-making. The orientation towards stability limits the possible consideration of other goals within the EMU framework, while the no-bailout clause of Article 125 TFEU would prohibit the Union and the Member States from taking over commitments of other Member States. The subjection of Member States' economic policies to budgetary norms similarly restricts the room for democratic politics. During the crisis, the GFCC appears to have contributed to upholding a particular contested economic ideology of austerity. Germany feared that any assistance to debtor states would not pass constitutional review in Karlsruhe unless such assistance could be shown to be a last resort and given under strict conditions. The threat of review by the GFCC helped to ensure that this vision was laid down in Article 136(3) TFEU. The analysis of German parliamentary debates during the euro crisis showed that this policy of austerity was deeply contested and that several parties forcefully opposed it in light of broader democratic considerations.

The subsequent judicial struggle over the powers of the ECB in the *OMT* and *PSPP* cases similarly underline the political stakes and contested nature of competence review. For example, in its ruling on the PSPP, the GFCC focused only on specific negative effects of the ECB's policy, while ignoring other positive effects of the ECB's programme. Such an assessment shows that the GFCC's reading of the competence division between the EU and the Member States is easily influenced by a partial view of the many interests and positions affected. The political debates surrounding the GFCC's *PSPP* ruling also affirmed that there was widespread disagreement among Germany's elected politicians concerning the merits of the GFCC's approach, the suitability of its constitutional interpretations, and the way in which the ECB's actions should be evaluated.

These findings cast significant doubts on the legitimacy of both constitutional identity and *ultra vires* review. Nonetheless, it should be emphasized that the current study has limitations that require future research. First, the case study does not exhaust the different constellations in which national constitutional courts' review of European law can take place. It could be that, in other instances, constitutional issues were disregarded in the prior political process, making intervention by constitutional courts more easily justifiable. In this respect, the case study does not establish that legislatures will always do a sufficiently good job in deliberating on constitutional principles in relation to European integration. In fact, I have argued that at times the *Bundestag* failed to properly protect its own position in relation to the executive, even though it did seriously consider many other constitutional issues later addressed by the GFCC.

Secondly, the quality of political debate may diverge in different Member States. What holds for Germany may not hold for political deliberations in other Member States. In other Member States it could be that constitutional issues play a far more limited role in the deliberations of its political institutions. In such conditions, constitutional courts, despite the shortcomings of their judgments, could still compensate for a lack of attention to constitutional issues in political debate and thus contribute to a better understanding of how constitutional ideals should be realized in the context of European integration. This issue requires further research.

Thirdly, it could also be that judgments from other Member States' constitutional courts are not given the same authority as the GFCC's judgments within German political debate. In other Member States, democratic contestation of constitutional court judgments may be more common, which could mean that such judgments can more easily be seen as contributions to an improved democratic debate on European integration instead of being viewed as a constraint. This topic also requires further study. It is likely that the GFCC does enjoy an exceptionally authoritative status in Germany, as constitutional interpretation is largely left to legal experts there.[7] That said, concerns about the judicialization of politics are not restricted to Germany but have been raised in a range of different legal systems.

A fourth issue that should be explored further is how the political power of a Member State translates into the effects that its national constitutional court judgments have on European decision-making. In this respect, the GFCC is probably an outlier, given the powerful position of Germany in EU decision-making. The effects on EU decision-making of constitutional courts' judgments from other Member States are likely to be more limited. This could in turn allow for a more

[7] Michaela Hailbronner, 'We the Experts. Die geschlossene Gesellschaft der Verfassungsinterpreten' (2014) 53 Der Staat 425. As Michaela Hailbronner notes elsewhere: 'The German emphasis on expert authority also excludes laymen from the task of constitutional interpretation, making German constitutional patriotism a rather Catholic affair and heightening risks of policy distortion.' Michaela Hailbronner, *Traditions and Transformations: The Rise of German Constitutionalism* (Oxford University Press 2015) 176.

positive appreciation of their role, seeing their interventions more as contributions than as impediments to ongoing democratic debate over constitutional principles.

Further research into these four issues could lead to a different and more positive assessment of the national constitutional courts' review of European law than the critical evaluation put forward here. Nonetheless, based on the critical findings of this book, the following subsection offers a number of ideas on how to improve the democratic legitimacy of constitutional courts' review of European law.

3.2 Weakening and Limiting Review

In light of the democratic problem posed by national constitutional courts' review of European law, the core challenge is to find out how the role of constitutional courts could respect legitimate political disagreement over constitutional norms, as well as potentially enhance the democratic process. I suggest that more deferential and weak review would be ways to improve the legitimacy of the national constitutional courts' role in relation to the EU. In special cases, constitutional courts would still be justified in exercising strong review, namely where their review addresses democratic legitimacy problems of the EU in way that is beyond reasonable disagreement.

The first idea is that when constitutional courts review European law, they should respect legitimate political disagreement on constitutional issues related to European integration. This consideration favours a deferential type of review, where constitutional courts leave it largely to political institutions to decide on constitutional questions related to European integration. In this respect, the approaches of the Czech Constitutional Court and the Danish Supreme Court on the issue of constitutional identity are more legitimate than that of its German counterpart.[8] These courts have expressly granted considerable leeway to their respective legislatures in determining the constitutional limits to transfers of competence to the EU. Such an approach rightly makes the determination of ultimate limits to European integration a largely political issue. The question of what powers the EU should have can only be answered through democratic politics in light of changing circumstances, knowledge, and political perspectives. This consideration favours that national constitutional courts leave questions of constitutional identity primarily to political institutions.

In this vein, rather than seeing constitutional identity as an absolute bar against European integration, national constitutional courts could also open up their judgments to arguments that have been brought forward in prior political debates.

[8] Supreme Court of Denmark (Højesteret), Case 361/1997, decision of 6 April 1998 (Maastricht) (summary translated in [1999] 3 CMLR 854); Constitutional Court of the Czech Republic (Ústavní soud), judgment of 3 November 2009, Pl ÚS 29/09 (*Treaty of Lisbon II*).

Instead of trying to determine constitutional identity autonomously, these courts could draw on the different arguments presented in political debate and consider whether political institutions have reasonably considered the constitutional concerns. In this respect, one could reimagine how the GFCC might have reviewed the Maastricht Treaty in a manner more open to arguments offered in the political debates on this Treaty. Rather than constructing the concept of democracy from an autonomous constitutional interpretation, the Court could have reflected on how the Treaty was justified in the prior political process, how the political institutions had considered the democratic shortcomings of the Treaty, and why, nonetheless, they still accepted it. The Court could then have noted the connection between German reunification and European integration and could have considered how the importance of European integration was appreciated politically. At the same time, it could have brought forward democratic concerns already voiced within political debate.

A second and related idea is that national constitutional courts should exercise weak review. Constitutional courts could continue to assess European law against their respective national constitutions. However, where they consider European law to be incompatible with national constitutional law, they could merely declare such an incompatibility without disapplying or invalidating European law.[9] Constitutional courts would then still be able to signal constitutional problems that, in their view, have received insufficient consideration, or were not anticipated when European laws were drafted. Yet, these courts would leave it to political institutions to address these problems. Weakening judicial review in this way would allow constitutional courts to contribute to an ongoing dialogue about constitutional issues, without constraining legitimate political decision-making.

In some respects, the GFCC's *PSPP* ruling offers an example of such weak review. The German Court pointed to democratic problems with the position of the ECB but left it to the German government and *Bundestag* to address them. In this way, as discussed in Chapter 7, the ruling did contribute to further democratic debate on the legitimacy of the ECB's actions. The *PSPP* ruling was strong, however, in the sense that the German judges set aside the CJEU's judgment and the primacy of EU law. It is widely acknowledged that such decentralized review poses a challenge to the uniformity of EU law and risks undermining the EU legal order.[10] As

[9] Oliver Garner proposed such weak review as a solution following the GFCC's *PSPP* judgment. Garner bases his ideas on the powers of the UK Supreme Court to issue declarations of incompatibility under s 4 of the UK Human Rights Act 1998. He also develops ideas for including in the EU Treaties a mechanism to politically resolve constitutional conflicts following a declaration of incompatibility by national constitutional courts. See Oliver Garner, 'Squaring the PSPP Circle' (*Verfassungsblog*, 22 May 2020) <https://verfassungsblog.de/squaring-the-pspp-circle/> accessed 2 August 2022.

[10] See eg Peter Meier-Beck, 'Ultra Vires?' (*D'Kart*, 11 May 2020) <www.d-kart.de/en/blog/2020/05/11/ultra-vires/> accessed 2 August 2022; R Daniel Kelemen and others, 'National Courts Cannot Override CJEU Judgments: A Joint Statement in Defense of the EU Legal Order' (*VerfBlog*, 26 May 2020) <https://verfassungsblog.de/national-courts-cannot-override-cjeu-judgments/> accessed 2 August 2022; Jürgen Basedow and others, 'European Integration: Quo Vadis? A Critical Commentary on the

Sarmiento and Weiler reiterated in a reflection on the *PSPP* judgment: 'If every constitutional or high court of each of our Member States were to emulate the German example, it would really spell the end of the EU as an integrated legal space of justice and the rule of law and fatally damage the single market.'[11] This concern has also been acknowledged by the GFCC itself, which stated in its *PSPP* judgment that '[i]f any Member State could readily invoke the authority to decide, through its own courts, on the validity of EU acts, this could undermine the precedence of application accorded to EU law and jeopardise its uniform application'.[12] Further weakening the constitutional courts' review presents a solution to this dilemma. As proposed by Oliver Garner in the wake of the *PSPP* ruling, constitutional courts should not declare EU law inapplicable, but instead issue declarations of incompatibility when they have serious constitutional concerns.[13] In this way, national courts could continue to voice their constitutional concerns and even signal disagreement with the CJEU, without undermining the primacy of EU law and the position of the CJEU. The preliminary reference procedure would be the natural starting point for national courts to voice such concerns. But even where they continue to disagree with the CJEU, they could still express such disagreement following the outcome of a preliminary reference without declaring EU law inapplicable. This would entail that national courts give up their power to sanction expansive and democratically problematic interpretations of EU primary law by the CJEU.[14] However, weakening such review would put the burden more squarely on the strength of the constitutional courts' reasoning.

A further advantage of weak review is that it would be compatible with a broad standing for individuals to contest European law on constitutional grounds and demand reasoned justification before an impartial court. Various theorists, considered in Chapter 2, see this feature of the judicial process as an intrinsic reason to value judicial review, quite apart from the outcomes that it produces.[15]

PSPP Judgment of the German Federal Constitutional Court of May 5, 2020' (2021) 19 International Journal of Constitutional Law 188.

[11] Daniel Sarmiento and Joseph HH Weiler, 'The EU Judiciary After Weiss' (*Verfassungsblog: On Matters Constitutional*, 2020) <https://verfassungsblog.de/the-eu-judiciary-after-weiss/> accessed 1 August 2022.

[12] Bundesverfassungsgericht, judgment of 5 May 2020, 2 BvR 859/15 (*PSPP*).

[13] Garner, 'Squaring the PSPP Circle' (n 9).

[14] The CJEU's democratically problematic interpretations of primary law can be seen as an important concern in Supreme Court of Denmark (Højesteret), Case 199/2012, decision of 20 February 2013 (Lisbon) (translation on <https://domstol.dk/media/0xebqufh/199-12-english.pdf> accessed 2 August 2022), as well as Constitutional Court of Italy (*Corte costituzionale*), order of 23 November 2016, no 24 (*Taricco I*) and Constitutional Court of Italy (*Corte costituzionale*), order of 10 April 2018, no 115 (*Taricco II*).

[15] Alon Harel, *Why Law Matters* (Oxford University Press 2014) ; Cristina Lafont, 'Philosophical Foundations of Judicial Review' in David Dyzenhaus and Malcolm Thorburn (eds), *Philosophical Foundations of Constitutional Law* (Oxford University Press 2016) ; Mattias Kumm, 'The Idea of Socratic Contestation and the Right to Justification: The Point of Rights-Based Proportionality Review' (2010) 4 Law & Ethics of Human Rights 142.

A transformation of national constitutional review of European law into weak review could justify the broad standing that the GFCC offers to litigants through its expansive interpretation of Article 38 BL. In this way, the GFCC could continue to provide an avenue for viewpoints that are less prominent in political institutions, while leaving the final say to elected politicians.

A third idea is that courts could still exercise strong review in limited cases, namely where their review aims to correct the democratic legitimacy problems of the EU's decision-making processes that are less subject to reasonable disagreement. As the case study indicated, a promising way for national constitutional courts to strengthen the democratic legitimacy of EU decision-making is to enhance the information and participation rights of national parliaments in EU affairs, as the GFCC has done in several judgments. Such review raises fewer problems from a democratic point of view, because it does not foreclose legitimate political disagreement about the best way to democratize the EU.

Especially where constitutional courts take into account possible legitimate reasons for restricting parliamentary oversight, this review seems to raise few democratic problems. The case on the *Neuner Gremium* discussed in Chapter 6 provides a good example.[16] In that case, the GFCC accepted political arguments for restricting the powers of the *Bundestag*'s plenary in individual bailouts if there was a legitimate need for confidentiality. However, the Court found that the reasons for confidentiality could not justify the full range of decisions for which secrecy was allowed. The need to take a number of public preparatory measures meant that there was no convincing argument to keep subsequent decisions secret. For that reason, the extent to which the legislative provision in question allowed for secrecy lacked reasonable justification. Where national constitutional courts review European law in this manner, they can enhance the democratic legitimacy of the EU by strengthening the national parliaments' oversight role over the national executive. Nonetheless, a full account of when and how constitutional courts would be justified in combating democratic legitimacy problems related to European integration requires further research.[17]

Finally, institutional changes may support these proposed modifications in the interpretive practice of constitutional courts. To institutionalize weak review, for example, Member States could create political overrides of constitutional court judgments on European integration or ease requirements for constitutional amendment in this context.[18] In this respect, European legal scholarship could still

[16] Bundesverfassungsgericht, judgment of 28 February 2012, 2 BvE 8/11 (*Neuner Gremium*).

[17] On this point, see recently also Michaela Hailbronner, 'Political Process Review: Beyond Distrust' (2020) 18 International Journal of Constitutional Law 1458; who responds to Stephen Gardbaum, 'Comparative Political Process Theory' (2020) 18 International Journal of Constitutional Law 1429.

[18] I understand that this may not be possible in all Member States, Germany being a prime example, given the eternity clause.

learn more from existing comparative constitutional studies on different forms of judicial review.[19]

Yet, when debating institutional changes, it is crucial to think beyond the role of constitutional courts. In light of the legitimacy problems posed by national constitutional courts' *ultra vires* and identity review, political solutions should be considered. Thus, instead of relying on *ultra vires* review by national constitutional courts to protect the prerogatives of national parliaments, it seems more sensible to invest in strengthening political safeguards that prevent unwanted expansions of the EU's powers. This could be achieved by ensuring better parliamentary oversight of the executive by national parliaments. An additional option is to consider strengthening the existing Early Warning Mechanism and explore additional ways of directly involving national parliaments in European decision-making. Such a strengthening of the national parliaments' position in EU affairs could also put them in a better position to bring forward specific constitutional issues. Similar ideas may apply to the democratic concerns posed by the CJEU's position. Although *ultra vires* review could in some cases be seen as a legitimate response to the role of the CJEU, alternatives to review by national constitutional courts may be more effective and legitimate. One solution is to create a political override at the EU level of the CJEU's interpretations of primary EU law, as has been proposed by Scharpf.[20] A more far-reaching idea would be to de-constitutionalize the EU Treaties, as proposed by Grimm.[21] Further research on these options is needed.

Should Member States with limited or no institutions for judicial review of European law set up such institutions? Given the legitimacy problems with national constitutional review of European law, this study suggests that the reasons for doing so are weak. The German example shows that allowing such review comes with several risks. Setting up a constitutional court to allow it to review European law or extending an existing Court's jurisdiction to do so, risks that such a court will end up interpreting the constitution in a way that is at odds with the legitimate views of political majorities. For such Member States, the more logical starting point would be to invest in strengthened constitutional scrutiny of European law within political institutions. In this respect, further research into political systems with such a model for constitutional review would be insightful.[22]

[19] Possible examples are: Mark Tushnet, *Weak Courts, Strong Rights* (Princeton University Press 2008); Maartje de Visser, *Constitutional Review in Europe: A Comparative Analysis* (Hart 2014).

[20] Fritz W Scharpf, 'Legitimacy in the Multi-Level European Polity' in Petra Dobner and Martin Loughlin (eds), *The Twilight of Constitutionalism?* (Oxford University Press 2010).

[21] Dieter Grimm, 'The Democratic Costs of Constitutionalisation: The European Case' (2015) 21 European Law Journal 460.

[22] The obvious comparison here would be with the constitutional law committee of the Finnish parliament.

4. In Defence of Politics: Judging European Democracy and its Contradictions

Since the review of the Maastricht Treaty by the GFCC, a significant body of EU constitutional scholarship has put the national constitutional courts' review of European law in a positive light. Discussions of constitutional pluralism, judicial dialogue, and constitutional identity convey the message that the national constitutional courts can help overcome the supposed excessive hierarchy of the EU legal order. As I have argued in this book, these ideas lack a clear perspective on the role of political institutions and the troubled democratic legitimacy of judicial review. Taking into account the role of these political institutions offers a more sobering perspective on the role of national constitutional courts: rather than introducing much-desired contestation in the EU, the constitutional courts' review risks stifling debate over the EU's future. The EU needs more room for political decision-making that allows for conflict and disagreement. Trying to remedy that shortcoming by allowing national constitutional courts to review European law was bound to be a difficult enterprise from the beginning. What the EU requires is more democratic politics, not more courts.

Constitutional courts that judge European democracy must ultimately take into account a fundamental aspect of democratic decision-making, namely its plurality of arguments and viewpoints, as well as its openness to change. It requires courts to accept that they cannot be the ultimate arbiters of what European democracy should look like, lest their position end up in a democratic contradiction. Constitutional pluralism, despite its name, has failed to heed this insight. By neglecting the role of political institutions and the way in which national constitutional courts' case law affects their role, constitutional pluralism seems to have never been pluralist enough. The manner in which democracy in the EU should be realized is a question that itself can only be answered in an ongoing democratic debate. It is here that the German Constitutional Court has ultimately failed to see the limitations of its own position.

Interviews

The details below provide an overview of the interviews conducted for this study. Some of these interviews served only as background information to the case studies and are not directly referred to in the text.

Respondents were offered the option of full anonymity, partial anonymity, or no anonymity. The details below are a reflection of these choices. In line with the revised guidelines of the Ethics Committee of the Law Faculty of the University of Amsterdam, respondents were given the additional option of non-attributability for the interviews conducted in 2021. This meant that publications would not attribute quotes and information to specific interviewees. As a result, some of the interviews below are not referred to in the text of the book.

Interview with Ingolf Pernice, Professor of Public Law, European Law and Public International Law Humboldt-Universität zu Berlin and representative of the German *Bundestag* in the *Lisbon* case (Berlin, Germany, 16 April 2015)

Interview with former judge at the German Federal Constitutional Court (Berlin, Germany, 20 April 2015)

Interview with Christoph Möllers, Professor of Public Law and Jurisprudence, Faculty of Law, Humboldt-University Berlin and representative of the German *Bundestag* in the *ESM* case (Berlin, Germany, 20 April 2015)

Interview with Peter Huber, Judge at the German Federal Constitutional Court and judge rapporteur in most EU-related cases (Karlsruhe, Germany, 23 April 2015)

Interview with German legal official (Karlsruhe, Germany, 23 April 2015).

Interview with Christian Hirte, *Bundestag* member for the CDU (Berlin, Germany, 24 April 2015)

Interview with Lothar Binding, former *Bundestag* member for the SPD (Berlin, Germany, 29 April 2015)

Interview with Otto Fricke, former *Bundestag* member for the FDP and chair of the *Bundestag*'s budget committee between 2005 and 2009 (Berlin, Germany, 6 May 2015)

Interview with Peter Danckert, former member of the *Bundestag* for the SPD (Berlin, Germany, 12 May 2015)

Interview with Christoph Thum, advisor for European politics to SPD Bundestagsfraktion (Berlin, Germany, 26 May 2015)

Interview with Gesine Lötzsch, *Bundestag* member for Die Linke and former chair of the *Bundestag*'s budget committee (Berlin, Germany, 27 May 2015)

Interview with Franz Mayer, Professor of Public Law at Universität Bielefeld and representative of the German *Bundestag* in the *Lisbon* and *EFSF* cases (Berlin, Germany, 28 May 2015)

Interview with Karl-Albrecht Schachtschneider, legal representative of Manfred Brunner in the *Maastricht* case and complainant in multiple other EU-related cases before the GFCC (Berlin, Germany, 29 May 2015)

Interview with former judge at the German Federal Constitutional Court (Bonn, Germany, 29 June 2015)

Interview with EU official #1 (Brussels, Belgium, 3 November 2015)

Interview with EU official #2 (Brussels, Belgium, 3 November 2015)

Interview with EU official # 3 (Brussels, Belgium, 4 November 2015)

Interview with Tom de Bruijn, former Permanent Representative of the Netherlands at the European Union (The Hague, the Netherlands, 18 November 2015)

Interview with Luuk van Middelaar, Professor of Foundations and Practice of the European Union and its Institutions and former speechwriter and advisor of the first permanent President of the European Council, H A Van Rompuy (2010–14) (Leiden, the Netherlands, 10 November 2015)

Interview with Jean-Paul Jacqué, former Director in the Legal Service of the Council of the European Union (Brussels, Belgium, 8 December 2015)

Interview with former Dutch politician involved in Maastricht negotiations (Amsterdam, the Netherlands, 20 January 2016)

Interview with Director in the Legal Service of the Council of the EU and with Legal Adviser in the Legal Service of the Council of the EU (Zoom interview, 25 May 2021)

Interview with member of the Eurogroup Working Group and of the Economic and Financial Committee (Zoom interview, 22 June 2021)

Interview with former member of the Eurogroup Working Group and of the Economic and Financial Committee (Zoom interview, 29 July 2021)

Interview with EU official (Zoom interview, 1 June 2021)

Interview with Dutch civil servant (Zoom interview, 1 June 2021)

Bibliography

—— 'Deficits and Finance' *The Economist* (2 September 2003)

—— 'Schäuble fordert Europäischen Währungsfonds', *Spiegel Online* (Hamburg, 6 March 2010) < <www.spiegel.de/politik/ausland/krise-in-griechenland-schaeuble-fordert-europaeischen-waehrungsfonds-a-682167.html> accessed 2 August 2022

—— 'Papandreou Tries to Prop up the Pillars' *The Economist* (London, 17 December 2009)

—— 'Now Comes the Pain' *The Economist* (London, 4 May 2010)

—— 'No Going Back' *The Economist* (London, 13 May 2010)

—— 'Die Angst der Abnicker' *Focus Magazin* (21 May 2010)

—— 'Merkel bleibt bei Euro-Bonds hart' *ZEIT ONLINE* (Berlin, 15 December 2010)

—— 'Merkel wehrt sich gegen Arroganz-Vorwürfe' *ZEIT ONLINE* (Berlin, 16 December 2010)

—— 'Bundestagspräsident blockiert Schäubles Blankoscheck-Pläne' *Handelsblatt* (24 August 2011)

—— 'Lammert fürchtet Entmündigung des Bundestags bei Euro-Rettung' *ZEIT ONLINE* (24 August 2011)

—— '"Urteil ist klare Absage an Euro-Bonds"' *Handelsblatt* (Düsseldorf, 7 September 2011)

—— 'Streit um Rederecht für Euro-Rettungskritiker' *Handelsblatt* (Düsseldorf, 30 September 2011)

—— 'Merkel Eyes Constitution Revamp to Boost EU Powers' *Spiegel Online* (Hamburg, 14 November 2011)

—— '"Mein Widerstand war grundsätzlich"' *Frankfurter Allgemeine Zeitung* (Frankfurt, 21 April 2012)

—— 'Rot-Grün distanziert sich von Hollandes Euro-Bonds' *Die Welt* (Hamburg, 24 May 2012)

—— 'SPD und Grüne schlagen Alternative zu Euro-Bonds vor' *ZEIT ONLINE* (Berlin, 24 May 2012)

—— 'Gauck unterzeichnet Fiskalpakt vorerst nicht' *Frankfurter Allgemeine Zeitung* (Frankfurt, 21 June 2012)

—— 'Merkel rechnet nicht mit baldiger Volksabstimmung' *Frankfurter Allgemeine Zeitung* (Frankfurt, 25 June 2012)

—— 'Seehofer unterstützt Schäubles Vorstoß' *Frankfurter Allgemeine Zeitung* (Frankfurt, 26 June 2012)

—— 'Lammert hält verfassungsgebende Versammlung für vorstellbar' *Süddeutsche Zeitung* (München, 1 July 2012)

—— 'Brüderle hält Volksabstimmung über EU-Zukunft für möglich' *Frankfurter Allgemeine Zeitung* (Frankfurt, 10 August 2012)

—— 'German Court Backs Eurozone's ESM Bailout Fund' (*BBC.com*, 12 September 2012) <www.bbc.com/news/world-europe-19567867> accessed 1 August 2022

—— 'Griechische Anleger feiern ESM-Urteil' *Spiegel Online* (12 September 2012) <www.spiegel.de/> accessed 1 August 2022

—— 'Commission Banking Union Plans Met with Scepticism' (11 July 2013) <http://openeuropeblog.blogspot.nl/2013/07/commission-banking-union-plans-met-with.html> accessed 2 August 2022

—— 'CDU will keine Volksabstimmungen auf Bundesebene' *Handelsblatt* (Düsseldorf, 12 November 2013)

—— 'Schäuble erwartet Volksabstimmung über neue Verfassung' *Handelsblatt* (24 June 2012)

—— 'Volksabstimmungen bundesweit geplant' *Die Welt* (Hamburg, 12 November 2013)

—— 'Grünen-Abgeordnete lehnt EU-Volksabstimmungen ab' *Spiegel Online* (8 April 2016) <www.spiegel.de/politik/ausland/referendum-in-den-niederlanden-harms-ist-gegen-volksabstimmungen-a-1086067.html > accessed 2 August 2022

—— 'Verfassungsrichter Dr. Ulrich Maidowski erklärt: Anders als die Polnische Regierung will das Bundesverfassungsgericht mehr Kontrolle durch den Europäischen Gerichtshof' (27 May 2020) <www.iustitia.pl/en/activity/informations/3856-verfassungsrichter-dr-ulrich-maidowski-erklaert-anders-als-die-polnische-regierung-will-das-bundesverfassungsgericht-mehr-kontrolle-durch-den-europaeischen-gerichtshof> accessed 2 August 2022

Adamski D, 'National Power Games and Structural Failures in the European Macroeconomic Governance' (2012) 49 Common Market Law Review 1319

Albi A and Bardutzky S (eds), *National Constitutions in European and Global Governance: Democracy, Rights, the Rule of Law* (TMC Asser Press 2019)

Alesina A and Summers LH, 'Central Bank Independence and Macroeconomic Performance: Some Comparative Evidence' (1993) 25 Journal of Money, Credit and Banking 151

Amtenbrink F, 'Economic and Monetary Union' in Pieter Jan Kuijper and others (eds), *The Law of the European Union* (Kluwer Law International 2018)

Armbruster A, 'Verfassungsgericht erlaubt EZB-Programm unter Auflagen' (Frankfurt 21 June 2016) *Frankfurter Allgemeine Zeitung* <www.faz.net/aktuell/wirtschaft/konjunktur/euro-krise-verfassungsgericht-erlaubt-ezb-programm-unter-auflagen-14299519.html> accessed 2 August 2022.

Armstrong K, 'The New Governance of EU Fiscal Discipline' (2013) 38(5) European Law Review 601

Arnold M, 'Splits at the ECB Top Table over Mario Draghi's Last Big Stimulus' *Financial Times* (27 September 2019)

—— 'Former Central Bankers Attack ECB's Monetary Policy' *Financial Times* (4 October 2019)

—— 'Christine Lagarde Says ECB Is "Undeterred" by German Court Challenge' *Financial Times* (Frankfurt, 7 May 2020) <www.ft.com/content/d93008c5-2b3c-4b2e-9499-5eabaaa959db> accessed 2 August 2022

—— 'German ECB Executive Shrugs off Court Ruling against Bond Buying' *Financial Times* (Frankfurt, 27 May 2020) <www.ft.com/content/a48b8982-3e75-4a35-8fb5-a66f4fb0fedc> accessed 2 August 2022

—— 'EU Recovery Fund Deal Revives Hopes for Eurozone Banking Union' *Financial Times* (Frankfurt, 24 July 2020)

Aroney N, 'Reasonable Disagreement, Democracy and the Judicial Safeguards of Federalism' (2008) 27 The University of Queensland Law Journal 129

Auel K, Rozenberg O, and Tacea A, 'Fighting Back? And, if so, How? Measuring Parliamentary Strength and Activity in EU Affairs' in Claudia Hefftler and others (eds),

The Palgrave Handbook of National Parliaments and the European Union (Palgrave Macmillan 2015)

Avbelj M and Komárek J, 'Introduction' in Matej Avbelj and Jan Komárek (eds), *Constitutional Pluralism in the European Union and Beyond* (Hart 2012)

—— 'Constitutional Pluralism and Authoritarianism' (2020) 21 German Law Journal 1023

Bakker F and Sterk K, 'Laat Rechters de Grondrechten van Burgers Beschermen' *NRC Next* (7 March 2014) <www.nrc.nl/nieuws/2014/03/07/laat-rechters-de-grondrechten-van-burgers-bescherm-1353312-a40579> accessed 1 August 2022

Bannas G, 'Auch Abweichler dürfen lange reden' *Frankfurter Allgemeine Zeitung* (Frankfurt, 16 April 2012)

Baquero Cruz J, 'The Legacy of the Maastricht-Urteil and the Pluralist Movement' (2007) EUI Working Papers RSCAS 2007/13 <https://cadmus.eui.eu/handle/1814/6760> accessed 2 August 2022

—— 'The Legacy of the Maastricht-Urteil and the Pluralist Movement' (2008) 14(4) European Law Journal 389

——, 'Another Look at Constitutional Pluralism in the European Union' (2016) 22 European Law Journal 356

Barber T, 'Saving the Euro: Dinner on the Edge of the Abyss' *Financial Times* (London, 10 October 2010) <www.ft.com/content/190b32ae-d49a-11df-b230-00144feabdc0> accessed 2 August 2022

—— 'Italy's Struggle with Coronavirus Threatens All of the Eurozone' *Financial Times* (13 March 2020) <www.ft.com/content/6d3b5ff4-646c-11ea-b3f3-fe4680ea68b5> accessed 2 August 2022

Barker A, 'Berlin Demands Treaty Change for Bank Reforms' *Financial Times* (Brussels, 14 April 2013) <www.ft.com/content/eea3918c-a51b-11e2-8777-00144feabdc0> accessed 2 August 2022

Bartl M, 'The Way We Do Europe: Subsidiarity and the Substantive Democratic Deficit' (2015) 21 European Law Journal 23

Barysch K, 'Germany, the Euro and the Politics of the Bail-Out' (2010) Centre for European Reform Briefing Note <www.cer.org.uk> accessed 2 August 2022

Basedow J and others, 'European Integration: Quo Vadis? A Critical Commentary on the PSPP Judgment of the German Federal Constitutional Court of May 5, 2020' (2021) 19 International Journal of Constitutional Law 188

Bast J, 'Don't Act Beyond Your Powers: The Perils and Pitfalls of the German Constitutional Court's Ultra Vires Review' (2014) 15 German Law Journal 147

Bateman W, *Public Finance and Parliamentary Constitutionalism* (Cambridge University Press 2020)

Baxter H, *Habermas: The Discourse Theory of Law and Democracy* (Stanford University Press 2011)

Baynes K, 'Democracy and the Rechtsstaat: Habermas' Faktizität Und Geltung' in Stephen K White (ed), *The Cambridge Companion to Habermas* (Cambridge University Press 1995)

Beesley A, 'Our Loss of Economic Sovereignty May Be Just the Beginning' *The Irish Times* (22 November 2011)

Bellamy R, *Liberalism and Pluralism* (Routledge 1999)

—— *Political Constitutionalism: A Republican Defence of the Constitutionality of Democracy* (Cambridge University Press 2007)

—— 'Political Constitutionalism and the Human Rights Act' (2011) 9 International Journal of Constitutional Law 86

—— 'Democracy as Public Law: The Case of Constitutional Rights' (2013) 14 German Law Journal 1017
—— 'The Democratic Qualities of Courts: A Critical Analysis of Three Arguments' (2013) 49 Representation 333
—— 'The Democratic Legitimacy of International Human Rights Conventions: Political Constitutionalism and the European Convention on Human Rights' (2014) 25 European Journal of International Law 1019
—— 'A European Republic of Sovereign States: Sovereignty, Republicanism and the European Union' (2017) 16 European Journal of Political Theory 188
—— 'The Republican Core of the Case for Judicial Review: A Reply to Tom Hickey. Why Political Constitutionalism Requires Equality of Power and Weak Review' (2019) 17 International Journal of Constitutional Law 317
—— *A Republican Europe of States: Cosmopolitanism, Intergovernmentalism and Democracy in the EU* (Cambridge University Press 2019) <www.cambridge.org/core/books/republican-europe-of-states/7C2EFBA3A89FB6E500160AF01A0A99C0> accessed 1 August 2022
Benvenisti E and Downs GW, 'The Democratizing Effects of Transjudicial Coordination' (2012) 8 Utrecht Law Review 158
Besselink LFM, 'Entrapped by the Maximum Standard: On Fundamental Rights, Pluralism and Subsidiarity in the European Union' (1998) 35 Common Market Law Review 629
—— 'National and Constitutional Identity Before and After Lisbon' (2010) 6 Utrecht Law Review 36
—— 'Case C-208/09, Ilonka Sayn-Wittgenstein v. Landeshauptmann von Wien, Judgment of the Court (Second Chamber) of 22 December, Nyr.' (2012) 49 Common Market Law Review 671
—— *National Constitutional Avenues for Further EU Integration* (Study requested by the European Parliament's Committee on Legal Affairs and Constitutional Affairs Committee of the European Parliament, DG for Internal Policies Study 2014) <www.europarl.europa.eu/RegData/etudes/etudes/join/2014/493046/IPOL-JURI_ET(2014)493046_EN.pdf> accessed 2 August 2022
Beukers T, 'The New ECB and its Relationship with the Eurozone Member States: Between Central Bank Independence and Central Bank Intervention' (2013) 50 Common Market Law Review 1579
—— 'Legal Writing(s) on the Eurozone Crisis' (2015) 11 EUI Working Papers <https://cadmus.eui.eu/handle/1814/35418> accessed 2 August 2022
Beuter R, 'Germany and the Ratification of the Maastricht Treaty' in Finn Laursen and Sophie Vanhoonacker (eds), *The Ratification of the Maastricht Treaty: Issues, Debates and Future Implications* (European Institute of Public Administration Maastricht 1994)
Bickel A, *The Least Dangerous Branch: The Supreme Court at the Bar of Politics* (2nd edn, Bobbs-Merrill 1986)
Biernat S, 'How Far Is It from Warsaw to Luxembourg and Karlsruhe: The Impact of the PSPP Judgment on Poland' (2020) 21 German Law Journal 1104
Bindseil U, *Monetary Policy Operations and the Financial System* (Oxford University Press 2014)
Blinder AS, *Central Banking in Theory and Practice, The Lionel Robbins Lectures* (MIT Press 1999)
Bobek M, 'Landtová, Holubec, and the Problem of an Uncooperative Court: Implications for the Preliminary Rulings Procedure' (2014) 10 European Constitutional Law Review 54

Bobić A, 'Constitutional Pluralism Is Not Dead: An Analysis of Interactions between Constitutional Courts of Member States and the European Court of Justice' (2017) 18 German Law Journal 1395

—— *The Jurisprudence of Constitutional Conflict in the European Union* (Oxford University Press 2022)

—— and Dawson M, 'Making Sense of the "Incomprehensible": The PSPP Judgment of the German Federal Constitutional Court' (2020) 57 Common Market Law Review 1953

Böckenförde EW, 'Kennt die europäische Not kein Gebot?' *Neue Zürcher Zeitung* (21 June 2010).

de Boer N, 'Addressing Rights Divergences under the Charter: Melloni' (2013) 50 Common Market Law Review 1083

—— 'The False Promise of Constitutional Pluralism' in M Avbelj and G Davies (eds), *A Research Handbook of Legal Pluralism and EU Law* (Edward Elgar 2018)

—— and van 't Klooster J, 'The ECB, the Courts and the Issue of Democratic Legitimacy after Weiss' (2020) 57 Common Market Law Review 1689

Bogdandy AV and Schill S, 'Overcoming Absolute Primacy: Respect for National Identity under the Lisbon Treaty' (2011) 48 Common Market Law Review 1417

Borger V, 'The ESM and the European Court's Predicament in *Pringle*' (2013) 14 German Law Journal 113

—— 'Outright Monetary Transactions and the Stability Mandate of the ECB: Gauweiler' (2016) 53 Common Market Law Review 139

Borio C, 'A Hundred Ways to Skin a Cat: Comparing Monetary Policy Operating Procedures in the United States, Japan and the Euro Area' (2001) BIS Working Papers No. 9 <www.bis.org/publ/bppdf/bispap09a.pdf> accessed 2 August 2022

van den Bos B, *Mirakel en Debacle* (PhD thesis, Universiteit Leiden 2008)

Bovens M, 'Analysing and Assessing Accountability: A Conceptual Framework' (2007) 13 European Law Journal 447

Bowles, S and others, Letter to the Greek Presidency of the EU of 15 January 2014, no 200209

Buiter Willem H, 'Germany's Judges Declare War on the ECB' (*Project Syndicate*, 6 May 2020) <www.project-syndicate.org/commentary/german-constitution-court-ecb-pspp-ruling-by-willem-h-buiter-2020-05>

Bündnis 90/Die Grünen, Zukunft der Währungsunion—Zukunft Europas, Konsequenzen aus der Schuldenkrise in Griechenland, Fraktionsbeschluss of 15 March 2010

Calliess C, 'Constitutional Identity in Germany: One for Three or Three in One?' in Christian Calliess and Gerhard van der Schyff (eds), *Constitutional Identity in a Europe of Multilevel Constitutionalism* (Cambridge University Press 2019)

—— and van der Schyff G (eds), *Constitutional Identity in a Europe of Multilevel Constitutionalism* (Cambridge University Press 2019)

Canotilho M, Violante T, and Lanceiro R, 'Austerity Measures under Judicial Scrutiny: The Portuguese Constitutional Case-Law' (2015) 11 European Constitutional Law Review 155

Carstens P, 'Knapper Sieg über Euro-Skeptiker' *Frankfurter Allgemeine Zeitung* (Frankfürt, 16 December 2011)

Cartabia M, 'Europe and Rights: Taking Dialogue Seriously' [2009] European Constitutional Law Review 5

Caspari L, 'Teambuilding-Maßnahme Europa' *ZEIT ONLINE* (Berlin, 29 October 2013)

CDU/CSU, 'Starker Beitrag für europäische Solidarität', Press release of 18 May 2020 <www.cducsu.de/presse/pressemitteilungen/starker-beitrag-fuer-europaeische-solidaritaet> accessed 2 August 2022

Chambers S, 'Behind Closed Doors: Publicity, Secrecy, and the Quality of Deliberation' [2004] The Journal of Political Philosophy 389

Charlemagne, 'Germany: Europe's Fed-up Sugar Daddy' (*Economist*, 20 May 2010) <www.economist.com/blogs/charlemagne/2010/05/euro_crisis_6> accessed 2 August 2022s

Charpy C, 'France. The Conseil d'Etat Abandons Its Cohn Bendit Case-Law; Conseil d'Etat, 30 October 2009, Mme Perreux' (2010) 6 European Constitutional Law Review 123

Chazan G, 'The Minds behind Germany's Shifting Fiscal Stance' *Financial Times* (Berlin, 9 June 2020) <www.ft.com/content/2503ce9c-cde9-4301-bba0-8301f7deaf3b> accessed 2 August 2022

—— and Arnold M, 'German Finance Minister Moves to Resolve Court Stand-off with ECB' *Financial Times* (Berlin and Frankfurt, 29 June 2020) <www.ft.com/content/443a14d9-b631-4609-9ad1-7ee98b8249c5> accessed 2 August 2022

Christiano T, 'Waldron on Law and Disagreement' (2000) 19 Law and Philosophy 513

—— 'Authority' in Edward N Zalta (ed), *The Stanford Encyclopedia of Philosophy* (Spring 2013 edition)

Cingranelli DL and Richards DL, The CIRI Human Rights Data Project (2014) <www.humanrightsdata.com/> accessed 1 August 2022

Claes M, 'The National Courts' Mandate in the European Constitution' (PhD thesis, Maastricht University 2004)

—— and Reestman J-H, 'The Protection of National Constitutional Identity and the Limits of European Integration at the Occasion of the Gauweiler Case' (2016) 16 German Law Journal 917

Cloots E, 'Constitutional Identity in Belgium: A Thing of Mystery' in Christian Calliess and Gerhard van der Schyff (eds), *Constitutional Identity in a Europe of Multilevel Constitutionalism* (Cambridge University Press 2019)

Cohen J, 'Deliberation and Democratic Legitimacy' in James Bohman and William Rehg (eds), *Deliberative Democracy: Essays on Reason and Politics* (The MIT Press 1997)

—— 'Procedure and Substance in Deliberative Democracy' in James Bohman and William Rehg (eds) (The MIT Press 1997)

—— 'For a Democratic Society' in Samuel Freeman (ed), *The Cambridge Companion to Rawls* (Cambridge University Press 2002)

Collings J, *Democracy's Guardians: A History of the German Federal Constitutional Court, 1951–2001* (Oxford University Press, 2015)

Comella VF, 'The Rise of Specialized Constitutional Courts' in Tom Ginsburg and Rosalind Dixon (eds), *Comparative Constitutional Law* (Edward Elgar 2011)

Committee for the Study of Economic and Monetary Union, 'Report on Economic and Monetary Union in the European Community (Delors Report)' Office for Official Publications of the EC (Luxembourg 1989)

Coutts S, 'Constitutional Change through Euro Crisis Law: Ireland' (2 March 2014) <http://eurocrisislaw.eui.eu/ireland> accessed 2 August 2022

Craig P, 'The ECJ and Ultra Vires Action: A Conceptual Analysis' (2011) 48 Common Market Law Review 395

—— 'The Stability, Coordination and Governance Treaty: Principle, Politics and Pragmatism' (2012) 37(3) European Law Review 231

—— and Búrca GD, *EU Law: Text, Cases and Materials* (Oxford University Press 2015)

Crespy A and Schramm L, 'Breaking the Budgetary Taboo: German Preference Formation in the EU's Response to the Covid-19 Crisis' [2021] German Politics 1

Crum B, 'Saving the Euro at the Cost of Democracy?' (2013) 51 Journal of Common Market Studies 614

Curtin D, 'Judging EU Secrecy' [2012] Cahiers de droit européen 459

—— 'Challenging Executive Dominance in European Democracy' (2014) 77 Modern Law Review 1

—— and Leino-Sandberg P, 'Openness, Transparency and the Right of Access to Documents in the EU' (European Parliament 2016) PE 556.973 <www.europarl.europa.eu/thinktank/en/document.html?reference=IPOL_IDA%282016%29556973> accessed 2 August 2022

Dahl R, 'Decision-Making in a Democracy: The Supreme Court as a National Policy-Maker' (1957) 6 Journal of Public Law 279

Daly E, 'Republicanizing Rights?: Proportionality, Justification, and Non-Domination' in Ester Herlin-Karnell, Matthias Klatt, and Héctor A Morales Zúñiga (eds), *Constitutionalism Justified: Rainer Forst in Discourse* (Oxford University Press 2019)

Dani M and others, '"It's the Political Economy . . .!" A Moment of Truth for the Eurozone and the EU' (2021) 19 International Journal of Constitutional Law 309

Darnstädt T, 'Das überforderte Gericht' *Spiegel Online* (12 September 2012) <www.spiegel.de/politik/deutschland/kommentar-zum-esm-urteil-das-ueberforderte-gericht-a-855377.html>

Darvas Z, 'The ECB's Magic Wand' (2012) 47 Intereconomics 266

Davies B, *Resisting the European Court of Justice. West Germany Confrontation with European Law, 1949–1979* (Cambridge University Press 2012)

—— 'Resistance to European Law and Constitutional Identity in Germany: Herbert Kraus and Solange in Its Intellectual Context' (2015) 21 European Law Journal 434

Davies G, 'Democracy and Legitimacy in the Shadow of Purposive Competence' (2015) 21 European Law Journal 2

—— 'Brexit and the Free Movement of Workers: A Plea for National Legal Assertiveness' (2016) 41 European Law Review 925

—— 'Does the Court of Justice Own the Treaties? Interpretative Pluralism as a Solution to Over-constitutionalisation' (2018) 24 European Law Journal 358

Dawson M, 'The Legal and Political Accountability Structure of "Post-Crisis" EU Economic Governance' (2015) 53 Journal of Common Market Studies 976

—— and Witte F de, 'Constitutional Balance in the EU after the Euro-Crisis' (2013) 76 The Modern Law Review 817

—— and Witte F de, 'From Balance to Conflict: A New Constitution for the EU' (2016) 22 European Law Journal 204

De Cabanes A and Fontan C, 'Why Germany's Far Right Wants Judges to Rule Europe's Monetary Policy' (*Jacobin*, 24 May 2020) <https://jacobin.com/2020/05/germany-europe-judges-afd-banks> accessed 2 August 2022

de Grauwe P, *Economics of Monetary Union* (Oxford University Press 2014)

De Gregorio Merino A, 'Legal Developments in the Economic and Monetary Union During the Debt Crisis: the Mechanisms of Financial Assistance' (2012) 49 Common Market Law Review 1614

—— 'The Recovery Plan: Solidarity and the Living Constitution' (*EU Law Live*, 6 March 2021) <https://eulawlive.com/long-read-the-recovery-plan-solidarity-and-the-living-constitution-by-alberto-de-gregorio-merino/> accessed 2 August 2022

De Larosière Group, 'The High-Level Group on Financial Supervision in the EU' (Brussels, 25 February 2009)

Della J and von Weizsäcker J, 'The Blue Bond Proposal' (2010) 3 Bruegel Policy Brief <http://bruegel.org/wp-content/uploads/imported/publications/1005-PB-Blue_Bonds.pdf> accessed 2 August 2022

Denker T, 'Lammert gegen alle' *Süddeutsche Zeitung* (Munich, 29 September 2011)

Dermine P, 'The Ruling of the Bundesverfassungsgericht in PSPP—An Inquiry into Its Repercussions on the Economic and Monetary Union' (2020) 16 European Constitutional Law Review 525

Deutsche Bundesbank, 'Stellungnahme gegenüber dem Bundesverfassungsgericht zu den Verfahren mit den Az. 2 BvR 1390/12, 2 BvR 1421/12, 2 BvR 1439/12, 2 BvR 1824/12, 2 BvE 6/12' <www.bundesbank.de/de/startseite/stellungnahme-gegenueber-dem-bundesverfassungsgericht-zu-den-verfahren-mit-den-az-2-bvr-1390-12-2-bvr-1421-12-2-bvr-1439-12-2-bvr-1824-12-2-bve-6-12-799684> accessed 2 August 2022

di Fabio U, 'Karlsruhe Makes a Referral' (2014) 15 German Law Journal 107

di Lorenzo G and Wefing H, '"Erfolg Ist Eher Kalt" (Interview with Andreas Voßkuhle)' *Die Zeit* (13 May 2020) <www.zeit.de/2020/21/andreas-vosskuhle-ezb-anleihenkaeufe-corona-krise> accessed 2 August 2022

Dijsselbloem J, *De Eurocrisis* (Prometheus 2018)

Dixon R, 'The Core Case for Weak-Form Judicial Review' (2017) 38 Cardozo Law Review 2193

Dowling S, 'Ireland's Budget Leak to Germany Brings Home Some Harsh Realities' *The Guardian* (18 November 2011)

Dreier H, 'Verfassungsreform: Ein neues Deutschland' *ZEIT ONLINE* (Berlin, 20 October 2011)

Dullien S and Guerot U, 'The Long Shadow of Ordoliberalism: Germany's Approach to the Euro Crisis' (2012) European Council of Foreign Relations Policy Brief <www.ecfr.eu/publications/summary/the_long_shadow_of_ordoliberalism_germanys_approach_to_the_euro_crisis> accessed 2 August 2022

Dworkin R, *Taking Rights Seriously* (Duckworth 1977)

—— 'The Forum of Principle' (1981) 56 New York University Law Review 469

—— *A Matter of Principle* (Harvard University Press 1985)

—— *Law's Empire* (Hart Publishing 1998)

—— *Freedom's Law: The Moral Reading of the American Constitution* (Oxford University Press 1996)

Dyevre A, 'Technocracy and Distrust: Revisiting the Rationale for Constitutional Review' (2015) 13 International Journal of Constitutional Law 30

Dyson K and Featherstone K, *The Road to Maastricht: Negotiating Economic and Monetary Union* (Oxford University Press 1999)

ECB, 'The Accountability of the ECB' [2002] Monthly Bulletin 45

—— 'Two Per Cent Inflation Target' <www.ecb.europa.eu/mopo/strategy/pricestab/html/index.en.html> accessed 1 August 2022.

—— 'Asset Purchase Programmes' <www.ecb.europa.eu/mopo/implement/app/html/index.en.html> accessed 2 August 2022

Editorial Comments, 'Whither the Stability and Growth Pact?' (2004) 41 Common Market Law Review 1193

—— 'On the Lissabon-Urteil: Democracy and a Democratic Paradox' (2009) 5 European Constitutional Law Review 341

—— 'Ultra Vires—Has the Bundesverfassungsgericht Shown Its Teeth?' (2013) 50 Common Market Law Review 925

Eichengreen B, 'Should the Maastricht Treaty be Saved?' (1992) 74 Princeton Studies in International Finance 12

Eisgruber CL, *Constitutional Self-Government* (Harvard University Press 2007)

Elster J, 'Introduction' in Jon Elster and Rune Slagstad (eds), *Constitutionalism and Democracy* (Cambridge University Press 1988)

Ely JH, *Democracy and Distrust: A Theory of Judicial Review* (Harvard University Press 1980)

Emerson M, Gros D, and Italianer A, *One Market, One Money: An Evaluation of the Potential Benefits and Costs of Forming an Economic and Monetary Union* (Oxford University Press 1992)

Epstein R and Rhodes M, 'The Political Dynamics Behind Europe's New Banking Union' (2016) 39(3) West European Politics 415

European Commission, 'Banking Union' <http://ec.europa.eu/finance/general-policy/banking-union/european-deposit-insurance-scheme/index_en.htm> accessed 8 August 2022

—— 'SURE' <https://ec.europa.eu/info/business-economy-euro/economic-and-fiscal-policy-coordination/financial-assistance-eu/funding-mechanisms-and-facilities/sure_en> accessed 2 August 2022

European Council and Council of the European Union, 'Economic and Financial Committee' <www.consilium.europa.eu/en/council-eu/preparatory-bodies/economic-financial-committee/> accessed 2 August 2022

European Parliament, 'The Political Bodies of the European Parliament' <www.europarl.europa.eu/about-parliament/en/organisation-and-rules/organisation/political-bodies> accessed 2 August 2022

Expert Group on Debt Redemption Fund and Eurobills, 'Final Report' (2014) <http://ec.europa.eu/economy_finance/articles/governance/2014-03-31-redemption_fund_and_eurobills_en.htm> accessed 2 August 2022

Fabbrini F, 'On Banks, Courts and International Law' (2014) 21(3) Maastricht Journal of European and Comparative Law 444

—— 'The Euro-Crisis and the Courts: Judicial Review and the Political Process in Comparative Perspective' (2014) 32(1) Berkeley Journal of International Law 64

—— and Pollicino O, 'Constitutional Identity in Italy: Institutional Disagreements at a Time of Political Change' in Christian Calliess and Gerhard van der Schyff (eds), *Constitutional Identity in a Europe of Multilevel Constitutionalism* (Cambridge University Press 2019)

—— and Sajó A, 'The Dangers of Constitutional Identity' (2019) 25 European Law Journal 457

Fallon RH, 'Legitimacy and the Constitution' (2005) 118 Harvard Law Review 1787

—— 'The Core Of An Uneasy Case For Judicial Review' (2008) 121 Harvard Law Review 1693

Faraguna P, 'Taking Constitutional Identities Away from the Courts' (2016) 41 Brooklyn Journal of International Law 491

Fasone C and Lupo N, 'Constitutional Review and the Powers of National Parliaments in EU Affairs' in Davor Jancic (ed), *National Parliaments after the Lisbon Treaty and the Euro Crisis: Resilience or Resignation?* (Oxford University Press 2017)

Feichtner I, 'The German Constitutional Court's PSPP Judgment: Impediment and Impetus for the Democratization of Europe' (2020) 21 German Law Journal 1090

Feldstein M, 'Europe's Monetary Union: The Case Against EMU' *The Economist* (13 June 1992)

Fleming S and Arnold M, 'EU's Top Court Reasserts Primacy after German Challenge' *Financial Times* (Brussels and Frankfurt, 8 May 2020) <www.ft.com/content/894369cd-9631-43cc-8844-d6cd515e874b> accessed 2 August 2022

—— and Johnson M, 'Giuseppe Conte Prepares for Toxic Choice on Eurozone Rescue Fund' *Financial Times* (Brussels and Rome, 21 April 2020) <www.ft.com/content/e5bc46a8-8317-4876-acb9-0bcc5b67dedd> accessed 2 August 2022

—— and Khan M, 'Eurozone Strikes Emergency Deal on Coronavirus Rescue' *Financial Times* (Brussels, 10 April 2020) <www.ft.com/content/b984101a-42b8-40db-9a92-6786aec2ba5c> accessed 2 August 2022

—— and Khan M, 'EU Fails to Settle Rifts over Size and Shape of "Recovery Fund" ' Financial Times (24 April 2020) <www.ft.com/content/cee2c14a-fa59-4684-a335-27cef1260fa6> accessed 2 August 2022

—— Mallet V, and Chazan G, 'Germany and France Unite in Call for €500bn Europe Recovery Fund' *Financial Times* (Brussels, Paris, and Berlin, 18 May 2020) <www.ft.com/content/c23ebc5e-cbf3-4ad8-85aa-032b574d0562> accessed 2 August 2022

—— Shotter J and Hopkins V, 'Eastern European States Sense Opportunity in German Court Ruling' *Financial Times* (10 May 2020)

Flynn T, 'Constitutional Pluralism and Loyal Opposition' (2021) 19 International Journal of Constitutional Law 241

Føllesdal A, 'Survey Article: The Legitimacy Deficits of the European Union' (2006) 14(4) Journal of Political Philosophy 441

—— 'Why the European Court of Human Rights Might Be Democratically Legitimate—A Modest Defense' (2009) 27 Nordisk Tidsskrift for Menneskerettigheter 289

—— and Hix S, 'Why There Is a Democratic Deficit in the EU: A Response to Majone and Moravscik' (2006) 44 Journal of Common Market Studies 533

Fontan C and De Cabanes A, 'La Cour de Justice face à Gauweiler. La mise en récit de l'indépendance de la BCE' in Antoine Bailleux, Elsa Bernard, and Sophie Jacquot (eds), *Les récits judiciaires de l'Europe: concepts et typologie* (Bruylant 2019)

Forst R, *The Right to Justification* (Columbia University Press 2012)

Fox B, 'Brussels on Collision Course with Germany on Banking Union' *EU Observer* (Brussels 10 July 2013)

Fraser N, *Scales of Justice, Reimagining Political Space in a Globalizing World* (Columbia University Press 2010)

Freeman S, 'Constitutional Democracy and the Legitimacy of Judicial Review' (1990) 9 Law and Philosophy 327

Friedman B, 'The Birth of an Academic Obsession: The History of the Countermajoritarian Difficulty, Part Five' (2002) 112 The Yale Law Journal 153

—— *The Will of the People* (Farrar, Straus and Giroux 2010)

Friedman M, 'The Role of Monetary Policy' (1968) 58 American Economic Review 1

Fromage D and others, 'ECB Independence and Accountability Today: Towards a (Necessary) Redefinition?' (2019) 26 Maastricht Journal of European and Comparative Law 3

FT Reporters, 'EU Leaders Clash over Coronavirus Response' (26 March 2020) <www.ft.com/content/c3e4db7e-c45a-4113-9bf6-d5d5580fa0ba> accessed 2 August 2022

Fulbrook M, *A History of Germany 1918–2014: The Divided Nation* (Wiley-Blackwell 2014)

Fund EG on DR and Eurobills, 'Final Report' (2014) <http://ec.europa.eu/economy_finance/articles/governance/2014-03-31-redemption_fund_and_eurobills_en.htm> accessed 2 August 2022

Garben S, 'Confronting the Competence Conundrum: Democratising the European Union through an Expansion of Its Legislative Powers' [2014] Oxford Journal of Legal Studies 1

Gardbaum S, 'Comparative Political Process Theory' (2020) 18 International Journal of Constitutional Law 1429

Garner O, 'Squaring the PSPP Circle' (*Verfassungsblog*, 22 May 2020) <https://verfassungsblog.de/squaring-the-pspp-circle/> accessed 2 August 2022

Gaugele J, Malzahn C, and Sturm D, 'Seehofer fordert Volksabstimmung über Euro-Rettung' *Die Welt* (Hamburg, 12 February 2012)

Gauweiler P and Murswiek D, 'Sieg durch Niederlage' (2011) *Focus Magazin* <www.focus.de/politik/deutschland/sieg-durch-niederlage-politik_id_2278453.html> accessed 2 August 2022.

Gearty C, 'The Courts in Europe Today: Subverting or Saving Democracy?—Cristina E. Parau, Transnational Networking and Elite Self-Empowerment. The Making of the Judiciary in Contemporary Europe and Beyond (Oxford University Press 2018) Pp. 350.' (2020) 16 European Constitutional Law Review 770

Gelinsky K, 'Interview with Professor Dr. Christoph Möllers, Humboldt University, Berlin, Faculty of Law: On the Occasion Of the 60th Anniversary of the German Federal Constitutional Court ("Bundesverfassungsgericht")' (2012) 13 German Law Journal 165

Geuss R, *Philosophy and Real Politics* (Princeton University Press 2008)

Geyer F, 'The European Arrest Warrant in Germany—Constitutional Mistrust toward the Concept of Mutual Trust' in Elspeth Guild (ed), *Constitutional Challenges to the European Arrest Warrant* (Wolf Legal Publishers 2006)

Ginter C, 'Constitutionality of the European Stability Mechanism in Estonia: Applying Proportionality to Sovereignty' (2013) 9(2) European Constitutional Law Review 335

Glas O, 'SPD: Für Euro-Haftung und Rückübertragung von EU-Kompetenzen' *Euractiv* (23 July 2013) <www.euractiv.de/section/wahlen-und-macht/news/spd-fur-euro-haftung-und-ruckubertragung-von-eu-kompetenzen/> accessed 2 August 2022

—— 'Grüne: Für Eurobonds und europäischen Mindestlohn' *Euractiv* (31 July 2013) <www.euractiv.de/section/wahlen-und-macht/news/grune-fur-eurobonds-und-europaischen-mindestlohn/> accessed 2 August 2022

Gocaj L and Meunier S, 'Time Will Tell: The EFSF, the ESM, and the Euro Crisis' (2013) 35(3) Journal of European Integration 239

Godley W, 'Maastricht and All That' (1992) 14 (19) London Review of Books 3

Goldoni M, 'Politicising EU Lawmaking? The Spitzenkandidaten Experiment as a Cautionary Tale' (2016) 22 European Law Journal 279

Goldsworthy J, 'Structural Judicial Review and the Objection from Democracy' (2010) 60 The University of Toronto Law Journal 137

Goodhart C and Lastra R, 'Populism and Central Bank Independence' (2018) 29 Open Economies Review 49

Gordon M, 'The UK's Sovereignty Uncertainty' (*UK Constitutional Law Blog*, 11 February 2016) <https://ukconstitutionallaw.org/> accessed 1 August 2022

Götz V, 'Das Maastricht-Urteil des BVerfG' (1993) *Juristenzeitung* 48 (22) 1081

Grauwe P de, *Economics of Monetary Union* (Oxford University Press 2014)

—— and Moesen W, 'Gains for All: A Proposal for a Common Euro Bond' (2009) 3 Intereconomics 132

Greive M and Hildebrand J, 'Karlsruher Urteil zu EZB-Anleihekäufen: Bundesregierung hält EU-Vorwürfe für Unbegründet' *Handelsblatt* (Berlin, 10 August 2021) <www.handelsblatt.com/politik/deutschland/streit-ueber-geldpolitik-karlsruher-urteil-zu-ezb-anleihekaeufen-bundesregierung-haelt-eu-vorwuerfe-fuer-unbegruendet/27498622.html> accessed 2 August 2022

Greven L, 'Das Volk fragen—aber verantwortungsvoll' *ZEIT ONLINE* (Berlin, 14 August 2012)

Grimm D, 'Does Europe Need a Constitution?' (1995) 1 European Law Journal 282

—— 'Defending Sovereign Statehood Against Transforming the Union Into a State' (2009) 5 European Constitutional Law Review; European Constitutional Law Review 353

—— 'The Achievement of Constitutionalism and Its Prospects in a Changed World' in Petra Dobner and Martin Loughlin (eds) (Oxford University Press 2010)

—— 'The Democratic Costs of Constitutionalisation: The European Case' (2015) 21 European Law Journal 460

—— 'The Role of National Constitutional Courts in European Democracy' in Dieter Grimm (ed), The Constitution of European Democracy (Oxford University Press 2017)

—— 'A Long Time Coming' (2020) 21 German Law Journal 944

Gröpl C, 'Schritte zur Europäisierung des Haushaltsrechts' (2013) 52(1) Der Staat 1

Gros D and Mayer T, 'How to Deal with the Threat of Sovereign Default in Europe: Towards a Euro(pean) Monetary Fund' (2010) 2 Intereconomics 64

Guild E, 'Introduction' in Elspeth Guild (ed), *Constitutional Challenges to the European Arrest Warrant* (Wolf Legal Publishers 2006)

Gutman A and Thompson D, *Democracy and Disagreement* (The Belknap Press of Harvard University Press 1996)

—— Why Deliberative Democracy? (Princeton University Press 2004)

Gutschker T and Lohse E, 'Europa muss handlungsfähig sein—nach außen und innen' *Frankfurter Allgemeine Zeitung* (Berlin, 3 June 2018)

Guttenberg L, 'Un nouveau départ pur la zone euro?' (Jacques Delors Institute 2019) <https://institutdelors.eu/publications/a-new-approach-to-eurozone-reform-2/> accessed 1 August 2022

—— 'Time to Come Home if the ESM is to Stay Relevant, it Should Be Reinvented inside the EU' (Jacques Delors Institute & Bertelsmann Stiftung 2020) Policy Brief <www.delor scen tre.eu/ en/ publi cati ons/ det ail/ publ icat ion/ time- to- come- home> accessed 1 August 2022

—— and Rubio E, 'The Future of the Eurozone: Cross-Perspective from France and Germany' (Jacques Delors Institute 2018) Policy Brief <https://institutdelors.eu/wp-content/uploads/2020/08/RencontresdEvian-EMU-GuttenbergRubio-Sept2018-3.pdf> accessed 1 June 2022

Habermas J, 'Remarks on Dieter Grimm's "Does Europe Need a Constitution?"' (1995) 1 European Law Journal 303

—— *Between Facts and Norms* (Polity Press 1996)

—— *The Inclusion of the Other: Studies in Political Theory* (The MIT Press 1998)

—— *The Postnational Constellation* (The MIT Press 2001)

—— 'Constitutional Democracy: A Paradoxical Union of Contradictory Principles?' [2011] Political Theory 766

—— *The Crisis of the European Union: A Response* (English Edition, Polity 2012)

—— 'Democracy in Europe: Why the Development of the EU into a Transnational Democracy Is Necessary and How It Is Possible' (2015) 21 European Law Journal 546

Hahn HJ, 'The Stability Pact for European Monetary Union: Compliance with Deficit Limit as a Constant Legal Duty' (1998) 35 Common Market Law Review 77

Hailbronner M, 'We the Experts. Die geschlossene Gesellschaft der Verfassungsinterpreten' (2014) 53 Der Staat 425

—— *Traditions and Transformations: The Rise of German Constitutionalism* (Oxford University Press 2015)

—— 'Political Process Review: Beyond Distrust' (2020) 18 International Journal of Constitutional Law 1458

Halberstam D, 'Constitutional Heterarchy: The Centrality of Conflict in the European Union and the United States' (2008) *U of Michigan Public Law Working Paper No. 111*<http://ssrn.com/abstract=1147769> accessed 1 August 2022

—— and Möllers C, 'The German Constitutional Court Says "Ja zu Deutschland!"' (2009) 10 German Law Journal 1241

Hall B and Arnold M, 'German Court Ruling Casts Doubt on European Monetary Policy' *Financial Times* (London and Frankfurt, 6 May 2020) <www.ft.com/content/07f19a1b-7494-439d-9765-7fd7ddf09860> accessed 2 August 2022

—— Fleming S, and Chazan G, 'Is the Franco-German Plan Europe's "Hamiltonian" Moment?' *Financial Times* (London, Brussels and Berlin, 21 May 2020) <www.ft.com/content/2735a3f1-bc58-477c-9315-c98129d12852> accessed 2 August 2022

Halmai G, 'Abuse of Constitutional Identity. The Hungarian Constitutional Court on Interpretation of Article E) (2) of the Fundamental Law' (2018) 43 Review of Central and East European Law 23

Haltern U, 'High Time for a Check-up: Progressivism, Populism and Constitutional Review in Germany' (1996) Jean Monnet Working Papers <http://jeanmonnetprogram.org/1996-jean-monnet-working-papers/> accessed 1 August 2022

Hancox E, 'The Meaning of "Implementing" EU Law under Article 51(1) of the Charter: Åkerberg Fransson' (2013) 50 Common Market Law Review 1411

Hannoun H and others, 'Memorandum on the ECB's Monetary Policy' (2019) <www.hanswernersinn.de/en/memorand-ecb-monetary-policy-04102019> accessed 2 August 2022

Harel A, *Why Law Matters* (Oxford University Press 2014)

—— and Kahana T, 'The Easy Core Case for Judicial Review' (2010) 2 Journal of Legal Analysis 227

—— and Shinar A, 'Between Judicial and Legislative Supremacy: A Cautious Defense of Constrained Judicial Review' (2012) 10 International Journal of Constitutional Law 950

Hart HLA, *Rawls on Liberty and Its Priority* (Oxford University Press 1983)

Heipertz M and Verdun A, *Ruling Europe: The Politics of the Stability and Growth Pact* (Cambridge University Press 2010)

Held D, *Models of Democracy* (3rd edn, Stanford University Press 2006)

Henning CR and Kessler M, 'Fiscal Federalism: US History for Architects of Europe's Fiscal Union' (Bruegel 2012) <www.bruegel.org/comment/fiscal-federalism-us-history-architects-europes-fiscal-union> accessed 2 August 2022

Herbst T, 'Legale Abschaffung Des Grundgesetzes Nach Art. 146 GG?' [2012] Zeitschrift für Rechtspolitik 33

Herdegen M, 'Maastricht and the German Constitutional Court—Constitutional Restraints for an Ever Closer Union' (1994) 31 Common Market Law Review 235

—— 'Price Stability and Budgetary Restraints in the Economic and Monetary Union: The Law as Guardian of Economic Wisdom' (1998) 35 Common Market Law Review 9

Hickey T, 'The Republican Core of the Case for Judicial Review' (2019) 17 International Journal of Constitutional Law 288

Hillebrandt M, 'Living Transparency: The Development of Access to Documents in the Council of the EU and Its Democratic Implications' (PhD thesis, Amsterdam University 2017)

Hinarejos A, 'Fiscal Federalism in the European Union: Evolution and Future Choices for EMU' (2013) 50 Common Market Law Review 1621

—— *The Euro Area Crisis in Constitutional Perspective* (Oxford University Press 2015)

Hipp D, 'Fehler Im Denksystem' *Der Spiegel* (27 April 2005) <www.spiegel.de/spiegel/print/d-40077635.html> accessed 2 August 2022

—— and Darnstädt T, '"Der Bundesstaat ist ein Irrtum"' *Der Spiegel* (22 December 2011) <www.spiegel.de/politik/der-bundesstaat-ist-ein-irrtum-a-205029f4-0002-0001-0000-000083328883> accessed 2 August 2022

Högenauer A-L, 'The Politicisation of the European Central Bank and the Bundestag' (2019) 7 Politics and Governance 291

Höing O, 'Differentation of Parliamentary Powers: The German Constitutional Court and the German Bundestag within the Financial Crisis' (2012) 9 OPAL Online Paper Series

—— 'With a Little Help of the Constitutional Court: The Bundestag on Its Way to an Active Policy Shaper' in Claudia Hefftler and others (eds), *The Palgrave Handbook of National Parliaments and the European Union* (Palgrave Macmillan 2015)

Holmes S, 'Precommitment and Disagreement' in Jon Elster and Rune Slagstad (eds), *Constitutionalism and Democracy* (Cambridge University Press 1988)

Hooghe L and Marks G, 'A Postfunctionalist Theory of European Integration: From Permissive Consensus to Constraining Dissensus' (2009) 39(1) British Journal of Political Science 1

Horn H-D, 'Antrag auf Erlass einer einstweiligen Anordnung' <www.uni-marburg.de/de/fb01/professuren/oeffrecht/prof-dr-hans-detlef-horn/vb-gg-eratg-ea_publ.pdf> accessed 2 August 2022

Howarth D and Quaglia L, 'The Steep Road to European Banking Union: Constructing the Single Resolution Mechanism' (2014) 52 Journal of Common Market Studies 125

—— and Schild J, 'Nein to "Transfer Union": The German Brake on the Construction of a European Union Fiscal Capacity' (2021) 43 Journal of European Integration 209

Hrbek R, 'Kontroversen und Manifeste zum Vertrag von Maastricht' (1992) 4 Integration 225

Huber PM, 'Art. 19 IV GG' in Hermann von Mangoldt and others (eds), *GG Kommentar* (6th edn, 2010)

Ioannidis M, 'Europe's New Transformations: How the EU Economic Constitution Changed During the Eurozone Crisis' (2016) 53 Common Market Law Review 1237

Jackson V and Tushnet M, *Comparative Constitutional Law* (Foundation Press 2014)

James H, *Making the European Monetary Union* (Harvard University Press 2012)

Janisch W and Kornelius S, '"Wir Haben Applaus von Der Falschen Seite Bekommen" (Interview with Peter Huber)' *Süddeutsche Zeitung* (Karlsruhe, 12 May 2020) <www.sueddeutsche.de/politik/ezb-urteil-bundesverfassungsgericht-anleihenkaeufe-peter-michael-huber-1.4905311?reduced=true> accessed 2 August 2022

—— and Prallt H '"Keine europaïsche Wirtschaftsregierung ohne Änderung des Grundgesetzes"' *Süddeutsche Zeitung* (München, 19 September 2011)

Janssen R, *De Euro* (De Bezige Bij 2012)

Jaraczewski J, 'Gazing into the Abyss: The K 3/21 Decision of the Polish Constitutional Tribunal' (*Verfassungsblog*, 12 October 2021) <https://verfassungsblog.de/gazing-into-the-abyss/> accessed 2 August 2022

Jefferson T, 'Letter to Samuel Kercheval' (12 July 1816) <https://founders.archives.gov/> accessed 1 August 2022

Jestaedt M, 'Warum in Die Ferne Schweifen Wenn Der Masstab Liegt so Nah?' (2009) 48 Der Staat 497

—— and others (eds), *Das Entgrenzte Gericht. Eine Kritische Bilanz Nach Sechzig Jahren Bundesverfassungsgericht* (Suhrkamp 2011)

Joerges C, 'Where the Law Ends' (2014) *Verfassungsblog* <http://verfassungsblog.de/where-the-law-ends/> accessed 1 August 2022

Jones C and Wagstyl S, 'The Eurozone: A Strained Bond' *Financial Times* (18 January 2015)

Judt T, *Postwar: A History of Europe since 1945* (Penguin Books 2005)

Juncker J-C, 'Completing Europe's Economic and Monetary Union (Five Presidents' Report)' (European Commission 2015) <https://ec.europa.eu/info/publications/five-presidents-report-completing-europes-economic-and-monetary-union_en> accessed 2 August 2022

—— and Tremonti G, 'E-bonds Would End the Crisis' *Financial Times* (London, 6 December 2010)

Kahl W, 'Bewältigung der Staatsschuldenkrise unter Kontrolle des Bundesverfassungsgerichts' [2013] Deutsches Verwaltungsblatt 197

Karatzia A and Markakis M, 'Court of Justice Financial Assistance Conditionality and Effective Judicial Protection: Chrysostomides' [2022] Common Market Law Review 501

Karpenstein U and Steinbeis M, 'Die Stunde des Gesetzgebers' (*Verfassungsblog: On Matters Constitutional*, 19 July 2021) <https://verfassungsblog.de/die-stunde-des-gesetzgebers/>

Kaupa C, 'Has (Downturn-)Austerity Really Been "Constitutionalized" in Europe? On the Ideological Dimension of Such a Claim' (2017) 44(1) Journal of Law and Society 32

Kavanagh A, 'Participation and Judicial Review: A Reply to Jeremy Waldron' (2003) 22 Law and Philosophy 451

Keating D, 'MEPs Cry Foul Over Council Plans for Banking Union that Bypass EU' *Politico* (Brussels, 12 November 2013)

Kelemen RD, 'On the Unsustainability of Constitutional Pluralism' (2016) 23 Maastricht Journal of European and Comparative Law 136

—— 'National Courts Cannot Override CJEU Judgments: A Joint Statement in Defense of the EU Legal Order' (*VerfBlog*, 26 May 2020) <https://verfassungsblog.de/national-courts-cannot-override-cjeu-judgments/>

—— and Pech L, 'The Uses and Abuses of Constitutional Pluralism: Undermining the Rule of Law in the Name of Constitutional Identity in Hungary and Poland' (2019) 21 Cambridge Yearbook of European Legal Studies 59

Kelsen H, 'La Garantie juridictionelle de la constitution (la justice constitutionnelle)' [1928] Revue de droit public 197

—— 'Judicial Review of Legislation: A Comparative Study of the Austrian and American Constitution' (1942) 4 Journal of Politics 183

Kennedy D, *A Critique of Adjudication* (Harvard University Press 1997)

Kerber MC, 'Letter: Those Challenging the ECB's Rescue Measures Are Not Mad' *Financial Times* (27 April 2020)

Khan M, 'Straining the Ties That Bind the Eurozone' *Financial Times* (Brussels, 26 March 2020) <www.ft.com/content/f54d21cf-0701-492e-8516-8f60d000d68f> accessed 2 August 2022

—— and Chazan G, 'Brussels Takes Legal Action against German Constitutional Court' *Financial Times* (Brussels and Berlin, 9 June 2021) <www.ft.com/content/76aabe45-883f-4e3a-80d8-95928db47063> accessed 2 August 2022

Kietz D, *Politisierung trotz Parteienkonsens: Bundestag, Bundesrat und die Euro-Krise* (Bertelsmann Stiftung 2013)

Kiiver P, 'The Lisbon Judgment of the German Constitutional Court: A Court-Ordered Strengthening of the National Legislature in the EU' (2010) 16 European Law Journal 578

Kilpatrick C, 'Are the Bailouts Immune to EU Social Challenge Because They Are Not EU Law?' (2014) 10 European Constitutional Law Review 393

—— 'On the Rule of Law and Economic Emergency: The Degradation of Basic Legal Values in Europe's Bailouts' (2015) 35 Oxford Journal of Legal Studies 325

—— and De Witte B, 'A Comparative Framing of Fundamental Rights Challenges to Social Crisis Measures in the Eurozone' (2014) 7 Sieps European Policy Analysis <www.sieps.se/en/publications/2014/a-comparative-framing-of-fundamental-rights-challenges-to-social-crisis-measures-in-the-eurozone-20147epa/> accessed 2 August 2022

—— and De Witte B (eds), 'Social Rights in Times of Crisis in the Eurozone: The Role of Fundamental Rights' Challenges' (2014) EUI Working Paper LAW 2014/05 <https://cadmus.eui.eu/handle/1814/31247> accessed 2 August 2022

King J, 'On the Proposal for a UK Constitutional Court' (*UK Constitutional Law Blog*, 8 February 2016) <https://ukconstitutionallaw.org/> accessed 1 August 2022

Kirchhof P, 'Deutsches Verfassungsrecht und Europaisches Gemeinschaftsrecht' [1991] Europarecht-Beiheft 1 11

—— 'The Politics of the ECB's Market-Based Approach to Government Debt' [2022] Socio-Economic Review <doi.org/10.1093/ser/mwac014> accessed o1 August 2022

—— and de Boer N, 'What to Do with the ECB's Secondary Mandate' (2022) 61 Journal of Common Market Studies 730

Knoben R, 'Public Opinion in the European Union' in Finn Laursen and Sophie Vanhoonacker (eds), *The Ratification of the Maastricht Treaty: Issues, Debates and Future Implications* (European Institute of Public Administration Maastricht 1994)

Knook A, 'The Court, the Charter, and the Vertical Division of Powers in the European Union' (2005) 42 Common Market Law Review 367

Koedooder C, 'The *Pringle* Judgment: Economic and/or Monetary Union' (2013) 37(1) Fordham International Law Journal 112

Kohl H, *Erinnerungen 1990–1994* (Droemer 2007)

Kokott J, 'Report on Germany' in Joseph Weiler, Anne-Marie Slaughter, and Alec Stone Sweet (eds), *The European Court and National Courts—Doctrine and Jurisprudence* (Hart 1998)

Komárek J, 'European Constitutionalism and the European Arrest Warrant: In Search of the Limits of "Contrapunctual Principles"' (2007) 44 Common Market Law Review 9

—— 'The Place of Constitutional Courts in the EU' (2013) 9 European Constitutional Law Review 420

—— 'National Constitutional Courts in the European Constitutional Democracy' (2014) 12 International Journal of Constitutional Law 525

—— 'Why National Constitutional Courts Should Not Embrace EU Fundamental Rights' (2014) LSE Law, Society and Economy Working Papers <https://papers.ssrn.com/sol3/papers.cfm?abstract_id=2510290>

Kommers D and Miller R, *The Constitutional Jurisprudence of the Federal Republic of Germany* (Duke University Press 2012)

König D, *Die Übertragung von Hoheitsrechten Im Rahmen Des Europäischen Integrationsprozesses—Anwendungsbereich Und Schranken Des Art. 23 Des Grundgesetzes* (Duncker & Humblot 2000)

Kosař D and Vyhnánek L, 'Constitutional Identity in the Czech Republic: A New Twist on an Old-Fashioned Idea?' in Christian Calliess and Gerhard van der Schyff (eds), *Constitutional Identity in a Europe of Multilevel Constitutionalism* (Cambridge University Press 2019)

Kramer LD, 'Putting the Politics Back into the Political Safeguards of Federalism' (2000) 100 Columbia Law Review 215

—— 'Popular Constitutionalism, circa 2004' (2004) 92 California Law Review 959

—— *The People Themselves* (Oxford University Press 2006)

Kreilinger V, 'The Making of a New Treaty: Six Rounds of Political Bargaining' (2012) 32 Notre Europe Policy Brief V

Krisch N, *Beyond Constitutionalism: The Pluralist Structure of Postnational Law* (Oxford University Press 2010)

Kröger S and Bellamy R, 'Beyond a Constraining Dissensus: The Role of National Parliaments in Domesticating and Normalising the Politicization of European Integration' (2016) 14 Comparative European Politics 131

Krotz U and Schramm L, 'Embedded Bilateralism, Integration Theory, and European Crisis Politics: France, Germany, and the Birth of the EU Corona Recovery Fund' (2022) 60 Journal of Common Market Studies 526

Krunke H, 'The Danish Lisbon Judgment—Danish Supreme Court, Case 199/2012, Judgment of 20 February 2013' (2014) 10 European Constitutional Law Review 542

—— and Klinge S, 'The Danish Ajos Case: The Missing Case from Maastricht and Lisbon' (2018) 3 European Papers 157

Kumm M, 'The Jurisprudence of Constitutional Conflict: Constitutional Supremacy in Europe Before and After the Constitutional Treaty' (2005) 11 European Law Journal 262

—— 'Institutionalising Socratic Contestation: The Rationalist Human Rights Paradigm, Legitimate Authority and the Point of Judicial Review' (2007) 1 European Journal of Legal Studies 1

—— 'The Idea of Socratic Contestation and the Right to Justification: The Point of Rights-Based Proportionality Review' (2010) 4 Law & Ethics of Human Rights 142

—— 'The Moral Point of Constitutional Pluralism' in Julie Dickson and Pavlos Eleftheriadis (eds), *Philosophical Foundations of Law* (Oxford University Press 2012)

—— 'Rethinking Constitutional Authority: On the Structure and Limits of Constitutional Pluralism' in Matej Avbelj and Jan Komárek (eds), *Constitutional Pluralism in the European Union and Beyond* (Hart Publishing 2012)

—— 'The Cosmopolitan Turn in Constitutionalism: An Integrated Conception of Public Law' (2013) 20 Indiana Journal of Global Legal Studies 629

—— 'What Kind of a Constitutional Crisis Is Europe In and What Should Be Done About It?' (2013) WZB Discussion Paper SP IV <https://bibliothek.wzb.eu/pdf/2013/iv13-801.pdf> accessed 2 August 2022

—— 'Rebel Without a Good Cause: Karlsruhe's Misguided Attempt to Draw the CJEU into a Game of "Chicken" and What the CJEU Might Do About It' (2014) 15 German Law Journal 203

—— 'The Turn to Justification: On the Structure and Domain of Human Rights Practice' in Adam Etinson (ed), *Human Rights: Moral or Political?* (Oxford University Press 2018)

—— and Comella VF, 'The Primacy Clause of the Constitutional Treaty and the Future of Constitutional Conflict in the European Union' (2005) 3 International Journal of Constitutional Law 473

Kydland FE and Prescott EC, 'Rules Rather than Discretion: The Inconsistency of Optimal Plans' (1977) 85 Journal of Political Economy 473

Lafont C, 'Philosophical Foundations of Judicial Review' in David Dyzenhaus and Malcolm Thorburn (eds), *Philosophical Foundations of Constitutional Law* (Oxford University Press 2016)

Landau D, 'The Reality of Social Rights Enforcement' (2012) 53 Harvard International Law Journal 189

Lasek-Markey M, 'Poland's Constitutional Tribunal on the Status of EU Law: The Polish Government Got All the Answers It Needed from a Court It Controls' (*European Law Blog*, 21 October 2021) <https://europeanlawblog.eu/2021/10/21/polands-constitutional-tribunal-on-the-status-of-eu-law-the-polish-government-got-all-the-answers-it-needed-from-a-court-it-controls/> accessed 2 August 2022

Lastra R, 'The Independence of the European System of Central Banks' (1992) 33 Harvard International Law Journal 475

—— *International Financial and Monetary Law* (Oxford University Press 2015)

Laursen F, 'The Not-So-Permissive Consensus: Thoughts on the Maastricht Treaty and the Future of European Integration' in Finn Laursen and Sophie Vanhoonacker (eds), *The Ratification of the Maastricht Treaty: Issues, Debates and Future Implications* (European Institute of Public Administration Maastricht 1994)

—— Vanhoonacker S, and Wester R, 'Overview of the Negotiations' in Finn Laursen and Sophie Vanhoonacker (eds), *The Intergovernmental Conference on Political Union* (European Institute of Public Administration Maastricht 1992)

Leino-Sandberg P, 'Who Is Ultra Vires Now? The EU's Legal U-Turn in Interpreting Article 310 TFEU' (*Verfassungsblog: On Matters Constitutional*, 18 June 2020) <https://verfassungsblog.de/who-is-ultra-vires-now-the-eus-legal-u-turn-in-interpreting-article-310-tfeu/> accessed 2 August 2022

—— 'Between European Commitment and "Taking the Law Seriously"' (*Verfassungsblog: On Matters Constitutional*, 29 April 2021) <https://verfassungsblog.de/between-european-commitment-and-taking-the-law-seriously/> accessed 2 August 2022

—— and Ruffert M, 'Next Generation EU and Its Constitutional Ramifications: A Critical Assessment' (2022) 59 Common Market Law Review 433

Leterme Y, 'Pour une agence européenne de la dette' *Le Monde* (Paris, 5 March 2010) <www.lemonde.fr/idees/article/2010/03/05/pour-une-agence-europeenne-de-la-dette-par-yves-leterme_1314894_3232.html> accessed 2 August 2022

Lindseth P, *Power and Legitimacy: Reconciling Europe and the Nation-State* (Oxford University Press 2010)

Loughlin M, 'Constitutional Pluralism: An Oxymoron?' (2014) 3 Global Constitutionalism 9

Louis J, 'The Review of the Stability and Growth Pact' (2006) 43 Common Market Law Review 85

—— 'Guest Editorial: The No-Bailout Clause and Rescue packages' (2010) 47 Common Market Law Review 971

Lucarelli B, *Endgame for the Euro: A Critical History* (Palgrave Pivot 2013)

Ludlow P 'In the Last Resort: The European Council and the euro crisis' (2010) 7(7/8) Eurocomment Briefing Note

—— 'The Euro Crisis Once Again' (2010) 8(3) Eurocomment Briefing Note

—— 'Doing Whatever is Required? The European Council of 16–17 December 2010' 8(4) Eurocomment Briefing Note (Brussels 2011)

MacCormick N, 'Beyond the Sovereign State' (1993) 56 The Modern Law Review 1

—— 'The Maastricht-Urteil: Sovereignty Now' (1995) 1 European Law Journal 259

Macdougall D, 'Report of the Study Group on the Role of Public Finance in European Integration, Volume I: General Report (The MacDougall Report)' (Brussels, April 1977)

McNamara K, *The Currency of Ideas: Monetary Politics in the European Union* (Cornell University Press 1999)

Macron E, 'Sorbonne Speech' (26 September 2017) <http://international.blogs.ouest-france.fr/archive/2017/09/29/macron-sorbonne-verbatim-europe-18583.html> accessed 2 August 2022

Madsen MR, Olsen HP, and Šadl U, 'Competing Supremacies and Clashing Institutional Rationalities: The Danish Supreme Court's Decision in the Ajos Case and the National Limits of Judicial Cooperation' (2017) 23 European Law Journal 140

Maduro MP, 'Contrapunctual Law: Europe's Constitutional Pluralism in Action' in Neil Walker (ed), *Sovereignty in Transition* (Hart Publishing 2003)

—— 'Europe and the Constitution: What If This Is as Good as It Gets?' in JHH Weiler and Marlene Wind (eds), *European Constitutionalism Beyond the State* (Cambridge University Press 2003)

—— 'Some Preliminary Remarks on the PSPP Decision of the German Constitutional Court' (*Verfassungsblog*, 6 May 2020) <https://verfassungsblog.de> accessed 21 July 2020

Magnette P, 'Towards "Accountable Independence"? Parliamentary Controls of the European Central Bank and the Rise of a New Democratic Model' (2000) 6 European Law Journal 326

Mair S and Kröge M, 'Constitutional Change through Euro Crisis Law: Germany' (28 December 2015) <http://eurocrisislaw.eui.eu/germany/> accessed 2 August 2022

Majastre C, 'Penser l'état contre l'Europe: la genèse d'une orthodoxie juridique dans la République Fédérale d'Allemagne de 1949 à l'arrêt Maastricht' (2019) 69 Revue française de science politique 117

Mallet V, Chazan G, and Fleming S, 'The Chain of Events That Led to Germany's Change over Europe's Recovery Fund' *Financial Times* (Brussels, 22 May 2020) <www.ft.com/content/1d8853f4-726d-4c06-a905-ed2f37d25eee> accessed 2 August 2022

Mallien J 'Weidmann soll den Bundestag regelmäßig über EZB-Beschlüsse informieren' *Handelsblatt* (Frankfurt, 19 June 2020) < www.handelsblatt.com/finanzen/geldpolitik/bundesbank-praesident-weidmann-soll-den-bundestag-regelmaessig-ueber-ezb-beschluesse-informieren/25932334.html> accessed 2 August 2022

Manin B, 'On Legitimacy and Political Deliberation' (1987) 15 Political Theory 338

Mann M and Kloepfer I, 'Mehr Europa lässt das Grundgesetz kaum zu' (2011) *Frankfurter Allgemeine Zeitung* (25 September 2011) <www.faz.net/aktuell/wirtschaft/eurokrise/im-gespraech-andreas-vosskuhle-mehr-europa-laesst-das-grundgesetz-kaum-zu-11369184.html> accessed 2 August 2022

Mansbridge J and others, 'The Place of Self-Interest and the Role of Power in Deliberative Democracy' (2010) 18 The Journal of Political Philosophy 64

Markakis M, *Accountability in the Economic and Monetary Union: Foundations, Policy, and Governance* (Oxford University Press 2020)

Marsh D, 'Fresh German Legal Battle over ECB Easing' (*OMFIF*, 17 June 2020) <www.omfif.org/2020/06/fresh-german-legal-battle-over-ecb-easing/> accessed 2 August 2022

——and Meyer-Schwickerath A, 'German Litigation May Trap ECB in Pincer' (*OMFIF*, 31 March 2021) <www.omfif.org/2021/03/german-litigation-may-trap-ecb-in-pincer/> accessed 2 August 2022

Matthijs M, 'Hegemonic Leadership Is What States Make of It: Reading Kindleberger in Washington and Berlin' (2022) 29 Review of International Political Economy 371

Matthijs M and McNamara K, 'The Euro Crisis' Theory Effect: Northern Saints, Southern Sinners, and the Demise of the Eurobond' (2015) 37(2) Journal of European Integration 229

May KO, 'A Set of Independent Necessary and Sufficient Conditions for Simple Majority Decision' (1952) 10 Econometrica 680

Mayer F, 'Kompetenzüberschreitung und Letzentscheidung' (PhD thesis, Ludwig-Maximillians-Universität München 2000)

—— 'Rebel Without a Cause? A Critical Analysis of the German Constitutional Court's OMT Reference' (2014) 15 German Law Journal 111

—— 'Auf dem Weg zum Richterfaustrecht?' (*Verfassungsblog*, 7 May 2020) <https://verfassungsblog.de/auf-dem-weg-zum-richterfaustrecht/> accessed 2 August 2022

—— 'The Ultra Vires Ruling: Deconstructing the German Federal Constitutional Court's PSPP Decision of 5 May 2020' (2020) 16 European Constitutional Law Review 733

—— and Heidfeld C, 'Verfassungs- und europarechtliche Aspekte der Einführung von Eurobonds' [2012] Neue Juristische Wochenschrift 422

Mayer, T, 'The Case for a European Monetary Fund' (2009) 3 *Intereconomics* 138

—— *Europe's Unfinished Currency* (Anthem Press 2012)

Meier-Beck P, 'Ultra Vires?' (*D'Kart*, 11 May 2020) <www.d-kart.de/en/blog/2020/05/11/ultra-vires/> accessed 2 August 2022

Mendes CH, 'Neither Dialogue Nor Last Word—Deliberative Separation of Powers 3' (2011) 5 Legisprudence 1

Menéndez AJ, 'The Existential Crisis of the European Union' (2013) 14 German Law Journal 453

Mersch Y, 'In the Spirit of European Cooperation' <www.ecb.europa.eu/press/key/date/2020/html/ecb.sp200702~87ce377373.en.html> accessed 2 August 2022

Michalopoulos S, 'Nine Member States Ask for Eurobonds to Face Coronavirus Crisis' *Euractiv* (25 March 2020) <www.euractiv.com/section/economy-jobs/news/nine-member-states-ask-for-eurobonds-to-face-coronavirus-crisis/> accessed 2 August 2022

Michelman FI, 'Rawls on Constitutionalism and Constitutional Law' in Samuel Freeman (ed), *The Cambridge Companion to Rawls* (Cambridge University Press 2002)

—— 'Why Not Just Say No? An Essay on the Obduracy of Constitutional Fixation' (2014) 94 Boston University Law Review 1141

—— 'Legitimacy, The Social Turn and Constitutional Review: What Political Liberalism Suggests' (2015) 98 Kritische Vierteljahresschrift für Gesetzgebung und Rechtswissenschaft 183

Middelaar L van, *Een Europees Pandemonium* (Historische Uitgeverij 2021)

Miller D, *On Nationality* (Clarendon Press 1995)

—— *Citizenship and National Identity* (Polity Press 2000)

Millet F-X, *L'Union Européenne et l'identité constitutionnelle des États membres* (LGDJ, Lextenso éditions 2013)

—— 'Constitutional Identity in France: Vices and—Above All—Virtues' in Christian Calliess and Gerhard van der Schyff (eds), *Constitutional Identity in a Europe of Multilevel Constitutionalism* (Cambridge University Press 2019)

Möller K, *The Global Model of Constitutional Rights* (Oxford University Press 2012)

Möllers C, *Der vermisste Leviathan—Staatstheorie in der Bundesrepublik* (Suhrkamp 2008)

—— 'Constitutional Ultra Vires Review of European Acts Only Under Exceptional Circumstances; Decision of 6 July 2010, 2 BvR 2661/06, Honeywell' (2011) 7 European Constitutional Law Review 161

—— 'Legalität, Legitimität und Legitimation des Bundesverfassungsgerichts' in Matthias Jestaedt and others (eds), *Das entgrenzte Gericht. Eine kritische Bilanz nach sechzig Jahren Bundesverfassungsgericht* (Suhrkamp 2011)

—— *The Three Branches: A Comparative Model of Separation of Powers* (Oxford University Press 2013)

Moloney N, 'EU Financial Market Regulation after the Global Financial Crisis: "More Europe" or More Risks?' (2010) 47 Common Market Law Review 1317

—— 'European Banking Union: Assessing its Risks and Resilience' (2014) 51 Common Market Law Review 1609

Moravcsik A, *The Choice for Europe: Social Purpose and State Power from Messina to Maastricht* (Routledge 1998)

Morgan R and Christiansen T, 'The New Germany and European Union after Maastricht: The Difficult Way Ahead' in Stephen Martin (ed), *The Construction of Europe: Essays in Honour of Emile Noël* (Kluwer 1994)

Mouffe C, *The Democratic Paradox* (Verso 2000)

Müller JW, 'In the Shadows of Statism: Peculiarities of the German Debates on European Integration' in Justine Lacroix and Kalypso Nicolaïdis (eds), *European Stories* (Oxford University Press 2010)

—— *Contesting Democracy* (Yale University Press 2011)

Müller P, 'FDP Mitgliederentscheid soll Rettungsschirm stoppen' *Spiegel Online* (Hamburg, 9 September 2011)

Müller R, 'Wie demokratisch ist direkte Demokratie?' *Frankfurter Allgemeine Zeitung* (Frankfurt, 7 November 2011) <www.faz.net/aktuell/politik/volksentscheide-wie-demokratisch-ist-direkte-demokratie-11520785.html> accessed 2 August 2022

—— '"Das EZB-Urteil war zwingend"' *Frankfurter Allgemeine Zeitung* (12 May 2020) <www.faz.net/aktuell/politik/inland/peter-huber-im-gespraech-das-ezb-urteil-war-zwingend-16766682.html> accessed 2 August 2022

Münchau W, 'Eurozone Stability Is under Threat Again' *Financial Times* (15 March 2020) <www.ft.com/content/d8086302-6545-11ea-a6cd-df28cc3c6a68> accessed 2 August 2022

Münchrath J, 'Finanzhilfe für Griechenland: "Wir ziehen wieder nach Karlsruhe"' *Handelsblatt* (Düsseldorf, 22 February 2010) <www.handelsblatt.com/politik/konjunktur/oekonomie/nachrichten/finanzhilfe-fuer-griechenland-wir-ziehen-wieder-nach-karlsruhe/3374780.html> accessed 2 August 2022

Mundell R, 'A Theory of Optimum Currency Areas' (1961) 51(4) The American Economic Review 657

Murkens JEK, 'The Future of Staatsrecht: Dominance, Demise or Demystification?' (2007) 70 The Modern Law Review 731

—— *From Empire to Union: Conceptions of German Constitutional Law Since 1871* (Oxford University Press 2013)

Murswiek D, 'ECB, ECJ, Democracy, and the Federal Constitutional Court: Notes on the Federal Constitutional Court's Referral from 14 January 2014' (2014) 15(2) German Law Journal 147

—— 'Eurokrise—Materialien zu den Prozessen' <www.dietrich-murswiek.de/materialien.html> accessed 2 August 2022

Nanclares JMYP de, 'Constitutional Identity in Spain: Commitment to European Integration without Giving Up the Essence of the Constitution' in Christian Calliess and Gerhard van der Schyff (eds), *Constitutional Identity in a Europe of Multilevel Constitutionalism* (Cambridge University Press 2019)

Naurin D, 'Dressed for Politics' (PhD thesis, Göteborg University 2004)

Nettesheim M, 'Das Ende eines epochalen Verfassungsstreits' (*Verfassungsblog*, 18 May 2021) <https://verfassungsblog.de/das-ende-eines-epochalen-verfassungsstreits/> accessed 2 August 2022

Nguyen T, 'A Matter of Principle' (*Verfassungsblog*, 11 June 2021) <https://verfassungsblog.de/a-matter-of-principle/> accessed 2 August 2022

Öberg J, 'National Parliaments and Political Control of EU Competences: A Sufficient Safeguard of Federalism?' (2018) 24 European Public Law 965

Offe C, 'Europe Entrapped: Does the EU Have the Political Capacity to Overcome its Current Crisis?' (2013) 19(5) European Law Journal 595

Oppenheimer A (ed), *The Relationship between European Community Law and National Law: The Cases* (Cambridge University Press 2003)

Palmstorfer R, 'To Bail Out or Not to Bail Out? The Current Framework of Financial Assistance for Euro Area Member States Measured against the Requirements of EU Primary Law' (2012) 6 European Law Review 771

Papadopoulos Y, *Democracy in Crisis? Politics, Governance and Policy* (Palgrave Macmillan 2013)

Payandeh M, 'Constitutional Review of EU Law after Honeywell: Contextualizing the Relationship between the German Constitutional Court and the EU Court of Justice' (2011) 48 Common Market Law Review 9

Peel Q, 'Merkel Warns of Hurdles in EMF Plan' *Financial Times* (London, 8 March 2010) <www.ft.com/content/6fdeed16-2ad9-11df-886b-00144feabdc0> accessed 2 August 2022

—— 'German Court Backs ESM Bailout Fund' *Financial Times* (Berlin, 12 September 2012)

Peeperkorn M, 'Hoekstra Stribbelt Tegen Bij Steunpakket EU: "Een Nederlandse Middelvinger Naar Het Zuiden"' *de Volkskrant* (24 March 2020)

Pérez AT, *Conflicts of Rights in the European Union, A Theory of Supranational Adjudication* (Oxford University Press 2009)

Peter F, 'Political Legitimacy' in Edward N Zalta (ed), *The Stanford Encyclopedia of Philosophy* (Summer 2010 edition)

Petersen N, 'Karlsruhe's Lochner Moment? A Rational Choice Perspective on the German Federal Constitutional Court's Relationship to the CJEU After the PSPP Decision' (2020) 21 German Law Journal 995

—— and Chatziathanasiou K, 'Primacy's Twilight?' (European Parliament 2021) PE 692.276 <www.europarl.europa.eu/thinktank/en/document/IPOL_STU(2021)692276> accessed 1 August 2022

Pipkorn J, 'Legal Arrangements in the Treaty of Maastricht for the Effectiveness of the Economic and Monetary Union' (1994) 31 Common Market Law Review 263

Pisani-Ferry J, *The Euro Crisis and its Aftermath* (Oxford University Press 2013)

Pistor K, 'Germany's Constitutional Court Goes Rogue' (*Project Syndicate*, 8 May 2020) <www.project-syndicate.org> accessed 1 August 2022

Pogge TW, *Realizing Rawls* (Cornell University Press 1989)

Poiares Maduro M, 'A New Governance for the European Union and the Euro: Democracy and Justice' (2012) 11 RCSAS Policy Papers

Polzin M, 'Constitutional Identity, Unconstitutional Amendments and the Idea of Constituent Power: The Development of the Doctrine of Constitutional Identity in German Constitutional Law' (2016) 14 International Journal of Constitutional Law 411

Postema GJ, *Legal Philosophy in the Twentieth Century: The Common Law World* (Springer 2011)

Poulou A, 'Financial Assistance Conditionality and Human Rights Protection: What Is the Role of the EU Charter of Fundamental Rights?' (2017) 54 Common Market Law Review 991

Proissl W, 'Why Germany Fell Out of Love with Europe' (2010) Bruegel Essay and Lecture Series <http://bruegel.org/2010/06/why-germany-fell-out-of-love-with-europe/> accessed 2 August 2022

Ragnarsson KH, 'The Counter-Majoritarian Difficulty in a Neloiberal World: Socio-Economic Rights and Deference in Post-2008 Austerity Cases' (2019) 8 Global Constitutionalism 605

Rasmussen M, 'Revolutionizing European Law: A History of the Van Gend En Loos Judgment' (2014) 12 International Journal of Constitutional Law 136

Rauchegger C, 'National Constitutional Rights and the Primacy of EU Law: M.A.S.' (2018) 55 Common Market Law Review 1521

Rawls J, *A Theory of Justice* (rev edn, Oxford University Press 1999)

—— *Political Liberalism* (Columbia University Press 2005)

Reestman J-H, 'The Franco-German Constitutional Divide, Reflections on National and Constitutional Identity' (2009) 5 European Constitutional Law Review 374

—— 'Legitimacy through Adjudication: The ESM Treaty and the Fiscal Compact before the National Courts' in Thomas Beukers, Bruno De Witte, and Claire Kilpatrick (eds), *Constitutional Change Through Euro-Crisis Law* (Cambridge University Press 2017)

—— and Besselink LFM, 'Spitzenkandidaten and the European Union's System of Government' (2019) 15 European Constitutional Law Review 609

Risse T, 'No Demos? Identities and Public Spheres in the Euro Crisis' (2014) 52 Journal of Common Market Studies 1207

Rodrik D, *The Globalization Paradox: Democracy and the Future of the World Economy* (WW Norton & Company 2011)

Rompuy H van, 'Towards a Genuine Economic and Monetary Union (Four Presidents' Report)' (2012) EUCO <www.consilium.europa.eu/media/23818/134069.pdf> accessed 2 August 2022

Roßmann, R, 'Union und SPD wollen bundesweite Volksabstimmungen' *Süddeutsche Zeitung* (München, 12 November 2013)

Roth, M, 'Für eine Volksabstimmung über Europa' *Euractiv* (14 November 2011) <www.euractiv.de/section/prioritaten-der-eu-fur-2020/opinion/fur-eine-volksabstimmung-uber-europa/> accessed 2 August 2022

Roux T, 'In Defence of Empirical Entanglement: The Methodological Flaw in Waldron's Case against Judicial Review' in Graeme Orr and others (eds), *The Cambridge Handbook of Deliberative Constitutionalism* (Cambridge University Press 2018)

Rozenberg O and Hefftler C, 'Introduction' in Claudia Hefftler and others (eds), *The Palgrave Handbook of National Parliaments and the European Union* (Palgrave Macmillan 2015)

Ruffert M, 'The European Debt Crisis and European Union Law' (2011) 48(6) Common Market Law Review 1777

Rytter JE and Wind M, 'In Need of Juristocracy? The Silence of Denmark in the Development of European Legal Norms' (2011) 9 International Journal of Constitutional Law 470

Sachverständigenrat zur Begutachtung der gesamtwirtschaftlichen Entwicklung, 'Jahresgutachten 2011/12 "Verantwortung für Europa wahrnehmen"' Bonifatius GmbH Buch-Druck-Verlag (Paderborn)

Sadch T and Verdun A, 'Explaining Europe's Monetary Union: A Survey of the Literature' (2009) 11 International Studies Review 277.

Šadl U and Mair S, 'Mutual Disempowerment: Case C-441/14 Dansk Industri, Acting on Behalf of Ajos A/S v Estate of Karsten Eigil Rasmussen and Case No. 15/2014 Dansk Industri (DI) Acting for Ajos A/S v The Estate Left by A' (2017) 13 European Constitutional Law Review 347

Sadurski W, *Poland's Constitutional Breakdown* (Oxford University Press 2019)

Sandbu M, *Europe's Orphan: The Future of the Euro and the Politics of Debt* (Princeton University Press 2016)

—— 'German Court Has Set a Bomb under the EU Legal Order' *Financial Times* (5 May 2020) <www.ft.com/content/79181c01-b66b-4f81-bdc6-fd4dcf940821> accessed 1 August 2022

——, 'The Eurozone's Bailout Fund Remains Unfairly Toxic' *Financial Times* (20 May 2020) <www.ft.com/content/2741caf1-5758-4a26-ac88-0cab6cf63500> accessed 2 August 2022

Sarmiento D and Weiler JHH, 'The EU Judiciary After Weiss' (*Verfassungsblog: On Matters Constitutional*, 3 June 2020) <https://verfassungsblog.de/the-eu-judiciary-after-weiss/> accessed 1 August 2022

Schaart E, 'Dutch Finance Minister Acknowledges Lack of Empathy on Corona Bonds' *Politico* (31 March 2020) <www.politico.eu/article/dutch-finance-minister-acknowledges-lack-of-empathy-on-corona-bonds/> accessed 2 August 2022

Schäfers M and Seidenbiedel C, 'Bundesregierung: EZB hat Urteil aus Karlsruhe erfüllt' *Frankfurter Allgemeine Zeitung* (29 June 2020) <www.faz.net/aktuell/wirtschaft/bundesregierung-ezb-hat-urteil-aus-karlsruhe-erfuellt-16837926.html> accessed 2 August 2022

Scharpf FW, 'The Asymmetry of European Integration, or Why the EU Cannot Be a "Social Market Economy"' (2010) 8 Socio-Economic Review 211

—— 'Legitimacy in the Multi-Level European Polity' in Petra Dobner and Martin Loughlin (eds), *The Twilight of Constitutionalism?* (Oxford University Press 2010)

—— 'Monetary Union, Fiscal Crisis and the Disabling of Democratic Accountability' in Armin Schäfer and Wolfgang Streeck (eds), *Politics in the Age of Austerity* (Polity Press 2013)

Schäuble W, 'Banking Union Must Be Built on Firm Foundations' *Financial Times* (London, 12 May 2013)

—— 'After the Crash: A Perspective on European Multilevel Democracy' (2015) 21 European Law Journal 384

Scheller HK, *The European Central Bank: History, Role and Functions* (2nd edn, European Central Bank 2006)

Schepel, H, 'The Bank, the Bond, and the Bail-out: On the Legal Construction of Market Discipline in the Eurozone' (2017) 44(1) Journal of Law and Society 79

Schermers HG, 'The Scales in Balance: National Constitutional Court v. Court of Justice' (1990) 27 Common Market Law Review 97

Schertzer R, 'Federal Arbiters as Facilitators: Towards an Integrated Federal and Judicial Theory for Diverse States' (2017) 15 International Journal of Constitutional Law 110

Schimmelfennig F, Leuffen D, and Ritterger B, 'The European Union as a System of Differentiated Integration: Interdependence, Politicization and Differentiation' (2015) 22 Journal of European Public Policy 764

Schoeller MG and Karlsson O, 'Championing the "German Model"? Germany's Consistent Preferences on the Integration of Fiscal Constraints' (2021) 43 Journal of European Integration 191

Scholz R, 'Grundgesetz und europäische Einigung—Zu den reformpolitischen Empfehlungen der Gemeinsamen Verfassungskommission' (1992) Neue Juristische Wochenschrift 2593

Schönberger C, 'Lisbon in Karlsruhe: Maastricht's Epigonies at Sea' (2009) 10 German Law Journal 1201

Schorkopf F, 'Verfassungsrechtliche Grenzen und Möglichkeitenfür eine Umsetzung des Schuldentilgungspaktes des Sachverständigenrates' Sachverständigenrat zur Begutachtung der gesamtwirtschaftlichen Entwicklung, Gutachten of 20 July 2012 <www.sachverstaendigenrat-wirtschaft.de/fileadmin/dateiablage/download/publikationen/rechtsgutachten_schuldentilgungspakt.pdf> accessed 2 August 2022.

Schrag Sternberg C, *The Struggle for EU Legitimacy: Public Contestation, 1950–2005* (Palgrave Macmillan 2013)

Schramm L, 'Economic Ideas, Party Politics, or Material Interests? Explaining Germany's Support for the EU Corona Recovery Plan' [2021] Journal of European Public Policy 1

Schulz M, Letter to Mr José Manuel Barroso, President of the European Commission, of 20 January 2014, no 301049

Schutte C, 'Spain Tribunal Constitucional on the European Constitution. Declaration of 13 December 2004' (2005) 1 European Constitutional Law Review 281

Schyff G van der, 'Member States of the European Union, Constitutions, and Identity: A Comparative Perspective' in Christian Calliess and Gerhard van der Schyff (eds), *Constitutional Identity in a Europe of Multilevel Constitutionalism* (Cambridge University Press 2019)

Scialom L, Quang GL, and Deyris J, 'Shaky Foundations Central Bank Independence in the 21st Century' (2022) University of Paris Nanterre, EconomiX Working Papers 2022–16 <https://ideas.repec.org/p/drm/wpaper/2022-16.html> accessed 2 August 2022

Seikel D and Truger A, 'The Blocked Completion of the European Monetary Union', WSI Institute of Economic and Social Research 2019, WSI Report 52 <www.boeckler.de/en/faust-detail.htm?sync_id=8520> accessed 1 June 2022

Shklar JN, *Legalism* (Harvard University Press 1964)

Simon S and Rathke H, '"Simply Not Comprehensible." Why?' (2020) 21 German Law Journal 950

Smits R, 'Accountability of the European Central Bank' [2019] Ars Aequi 27

Smyth J, and Spiegel P, 'Irish Angry Over Budget Leak to Germany' *Financial Times* (18 November 2011)

Snell J, 'The Trilemma of European Economic and Monetary Integration, and Its Consequences' (2016) 22 European Law Journal 157

SPD, *Das wir entscheidet, das Regierungsprogramm 2013–2017* (2013) <www.spd.de/fileadmin/Dokumente/Beschluesse/Bundesparteitag/20130415_regierungsprogramm_2013_2017.pdf> accessed 2 August 2022

Spiegel P, 'If the Euro Falls, Europe Falls' *Financial Times* (15 May 2020) <www.ft.com/content/b4e2e140-d9c3-11e3-920f-00144feabdc0> accessed 2 August 2022

Spieker LD, 'Framing and Managing Constitutional Identity Conflicts: How to Stabilize the Modus Vivendi between the Court of Justice and National Constitutional Courts' (2020) 57 Common Market Law Review 361

Steiner J, *Deliberative Politics in Action: Analyzing Parliamentary Discourse* (Cambridge University Press 2004)

—— *The Foundations of Deliberative Democracy: Empirical Research and Normative Implications* (Cambridge University Press 2012)

Steinmeier, F and Steinbrück P, 'Germany Must Lead Fightback' *Financial Times* (London, 14 December 2010)

Stone A, 'Judicial Review Without Rights: Some Problems for the Democratic Legitimacy of Structural Judicial Review' (2008) 28 Oxford Journal of Legal Studies 1

—— 'Democratic Objections to Structural Judicial Review and the Judicial Role in Constitutional Law' (2010) 60 The University of Toronto Law Journal 109

Stone Sweet A, *Governing with Judges: Constitutional Politics in Europe* (Oxford University Press 2000)

—— 'Why Europe Rejected American Judicial Review—and Why It May Not Matter' (2002) 101 Michigan Law Review 2744

Streeck W, *Buying Time: The Delayed Crisis of Democratic Capitalism* (Verso 2014)

Stubbington T, 'Rise in Italian Yields Has Echoes of Eurozone Debt Crisis' *Financial Times* (17 March 2020) <www.ft.com/content/3e372b66-684a-11ea-800d-da70cff6e4d3> accessed 2 August 2022

Szász A, *The Road to European Monetary Union* (Macmillan & St Martin's Press 1999)

Tesche T, 'Pandemic Politics: The European Union in Times of the Coronavirus Emergency' (2022) 60 Journal of Common Market Studies 480

Thompson D, 'Deliberative Democratic Theory and Empirical Political Science' (2008) 11 Annual Review of Political Science 497

Thym D, 'In the Name of Sovereign Statehood: A Critical Introduction to the Lisbon Judgment of the German Constitutional Court' (2009) 46 Common Market Law Review 1795

Timmermans C, 'Voorrang van Het Unierecht Door Multilevel Rechterlijke Samenwerking' [2012] Sociaal-Economische Wetgeving 50

Tomuschat C, 'Die Europaïsche Union unter der Aufsicht des Bundesverfassungsgerichts' (1993) 20 Europäische Grundrechte-Zeitschrift 489

—— 'The Ruling of the German Constitutional Court on the Treaty of Lisbon' (2009) 10 German Law Journal 1259

Tooze A, 'The Death of the Central Bank Myth' *Foreign Policy* (13 May 2020) <https://foreignpolicy.com/2020/05/13/european-central-bank-myth-monetary-policy-german-court-ruling/> accessed 2 August 2022

—— *Shutdown: How Covid Shook the World's Economy* (Penguin 2021)

—— 'Debating Central Bank Mandates' (2022) Forum for a New Economy Working Papers 01 <www.newforum.org> accessed 2 August 2022

Tribe L, *The Puzzling Persistence of Process-Based Constitutional Theories* (1980) <http://hdl.handle.net/20.500.13051/15960> accessed 1 August 2022

Tuominen T, 'Aspects of Constitutional Pluralism in Light of the Gauweiler Saga' (2018) 43 European Law Review 186

—— *The Euro Crisis and Constitutional Pluralism* (Edward Elgar 2021)

Tuori K and Tuori K, *The Eurozone Crisis. A Constitutional Analysis* (Cambridge University Press 2014)

Tushnet M, 'Darkness on the Edge of Town: The Contributions of John Hart Ely to Constitutional Theory' (1980) 89 The Yale Law Journal 1037

—— *Taking the Constitution Away from the Courts* (Princeton University Press 2000)

—— *Weak Courts, Strong Rights* (Princeton University Press 2008)

—— 'The Relation Between Political Constitutionalism and Weak-Form Judicial Review' (2013) 14 German Law Journal 2249

Tusseau G, 'A Plea for a Hint of Empiricism in Constitutional Theory: A Comment on Cesare Pinelli's Constitutional Reasoning and Political Deliberation' (2013) 14 German Law Journal 1184

van den Brink M, 'Justice, Legitimacy and the Authority of Legislation within the European Union' (2019) 82 The Modern Law Review 293

Van Malleghem P-A, '*Pringle*: A Paradigm Shift in the European Union's Monetary Constitution' (2013) 14 (1) German Law Journal 141

van 't Klooster J 'Democracy and the European Central Bank's Emergency Powers' (2018) 42 Midwest Studies in Philosophy 270

—— 'The Politics of the ECB's Market-Based Approach to Government Debt' [2022] Socio-Economic Review <https://doi.org/10.1093/ser/mwac014> accessed 1 August 2022

—— and de Boer N, 'What to Do with the ECB's Secondary Mandate' (2022) 61 Journal of Common Market Studies 730

van Wijnbergen C, 'The Federal Republic of Germany' in Finn Laursen and Sophie Vanhoonacker (eds), *The Intergovernmental Conference on Political Union* (European Institute of Public Administration Maastricht 1992)

Venzke I, *How Interpretation Makes International Law* (Oxford University Press 2012)

Verdun A, 'The Role of the Delors Committee in the Creation of EMU: An Epistemic Community?' (1999) 6(2) Journal of European Public Policy 308

Violante T, 'Bring Back the Politics: The PSPP Ruling in Its Institutional Context' (2020) 21 German Law Journal 1045

Visser M de, *Constitutional Review in Europe: A Comparative Analysis* (Hart 2014)

—— and Claes M, 'Are You Networked Yet? On Dialogues in European Judicial Networks' (2012) 8 Utrecht Law Review 100

Von Altenbockum J, 'Schwache Chefs' *Frankfurter Allgemeine Zeitung* (Frankfurt, 17 April 2012)

Von der Burchard H, Oliveira I, and Schaart E, 'Dutch Try to Calm North-South Economic Storm over Coronavirus' *Politico* (27 March 2020) <www.politico.eu/article/netherlands-try-to-calm-storm-over-repugnant-finance-ministers-comments/> accessed 2 August 2022

Voßkuhle A, 'Multilevel Cooperation of the European Constitutional Courts: Der Europäische Verfassungsgerichtsverbund' (2010) 6 European Constitutional Law Review 175

—— '"European Integration Through Law": The Contribution of the Federal Constitutional Court' (2017) 58 European Journal of Sociology 145

Waldron J, 'A Right-Based Critique of Constitutional Rights' (1993) 13 Oxford Journal of Legal Studies 18

—— 'Rights and Majorities: Rousseau Revisited' in Jeremy Waldron (ed), *Liberal Rights* (Cambridge University Press 1993)

—— *The Dignity of Legislation* (Cambridge University Press 1999)

—— *Law and Disagreement* (Oxford University Press 1999)

—— 'The Core of the Case Against Judicial Review' (2006) 115 The Yale Law Journal 1346

—— 'Judges as Moral Reasoners' (2009) 7 International Journal of Constitutional Law 2

—— 'Democracy' in David Estlund (ed), *The Oxford Handbook of Political Philosophy* (Oxford University Press 2012)

—— 'Political Political Theory: An Inaugural Lecture' (2013) 21 The Journal of Political Philosophy 1

—— 'Constitutionalism: A Skeptical View' in Jeremy Waldron (ed), *Political Political Theory* (Harvard University Press 2016)

Walker N, 'The Idea of Constitutional Pluralism' (2002) 65 The Modern Law Review 317

—— 'Constitutional Pluralism Revisited' (2016) 22 European Law Journal 333

Waluchow W, 'Constitutionalism' in Edward N Zalta (ed), *The Stanford Encyclopedia of Philosophy* (Winter 2012 edition)

Wechsler H, 'The Political Safeguards of Federalism: The Role of the States in the Composition and Selection of the National Government' (1954) 54 Columbia Law Review 543

Weidmann J, 'Eingangserklärung anlässlich der mündlichen Verhandlung im Hauptsacheverfahren ESM/EZB' (11 June 2013) <www.bundesbank.de/de/presse/stellungnahmen/eingangserklaerung-anlaesslich-der-muendlichenverhandlung-im-hauptsacheverfahren-esm-ezb-662878> accessed 2 August 2022

Weiler JHH, 'Eurocracy and Distrust: Some Questions Concerning the Role of the European Court of Justice in the Protection of Fundamental Human Rights within the Legal Order of the European Communities' (1986) 61 Washington Law Review 1103

—— 'The Transformation of Europe' (1991) 100 The Yale Law Journal 2403

—— 'Does Europe Need a Constitution? Demos, Telos and the German Maastricht Decision' (1995) 1(3) European Law Journal 219

—— 'In Defence of the Status Quo: Europe's Constitutional Sonderweg' in JHH Weiler and Marlene Wind (eds), *European Constitutionalism Beyond the State* (Cambridge University Press 2003)

—— *The Constitution of Europe: 'Do the New Clothes Have an Emperor?' And Other Essays on European Integration* (Cambridge University Press 1999)

—— 'Fundamental Rights and Fundamental Boundaries: On the Conflict of Standards and Values in the Protection of Human Rights in the European Legal Space' in JHH Weiler (ed) *The Constitution of Europe: 'Do the New Clothes Have an Emperor?' And Other Essays on European Integration* (Cambridge University Press 1999)

——, 'Prologue: Global and Pluralist Constitutionalism - Some Doubts' in Gráinne d. Búrca and JHH Weiler (eds) (Cambridge University Press 2012)

—— 'Van Gend En Loos: The Individual as Subject and Object and the Dilemma of European Legitimacy' (2014) 12 International Journal of Constitutional Law 94

—— Haltern UR, and Mayer F, 'European Democracy and Its Critique' (1995) EUI Working Paper RSC No 95/11 <http://cadmus.eui.eu/bitstream/handle/1814/1386/95_11.pdf>

—— Slaughter A-M, and Sweet AS, 'Prologue—The European Court of Justice' in Joseph Weiler, Anne-Marie Slaughter, and Alec Stone Sweet (eds), *The European Court and National Courts* (Hart 1998)

Wendel M, 'Lisbon Before the Courts: Comparative Perspectives' (2011) 7 European Constitutional Law Review 96

—— *Permeabilität im Europäischen Verfassungsrecht* (Mohr Siebeck 2011)

—— 'Comparative Reasoning and the Making of a Common Constitutional Law: EU-Related Decisions of National Constitutional Courts in a Transnational Perspective' (2013) 11 International Journal of Constitutional Law 981

—— 'Judicial Restraint and the Return to Openness: The Decision of the German Federal Constitutional Court on the ESM and the Fiscal Treaty of 12 September 2012' (2013) 14 German Law Journal 21

—— 'Exceeding Judicial Competence in the Name of Democracy: The German Federal Constitutional Court's OMT Reference' (2014) 10 European Constitutional Law Review 263

—— 'Paradoxes of Ultra-Vires Review: A Critical Review of the PSPP-Decision and Its Initial Reception' (2020) 21 German Law Journal 979

—— 'The Two-Faced Guardian: Or How One Half of the German Federal Constitutional Court Became a European Fundamental Rights Court' (2020) 57 Common Market Law Review 1383

—— 'The Fog of Identity and Judicial Contestation: Preventive and Defensive Constitutional Identity Review in Germany' (2021) 27 European Public Law 465

—— 'Next Generation EU and the German Federal Constitutional Court—The Decision on Preliminary Injunctions of 15 April 2021' (*BRIDGE Network Blog*, 17 May 2021) <https://bridgenetwork.eu/2021/05/17/next-generation-eu-and-the-german-federal-constitutional-court-the-decision-on-preliminary-injunctions-of-15-april-2021/> accessed 2 August 2022

Werner P and others, 'Report to the Council and the Commission on the realisation by stages of Economic and Monetary Union in the Community, "Werner Report"' (Council—Commission of the European Communities, Luxembourg 1970)

Wessels W and others, 'Democratic Control in the Member States of the European Council and the Euro Zone Summits' (Study requested by the Constitutional Affairs Committee of the European Parliament, DG for Internal Policies Study 2013)

Wetenschappelijke Raad voor het Regeringsbeleid, *Europa in Nederland* (Amsterdam University Press 2007)

White J, 'Emergency Europe' (2015) 63 Political Studies 300

Wieczorek-Zeul H, 'Der Vertrag von Maastricht im Deutschen Bundestag' (1993) 48(13–14) Europa-Archiv 405

Wilkinson MA, 'Economic Messianism and Constitutional Power in a "German Europe": All Courts Are Equal, but Some Courts Are More Equal than Others' (2014) LSE Law, Society and Economy Working Papers <https://papers.ssrn.com/sol3/papers.cfm?abstract_id=2522919> accessed 1 August 2022

Willis A, 'Revised Greek Deficit Figures Cause Outrage' *EU Observer* (20 October 2009) <https://euobserver.com/economic/28853> accessed 1 August 2022

Willsch KP and others, 'Allianz gegen den ESM' (23 May 2012) on file with the author

Wilmès S and others, 'Letter to President of the European Council, Charles Michel' (25 March 2020) <https://twitter.com/Shahinvallee/status/1242790458926993409/photo/1> accessed 2 August 2022

Winkelmann I (ed), *Das Maastricht-Urteil des Bundesverfassungsgerichts vom 12. Oktober 1993, Dokumentation des Verfahrens mit Einführung* (Dunckler & Humblot 1994)

Winzen T, 'Political Integration and National Parliaments in Europe' (2010) 2 Living Reviews in Democracy <https://ethz.ch/content/dam/ethz/special-interest/gess/cis/cis-dam/CIS_DAM_2015/WorkingPapers/Living_Reviews_Democracy/Winzen.pdf> accessed 2 August 2022

—— 'European Integration and National Parliamentary Oversight Institutions' (2012) 14 European Union Politics 297

Witte B de, 'Using International Law in the Euro Crisis' (2013) No 4 ARENA Working Paper 20 December 2016 <www.arena.uio.no> accessed 2 August 2022

—— 'The European Union's Covid-19 Recovery Plan: The Legal Engineering of an Economic Policy Shift' (2021) 58 Common Market Law Review 635

Wittrock P, 'CDU beerdigt Pläne für Volksabstimmungen' *Spiegel Online* (Hamburg, 12 November 2013)

Wohlfahrt C, 'The Lisbon Case: A Critical Summary' (2009) 10(8) German Law Journal 1277

Wolf M, 'German Court Decides to Take Back Control with ECB Ruling' *Financial Times* (16 May 2020) <www.ft.com/content/37825304-9428-11ea-af4b-499244625ac4> accessed 1 August 2022

Zschäpitz H, '"Krasser Fall von Staatsfinanzierung"—EZB wird an Grenzen ihres Mandats Erinnert' *Die Welt* (11 March 2021) <www.welt.de/wirtschaft/article228033723/EZB-Notfallprogramm-PEPP-Klaeger-ziehen-vor-Bundesverfassungsgericht.html> accessed 2 August 2022

Zurn CF, 'Deliberative Democracy and Constitutional Review' (2002) 21 Law and Philosophy 467

—— *Deliberative Democracy and the Institutions of Judicial Review* (Cambridge University Press 2007)

Documents

European Union

Conclusions of the European Council of 14 and 15 December 1990 <www.consilium.europa.eu/media/20537/1990_december_-_rome__eng__part_i.pdf> accessed 1 August 2022

Conclusions of the Extraordinary European Council of 29 October 1993 <www.europarl.europa.eu/summits/brussels2/default_en.htm> accessed 1 August 2022

Conclusions of the Council of the European Union, Economic and Financial Affairs Council, Extraordinary meeting of 9/10 May 2010 <www.consilium.europa.eu/uedocs/cms_data/docs/pressdata/en/ecofin/114324.pdf> accessed 2 August 2022

Conclusions of the European Council of 28–29 October 2010, doc no EUCO 25/1/10, REV 1 <www.consilium.europa.eu/uedocs/cms_data/docs/pressdata/en/ec/117496.pdf> accessed 2 August 2022

Conclusions of the European Council of 16–17 December 2010, doc no EUCO 30/1/10 <www.consilium.europa.eu/uedocs/cms_data/docs/pressdata/en/ec/118578.pdf> accessed 2 August 2022

Council of the European Union, Press Release 9596/10, 9/10 May 2010 <www.consilium.europa.eu/uedocs/cms_data/docs/pressdata/en/ecofin/114324.pdf> accessed 2 August 2022

Council of the European Union, 'Council Agrees General Approach on Single Resolution Mechanism', Brussels, 18 December 2013 <www.consilium.europa.eu/uedocs/cms_data/docs/pressdata/en/ecofin/140190.pdf> accessed 2 August 2022

Council of the European Union, 'Report on Single Resolution Mechanism', 7 February 2014, no 6187/14

Council of the European Union, 'Member States Sign Agreement on Bank Resolution Fund', Brussels, 21 May 2014 <http://register.consilium.europa.eu/doc/srv?l=EN&f=ST%2010088%202014%20INIT> accessed 2 August 2022

Council of the European Union, 'Opinion of the Legal Service' (Brussels, 24 June 2020) 9062/20 <https://data.consilium.europa.eu/doc/document/ST-9062-2020-INIT/en/pdf> accessed 2 August 2022

Council of the European Union, 'Statement of EU Ministers of Finance on the Stability and Growth Pact in Light of the COVID-19 Crisis of 23 March 2020' <www.consilium.europa.eu/en/press/press-releases/2020/03/23/statement-of-eu-ministers-of-finance-on-the-stability-and-growth-pact-in-light-of-the-covid-19-crisis/> accessed 2 August 2022

Court of Justice of the European Union Press Release 58/20, Press release following the judgment of the German Constitutional Court of 5 May 2020 (8 May 2020)

Court of Justice of the European Union Press Release 63/22, Broadcast by streaming of hearings and the handing down of judgments and opinions of the Court of Justice (22 April 2022)

ECB, 'ECB decides on measures to address severe tensions in financial markets', Press release, 10 May 2010 <www.ecb.europa.eu/press/pr/date/2010/html/pr100510.en.html> accessed 2 August 2022

ECB, 'Technical features of Outright Monetary Transactions', Press release, 6 September 2012 <www.ecb.europa.eu/press/pr/date/2012/html/pr120906_1.en.html> accessed 2 August 2022

ECB, 'ECB announces €750 billion Pandemic Emergency Purchase Programme (PEPP)', Press release, 18 March 2020 <www.ecb.europa.eu/press/pr/date/2020/html/ecb.pr200318_1~3949d6f266.en.html> accessed 2 August 2022

ECB, 'Account of the monetary policy meeting of the Governing Council of the European Central Bank held in Frankfurt am Main on Wednesday and Thursday, 3–4 June 2020' <www.ecb.europa.eu/press/accounts/2022/html/ecb.mg220519~c9200dba08.en.html> accessed 2 August 2022.

ECB, 'Monetary policy decisions', Press release, 4 June 2020 <www.ecb.europa.eu/press/pr/date/2020/html/ecb.mp200604~a307d3429c.en.html> accessed 2 August 2022

ECB, 'Press Conference Christine Lagarde, President of the ECB, Luis de Guindos, Vice-President of the ECB,Frankfurt am Main, 4 June 2020' <www.ecb.europa.eu/press/pressconf/2020/html/ecb.is200604~b479b8cfff.en.html> accessed 2 August 2022

ECB, 'Monetary policy decisions', Press release, 10 December 2020 <www.ecb.europa.eu/press/pr/date/2020/html/ecb.mp201210~8c2778b843.en.html> accessed 2 August 2022

ECB, 'The ECB's monetary policy strategy statement', 8 July 2021 <www.ecb.europa.eu/home/search/review/html/ecb.strategyreview_monpol_strategy_statement.en.html> accessed 2 August 2022

ESM, 'ESM Board of Governors backs Pandemic Crisis Support', Press release, 15 May 2020 <www.esm.europa.eu/press-releases/esm-board-governors-backs-pandemic-crisis-support> accessed 2 August 2022

ESM, 'ESM direct bank recapitalisation instrument adopted', Press Release, 8 December 2014 <www.esm.europa.eu/press-releases/esm-direct-bank-recapitalisation-instrument-adopted> accessed 2 August 2022

Eurogroup, 'Report on the comprehensive economic policy response to the COVID-19 pandemic', Press release, 9 April 2020 <www.consilium.europa.eu/en/press/press-releases/2020/04/09/report-on-the-comprehensive-economic-policy-response-to-the-covid-19-pandemic/> accessed 2 August 2022

Eurogroup, 'Eurogroup Statement on the Pandemic Crisis Support', Press release, 8 May 2020 <www.consilium.europa.eu/nl/press/press-releases/2020/05/08/eurogroup-statement-on-the-pandemic-crisis-support/> accessed 2 August 2020

Eurogroup, 'Videoconference of 8 May 2020', Brussels, 14 May 2020 <www.consilium.europa.eu/media/43992/2020-05-08-summing-up-letter-rev01.pdf> accessed 2 August 2022

European Commission Legal Service, 'Analysis of the judgment of the German Constitutional Court of 30 June 2009 on the Treaty of Lisbon, and of the German legislation adopted thereupon' (Brussels, 18 September 2009) JUR(2009) 55096 LRR/CL/FH/bds

European Commission, 'Report on Greek Government Deficit and Debt Statistics' (Brussels, 8 January 2010) COM(2010) 1 final

European Commission, 'Proposal for a Council Regulation establishing a European financial stabilization' (Brussels, 9 May 2010) COM(2010) 2010 final

European Commission, 'A blueprint for a deep and genuine economic and monetary union' (Brussels, 28 November 2012) COM(2012) 777 final

European Commission, 'Commissioner Michel Barnier's remarks at the ECOFIN Council press conference' (Brussels, 19 December 2013) MEMO/13/1186

Commissioner Barnier 2013 <https://ec.europa.eu/commission/presscorner/detail/en/MEMO_13_1186> accessed 2 August 2022

European Commission, 'Proposal for a Regulation of the European Parliament and of the Council establishing uniform rules and a uniform procedure for the resolution of credit institutions and certain investment firms in the framework of a Single Resolution Mechanism and a Single Bank Resolution Fund and amending Regulation (EU) 1093/2010 of the European Parliament and of the Council' COM(2013) 520 final

European Commission, 'Proposal for a regulation of the European Parliament and of the Council amending Regulation (EU) 806/2014 in order to establish a European Deposit Insurance Scheme' COM(2015) 586 final

European Commission, 'Reflection Paper on the Deepening of the Economic and Monetary Union' (Brussels, 31 May 2017) COM(2017) 291

European Commission, 'State aid: Commission adopts Temporary Framework to enable Member States to further support the economy in the COVID-19 outbreak', Press release, Brussels, 19 March 2020 <https://ec.europa.eu/commission/presscorner/detail/en/IP_20_496> accessed 2 August 2022

European Commission 'Proposal for a Council Regulation on the establishment of a European instrument for temporary support to mitigate unemployment risks in an emergency (SURE) following the COVID-19 outbreak' (Brussels 2 April 2020) COM(2020) 139 final <https://eur-lex.europa.eu/legal-content/EN/TXT/?uri=COM%3A2020%3A0139%3AFIN> accessed 2 August 2022

European Commission, 'Statement by President Von der Leyen', Brussels, 10 May 2020 <https://ec.europa.eu/commission/presscorner/detail/en/statement_20_846> accessed 2 August 2022

European Commission, 'Communication from the Commission to the Council on the Activation of the general escape clause of the Stability and Growth Pact', COM(2020) 123 final <https://ec.europa.eu/info/sites/default/files/economy-finance/2_en_act_part1_v3-adopted_text.pdf> accessed 2 August 2022

European Commission, 'Temporary Framework for State aid measures to support the economy in the current COVID-19 outbreak (Communication)', (Brussels, 19 March 2020) COM(2020) 1863 final <https://ec.europa.eu/competition/state_aid/what_is_new/sa_covid19_temporary-framework.pdf> accessed 2 August 2022

European Commission, 'The EU budget powering the recovery plan for Europe', COM(2020) 442 final https://eur-lex.europa.eu/resource.html?uri=cellar:4524c01c-a0e6-11ea-9d2d-01aa75ed71a1.0003.02/DOC_1&format=PDF> accessed 2 August 2022

European Commission, 'Amended proposal for a Council decision on the system of Own Resources of the European Union', COM(2020) 445 final 1 <https://ec.europa.eu/info/sites/default/files/about_the_european_commission/eu_budget/com_2020_445_en_act_v8.pdf> accessed 2 August 2022

European Commission, 'June infringements package: key decisions', Brussels, 9 June 2021 <https://ec.europa.eu/commission/presscorner/detail/en/inf_21_2743> accessed 2 August 2022

European Parliament, Press Release of 5 March 2014, 'MEPs lay out final offer on bank single resolution mechanism' <www.europarl.europa.eu/news/en/press-room/20140305IPR37601/meps-lay-out-final-offer-on-bank-single-resolution-mechanism> accessed 2 August 2022

European Parliament, Press Release of 20 March 2014, 'Parliament negotiators rescue seriously damaged bank resolution system' <www.europarl.europa.eu/news/en/news-room/20140319IPR39310/parliament-negotiators-rescue-seriously-damaged-bank-resolution-system> accessed 2 August 2022

European Parliament, 'Committee on Economic and Monetary Affairs Monetary Dialogue with Christine Lagarde, President of the European Central Bank', Brussels, 8 June 2020

Priority question for written answer P-004295/20 to the Commission Domènec Ruiz Devesa (S&D), Juan Fernando López Aguilar (S&D), Charles Goerens (Renew), Guy Verhofstadt (Renew), Sandro Gozi (Renew), Damian Boeselager (Verts/ALE) (20 July 2020)

Question for written answer E-004215/20 to the Commission Jean-Paul Garraud (ID), Gilles Lebreton (ID) (15 July 2020)

Question for written answer E-002887/20 to the Commission Vangelis Meimarakis (PPE) (11 May 2020)

Question for written answer Z-035/2020 to the European Central Bank Nuno Melo (PPE) (29 May 2020)

Question for written answer E-003385/20 to the Council Hélène Laporte (ID) (5 June 2020)

Statement by the Heads of State or Government of the European Union of 11 February 2010 <www.consilium.europa.eu/media/20485/112856.pdf> accessed 2 August 2022

Statement by the Heads of State and Government of the Euro Area of 25 March 2010 <www.consilium.europa.eu/media/21429/20100325-statement-of-the-heads-of-state-or-government-of-the-euro-area-en.pdf> accessed 2 August 2022

Statement by the Eurogroup of 2 May 2010 and Joint statement on financial support programme for Greece by Commissioner Olli Rehn and IMF Managing Director Dominique Strauss-Kahn of 2 May 2010 <http://ec.europa.eu/economy_finance/articles/eu_economic_situation/2010-05-03-statement-commissioner-rehn-imf-on-greece_en.htm> accessed 2 August 2022

Statement by the Heads of State or Government of the Euro Area of 7 May 2010 <www.consilium.europa.eu/media/21430/20100507-statement-of-the-heads-of-state-or-government-of-the-euro-area-en.pdf> accessed 2 August 2022

Statement by the Heads of State or Government of the Euro Area and EU Institutions, of 21 July 2011 <www.consilium.europa.eu/media/21426/20110721-statem

ent-by-the-heads-of-state-or-government-of-the-euro-area-and-eu-institutions-en.pdf> accessed 2 August 2022

Statement on Banking Union and bridge financing arrangements for the Single Resolution Fund adopted by Ministers of the 28 Member States meeting in the margins of the Council (ECOFIN) of 8 December 2015 <www.consilium.europa.eu/nl/press/press-releases/2015/12/08/statement-by-28-ministers-on-banking-union-and-bridge-financing-arrangements-to-srf/pdf> accessed 25 August 2021

Germany

Plenary Parliamentary Debates

Plenarprotokoll 12/110, Stenografischer Bericht der 110. Sitzung des Deutschen Bundestages am 8. Oktober 1992 (Maastricht first plenary)

Plenarprotokoll 12/126, Stenografischer Bericht der 126. Sitzung des Deutschen Bundestages am 2. Dezember 1992 (Maastricht second plenary)

Plenarprotokoll 650, Stenografischer Bericht der 650. Sitzung des Deutschen Bundesrates am 18. Dezember 1992 (Maastricht final debate)

Plenarprotokoll 12/181, Stenografischer Bericht der 181. Sitzung des Deutschen Bundestages am 20. Oktober 1993

Plenarprotokoll 17/39, Stenografischer Bericht der 39. Sitzung des Deutschen Bundestages am 5. Mai 2010 (Greek loan facility first plenary)

Plenarprotokoll 17/42, Stenografischer Bericht der 42. Sitzung des Deutschen Bundestages am 19. Mai 2010 (EFSF first plenary)

Plenarprotokoll 17/44, Stenografischer Bericht der 44. Sitzung des Deutschen Bundestages am 21. Mai 2010 (EFSF second plenary)

Plenarprotokoll 17/80, Stenografischer Bericht der 80. Sitzung des Deutschen Bundestages am 15. Dezember 2010 (debate on European Council of 16–17 December 2010)

Plenarprotokoll 17/123, Stenografischer Bericht der 123. Sitzung des Deutschen Bundestages am 7. September 2011 (debate on 2012 budget)

Plenarprotokoll 17/124, Stenografischer Bericht der 124. Sitzung des Deutschen Bundestages am 8. September 2011 (EFSF extension first plenary)

Plenarprotokoll 17/130, Stenografischer Bericht der 130. Sitzung des Deutschen Bundestages am 29. September 2011 (EFSF extension second plenary)

Plenarprotokoll 17/172, Stenografischer Bericht der 172. Sitzung des Deutschen Bundestages am 29. März 2012 (ESM and Fiscal Compact first plenary)

Plenarprotokoll 17/176, Stenografischer Bericht der 176. Sitzung des Deutschen Bundestages am 27. April 2012 (Neuner Gremium second plenary)

Plenarprotokoll 17/188, Stenografischer Bericht der 188. Sitzung des Deutschen Bundestages am 29. Juni 2012 (ESM and Fiscal Compact second plenary)

Plenarprotokoll 17/232, Stenografischer Bericht der 232. Sitzung des Deutschen Bundestages am 22. März 2013 (EUZBBG revision first plenary)

Plenarprotokoll 17/234, Stenografischer Bericht der 234. Sitzung des Deutschen Bundestages am 18. April 2013 (EUZBBG revision second plenary)

Plenarprotokoll 19/158, Stenografischer Bericht der 158. Sitzung des Deutschen Bundestages am 7. Mai 2020 (hereafter Plenarprotokoll 19/158)

Plenarprotokoll 19/163, Stenografischer Bericht der 163. Sitzung des Deutschen Bundestages am 28. Mai 2020

Plenarprotokoll 19/166, Stenografischer Bericht der 166. Sitzung des Deutschen Bundestages am 18. Juni 2020.

Plenarprotokoll 19/170, Stenografischer Bericht der 170. Sitzung des Deutschen Bundestages am 2. Juli 2020
Plenarprotokoll 19/212, Stenografischer Bericht der 212. Sitzung des Deutschen Bundestages am 25 Februar 2021

Parliamentary Documents

BT-Dr. 12/3322 of 30.09.1992: Antrag der Gruppe der PDS/Linke Liste—Maastrichter Vertrag über die Europäische Union
BT-Dr. 12/3353 of 06.10.1992: Gesetzentwurf der Abgeordneten Dr Gregor Gysi, Andrea Lederer und der Gruppe der PDS/Linke Liste—Entwurf eines Gesetzes zur Durchführung eines Volksentscheids über die Mitgliedschaft der Bundesrepublik Deutschland in einer Europäischen Union und die Ratifizierung des Maastrichter Vertrages über eine Europäische Union (Europa-Abstimmungsgesetz)
BT-Dr. 12/3334 of 01.10.1992 Gesetzentwurf der Bundesregierung Entwurf eines Gesetzes zum Vertrag vom 7. Februar 1992 über die Europäische Union
BT-Dr. 12/3338 of 02.10.1992 Gesetzentwurf der Bundesregierung Entwurf eines Gesetzes zur Änderung des Grundgesetzes
BT-Dr. 12/3366 of 7.10.1992: Antrag der Fraktion SPD
BT-Dr. 12/3367 of 07.10.1992: Antrag der Abgeordneten Gerd Poppe, Werner Schulz (Berlin), Dr Wolfgang Ullmann, Konrad Weiß (Berlin), Vera Wollenberger und der Gruppe Bündnis 90/Die Grünen
BT-Dr. 12/3895 of 01.12.1992: Beschlußempfehlung und Bericht des Sonderausschusses "Europäische Union (Vertrag von Maastricht)"
BT-Dr. 12/3896 of 01.12.1992: Beschlußempfehlung und Bericht des Sonderausschusses "Europäische Union (Vertrag von Maastricht)"
BT-Dr. 12/3906 of 02.12.1992: Entschließungsantrag der Fraktionen der CDU/CSU, SPD und FDP zu dem Gesetzentwurf der Bundesregierung—Drucksachen 12/3334,12/3895—Entwurf eines Gesetzes zum Vertrag vom 7. Februar 1992 über die Europäische Union
BT-Dr. 12/6000 of 05.11.1993: Bericht der Gemeinsamen Verfassungskommission gemäß Beschluß des Deutschen Bundestages—Drucksachen 12/1590, 12/1670—und Beschluß des Bundesrates—Drucksache 741/91 (Beschluß)
BT-Dr. 12/6520 of 29.12.1993: Antwort der Bundesregierung auf eine kleine Anfrage aus dem Deutschen Bundestag zu den Konsequenzen aus dem Urteil des Zweiten Senats des Bundesverfassungsgericht vom 12. Oktober 1993 (Maastricht-Urteil)
BT-Dr. 17/1639 of 06.05.2010: Entschließungsantrag der Fraktion der SPD zu der dritten Beratung des Gesetzentwurfs der Fraktionen der CDU/CSU und FDP—Drucksachen 17/1544, 17/1561, 17/1562—Entwurf eines Gesetzes zur Übernahme von Gewährleistungen zum Erhalt der für die Finanzstabilität in der Währungsunion erforderlichen Zahlungsfähigkeit der Hellenischen Republik (Währungsunion-Finanzstabilitätsgesetz—WFStG)
BT-Dr. 17/1685 of 11.05.2010: Gesetzentwurf der Fraktionen der CDU/CSU und FDP Entwurf eines Gesetzes zur Übernahme von Gewährleistungen im Rahmen eines europäischen Stabilisierungsmechanismus
BT-Dr. 17/1740 of 19.05.2010: Beschlussempfehlung des Haushaltsausschusses (8. Ausschuss) zu dem Gesetzentwurf der Fraktionen der CDU/CSU und FDP—Drucksache 17/1685—Entwurf eines Gesetzes zur Übernahme von Gewährleistungen im Rahmen eines europäischen Stabilisierungsmechanismus
BT-Dr. 17/1741 of 20.05.2010: Bericht des Haushaltsausschusses (8. Ausschuss) zu dem Gesetzentwurf der Fraktionen der CDU/CSU und FDP—Drucksache 17/1685—Entwurf

eines Gesetzes zur Übernahme von Gewährleistungen im Rahmen eines europäischen Stabilisierungsmechanismus

BT-Dr. 17/1808 of 20.05.2010: Entschließungsantrag der Abgeordneten Jürgen Trittin, Renate Künast, Fritz Kuhn, Dr Frithjof Schmidt, Dr Gerhard Schick, Kerstin Andreae, Lisa Paus und der Fraktion Bündnis 90/Die Grünen zu der dritten Beratung des Gesetzentwurfs der Fraktionen der CDU/CSU und FDP—Drucksachen 17/1685, 17/1740, 17/1741—Entwurf eines Gesetzes zur Übernahme von Gewährleistungen im Rahmen eines europäischen Stabilisierungsmechanismus

BT-Dr. 17/1810 of 20.05.2010: Entschließungsantrag der Fraktion der SPD zu der dritten Beratung des Gesetzentwurfs der Fraktionen der CDU/CSU und FDP—Drucksachen 17/1685, 17/1740, 17/1741—Entwurf eines Gesetzes zur Übernahme von Gewährleistungen im Rahmen eines europäischen Stabilisierungsmechanismus

BT-Dr. 17/1811 of 20.05.2010: Entschließungsantrag der Abgeordneten Michael Schlecht, Sahra Wagenknecht, Dr. Axel Troost und der Fraktion DIE LINKE zu der dritten Beratung des Gesetzentwurfs der Fraktionen der CDU/CSU und FDP—Drucksachen 17/1685, 17/1740, 17/1741—Entwurf eines Gesetzes zur Übernahme von Gewährleistungen im Rahmen eines europäischen Stabilisierungsmechanismus

BT-Dr. 17/4183 of 14.12.2010: Entschließungsantrag der Fraktion der SPD zu der Abgabe einer Regierungserklärung durch die Bundeskanzlerin zum Europäischen Rat am 16./17. Dezember 2010 in Brüssel

BT-Dr. 17/4881 of 22.02.2011: Antrag der Fraktion der SPD zum Entwurf eines Beschlusses des Europäischen Rates zur Änderung des Vertrags über die Arbeitsweise der Europäischen Union hinsichtlich eines Stabilitätsmechanismus für die Mitgliedstaaten, deren Währung der Euro ist—Ratsdok. 17620/10 (EUCO 30/10), Anlage I

BT-Dr. 17/6916 of 05.09.2011: Gesetzentwurf der Fraktionen der CDU/CSU und FDP Entwurf eines Gesetzes zur Änderung des Gesetzes zur Übernahme von Gewährleistungen im Rahmen eines europäischen Stabilisierungsmechanismus

BT-Dr. 17/6945 of 07.09.2011: Antrag der Fraktionen der CDU/CSU und FDP Parlamentsrechte im Rahmen zukünftiger europäischer Stabilisierungsmaßnahmen sichern und stärken.

BT-Dr. 17/7130 of 26.09.2011: Bericht des Haushaltsausschusses (8. Ausschuss) a) zu dem Gesetzentwurf der Fraktionen der CDU/CSU und FDP—Drucksache 17/6916—Entwurf eines Gesetzes zur Änderung des Gesetzes zur Übernahme von Gewährleistungen im Rahmen eines europäischen Stabilisierungsmechanismus b) zu dem Antrag der Fraktionen der CDU/CSU und FDP—Drucksache 17/6945—Parlamentsrechte im Rahmen zukünftiger europäischer Stabilisierungsmaßnahmen sichern und stärken

BT-Dr. 17/9046 of 20.03.2012: Gesetzentwurf der Fraktionen der CDU/CSU und FDP, Entwurf eines Gesetzes zu dem Vertrag vom 2. März 2012 über Stabilität, Koordinierung und Steuerung in der Wirtschafts- und Währungsunion

BT-Dr. 17/9145 of 27.03.2012: Gesetzentwurf der Fraktionen CDU/CSU, SPD, FDP und Bündnis 90/Die Grünen Entwurf eines Gesetzes zur Änderung des Stabilisierungsmec hanismusgesetzes

BT-Dr. 17/9146 of 27.03.2012: Antrag der Abgeordneten Dr Gesine Lötzsch, Dr Kirsten Tackmann, Dr Dietmar Bartsch, Herbert Behrens, Karin Binder, Heidrun Bluhm, Steffen Bockhahn, Roland Claus, Katrin Kunert, Caren Lay, Sabine Leidig, Michael Leutert, Thomas Lutze, Kornelia Möller, Wolfgang Neskovic, Jens Petermann, Ingrid Remmers, Dr Ilia Seifert, Kersten Steinke, Sabine Stüber, Alexander Süßmair und der Fraktion Die Linke

BT-Dr. 17/9148 of 27.03.2012: Antrag der Abgeordneten Dr Diether Dehm, Andrej Hunko, Thomas Nord, Alexander Ulrich, Wolfgang Gehrcke, Jan van Aken, Christine Buchholz,

Sevim Dağdelen, Werner Dreibus, Annette Groth, Heike Hänsel, Inge Höger, Harald Koch, Niema Movassat, Wolfgang Neskovic, Paul Schäfer (Köln), Michael Schlecht, Kathrin Vogler, Sahra Wagenknecht, Katrin Werner und der Fraktion Die Linke

BT-Dr. 17/9435 of 25.04.2012: Beschlussempfehlung und Bericht des Haushaltsausschusses (8. Ausschuss) zu dem Gesetzentwurf der Fraktionen CDU/CSU, SPD, FDP und Bündnis 90/Die Grünen—Drucksache 17/9145—Entwurf eines Gesetzes zur Änderung des Stabil isierungsmechanismusgesetzes

BT-Dr. 17/10152 of 27.06.2012: Entschließungsantrag der Fraktionen CDU/CSU, SPD, FDP und Bündnis 90/Die Grünen zu der dritten Beratung des Gesetzentwurfs der Fraktionen der CDU/CSU und FDP—Drucksachen 17/9046, 17/10125—Entwurf eines Gesetzes zu dem Vertrag vom 2. März 2012 über Stabilität, Koordinierung und Steuerung in der Wirtschafts- und Währungsunion

BT-Dr. 17/10125 of 27.06.2012: Beschlussempfehlung des Haushaltsausschusses (8. Ausschuss)

BT-Dr. 17/10171 of 28.06.2012: Bericht des Haushaltsausschusses (8. Ausschuss) a) zu dem Gesetzentwurf der Fraktionen der CDU/CSU und FDP—Drucksache 17/9046—Entwurf eines Gesetzes zu dem Vertrag vom 2. März 2012 über Stabilität, Koordinierung und Steuerung in der Wirtschafts- und Währungsunion (and other matters)

BT-Dr. 17/10172 of 28.06.2012: Bericht des Haushaltsausschusses (8. Ausschuss)—a) zu dem Gesetzentwurf der Fraktionen der CDU/CSU und FDP—Drucksache 17/9045—Entwurf eines Gesetzes zu dem Vertrag vom 2. Februar 2012 zur Einrichtung des Europäischen Stabilitätsmechanismus

BT-Dr. 17/12816 of 19.03.2013: Gesetzentwurf der Fraktionen CDU/CSU, SPD, FDP, Die Linke und Bündnis 90/Die Grünen Entwurf eines Gesetzes über die Zusammenarbeit von Bundesregierung und Deutschem Bundestag in Angelegenheiten der Europäischen Union (EUZBBG)

BT-Dr. 17/13142 of 17.04.2013: Beschlussempfehlung und Bericht des Ausschusses für die Angelegenheiten der Europäischen Union (21. Ausschuss) a) zu dem Gesetzentwurf der Fraktionen CDU/CSU, SPD, FDP, Die Linke und Bündnis 90/Die Grünen—Drucksache 17/12816—Entwurf eines Gesetzes über die Zusammenarbeit von Bundesregierung und Deutschem Bundestag in Angelegenheiten der Europäischen Union (EUZBBG) b) zu dem Antrag der Fraktionen der CDU/CSU und FDP—Drucksache 17/8137—Begleitgesetzgebung zum Vertrag von Lissabon konsequent anwenden—Mitwirkungsrechte des Bundestages in Angelegenheiten der Europäischen Union weiter stärken

BT-Dr. 18/298 of 17.01.2014: Schriftliche Fragen mit den in der Woche vom 13. Januar 2014 eingegangenen Antworten der Bundesregierung.

BT-Dr. 18/1340 of 07.05.2014: Antrag der Abgeordneten Dr Gerhard Schick, Manuel Sarrazin, Kerstin Andreae, Dieter Janecek, Uwe Kekeritz, Sven-Christian Kindler, Dr Tobias Lindner, Beate Müller-Gemmeke, Claudia Roth (Augsburg), Dr Frithjof Schmidt, Dr Wolfgang Strengmann-Kuhn, Jürgen Trittin und der Fraktion Bündnis 90/Die Grünen

BT-Dr. 19/19516 of 27.05.2020: Antrag der Abgeordneten Peter Boehringer et al. und der Fraktion der AfD—Rechtskonforme Zustände herstellen—PEPP-Anleihekäufe sofort beenden

BT-Dr. 19/20552 of 30.06.2020: Antrag der Abgeordneten Fabio De Masi et al. und der Fraktion Die Linke—Konflikt um die Geldpolitik der Europäischen Zentralbank politisch lösen—EU-Verträge ändern und geldpolitischen Dialog mit der Bundesbank verankern

BT-Dr. 19/20553 of 01.07.2020: Antrag der Abgeordneten Christian Dürr et al. und der Fraktion der FDP—Verhältnismäßigkeitsprüfung fristgerecht dargelegt—Kontrolle der Grenzen der Geldpolitik als Daueraufgabe ernstnehmen,

BT-Dr. 19/20616 of 01.07.2020: Antrag der Abgeordneten Tobias Matthias Peterka et al. und der Fraktion der AfD—Kritische und effektive Ausübung der sogenannten Integrationsverantwortung des Deutschen Bundestages im Zusammenhang mit Entscheidungen des Rates der Europäischen Zentralbank

BT-Dr. 19/20621 of 01.07.2020: Antrag der Fraktionen CDU/CSU, SPD, FDP und Bündnis 90/Die Grünen—Urteil des Bundesverfassungsgerichts zum Anleihekaufprogramm PSPP der Europäischen Zentralbank

BT-Dr. 19/22587 of 16.09.2020: Beschlussempfehlung und Bericht des Haushaltsausschusses zu dem Antrag der Abgeordneten Peter Boehringer, Marcus Bühl, Martin Hohmann, weiterer Abgeordneter und der Fraktion der AfD—Drucksache 19/19516

BT-Dr. 19/26877 of 23.02.2021: Gesetzentwurf der Abgeordneten Otto Fricke et al. und der Fraktion der FDP—Entwurf eines Gesetzes zur Änderung Gesetzes über die Zusammenarbeit von Bundesregierung und Deutschem Bundestag in Angelegenheiten der Europäischen Union zur Stärkung der Beteiligungsrechte des Bundestages in Angelegenheiten des Aufbauinstruments Next Generation EU (Next-Generation-EUZBBG—NG-EUZBBG)

BT-Dr. 19/27824 of 23.03.2021: Antrag der Abgeordneten Dr Franziska Brantner et al. und der Fraktion Bündnis 90/Die Grünen zu dem Beschluss (EU, Euratom) 2020/2053 des Rates vom 14. Dezember 2020 über das Eigenmittelsystem der Europäischen Union und zur Aufhebung des Beschlusses 2014/335/ EU, Euratom

BT-Dr. 19/2793 of 24.03.2021: Antrag der Abgeordneten Otto Fricke et al. und der Fraktion der FDP zu der dritten Beratung des Gesetzentwurfs der Bundesregierung—Drucksachen 19/26821, 19/27901—Entwurf eines Gesetzes zum Beschluss des Rates vom 14. Dezember 2020 über das Eigenmittelsystem der Europäischen Union und zur Aufhebung des Beschlusses 2014/335/EU, Euratom (Eigenmittelbeschluss-Ratifizierungsgesetz—ERatG)

BT-Dr. 19/27901 of 24.03.2021: Beschlussempfehlung und Bericht des Haushaltsausschusses zu dem Gesetzentwurf der Bundesregierung—Drucksache 19/26821—Entwurf eines Gesetzes zum Beschluss des Rates vom 14. Dezember 2020 über das Eigenmittelsystem der Europäischen Union und zur Aufhebung des Beschlusses 2014/335/EU, Euratom (Eigenmittelbeschluss-Ratifizierungsgesetz—ERatG)

Bewerting des Urteils durch die Bundesregierung, Runderlaβ des Auswärtigen Amts vom 30.11.1993 reprinted in Winkelmann I (ed), *Das Maastricht-Urteil des Bundesverfassungsgerichts vom 12. Oktober 1993, Dokumentation des Verfahrens mit Einführung* (Berlin: Dunckler & Humblot 1994)

Deutscher Bundestag, 'Kanzleramt soll "parlamentsfreundlicher" arbeiten' <www.bundestag.de/dokumente/textarchiv/2011/33702982_kw11_pa_europa/204826> accessed 2 August 2022

Deutscher Bundestag Wissenschaftliche Dienste, Sind Finanzhilfen der EU an Griechenland durch deutsche Zustimmungsakte zu den Europäischen Verträgen gedeckt und könnte dies vom Bundesverfassungsgericht überprüft werden?, no 3—3000—143/10, 4 May 2010 <www.bundestag.de/resource/blob/407314/6ffb62a01ca31240bc1a3a66f56d92ed/WD-3-143-10-pdf-data.pdf> accessed 2 August 2022

Gemeinsames Papier der Bundesregierung und der Fraktionen CDU/CSU, FDP, SPD und Bündnis 90/Die Grünen im Deutschen Bundestag vom 21. Juni 2012, 'Pakt für nachhaltiges Wachstum und Beschäftigung' <https://archiv.bundesregierung.de/Conten

tArchiv/DE/Archiv17/_Anlagen/2012/06/2012-06-21-wachstum-pakt.pdf?__blob=publicationFile&v=3> accessed 2 August 2022

German Government, 'A French-German Initiative for the European Recovery from the Coronavirus Crisis', Press release 18 May 2020 <www.bundeskanzler.de/resource/blob/1830100/1753772/414a4b5a1ca91d4f7146eeb2b39ee72b/2020-05-18-deutsch-franzoesischer-erklaerung-eng-data.pdf?download=1> accessed 2 August 2022

German Government, 'Mitteilung der Regierung der Bundesrepublik Deutschland an die Europäische Kommission vom 3. August 2021', 3 August 2021 <www.asktheeu.org/en/request/10318/response/35463/attach/2/doc%202%20DE%20reply%20to%20LFN%20de.pdf?cookie_passthrough=1> accessed 2 August 2022

Presseerklärung des Bundeskanzlers, Nr 386/93 v 12. Oktober 1993, a Abgedr in BullBReg Nr 87 v 16. Oktober 1993, S 990 f, reprinted in Winkelmann I (ed), *Das Maastricht-Urteil des Bundesverfassungsgerichts vom 12. Oktober 1993, Dokumentation des Verfahrens mit Einführung* (Dunckler & Humblot 1994)

Netherlands

Handelingen II, 2010/2011, nr 64, item 5

Kamerstukken II, 2001-2002, 28 331, nr 2 (legislative proposal by MP Halsema)

Kamerstukken II, 2001-2002, 28 331, nr 3 (Explanatory memorandum—legislative proposal by MP Halsema)

Kamerstukken II, 2011/2012, 33 319, nr 4 (Advies Raad van State en Nader Rapport)

Kamerstukken II, 2011/2012, 33 220, nr 4 (Advies Raad van State en Nader Rapport)

Kamerstukken II, 2011/2012, 33 221, nr 4 (Advies Raad van State en Nader Rapport)

Letter of the Dutch Minister of the Interior and Kingdom Relations and the Minister for Legal Protection of 1 July 2022, 2022-0000321093 <www.rijksoverheid.nl/documenten/kamerstukken/2022/07/01/kamerbrief-over-hoofdlijnen-constitutionele-toetsing> accessed 2 August 2022

Index

For the benefit of digital users, indexed terms that span two pages (e.g., 52–53) may, on occasion, appear on only one of those pages.